D1265238

LIFE OF JOHN RANDOLPH.

ENGRAVED BY J.SARTAIN.

JOHN RANDOLPH.

THE LIFE

OF

JOHN RANDOLPH

OF ROANOKE.

BY

HUGH A. GARLAND

VOL. I.

TWELFTH EDITION.

GREENWOOD PRESS, PUBLISHERS
NEW YORK

E 302.6

.R2 G25

1969b
C.2

INDIANA-
PURDUE
LIBRARY

WITHDRAWN

FORT WAYNE

Originally published in 1859
by D. Appleton & Company

First Greenwood Reprinting 1969

Library of Congress Catalogue Card Number 68-57603

SBN 8371-1971-5

PRINTED IN UNITED STATES OF AMERICA

PREFACE.

THE author of this book has had, perhaps, as good an oppor
tunity as any other man, who was not a contemporary and
intimate friend, to form a just estimate of Mr. Randolph's
character, and also to collect valuable and copious materials
for his biography. He was educated in Mr. Randolph's
district, was familiar with all the local associations of that
devoted son of the Old Dominion, often saw him among
his beloved constituents, and heard him under most favorable circumstances both on the hustings and in the Virginia
Convention. The writer was then but a youth, full of all
the eager interest and curiosity that would naturally be
excited by so extraordinary a man. Since Mr. Randolph's
death, it has been his good fortune to have been thrown into
the circle of his most intimate and confidential friends, some
of whom the writer feels justified in saying he also may claim
as his friends. While the thought of writing a life of Mr.
Randolph is of recent date, the character of the man and the
incidents of his life have been for many years the subject of
interest and of inquiry, which were abundantly gratified by
those who knew him and delighted to discourse on the
peculiarities and eccentricities of their departed friend.

Some ten or twelve years before his death, Mr. Randolph

APR 2 1 1970

made a will liberating his slaves; a short time before his decease, while under the influence of utter debility and disease, he made various and conflicting dispositions of his property. Here, of course, was a fruitful theme for the Courts. Was Mr. Randolph capable of making a will in the latter part of his life? was the subject of inquiry. Nearly every body who had known him, or who had had any dealings with him, from the earliest period, were summoned to give testimony. Many interesting and important facts, that would properly find a place in his biography, were elicited on that occasion. The whole testimony was taken down by an accurate stenographer, and the most important parts afterwards were written out in full. These valuable materials were placed in the hands of the writer of this memoir. In 1845, the whole subject again underwent a thorough investigation before the Circuit Court of Petersburg, many additional witnesses were summoned, and much new and important information elicited. The writer was a personal attendant on that Court during the trial.

To Mrs. Elizabeth Bryan, who is the niece of Mr. Randolph, and to Mr. Bryan himself, who is the son of his earliest friend, we are indebted for the interesting correspondence to be found in the first volume of this work. To Mrs. Dudley, Judge Beverly Tucker, the Hon. John Taliaferro, and Governor Tazewell, who were the youthful companions and schoolmates of Mr. Randolph, we are indebted for the incidents of his early life. By far the most interesting and important part of the work is the copious and unreserved correspondence of Mr. Randolph with the late and much lamented Francis S. Key, Esq., of Washington, and Dr. John Brockenbrough, of Virginia. This latter gentleman was, *par excellence*, the friend of his bosom. Not a thought or a feeling was concealed from him, and from 1811 to May, 17, 1833 ,but a few days before his death, Mr. Randolph wrote constantly, many times daily, to this invaluable friend. The entire correspondence is now in the hands of the writer. Without these materials and this unreserved confidence on the part of one who most valued the reputation of his departed friend, the author would never have undertaken the difficult task of writing the life of John Randolph. Very many of the letters have been inserted in their proper places—and many of the facts and incidents interwoven into the narrative, were obtained from others which have been suppressed—the author's chief study has been to use discreetly the unbounded confidence that was reposed in his prudence and judgment. It would be almost impossible to enumerate all the persons to whom we are indebted for many of the incidents narrated in this biography; every body knows something of the extraordinary man who is the subject of it; but we have given each one, we trust, credit for his contribution in its proper place. Many of the anecdotes and witticisms commonly attributed to Mr. Randolph are not found in this work, because there is no authority for them. "All the bastard wit of the country," said he to a friend, "has been fathered on me."

As to the *printed sources* of information connected with Mr. Randolph's public career, besides a valuable collection of pamphlets obtained from the estate of the late John Clopton, the author has had free access to the library of Congress, which, having been collected by Mr. Jefferson, is very copious on all subjects connected with the history and politics of the country. Besides these, Mr. Ritchie was so kind as to lend the only full file of the Enquirer in his possession. The reader needs not to be informed that the Richmond Enquirer contains a full chronicle of every thing that has been said and done in Virginia, worthy of being recorded in history, from 1804 to the present time.

Such were the materials in possession of the author. The difficulty was not to obtain—but to sift, digest, and arrange the abundant treasures in his possession. The book was commenced when the author had leisure to write to his satisfaction; it has been finished in the intervals of a laborious profession, and he feels that there are many defects which more time and leisure would have enabled him to correct. Many of the chapters were written under feelings of depression and anxiety while that dread pestilence, the cholera, had overshadowed with gloom and made desolate our devoted city. Whatever may be the defects of the book, however, the reader may be assured that nothing will be found in it that the author has not good reason to believe is true.

H. A. GARLAND.

Saint Louis, August, 1850.

CONTENTS OF VOL. I.

CONTENTS.

CONTENTS.

CHAPTER I

BIRTHPLACE.

CAWSONS, situated on a commanding promontory, near the mouth of Appomatox river, was the family seat of Colonel Theodorick Bland, Senior, of Prince George. After winding amidst its woody islands. around the base of this hill, the river spreads out into a wide bay; and, together with the James, into which it empties, makes towards the north and east a magnificent water prospect, embracing in one view Shirley, the seat of the Carters, Bermuda Hundred, with its harbor and ships, City Point, and other places of less note. In the midst of this commanding scene, the old mansion-house reared its ample proportions, and, with its offices and extended wings, was not an unworthy representative of the baronial days in which it was built— when Virginia cavaliers, under the title of gentlemen, with their broad domain of virgin soil, and long retinue of servants, lived in a style of elegance and profusion, not inferior to the barons of England, and dispensed a hospitality which more than half a century of subdivision, exhaustion, and decay, has not entirely effaced from the memory of their impoverished descendants.

At Cawsons, scarcely a vestige now remains of former magnificence. The old mansion was burnt down many years ago. Here and there a solitary out-dwelling, which escaped the conflagration, like the old servants of a decayed family, seem to speak in melancholy pride of those days, when it was their glory to stand in the shadow of loftier walls, and reflect back their loud revelry, when

> " The misletoe hung in the castle hall,
> The holly branch shone on the old oak wall;
> And the baron's retainers were blithe and gay,
> And keeping their Christmas holiday."

The serpentine paths, the broad avenues, and smooth gravel, the mounds, the green turf, and the shrubbery of extended pleasure-grounds, are all mingled with the vulgar sod. The noble outlines of nature are still there; but the handiwork of man has disappeared.

In a letter to his friend, F. S. Key, dated March 20, 1814, John Randolph says:—"A few days ago I returned from a visit to my birthplace, the seat of my ancestors on one side—the spot where my dear and honored mother was given in marriage, and where I was ushered in this world of woe. The sight of the broad waters seemed to renovate me. I was tossed in a boat, during a row of three miles across James river, and sprinkled with the spray that dashed over her. The days of my boyhood seemed to be renewed; but at the end of my journey I found desolation and stillness as of death—the fires of hospitality long since quenched; the parish church, associated with my earliest and tenderest recollections, tumbling to pieces; not more from natural decay than sacrilegious violence! What a spectacle does our lower country present! Deserted and dismantled country-houses, once the seats of cheerfulness and plenty, and the temples of the Most High ruinous and desolate, 'frowning in portentous silence upon the land.' The very mansions of the dead have not escaped violation. Shattered fragments of armorial bearings, and epitaphs on scattered stone, attest the piety and vanity of the past, and the brutality of the present age."

Colonel Bland was an active promoter of the Revolution. When Lord Dunmore, in the spring of 1775, under instructions from England, undertook to disarm the people, by secretly withdrawing the muskets and powder from the Magazine in Williamsburg, Colonel Bland was among the first to rouse the country to resistance. As munitions of war were scarce, he, his son Theodorick Bland, Jun., and his son-in-law, John Randolph, father of the late John of Roanoke, sold forty negroes, and with the money purchased powder for the use of the colony. Endowed with an ample fortune and a manly character, having been for a series of years in succession lieutenant of the county of Prince George, clerk of the court, and representative in the House of Burgesses, he possessed a commanding influence among the people. His house was the centre of a wide circle of friends and relations, who had pledged their lives, fortunes, and sacred honor, to the cause of independence. Though they did not rise to be master-spirits in that eventful struggle, the Blands, the Banisters, the Bollings, and the Eatons, were inferior to none in zeal, devotion, and heroic sacrifice.

The political spirit of the times may be inferred from the following incident:—The old man growing weary of a solitary life of widowhood, was advised by his son to look for a matrimonial connection in a certain quarter. After spying out the land, he wrote to his son: " Our politics differed so much that we parted by mutual consent ;" and in allusion to his own choice, he says: " the person I have thought of, is a lady of great goodness, sensible, and a true whig."

Among those who frequented Cawsons at this time, and partook of its welcome and generous hospitality, and shared with its inmates a proud defiance of the encroachments of England, was a young foreigner—though he can scarcely be called a foreigner who speaks our own mother tongue, and was bred up almost in sight of the American shores.

St. George Tucker was born of respectable parents in the island of Bermuda, where he commenced the study of law, but came to Virginia, before the Revolution, in order to complete his academic exercises in William and Mary College. His urbanity, social disposition, and literary attainments, introduced him into the best company and fashionable circles of the city. His general good conduct and deportment procured him the favor of most of the distinguished gentlemen of that place. When he had completed his college courses. he resumed the study of law, and settled permanently in Williamsburg ; but, on the breaking out of the disturbances with Great Britain, he took part with his adopted country, laid aside his legal pursuits, and engaged in other occupations. It doubtless was his intention to have served in the tented field ; but what he might have done in the way of military achievement, is left only to conjecture. That he might have rivalled Kosciusko, or Pulaski, or De Kalb, he afterwards gave ample proof on the field of Guilford ; but the glittering butterfly of military glory was destined to fade before the more substantial charms of female beauty.

Though Cawsons was a pleasant place, its chief magic lay in the Colonel's youngest daughter, Mrs. Frances Randolph, who, in her " unhappy widowhood," (to use her own expressive language,) had for the most part forsaken her own solitary home, and sought society and consolation beneath her father's roof. Mrs. Randolph was possessed of high mental qualities and extraordinary beauty. Though one might suppose she was endowed with little personal attraction, from an expression of her brother, Colonel Theodorick Bland, Jun., who was accustomed to call her, "my tawny sister." But tradition, confirmed by the portraits extant, speaks in admiration of her uncommon charms. The high, expanded forehead; smooth, arched brow, and brilliant dark eyes; the well-defined nose, and full, round, laughing lips, pregnant with wit and mirthfulness; the tall figure and expanded chest; the dark hair, winding in massy folds around the neck and bosom; an open, cheerful countenance—all suffused with that deep, rich, oriental tint that never fades—made her the most beautiful, sprightly, and attractive woman of her age.

Though clad in widow's garments, and on her brow lay a pensive stillness, as of one dreaming, she was yet young and beautiful. By her side, or on her knee, as inseparable as her own shadow, was a child—her youngest child—a little boy, her favorite John, the very image of his mother. In his dark eyes were reflected the sadness of her own soul; on his orphan brow was imprinted a kiss, that ever and anon a tear washed away. So much of subdued loveliness could not fail to win the sympathy of old and young, and to call forth sighs of pity and regret.

St. George Tucker, the first time he beheld the mother and her child, was filled with that mingled sentiment which more agitates the soul, and takes deeper hold on the affections, than any single passion. He soon found himself an ardent lover at the feet of the charming widow. A wife at sixteen, she was not long to be persuaded at six-and-twenty to abandon her unhappy widowhood. In an old family Prayer Book, in her own handwriting, is found the following record:

The unhappy widowhood of Frances Randolph commenced on the 28th day of Oct., in the year 1775.

John Randolph and Frances Bland were married the 9th of March, 1769.

Richard Randolph, their first son, was born the 9th of March, 1770.

Theodorick Bland Randolph, their second son, was born the 22d of January, 1771.

John Randolph, their third son, was born the 2d of June, 1773.

Jane Randolph, their first daughter, was born Nov. 10th, 1774, and died on the 26th of Nov., 1774.

The following additions to the above record is found in the hand-writing of the late John Randolph of Roanoke:

John Randolph, Junior, fourth son of Richard Randolph, of Curles, in the County of Henrico, was born on the 29th of June, 1742, O. S.,—answering to the 10th of July, N. S.

Frances Bland, fifth and youngest daughter of Theodorick Bland, of Cawsons, in the county of Prince George, was born on the 24th of Sept., 1752, N. S.

John Randolph, Esq., died at Matoax, on the 28th of October 1775; and on the 23d of Sept., 1778, his widow married St. George Tucker, of Bermuda.

———•••———

CHAPTER II.

MATOAX—GENEALOGY.

MATOAX, the residence of John and Frances Randolph during his life, of Mrs. Randolph in her widowhood, and of herself and Mr. Tucker, her second husband, till the time of her death, was situated on Appomatox, about two miles above Petersburg, on the opposite side; midway the falls, and on a high bluff, commanding a wide prospect of the surrounding country. At the time Mr. Tucker was introduced there by his elegant and accomplished bride, it was the centre of a populous, wealthy, and fashionable neighborhood. To say nothing of the town, there were Battersea, Mayfield, Burlington, Mansfield, Olive Hill, Violet Hill, Roslin, all on the same river; many in sight, and none more than two miles distant. These were the residences of gentlemen of ample fortunes, liberal education, polished manners, refined hospitality, and devoted patriotism. They have all since passed into other hands; some have gone down entirely; and the wild pine and the broom sedge have made such steady encroachments, that a wilderness has grown up in the place of fruitful fields, and more wild deer can be caught within a circuit of ten miles around the second most populous city in the State, than in a similar space in the prairies of the West. A statue of Niobe, in her own capitol—of Niobe weeping for her children—would be no unfit emblem of Old Virginia; her sons gone, her hearths cold, her fields desolate.

The mansion house at Matoax, like that at Cawsons, was burnt down many years ago. Nothing now remains but a heap of ruins. When we visited the spot, the factory boys, with their hounds, were chasing the hares over those solitary hills where once the proud sons of a proud race pursued the same light-footed game. A high hill to the eastward of that on which the mansion was, and separated from it by a deep ravine, is crowned by a thick cluster of oaks and other trees. At the foot, and under the shadow of those trees, are two graves, covered with simple marble slabs, level with the earth,—containing the following inscriptions:

Johannes Randolph, Arm:
Ob. xxviii. Octo,
MDCCLXXV,
Æt. xxxiv.
Non opibus urna, nec mens
virtutibus absit.

(*Translated.*)

John Randolph, Esq., died Oct. 28th, 1775, aged 34. Let not a tomb be wanting to his ashes, nor memory to his virtues.

I. H. S.
Francescæ Tucker Blandæ,
Conjugio
Sti Georgii Tucker.
Quis desiderio sit modus?
Obiit xviii. Januarii,
MDCCLXXXVIII,
Æt. xxxvi.

(*Translated.*)
Jesus, Saviour of mankind.

When shall we cease to mourn for Frances Bland Tucker, wife of St. George Tucker? She died 18th January, 1788, aged 36.

The father and the mother of the late John Randolph of Roanoke! It was his wish to be buried by their side. In a letter dated London, Dec. 19, 1830, he says: "I have personally but one wish; it is to be buried by the side of my honored parents at old Matoax, and I have taken measures to effectuate it. It is not long since this desire sprung up in my heart, where all else is withered, hard and dry."

Matoax was a part of the vast inheritance which descended from Richard Randolph of Curles, to his four sons, Richard, Brett, Ryland, and John.

His will is still extant, and bears date about the time of the birth of his youngest son, John, and a short time before his own death, 1742. It makes disposition of not less than forty thousand acres of the choicest lands on the James, Appomatox, and Roanoke rivers. Most of this vast estate was accumulated by his own industry and economy," as we learn from a monument erected to his memory at Turkey Island by his third son, Ryland. To his daughters—Mary, who married Archibald Cary, of Ampthill; Jane, who married Anthony Walke, of Princess Anne; and Elizabeth, who married Richard Kidder Meade—he left only personal property. All the lands were divided among the four sons. Those on Appomatox fell to John; those on Roanoke, jointly to John and Ryland. Ryland died without heir, and his portion descended to his brother; so that John, at the time of his death in 1775, was possessed of large and valuable estates on Appomatox and Roanoke.

Richard Randolph of Curles, was the fourth son of Col. Wm. Randolph, of Warwickshire, England, who was the first of the name that emigrated to Virginia, and settled at Turkey Island. He died April 11th, 1711. That he was of Warwickshire, we learn from a monument at Turkey Island; but the late John Randolph, who took great pride in searching into the genealogy of his family, says that he was of Yorkshire. Between the researches of the Hon. John, and the monument at Turkey Island, we leave the reader to judge. William Randolph was the father of seven sons and two daughters, who became the progenitors of a widespread and numerous race, embracing the most wealthy families, and many of the most distinguished names in Virginia history.

We will not cumber our pages with their complicated and unintelligible genealogy. In the course of our narrative, we shall give such portions as may become necessary for its elucidation. At present, we are only concerned with Richard Randolph of Curles, the fourth son. He married Jane Bolling, who was the daughter of John Bolling, who was the son of Robert Bolling and Jane Rolfe his wife, who was the granddaughter of Pocahontas, the beautiful Indian princess, daughter of Powhatan, whose pathetic story is so well known.

The portrait of Mrs. Randolph (Jane Bolling) is still extant. A more marked and commanding countenance is rarely to be met with. A perfect contrast to the luxurious ease, graceful manners, fluent and courtly conversation, betrayed by the full round face, ruddy complexion, low projecting eyes, smooth brow, and the delicate person and features of her husband. If the portrait be true to nature, none of the Indian complexion can be traced in her countenance. Her erect and firm position, and square broad shoulders, are the only indications of Indian descent. The face is decidedly handsome; while the lofty, expanded, and well marked forehead, the great breadth between the eyes, the firm distended nostril, compressed lips, and steady eye, display an intellect, a firmness, and moral qualities, truly heroic and commanding. Worthy descendant of the daughter of Powhatan.

Placing the two portraits side by side, one cannot fail to trace in the general contour of countenance, and cranial development, a striking resemblance between this lady and her grandson, the late John Randolph of Roanoke.

CHAPTER III.

CHILDHOOD.

A WISE poet and philosopher has said, "The child is father of the man," and that our days are "Bound each to each in natural piety." Who has not felt the force of this truth, so beautifully expressed? Who is not conscious that his personal identity cannot be measured by time—that he is the same to-day he was yesterday, and as far back as memory can reach? Though covered with years and busied with graver trifles, who does not feel that he is the same being that once gambolled on the plain with his school-fellows, and sought childish sports with cheerful heart by flood and field? Life is a continuous growth. The outspreading oak that shades the venerable old man at its root, is but the gradual development of the little nut that lay concealed in the acorn, which in his childhood he carelessly planted there. Had it been planted in a more genial soil, it might have attained a prouder growth. In a Siberian clime it would have been stunted and mean. Circumstances, therefore, do not make, but they develope the man. To know one thoroughly as he is; why he is thus and not otherwise; the man he is and not another; we must go back to his childhood. We must go to the salient point, to take the scope and direction of his character. We must see him surrounded by the circumstances that gave the first impulse; the influences that first stamped their impress on the plastic clay; we must know by what scenes he was surrounded; was he reared by the mountain-side, the running stream, or on the ocean's shore? was he in daily converse with the tamer scenes of nature, or with the grand, or the beautiful? what sort of people were his father and mother, his brothers and sisters, his playmates, and the men and women that went in and out before him? what books lay in his way? what lessons were taught him, not in the school-house, but the nursery, and by the domestic fireside? what were the traditions, opinions, passions, prejudices, that constituted a part of his heritage far more important than lands or merchandise?

Could we but know these things about the heroes, the statesmen, the orators and the poets, who excite our wonder and admiration, and have stamped the impress of their character not only on their own age, but on the world's history, how different would be our judgment in regard to them! We behold the outside alone; we are only made acquainted with the histrionic, the acted part of their life. What we see is but a masquerade, a succession of magnified and illuminated faces passing before the disk of a magic lantern. What we wish to see and long to know is far otherwise. Each, like Mephistopheles, has caught up some garment best suited to his nature or his purpose, and strives to *personate* (*persona* originally meant an actor's *mask*), to seem what he is not. Could we but draw aside the coverings by which they strive to conceal their motives, how many a sigh should we hear escape from heroic bosoms; how many a wail from the proud and silent spirit! The wounded pride of authorship gave birth to Manfred and Don Juan. The want of bread has caused many a swanlike strain to pour from the lips of the famishing author. More than one Helen or Cleopatra has set the heroes of the world in motion.   Pericles governed Athens, his wife Pericles; the son the mother—the schoolmaster the son, and he in his turn—but where would this end?   Oh the subtlety and complexity of human motives!

And yet without some tolerable insight into these, history is but an empty cloud-castle, built of mist, and shadow, and sunbeams. There are two kinds of history—the outward acted history, which is false, and the inner, secret history of causes and influences; this alone is true and worth knowing, and without it we know nothing; it matters not how learned we may be in facts and dates.   It is said that Dr. Johnson would insult any man who began to talk to him about the Punic wars.   What does the wise man care to know about battles or the marching and counter-marching of a multitude with swords, and battle-axes in their hands.   He wants to know the condition and circumstances of the people that made war necessary; the train of secret causes that brought it on; the master-spirits that controlled it, and the motives that influenced them.   He is not dazzled by the helmet or the martial dress, but lends a willing ear to the murmurings of the mad Achilles in his tent, for it is there, in those breathings of discontent, in those outpourings of a genuine living man, that he hopes to find some glimmering of the truth.   A little insight into the private life of the humblest Roman would be worth all we know of the Punic wars, its galleys, and battles of Cannæ.   A mere narrative of events abstracted from the man who wrought them, is like the human body when the life has gone out of it—cold, stiff, and cumbrous.   All true history consists in biography.   And there can be no biography where the author does not forget the hero, and write of the man.   It is not a history of the Revolution that we want, but the Life of Washington.   Under the influence of these opinions, we have commenced the task of writing the Life of John Randolph.

John Randolph was born at Cawsons, the second day of June, 1773.   The fiery star was in the ascendant at his birth, and pursued him through life; both as a destroying element, and a subtle Promethean flame consuming the soul.   It is a remarkable coincidence, that his birthplace, the cherished home of his childhood, and the house in which he spent the first fifteen years of his manhood, Cawsons, Matoax, and Bizzarre, were all in succession destroyed by fire.

Shortly after the destruction of Bizzarre, which was complete—involving his books and papers—he was asked by a friend why he did

not write something to leave behind him. " Too late, sir, too late,"
was the reply ; " all I ever wrote perished in the flames ; it is too late
to restore it now." He felt himself to be a child of destiny ; he had
a work given him to do, but some cross fate prevented ; he failed to
fulfil his destiny, and was wretched. " My whole name and race," he
has been known to say, " lie under a curse. I am sure I feel the
curse cleaving to me." He was not two years and a half old when
his father died. What could he know of death ? He only grieved
in sympathy with his mother's tears. It was not till long after, that
he learned the value of the treasure that lay buried beneath the marble slab on the hill under the old oak tree.

Much of the time of her " unhappy widowhood" was spent by
Mrs. Randolph at Cawsons. Here the little John was always a
welcome guest. He was a great favorite with the whole household,
especially with his grandfather and his cousin Anna Eaton, about
ten years older than himself, now the venerable Mrs. Anna Bland
Dudley, of Franklin, Tennessee. He was so delicate, reserved, and
beautiful, that he attracted the notice of all who frequented the
house. His skin was as soft and delicate as a female. " There is no
accounting for thinness of skins in different animals, human or
brute," says he in a letter dated January 31, 1826. " Mine I believe to be more tender than many infants of a month old. Indeed,
I have remarked in myself, from my earliest recollection, a delicacy
or effeminacy of complexion, that, but for a spice of the devil in my
temper, would have consigned me to the distaff or the needle." A
spice of the devil in his temper ! Well might he say that. Before
he was four years old, Mrs. Dudley has known him to swoon away in
a fit of passion, and with difficulty could be restored : an evidence
of the extreme delicacy of his constitution, and the uncontrollable ardor of a temper that required a stronger frame to repress and restrain it. Notwithstanding his excitable nature, he was always devoted to his mother; would hang fondly about her neck, and could
only be soothed by her caresses. Of her Mrs. Dudley thus speaks :
—" She was a woman, not only of superior personal attractions, but
excelled all others of her day in strength of intellect, for which she
was so justly celebrated." This excellent and highly gifted lady
trained up her child in the way he should go. He was allowed to
come in contact with nothing low, vulgar or mean. Mrs. Dudley,

Governor Tazewell, and the Hon. John Talliaferro, who remember him well in childhood, speak with admiration of his moral purity, and entire exemption from all vicious habits. His mother early taught him to read, and impressed on his mind the best lessons. She was a member of the Church of England, a faith from which her son never long departed. On her bended knees, with him by her side, she repeated day after day the prayers and collects of that admirable litany, which were never effaced from his tenacious memory. Often through life has he been known, in mental agony, to ejaculate them with an earnestness that called forth tears from all who heard him.

"When I could first remember," says he to a friend, "I slept in the same bed with my widowed mother—each night, before putting me to bed, I repeated on my knees before her the Lord's Prayer and the Apostle's Creed—each morning kneeling in the bed I put up my little hands in prayer in the same form. Years have since passed away; I have been a skeptic, a professed scoffer, glorying in my infidelity, and vain of the ingenuity with which I could defend it. Prayer never crossed my mind, but in scorn. I am now conscious that the lessons above mentioned, taught me by my dear and revered mother, are of more value to me than all that I have learned from my preceptors and compeers. On Sunday I said my catechism, a great part of which at the distance of thirty-five years I can yet repeat."

------ • • • ------

CHAPTER IV.

FAMILY CIRCLE.

IN the autumn of 1778, the family circle at Matoax consisted of Mr. and Mrs. Tucker, and her three sons, Richard, Theodorick, and John Randolph. Richard was in his ninth year, Theodorick was nearly eight, and John was in the sixth year of his age. They were all sprightly and interesting boys; and cheerfulness was once more restored to this happy family. A more amiable and exemplary step-father than Mr. Tucker could not be found. This trait in his character was proverbial among his acquaintance every where. "I remember to have heard a brother of mine," says the late Daniel Call, "who

married a niece of Mrs. Randolph of Curles, and was thus occasionally thrown into circles, where he sometimes met the Matoax family,
once say, that 'Mr. Tucker must be the best father-in-law in the
world, or his step-children would not be so fond of him.'" Up to
this time the boys had never been to school. All of their instruction
had been received at the hands of their mother. Mr. Tucker now
undertook their education. But it cannot be supposed that he devoted himself to school-keeping with the rigid discipline of a pedagogue. The life of ease and elegance which he is known to have
lived, amidst literary pursuits to which he was devoted, and in the
society of wealthy and fashionable neighbors, of which he and his
accomplished lady were the chief ornament, would not justify such a
conclusion. His leisure was given to their instruction ; and he at all
times took a lively interest in their improvement. In his letters to
Colonel Bland, Jr., who was stationed with a regiment at Charlottesville to guard the captured troops of Burgoyne's army, he often men-
tions them, and always with great solicitude. In one dated Matoax,
July 20, 1779, not ten months after his connection with the family,
he writes :—" What you wrote about Bob (Robert Banister, a cousin,
then with his uncle, Colonel Bland) has inspired the boys with the
spirit of emulation, which I hope will be productive of some benefit
to them. I find he serves as a very good spur to them when they are
growing a little negligent. Two of them appear to be blessed with
excellent capacities, but I confess I am afraid that the genius of your
namesake (Theodorick), though possessed of great quickness and
acuteness in many respects, does not lie in the literary line.   *   *
*   *   I shall continue to give them all the assistance that leisure
will permit."

John was too young and too delicate to be confined. We may
imagine also that, with so indulgent a teacher and so amiable a man,
having a spice of the devil withal in his own temper, he could not
have learnt much. He was not boisterous, nor inclined to the athletic
out-door sports of which boys are so fond. He sought amusements
within. When any of the boys and girls from the neighborhood
came to Matoax, he introduced the play of " Ladies and Gentlemen,"
in which each one personated some known or imagined character,
male or female, and acted as they supposed such persons would under
similar circumstances have acted. He was decidedly of a dramatic

turn. And his ardent temper and oriental imagination, precociously developed, invested with an earnestness and a reality all the sports and pastimes of his childhood. But he was not idle.

There was a certain closet to which he stole away and secreted himself whenever he could. It was not redolent—that closet—of cakes or the perfume of sweetmeats, but the odor of books,—of old musty tomes arranged along its shelves. With a mysterious awe,—as if about to commune with mighty spirits and beings of another world, as he really was—would he close the door upon himself, and devour, with " more eagerness than gingerbread," the contents of those old volumes. His mind, young as he was. craved after ethereal food, and there he found the richest repast.

The first book that fell in his way was Voltaire's History of Charles XII. of Sweden. An admirable writer on education has said, that "whatever the young have to read ought to be *objective*, clear, simple, and precise; ought to be the thing itself, and not round-about dialogues about the thing." No book could fill this description more completely than the above-mentioned History—full of stirring incidents, with a style of simple narrative as rapid and perspicuous as that master of style could make it. How his young heart must have burned within him as he pursued the eventful career of the bold, reckless and indomitable Charles! Feeling the impulses of a kindred spirit, his sympathy must have been intense for the wild, stout-hearted Scandinavian. The next book he read was the Spectator; but only the narrative and dramatic parts as we might suppose. The young mind can only be interested in things, objects, and not in roundabout dialogues about things. He delighted in Humphrey Clinker—Reynard the Fox came next; then Tales of the Genii and Arabian Nights. What a field of delight was opened here—what a world of glory in those old tales of wonder, the genuine poetry for children! The Arabian Nights and Shakspeare were his idols. He had read Goldsmith's Roman History, and an old History of Braddock's War. When not eight years old, he used to sing an old ballad of his defeat:

> " On the sixth day of July, in the year sixty-five,
>   At two in the morning did our forces arrive;
>   When the French and the Indians in ambush did lay,
>   And there was great slaughter of our forces that day."

But the "Thousand and One Tales" and Shakspeare were his idols! All others were in a sense shallow and limited—had bounds that could be measured—but these were fathomless, boundless; opening up to the rapt vision a world of enchantment, ever varying, ever new. He was a poet, a born poet, *nascitur non fit.* He did not write poetry; but he spoke it, he felt it, he lived it. His whole life was a poem, of the genuine epic sort; sad, mournful, true. "For poetry," says he, "I have had a decided taste from my childhood; this taste I have sedulously cultivated." Let that old closet tell! Only think of the boy who had read the books we have cited, and Don Quixotte, Gil Blas, Quintus Curtius, Plutarch, Pope's Homer, Robinson Crusoe, Gulliver, Tom Jones, Orlando Furioso, and Thomson's Seasons, before he was eleven years of age!

For more than two years the old closet was to that young genius the cave of Aladdin: and those old tomes the magic lamp by whose aid he could summon to his presence the giants and the genii, the dwarfs and the fairies, the Calibans and the Mirandas, and all the wonderful creations of fancy and imagination. With the clear, open sense and loving heart of childhood, he devoured those narrations and tales, which as he grew up became the themes of reflection, the objects of his aptest illustrations, and the sources whence he drew his lessons of profoundest wisdom. What a force of illustration, and even of argument, is found in his beautiful allusions to the marriage of Sinbad the Sailor to the corpse of his wife; the Old Man of the Sea; and the Vision of Alnascar! As to Shakspeare, he was so thoroughly imbued with his spirit, his own genius so akin to the Avon bard, that he thought and spoke as Shakspeare in his station would have thought and spoken.

He lamented in after life his rambling way of reading. But it could not have been otherwise. He belonged to the *irritabile genus* —was a born poet, and could not brook the restraint or the gin-horse routine of a grammar school. "I have been all my life," says he, "the creature of impulse, the sport of chance, the victim of my own uncontrolled and uncontrollable sensations; of a poetic temperament. I admire and pity all who possess this temperament" Poor fellow! What could mother or step-father do with such a thin-skinned, sensitive, impulsive, imaginative boy? With his fits of passion and swooning, what could they do? Nature is her own best guide. Develope nature according to her own instincts, and the best has been done that the case will admit of. So thought the kind parents of this delicate boy. They put no restraint upon him. Gentleness and tender care followed all his footsteps. He was suffered to roam freely over the hills and by the waterfalls of Appomatox. The quiet sport of angling was his chief source of amusement. When tired, he stole away into the closet, and none took heed of him. In this happy, ever-remembered dream of childhood, two years and a half passed away. Christmas, in the year seventeen hundred and eighty, was destined to be the last Christmas he would ever spend at Matoax as his home—as his home and dwelling-place.

———••———

CHAPTER V.

FLIGHT FROM MATOAX.

THE new year seventeen hundred and eighty-one commenced with the invasion of Virginia by the traitor Arnold. He had been intrusted with an expedition to that province, not with the hope of conquest, or with the expectation of achieving any important military enterprise, but solely for the purpose of plunder and devastation. What the proud soldier scorned to do was fit work for the betrayer of his country. The name of Arnold, before it became a by-word of reproach, was a sound of terror, not to armed men, but to defenceless women and children. The fame of his rapine and murder in his native State had preceded his arrival in Virginia. On the 3d of January, it was rumored at Matoax that the enemy were coming up James river, and that they were destined for Petersburg or Richmond. Mrs. Tucker had then been but five days mother to her last child, the present eminent jurist, Judge Henry St. George Tucker, of the University. "The first time I ever saw that gentleman," said John Randolph once in a speech, "we were trying to get out of the way of the British." The enemy that night landed at Hood's, of which being apprised early next morning, and hearing that they had marched as far as Bland's Ordinary, in their

way to Petersburg, Mr. Tucker came to the conclusion, whatever
might be the consequence, to remove his family out of the way of
danger, if possible. Hasty preparations were ordered for their
immediate departure. What bustle and confusion that frosty morning reigned through the halls at Matoax—each hurrying into trunks
or boxes, or loaded wagons, such articles as to them seemed most
valuable, heaping imprecations at the same time on that new name
of dread, Benedict Arnold. Whether John stole into the old closet
for the last time, and took out such volumes as pleased him, we are
not informed. Early next morning, the 5th of January, Syphax
drove off with the mother and her child; Essex and the boys
brought up the rear; and in a few hours Matoax, solitary and alone,
with all its effects, was abandoned to its fate. Mrs. Tucker met
with a most kind and hospitable reception at the house of Mr. Ben.
Ward, Jun'r, at Wintopoke : an ominous name in conjunction with
that of John Randolph. It was the daughter of this gentleman
to whom in after years he became so much attached. The un-
smooth current of their loves (as all true love is) greatly affected his
sensitive nature, and had no little influence on the most important
events of his life. Those children, when they first met together
around the fireside at Wintopoke, and joined in the innocent plays
of childhood, how unconscious were they of the deep drama of life
in which they were destined to play so sad a part! After recruiting
her health and strength a few days, which had been somewhat impaired by fatigue and hurry of spirits, Mrs. Tucker pursued her
journey to Bizarre, a large and valuable estate on both sides of the
Appomatox, where she and the boys were destined to spend alone
the remainder of this stirring and eventful year. So soon as his
family were in a place of safety, Mr. Tucker hastened back to the
scene of action to assist old Col. Bland in his escape, and to secure
such property, belonging to himself and friends, as had not been
destroyed by the enemy. This done, he threw himself at the head
of the Chesterfield regiment of militia and joined General Greene,
then manœuvring before Cornwallis's army on the borders of North
Carolina and Virginia. He was at the battle of Guilford, which
took place the 8th of March, where he behaved very gallantly.
When Gen. Greene marched into South Carolina after this engagement, he returned to Virginia, spent a few weeks with his family at

Bizarre, then joined General La Fayette, with whom he continued till the capture of Cornwallis, the 19th of October, at Yorktown.

Notwithstanding his active participation in the military operations of that period, his solicitude for the education of the boys was unabated. From Bizarre, May the 23d, he wrote to Colonel Bland: "Lose no opportunity of procuring a tutor for the boys, for the exigency is greater than you can imagine." Again, from Richmond, July 17th, he writes on the same subject; and then from Williamsburg, amidst the active preparations for that great event which was to end the war, and secure the independence of the country. In a letter dated Williamsburg, Sept. 21st, he says: "The boys are still without, and more than ever in want, of a tutor. Walker Maury has written to me lately, and given me such a plan of his school, that unless you procure a tutor before Christmas, I would at all events advise sending them to him immediately after. I know his worth; I know that his abilities are equal to the task; and I know that his assiduity will be equally directed to improve their morals and their understandings, as their manners. With this prospect, I would not advise the providing any but a man of superior talents as a private tutor." The year '81 was full of stirring life to the men, but of idleness to the boys; yet we are not to suppose that because the young Randolphs had not the benefit of a tutor to teach them the Latin and Greek languages, they were entirely destitute of instruction: with such a mother as they were blessed, they could not grow up in vice or idleness. Her sprightly wit, sound judgment, good temper, and pious example, impressed their character more favorably than all the learning of the schools. Her precepts were law to their plastic minds; and they ever afterwards retained a lively recollection of their wisdom and truth. When riding over the vast Roanoke estates one day, she took John up behind her, and, waving her hand over the broad acres spread before them, she said: "Johnny, all this land belongs to you and your brother Theodorick; it is your father's inheritance. When you get to be a man you must not sell your land; it is the first step to ruin for a boy to part with his father's home: be sure to keep it as long as you live. Keep your land and your land will keep you." In relating this anecdote, Mr. Randolph said it made such an impression on his mind that it governed his future life. He was confident it saved him from many errors. He never did part from his father's home. His attachment to the soil, the old English law of inheritance, and a landed aristocracy (we have no other word to express our meaning), constituted the most remarkable trait in his character. The Virginia law of descents, framed by Pendleton, Wythe, and Jefferson, never found favor in his eyes. While descanting on its evils, he has been heard to say, " Well might old George Mason exclaim, that the authors of that law never had a son !" In a letter addressed to a friend at a very late period of life, he says: " The old families of Virginia will form connections with low people, and sink into the mass of overseers' sons and daughters; and this is the legitimate, nay, inevitable conclusion to which Mr. Jefferson and his levelling system has brought us. They know better in New-York, and they feel the good effects of not disturbing the rights of property. The patroon is as secure in his rents as any man in the community. The great manor of Philipsburg was scandalously confiscated, and the Livingstons have lost their influence by subdivision. Every now and then our old acquaintance, Burr, finds out some flaw in the titles of the usurpers, and a fine estate is restored to its legitimate owners." In this passage the reader will find " the key words," to use his own expression, that decipher every thing in the character of John Randolph.

The subdivision or alienation of his father's inheritance was a subject he could not contemplate. Like Logan, he was alone—all alone—and no one of his father's house after him to inherit his father's home ; hence the apparent inconsistency in the disposition of his estates, the facility with which he made and unmade wills—in short, the monomania with which he was charged on the subject of property.

CHAPTER VI.

AT SCHOOL.

AFTER Christmas the boys were sent to Walker Maury's school in Orange county. Before he was nine years of age, John was separated from the brooding watchfulness of a devoted mother, and exposed to the dangers, evil examples, and vices of a public school. Tender and delicate as a female, he was forced out on the society of ruder boys, to endure or to resist as he might their kicks, cuffs, and bruises. Early did he begin among his equals to learn that personal merit is of more avail than birth or riches; and that truth, fortitude, and courage, are more to be valued than much learning.

At the school in Orange. the young Randolphs remained until about the middle of October, 1782, when it was broken up, and Mr. Maury removed to the city of Williamsburg.

He had been invited to that place to establish a Grammar School as an appendage to William and Mary College, in which there was no professorship of Humanity existing at that time. The school was regulated most judiciously; and was soon attended by more pupils than any other Grammar School that had been before established or has since existed in Virginia. More than one hundred, at one time, were in attendance, including boys from every State in the Union, from Georgia to Maryland, both inclusive. Such a number of pupils made it necessary that they should be divided into classes. The greater proportion of these classes were consigned to assistants, of whom there were four. Soon after Mr. Maury was established in Williamsburg, the young Randolphs followed him there, and again became members of his school. Richard, the eldest, was placed in the second class, under the immediate direction of Mr. Maury himself. Theodorick and John were placed in the fourth class, which was the head class assigned to the superintendence of the chief usher, a Mr. Elliot. When the class was so augmented, it was reading, and had nearly finished, Eutropius. One of the books then used by a class-mate, with a class-roll written on the fly-leaf, is still extant. In a short time after the young Randolphs joined it, the class had made such progress that it was transferred from the usher's department to that of the principal. It then became the third class. While John Randolph continued a member of it, which was more than a year, it was engaged in reading Sallust and Virgil, and had made some progress in learning the Greek and French languages, and the elements of Geometry. Though he complained of having learned but little at this school, his attainments for the short time he was connected with it must have been very considerable. While there he learned to repeat the Westminster Greek Grammar by heart, as he could the alphabet.

It was around the base of Lord Bottetourt's statue, in the old Capitol, the great clock, now removed to the church in Williamsburg, vibrating overhead, that he committed his lessons to memory. His attainment in Latin also must have been considerable. The boys were in the habit of acting plays in the original language from Plautus and Terrence. He was always selected to perform the female parts. His feminine appearance, and the "spice of the devil in his temper," rendered him peculiarly fitted for that purpose, and his performance was admirable. One who remembers his personal appearance at that time, in speaking of him, lifted up both hands, and exclaimed, "he was the most beautiful boy I ever beheld!" He was, indeed, the admiration of all who saw him, was a great favorite with the ladies, but his proud temper and reserved manners prevented him from forming any intimate associations with his school-fellows. Though a promiscuous intercourse was repugnant to his feelings, no one was capable of appreciating true merit, and of forming closer, more unreserved, warmer, and lasting attachments than John Randolph. Shunning vulgar society and repelling familiarity, he was the more open and devoted to those who were honored with his friendship. He had a natural instinct for discovering character; and was remarkable in earliest youth for his discernment and scrutiny into motives.

Among the hundreds of boys with whom he came in daily contact, he associated with, and formed an attachment to, one class-mate alone. That class-mate was Littleton Waller Tazewell. With a genius as brilliant as his own, a heart as warm, and a person as prepossessing, young Tazewell was worthy of the distinction. A mutual respect and friendship grew up between them, which lasted to the end of Mr. Randolph's life ; and the recollection of which is still warmly preserved by the noble survivor. In a manner peculiar to John Randolph, this early attachment was often called to remembrance, and cherished. Near forty years afterwards, when he had heard a lady sing some Scotch airs, he wrote to a friend : " Among others she sang ' There's nae luck aboot the house' very well, and ' Auld Lang Syne.' When she came to the lines:

> ' We twa ha'e paidlet in the burn,
> Frae morning sun till dine,'

I cast my mind's eye around for such a " trusty feese," and could light only on Tazewell (who, God be praised, is here), and you may judge how we met."

In the spring of 1784, after he had been in Williamsburg a little more than one year, John Randolph was taken away from school. His parents went on a visit to Mr. Tucker's friends in the island of Bermuda, and as John's health was very delicate, they took him along with them. When about to take his leave, he proposed to young Tazewell that they should exchange class-books, that each might have some testimonial of their mutual friendship and of its origin.

They accordingly exchanged Sallusts. Not many years since, while he was in Norfolk, preparing to depart on his mission to Russia, he showed Mr. Tazewell the identical Sallust he (Tazewell) had given him. On the fly-leaf of the book he had written, at the time he received it, how, when, and from whom he had acquired it. To this he had added this hexameter : " Cœlum non animum mutant qui transmare currunt."

He continued abroad more than eighteen months, and not having the advantage of daily recitation, the Greek language, which he had begun so successfully to acquire in his promenades around Lord Bottetourt's statue, was entirely effaced from his memory; and he barely kept alive the more extensive knowledge he had acquired of the Latin. Though these newly acquired elements of learning were readily abandoned, and easily effaced, pursuits more genial to his taste were followed with unabated vigor. Poetry continued to be the charm of his life. While abroad, he read Chatterton and Rowley, and Young and Gay. Percy's Reliques and Chaucer then became his great favorites. On his return to Virginia, in the latter part of 1785 we do not learn that he returned to Walker Mauray's school in Williamsburg; on the contrary, we presume he did not, for he then would have formed an acquaintance in early youth with John Brockenbrough, the most intimate friend of his after life.

The letter from which the above paragraph was taken continues in this wise: "During the time that Dr. Brockenbrough was at Walter Mauray's school (from the spring of 1784, to the end of 1785), I was in Bermuda; and (although he was well acquainted with both my brothers) our acquaintance did not begin until nearly twenty years afterwards. Do you know that I am childish enough to regret this very sensibly? for, although I cannot detract from the esteem or regard in which I hold him, or lessen the value I set upon his friendship, yet, had I known him then, I think I should enjoy 'Auld Lang Syne' more, when I hear it sung, or hum it to myself, as I often do."

How he spent the next twelve or eighteen months after his return from Bermuda, we have not been able to learn. When we see him again it is at Princeton College, in the autumn of 1787. The manner in which he spent his time there and at Columbia College, New-York, shall be given in his own words.

"My mother once expressed a wish to me, that I might one day or other be as great a speaker as Jerman Baker or Edmund Randolph! That gave the bent to my disposition. At Princeton College, where I spent a few months (1787), the prize of elocution was borne away by mouthers and ranters. I never would speak if I could possibly avoid it, and when I could not, repeated, without gesture, the shortest piece that I had committed to memory. I remember some verses from Pope, and the first anonymous letter from Newberg, made up the sum and substance of my spoutings, and I can yet repeat much of the first epistle (to Lord Chatham) of the former, and a good deal of the latter. I was then as conscious of my superiority over my competitors in delivery and elocution, as I am now that they are sunk in oblivion; and I despised the award and the umpires in the bottom of my heart. I believe that there is no-where such foul play as among professors and schoolmasters; more especially if they are priests. I have had a contempt for college honors ever since.

My mother's death drew me from Princeton, (where I had been

forced to be idle, being put into a noisy wretched grammar school for Dr. Witherspoon's emolument: I was ten times a better scholar than the master of it,) and in June, 1788, I was sent to Columbia College, New-York; just then having completed my fifteenth year. Never did higher literary ambition burn in human bosom. Columbia College, New-York, was just rising out of chaos; but there was an Irishman named Cochran, who was our humanity professor.

I now (July, 1788) mastered the Eaton grammar, and gave Cochran, who was a scholar, "and a ripe and good one," a half-joe, out of my own pocket, for months, to give me private lessons. We read Demosthenes together, and I used to cry for indignation at the success of Philip's arts and arms over the liberties of Greece. But some disgust induced my master to remove to Nova Scotia, where a professor's chair was offered him, about three months after I became his pupil. Next to the loss of my mother, and my being sent to Walker Mauray's school (and one other that I shall not name), this was the greatest misfortune of my life.

"Unhappily, my poor brother Theodorick, who was two years older than myself, had a strong aversion to books and a decided taste for pleasure. Often when I had retreated from him and his convivial associates to my little study, has he forced the lock, taken away my book, and rendered further prosecution of my purpose impossible. From that time forward I began to neglect study (Cochran left no one but Dr. Johnson, the president, of any capacity behind him, and he was in the Senate of the United States from March, 1789), read only the trash of the circulating library, and never have read since, except for amusement, unless for a few weeks at Williamsburg at the close of 1793; and all my dear mother's fond anticipations and all my own noble and generous aspirations have been quenched; and if not entirely—if a single spark or languid flame yet burns—it is owing to my accidental election to Congress five and twenty years ago."

He was recalled from Princeton by the death of his mother, That sad event took place the 18th of January, 1788. She was but thirty-six years old when she died. Cut off in the bloom of youth and beauty, he ever retained a most vivid and impassioned remembrance of her person, her charms, and her virtues. He always kept her portrait hanging before him in his chamber. Though he was not yet fifteen years old, the loss to him was irreparable. She knew him; she knew the delicacy of his frame, the tenderness of his heart, the irritability of his temper; and she alone could sympathize with him. Many years after this event—the day after his duel with Mr. Clay—while reflecting on the narrow escape he had made with his life, and the professions of men who disappear in such an hour ot trial, his mind naturally reverted to his dear mother, who understood and never forsook him; he wrote thus to a friend: " I am a fatalist. I am all but friendless. Only one human being ever knew me. *She* only knew me." That human being was his mother! The loss to him was irreparable; nor did he ever cease to mourn over it. Rarely did he come to Petersburg or its vicinity, that he did not visit old Matoax, in its wasted solitude, and shed tears over the grave of those honored parents, by whose side it was the last wish of his heart to be buried.

The spring of the year 1788 was spent in Virginia. It does not appear that he was engaged in any regular course of study. Much of his time, as was his custom whenever he could, was devoted to friendship. He spent several weeks of this vacation with young Tazewell, at his father's house, in Williamsburg. While there, he discoursed at large on the various incidents he had met with while abroad in Bermuda, and at college in Princeton, thus early displaying that faculty of observation and fluent narrative that in after years rendered his conversation so brilliant and captivating. After his departure on the present occasion, he commenced a correspondence, which, with short intervals, was kept up through life. Such was Mr. Tazewell's reputation for profound learning on all subjects touching the laws and the Constitution of the country, that Mr. Randolph consulted him on every important occasion as it arose in Congress. Often in one line would he propound an inquiry that cost his friend weeks of investigation to answer. His own early letters displayed an inquiring mind far beyond his years. In his first letter, written on his arrival in New-York (June, 1788), he stated that alien duties had been exacted by the custom-house there, not only upon the vessel in which he had taken his passage, which was owned in Virginia, but upon the passengers on board of her, all of whom were natives of Virginia. This statement was accompanied by many reflections, designed to show the impolicy of such exactions on the

part of New-York, and the ill effects that would result from persist
ing in such a course. This incident took place before the adoption
of the present Constitution of the United States, and when the subject of it was just fifteen years old. It is mentioned merely to show
" the precocious proclivity" of John Randolph to the investigation of
political subjects.

Another letter addressed to the same friend, was confined to an
account of the first inauguration of General Washington as President
of the United States, which took place the 30th of April, 1789, in
the city of New-York. John Randolph was an eye-witness of the
scene. His letter contained a narrative of many minute but very
interesting incidents that do not appear in any of our public records
or histories. This narrative, being written at the moment such incidents occurred, by an ingenuous youth, an eye-witness of the events,
had an air of freshness and truthfulness about it that was most captivating. As the letter related to nothing but matters of general
interest, young Tazewell showed it to his father, who was so much
·leased with it, that shortly afterwards he requested his son to read
it to a party of friends who were dining with him. The late Colonel
James Innis, the attorney-general, was one of the party. He was
considered, at that time, the most eloquent speaker, and the best belles-
lettres scholar in Virginia. Colonel Innis was so much pleased with
the letter, that he took it from the hands of the owner, and read it
over and over again, pronouncing it to be a model of such writing,
and recommended to the young man to preserve it, and study its style.

CHAPTER VII.

THE CONSTITUTION IN ITS CHRYSALIS STATE.

No man with a growing intellect was ever content with his early
education. The boy turns a contemptuous look on the swaddlings of
infancy. The wisest instruction is so inadequate to the wants of the
human mind, that when one grows up to manhood he looks back with
mortification on the dark gropings of youthful ignorance, and with

disgust on the time and effort wasted in pursuing barren paths, where experience taught him no truth could be found. John Randolph was not singular in lamenting that he had disappointed the fond anticipations of his friends, and mourning that " all his noble and generous aspirations had been quenched." Had Theodorick and his noisy companions left the ambitious student alone to his books and his closet, we should still have heard the same complaint. No attainment can satisfy the aspirations of genius. But it is true he was not without just cause of discontent. His frequent changes of school, not less than five times in as many years; the long interruptions thereby occasioned—by his travels abroad, the death of his mother, and the daily vexations of ill health and of noisy companions, with whom he was compelled to associate—rendered it impossible for him to give that continuous and ardent devotion to study which is indispensable to mental discipline, and the acquisition of learning. In disgust he gave up the effort, and abandoned himself to the loose habit of promiscuous reading. His classical studies, so often interrupted, were finally closed before he was sixteen years of age. " I am an ignorant man, sir !" though sounding like sarcasm from his lips, was uttered with sincerity. Though the broad foundation of solid learning was wanting to him, his active and inquiring mind was scarcely conscious of the deficiency. Nature had designed him for a statesman ; he was eminently a practical man, and drew his lessons of wisdom from experience and observation. He was, while yet a youth, in daily intercourse with statesmen and men of learning. He enjoyed great and rare opportunities for acquiring information on those subjects towards which his mind had " a precocious proclivity." Practical politics, and the science of government, were the daily themes of the statesmen with whom he associated. He was a constant attendant on the sittings of the first Congress. He was in Federal Hall, the 4th of March, 1789, when only thirteen members of the new Congress under our present Constitution appeared and took their seats. Two only presented themselves from the south side of the Potomac ; Alexander White, from Virginia, and Thomas Tudor Tucker, from South Carolina. Mr. Tucker was the brother of St. George Tucker, the father-in-law of John Randolph. The 14th of March, Richard Bland Lee, a cousin of John Randolph, Mr. Madison, and John Page, from Virginia, entered the hall, and cheered the hearts of those who had assembled from day to day for more than a week without a quorum, and were beginning to despond and doubt lest this new government might prove a failure. The 30th of March, Col. Theodorick Bland, the uncle of John Randolph, made his appearance. It was not till the 1st of April, nearly a month after the time appointed by the Constitution, that a quorum was obtained, and the House organized for business. Such was the feeble and doubtful infancy of this great and growing Republic. "I was at Federal Hall," said Randolph once in a speech to his constituents; "I saw Washington, but could not hear him take the oath to support the Federal Constitution. The Constitution was in its chrysalis state. I saw what Washington did not see; but two other men in Virginia saw it—George Mason and Patrick Henry—*the poison under its wings.*" That this was no vain boasting in a boy of sixteen, the reader will soon see.

The arduous and responsible task of organizing a new government devolved on the first Congress. In that body were a number of men who preferred the Old Confederation, with some modifications to give it energy; and were strenuously opposed to a strong centralizing system, such as they apprehended the new government to be. They, therefore, looked with watchfulness and jealousy on every step that was taken in its organization. The most prominent among those who thus early opposed the assumptions of federal power, were Theodorick Bland and Thomas Tudor Tucker, the two uncles of John Randolph. Col. Bland was a great admirer and follower of Patrick Henry. He was a member of the Convention that met, June, 1788, in Richmond, to ratify the new Constitution. It is well known that Patrick Henry opposed the ratification with all his eloquence. The very day in which he shook the capitol with a power not inferior to that with which he set the ball of Revolution in motion, Col. Bland, writing to a friend, says: "I see my country on the point of embarking and launching into a troubled ocean, without chart or compass, to direct her; one half of her crew hoisting sail for the land of *energy,* and the other looking with a longing aspect on the shore of *liberty.*" After declaring that the Convention which framed the Constitution had transcended its powers, Patrick Henry exclaimed: 'It is most clearly a consolidated government. I need not take much pains to show that the principles of this system are extremely pernicious, impolitic, and dangerous. We have no detail of those great considerations which, in my opinion, ought to have abounded before we should recur to a government of this kind. Here is a revolution as radical as that which separated us from Great Britain. It is as radical, if in this transition our rights and privileges are endangered, and the sovereignty of the States be relinquished: and cannot we plainly see that this is actually the case? Is this tame relinquishment of rights worthy of freemen? Is it worthy of that manly fortitude that ought to characterize republicans? The Confederation—this same despised government—merits, in my opinion, the highest encomium: it carried us through a long and dangerous war; it rendered us victorious in that bloody conflict with a powerful nation; it has secured us a territory greater than any European monarch possesses: and shall a government which has been thus strong and vigorous, be accused of imbecility, and abandoned for want of energy? Consider what you are about to do before you part with this government." "It is now confessed that the new government is national. There is not a single federal feature in it. It has been alleged within these walls, during the debates, to be national and federal, as it suited the arguments of gentlemen. But now when we have the definition of it, it is purely national. The honorable member was pleased to say, that the sword and purse included every thing of consequence. And shall we trust them out of our hands without checks and barriers? The sword and purse are essentially necessary for the government. Every essential requisite must be in Congress. Where are the purse and sword of Virginia? They must go to Congress. What is become of your country? The Virginian government is but a name. We should be thought unwise indeed to keep two hundred legislators in Virginia, when the government is, in fact, gone to Philadelphia, or New-York. We are as a State to form no part of the government. Where are your checks? The most essential objects of government are to be administered by Congress. How then can the State governments be any check upon them? If we are to be a republican government, it will be consolidated, not confederated. This is not imaginary; it is a formidable reality. If consolidation proves to be as mischievous to this country as it has been to other countries, what will the poor inhabitants of this country do? This government will operate like an ambuscade. It will destroy the State governments, and swallow the liberties of the people, without giving them previous notice. If gentlemen are willing to run the hazard, let them run it; but I shall exculpate myself by my opposition, and monitory warnings, within these walls. Another gentleman tells us that no inconvenience will result from the exercise of the power of taxation by the general government. A change of government will not pay money. If from the probable amount of the import, you take the enormous and extravagant expenses, which will certainly attend the support of this great consolidated government, I believe you will find no reduction of the public burdens by this new system. The splendid maintenance of the President, and of the members of both Houses; and the salaries and fees for the swarm of officers and dependents on the Government, will cost this continent immense sums. After satisfying their uncontrolled demands, what can be left for the States? Not a sufficiency even to defray the expense of their internal administration. They must, therefore, glide imperceptibly and gradually out of existence. This, Sir, must naturally terminate in a consolidation. If this will do for other people, it will never do for me. I never will give up that darling word *requisition;* my country may give it up; a majority may wrest it from me; but I never will give it up till my grave. The power of direct taxation was called by the honorable gentleman the soul of the government: another gentleman called it the lungs of the government. We all agree that it is the most important part of the body politic. If the power of raising money be necessary for the general government, it is no less so for the States. Must I give my soul—my lungs to Congress? Congress must have our souls; the State must have our souls. These two co-ordinate, interfering, unlimited powers of harassing the community are unexampled; it is unprecedented in history; they are the visionary projects of modern politicians. Tell me not of imaginary means, but of reality: this political solecism will never tend to the benefit of the community. It will be as oppressive in practice as it is absurd in theory. If you part from this, which the honorable gentleman tells you is the soul of Congress, you will be inevitably ruined. I tell you they shall not have the soul of Virginia."

After speaking of the "awful squinting towards monarchy" in the executive ; and of the great powers conferred on the judiciary, Mr. Henry concluded in one of those bursts of rapt eloquence, which can only be compared to the eloquence of Demosthenes, when on a similar occasion—in a last appeal to his countrymen to defend themselves against the invasion of Philip—he called on the spirits of the mighty dead, those who fell at Thermopylæ, at Salamis, and at Marathon, to rise and protect their country against the arts and arms of the Macedonian Tyrant.

" The gentleman, tells you, said Mr. Henry, " of important blessings which he imagines will result to us, and to mankind in general, from the adoption of this system. I see the awful immensity of the dangers with which it is pregnant. I see it,—I feel it. I see beings of a far higher order anxious concerning our decision. When I see beyond the horizon that bounds human eyes, and look at the final consummation of all human things, and see those intelligent beings which inhabit the ethereal mansions, reviewing the political divisions and revolutions which in the progress of time will happen in America, and the consequent happiness or misery of mankind, I am led to believe, that much of the account, on one side or the other, will depend on what we now decide. Our own happiness alone is not affected by the event. All nations are interested in the determination. We have it in our power to secure the happiness of one half of the human race. Its adoption may involve the misery of the other hemispheres."

When the vote was about to be taken on the ratification, Patrick Henry, seconded by Theodorick Bland, moved a resolution, " That previous to the ratification of the new constitution of government recommended by the late Federal Convention, a declaration of rights asserting and securing from encroachment the great principles of civil and religious liberty, and the inalienable rights of the people, together with amendments to the most exceptionable parts of the said constitution of government, ought to be referred by this convention to the other States in the American confederacy for their consideration." This resolution was lost by a majority of *eight votes*. Many who voted for it were members of the first Congress ; and some of them were among the most influential and distinguished men in Virginia. William Cabell, Samuel Jordan Cabell, Benjamin Harrison, John Tyler, father of the late President, Isaac Coles, Stephen Thompson Mason, Abraham Twigg, Patrick Henry, Theo-

dorick Bland, William Grayson, James Monroe, and George Mason
These same persons voted against the adoption of the Constitution,
which was only carried by a majority of *ten*.   So great was the impression made on the public mind by the arguments in the Convention against the evil tendencies of the Constitution, that a majority
of the Virginia Legislature that met the ensuing October, to appoint
senators, and pass laws for electing members of Congress, was decidedly anti-federal; that is, opposed to the Constitution, as it came
from the hands of its framers, without important modifications.
Patrick Henry was the master spirit of that assembly. He was
offered a seat in the Senate of the United States; but he declined it,
as he had previously declined a seat in the Federal Convention.
Through his influence the appointment of senator was conferred on
William Grayson, and on Richard Henry Lee.

Mr. Grayson distinguished himself in the Virginia Convention
by a very elaborate analysis of the new Constitution, pointing
out its defects, and illustrating by history its dangerous tendencies
He gave utterance to a prediction, which many believe has been
in the daily process of fulfilment from that time to the present
moment.   " But my greatest objection is," says he, speaking of
the Constitution, "that it will, in its operation, be found unequal, grievous, and oppressive.   If it have any efficacy at all, it
must be by a faction—a faction of one part of the Union against
the other.   There is a great difference of circumstances between the
States.   The interest of the carrying States (since manufacturing
States) is strikingly different from that of the producing States.   I
mean not to give offence to any part of America, but mankind are
governed by interest.   The carrying States will assuredly unite, and
our situation will then be wretched indeed.   Every measure will
have for its object their particular interest.   Let ill-fated Ireland be
ever present to our view.   I hope that my fears are groundless, but
I believe it as I do my creed, that this government will operate as
a faction of seven States to oppress the rest of the Union.   But it
may be said, that we are represented, and cannot therefore be injured—a poor representation it will be!   The British would have
been glad to take America into the Union like the Scotch, by giving
us a small representation.   The Irish might be indulged with the
same favor by asking for it.   (As they have done, and with what

result?)   Will that lessen our misfortunes?   A small representation
gives a pretence to injure and destroy.   But, sir, the Scotch Union
is introduced by an honorable gentleman as an argument in favor of
adoption.   Would he wish his country to be on the same foundation
with Scotland?   They have but 45 members in the House of Commons, and 16 in the House of Lords.   They go up regularly in order
to be bribed.   The smallness of their number puts it out of their
power to carry any measure.   And this unhappy nation exhibits the
only instance, perhaps, in the world, where corruption becomes a
virtue.   I devoutly pray, that this description of Scotland may not
be picturesque of the Southern States, in three years from this time."

The other senator from Virginia was Richard Henry Lee.   He
stood by Patrick Henry from the commencement of our revolutionary
struggles to their end.   He was one of the first delegates to the first
Congress.   His name appears on almost all the important committees
of that body.   He was selected by the Virginia delegation to move
the declaration of independence.   For his patriotism, statesmanship,
and oratory, he was regarded as the Cicero of his age.   His classical
and chaste elocution possessed a tone of depth and inspiration that
charmed his auditory.   While his great compatriot poured down
upon agitated assemblies a cataract of mingled passion and logic, he
awakened the attention, captivated the heart, and convinced the understanding of his hearers by a regulated flow of harmonious language, generous sentiment, and lucid argument.   "In his personal
character, he was just, benevolent, and high-spirited, domestic in his
tastes, and too proud to be ambitious of popularity."   This distinguished patriot and statesman was strenuously opposed to the Constitution as it came from the hands of its framers.   He was a member
of Congress to whom it was referred, and by whom it was expected
to be recommended to their respective States.   "When the plan of a
Constitution," says Mr. Madison, "proposed by the Convention came
before Congress for their sanction, a very serious effort was made by
Richard Henry Lee to embarrass it.   It was first contended that
Congress could not properly give any positive countenance to a measure
which had for its object the subversion of the Constitution under
which they acted.   This ground of attack failing, he then urged the
expediency of sending out the plan with amendments, and proposed
a number of them corresponding with the objections of Col. Mason."

He then addressed a letter to Governor Edmund Randolph, of Virginia, who as a member of the Convention had refused to sign the Constitution. After giving his objections in detail, he says: "You are, therefore, sir, well warranted in saying, either a monarchy or aristocracy will be generated—perhaps the most grievous system of government will arise. It cannot be denied with truth, that this new Constitution is, in its first principles, highly and dangerously oligarchic; and it is a point agreed, that a government of the few, is, of all governments, the worst."

"The only check to be found in favor of the democratic principle, in this system, is the House of Representatives; which, I believe, may justly be called a mere shred or rag of representation; it being obvious to the least examination, that smallness of number, and great comparative disparity of power, render that house of little effect to promote good, or restrain bad government. But what is the power given to this ill-constructed body? To judge of what may be for the general welfare, seems a power coextensive with every possible object of human legislation." Such were the first senators from Virginia, and of a like complexion were a majority of those returned to the House of Representatives. For devoting himself so ardently to the election of men known to be hostile to the Constitution as it stood, Mr. Henry was charged with a design of subverting that which he could not prevent. It is said that his avowed attachment to the confederation was mere hypocrisy; that he secretly rejoiced in its imbecility, and did not desire a union of the States under any form of government. He was attacked in a most virulent and personal manner by a writer who signed himself Decius. He charged Mr. Henry with a design of forming Virginia and North Carolina into one republic, and placing himself at the head as their dictator. "Were I to draw the picture of a tyrant for this country," says Decius, "it should be very different from that which some others have sketched out. He should be a man in every instance calculated to soothe and not to threaten the populace; possessing a humiliating and not an arrogant turn; affecting an entire ignorance and poorness of capacity, and not assuming the superiorities of the illumined; a man whose capacity should be calculated to insinuate itself into the good esteem of others by degrees, and not to surprise them into a compliance on a sudden · whose plainness of manners and meanness of address first should move our compassion, steal upon our hearts, betray our judgments, and finally run away with the whole of the human composition."

This description of the demagogue winning his way by affected humility and low cunning to the supreme command, was intended to be applied to Mr. Henry. Many of his own expressions are used in drawing the portrait, but no man less deserved the epithet of ambitious. There can be no doubt that he delighted to sway the passions of the multitude, and to influence the decision of legislative bodies by the powers of his eloquence; but that his ambition extended to the acquisition of supreme executive command, there is not the slightest ground of suspicion.

The virulence with which he was assailed must be attributed to the high party excitement of the times, which indiscriminately assaulted the most spotless characters, and paid no respect to exalted services or venerable age.

CHAPTER VIII.

GEORGE MASON.

GEORGE MASON was a wise man. He was at once the Solon and the Cato, the lawgiver and the stern patriot of the age in which he lived. At a period when republics were to be founded, and constitutions of government ordained for growing empires, he was the first to define and to guard with watchful care the rights of the people—to prescribe limitations to the different departments of government, and to place restrictions on their exercise of power. The Bill of Rights, and the Constitution of Virginia, are lasting monuments to his memory. One sentence of the former contains more wisdom and concentration of thought, than all former writings on the subject of government. The sentence is this; " that no man or set of men is entitled to exclusive or separate emoluments, or privileges from the community, but in consideration of public services; which, not being descendible, neither ought the offices of magistrate, legislator, or judge, to be hereditary." Here is a volume of truth and wisdom, says an eminent writer, a lesson for the study of nations, embodied in a single sentence, and expressed in the plainest language. If a deluge of despotism were to overspread the world, and destroy those institutions under which freedom is yet protected, sweeping into oblivion every vestige of their remembrance among men, could this single sentence of Mason be preserved, it would be sufficient to rekindle the flame of liberty, and to revive the race of freemen. Though Mr. Mason did not object to a union of the States for their mutual defence and welfare, he yet regarded the commonwealth of Virginia as his country, and her government as the only one that could guarantee his rights or protect his interests. So far back as 1783, Mr. Madison, speaking of him, says, "his heterodoxy lay chiefly in being too little impressed with the necessity or the proper means of preserving the confederacy." Virginia was a great empire within herself, and had every thing to sacrifice in surrendering her sovereignty to a central government. On the independence of the States also rested his only hope of preserving the liberties of the people. He entered the Federal Convention, therefore, in 1787, with a stern resolution never to surrender the sovereignty of the States. Others, on the contrary, could conceive of no other plan but a consolidated government, by which the States should be reduced from political societies to mere municipal corporations. The middle ground of compromise had not yet been thought of. Mr. Madison had but a dim perception of its possibility. Even he was for a strong government. In a letter addressed to Edmund Randolph, dated New-York, April 8th, 1787, he says: "I hold it for a fundamental point, that an individual independence of the States is utterly irreconcilable with the idea of an aggregate sovereignty. I think, at the same time, that a consolidation of the States into one simple republic, is not less unattainable than it would be inexpedient. Let it be tried, then, whether any middle ground can be taken." To the untiring exertions of Mr. Madison, both in the Federal Convention and in the Convention of Virginia, are we indebted for the existence of the Constitution. But to Colonel Mason are we indebted for the only democratic and federal features it contains. But for Madison we should have been without a government; but for Mason, that government would have crushed the States, and swallowed up the liberties of the people. To Mason are we indebted for the popular election of members of the House of Representatives, the election of senators by the State Legislatures, and the equal representation of the States in the Senate. In the first, there is some guarantee for the rights of the people; in the second, some protection to the sovereignty and independence of the States. So important were Mr. Mason's services, that we must detain the reader by a few quotations from his speeches to establish his claim to the high distinction here awarded him. When the question of electing members to the House of Representatives by the State Legislatures instead of the people, was before the Convention, Mr. Mason said: " Under the existing Confederacy Congress represent the *States*, and not the *people* of the States; their acts operate on the *States*, and not on the *individuals*. The case will be changed in the new plan of government. The people will be represented; they ought therefore to choose the representatives. Much," he said, " had been alleged against democratic elections. He admitted that much might be said; but it was to be considered that no government was free from imperfections and evils, and that improper elections, in many instances, were inseparable from republican governments. But compare these with the advantage of this form, in favor of the rights of the people, in favor of human nature !" Mr. Mason urged the necessity of retaining the election by the people. " Whatever inconvenience may attend the democratic principle, it must actuate one part of the government. It is the only security for the rights of the people."

When the organization of the Senate was under consideration, Mr. Mason said, " he never would agree to abolish the State Governments, or render them absolutely insignificant. They were as necessary as the General Government, and he would be equally careful to preserve them. He was aware of the difficulty of drawing the line between them, but hoped it was not insurmountable. It has been argued on all hands, that an efficient government is necessary; that to render it such, it ought to have the faculty of self-defence; that to render its different branches effectual, each of them ought to have the same power of self-defence. He did not wonder that such an argument should have prevailed on these points. He only wondered that there should be any disagreement about the necessity of allowing the State governments the same self-defence. If they are to be preserved, as he conceived to be essential, they certainly ought to have this power; and the only mode left of giving it to them, was by allowing them to appoint the second branch of the National Legislature." Dr. Johnson said: "The controversy must be endless while gentlemen differ in the grounds of their arguments; those on one side considering the States as districts of people composing one political society; those on the other, considering them as so many political societies. The fact is, that the States do exist as political societies, and a government is to be formed for them in their political capacity, as well as for the individuals composing them. Does it not seem to follow, that if the States, as such, are to exist, they must be armed with some power of self-defence? *This is the idea of Colonel Mason, who appears to have looked to the bottom of this matter.* Besides the aristocratic and other interests, which ought to have the means of defending themselves, the States have their interests as such, and are equally entitled to like means. On the whole he thought, that, as in some respects the States are to be considered in their political capacity, and in others as districts of individual citizens, the two ideas embraced on different sides, instead of being opposed to each other, ought to be combined; that in *one* branch the *people* ought to be represented, in the *other* the *States*."

Notwithstanding Col. Mason labored to modify the Constitution through its various stages, as much as he could in favor of liberty and the independence of the States, he finally voted against it. His objections were radical, extending to every department of government. He objected to the unlimited powers of taxation, conferred on a House of Representatives, which was but the shadow of representation, and could never inspire confidence in the people. He objected to the marriage, as he called it, between the President and the Senate, and the extraordinary powers conferred on the latter. He insisted that they would destroy any balance in the government, and would enable the President and the Senate, by mutually supporting and aiding each other, to accomplish what usurpations they please upon the rights and liberties of the people. He objected to the judiciary of the United States being so constructed and extended as to absorb and destroy the judiciaries of the several States, thereby rendering the administration of laws tedious, intricate, expensive, and unattainable by a great part of the community. He objected to the

Executive because the President of the United States has no constitutional counsel (a thing unknown in any safe and regular government); he will therefore be unsupported by proper information and advice; and will generally be directed by minions and favorites—or he will become a tool to the Senate—or a council of state will grow out of the principal officers of the great departments—the worst and most dangerous of all ingredients for such a council in a free country; for they may be induced to join in any dangerous and oppressive measures to shelter themselves, and prevent an inquiry into their own misconduct in office.

In a word, said Col. Mason, the Confederation is converted to one general consolidated government, which, from my best judgment of it, is one of the worst curses that can possibly befall a nation.

Such was George Mason—the champion of the States, and the author of the doctrine of State Rights. Many of the prophecies of this profound statesman are recorded in the fulfilments of history—many of the ill forebodings of the inspired orator are daily shaping themselves into sad realities. To the indomitable courage, Roman energy, and inspiring eloquence of Mason and of Henry, we are as much indebted for our independence, as to the sword of the warrior. To their wisdom and sagacity we owe the preservation and the future safety of the ship of state, which, without their forewarning, would have long since been dashed to pieces against the rocks and the quicksands that lay concealed in its pathway. While the eyes of many good and wise men were dazzled with the strength and brilliancy of the young eagle, now pluming himself for a bold and arduous flight, they with keener vision saw the *poison under his wing*, and sought to extract it, lest, in his high career, he might shed pestilence and death on the country which it was his destiny to overshadow and protect.

CHAPTER IX.

EARLY POLITICAL ASSOCIATES.

In the foregoing chapters we may have gone more into detail, and dwelt more on collateral subjects than might appear consistent with a work of this kind. But it was necessary to give the reader a clue to the political opinions of John Randolph. No one can fail to ponder over those chapters, and study the character of those men we have briefly attempted to portray, and do justice to the subject of this memoir. He was bred up in the school of Mason and of Henry. His father-in-law, his uncles, his brother, and all with whom he associated, imbibed the sentiments of those great statesmen, shared their devotion to the principles and the independence of the Commonwealth of Virginia, and participated in all their objections to the new government. Randolph, as we have seen, was a constant attendant on the debates of the first Congress, which had devolved on it the delicate task of organizing the government, and setting its wheels in motion. A majority of the members in that body, from Virginia, belonged to the political school of Mason and of Henry. They owed their appointment to the influence of those men and the alarms excited in the public mind by their predictions. Many of them were the blood relations of John Randolph, and all of them his intimate friends. With these he associated. For the sage delights to take ingenuous youth by the hand, and address to his attentive ear words of truth and of wisdom. When Richard Henry Lee, and Grayson, and Bland, and Tucker, and Page, were seated around the domestic fireside, holding free and familiar discourse on those great questions involved in founding a Republic, we may well conceive that their young friend and kinsman was a welcome and an attentive listener to those high themes, teaching

"What makes a nation happy and keeps it so,
 What ruins kingdoms and lays cities flat."

We may well conceive how his bosom dilated, and his eye kindled with unwonted fire, as they narrated the great battle of giants in the Convention, told of the many-sided wisdom of George Mason.

who in majestic unaffected style better taught the solid rules of civil government than all the oratory of Greece and Rome, and spoke of the deep-toned awful eloquence of Patrick Henry, which rivalled the thunders that rolled over their heads, as he uttered his words of warning. From these familiar communings he daily repaired to Federal Hall, there to hang upon the bar of the House of Representatives, and with keen vision see enacted before him the fulfilment of the statesman's prophecy.

The great subject of taxation was the first to attract his atten. tion. No sooner had Congress been organized, than they com. menced, as he conceived, the work of oppression. The unlimited powers conferred on Congress to tax the people, excited the alarm of those who looked to the independence of the States as the only protection to liberty. They sought a modification of this power in the Convention. Failing there, they asked an amendment of the Constitution. But all their efforts to place restrictions on this all-absorbing power of government, were unavailing. The first exercise of it justified, in their opinion, the worst suspicions which had been excited as to its dangerous and oppressive tendency. They declared that no duty or tax had been imposed, that did not operate as a bounty to one section and a burden on another. While the import and tonnage bills were under discussion, Mr. Smith of South Carolina said, " that the States which adopted the Constitution, expected its administration would be conducted with a favorable hand. The manufacturing States wished the encouragement of manufactures ; the maritime States the encouragement of ship building, and the agricultural States the encouragement of agriculture. Let us view the progress we have made in accommodating their interests :—We have laid heavy duties upon foreign goods to encourage domestic manufactures ; we are now about to lay a tonnage duty, for the encouragement of commerce ; but has any one step been taken to encourage the agricultural States ? So far from it, that all that has been done operates against their interest : every duty we have laid will be heavily felt by South Carolina, while nothing has been done to assist or even encourage her or her agriculture." Mr. Tucker said : " I am opposed to high duties, because they tend to the oppression of certain citizens and States, in order to promote the benefit of other States and other classes of citizens." Mr. Bland laid it down as an incontrovertible truth, "that the agricultural interest is the permanent interest of this country, and therefore ought not to be sacrificed to any other." Mr. Jackson of Georgia, who had accustomed himself, as he said, to a blunt integrity of speech, that attested his sincerity, exclaimed: " They call to my mind a passage of Scripture, where a king, by the advice of inexperienced counsellors, declared to his people, ' my father did laden you with a heavy yoke, but I will add to your burdens.' " Follow those men through all their legislative career and it will be found, though history has given them little credit for it, that they steadily pursued one object as their polar star—resistance to the encroachments of power, and protection to the rights of the people.

The awful squinting towards monarchy which Henry saw in the Executive, made them particularly jealous of that department of government, and caused them to oppose every measure that might tend to increase its power or patronage. On the much mooted question, for example, of removal from office, they insisted that the Senate should be associated with the President. Mr. Bland was the first to give expression to opinions which have since been so often repeated, and the policy of which is still a question. He thought the power given by the Constitution to the Senate, respecting the appointments to office, would be rendered almost nugatory if the President had the power of removal. He thought it consistent with the nature of things, that the power which appointed, should remove; and would not object to a declaration in the resolution, that the President shall remove from office by and with the advice and consent of the Senate.

The bill to establish the Treasury Department contained a clause making it the duty of the Secretary, "to digest and report plans for the improvement and management of the revenue and for the support of public credit."

Mr. Page moved to strike out these words, observing, that to permit the Secretary to go farther than to prepare estimates, would be a dangerous innovation on the constitutional privilege of that house. It would create an undue influence within those walls, because members might be led by the deference commonly paid to men of abilities, who gave an opinion in a case they have thoroughly considered, to support the plan of the minister even against their own judgment. Nor would the mischief stop there. A precedent would be established, which might be extended until ministers of the government should be admitted on that floor, to explain and support the plans they had digested and reported, thereby laying a foundation for an aristocracy or a detestable monarchy.

Mr. Tucker seconded the motion of Mr. Page. He hoped the house was not already weary of executing and sustaining the powers vested in them by the Constitution ; and yet the adoption of this clause would argue that they thought themselves less adequate than an individual to determine what burdens their constituents were able to bear. This was not answering the high expectations that had been formed of their exertions for the general good, or of their vigilance in guarding their own and the people's rights.

But nothing could equal the ferment and disquietude occasioned throughout the country by the proposition which came from the Senate, to confer titles on the President and other officers of government. The committee of the Senate reported, that it was proper to style the President *his highness the President of the United States of America, and Protector of their liberties.* In some of the newspapers the President was called *his highness the President General.* Some even went farther, and declared that as he represented the *majesty of the people,* he might even be styled " *His Majesty,*" without reasonable offence to republican ears. The Senate was denominated *most honorable,* and the same epithet was applied to the members of that body. For instance, it was published that *the most honorable* Rufus King and *the most honorable* Philip Schuyler were appointed senators. And when Mrs. Washington came to New-York, she was accompanied by the " lady of the most honorable Robert Morris." The representatives, and even the secretaries of the executive departments were favored with no higher title than honorable. This habit of conferring titles and drawing distinctions between the different departments of government, and extending those titles and distinctions to persons no way connected with the government, had become very common, and would unquestionably have grown into something worse, but for the debates called forth in the House of Representatives, and the indignation shown by the leading members of that body against such proceedings. " What, sir," said Mr. Tucker, " is the intention of this business? Will it not alarm our fellow-citizens? will it not give them just cause of alarm? Will they not say, that they have been deceived by the Convention that framed the Constitution? That it has been contrived with a view to lead them on by degrees to that kind of government which they have thrown off with abhorrence? Shall we not justify the fears of those who are opposed to the Constitution, because they considered it as insidious and hostile to the liberties of the people?"

"Titles, sir," said Mr. Page, "may do harm and have done harm. If we contend now for a right to confer titles, I apprehend the time will come when we shall form a reservoir for honor, and make our President the fountain of it. In such case may not titles do an injury to the Union? They have been the occasion of an eternal faction in the kingdom we were formerly connected with, and may beget like inquietude in America; for I contend, if you give the title, you must follow it with the robe and the diadem, and then the principles of your government are subverted."

Such were the men with whom John Randolph daily associated, such were the high-toned principles of liberty he was daily accustomed to hear. It was not from the reading of books in his closet, nor from second-hand that he acquired his knowledge of politics, and that extensive acquaintance with the leading characters of the country for which he was so remarkable, but from familiar intercourse with the statesmen and sages who laid the foundations of the government, and commenced the first superstructure of laws and precedents to serve as guides and examples to the statesmen who should come after them.

It was the fortune of this young man to behold the Government in its feeble beginnings, like the simple shepherds on the snowy Vesolo, gazing in the overshadowed fountain of the Po with his scanty waters.

> Mirando al fonte ombroso
> Il Po con pochi umori.

It was his destiny also never to lose sight of it, but to follow it through near half a century of various fortune, now enfeebled by war and faction, now strengthened and enlarged by new States and new powers. How like the Po! he receives as a sovereign the Adda and the Tessino in his course, how ample he hastens on to the sea, how he foams, how mighty his voice, and to him the crown is assigned.

Che 'l Adda, che 'l Tessino
Soverchia in suo cammimo,
Che ampio al Mar' s'affretta
Che si spuma, e si suona,
Che gli si da corona!

———•••———

CHAPTER X.

THOMAS JEFFERSON.

IN the winter of the year 1790–1, Philadelphia had again become, as in times of the old Continental Congress, the great centre of attraction.   By a recent Act it had been made the seat of the Federal Government for *ten* years.   The national legislature, adjourning the 12th of August in New-York, were to assemble the first Monday in December in the new Capitol.   The papers and officers of all the Executive Departments were removed thither early in October, under the conduct of Col. Hamilton, the Secretary of the Treasury.   The President returning from Mount Vernon about the 1st of December, took up his lodgings in a house belonging to Robert Morris, which had been hired and fitted up for the purpose.   And Tuesday, the 7th of December, the 3d session of the 1st Congress was organized in the new Court House of the city, which had been tendered to the government by the town authorities.   We find also our young friend, in this general removal, transferred to the city of Philadelphia.   He took up his residence at No. 154 Arch-street, where he continued with short intervals, till the spring of 1794, when he returned to Virginia.

He was attached to the family of Edmund Randolph, the Attorney General of the United States—the same person his mother pointed him to as the model of an orator, worthy of his imitation. Edmund Randolph was a kinsman in the collateral line.   He was the son of John Randolph, the King's Attorney General about the time of the Revolution.

" Mr. Randolph," says Wirt, " was, in person and manners, among the most elegant gentlemen in the colony, and in his profession one of the most splendid ornaments of the bar." He was the son of Sir John (Knight), who was the son of William of Turkey Island, the great American progenitor of the family. Edmund Randolph inherited many of the accomplishments of his father. But he was more showy than solid. He was also of a vacillating character; voting against the Constitution, then violent in its favor; striving at first to steer above the influence of party, he was at length ingulfed and swept away by its current. "Friend Edmund," said John Randolph years afterwards, "was like the aspen, like the chameleon, ever trembling, ever changing." We may, therefore, suppose that his influence over the mind and character of his pupil was not so great as that of another kinsman who was also a member of General Washington's Cabinet. We allude to Thomas Jefferson, the first cousin of John Randolph's father, and the intimate friend of his youth.

Mr. Jefferson had been abroad some years as Minister to France. Returning on a visit to America, he was invited by General Washington to take charge of the State Department. The invitation was accepted, and he was no sooner installed in office in the spring of 1790, than he became the head and leader of the Republican State-Rights Party, then struggling into existence. Is was not the exalted station alone, but other circumstances that forced him into this unenviable and critical position. The author of the doctrine of State Rights and its eloquent defender, George Mason, and Patrick Henry, were both in retirement. The latter had been offered a seat in the Senate at its organization, but declined. It was tendered to him the second time, on the death of Col. Grayson; he again declined on the ground that he was *too old to fall into those awkward imitations which have now become fashionable*, spoken in allusion to the levees of Mrs. Washington, and the etiquette observed in presentations at the Executive Mansion.

Richard Henry Lee was still in the Senate. He was the gentleman, the scholar, and the orator, but his thoughts ran too much in the smooth channel of established forms, his oratory too elaborate and polished, his disposition too indolent and unambitious to make him the fit leader of a party just coming into existence in a new era, with new thoughts, new principles, and an untried experiment before them. Thomas Jefferson was the man. The qualities of his mind, his education and previous course of life, fitted him to be the bold and intrepid pioneer of that untried course the people had entered upon.

His mind, not of the Platonic cast, was eminently perceptive. The abstract had no charms for him—the spiritual no existence. Devoted to the natural sciences, his metaphysics savored of materialism. Locke's Philosophy of the Senses bounded his conceptions of the human understanding. And the French Disciples, who pursued the doctrines of their master, to the legitimate consequence of sensualism and infidelity, were his chief authorities on all questions of morality and religion.

He was a bold, free thinker, bound to no school. " I never submitted the whole system of my opinions," says he, " to the creed of any party of men whatever, in religion, in philosophy, in politics, or in any thing else."

He was born in a country in the vigor of its youth, untrammelled by habit, and new in all its social relations. He was a child of the Revolution. His ardent temper was kindled by its stormy passions, and his bold intellect grasped the master idea of that great popular movement, which was unfettered freedom to mind, body, and estate. By him the law of primogeniture was destroyed in Virginia, religious freedom established, and universal liberty and equality proclaimed in the Declaration of Independence.

His ruling desire to strike the padlock from the mind, and the fetter from the limbs of mankind, was rather strengthened than abated by his long residence abroad under a despotic government. Being a man of letters and of taste, he was in intimate association with the great writers and master spirits that set the ball of the French Revolution in motion. In boldness and freedom of discussion they surpassed even himself. Speaking of them he says, " the writers of this country (France) now taking the field freely, and unrestrained, or rather revolted by prejudice, will rouse us all from the errors in which we have been hitherto rocked."

A witness of the assembling of the States General, May, 1789, he rejoiced in the downfall of the worn-out French monarchy, of which that was the signal; and was the friend and adviser of those who sought to rebuild on its ruins a freer government, with broader and deeper foundations. He heard the rights of man, the origin of government, the abuses and limitations of power, more freely discussed in the cafés and saloons of Paris than in the court-yards of Virginia.

When the usages and precedents of past times, and of other governments, were scornfully rejected, he saw our own proceedings pointed to as a model, and regarded with an authority like that of the Bible, *open to explanation, but not to question.*

Coming from those scenes of enthusiasm in which he so warmly participated; coming from a land where old prejudices and long established abuses were vanishing away; where the titles of feudalism and the privileges of despotism had been swept away in a night, and a great nation was rejoicing in the dawn of a new era of freedom; he expressed himself astonished to find his own government, which was regarded by others as a model and an example, possessed with a spirit that seemed to him so anti-republican.

This false direction of the government he mainly attributed to the financial schemes of Alexander Hamilton, Secretary of the Treasury.

It is well known that Hamilton advised a Constitution far different from the one adopted. His was a plan of consolidation, with a strong infusion of the aristocratic principle. Having experienced the imbecility of the Confederation, he did not believe the new government practicable. Without a successful example in history, he did not believe in the capacity of the people for self-government. Judging of mankind by the oppressed and degraded specimens of the army and of the Old Country, he did not duly appreciate the intelligent and manly character of his own countrymen, nor did he comprehend the nature of that government of specified powers and divided sovereignty which was the embodiment of their spirit and principles. Placed at the head of the Financial Department of a new government, he was surrounded with many difficulties. The war had left the Confederation and the States burdened with debt; and, exhausted of resources, it became his duty to devise means to resuscitate the one, and to pay off the other. With no experience in his own country, it was natural he should look to the successful example of others. He is considered a wise statesman, who is guided by established precedents, does not strike into unknown paths, but prudently follows the course that has been pursued before him. Judging him by this rule, it would be hard to say how far he ought to have acted otherwise than he did, without hazarding the censure of rashness. " The chief outlines of these plans," says he, in his report on public credit, "are not original, but it is no ill recommendation that they have been tried with success." He recommended that the debts which had been contracted by the several States in the War of Independence, and for which they were bound, as independent sovereignties, should be assumed by the new government,—that these assumed debts, and those contracted by the Confederation, amounting in all to some eighty millions of dollars, though greatly depreciated, and passed from the hands of the original owner, should be funded at their par value ; the interest to be paid regularly by an excise and an impost duty, but the capital to be viewed in the light of an annuity, at the rate of six per centum per annum, redeemable at the pleasure of the government. He also advised the incorporation of a National Bank, as " an institution of primary importance to the prosperous administration of the finances, and of the greatest utility in the operations connected with the support of the public credit." In his Reports, he labors, at great length, to prove the utility of a well-funded National Debt. " It is a well known fact," says he, " that in countries where the national debt is properly funded, it answers most of the purposes of money. Transfers of stock, or public debt, are there equivalent to payments in specie ; or, in other words, stock in the principal transactions of business passes current as specie. Trade is extended by it, because there is a larger capital to carry it on. Agriculture and manufactures are promoted by it for a like reason. The interest of money will be lowered by it, for this is always in ratio to the quantity of money, and to the quickness of circulation. From the combination of these effects, additional aids will be furnished to labor, to industry, and to arts of every kind. But these good effects of a public debt are only to be looked for when, by being well funded, it has acquired an adequate and stable value." These arguments, viewed in connection with the obvious tendency of his policy, led the enemies of Hamilton to declare that he regarded a national debt as a national blessing. Though this inference might be drawn from his doctrine and policy, he yet, in express terms, declared himself against it. " Persuaded as the Secretary is," says he, " that the proper funding of the present debt will render it a national blessing, yet he is so far from acceding to the proposition, in the latitude in which it is sometimes laid down, that 'public debts are public benefits'—a position inviting to prodigality, and liable to dangerous abuse—that he ardently wishes to see it incorporated, as a fundamental maxim, in the system of public credit of the United States, that the creation of debt should always be accompanied with the means of extinguishment." Had those schemes of Hamilton been laid before a British Parliament, they would have been viewed as clearly and ably expressed, and adopted as practicable and expedient; but with us, far other and higher considerations than those of expediency or practicability had to be weighed before the adoption of any measure. The British Parliament was omnipotent; the American Congress limited to a few, well defined, and specified powers. Parliament was only guided by precedent and usage; Congress were controlled by the words of a written Constitution. There was with us, therefore, a primary and fundamental inquiry to be made on all subjects of legislation, unknown to the British statesman. Whenever a measure is proposed, the first question should be, Is it constitutional? Is it authorized by the specified powers laid down in the Charter? or does it encroach on the reserved rights of the States? How does it affect the balance of power between the Executive, Legislative, and Judiciary Departments, or how does it operate on the morals and integrity of the people, upon whose purity depends the existence of a free government? Unless these preliminary questions are always honestly and fairly settled, it is obvious that a republican and a written Constitution cannot long be of any avail. But these considerations did not occur to the mind of Hamilton, in projecting his schemes of finance; they are never started, nor is the slightest allusion made to them in his Reports. He views every subject in its financial aspect, without regard to its political bearing on the new, peculiar, and delicately balanced institutions of his country. This was his great and fatal error. Thomas Jefferson perceived it, and battled against all his schemes as unconstitutional, destructive to the independence of the States, and corrupting to the rulers and to the people.

Posterity, therefore, in pronouncing judgment on these great rivals, would be constrained to say that Hamilton was the able financier, but Jefferson the profound statesman. While the one, with averted countenance, looked back upon the lights the world had already *passed ;* the other, with prophetic vision, caught the rays of a new constellation, just dawning upon it. Gathering up in his capacious mind the tendency and influences of those feelings and opinions, recently developed in American history and institutions, Jefferson conceived a theory of government that embodied the growing sentiments of the people, and fulfilled their idea of what free Republic should be. He stands in relation to the Constitution as Aristotle to the Iliad ; Homer wrote the poem, the philosopher deduced thence the rules of poetry. Mason and other sages made the Constitution, the statesman abstracted from it the doctrines of a federative, representative, republican government; and demonstrated that they alone are adapted to a wide-spread and diversified country, and suited to the genius of a free and enlightened people. Were the question asked, What has America done for the amelioration of mankind ? the answer would not be found in her discoveries in science or improvements in art, but in her political philosophy, as conceived by Jefferson, and developed by his disciples. Though he was the acknowledged leader of what may be called the great American movement, he never spoke in public, and never wrote an essay for the newspapers. His great skill lay in infusing his sentiments into the minds of others by conversation, or correspondence, and making them the instruments of their propagation. Gathering about him the influential men of the new party, he imparted to them more comprehensive views of their own doctrines, and made them the enthusiastic defenders of those principles, the importance of which they had but dimly perceived. Over no one did he exert a greater influence than the young and ardent subject of this memoir. His connection with the family of Edmund Randolph, and his near relationship to Mr. Jefferson himself, brought him frequently within the sphere of that fascinating conversation, which was never spared in the propagation of his opinions. But John Randolph, although a youth, was not the character to yield a blind allegiance to any leader. The disciple differed widely in many doctrines from the master. The grounds of that difference may be found in the writings of another great statesman that begun about that time to take hold on his mind, and deeply impress his character. So great was their influence in after life, that the writings of Edmund Burke became the key to the political opinions of John Randolph. With him Edmund Burke was the great master of political philosophy.

CHAPTER XI.

SMALL BEGINNINGS—EDMUND BURKE—THOMAS PAINE.

Soon after the adjournment of Congress, the 4th of March, 1791, General Washington left the seat of government, and commenced his tour through the Southern States. The secretaries at the head of the different departments, were left as a kind of committee to conduct affairs in his absence.

About this time the public mind began to be greatly agitated not only by the wonderful events of the French Revolution, but the various speculations on those extraordinary occurrences that daily teemed from our own political press. The two leading productions, that were held up on both sides as setting forth most clearly and fully the views they respectively entertained, proceeded from men who were well and favorably known in America as the friends of liberty.

Edmund Burke had not only defended the colonies, in the British Parliament, against the unjust and oppressive taxation of the ministry, but had nobly vindicated their character and their motives. Throughout America his name was venerated and beloved. Well might he exclaim, " I love a manly, moral, regulated liberty as well as any man, be he who he will; and perhaps I have given as good proofs of my attachment to that cause in the whole course of my public conduct."

Thomas Paine was in America during the struggle of the Colonies for independence, and greatly aided the cause by his spirited and patriotic essays. It was generally conceded that in the darkest hour of the Revolution. when our armies were disbanded, and the hearts of the people despondent, he helped to rally the one, and to animate the other by his bold and patriotic appeals. The first men of the nation forgot his many vices, and cherished his person and his reputation in grateful remembrance of his valuable services

General Washington was his constant correspondent while abroad, and while in America the house of Jefferson was his home.

In the great struggle for liberty which had now commenced on the other side of the Atlantic, these two champions of the cause took opposite sides.   Burke expressed a hearty wish that France might be animated by a spirit of rational liberty, and provide a permanent body in which that spirit might reside, and an effectual organ by which it might act; but, he said, it was his misfortune to entertain great doubts concerning several material points in their late transactions.   Paine, on the other hand, had no doubts; inflamed by the spirit of liberty, suddenly burst forth in the hearts of the French people, and dazzled by its brilliant achievements, he threw himself warmly into the popular cause without knowing or caring for the consequences.

The habits, education, social position, and natural temperament of the two men led to this wide difference.   Burke had been long trained in the school of experience, Paine was the mere speculative theorist.   The one judged of the future by the past, the other projected the future not from the solid ground of experience, but the hopeful theories of his own sanguine imagination.   Burke was the cautious statesman, Paine the enthusiastic patriot.

The statesman cannot stand forward and give praise or blame to any thing which relates to human actions, and human concerns, on a simple view of the object, as it stands stripped of every relation, in all the nakedness and solitude of metaphysical abstraction.   Circumstances which with some pass for nothing, give in reality to every political principle its distinguishing color, and discriminating effect.   The circumstances are what render every civil and political scheme beneficial or noxious to mankind.   Burke was guided by this great political maxim, the truth of which he had been taught by long experience.   " I must be tolerably sure," said he, " before I venture publicly to congratulate men upon a blessing, that they have really received one.   Flattery corrupts both the receiver and the giver; and adulation is not of more service to the people than to kings.   I should therefore suspend my congratulations on the new liberty of France, until I was informed how it had been combined with government, with public force, with the discipline and obedience of armies, with the collection of an effective and well distributed revenue, with morality and religion, with solidity and property, with peace and order, with civil and social manners. The effect of liberty to individuals is, that they may do what they please; we ought to see what it will please them to do, before we risk congratulations, which may soon be turned into complaints. Prudence would dictate this in the case of separate insulated private men; but liberty, when men act in bodies, *is power*. Considerate people, before they declare themselves, will observe the use which is made of power; and particularly of so trying a thing as *new* power in *new* persons, of whose principles, tempers, and dispositions, they have little or no experience. Better to be despised for too anxious apprehensions, than ruined by too confident a security."

Paine, on the other hand, with all the inexperienced statesmen of France, followed a transcendental idea. He saw a great and powerful nation burst the oppressive and galling fetters of feudal ages, and proclaim themselves a free people. With all the lovers of mankind through the world, he lifted up his hands and clapped for joy. He beheld the event and rejoiced. But how this new power might be used by the new men, of whose principles, tempers, and dispositions he had no experience, he did not stop to inquire; he did not consult the maxims of prudence, or the principles of reason, but obeyed the impulses of a warm, enthusiastic and patriotic heart. Dictated by such a spirit, his writings might serve to animate, but not to instruct, to inspire a kindred enthusiasm, but to afford no nourishment to the hungering mind. They have perished with the occasion that gave them birth, while the immortal truths scattered as gems through the writings of Edmund Burke, are set like stars in the firmament for lights and guides to mankind.

Burke wrote his reflections on the Revolution in France in the month of May, 1790; and some short time thereafter gave them to the public. Paine's answer, entitled the Rights of Man, soon followed. The first and only copy of this latter production made its appearance in Philadelphia about the first of May, 1791; it was in the hands of Beckley. He lent the pamphlet to Mr. Jefferson, with a request, that when he should have read it, he would send it to Smith the printer, who wished it for re-publication. As he was a stranger to Smith, Mr. Jefferson, in sending the pamphlet, wrote him a note, stating why he, a stranger, had sent it, namely, that Mr.

Beckley had desired it; and, to take off a little of the dryness of a note, he added, that he was glad to find it was to be reprinted, that something would at length be publicly said against the political heresies which had lately sprung up amongst us, and that he did not doubt our citizens would rally again around the standard of Common Sense In these allusions, Mr. Jefferson had reference to the *Discourses on Davila*, which had filled Fenno's paper for a twelvemonth without contradiction. Mr. Adams, the Vice-President, was the reputed author of those Discourses. When the reprint of Paine's pamphlet appeared, it had prefixed to it the note of Mr. Jefferson, which the printer had appended without giving him the slightest intimation of such an intention. In this unexpected way was the .eader of the new and rising Democratic Party identified with the political doctrines of Paine, the principles of the French Revolution, and made publicly to avow his hostility to the political heresies which had lately sprung up in our own country. In addition to this, Paine's pamphlet, though without authority, had been dedicated to General Washington. The pamphlet, accompanied with these circumstances, produced a considerable excitement in the political circles of Philadelphia. Major Beckwith, an unofficial British agent, made it a subject of formal complaint to the private secretary of the President. He expressed surprise that the pamphlet should be dedicated to the President of the United States, and averred that it had received the unequivocal official sanction of the Secretary of State, not as Mr. Jefferson, but as the Secretary of State.

On the other hand, Mr. Adams was not slow in declaring his opposition to the sentiments expressed in Paine's pamphlet. In the most pointed manner, he expressed his detestation of the book and its tendency. "I was at the Vice-President's house," says the private secretary, writing to General Washington, "and while there, the Doctor and Mrs. Rush came in. The conversation turned on this book, and Dr. Rush asked the Vice-President what he thought of it. After a little hesitation, he laid his hand upon his breast, and said in a very solemn manner, 'I detest that book and its tendency, from the bottom of my heart.'"

Mr. Jefferson, in writing to the President about the same time, says: "Paine's answer to Burke's pamphlet begins to produce some squibs in our public papers. In Fenno's paper they are Burkites;

in the others, they are Painites. One of Fenno's was evidently from the author of the *Discourses on Davila.* I am afraid the indiscretion of a printer has committed me with my friend Mr. Adams, for whom, as one of the most honest and disinterested men alive, I have a cordial esteem, increased by long habits of concurrence in opinion in the days of his republicanism; and ever since his apostasy to hereditary monarchy and nobility, though we differ, we differ as friends should do.

" Mr. Adams will unquestionably take to himself the charge of political heresy, as conscious of his own views of drawing the present government to the form of the English constitution, and, I fear, will consider me as meaning to injure him in the public eye. I certainly never made a secret of my being anti-monarchical, and anti-aristocratical; but I am sincerely mortified to be thus brought foward on the public stage, where to remain, to advance, or to retire, will be equally against my love of silence and quiet, and my abhorrence of dispute."

We have given the minute history of this transaction, not only because of its important bearing on the subject of this memoir, but because it traces up to the fountain head one of the many streams which, flowing together in after times, have conspired to swell the mighty tide of party spirit that now sweeps through the land.

John Randolph was in Philadelphia during this time; participated in the interest and excitement of the occasion; heard the discussions in the various circles into which he was freely admitted; saw people become inflamed with the Anglomania or the Gallomania, and arrange themselves under the banners of their respective champions as Burkites or Painites, according as they were inclined to admire the British Constitution, or the more free and levelling doctrines of the French Revolution, and plainly perceived that that great event was destined to swallow up every minor consideration, and to give character and complexion to the politics of his own country. But while he was a democratic republican, a follower of Jefferson in all that pertained to his political doctrines and interpretation of the Constitution, pre-eminently a disciple of the Mason and Henry school of States' rights, yet he did not become a Painite in the sense that term was used by Mr. Jefferson. In the expressive language of Governor Tazewell, he could not bear Tom Paine; he ad

mired Burke, though himself a jacobin ! While he rejoiced in the overthrow of despotism by the French people, he could not fail to perceive
that they were better fitted to destroy tyrants than obey the laws ; and
hastened to learn those lessons of wisdom that fell from the lips of
the great master of political philosophy, who, from the few events already transpired, foretold with the clearness of a Hebrew prophet,
the wretched end to which they were hastening. We regard this as
a most remarkable fact in the history of that young man. The design of Burke was eminently conservative. He saw the consequences of a dissemination of French revolutionary doctrines among
the English people; his purpose was to shut out from England
what the kings of Europe called the *French evil.*

With this design, he gives a most beautiful and masterly exposition of the British Constitution, from Magna Charta to the
declaration of rights. He calls it an entailed inheritance, derived to
us (the people of England) from our forefathers, and to be transmitted
to our posterity ; as an estate specially belonging to the people of
this kingdom—an inheritable crown—an inheritable peerage ; and a
House of Commons, and a people inheriting privileges, franchises,
and liberties from a long line of ancestors.

With the same masterly hand he makes bare the composition of
the French National Assembly—the characters that compose it—the
few acts they had already performed during a single year; and then
predicts, from these elements of calculation, that France will be
wholly governed by the agitators in corporations, by societies in the
towns formed of directors in assignats, and trustees for the sale of
church lands, attorneys, agents, money-jobbers, speculators, and adventurers, composing an ignoble oligarchy, founded on the destruction of the crown, the church, the nobility, and the people. Here
end all the deceitful dreams and visions of this equality, and the
rights of man. In the *Serbonian bog* of this base oligarchy, they are
all absorbed, sunk, and lost for ever. The present form of the
French commonwealth, he says, cannot remain ; but before its final
settlement it may be obliged to pass, as one of our poets says,
" through great varieties of untried being ;" and in all its transmi
grations to be purified by fire and blood !

It is not surprising that such a book as this should be seized
pon by the partisans of England, and held up as a justification of

their doctrine that the British Constitution, with all its corruptions, was the best model of a government the world ever saw; and as a vindication of the abhorrence they had expressed for the doctrines of the French Revolution, and their tendency.

But it is a matter of no little surprise that a mere stripling, a youth of some eighteen or twenty years of age, himself a republican and a jacobin, with an ardent temperament and a lively imagination, should have the independence to ponder over the pages of a book condemned by his associates; the judgment to perceive its value, and the discrimination to leave out that which peculiarly belonged to England or to France, without being inflamed by its arguments, and to appropriate to himself those rich treasures of wisdom to be found in its pages : the massive ingots of gold that constitute the greater part of that magnificent monument of human intellect. As we have said, the writings of Edmund Burke are the key to the political opinions of John Randolph.

In after life, as he grew in experience, those opinions became more and more assimilated to the doctrines of his great master.

His position in society, his large hereditary possessions, his pride of ancestry, his veneration for the commonwealth of Virginia, her ancient laws and institutions; his high estimation of the rights of property in the business of legislation,—all conspired to shape his thoughts, and mould them in matters pertaining to domestic polity after the fashion of those who have faith in the old, the long-established, and the venerable. No one can trace his course in the Virginia Convention, or read his speeches, which had a remarkable influence on the deliberations of that body, without perceiving that his deep and practical wisdom is of the same stamp, and but little inferior to the great Gamaliel at whose feet he was taught.

CHAPTER XII.

YOUTHFUL COMPANIONS.

WE are not to suppose that a youth, in the joyous hours of his dawning faculties, devoted his time, or any great portion of it, to the society of sober statesmen, or to the grave study of political science. Far other were the associates and companions of John Randolph during his residence in the Quaker city, even at that day renowned for its intelligent, polished, gay, and fashionable society.

With occasional visits to Virginia, and a short residence of a few weeks in Williamsburg during the autumn of 1793, Philadelphia, till the spring of 1794, continued to be his place of abode. His companions were Batte, Carter, Epps, Marshall, and Rose of Virginia; Bryan of Georgia, and Rutledge of South Carolina. Most of these were young men of wealth, education, refined manners, high sense of honor, and of noble bearing. John W. Epps afterwards became a leading member of Congress, married the daughter of Mr. Jefferson, and in 1813 was the successful rival of Randolph on the hustings before the people. Joseph Bryan likewise in a short time became a leading character in Georgia, was a member of Congress from that State, and to the day of his untimely death continued to be the bosom friend of the associate of his youth. Most of the others, though unknown to fame, adorned the social sphere in which they moved, and were noble specimens of the unambitious scholar and the gentleman. Thomas Marshall, the brother of the Chief Justice, and father of Thomas Marshall, the late member of Congress, is still living. He is a man of extraordinary powers, and great learning: his wit and genial humor are not to be surpassed. Those who knew them well agree that his natural talents surpass those of his late illustrious brother, the Chief Justice. Robert Rose was a man of genius; he married the sister of Mr. Madison, and might have risen to any station in his profession (which he merely studied as an ornament), in letters, or in politics, that he aspired to; but, like too many in his sphere and station in society, he lived a life of inglorious ease, and wasted his gifts, like the rose its sweets, on the desert air. With such companions, we may readily suppose there was fun and frolic enough; but nothing low or mean, or vulgar or sordid, in all their intercourse. The correspondence of some of those young men at that period is now before the writer. It is very clear that Randolph was the centre of attraction in that joyous circle of boon companions. And while there can be no doubt that they indulged in all the license allowed at that time to young men of their rank and fortune, yet he passed through that critical period of life without the contamination of a single vice. Though many years afterwards, he said, " I know by fatal experience the fascinations of a town life, how they estrange the mind from its old habits and attachments." Bryan, in February, 1794, wishes him all the happiness that is attendant on *virtue and regularity*. Again, in speaking of one of their companions, to whom Randolph had become strongly attached, he expresses a hope that he may prove worthy of the friendship,—" possessing as you do," says he, " a considerable knowledge of mankind, your soul would not have knit so firmly to an unworthy object."

Most of those young men were students of medicine. Randolph also attended with them several courses of lectures in anatomy and physiology—sciences that are indispensable not only to a professional, but to a liberal and gentlemanly education. We do not learn, as many have supposed, that he studied law at that time in the office of his relation, Edmund Randolph, the Attorney General. Two years after leaving Philadelphia, Bryan writes that he is rejoiced to hear his friend has serious thoughts of *attacking the law*. He tells us himself that he never, after Theodorick broke up his regular habits at New-York, devoted himself to any systematic study, except for the few weeks he was in Williamsburg, in the autumn of 1793. So we conclude that he never made the law a matter of serious study, certainly never with the view of making it a profession.

In April, 1794, he returned to Virginia. In June he was twenty-one years of age, and then took upon himself the management of his patrimonial estates, which were heavily encumbered with a British debt. Matoax was still in the family, but was sold about this time for *three thousand pounds sterling*, to pay off a part of the above debt. The mansion house has since been burnt, but the same estate now would not bring three hundred dollars, although it is within three miles of Petersburg.

Richard Randolph, the elder brother, lived at Bizarre, an estate on the Appomatox, about ninety miles above Petersburg. It is near Farmville, but on the opposite side of the river, in Cumberland county. John made his brother's house his home, while his own estate, called Roanoke, lay about thirty miles south on the Roanoke river, in the county of Charlotte.

CHAPTER XIII

RICHARD RANDOLPH.

With Richard the reader has already formed some slight acquaintance. In 1789 he married Judith Randolph, the daughter of Thomas Mann Randolph, of Tuckahoe. Judith was a relation in both the direct and collateral lines. Her father, Thomas Mann, was the son of William, who was the son of Thomas of Tuckahoe, the son of William, the first founder of the family in Virginia. Her mother was Anne Cary, the daughter of Mary Cary, who was the daughter of the first Richard of Curles, and the sister of the second Richard of Curles, the grandfather of Richard her husband. This lady was remarkable for her great strength of mind, for her many virtues, and high accomplishments. Richard was regarded as the most promising young man in Virginia. His talents were only surpassed by his extraordinary goodness of character.

Let his own grateful acknowledgments to his father-in-law, Judge Tucker, speak for him. "Accept," says he, "once more, my beloved father, the warmest effusions of a heart that knows but one tie superior to that which binds him to the .best of parental friends. When I look back to those times wherein I was occupied in forming my mind for the reception of professional knowledge, and indeed to whatever period of my life I cast my eyes, something presents itself to remind me of the source whence sprung all my present advantages and happiness. Something continually shows my father to me in the double light of parent and friend. While I recognize all the attention I have received from him, all the precepts inculcated by him; while I feel that if I have any virtuous emotions or pleasures, they are all derived from him, that to him I owe whatever capacity I possess of being useful in the world I am in—while all these reflections are crowding into my mind, I feel a sensation that all are strangers to, who have not known such a friend. The feelings which arise from a sense of gratitude for the kindness and friendship of my father—the tender affection inspired by his virtues and his love, are as delightful to my soul, as the knowledge of being obliged by those we despise is painful and oppressive." A grateful heart obliged by a worthy and beloved object, as Milton finely says, "*by owing owes not*, but finds itself at once indebted and discharged." And again:—" The time is now at hand, when I hope you will be relieved from all further anxiety, and the embarrassments you have too long endured in the management of our patrimony; when my brother and myself will take on ourselves our own troubles, and when the end of your administration of our little affairs will furnish the world with one complete and perhaps solitary example, shall I only say, of an unerring guardian of infant education and property? An example, I glory in boasting it, of an adopted father surpassing in parental affection, and unremitted attention to his adopted children, all the real fathers who are known to any one. I can most sincerely and truly declare, that in no one moment of my whole life, have I ever felt the loss in the least trifle."

One of the debts owing by the father to creditors in England was a simple open account, that might have been easily avoided, as it was not binding on the estate devised to the sons. But Richard wrote to Judge Tucker, " I urge the propriety, indeed necessity, of paying the open account which my mother always said was recognized by my father as a true one, and ought therefore honestly to be discharged. For myself I can never bear the idea of a just debt due from my father to *any* one, remaining unsatisfied while I have property of his, firmly convinced as I am that he had no equitable right, whatever power the law may have given him, of devising me land or any thing else, to the loss of any of his just creditors, and that under this conviction, it will be equally iniquitous in me to retain such property, suffering these just claims to pass unnoticed."

Nor did this noble-minded man stop here in his high sense of right and justice. He again writes to his late guardian :—" With regard to the division of the estate, I have only to say, that I want not a single negro for any other purpose than his immediate liberation. I consider every individual thus unshackled as the source of future generations, not to say nations of freemen ; and I shudder when I think that so insignificant an animal as I am, is invested with this monstrous, this horrid power. For the land I care not a jot. I am ready to yield all my claim to it. I am ready to yield Matoax or its profits, and all of my Prince Edward and Cumberland land, except a bare support, rather than see those wretches sacrificed at the shrine of unjust and lawless power."

Richard was bred to the profession of law, but never could be induced to engage in the practice. Nothing but necessity, he declared, could overcome his disinclination. It was not the fatigue and disgust that repelled him so much as the chicane and low cunning, which his observation led him to conclude were the essential qualifications of a county court lawyer. " What inducement," exclaimed he, " have I to leave a happy and comfortable home to search for bustle, fatigue and disappointment ? I have a comfortable subsistence, which is enough to make me happy."

The family circle was composed of Richard, his wife, Nancy the sister of Mrs. Randolph, John (Theodorick had died in February, 1791), and Mrs. Anna Bland Dudley and her children. Mrs. Dudley was the daughter of Mrs. Eaton, the sister of John Randolph's mother. They lived in North Carolina. Her husband was unfortunate, had died and left his family poor and dependent on their friends. Richard went himself to North Carolina, brought Mrs. Dudley and her children to Virginia, and gave them an asylum under the hospitable roof of Bizarre.

John did not confine himself much to home or business. He kept up a regular correspondence with many of his old companions ; amused himself with his dog and gun, and visited from place to place among his friends. As a specimen of his wanderings, we give the following memorandum made by himself :

November, 1795.
Monday, 30.—Bizarre to D. Meade's.

December.

Tuesday, 1.—Capt. Murray's.
          3.—Richmond.
Wednesday, 9.—Petersburg.
Thursday, 17.—Left Petersburg to Jenito.
Friday, 18.—To F. Archer's and D. Meade's.
Saturday, 19.—D. Meade's to Bizarre; received letter from Rutledge.
Sunday, 20.—Roanoke.
Sunday, 27.—From Roanoke to Bizarre.
Tuesday, 29.—To Roanoke.
Thursday, 31.—To Bizarre.
January, '96, New-Year's day at Bizarre.
Saturday, 2.—To Major Eggleston's.
Sunday, 3.—Colonel Botts.
Monday, 4.—Petersburg.
Friday, 15.—At Jenito Bridge.
Saturday, 16.—At D. Meade's. } rain.
Sunday, 17.—At D. Meade's.

———•••———

CHAPTER XIV.

VISIT TO CHARLESTON AND GEORGIA.

His old friends, Bryan and Rutledge, had for some time been urging him to pay them a visit. Bryan directed his letters to "Citizen John Randolph, of Charlotte county, Virginia," and says, "I am happy to hear you are settled in a healthy part of Virginia, but I am almost inclined to think my friend premature in settling so early, as you will in a great measure be deprived of that freedom you know so well how to enjoy." He then urges him to visit Georgia. "You will find me on the sea-coast," says he, "and as you bribe me with a pipe, I can promise in return best Spanish segars and the best of liquors—good horses, deer-hunting in perfection—good companions, that is to say, not merely bottle crackers, Jack, but good, sound, well-informed Democrats."

This long-expected visit was made in the spring of 1796. On the back of a letter received from Rutledge, he lays out the programme of his journey, with the various distances and stages, from Bizarre to Charleston; then concludes the memorandum with these words: " Where I hope to embrace the friend of my youth; the sight of whom will ten thousand times repay this tedious journey."

E. S. Thomas, in his Reminiscences of the last Sixty-five Years, printed at Hartford, in 1840, thus speaks of him: " On a bright sunny morning, early in February, 1796, might have been seen entering my bookstore in Charleston, S. C., a fine-looking, florid complexioned old gentleman, with hair white as snow, which, contrasted with his own complexion, showed him to have been a free liver, or *bon-vivant* of the first order. Along with him was a tall, gawky-looking flaxen-haired stripling, apparently of the age from sixteen to eighteen, with a complexion of a good parchment color, beardless chin, and as much assumed self-consequence as any two-footed animal I ever saw. This was John Randolph. I handed him from the shelves volume after volume, which he tumbled carelessly over, and handed back again. At length he hit upon something that struck his fancy. My eye happened to be fixed upon his face at the moment, and never did I witness so sudden, so perfect a change of the human countenance. That which before was dull and heavy, in a moment became animated and flushed with the brightest beams of intellect. He stepped up to the old gray-headed gentleman, and, giving him a thundering slap on the shoulder, said, " Jack, look at this ! !" I was young, then, but I never can forget the thought that rushed upon my mind at the moment, which was that he was the most impudent youth I ever saw. He had come to Charleston to attend the races. There was then living in Charleston a Scotch Baronet, by the name of Sir John Nesbit, with his younger brother Alexander, of the ancient house of Nesbits, of Dean Hall, some fifteen miles from Edinburgh. Sir John was a very handsome man, and as ' gallant gay Lothario' as could be found in the city. He and Randolph became intimate, which led to a banter between them for a race, in which each was to ride his own horse. The race came off during the same week, and Randolph won; some of the ladies exclaiming at the time, ' though Mr. Randolph had won the race, Sir John had won their hearts.' This was not so much to be wondered at, when you contrasted the elegant form and graceful style of riding of the Baronet, with the uncouth and awkward manner of his competitor."

From Charleston, Randolph pursued his journey into Georgia, and spent several months with his friend Bryan.

We cannot doubt that these young men enjoyed themselves in the manner that young men usually enjoy themselves on such occasions. Bryan, in his subsequent letters, frequently alludes to some amusing incident that occurred during the sojourn of his friend in Georgia. " My eldest brother," says he, " still bears a friendly remembrance of the *rum ducking* you gave him."

But the all-absorbing subject in Georgia, at the time of Randolph's visit, was the Yazoo question.

On the 7th day of February, 1795, the Legislature of Georgia passed an act authorizing the sale of four tracts of land, therein described, and comprehending the greater part of the country west of the Alabama river, to four companies, called the Georgia, the Georgia Mississippi, the Upper Mississippi, and the Tennessean Companies, for which they were to pay five hundred thousand dollars. The land contained within the boundaries of the several companies was estimated by the claimants at *forty millions* of acres. The sale of a country so extensive, for a sum so far below its value, excited immediate and universal indignation in the State of Georgia. The motives of the Legislature were questioned and examined. Their corruption was established on the most indisputable evidence. Upwards of sixty-four depositions were taken, that developed a scene of villany and swindling unparalleled in the history of any country. On comparing a list of the names of the companies with the names of the persons who voted for the land, it appeared that all the members in the Senate and House of Representatives of Georgia, who voted in favor of the law, were, with one single exception, interested in and parties to the purchase. Every member who voted for the law received either money or land for his vote. The guardians of the rights of the people united with swindlers, defrauded their constituents, sold their votes, betrayed the delegated trust reposed in them, and basely divided among themselves the lands of the people of Georgia. This flagrant abuse of power, this enormous act of corruption, was viewed with abhorrence by every honest man. The press through the country burst out in a blaze of indignation. All the grand juries of the State (except in two counties, where there were corrupt majorities of Yazoo men,) presented this law as a public robbery. and a deliberate fraud. The Convention which met in the month -▴ May, 1795, at Louisville, was crowded with petitions from every part of the State, which, by an order of the Convention, was referred to the succeeding Legislature. This Legislature was elected solely with reference to that question. Repeal or no repeal, Yazoo and anti-Yazoo, was the only subject canvassed before the people. On the 30th of January, 1796, an act was passed, with only three dissenting voices, declaring the usurped act of February, 1795, void, and expunging the same from the public records. At a subsequent period, this expunging act was engrafted on the Constitution, and made a fundamental law of the land.

Randolph arrived in Georgia in the midst of this excitement, and shared with his friends their indignation at that flagrant act of corruption on the part of the agents of the people. The famous Yazoo claim, which afterwards made such a noise in Congress, was preferred by the New England Mississippi Land Company, to recover from Congress the value of the lands thus fraudulently obtained. It was in opposition to this application, that Randolph immortalized himself in speeches that will stand the test of time, and of criticism the severest scrutiny. It was among those who had been betrayed, in the midst of the people who were burning with shame at the insult and indignity offered them, that he caught the fire of inspiration that winged his words with such a withering power as to drive from the halls of Congress for more than ten years, so long as he had a seat there, all those who were interested in the nefarious scheme.

John Randolph returned from this visit of friendship, and arrived in Virginia about the first of July. He was destined to experience a shock such as he had never felt before. His brother Richard died the 14th of June, on Tuesday, about 4 o'clock in the morning; such was the minute record made of it himself. This sudden and unexpected calamity crushed him down.

Next to the death of his mother this was the severest blow he had ever received. His mother died when he was a child. Though mournful, yet sweet was the memory of her image, associated with those days of innocence and brightness. But the strong bonds of fraternal affection in grown up men, were now torn asunder; the much prized treasure of a brother's love is suddenly taken from him, leaving no pleasant memories to soothe the pain of so deep a wound. His best friend and counsellor, the first born of his father's house, its pride, and cherished representative, hurried away in his absence to an untimely grave—he not present to receive his last breath, and to close his lifeless eyes. He never recovered from this stroke. The anguish of his heart was as fresh on the fiftieth anniversary of the birthday of that brother, as when first he experienced the desolation made in the domestic circle at Bizarre by the hand of death. How touching is the following simple note addressed to his brother, Henry St. George Tucker, many, many years after this sad event ! " Dear Henry :—Our poor brother Richard was born 1770. He would have been fifty-six years old on the 9th of this month. I can no more. J. R. of R." In the deep solitude of his heart, the only green spot was the memory of the days of his youth.

Few events exerted a greater influence over the mind and character of John Randolph than the death, the untimely and sudden death, of his brother. Richard, as we have said, was the most promising man in Virginia. John Thompson, himself a man of brilliant genius, nipped also in the blooming, thus writes: " Grief like yours, my dear friend, is not to be alleviated by letters of condolence. The anguish of hearts like yours cannot be mitigated by the maxims of an unfeeling and unnatural philosophy. Let such consolation be administered to the insensible being, who mourns without sorrow, whose tears fall from a sense of decorum, and whose melancholy ceases the instant fashion permits. Let some obdurate moralist instruct this selfish being, that the death of a friend is not a misfortune, and that sensibility is weakness. Nothing but sympathy ought to be offered to you. Accept that offering from one of your sincerest friends. My heart was long divided between you and your brother. His death has left a void which you will occupy. I will fondly cher ish his memory. Painful as the retrospect is, I will often contemplate his virtues and his talents. Never shall I perform that holy exercise without feeling new virtue infused into my soul. To you I will give that friendship, of which he can no longer be sensible. Take it, and return it if you can. I cannot write your brother's eulogium. Although his fame was only in the dawn, although like a meteor he perished as soon as he began to dazzle, I cannot sound his praise. His life would be a pathetic tale of persecuted genius and oppressed innocence. The fictions of romance cannot present so affecting a story. When his country was preparing to do him ample justice, and to recompense his sufferings by her warmest admiration,

Death marked him for his victim. Modern degeneracy had not reached him.

"Nervous eloquence and dauntless courage fitted him to save his sinking country. He has left no memorial of his talents behind. He was born to enlighten posterity, but posterity will not hear of him.

"O Providence, thy dispensations are dark! We cannot comprehend them! His amiable wife, his children—but here my heart begins to bleed—I cannot go on."

----●●----

CHAPTER XV.

AT HOME.

JOHN RANDOLPH, now became the head of a large household, was suddenly thrown into a position of great responsibility. His own estate was very large; so was his brother's—and both were heavily encumbered with a British debt, contracted by the father many years before.

Richard liberated his slaves. This was a mark of his great benevolence of feeling and nobleness of character. But it proved in the end to be a mistaken philanthropy. Left in the country where they had been slaves, those negroes soon became idle and profligate vagabonds and thieves; a burthen to themselves, and a pest to the neighborhood. The family at Bizarre consisted of Mrs. Randolph, her two infant children, St. George and Tudor, Mrs. Dudley and her children, Nancy and John Randolph. For nearly fifteen years, till Bizarre was destroyed by fire, he continued at the head of the household. Though twenty-three years of age at the death of his brother, he had the appearance of a youth of sixteen, and was not grown. He grew a full head taller after this period.

His extreme sensibility had been deeply touched—the quick irritability of his temper exasperated by the tragic events of his family. A father's face he had never seen, save what his lively imagination would picture to itself from the lines of a miniature likeness which he always wore in his bosom. The fond caresses of a tender

mother, *who alone knew him,* were torn from him in his childhood
The second brother had died in his youth ; and now the oldest, the
best, the pride and hope of the family, after years of suffering and
persecution, just as he had triumphed over calumny and oppression,
was suddenly called away. We may well imagine how deep, how
poignant was his grief, when thirty years thereafter, in the solitude
of his hermitage at Roanoke, his lively fancy brought back those
early scenes with all the freshness of recent events, and caused him
to exclaim with the Indian Chief, who had been deprived of all his
children by the white man's hand—" Not a drop of Logan's blood—
father's blood except St. George, the most bereaved and pitiable of
the step-sons of nature !"

His room at Bizarre was immediately under the chamber of
Mrs. Dudley. She never waked in the night that she did not hear
him moving about, sometimes striding across the floor, and exclaiming, " *Macbeth hath murdered sleep !* Macbeth hath murdered
sleep !" She has known him to have his horse saddled in the dead
of night, and ride over the plantation with loaded pistols.

His natural temper became more repulsive ; he had no confidential friend, nor would any tie, however sacred, excuse inquiry. Why
should it ? for who can minister to a mind diseased, or pluck from
the heart its rooted sorrow ? Why then expose, even to friendship's
eye, the lacerated wounds that no balm can cure ?

He grew more restless than ever, though his home had every
external arrangement to make it agreeable. Hear him describe it :
" Mrs. Randolph, of Bizarre, my brother's widow, was, beyond all
comparison, the nicest and best housewife that I ever saw. Not one
drop of water was ever suffered to stand on her sideboard, except
what was in the pitcher ; the house, from cellar to garret, and in
every part, as clean as hands could make it ; and every thing as it
should be to suit even my fastidious taste. Never did I see or
smell any thing to offend my senses, or my imagination." Those
who lived there had been taught in the school of affliction. Chastened and subdued by their own sorrows, they had learned to feel
for the misfortunes of others. That home, which could not fill the
aching void of its youthful master's heart, or soothe the earnest
longings of his wounded soul, was made the delightful retreat and

asylum of the distressed and the unfortunate. There could they find sympathy and encouragement.

To escape from the burden and pain of his own thoughts, John Randolph often fled to his friends in distant parts of the country. For the next three years he was frequently found at the residence of his father-in-law, in Williamsburg. He often visited Mr. Wickham, who lived in the same city. That gentleman had taken a great liking to him. He was the agent of the British creditors, who held a mortgage on the Randolph estates. His forbearance and indulgence were highly appreciated by him on whom the whole burthen of payment had now fallen. He returned this act of kindness by an ardent affection for the man, and a high admiration of his character. He has said, " John Wickham was my best of friends without making any professions of friendship for me ; and the best and wisest man I ever knew except Mr. Macon."

When interrogated by Mr. Wickham as to what he had been doing, Governor Tazewell, who was his youthful companion on those visits, says his answer was—*Nothing, sir, nothing !* Yet he showed that he had been reading, and that he had digested well what he had read. The conversation was generally on the politics of the day— the French Revolution, and Burke, which was his political Bible.

That he pursued no systematic course of reading at this time is certain. Mrs. Dudley says his habits of study one could not ascertain, as he was never long enough in one place to study much. She has frequently heard him lament that he was fond of light reading— has known him to seat himself by the candle, where she and Mrs. Randolph were knitting, turn over the leaves of a book carelessly, like a child, without seeming to read, and then lay it down and tell more about it than those who had studied it. He had a fine taste for music, but it was uncultivated. " I inherited from your grandmother," says he, writing to his niece, Mrs. Bryan, " an exquisite ear, which has never received the slightest cultivation. This is owing in a great measure to the low estimate that I saw the fiddling, piping gentry held in when I was young ; but partly to the torture that my poor brother used to inflict upon me, when essaying to learn to play upon the violin, now about forty years ago. I have a taste for painting, but never attempted drawing. I had read a great deal upon it and had seen a few good pictures before I went to England : there I as-

tonished some of their connoisseurs as much by the facility
which I pointed out the hand of a particular master, without re.
ence to the catalogue (I never mistook the hand of Van Dyke—ı
had seen specimens of his and Reuben's pencil, and some other great
masters, at Mr. Geo. Calvert's, near Bladensburg—they were since
sold in Europe), as by my exact knowledge of the geography, topo-
graphy and statistics of the country.

" For poetry I have had a decided taste from my childhood, yet
never attempted to write one line of it. This taste I have sedulously
cultivated. I believe that I was deterred from attempting poetry by
the verses of Billy Mumford, and some other taggers of rhyme,
which I heard praised (I allude to epistles in verse, written at 12 or
13 years old), but secretly in my heart despised. I also remember
to have heard some poetry of Lord Chatham and of Mr. Fox, which
I thought then, and still think, to be unworthy of their illustrious
names—and before Horace had taught me that ' neither gods, nor
men, nor booksellers' stalls could endure middling poetry,' I thought
none but an inspired pen should attempt the task."

Among the youthful companions that he most valued and cherished about this time, were John Thompson, the author of the letter
in a preceding chapter, and his brother William Thompson. The
following is a memorandum in his own handwriting, and found among
his papers : " John Thompson, Jr., son of John and Anne Thompson, of Sussex, born 3d Nov. 1776, died 25th January, 1799. He
was the author of Graccus, Cassius, Curtius, written on the subject
of American politics—*speak they for him.*" And surely for one of
his age they were remarkable productions, especially the latter addressed to General Marshall, afterwards Chief Justice, then a candidate for Congress on the Federal side of politics. William Thompson was born the 20th of August, 1778. In the year 1798 he and
his friend John Randolph undertook a pedestrian tour to the Mountains, to visit Richard Kidder Meade, a relation of the latter. They
started from Bizarre, each with a small bundle on a cane. Mrs.
Dudley was an eye-witness of their departure and of their return.
She was informed that they performed the whole journey on foot.
They both returned in fine health and spirits. Soon after this
Thompson went to Europe, wandered over Germany, studied medicine, then abandoned it for the law, returned to Virginia, went on

foot to Canada in the fall of 1801. Having squandered his patrimony, falling into dissipated habits, with a genius equally as brilliant, though far more eccentric than his deceased brother, he was rapidly throwing away the great gifts of nature, and sinking into a hopeless vagabond and outcast, when his friend Randolph took him by the hand, brought him to Bizarre, made it his home, encouraged him, and cherished him with the affection of a brother so long as he could be persuaded to remain in Virginia. With him hereafter the reader will become more intimately acquainted. Writing from Bizarre to Randolph, in his absence, he says : " My dear brother—Since you left us I have been deeply engaged in what you advised. I have reviewed the Roman and the Grecian History. I have done more; I have reviewed my own. Believe me, Jack, that I am less calculated for society than almost any man in existence. I am not, perhaps, a vain fool, but I have too much vanity, and I am too susceptible of flattery. I have that fluency which will attract attention and receive applause from an unthinking multitude. Content with my superiority, I should be too indolent to acquire real, useful knowledge. I am stimulated by gratitude, by friendship, and by love, to make exertions now. I feel confident that you will view my foibles with a lenient eye—that you will see me prosper, and in my progress be delighted."

CHAPTER XVI.

CANDIDATE FOR CONGRESS—HISTORY OF THE TIMES.

WE have now approached an important period in the life of John Randolph. In the winter of 1799, in the twenty-sixth year of his age, he was announced as a candidate for Congress in the district which afterwards became so celebrated as the Charlotte district.

John Thompson, writing to his brother, then in Europe, says. " Our friend John Randolph *offers* for Congress, and will probably be elected. He is a brilliant and noble young man. He will be an object of admiration and terror to the enemies of liberty." In 1831, in the last political speech he ever made, he is reported to have said that when he commenced his political career he had waged a warfare, remarkable for its fierceness—he had almost said for its ferocity—against certain principles, and those who advocated them. When he drew his sword to carry on that warfare, he had thrown away the scabbard, and as he never asked for quarter, so he did not always give it. It becomes necessary, therefore, in order to understand his position, to give a brief and general outline of the most important events which had occurred up to the time that he made his appearance on the political stage. We have already seen that the source of party division is to be traced to the Federal Convention; that those elements of discord which have continued to agitate the country up to this day, had their birth in the cradle of the Constitution. Patrick Henry and George Mason were the fathers of the doctrine of States-rights. At a subsequent period, under the auspices of Thomas Jefferson, those doctrines were digested into the canon of a regularly organized party that exerted a powerful influence on the administration of government. The difference between the two parties, Federalist and Republican, as they respectively called themselves at that time, was not confined to the interpretation of the Constitution.

While the one desired and the other deprecated a strong government, the spirit that inclined them to bend that instrument to their wishes, is to be found in the mental and moral organization of the men themselves. Those who doubted the capacity of the people for self-government (and there were many at that time when our experiment was untried), and believed that the only efficient control was to be found in a strong government in the hands of the *rich and well born*, naturally inclined to an interpretation that would authorize such measures as might bring about such a state of things. Those, on the other hand, who had full faith in the capacity of the people, combatted every doctrine which in their judgment tended to steal power from the many and place it in the hands of the few. This radical difference of sentiment, which originated in natural temperament, and was modified by education and position in society, influenced the judgment in its interpretation of every measure of government, and men inclined to the one or the other side, according as they believed the measure originated in the one or the other doctrine above mentioned. The Republicans accused the other party of being monarchists in principle, and of a design so to shape the administration of affairs, that in time the government might assume that form.

The Republicans again were charged by their opponents with being disorganizing levellers, and the enemies of all government. The first great questions on which they divided were the financial schemes of Alexander Hamilton, then Secretary of the Treasury. With these the reader has already been made acquainted. The legislative measures enacted from time to time to carry them into effect, finally brought on a crisis in the whisky insurrection, as it was called, when the people in the western counties of Pennsylvania, by armed force, resisted the execution of the excise law. The Federalists were accused of goading on this rebellion, that they might have a pretext to raise a standing army, to be used as an instrument for forcing their schemes on the country. The Republicans were charged with promoting discontent and insurrection, that they might destroy all government. Unhappily, neither party gave the other credit for honesty or patriotism; and the people, in the heat of the contest, were well nigh driven, in blindness and in rage, on the bayonets of each other. The occasion, however, passed away without serious difficulty; but the bitter and hostile feelings engendered by so violent a contest still remained, and were ready to expand themselves with increased fury on any other occasion that might arise.

In the mean time the French Revolution had made rapid progress. When the news of that event was first wafted across the Atlantic, it was hailed with acclamation as the effort of a great nation to shake off the yoke of despotism, and to assume their position among people with a free and enlightened government. The events of a single year led many to doubt the success of the experiment, and to predict that the whole would end in anarchy. Among the prophets of evil omen was Edmund Burke, the great master of political philosophy. We have already seen how his great work was seized upon by the Federalists as the ablest expounder of their general doctrines, and of their views in particular in regard to the tendency of the principles of the French Revolution. This was to throw the other party to the other extreme: for true it is that the great masses are more influenced by impulses of the heart, than the judgments of the understanding. Paine's "Rights of Man" was set forth as the exponent of the doctrines of the Republicans. Burke, in his spirit of conservatism, pronounced a glowing eulogy on the British Constitution. Paine denounced it as the instrument of oppression and tyranny. It is easy to perceive the bias in the minds of those who took Burke and those who took Paine as their standard of orthodoxy. When these great masters wrote, the monarchy in France was still in existence. It was soon overturned, and a republic, one and indivisible, proclaimed in its stead. This event, more than any thing that had transpired before, stirred up the elements of party-strife in the United States. Free and republican themselves, the American people did not pause on the horrors that were perpetrated, did not consider the consequences of the doctrines that were brought into practice by the rash theorists of France; they only saw a great people, taking themselves as a model, struggling for their independence. Their sympathies were awakened, and all their feelings enlisted in behalf of the republican cause in France. Those who paused—those who suggested a doubt—were denounced as enemies of the people. The deep enthusiasm of a free people in favor of those who, however erroneous, were, like themselves, seeking freedom, did more than any other cause to build up the Republican party in America. The cautions of a cold judgment, however true, cannot weigh against the generous impulses of a warm heart. What is true of individuals in this particular, is ten thousand times more true of the multitude.

But the elastic spirit of freedom could not be restrained within the limits of France. It began to spread to other kingdoms, and to alarm, by its rapid diffusion, the monarchs of Europe. They combined to suppress what they called the *French evil.* England was at the head of the coalition. A furious war commenced—a desperate death-struggle for existence. One or the other must be crushed and destroyed. Republicanism and monarchy could not exist together on the same continent. All the deep passions of the human heart were aroused—all the elements of destruction brought into active operation. It was a war of Titans, and nature groaned under the mighty toils of her warring sons. There could be no neutrality in such a contest. Their wide-sweeping arms drew in, as instruments or agents of strife, the remotest nations. America, though remote, could not hope to escape.

Her position was too conspicuous—her example in producing the present state of things in France too well known for her to escape. England sought to drag her into the contest on the side of the allies. France stretched forth her arms to embrace her ancient ally, and to stand by her side on the hills of Ardenne in the same cause that had seen them side by side on the plains of Yorktown.

The true policy of the United States was to pursue a line of strict neutrality. In accordance with the unanimous vote of his cabinet, Thomas Jefferson at the head as Secretary of State, General Washington issued his proclamation, April 22d, 1793, declaring that a state of war exists between Austria, Prussia, Sardinia, Great Britain, and the United Netherlands, on the one part, and France on the other; and that the duty and interest of the United States require that they should with sincerity and good faith adopt and pursue a conduct friendly and impartial toward the belligerent powers. The citizens of the United States at the same time were warned carefully to avoid all acts and proceedings whatsoever, which might in any manner tend to contravene such disposition. It was impossible, however, to repress the enthusiasm of the people in favor of the French cause. When their minister landed at Charleston, about the time of the above proclamation, he was marched in triumph through the Southern States and principal towns to the capitol at Philadelphia. Presuming on certain privileges which he assumed to have been granted to France in her treaty of alliance with the United States, 1778,— emboldened by the ardent devotion of the people to the cause of liberty, so eagerly manifested towards himself as the representative of a sister republic, he soon threw off all restraint, treated the government with contempt, and assumed acts of sovereignty not only inconsistent with our rights of neutrality, but our existence as an independent and respectable nation. This conduct led to correspondence, remonstrance, and irritation on both sides.

Great Britain at all times doubted the sincerity of our declaration of impartiality, and treated with the utmost contempt our rights of neutrality. Her naval officers insulted and menaced us in our own ports—violated our national rights, by searching vessels and impressing seamen within our acknowledged jurisdiction, and in an outrageous manner seizing *entire crews* in the West Indies, and other parts of the world. Her licensed privateers committed the most atrocious depredations and violences on our commerce, both in the capture and in the after-adjudication, such as were never tolerated in any well organized and efficient government. The Governor of Upper Canada, in an official and formal manner, ordered settlers within our own territory, and far removed from the posts they had unjustly withheld from us, to withdraw, and forbade others to settle on the same. The persons to whom their Indian affairs were intrusted took unusual pains and practised every deception to keep those people in a temper of hostility towards us.

The agents sent amongst us, as with a design to insult the country, were ungracious and obnoxious characters, rancorous refugees, who retaining all their former enmity, could see nothing through a proper medium, and were the source of constant misrepresentation and falsehood. The government were encouraged to permit all these outrages, because they were told there was a British party in America that would not suffer the country to be involved in a war with England.

France, seeing with what boldness and impunity England committed her depredations, was not slow in doing the same. She avowed her purpose, and fulfilled it to the letter, of treating us in the same manner we permitted her enemies to treat us. Such was the deplorable condition of things within one year from the proclamation of neutrality. As the last resort, willing to exhaust all the means of conciliation before a declaration of war, the administration, on the 19th of April, 1794, commissioned John Jay as minister extraordinary to the court of London, with instructions to demand redress for our grievances, and if occasion suited, to negotiate a treaty of amity and commerce. A few weeks thereafter, the 28th of May, James Monroe was sent as minister plenipotentiary to the French government, with similar instructions. The occasion was most favorable for a negotiation with England. The campaign of 1793–4 proved disastrous to the allied powers. The coalition was dissolved. The hot lava fires France poured forth from her volcanic bosom consumed her enemies. The star of the republic was in the ascendant. At such a moment it seemed plain to the ministry that it would not do to break with the United States. If they should drive the two republics into a close alliance, events had already proved that the two united would be invincible. A different line of policy, therefore, must be pursued. Hence, when Mr. Jay arrived at the Court of St. James, he was most graciously received. Lord Granville was all conciliation and compromise. He had not been engaged in the business of negotiation many days, when the King—tough old George, who was the last to surrender in the Revolution—said to him, " Well, sir, I imagine you begin to see that your mission will probably be successful." " I am happy, may it please your majesty, to find that you entertain that idea." " Well, but don't you perceive that it is likely to be so ?" " There are some recent circumstances (the answer to Jay's representations) which induce me to flatter myself that it will be so." The king nodded with a smile, signifying that it was to those circumstances that he alluded. It was a foregone conclusion. Peace with the United States had now become essential to England : and that wise nation never stands on trifles when an important object is to be attained.

Never did negotiator, beginning with such anxious forebodings, find himself proceeding so smoothly, so satisfactorily. The treaty was concluded and signed in London, on the 19th of November, 1794 ; was received by the President the 7th of March following, and on the 8th of June was submitted to the Senate for their consideration. On the 24th, by precisely a constitutional majority, they advised and consented to its ratification. Although in the mind of the President several objections had occurred, they were overbalanced by what he conceived to be its advantages ; and before transmitting it to the Senate he had resolved to ratify it, if approved by that body. But before he had given his signature to the treaty, it was well ascertained that the British order in council of the 8th of June, 1793, for the seizure of provisions going to French ports, had been renewed. Apprehensive that this might be regarded as a practical interpretation of an article in the treaty in regard to provisions not being contraband of war unless in particular cases, the President wisely determined to reconsider his decision. Marshall, in his Life of Washington, says : " Of the result of this reconsideration there is no conclusive testimony." It has become a matter of importance in history to determine this fact.

It was charged that a war with France, and a consequent alliance with England, had been the object of the executive council, from the commencement of hostilities between those two great European powers. The treaty, it was alleged, originated in that spirit. And the circumstances and manner of its consummation were confidently alluded to as evidence of that fact. It was well known that the President made up his judgment with great deliberation; and that when once fixed he was unalterable; he had an invincible repugnance to retract an opinion, or retrace a step once taken.

While he was deliberating on the treaty—when in fact, as it was alleged, he had determined not to sign for the present, an intercepted letter addressed by the French minister to his government, was placed in the President's hands. This letter contained many facts bearing on the character of the President, the influences that were working on him, and deeply implicating the reputation of the Secretary of State. It was alleged that the other Secretaries, into whose hands the letter had fallen, made an unwarrantable use of it to prejudice the mind of the President against their obnoxious colleague and the French cause, and thereby to induce him hastily to ratify the treaty contrary to his better judgment—to drive from his cabinet the only republican remaining in office, and to lend his aid, though unconsciously and indirectly, to the destruction of the republican cause in the United States.

Mr. Jefferson retired from the State Department in 1794, early in January. He says that he suffered martyrdom all the time he was in office—alluding to his single-handed and unaided efforts to combat the heresies of Hamilton, and to resist the tendencies of the government to yield to British influence. He was succeeded by the Attorney General, Edmund Randolph, whose relationship to the subject of this memoir has already been made known to the reader. That gentleman professed to be of no party, but was understood to be a Republican in principle, and favorably inclined to the French cause. "The fact is," says Jefferson, "he has generally given his principles to the one party, and his practice to the other—the oyster to one, the shell to the other. Unfortunately, the shell was generally the lot of his friends, the French and Republicans, and the oyster, of their antagonists. Had he been firm to the principles he professed, in the year 1793, the President would have been kept from an habitual concert with the British and anti-republican party."

Randolph declared that long before the Fauchet letter made its appearance, the British partizans had been industrious in disseminating the most poisonous falsehoods concerning him, and in his absence seized the advantage of uttering uncontradicted slanders; boasting and insisting that in a controversy between them, he (Randolph) must be sacrificed. Hamilton had retired, but was in constant communication with the President on all subjects of importance. The British partisans alluded to, were Pickering and Wolcott, the Secretary of War and of the Treasury.

With these facts before us we can now proceed with the subject in hand. We have said that the President had determined to ratify the treaty, if so advised by the Senate. But soon after their adjournment he became satisfied that the *provision order*, as it was called, had been renewed by the British government. He then began to balance whether to ratify or not. In this state of mind, he required the Secretary of State to hold a conversation with the British Minister on the 29th June, 1795, and to tell him that by the constitution the treaty now rested with the President, and that he had entered into the consideration of the subject. A letter was written to the American Minister at Paris, on the 2d of July, under the President's eye and special correction, in which it was stated that the " President has not yet decided upon the final measure to be adopted by himself." He consulted with all the officers of government on several collateral points in the treaty—consulted, as it was believed, with Hamilton on the treaty at large—and required the Secretary of State to give his written opinion. This opinion of the Secretary was handed in the 12th of July, 1795. Among other things, he says : " I take the liberty of suggesting that a personal interview be immediately had between the Secretary of State and Mr. Hammond, and that the substance of the address to him be this "—(after some preliminary remarks) : " But we are informed by the public gazettes, and by letters tolerably authentic, that vessels, even American vessels, laden with provisions for France, may be captured and dealt with as carrying a kind of contraband. Upon the supposition of its truth, the President cannot persuade himself that he ought to ratify during the existence of the order. His reasons will be detailed in a proper representation through you (Mr. Hammond) to his Britannic Majesty. At the same time, that order being removed, he will ratify without delay or further scruple." In the morning of the 13th of July, the President instructed the Secretary to have the proposed interview immediately with Mr. Hammond, and to address him as had been suggested.

Mr. Hammond asked, in the course of the interview, if it would not be sufficient to remove the order out of the way; and after the ratification to rescind it?

The Secretary replied with some warmth, that this would be a mere shift, as the principle was the important thing. He then asked, if the President was irrevocably determined, not to ratify, if the provision order was not removed? The Secretary answered, that he was not instructed upon that point. This conversation was immediately related to the President. He told the Secretary *that he might have informed Mr. Hammond that he never would ratify, if the provision order was not removed out of the way.*

The President left Philadelphia for Mount Vernon, the 15th day of July, 1795; and soon afterwards, the Secretary commenced drafting the memorial that was to be addressed to his Britannic Majesty. After discussing the article of the treaty in reference to provisions, and showing the inconsistency of the order of the 8th of June, 1793, with that article, the memorial concludes : " The chief obstacle, which is dependent for its removal on his Britannic Majesty, is the order above stated. The President is too much deprived of its particulars, to declare what shall be his irrevocable determination: but the sensibility which it has excited in his mind, cannot be allayed without the most unequivocal stipulation, to reduce to the only construction in which he can acquiesce, the article of the treaty."

Before the President had received the memorial which he had ordered to be drafted, he wrote to the Secretary on the 22d July, from Mount Vernon, thus : " In my hurry I did not signify the propriety of letting those gentlemen (the Secretaries of War and the Treasury, and the Attorney General) know fully my determination with respect to the ratification of the treaty, and the train it was in; but as this was necessary, in order to enable them to form their opinions on the subject submitted, I take it for granted, that both were communicated to them by you, as a matter of course. The first, that is the conditional ratification, (if the late order, which we have heard of respecting provision-vessels, is not in operation,) may on all fit occasions be spoken of as my determination, unless from any thing you have heard, or met with since I left the city, it should be thought more advisable to communicate with me on the subject. My opinion respecting the treaty is the same now that it was; that is, not favorable to it; but that it is better to ratify it in the manner the Senate have advised, (*and with the reservation already mentioned*,) than to suffer matters to remain as they are—unsettled."

In answer to this the Secretary writes: "I had communicated fully your determination with respect to the ratification. I have no doubt that the order for seizing provision-vessels exists. Nothing has occurred to prevent the speaking of that determination."

On the 29th July the President writes: "I also return, under cover of this letter, the draft of the *memorial*, and the rough draft of a *ratification*. These are very important papers, and, with the instructions which follow, will require great attention and consideration, and are the primary cause of my returning to Philadelphia."

On the 31st he writes: "The *memorial* seems well designed to answer the end proposed."

While the memorial was in the hands of the President at Mount Vernon, it became the subject of conversation with the Heads of Departments. Wolcott and Pickering were both opposed to any delay in concluding the business. Wolcott observed that it would give the French Government an opportunity of professing to make very extensive overtures to the United States, and thus embarrass the treaty with Great Britain.

Pickering, on hearing the memorial, exclaimed, "This, as the sailors say, is throwing the whole up in the wind."

The President returned to Philadelphia on the 11th of August. The same evening, in presence of Pickering and Bradford, the Secretary of State observed, "that the sooner the memorial was revised by the gentlemen jointly, who were prepared with their opinions, the better." The President replied, "that he supposed every thing of this sort had been settled. The Secretary said that it was not so, as Colonel Pickering was for an immediate ratification. To this Pickering responded: "I told Mr. Randolph that I thought the postponement of ratification was a ruinous step."

On the morning of the 13th of August, the letters which had been written to foreign ministers in his absence, were laid before the President. The one addressed to Mr. Monroe was in these words: —"The treaty is not yet ratified by the President; nor will it be ratified, I believe, until it returns from England—if then. The late British order for seizing provisions, is a weighty obstacle to a ratification. I do not suppose that such an attempt to starve France will be countenanced." Other letters were written of the same tenor, and laid before the President. He made no objection to the strong expressions contained in them.

There can be no question from the evidence, that up to the 13th of August, 1795, and for a month previous, the President had deliberately made up his mind not to sign the treaty so long as the provision order was in existence. What caused the great change between that time and the 18th; for on that day he gave to the treaty an unconditional ratification? Marshall, in his Life of Washington, intimates, that the great clamor raised against the treaty in the commercial towns, was the cause of this change in the mind of the President. He thought that by signing the treaty at once he would put an end to all hope of influencing the executive will by agitation. This solution is not consistent with the character of the man. No one despised mere popular clamor more than he did; no one valued more the opinion of his fellow-citizens. With a mind not suggestive but eminently judicious, he sought for counsel in all quarters, and profited more by advice than any other man that ever held a public station.

He considered that the occasion called for wise and temperate measures. In his letter of the 31st of July, to the Secretary of State, he says: "In time, when passion shall have yielded to sober reason, the current may possibly turn; but in the mean while, this Government, in relation to France and England, may be compared to a ship between the rocks Scylla and Charybdis. If the treaty is ratified, the partisans of the French (or rather of war and confusion) will excite them to hostile measures, or at least to unfriendly sentiments: if it is not, there is no foreseeing all the consequences which may follow, as it respects Great Britain. It is not to be inferred from hence, that I am, or shall be disposed to quit the ground I have taken, unless circumstances more imperious than have yet come to my knowledge, should compel it; for there is but one *straight* course in these things, and that is, to seek truth and pursue it steadily." He then instructs the Secretary to be attentive to all the resolutions that might come in, and to all the newspaper publications, that he might have all the objections against the treaty which had any weight in them, embodied in the *memorial* addressed to the British king, or in the instructions to the American Minister at London. It cannot be presumed, therefore, that the excitement in the country against the treaty, was the cause, or at least the principal cause of the sudden change in the determination of the President. We must look to some other source for a solution of this difficulty.

———•♦•———

CHAPTER XVII.

THE FAUCHET LETTER.

ON the 31st day of October, 1794, about the time of the whisky insurrection, and Jay's negotiation in London, the French Minister forwarded a dispatch to his government, entitled " Private Correspondence of the Minister on Politics, No. 10."

This letter on its way was captured by a British cruiser, placed in the hands of Lord Grenville, and by him forwarded to the Minister here (Mr. Hammond), with instructions to use it for the benefit of his Majesty's service. When the letter came to Hammond, he made known the contents to Mr. Wolcott, Secretary of the Treasury, but did not intimate a desire that it might be communicated to the President. Wolcott himself suggested it, and asked that it might be placed in his hands for that purpose. Hammond at first declined, but finally consented, on condition that a certified copy should be left in his hands. Wolcott received the letter the 28th day of July, 1795, while the President was at Mount Vernon. He immediately showed it to Mr. Pickering. It was their opinion that its contents were of so delicate and important a nature that they ought to be imparted to the President without delay, *and with the utmost secrecy.* Any open attempt to effect this end, they thought *might excite the suspicion of Mr. Randolph.* The first hint of the matter was communicated to the President in a letter from Mr. Pickering in the following words : " July 31st—On the subject of the treaty, I confess I feel extreme solicitude, and, *for a special reason,* which can be communicated to you only in person. I entreat, therefore, that you will return with all convenient speed to the seat of government. In the mean time, for the reason above referred to, I pray you to decide on no important political measure in whatever form it may be presented to you. Mr. Wolcott and I (Mr. Bradford concurring) waited on Mr. Randolph, and *urged his writing to request your return. He wrote in our presence.*" Just the day before, Randolph had written to the President—"As soon as I had the honor of receiving your letter of the 24th instant, I conferred with the Secretaries of the Treasury and of War upon the necessity or expediency of your return hither at this time. *We all concurred* that neither the one nor the other existed, and that the circumstance would confer upon the things which had been and are still carried on, an importance which it would not be convenient to give them." After receiving the above mysterious letter from Pickering, which perhaps arrived the same day with Randolph's, the President hastened to the seat of government. He arrived on the 11th of August, and the contents of Fauchet's intercepted letter were made known to him the same day.

In this *private correspondence,* after stating that the dispatches of himself and colleagues had been confined to a naked recital of facts, the Minister thus proceeds:—"I have reserved myself to give you, as far as I am able, a key to the facts detailed in our reports. * * * The previous confessions of Mr. Randolph alone throw a satisfactory light upon every thing that comes to pass. * * * I shall, then, endeavor to give you a clue to all the measures, of which the common dispatches give you an account; and to discover the true causes of the explosion, which it is *obstinately* resolved to repress with great means (the whisky insurrection), although the state of things has no longer any thing alarming." * * * He then undertakes to give a history of the primitive division of parties—Federalists and Anti-Federalists. Speaks of the whimsical contrast between the name and the real opinion of the parties—the former aiming with all their power to *annihilate Federalism,* while the latter were striving to preserve it. These divisions, he proceeds to say, originated in the system of finances, which had its birth in the cradle of the constitution. It created a financiering class, who threaten to become the aristocratical order of the State. He then continues, in the fifth paragraph, in these words: "It is useless to stop longer to prove that the monarchical system was interwoven with those novelties of finance, and that the friends of the latter favored the attempts which were made, in order to bring the constitution to the former by insensible gradations. The writings of influential men of this party prove it (alluding to Mr. Adams's Discourses on Davila); their real opinions, too, avow it, and the journals of the Senate are the depository of the first attempts."

He speaks of the sympathy of this party with the regenerating movements of France, *while running in monarchical paths;* and after an account of the rapid increase and consolidation of the Anti-Federal party, under the name of patriots and republicans, he thus proceeds:—"In every quarter are arraigned the imbecility of the Government towards Great Britain, the defenceless state of the country against possible invasions, the coldness towards the French Republic—the system of finance is attacked, which threatens eternizing the debt, under pretext of making it the guarantee of public happiness; the complication of that system which withholds from general inspection all its operations—the alarming power of the influence it procures to a man whose principles are regarded as dangerous—the preponderance which that man acquires from day to day in public measures, and, in a word, the *immoral* and impolitic modes of taxation which he at first presents as expedients, and afterwards raises to permanency."

He then speaks of the *excise law*—the navigation of the Mississippi, and the system for the sale of public lands, as being the principal sources of discontent to the Western people, and the cause of their rebellion. "At last," says he, "the local explosion is effected. * * * The Government which had foreseen it, reproduced, under various forms, the demand of a disposable force which might put it in a state of respectable defence. Defeated in this measure, who can aver that it may not have hastened the local eruption, in order to make an advantageous diversion, and to lay the more general storm which it saw gathering? Am I not authorized in forming this conjecture from the conversation which the Secretary of State had with me and Le Blanc, above, an account of which you have in my dispatch, No. 3? But how may we expect that this new plan will be executed?—By exasperating and severe measures, authorized by a law which was not solicited till the close of the session. This law gave to the one already existing for collecting the *excise*, a coercive force which hitherto it had not possessed, and a demand of which was not before ventured to be made. * * * * This was undoubtedly what Mr. Randolph meant in telling me *that under pretext of giving energy to the Government, it was intended to introduce absolute power, and to mislead the President in paths which would conduct him to unpopularity.*"

He then proceeds to describe the successful efforts to raise an army, and to gain over certain influential characters, and continues thus : " The Secretary of this State possessed great influence in the popular societies of Philadelphia, which in its turn influenced those of other States : of course he merited attention. It appears, therefore, that those men, with others unknown to me, all having, without doubt, Randolph at their head, were balancing to decide on this party. Two or three days before the proclamation was published (in reference to the whisky insurrection 25th September, 1794), and of course before the cabinet had resolved on its measures, Mr. Randolph came to see me with an air of great eagerness, and made to me the overtures of which I have given you an account in my No. 6. Thus, with some thousands of dollars, the republic would have decided on civil war, or on peace. Thus the consciences of the pretended patriots of America have already their prices. * * * What will be the old age of this Government if it is thus early decrepit. Such, citizen, is the evident consequence of the system of finances conceived by Mr. Hamilton. He has made of a whole nation, a stock-jobbing, speculating, selfish people. * * * * Still, there are patriots of whom I delight to entertain an idea worthy of that imposing title. Consult Monroe—he is of this number; he had apprised me of the men whom the current of events had dragged along as bodies devoid of weight. His friend Madison is also an honest man. Jefferson, on whom the patriots cast their eyes to succeed the President, had foreseen these crises. He prudently retired, in order to avoid making a figure against his inclination in scenes, the secret of which will soon or late be brought to light."

These are the leading and essential facts in the intercepted letter. And they certainly contain very grave charges. The men in power are accused of a design of changing the government into a monarchy; clothing the President with absolute power, and fomenting a rebellion, that they might have a pretext to raise a standing army to enforce their designs. The pretended patriots of the country are accused of venality and corruption—the highest officer under Government charged with making overtures to the minister of a foreign power for money; and it is alleged that none but those who are opposed to the Administration are trustworthy and honest.

It is not surprising that a communication of this sort, addressed by a foreign minister to his Government, whose feeling of friendship to our own was extremely questionable, falling into the hands of one of the parties implicated, should excite his indignation and create in him a desire to have the truth of the charges investigated. But the use made of that letter by the triumvirate, Wolcott, Pickering, and Bradford, to destroy an obnoxious rival and to crush the rising energies of a hateful party, cannot be justified. The wicked and jesuitical doctrine, that *all is fair in politics*, may sanction the means in the end; but the pen of the historian must condemn, under all circumstances, both the principle and its application. Randolph was a colleague of those men—held the highest station in the executive department of Government—was in the most intimate relations with them, holding daily and hourly communications on the gravest subjects of state. He was reputed to be among the first gentlemen of his age—possessed a high reputation, and an unblemished character for integrity and honor. A paper falls into the hands of his intimate and daily associates, written by an ignorant and prejudiced foreigner, in which this man is charged with being accessible to a bribe. What line of conduct do they pursue? It seems that in a formal dispatch of the foreign minister, No. 6, the facts are stated from which he draws his injurious inference. Did the triumvirate call for that document so obviously necessary as a means of explaining the injurious charges? It was in the hands of the same individual from whom they had obtained the first communication. But they made no inquiry for it; did not seem to wish to know that the means of explanation were in their reach, or in existence. Did they communicate the contents of the letter to their implicated colleague, that he might exculpate himself from its charges? They kept it a profound secret from him—held frequent conclaves over it—considered it extremely important, and concluded that the President must be informed of it, but in the most secret manner, lest the implicated person might take the alarm. They even go to him, and induce him in their presence to write to the President, requesting his immediate return to the seat of government. Not content with this, one of the party writes himself, stating that he is very solicitous about the treaty, and *for a special reason*, thus connecting the fate of the treaty with the contents of the intercepted letter. Was this acting fairly towards their colleague? It was not treating him even as a gentleman. Their conduct can only be compared to that of a bailiff or town beadle, who has gotten some clue on a suspected character, towards whom he must act with the utmost caution and secrecy, lest he might snuff suspicion in the wind and take to flight.

Nor was their conduct at all mitigated by the return of the President. They beset him the moment of his arrival; the intercepted letter was placed in his hands the same evening; a cabinet council was called the next morning to deliberate on the treaty. Not a breath was uttered to Randolph by the President, that he was suspected of treachery to himself, and of having made overtures for a bribe to betray his country. On the contrary, an unusually cordial manner is observed towards him. He is called on to give his opinion on the subject of ratification. He repeats the same arguments he had used before; he contended that the treaty did not warrant the provision order, and that the President could not sign the treaty so long as the order existed; because we had already acknowledged, on the 7th of September, 1793, that a permission to Great Britain to exercise such a power, would be a just cause of war to France; that we should be inconsistent in our discussions with the French minister; because when he remonstrated upon the extension of contraband by the treaty, it was answered that we did not alter the law of nations; but now we should desert what was contended to be the law of nations, in two letters to Mr. Hammond; that we should run the hazard of a war with France, by combining to starve her; and that her discontents were the only possible chance remaining to the British partisans for throwing us into the arms of Great Britain, by creating a seeming necessity of an alliance with the latter power. These cogent arguments had already been urged on the President; he felt their force, and had determined, as the reader cannot doubt, not to sign so long as the provision order existed, and had taken his measures accordingly. How are these arguments met now? Let it be remembered that on the morning of this very day, it was circulated in the coffee-houses by Hammond, the British minister, and his partisans, that Randolph was at the bottom of the town meetings which had been gotten up to denounce the treaty (and which actually burnt a copy of the treaty in front of Hammond's house, by the hands of the common hangman), and that there was a conspiracy, of which Randolph was a member, to destroy the popularity of the President, and to thrust Mr. Jefferson into his chair. No one can doubt that these rumors designedly put afloat, were carefully related to the President by his faithful and disinterested ministers, so that when Randolph concluded his speech, the very arguments that had weighed with the President before, were now evidences of his guilt—*confirmations strong as proofs of Holy Writ*. Pickering and Wolcott answered in the most excited and intemperate manner; urged the immediate ratification of the treaty, and charged that the struggle to defeat it was the act of a *detestable and nefarious conspiracy*. There was a unanimous vote for immediate unconditional ratification, so far as the provision order was concerned; but to be accompanied with a remonstrance on that subject. The President receded from his determination, and consented to ratify. The necessary papers were prepared, and on the 18th of August, 1795, the President affixed his signature to the treaty. All this struck the Secretary of State with astonishment. He did not know how to account for it. All the while he was treated with unusual courtesy. Two days after the President had determined to sign the treaty, on the 14th of the month, he paid a private and friendly visit to Mr. Randolph's house; invited him next day in the most cordial manner to dine with a party of chosen friends, and placed him at the foot of the table as a mark of respect and confidence. On the 18th, the day of the ratification, the same air of cordiality was assumed. But good, easy man, while his honors were thus ripening, next day there came a nipping frost.

On Wednesday, the 19th of August, 1795, while going to the President's at the usual hour, *nine o'clock* in the morning, he was met by the steward, who informed him that the President desired him to postpone his visit till half past ten. On reaching the door at the appointed hour, he was surprised to learn that the President had been closeted with his colleagues for more than an hour. On entering the room, the President rose from his chair, and received him with marked formality. After a few words, the President drew a letter from his pocket, and said: " Mr. Randolph, here is a letter which I desire you to read, and make such explanations as you choose."

After he had read the letter, and some little conversation had ensued, the President requested Messrs. Wolcott and Pickering to interrogate him! In a short time he was requested to leave the room, that they might consult on what had been said! Can the reader come to any other conclusion, than that the mind of the President had been worked up to prejudge the case? Can any one believe that the great and good Washington would have acted in a manner so precipitate in itself, so injurious and humiliating to a long tried friend, and a faithful, confidential officer, unless his passions had been excited by some undue influence, exerted over his peculiar temper and character?

Who can doubt, after a review of all the facts connected with this transaction, that Randolph, as he declared himself, *was the meditated victim of party spirit?* Who can doubt that Wolcott and Pickering, by their artful insinuations, and earnest commentaries on the intercepted letter, had induced the President to believe that there was in truth a *detestable* and *nefarious* conspiracy to defeat the treaty?—that there was a dark design of replacing him by another President; and that his Secretary of State, in whom he had placed the most unbounded confidence, had been convicted of a corrupt attachment to France, and of perfidy to himself. The more we read and learn of Washington and his acts, the more exalted our judgment becomes of his virtue and purity. The more the days of his mortality recede from us, the more sublime and godlike his character appears. But when we go back to the times when he wrought on earth with other men, and performed his part on the public stage, we perceive that he had like passions with ourselves, and like us, was liable to err.

The ratification of such a treaty would at any time have created a strong hostility to the administration that advised it. It was certainly very defective. We say nothing about the objections raised against it, under the influence of the party excitement of the times. Much allowance must be made for them; but the negotiator himself admitted that the subjects of difficulty were merged in the treaty, but not settled. Time has proved the truth of his admission. The late war with Great Britain—the more recent difficulties on the boundary question, all grew out of the unsettled questions of dispute merged in the treaty. It was evidently made for a temporary purpose—*to serve the nonce*—and perhaps that was all that could have been expected. The President did not approve it. The more he thought of it, the less he liked it. But that there might be some settlement of the perplexing and threatening difficulties between the two nations, he consented to ratify, if the Senate advised. The ratification of such a treaty, under any circumstances, would have encountered formidable opposition. But when it was made known that the President, under the influence of a party intrigue, had been hurried into a premature ratification, contrary to his better judgment, with the British order in council staring him in the face, which s eemed to have been issued in contempt of the treaty, as a license to plunder our defenceless commerce, the storm that was raised cannot well be imagined. The great Washington rose into the pure empyrean of a clear conscience; but the guilty beings below were swept away by the tempest. All who had any thing to do with this business were *treaty-foundered*, and ingulfed in the torrent that soon swept over the land.

It was predicted, as a sequel to these transactions, that Monroe would be recalled from Paris. In December, 1795, only three months after the ratification, Mr. Jefferson writes: " I should not wonder if Monroe were to be recalled, under the idea of his being of the partisans of France, whom the President considers as the partisans of *war and confusion*, in his letter of July 31st, and as disposed to excite them to hostile measures, or at least to unfriendly sentiments; a most infatuated blindness to the true character of the sentiments entertained in favor of France." Sure enough, the subject was soon made the theme of cabinet consultation; and on the 2d day of July, 1796, it was resolved to recall him. " We think," said the Heads of Department, in their communication to the President, " the great interests of the United States require that they have near the French government some faithful organ to explain their real views, and to ascertain those of the French. Our duty obliges us to be explicit. Although the present Minister Plenipotentiary of the United States at Paris has been amply furnished with documents to explain the views and conduct of the United States, yet his own letters authorize us to say, that he has omitted to use them, and thereby exposed the United States to all the mischiefs which would flow from jealousies and erroneous conceptions of their views and conduct. Whether this dangerous omission arose from such an attachment to the cause of France as rendered him too little mindful of the interests of his own country, or from mistaken views of the latter, or from any other cause, the evil is the same." After speaking of his confidential correspondence with the *notorious enemies of the whole system of government*, and of certain anonymous letters, which they entertained no doubt were written with the privity of Mr. Monroe, they proceed: "The anonymous communications from officers of the United States in a foreign country, on matters of a public nature, and which deeply concern the interests of the United States in relation to that foreign country, *are proofs of sinister designs*, and show that the public interests are no longer safe in the hands of such men." On the 8th of July, from Mount Vernon, the President invited Charles Cotesworth Pinkney, of Charleston, to succeed Mr. Monroe. In his private and confidential letter to that gentleman, he says: "The situation of affairs, and the interests of this country, as they relate to France, render it indispensably necessary, that a *faithful organ* near that Government, able and willing to explain its views and to ascertain those of France, should immediately fill the place of our present Minister Plenipotentiary at Paris."

From this period not a friend of the French cause remained in the administration of affairs. Jefferson, foreseeing the tendency of events, had prudently retired, after having suffered a three years' martyrdom. Randolph had been ignominiously driven from the cabinet; and Monroe recalled, not only with the charge of infidelity to his Government, but under the accusation of *sinister designs* against his country.

It was proclaimed in the newspapers, in political meetings, on the hustings, every where, *that the friends of liberty are for an intimate union with France. The partisans of slavery prefer an alliance with England.* On the other hand, the President had declared and acted on the belief, that the friends of France were the partisans of *war and confusion.* " *A most infatuated blindness,*" said Jefferson, " *to the true character of the sentiments entertained in favor of France !*"

The reader cannot mistake, at this rate, how things were tending.

The person and character of the President were no longer respected. The Republicans were resolved that their opponents should not shelter themselves behind the *ægis* of his fame. They considered that he had descended into the arena of strife, and were determined that he should share the fate of other combatants.

Happily for him, he soon sought repose in voluntary retirement. The reins of government fell into other hands. On the 4th of March, 1797, this pure patriot entered the shades of Mount Vernon with infinitely more pleasure than he had ever passed the threshold into the cabinet of power. However much some of the measures of his administration may be condemned, his own motives are above suspicion. If ever a man had in view the exaltation of the character of his own country, impressing on it a pure American stamp, free from all foreign alloy, he had. Whether all the measures advocated by him tended to that end is another question. The historian must not be deterred from a critical examination into them from the fear of tarnishing his great name. That is impossible! From the clouds of party it has come out all the brighter for the mists by which it was temporarily enveloped.

CHAPTER XIX.

MR. MONROE—FRANCE—MR. ADAMS ELECTED PRESIDENT.

THE charges against Mr. Monroe were unjust, and his recall an impolitic measure, unless the Government had determined not to send a successor, for which there was sufficient reason. Nothing but the intemperate zeal of such partisans as Pickering and Wolcott could have advised the course pursued. The strangest part of the business is that General Washington should have yielded so completely to their views. He speaks more harshly, if possible, than they do, not only of Mr. Monroe's conduct, but of his motives. He charges him with misrepresenting his own Government, an undue condescension to that of France, and alleges that he was promoting the views of a party in his own country, that were obstructing every measure of the

Administration, and, by their attachment to France, were hurrying it (*if not with design*, at least in its consequences), into a war with Great Britain, in order to favor France. He further charges that this *French party* had brought the country to a most degraded and humiliating condition ; and that our Minister at Paris had been the principal actor in its accomplishment. That he was timid in his demands of justice, and over zealous in his efforts to conciliate the French people, cannot be doubted. But he had a most difficult part to perform. His open reception by the National Convention—the fraternal embrace in the midst of shouts and acclamation, and his unreserved declarations of attachment to the French cause, were not at all diplomatic. The people of Paris, who were the Government in fact, would have consented to no other kind of reception. Fond of exhibition and excitement at all times, they could not let an occasion of that sort pass quietly by without considering that they had cast a slight on the representative of a sister Republic. At the same time, the whole nation were thoroughly impressed with the belief that we owed our existence to them ; that their timely alliance had sustained our cause against the arms of England, and their powerful influence in negotiation had secured our Independence. They were taught this lesson not only by their own Government, and the thousands of Frenchmen who fought in our armies, but they were taught it by the statesmen of America, her orators, her poets, her historians, and all her diplomatic agents abroad. All France was penetrated with a belief that we owed them a debt of gratitude that no service could repay. Whether right or wrong, such was the national faith. They were now engaged in a war with the very nation from whose tyrannous oppression they had plucked us—their own hereditary enemy of a thousand years—a war destructive, vindictive, exterminating. So soon, therefore, as it was known that the United States had sent an envoy to negotiate a treaty with England, their suspicions were awakened. They doubted the sincerity of our declarations of friendship, and insisted that Mr. Monroe was merely sent to blind and lull them into repose, while the real design was a close alliance with their mortal foe. In vain did the Minister declare that no treaty would be made with England that would affect the rights of France. There is no reasoning in detail with the multitude ; special facts make but a slight impression, they are governed by broad and universal truths.

It was impossible to persuade the French mind that the United States meant well in seeking to form a treaty with their enemies, while they were impressed with the belief that they owed their existence, independence, and an immense debt of gratitude to France. Whenever Mr. Monroe made a demand for the redress of our many grievances, he was at once met with the charge of ingratitude, and was threatened with the displeasure and hostility of France, if the treaty then in progress at London should be consummated. So soon as it was known that a treaty had been made, and that it had been advised by the Senate and ratified by the President, the hostility of the French Government and the indignation of the people knew no bounds. The harassing decrees of Government, the depredations on American commerce, the atrocious cruelties committed on her seamen and citizens were worse than if there had been an open declaration of war ; for then all merchant vessels would have been kept at home. It was declared by the Government that these things were done in consequence of the British treaty. They now began to draw a distinction between the Administration and the people of the United States. They imagined that a large majority were friendly to an alliance with France. The first appeal was made by the minister Adet, in the autumn of 1796, with a view of influencing the presidential election. Mr. Adams was considered as the representative of the Administration, or English party, and Mr. Jefferson the representative of the French party. The next occasion on which this spirit was manifested in the most remarkable degree, was in the month of December, 1796, by the Directory. When Mr. Monroe presented his letters of recall, and the letters of credence of General Pinckney, who the reader knows had been appointed to succeed him, he was told that the Directory would not acknowledge nor receive another Minister Plenipotentiary from the United States, until after the redress of grievances demanded of the American Government, and which the French Government had a right to expect from it. He was, at the same time, told that this determination allowed to subsist between the French Republic and the *American people*, the affection founded upon former benefits and reciprocal interests, and that he himself had cultivated this affection by every means in his power. And to his valedictory address, the President of the Executive Directory thus replied :—" Mr. Minister Plenipotentiary of the

United States of America, by presenting to-day your letters of recall to the Executive Directory, you give to Europe a very strange spec tacle. France, rich in her liberty, surrounded by a train of victories, strong in the esteem of her allies, will not abase herself by calcula ting the consequences of the condescension of the *American Govern ment to the suggestions of her former tyrants.* Moreover, the French Republic hopes that the successors of Columbus, Raleigh, and Penn— always proud of their liberty—*will never forget that they owe it to France.* They will weigh in their wisdom the magnanimous benevo lence of the French people, with the crafty caresses of certain perfidi ous persons who meditate bringing them back to their former slavery. Assure the good American people, sir, that, like them, we adore liberty ; that they will always have our esteem, and that they will find in the French people republican generosity, which knows how to grant peace, as it does to cause its sovereignty to be respected."

While Mr. Monroe was assured that he had combated for prin ciples, had known the true interests of his country, and that they parted from him with regret, General Pinckney was treated in the most disrespectful manner. In no manner was he recognized in his official capacity,—was refused the usual cards of hospitality on which his personal safety depended, and like an ordinary stranger, was left wholly to the regulations of the Paris police. And about the first of February, 1797, the very day that Bonaparte's brilliant termination of the Italian campaigns was announced, he was ordered to quit Paris, and to pass beyond the confines of France.

The news of the election of Mr. Adams to the presidency, arrived in Paris about the first of March. This filled the measure of hos tile feelings on the part of the Directory : they were now ready for any extremity. The unfriendly sentiments of Mr. Adams were well known in France; and they were cordially reciprocated. Those feelings began to develope themselves at an early period. And it is important at this point of our history, that the reader should know their origin.

In the summer of 1780 Mr. Adams was in Paris, charged with three distinct commissions from the Congress of the Confederation : first, to take a share in any future negotiations for peace ; second, to conclude a treaty of commerce with Great Britain; third, to re present the United States at the Court of London. At that time there was not the slightest prospect of peace. Cornwallis was marching triumphantly through the southern provinces, and England was in high hopes of subjugating her revolted colonies. At this conjuncture, Mr. Adams proposed to make known to the Court of London that he held a commission to conclude a treaty of commerce with Great Britain, and to represent the United States at the Court of London. As he was required to do, he consulted the Count de Vergennes on the subject. That nobleman, the Secretary for Foreign Affairs, ridiculed it as an ill-timed and visionary proposition. To be solicitous about a treaty of commerce, before independence was established, he thought was like being busy about furnishing a house before the foundation was laid. He told Mr. Adams that the British ministry would consider the communication as ridiculous, and would either return no answer, or an insolent one.

Mr. Adams still insisted on the propriety of his course, entered into an elaborate argument to prove it, and was very intemperate in his language and insinuations as to the motives of France, and showed an overweening desire either to figure himself in the Court of London, or to form a close commercial alliance with England as the best means of securing independence to his country. He evidently showed no disposition to rely on the good intentions of France in the business.

The Count de Vergennes at length inclosed a copy of his correspondence with Mr. Adams, to Dr. Franklin, accompanied with these remarks :—" You will find, I think, in the letters of that plenipotentiary, *opinions and a tone* which do not correspond either with the manner I explained myself to him, or with the intimate connection which subsists between the king and the United States. You will make that use of these pieces which your prudence shall suggest. As to myself, I desire that you will transmit them to Congress, that they may know the line of conduct which Mr. Adams pursues with regard to us, and that they may judge whether he is endowed, as Congress no doubt desires, *with that conciliating spirit* which is necessary for the important and delicate business with which he is in trusted."

The communication was made to Congress ; and that body responded to Mr. Adams, that they did not doubt his correspondence with the Count de Vergennes flowed from his zeal and assiduity in the service of his country, but that the opinions of that minister were well-founded, and that he must be more cautious in future. Mr. Adams never forgot or forgave this insult to his vanity and self-esteem, which were ruling traits in his character. He soon left for Holland, where he remained till negotiations for peace had commenced in Paris, in November, 1782. When he arrived on the scene of action, Mr. Jay and Dr. Franklin, two of the associate commissioners, had made considerable progress in the negotiation. The whole matter was talked over to him, and he very soon displayed his suspicions of the sincerity and motives of France. In his correspondence he thus writes :—" Paris, Nov. 1782. When I speak of this (French) Court, I know not that any other minister (Count de Vergennes) is included than that of Foreign Affairs. A whole system of policy is now as glaring as the day, which perhaps Congress and the people of America have little suspicion of. The evidence now results from a large view of all our European negotiations. The same principle and the same system have been uniformly pursued from the beginning of my knowledge in Europe, in April, 1778, to this hour. In substance it has been this :—In assistance afforded us in naval force and in money, to keep us from succumbing, and nothing more : To prevent us from ridding ourselves wholly of our enemies, and from growing rich and powerful : To prevent us from obtaining acknowledgments of our independence by other foreign powers, and from acquiring consideration in Europe, or any advantage in the peace, but what is expressly stipulated in the treaties : To deprive us of the Grand Fishery, the Mississippi river, the Western lands, and to saddle us with the tories." The friends of Mr. Adams even went so far as to say, that Dr. Franklin favored, or did not oppose the designs of France against the United States ; and that it was entirely owing to the firmness, sagacity, and disinterestedness of Mr. Adams, with whom Mr. Jay united, that we had obtained those important advantages. Dr. Franklin, in allusion to this subject, says : " He (Mr. Adams) thinks the French minister one of the greatest enemies of our country ; that he would have straitened our boundaries, to prevent the growth of our people ; contracted our fishery to obstruct the increase of our seamen ; and retained the royalists amongst us, to keep us divided ; that he privately opposed all our negotiations with foreign courts, and afforded us, during the war, the assistance we received, only to keep it alive, that we might be so much the more weakened by it; that to think of gratitude to France is the greatest of follies, and that to be influenced by it would ruin us. He makes no secret of his having these opinions—expresses them publicly, sometimes in presence of the English ministers, and speaks of hundreds of instances, which he could produce in proof of them. If I were not convinced of the real inability of this Court to furnish the further supplies we asked, I should suspect these discourses of a person in his station might have influenced the refusal—(at that very moment, the king of France had postponed his own creditors, that he might furnish means to sustain the credit of the United States;)— but I think they have gone no further than to occasion a suspicion, *that we have a considerable party of anti-Gallicans* in America, who are not tories, and consequently, to produce some doubts of the continuance of our friendship. As such doubts may hereafter have a bad effect, I think we cannot take too much care to remove them; and it is, therefore, I write this to put you on your guard (believing it my duty, though I know I hazard by it a mortal enmity), and to caution you respecting the insinuations of this gentleman against this Court, and the instances he supposes of their ill will to us, which I take to be as imaginary as I know his fancies to be, that Count de Vergennes and myself are continually plotting against him, and employing the news-writers of Europe to depreciate his character. But as Shakspeare says, " Trifles light as air," &c. I am persuaded, however, that he means well for his country, is always an honest man, often a wise one, but sometimes, and in some things, absolutely out of his senses."

This was the man elected President of the United States. Such were the opinions and sentiments entertained by him in regard to France, which time and the revolution in that country had only developed and strengthened.

So soon as this election was known, and avowedly in consequence of it, the Executive Directory, on the 2d of March, 1797, decreed that the treaty concluded on the sixth of February, 1778, between France and the United States, was modified of full right by that which had been concluded at London on the nineteenth of November, 1794, between the United States of America and England; and in consequence thereof, decreed further, that all merchandise of the enemy's, all merchandise not sufficiently ascertained to be neutral, conveyed under American flags, shall be confiscated; that every thing which serves directly or indirectly to the arming and equipping of vessels, shall be contraband—that every American who shall hold a commission from the enemies of France, as well as every seaman of that nation, composing the crew of the ships and vessels, shall, by this fact alone, be declared piratical, and treated as such, without suffering the party to establish that the act was the consequence of threats or violence; that every American ship shall be deemed a lawful prize, which shall not have on board a bill of lading (*role d'equipage*) in due form, according to the plan annexed to the treaty of the sixth of February, 1778. This was in fact a declaration of war in disguise. It was so intended. The Government avowed their determination to *fleece* the American citizens of their property, to a sufficient degree to bring them to their feeling in the only nerve in which it was presumed their sensibility lay, which was their pecuniary interest.

When Mr. Adams was inaugurated on the fourth of March, 1797, he was ignorant of this decree; he only knew that General Pinckney had been refused credence as Minister Plenipotentiary, and had been ordered to leave France.

Notwithstanding this, he expressed a desire for reconciliation. Meeting with Mr. Jefferson, who had come to Philadelphia to take upor himself the duties of Vice-President, to which office he had just been elected, Mr. Adams entered immediately on an explanation of the situation of our affairs with France, and the danger of rupture with that nation, a rupture which would convulse the attachments of this country; that he was impressed with the necessity of an immediate mission to the Directory, and had concluded to send one, which, by its dignity, should satisfy France, and by its selection from the three great divisions of the continent, should satisfy all parts of the United States; in short, that he had determined to join Gerry and Madison to Pinckney, and he requested Mr. Jefferson to consult Mr. Madison for him. On the *sixth of March*, when Mr. Jefferson reported the result of his negotiation with Mr. Madison, the President replied, that, on consultation, some objections to that nomination had been raised, which he had not contemplated; the subject was then dropped, and never afterwards resumed. The consultation alluded

to was with Pickering, Wolcott, McHenry and Lee, the late Cabinet of General Washington, which he had transmitted entire to his
successor. The feelings and opinions of those gentlemen are well
known to the reader. So that the kind intentions of Mr. Adams, in
the first enthusiasm of office, towards the Republican party, and his
spirit of conciliation towards France, were soon dissipated by the
advice of his counsellors. In less than three weeks from this date,
the President's proclamation was issued, requiring an extraordinary
session of Congress to be convened on the fifteenth day of May.

It is obvious that the President was *advised* to this measure, and
that the design of his advisers was to procure, if not a declaration of
war, at least the enactment of such strong retaliatory measures as
would lead to that result. There could have been no other motive
in convening the legislative department at that unusual season ; and
when the decree of the 2d of March was made known, there was no
other alternative left to the Administration. The President might
have dismissed his ministers, and taken into his Cabinet such men as
Madison, Gallatin and Gerry. With their advice he could have sent
to France, as he proposed at first, such envoys as would at once have
satisfied that nation, smothered every asperity, caused the repeal of
every obnoxious decree, and the institution of a tribunal to try all
questions of dispute between the two nations. But not choosing to
follow this course, there was no alternative in the line of policy to
be pursued but war or disgrace.

The President's opening speech on the 17th of May, was considered by his friends sufficiently spirited. After giving a history of
the rejection of the American Minister by the Executive Directory,
and the indignities offered to the nation through him, he thus proceeds : " With this conduct of the French Government, it will be
proper to take into view the public audience given to the late Minister of the United States on his taking leave of the Executive Directory—the speech of the President discloses sentiments more alarming than the refusal of a Minister, because more dangerous to our
independence and union ; and at the same time studiously marked
with indignities towards the Government of the United States : it
evinces a disposition to separate the people of the United States from
the Government, to persuade them that they have different affections,
principles, and interests, from those of their fellow-citizens whom they

themselves have chosen to manage their common concerns; and thus
to produce divisions fatal to our peace. Such attempts ought to be
repelled with a decision which shall convince France and the world,
that we are not a degraded people, humiliated under a colonial spirit
of fear and sense of inferiority, fitted to be the miserable instruments
of foreign influence, and regardless of national honor, character, and
interest."

While he intended to make another effort to adjust all our differences with France by amicable negotiation, the threatening aspect of
affairs rendered it his indispensable duty to recommend to the consideration of Congress *effectual measures of defence.* "The present
situation of our country," says he, in conclusion, "imposes an obligation on all the departments of Government to adopt an explicit and
decided conduct. . . . . It is impossible to conceal from ourselves, or
the world, what has been before observed, that endeavors have been
employed to foster and establish a division between the Government
and the people of the United States. To investigate the causes
which have encouraged this attempt is not necessary; but to repel,
by decided and united councils, insinuations so derogatory to the
honor, and aggressions so dangerous to the constitution, union, and
even independence of the nation, is an indispensable duty. . . . . Convinced that the conduct of this Government has been just and impartial to foreign nations; that those internal regulations which have
been established by land for the preservation of peace, are in their
nature proper, and that they have been fairly executed; nothing will
ever be done by me to impair the national engagements, to innovate
upon principles which have been so deliberately and uprightly established, *or to surrender in any manner the rights of the Government.*"

This energetic speech of the President was not responded to by
the Representatives in the same spirit. The original draft of the
address intending to be fully responsive to the speech, contained the
following clause: "Knowing as we do the confidence reposed by the
people of the United States in their Government, we cannot hesitate
in expressing our indignation at the sentiments disclosed by the
President of the Executive Directory of France in his speech to the
Minister of the United States. Such sentiments serve to discover
the imperfect knowledge which France possesses of the real opinions
of our constituents." This very pointed and spirited paragraph was

stricken out by a vote of *forty-eight* to *forty-six*, and the following substituted in its place : " Any sentiments tending to derogate from the confidence ; such sentiments, wherever entertained, serve to evince an imperfect knowledge of the real opinion of our constituents."

The address contained the following paragraph : " We therefore receive, with the utmost satisfaction, your information that a fresh attempt at negotiation will be instituted ; and we cherish the hope that a mutual spirit of conciliation, and a disposition on the part of the United States to place France on grounds similar to those of other countries, in their relation and connection with us, if any irregularities shall be found to exist, will produce an accommodation compatible with the engagements, rights, duties, and honor of the United States."   A motion was made to strike out the latter part of this clause, in regard to France.   It was negatived by a vote of *forty-nine* to *fifty*.   Thus it seems that there were forty-nine members opposed to placing France on similar grounds to those of other countries, in their relation and connection with us.

A motion was then made to strike out the whole paragraph. Only *forty-one* voted for this proposition ; so that there were at least that many opposed to any farther negotiation, or conciliation with France.

A motion was made to strike from the address the following paragraph : " Believing, with you, that the conduct of the Government has been just and impartial to foreign nations ; that the laws for the preservation of peace have been proper, and that they have been fairly executed, the representatives of the people do not hesitate to declare, that they will give their most cordial support to the execution of principles so deliberately and uprightly established."   This motion was made by Mr. Gallatin, who was a native of Geneva, and spoke English with a very broken accent.   It was opposed by Mr. Allen, who said he was sure such a motion could never pass while there was a drop of *American* blood in the House, and an American *accent* to say *no*.   *Forty-five* voted to strike out, thereby expressing their belief that the Government had not been just and impartial to foreign nations—that laws proper for the preservation of peace had not been enacted, nor fairly executed.

The House of Representatives was composed of one hundred members, leaving out the Speaker ; ninety-nine remained to vote on all questions. Fifty made the majority. Thus the reader will perceive that a very large and powerful minority were opposed to all the measures of the administration. Much the larger portion of its friends were desirous of no further attempts at negotiation with France, and were prepared to push matters to the extremity of war; but the two or three timid, vacillating, and as it was asserted, venal men, necessary to make the majority, could not be relied on. All the labors of Congress, after a two months' session, resulted in a perfect abortion. A few insignificant acts of a defensive character were passed, but nothing energetic or decisive was done.

The republican party, or French partisans as they were called, were reproached for this failure. General Washington had long before said they were the friends of war and confusion; it was now asserted that they were prepared to sacrifice the independence of their own country to the ambition of France. Had it been merely a subject of foreign policy that divided them from the administration, it might be a question how far they were justified in giving the least countenance to the indignities and the atrocities of the French Government. But it must be remembered that great principles, deep and radical, not only in regard to the interpretation of the Constitution, but the basis and design of all government, divided them from the party of the administration. They were firmly impressed with the belief that the latter desired to absorb all the powers distributed among the States, and left to the people, into the federal head; to concentrate them in the Executive, and then to consolidate and confirm these usurpations by a close alliance with Great Britain, whose government and policy were to be taken as a model for our own; and that all their measures, the British treaty, disgrace of Randolph, recall of Monroe, and unconciliating temper towards France, were taken with a view to the consummation of these great designs. Thus impressed, it could not be expected that those men would yield to the policy of the administration. The lasting welfare of the country was of more importance than the removal of a mere temporary shadow that overhung the shield of its fame. They saw the administration in a dilemma; they did not consider it their duty to extricate them from it, that they might pursue measures detrimental to the interests of the country.

Mr. Adams never pursued any well-digested plan of any sort.

He was the creature of impulse. His first impulse, as we have seen, was to send Madison and Gerry to France. This feeling he yielded to the wishes of his counsellors, who were evidently for war. The representatives of the people were called together to second these designs. But falling far short of the expectations of those who had advised the call, the President was compelled to fall back on his original plan, and resort once more to negotiation. But it was now too late. He found himself in this awkward position. He had said to France, I was indignant at your insults and malicious attempts to divide the people from their government, and intended to repel them with becoming spirit; but when I called on the popular branch of government, those who more immediately represented the feelings and wishes of the people, to furnish me the means, I found that a very formidable minority were of your way of thinking; very few prepared to retaliate your insults with war, and a large majority disposed to conciliate you by further negotiations. I am compelled to yield to their wishes, as they are the war-making power; and as a token of my sincerity, I send you three envoys—Messrs. Pinckney, Marshall, and Dana—gentlemen, one of whom you know, of high-toned character, great devotion to my administration and the policy of my predecessor—indignant at the insults you have offered their government, hostile to your principles, shocked at your merciless barbarities at home and abroad, and prepared with unyielding energy and spirit to demand redress for the depredations you have committed on our commerce, and the injuries you have done to our seamen.

What could have been expected from such a mission but disappointment and additional insult? It is true Mr. Dana resigned, and Gerry was put in his place; but the majority of the commission were precisely such men as were the least agreeable to the Directory. It was just as well known to Barras, Merlin, and Talleyrand, as it was to Gallatin, Madison, and Jefferson, that the administration were in a difficulty from which they could not easily escape. They saw plainly from the proceedings and the debates of Congress, that Mr. Adams would be compelled to yield to the republican party, or make war on France. and ally himself with England, or retire in disgrace. A war with France, and a consequent alliance with England, they knew would not be attempted with so formidable an opposition as the late Congress had displayed. They had every reason to expect, that by a steady resistance to the overtures of the administration, they would finally secure a triumph to their friends in America. Governments are conducted by men; men are influenced by human motives, too often by the basest passions and prejudices—(Quam parva sapientia regitur mundus.) Judging from these premises, it was preposterous in Mr. Adams to suppose that his embassy would be received by the Directory in any other than the haughtiest spirit. The defeat of such a mission must have been foreseen from the beginning. Pickering, Wolcott and Company had too much political sagacity not to have anticipated it. And perhaps it is not uncharitable to suppose, that it was projected with the view of creating additional causes of irritation on the part of France.

CHAPTER XIX.

THE X. Y. Z. BUSINESS.

THE envoys arrived in Paris about the first of October, 1797. On the *eighth* they were introduced to the minister, M. Talleyrand, and produced their letters of credence. The minister informed them that he was engaged in preparing for the Executive Directory, a report relative to the situation of the United States with regard to France; and that when it was finished he would let them know what steps were to follow. They then retired with the promise that cards of hospitality, in a style suitable to their official character, should be furnished them. No further notice was taken of them for ten days. They complained to unofficial persons that they had been treated with great slight and disrespect since their arrival. Talleyrand, on the other hand, complained that they had not been to see him. He sent his private secretary, Mr. Z., to wait on them. They had not yet been received by the Directory; and, of course, their Minister of Foreign Affairs could not recognize them publicly as ambassadors. But he did all in his power to do: he sent his secretary, who informed them that M. Talleyrand, Minister of Foreign Relations, professed to be well disposed towards the United States; had expected to have seen the American Ministers frequently in their private capacities; and to have conferred with them individually on the objects of their mission; and had authorized him to make the communication. This, from the circumstances in which the parties were placed, seems not to have been an unreasonable expectation on the part of M. Talleyrand. But two of the envoys excused themselves on the ground of etiquette. General Pinckney and General Marshall expressed their opinion, that, not being acquainted with M. Talleyrand, they could not, with propriety, call on him; but that, according to the custom of France, he might expect this of Mr. Gerry, from a previous acquaintance in America. This Mr. Gerry reluctantly complied with, and appointed a day for an interview. While thus standing off in this ceremonious manner, and unrecognized by the Government, our envoys had some strange adventures. In the morning of October the eighteenth, Mr. W * * * *, of the house of * * * * * * * *, called on General Pinckney, and informed him that a Mr. X. who was in Paris, and whom the General had seen, * * * * * * * *, was a gentleman of considerable credit and reputation, * * * * * * * *, and that we might place great reliance on him. In the evening of the same day, Mr. X., the gentleman so mysteriously announced, called on General Pinckney, and after having sat some time, whispered him, that he had a message from M. Talleyrand to communicate when he was at leisure. General Pinckney immediately withdrew with him into another room; and when they were alone Mr. X. said, that he was charged with a business in which he was a novice; that he had been acquainted with M. Talleyrand, * * * * * * * * * *, and that he was sure he had a great regard for America and its citizens; and was very desirous that a reconciliation should be brought about with France; that to effectuate that end, he was ready, if it was thought proper, to suggest a plan, confidentially, that M. Talleyrand expected would answer the purpose. General Pinckney said he would be glad to hear it. Mr. X. replied, that the Directory, and particularly two of the members of it, were exceedingly irritated at some passages of the President's speech at the opening of Congress in May, and desired that they should be softened; and that this step would be necessary previous to our reception; that, besides this, a sum of money was required for the pocket of the Directory and ministers (about fifty thousand pounds sterling), which would be at the disposal of M. Talleyrand; and that a loan would also be insisted on. Mr. X. said, if we acceded to these measures, M. Talleyrand had no doubt that all our difficulties with France might be accommodated. At the same time, he said his communication was not immediately with M. Talleyrand, but through another gentleman, in whom M. Talleyrand had great confidence.

Next day Mr. X., and Mr. Y., the confidential friend alluded to, called on the envoys. Mr. Y., having been introduced as the confidential friend of M. Talleyrand, commenced the conversation, and proceeded pretty much in the same strain as Mr. X. on the day preceding. He said the minister could not see them himself, as they had not been received by the Directory, but had authorized his friend Mr. Y. to communicate certain propositions, and to promise on his part, that if they could be considered as the basis of the proposed negotiation, he would intercede with the Directory to acknowledge them, and to give them a public audience. Mr. Y. stated explicitly and repeatedly that he was clothed with no authority; that he was not a diplomatic character; that he was not * * * * * * * *; he was only the friend of M. Talleyrand, and trusted by him. He then read tl e parts of the President's speech that were objectionable, and dilated very much upon the keenness of the resentment it had produced, and expatiated largely on the satisfaction he said was indispensably necessary as a preliminary to negotiation. "But," said he, "gentlemen, I will not disguise from you that this satisfaction being made, the essential part of the treaty remains to be adjusted : Il faut do l'argent—il faut beaucoup d'argent;" *you must pay money—you must pay a great deal of money.* He said that the reception of the money might be so disguised as to prevent its being considered a breach of neutrality by England; and thus save us from being embroiled with that power. Concerning the twelve hundred thousand livres (£50,000), little was said.

Next day (October 21st) Mr. X. and Mr. Y. again called on the envoys, and commenced their private and unofficial negotiation. It was explained more fully, how the loan might be accomplished by the purchase of certain Dutch inscriptions held by the French government ; and it was delicately intimated, that if the envoys would search a little, they might find means to soothe the angry feelings of Merlin and Company, and avert the demand concerning the President's speech.

The envoys replied, that the proposition of a loan in the form of Dutch inscriptions, or in any other form, was not within the limits of their instructions, and that upon this point the Government must be consulted; and one of the American ministers would, for the purpose, forthwith embark for America.

Mr. Y. seemed disappointed at this conclusion. He said the envoys treated the money part of the proposition as if·it had proceeded from the Directory; whereas, in fact, it did not even proceed from the minister, but was only a suggestion from himself, as a substitute to be proposed by them, in order to avoid the painful acknowledgment that the Directory had determined to demand.

These unofficial gentlemen, X. and Y., who, the envoys admitted, had brought no testimonials of their speaking any thing from authority, continued their visits from day to day, and urged their propositions with all the earnestness and eloquence they possessed. They told the envoys that France had just concluded a treaty with the Emperor of Austria; and that the Directory, since this peace, had taken a higher and more decided tone with respect to the United States, and all other neutral nations, than had been before taken; that it had been determined that all nations should aid them, or be considered and treated as their enemies. They expatiated on the power and violence of France, urged the danger of our situation, and pressed the policy of softening them, and of thereby obtaining time.

While these strange conferences were held with men unconnected with the Government, and one a foreigner, Mr. Gerry, on the 28th of October, according to appointment, paid his first visit to the minister since the day of their presentation. The others, standing on etiquette, refused to go. After the first introduction, M. Talleyrand began the conference. He said the Directory had passed an arrête, which he offered for perusal, in which they had demanded of the envoys an explanation of some parts, and a reparation for others, of the President's speech to Congress, of the 16th of May last. He was sensible, he said, that difficulties would exist on the part of the envoys relative to this demand; but that by their offering money, he thought he could prevent the effect of the arrête. It having been stated that the envoys had no such power, M. Talleyrand replied, they can in such case take a power on themselves, *and proposed that they should make a loan.* Mr. Gerry then stated that the uneasiness of the Directory resulting from the President's speech, was a subject unconnected with the objects of their mission; that the powers of the envoys, as they conceived, were adequate to the discussion and adjustment of all points of real difference between the two nations; that they could alter and amend the treaty, or, if necessary, form a new one; that as to a loan, they had no powers whatever to make one; but that they could send one of their number for instructions on this proposition, if deemed expedient. M. Talleyrand, in answer, said he should be glad to confer with the other envoys individually; but that this matter about the money must be settled directly, without sending to America; that he would not communicate the arrête for a week; and that if they could adjust the matter about the speech, an application would, nevertheless, go to the United States for a loan. In this private interview between M. Talleyrand and one of the envoys, that minister intimates that a loan will be asked, and will be expected to be granted on the part of the United States; but not the slightest allusion is made to a douceur for the use of the members of the Directory.

On the 11th of November the envoys transmitted an official letter for the first time to the Minister of Foreign Affairs, in which they state that his declaration at the time of their arrival, that a report on American affairs was then preparing, and would, in a few days be laid before the Directory, whose decision thereon should, without delay, be made known, had hitherto imposed silence on them. For this communication they had waited with that anxious solicitude which so interesting an event could not fail to excite, and with that respect which was due to the government of France. They disclosed their full powers to treat on all differences between the two nations; and expressed their anxiety to commence the task of restoring that friendship, that mutual interchange of good offices, which it was alike their wish and their duty to effect between the citizens of the two republics. Having received no answer, on the 21st they sent their secretary to wait on the minister, and inquire of him whether he had communicated the letter to the Directory, and whether an answer might be expected. He replied that he had submitted the letter, and that when he was directed what steps to pursue, they should be informed.

On the 24th of December the envoys wrote to the Secretary of State, that they had received no answer to their official letter to the Minister of Foreign Affairs, dated the 11th of November ; but that reiterated attempts had been made to engage them in negotiation with persons not officially authorized. They further stated it as their opinion, that if they were to remain six months longer, unless they were to stipulate the payment of money, and a great deal of it, in some shape or other, they would not be able to effectuate the object of their mission, nor would they even be officially received.

The President of the United States, in a message to Congress, March 19th, 1798, stated that the dispatches from the envoys extraordinary to the French Republic had been received, examined, maturely considered, and that he perceived no ground of expectation that the objects of their mission could be accomplished, on terms compatible with the safety, honor, or the essential interests of the nation.

On the 27th of January, 1798, the envoys addressed a letter to the Minister of Foreign Affairs, on the subject of a late law, authorizing the capture of neutral vessels, on board of which any productions of Great Britain or its possessions should be laden showing how incompatible such law was with the rights of neutral nations and the treaty between France and America, its direct tendency to destroy the remaining commerce of this country, and the particular hardships to which it would subject the agricultural as well as commercial interests of their countrymen, from the peculiar situation of the United States. They added, that under existing circumstances, they could no longer resist the conviction, that the demands of France rendered it entirely impracticable to effect the objects of their mission. On the 19th of February, having received no answer to this communication, they sent their secretary to know of the minister whether he had any response to make. He replied that he had none, as the Directory had taken no order on the subject. At length, on the 27th of February, for the first time since their arrival in Paris, the envoys solicited a personal interview on the subject of their mission. The minister promptly acceded to the request, and fixed on the 2d day of March for the interview. On that occasion, the minister said, that, without doubt, the Directory wished very sincerely, on the arrival of the envoys, to see a solid friendship established between France and the United States, and had manifested this disposition, by the readiness with which orders for their passports were given. That the Directory had been extremely wounded by the last speech of General Washington, made to Congress when about to quit the office of President of the United States; and by the first and last speech of Mr. Adams. That explanations of these speeches were expected and required of us. He said, that the original favorable disposition of the Directory had been a good deal altered by the coldness and distance which the envoys had observed. That instead of seeing him often, and endeavoring to remove the obstacles to a mutual approach, *they had not once waited on him.* In this state of things some proof, he said, would be required on the part of the United States, of a friendly disposition, previous to a treaty with them. The envoys ought to search for, and propose some means which might furnish this proof. In this he alluded very intelligibly to a loan. He said he must exact from them, on the part of his Government, some proposition of this sort; that to prove their friendship, there must be some immediate aid, or something which might avail them; that the principles of reciprocity would require it. This once done, he said, the adjustment of complaints would be easy; that would be matter of inquiry; and if France had done wrong, it would be repaired; but that if this was refused, it would increase the distance and coldness between the two republics. It was replied that the envoys had no power to make a loan. One of them, Mr. Gerry, then observed, that the Government of France must judge for itself; but that it appeared to him, that a treaty on liberal principles, such as those on which the treaty of commerce between the two nations was first established, would be infinitely more advantageous to France than the trifling advantages she could derive from a loan. Such a treaty would produce a friendship and attachment on the part of the United States to France, which would be solid and permanent, and produce benefits far superior to those of a loan, even if they had powers to make it. To this observation, M. Talleyrand made no reply. Nor did he express any sentiment as to the propriety of one of the envoys going home to consult the Government on the expediency of giving powers to negotiate a loan. He had already expressed his opinion that they had the power, or might assume it, without violating their instructions.

On the 18th of March, M. Talleyrand addressed a letter to the envoys in answer to theirs of the 17th January. In this he elaborately reviews the whole course of the two Governments, and justifies France in every particular. It might appear incredible, he said, that the Republic, and her alliance, were sacrificed at the moment when she had redoubled her regards for her ally; and that the corresponding demonstrations of the Federal Government had no other object but to keep her, as well as her Government, in a false security. And yet it is now known, that, at this very period, Mr. Jay, who had been sent to London solely, as it was then said, to negotiate arrangements relative to the depredations committed upon the American commerce by the cruisers of Great Britain, signed a treaty of amity, navigation and commerce, the negotiation and signing of which had been kept a profound secret at Paris and at Philadelphia. Observing that, in this treaty every thing having been calculated to turn the neutrality of the United States to the disadvantage of the French Republic, and to the advantage of England; that the Federal Government having in this act made to Great Britain concessions the most unheard of, the most incompatible with the interests of the United States, the most derogatory to the alliance which subsisted between the said States and the French Republic; the latter was perfectly free, in order to avoid the inconveniences of the treaty of London, to avail itself of the preservative means with which the laws of nature, the law of nations, and prior treaties furnished it. Such were the reasons which had produced the decrees of the Directory, of which the United States complained.

He then proceeded to declare that newspapers, known to be under the immediate control of the Cabinet, had, since the treaty, redoubled their invectives and calumnies against the Republic and against her principles, her magistrates and her envoys. Pamphlets, openly paid for by the minister of Great Britain, had reproduced in every form those insults and calumnies. The Government itself was intent on encouraging this scandal in its public acts. The Executive Directory had been denounced in a speech delivered by the President as endeavoring to propagate anarchy and division within the United States. In fine, he said, one could not help discovering in the tone of the speech and of the publications which had just been pointed to, a latent enmity that only wanted an opportunity to break out. Facts being thus established, it was disagreeable, he said, to be obliged to think that the instructions under which the commissioners acted, had not been drawn up with the sincere intention of attaining pacific ends. The intentions which he had attributed to the Government of the United States, were so little disguised, that nothing seemed to have been neglected at Philadelphia to manifest them to every eye. And it was probably with this view that it was thought proper to send to the French Republic, persons whose opinions and connections were too well known to hope from them dispositions sincerely conciliatory. Penetrated with the justice of these reflections, and their consequences, the Executive Directory had authorized him to express himself with all the frankness which became the French nation. It was only to smooth the way of discussions that he had entered into the preceding explanations. It was with the same view that he declared to the commissioners and envoys extraordinary, that, notwithstanding the kind of prejudice which had been entertained with respect to them, the Executive Directory was disposed to treat with that one of the three whose opinions, presumed to be more impartial, promised, in the course of the explanations, more of that reciprocal confidence which was indispensable.

To the communication of Talleyrand, the envoys returned a very elaborate reply, in which they reviewed all the points of difficulty raised by him, endeavored to disabuse his mind as to the motives of the Government of the United States, and the prejudices which he imagined to exist in the minds of the envoys themselves, and concluded by declaring that no one of them was authorized to take upon himself a negotiation indirectly intrusted by the tenor of their powers and instructions to the whole; nor were there any two of them who could propose to withdraw themselves from the task committed to them by their Government, while there remained a possibility of performing it.

The very day the answer of the envoys was sent to the minister (3d April) Mr. Gerry received a note from him in which he said:— "I suppose that Messrs. Pinckney and Marshall have thought it useful and proper, in consequence of the intimations given in the end of my note of the 28th Ventose last (18th March), and the obstacle which their known opinions have interposed to the desired reconciliation, to quit the territory of the Republic. On this supposition, I have the honor to point out to you the 5th or 7th of this decade, to resume our reciprocal communications upon the interests of the French Republic and the United States of America."

Mr. Gerry replied (April 4th), that as his colleagues were expected to quit the territory of France, he had no authority to act intheir absence. He could only confer informally, he said, and unaccredited, on any subject respecting their mission, and communicate to the Government of the United States the result of such conferences, being in his individual capacity unauthorized to give them an official stamp. Nevertheless, every measure in his power, he said, and in conformity with the duty he owed his country, should be zealously pursued, to restore harmony and a cordial friendship between the two republics.

In consequence of the above intimation from the minister, Messrs. Marshall and Pinckney soon left Paris. In a letter to the President, dated the 16th of April, Mr. Gerry said he had expected his passports with his colleagues, but was informed that the Directory would not consent to his leaving France ; and, to bring on an immediate rupture by adopting this measure, contrary to their wishes, would be in his mind unwarrantable, and therefore he concluded to remain.

Thus ended this extraordinary mission ; a conclusion which must have been foreseen—must have been anticipated by those who projected it. So soon as the dispatches containing those transactions, of which the above is intended to be a faithful though succinct narrative, were made known to the public, the political barometer at once rose to the storm point. At the time of their reception, Congress was debating the proposition, *that it is inexpedient to resort to war against the French Republic.* It was expected to be carried by a majority of two or three ; but it was now laid aside, and the most vigorous war measures introduced. " The most artful misrepresentations of the contents of those papers," says Mr. Jefferson, April 6th, " were published yesterday, and produced such a shock in the republican mind as had never been since our independence. We are to dread the effects of this dismay till their fuller information. The spirit kindled up in the towns is wonderful. These and New Jersey are pouring in their addresses, offering life and fortune. The answers of the President are more thrasonic than the addresses. Nor is it France alone, but his own fellow-citizens, against whom his threats are extended. *The delusions,* says he, *and misrepresen-*

tations which have misled so many citizens must be discountenanced by authority, as well as by the citizens at large. . . . . At present the warhawks talk of Septembrizing, deportation, and the examples of quelling sedition set by the French Executive. Early in April the war party, with passionate exclamation, declared that they would soon pass a citizens' bill, an alien bill, and a sedition bill, with the view of disfranchising such men as Gallatin, banishing Volney, Collot, and other unfortunate Frenchmen who had taken refuge in the country, and of silencing Bache, Carey, and other republican presses."

The excitement spread far and wide among the people. The cry was, *millions for defence, not a cent for tribute.* This broad, comprehensive, self-evident proposition to a brave and independent people, soon became the watchword of the multitude : *millions for defence, not a cent for tribute.* This happy and pithy appeal to the pride of a nation was level to the capacity of all; every body could understand it; and, what was more important, every body could feel it. 'Twas vain to attempt to reason down this excited feeling of national pride. 'Twas vain to tell the people that France had demanded no tribute—that our envoys had never held but one interview with the minister of foreign affairs, and that the only proposition on that occasion was the bare suggestion that the United States, as proof of her friendship, might make a loan to France in her present necessities, by way of reciprocity for a similar loan made to us in the war of revolution, when our credit and very existence were dependent on the timely aid then extended to us ; that the demand of tribute was made by a couple of swindlers, unconnected with the Government, who had imposed on the credulity of our envoys, and who, in fact, encouraged the intrigue, that they might make political capital, in order to create the very excitement it had occasioned ; that the only obstacle in the way of an amicable settlement of all our differences with France was the intemperate speeches of the President, the haughty, reserved and unconciliatory temper of the envoys themselves ; that France had only done what she had a right to do according to the laws of nations, to show her displeasure to ministers plenipotentiary who were disagreeable to her, who were hostile to her principles, unfriendly to her Government, and of such a temper as not to be able to secure her confidence; that she had only signified her desire that those envoys should depart, and the one in whom she had confidence might remain, with whom she was ready to negotiate on terms of the utmost fairness and equality. 'Twas vain to state the plain facts to an excited multitude. *Millions for defence, not a cent for tribute,* was the ready and comprehensive answer. The fever was up, and must run its course. The multitude are not only fond of broad and comprehensive phrases that will serve them on all occasions, and save the necessity of thought, but they must always have some sign, or outward symbol of their feelings. On this occasion the *black cockade* of England was mounted as a badge of hostility to the *tri-color* of France. The handwriting, it was said, at the bottom of an address is seen but by few persons; whereas a cockade will be seen by the whole city, by the friends and the foes of the wearer; it will be the visible sign of the sentiments of his heart, and will prove that he is not ashamed to avow those sentiments. Persons who marched to the President's house to present their warlike addresses were encouraged to wear the *American cockade.* Those who dare not designate themselves, they were told, by this lasting mark of resolution, may, indeed, walk up Market-street, but their part of the procession will only serve to recall to our minds the old battered French gasconade—

> "The King of France, with forty thousand men,
> Marched up the hill, and then—*marched down again.*"

Congress, under the war-excitement, passed in rapid succession, a stamp-act, an excise law, an act, entering into minute and vexatious details, laying a direct tax on lands, slaves, houses, and other property; two acts authorizing the President to borrow large sums of money at usurious interest; several acts authorizing the purchasing of vessels, creating a naval armament, and a navy department in the Government; acts prohibiting the exportation of arms, and authorizing the purchase of cannon, and the fortification of ports and harbors; acts creating additional regiments in the army, augmenting those in existence, and authorizing the President to call out and organize a *provisional* army of *ten thousand men,* if in his opinion there existed an imminent danger of invasion; acts prohibiting all intercourse with France or her dependencies, and authorizing the capture of all French armed vessels; an act making it lawful for the President of the United States to cause all such aliens as he shall judge dangerous to the peace and safety of the United States, or shall have reasonable grounds to suspect are concerned in any treasonable or secret machinations against the Government thereof, to depart out of the territory of the United States; and an act declaring, that if any person shall write, print, utter, or publish, or aid in the same, any false, scandalous, and malicious writings against the Government of the United States, Congress, or the President, with intent to defame, or bring them into contempt or disrepute, being thereof convicted before any court of the United States, shall be punished by fine and imprisonment. To crown all these vast military preparations, General Washington was appointed Commander-in-chief of the Army. " We must have your name," said the President, in a letter to him, " if you will in any way permit us to use it. There will be more efficiency in it than in many an army." Without waiting for an answer, on the 2d of July he nominated to the Senate, " George Washington, of Mount Vernon, to be Lieutenant-General and Commander-in-chief of all the armies, raised and to be raised in the United States."

Washington accepted the appointment; and in his reply to the President, said : " It was not possible for me to remain ignorant of, or indifferent to, recent transactions. The conduct of the Directory of France towards our country, their insidious hostilities to its Government, their various practices to withdraw the affections of the people from it, the evident tendency of their arts, and those of their agents, to countenance and invigorate opposition, their disregard of solemn treaties and the laws of nations, their war upon our defenceless commerce, their treatment of our minister of peace, and their demands, amounting to tribute, could not fail to excite in me corresponding sentiments with those which my countrymen had so generally expressed in their affectionate addresses to you. Believe me, sir, no one can more cordially approve of the wise and prudent measures of your administration. They ought to inspire universal confidence, and will no doubt, combined with the state of things, call from Congress such laws and means as will enable you to meet the full force and extent of the crisis. Satisfied, therefore, that you have sincerely wished and endeavored to avert war, and exhausted to the last drop the cup of reconciliation, we can with pure hearts appeal to Heaven for the justice of our cause, and may confidently trust the final result to that kind Providence, which has heretofore, and so often, signally favored the people of these United States."

The war excitement was kept up through the summer and autumn. The republican party found it difficult to separate in the public mind the principles for which they contended, from the acts of the French Directory. Having been regarded through the country as the French party, they had now to bear much of the odium that was attached to the French cause. The war fever began to abate as winter approached. Mr. Gerry, our envoy, who remained in France after the departure of his colleagues, and other eminent citizens of the United States, had now returned from Europe, and reported that the French Directory were in a most friendly temper towards the United States, and were prepared to treat with any minister they might send, on terms of perfect reciprocity. The Virginia legislature, early in the session of 1798-9, passed a series of resolutions denouncing the Alien and Sedition Laws as unconstitutional. The heavy taxes also began to work their usual effect on the public mind. It was soon perceived that some effort must be made to prevent the popular current from turning against the administration. The great object was to keep up the majority in Congress, so as to continue their war measures. The spring elections of 1799 were coming on, and every effort was made by both sides to influence them. It was perceived that the future destiny of the country depended on the result. Virginia was the great battle-ground: all eyes were turned in that direction.

There was the stronghold of republicanism—there were its renowned chiefs to be found—Jefferson, Madison, Monroe, Giles, Taylor, besides a host of others of less fame, but equal zeal in the cause. There, also, was Washington, who had thrown himself into the opposite scale, and, with energy, exerted all his influence to give preponderance to the side he espoused. No man did more to bring out influential characters to represent the State, both in Congress and the legislature. "At such a crisis as this," said he, "when every thing dear and valuable to us is assailed; when this party hangs upon the wheels of government as a dead weight, opposing every measure that is calculated for defence and self-preservation; abetting the nefarious views of another nation upon our rights; preferring, as long as they dare contend openly against the spirit and resentment of the people, the interest of France to the welfare of their own country; justifying the former, at the expense of the latter; when every act of their own government is tortured, by constructions they will not bear, into attempts to infringe and trample upon the constitution, with a view to introduce monarchy; when the most unceasing and the purest exertions, which were making to maintain a neutrality, proclaimed by the executive, approved unequivocally by Congress, by the State legislatures, nay, by the people themselves, in various meetings, and to preserve the country in peace, are charged with being measures calculated to favor Great Britain at the expense of France; and all those who had any agency in it, are accused of being under the influence of the former, and her pensioners; when measures are systematically and pertinaciously pursued, which must, eventually, dissolve the Union, or produce coercion; I say, when these things have become so obvious, ought characters who are best able to rescue their country from the pending evil, to remain at home? Rather ought they not to come forward, and, by their talents and influence, stand in the breach, which such conduct has made on the peace and happiness of this country ?"

By such persuasions as this, General Lee was induced to offer himself as a candidate for Congress in the Westmoreland district— Westmoreland, the birth-place of Washington! On the other hand, by the persuasions of Mr. Jefferson, Dr. Walter Jones came out in opposition to him. The canvass between these two champions of adverse wishes and sentiments, was very animated. In colloquial eloquence and irony, no man could surpass Dr. Jones; but he was overmatched by his antagonist, in popular address and public eloquence. In the Richmond district, John Clopton, the sitting member, and a republican, was opposed by General Marshall, the late envoy to France, and, by all odds, the ablest champion of the federal cause in Virginia. But the great field of contest—the citadel that must be carried—was the State legislature. That body had recently pronounced the Alien and Sedition Laws unconstitutional. The great object was now to obtain a majority to reverse that decision. It was well known that Mr. Madison would be in the next legislature, with his matchless logic, to develope, explain and enforce the doctrines of the resolutions recently passed. Some one must be found to oppose him. General Washington found the man—that man was Patrick Henry. And by him the trembling old warrior was induced to buckle on the harness for his last battle. In a confidential letter, dated 15th January, 1799, Washington says: "It would be a waste of time to attempt to bring to the view of a person of your observation and discernment, the endeavors of a certain party among us to disquiet the public mind with unfounded alarms; to arraign every act of the administration; to set the people at variance with their government; and to embarrass all its measures. Equally useless would it be to predict what must be the inevitable consequences of such a policy, if it cannot be arrested. Unfortunately, and extremely do I regret it, the State of Virginia has taken the lead in this opposition. I have said the *State*, because the conduct of its legislature in the eyes of the world will authorize the expression. I come now, my good sir, to the object of my letter, which is to express the hope, and an earnest wish, that you will come forward at the ensuing elections (if not for Congress, which you may think would take you too long from home) as a candidate for representative in the General Assembly of this Commonwealth. Your weight of character and influence in the House of Representatives would be a bulwark against such dangerous sentiments as are delivered there at present. It would be a rallying-point for the timid, and an attraction for the wavering. In a word, I conceive it to be of immense importance, at this crisis, that you should be there; and I would fain hope that all minor considerations will be made to yield to the measure." All minor considerations were made to yield; and the old veteran, bowed with age and disease, was announced as a candidate to represent the county of Charlotte in the General Assembly of Virginia. Powhatan Bolling was the candidate for Congress, on the federal side; he was opposed by John Randolph. On March court day, Patrick Henry and John Randolph met, for the first time, on the hustings at Charlotte Court House—the one the champion of the Federal—the other the champion of the Republican cause.

CHAPTER XX.

PATRICK HENRY.

PATRICK HENRY, the advocate of the Alien and Sedition Laws, the defender of federal measures leading to consolidation! Let the reader look back and contemplate his course in the Virginia Convention, called to ratify the Constitution—let him hear the eloquent defence of the Articles of Confederation, which had borne us safely through so many perils, and which needed only amendment, not annihilation—let him witness the ardent devotion to the State government as the bulwark of liberty—the uncompromising opposition to the new Government, its consolidation, its destruction of State independence, its awful squinting towards monarchy—let him behold the vivid picture drawn by the orator of the patriot of *seventy-six*, and the citizen of *eighty-eight;* then it was liberty, give me liberty! now the cry was energy, energy, give me a strong and energetic government—then let him turn and see the same man, in little more than ten years, stand forth, his prophecies all tending to rapid fulfilment, the advocate of the principles, the defender of the measures that had so agitated his mind and awakened his fears—let the reader meditate on these things, and have charity for the mutations of political opinion in his own day, which he so often unfeelingly denounces.

It is true that Patrick Henry had been in retirement since the adoption of the new Constitution, and had no part in the organization of those parties which had arisen under it, but it is certain that they took their origin in those principles which on the one side he so eloquently defended, and on the other so warmly deprecated. Federalist and Republican were names unknown in his day ; but from his past history no one could mistake the inclination of his feelings, or the conclusions of his judgment on the great events transpiring around him. Up to 1795 he was known to be on the republican side. In a letter, dated the 27th of June in that year, he says: " Since the adoption of the present Constitution I have generally moved in a narrow circle. But in that I have never omitted to inculcate a strict adherence to the principles of it. . . . . . Although a democrat myself, I like not the late democratic societies. As little do I like their suppression by law." On another occasion he writes: " The treaty (Jay's treaty) is, in my opinion, a very bad one indeed . . . . Sure I am, my first principle is, that from the British we have every thing to dread, when opportunities of oppressing us shall offer." He then proceeds to express his concern at the abusive manner in which his old commander-in-chief was treated; and that his long and great services were not remembered as an apology for his mistakes in an office to which he was totally unaccustomed.

A man of his talents, his eloquence, his weight of character and influence in the State, was well worth gaining over to the side of the administration. Some of the first characters in Virginia undertook to accomplish that end. Early in the summer of 1794, General Lee, then governor of Virginia, and commander-in-chief of the forces ordered out against the whisky insurrection, had frequent and earnest conferences with him on public affairs. He was at first very impracticable. It seems that the old man had been informed that General Washington, in passing through the State on his return from the South in the summer of 1791, while speaking of Mr. Henry on several occasions, considered him a *factious and seditious character*. General Lee undertook to remove these impressions, and combated his opinions as groundless; but his endeavors were unavailing. He seemed to be deeply and sorely affected. General Washington denied the charge. All he had said on the occasion alluded to was, that he had heard Mr. Henry was acquiescent in his conduct, and that, though he could not give up his opinion respecting the Constitution, yet, unless he should be called upon by official duty, he would express no sentiment unfriendly to the exercise of the powers of a government, which had been chosen by a majority of the people.

It was a long time before General Lee had an opportunity of communicating to Mr. Henry the kind feelings of Washington towards him. In June, 1795, about a year after the subject had been broached to him, Mr. Henry writes: " Every insinuation that taught me to believe I had forfeited the good will of that personage, to whom the world had agreed to ascribe the appellation of *good* and *great*, must needs give me pain; particularly as he had opportunities of knowing my character both in public and in private life. The intimation now given me, that there was no ground to believe I had incurred his censure, gives very great pleasure." In inclosing Mr. Henry's letter to General Washington for perusal, Lee thus writes (17th July, 1795): "I am very confident that Mr. Henry possesses the highest and truest regard for you, and that he continues friendly to the General Government, notwithstanding the unwearied efforts applied for the end of uniting him to the opposition; and I must think he would be an important official acquisition to the Government."

One month and two days from this date (19th August) as the reader remembers, Edmund Randolph resigned the office of Secretary of State. On the 9th of October it was tendered to Patrick Henry. In his letter of invitation General Washington stated that the office had been offered to others; but it was from a conviction that he would not accept it. But in a conversation with General Lee, that gentleman dropped sentiments that made it less doubtful. "I persuade myself, sir," said the President, "it has not escaped your observation that a crisis is approaching that must, if it cannot be arrested, soon decide whether order and good government shall be preserved, or anarchy and confusion ensue."

This letter of invitation was inclosed to Mr. Carrington, a confidential friend of Washington, with instructions to hold it back till he could hear from Colonel Innis, to whom the attorney-generalship had been offered. But on consultation with General Marshall, another confidential friend, they were so anxious to make an impression on Patrick Henry, and gain him over, if possible, by those marks of confidence, that they disobeyed orders, reversed the order in which the letters were to be sent, and dispatched Mr. Henry's first, by express.

"In this determination we were governed," say they, "by the following reasons." (We give the reasons entire, that the reader may see that great men and statesmen in those days were influenced by the same motives they are now, and that men are the same in every age.) "First, his non-acceptance, from domestic considerations may be calculated on. In this event, be his sentiments on either point what they may, he will properly estimate your letter, and if he has any asperities, it must tend to soften them, and render him, instead of a silent observer of the present tendency of things, in some degree active on the side of government and order. Secondly, should he feel an inclination to go into the office proposed, we are confident—very confident—he has too high a sense of honor to do so with sentiments hostile to either of the points in view. This we should rely on, upon general grounds; but under your letter a different conduct is, we conceive from our knowledge of Mr. Henry, impossible. Thirdly, we are fully persuaded that a more deadly blow could not be given to the faction in Virginia, and perhaps elsewhere, than that gentleman's acceptance of the office in question, convinced as we are of the sentiments he must carry with him. So much have the opposers of government held him up as their oracle, even since he has ceased to respond to them, that any event demonstrating his active support to government could not but give the party a severe shock."

A very good reason for disobeying instructions, and making the first demonstration on so important a personage. Mr. Henry did not accept the appointment, but the impression intended to be made was nearly as complete as the parties intended.

"It gives us pleasure to find," says Mr. Carrington, "that although Mr. Henry is rather to be understood as probably not an approver of the treaty, his conduct and sentiments generally, both as to the government and yourself, are such as we calculated on, and that he received your letter with impresssions which assure us of his discountenancing calumny and disorder of every description."

These great movements somehow got wind, and came to the ears of the leader of the faction they were designed to crush. In a letter addressed to Monroe, dated July 10th, 1796, Jefferson says: "Most assiduous court is paid to Patrick Henry. He has been offered every thing, which they knew he would not accept. Some impression is thought to be made: but we do not believe it is radical. If they thought they could count upon him, they would run him for their Vice-President, their first object being to produce a schism in this State." A move was now made to prevent the old man from going over altogether. In November following, the democratic legislature of Virginia elected him, for the third time, governor of the State. In his letter declining an acceptance of the office, he merely expresses his acknowledgments and gratitude for the signal honor conferred on him, excuses himself on the ground that he could not persuade himself that his abilities were commensurate to the duties of the office, but let fall no expression that could indicate his present political inclinations.

Early in January, 1799, soon after the passage of the resolutions declaring the alien and sedition laws unconstitutional, and before he had received the letter from Washington urging him to become a candidate for the Virginia legislature, Patrick Henry, in writing to a friend, thus expresses himself: " There is much cause for lamentation over the present state of things in Virginia. It is possible that most of the individuals who compose the contending factions are sincere, and act from honest motives. But it is more than probable that certain leaders meditate a change in government. To effect this, I see no way so practicable as dissolving the confederacy; and I am free to own that, in my judgment, most of the measures lately pursued by the opposition party directly and certainly lead to that end. If this is not the system of the party, they have none, and act *extempore.*"

In February following, the President nominated Mr. Henry as one of the Envoys Extraordinary and Ministers Plenipotentiary to the French Republic. Perhaps the very day he appeared before the people at Charlotte Court, he held the commission in his pocket. In his letter declining the appointment, he says: " That nothing short of absolute necessity could induce me to withhold my little aid from an administration whose abilities, patriotism, and virtue, deserve the gratitude and reverence of all their fellow-citizens."

In March, *eighty-nine*, Decius said, *I want to crush that anti-federal champion*—the cunning and deceitful Cromwell, who, under the guise of amendment, seeks to destroy the Constitution, break up the confederacy, and reign *the tyrant of popularity* over his own devoted Virginia. In *ninety-nine*, we find this anti-federal champion veered round to the support of doctrines he once condemned, and given in his allegiance to an administration, which a majority of his countrymen had declared, and all those who had followed him as their oracle declared, was rapidly hastening the Government into consolidation and monarchy.

Let no man boast of his consistency. Such is the subtlety of human motives, that, like a deep, unseen under-current, they unconsciously glide us into a position to-day different from that we occupied yesterday, while we perceive it not, and stoutly deny it.

Patrick Henry for years was sorely afflicted with the belief that the *greatest* and *best* of mankind considered him a *factious* and *seditious* character: to disabuse the mind of Washington, whose good opinion all men desired—to justify the flattering attentions of those distinguished men who had assiduously cultivated his society and correspondence, and showered bright honors on his head, he unconsciously receded from his old opinions, and embraced doctrines which he had, with the clearness and power of a Hebrew prophet, portrayed and made bare in all their naked deformity.

CHAPTER XXI.

MARCH COURT—THE RISING AND THE SETTING SUN.

IT was soon noised abroad that Patrick Henry was to address the people at March Court. Great was the political excitement—still greater the anxiety to hear the first orator of the age for the last time. They came from far and near, with eager hope depicted on every countenance. It was a treat that many had not enjoyed for years. Much the largest portion of those who flocked together that day, had only heard from the glowing lips of their fathers the wonderful powers of the man they were about to see and hear for the first time. The college in Prince Edward was emptied not only of its students, but of its professors. Dr. Moses Hogue, John H. Rice, Drury Lacy, eloquent men and learned divines, came up to enjoy the expected feast. The young man who was to answer Mr. Henry, if indeed the multitude suspected that any one would dare venture on a reply, was unknown to fame. A tall, slender, effeminate looking youth was he; light hair, combed back into a well-adjusted cue—pale countenance, a beardless chin, bright quick hazel eye, blue frock, buff small clothes, and fair-top boots. He was doubtless known to many on the court green as the little Jack Randolph they had frequently seen dashing by on wild horses, riding *a la mode Anglais*, from Roanoke to Bizarre, and back from Bizarre to Roanoke. A few knew him more intimately, but none had ever heard him speak in public, or even suspected that he could make a speech. "My first attempt at public speaking," says he, in a letter to Mrs. Bryan, his niece, "was in opposition to Patrick Henry at Charlotte March Court, 1799; for neither of us was present at the election in April, as Mr. Wirt avers of Mr. Henry." The very thought of his attempting to answer Mr. Henry, seemed to strike the grave and reflecting men of the place as preposterous. "Mr. Taylor," said Col. Reid, the clerk of the county, to Mr. Creed Taylor, a friend and neighbor of Randolph, and a good lawyer, "Mr. Taylor, don't you or Peter Johnson mean to appear for that young man to-day?" "Never mind," replied Taylor, "he can take care of himself." His friends knew his powers, his fluency in conversation, his ready wit, his polished satire, his extraordinary knowledge of men and affairs; but still he was about to enter on an untried field, and all those brilliant faculties might fail him, as they had so often failed men of genius before. They might well have felt some anxiety on his first appearance upon the hustings in presence of a popular assembly, and in reply to a man of Mr. Henry's reputation. But it seems they had no fear for the result—*he can take care of himself.* The reader can well imagine the remarks that might have been made by the crowd as he passed carelessly among them, shaking hands with this one and that one of his acquaintance. "And is that the man who is a candidate for Congress?" "Is he going to speak against Old Pat?" "Why, he is nothing but a boy—he's got no beard!" "He looks wormy!" "Old Pat will eat him up bodily!" There, also, was Powhatan Bolling, the other candidate for Congress, dressed in his scarlet coat—tall, proud in his bearing, and a fair representative of the old aristocracy fast melting away under the subdivisions of the law that had abolished the system of primogeniture.

Creed Taylor and others undertook to banter him about his scarlet coat. "Very well, gentlemen," replied he coolly, bristling up with a quick temper, "if my coat does not suit you, I can meet you in any other color that may suit your fancy." Seeing the gentleman not in a bantering mood, he was soon left to his own reflections. But the candidates for Congress were overlooked and forgotten by the crowd in their eagerness to behold and admire the great orator, whose fame had filled their imagination for so many years "As soon as he appeared on the ground," says Wirt, "he was surrounded by the admiring and adoring crowd, and whithersoever he moved, the concourse followed him. A preacher of the Baptist church, whose piety was wounded by this homage paid to a mortal, asked the people aloud, why they thus followed Mr. Henry about? " Mr. Henry," said he, " is not a god !" " No," said Mr. Henry, deeply affected by the scene and the remark, " no, indeed, my friend ; I am but a poor worm of the dust—as fleeting and unsubstantial as the shadow of the cloud that flies over your fields, and is remembered no more." The tone with which this was uttered, and the look which accompanied it, affected every heart, and silenced every voice.

Presently James Adams rose upon a platform that had been erected by the side of the tavern porch where Mr. Henry was seated, and proclaimed—" O yes ! O yes ! Colonel Henry will address the people from this stand, for the last time and at the risk of his life !" The grand-jury were in session at the moment, they burst through the doors, some leaped the windows, and came running up with the crowd, that they might not lose a word that fell from the old man's lips.

While Adams was lifting him on the stand, " Why Jimmy," says he, " you have made a better speech for me than I can make for myself." " Speak out, father," said Jimmy, " and let us hear how it is."

Old and feeble, more with disease than age, Mr. Henry rose and addressed the people to the following effect :—(Wirt's Life of Patrick Henry, page 393.) He told them that the late proceedings of the Virginia Assembly had filled him with apprehensions and alarm ; that they had planted thorns upon his pillow ; that they had drawn him from that happy retirement which it had pleased a bountiful Providence to bestow, and in which he had hoped to pass, in quiet, the remainder of his days ; that the State had quitted the sphere in which she had been placed by the Constitution ; and in daring to pronounce upon the validity of federal laws, had gone out of her jurisdiction in a manner not warranted by any authority, and in the highest degree alarming to every considerate mind ; that such opposition, on the part of Virginia, to the acts of the General Government, must beget their enforcement by military power ; that this would probably produce civil war ; civil war, foreign alliances ; and that foreign alliances must necessarily end in subjugation to the powers called in. He conjured the people to pause and consider well, before they rushed into such a desperate condition, from which there could be no retreat. He painted to their imaginations, Washington, at the head of a numerous and well appointed army, inflicting upon them military execution. "And where (he asked) are our resources to meet such a conflict? Where is the citizen of America who will dare to lift his hand against the father of his country?" A drunken man in the crowd threw up his arm and exclaimed that he dared to do it. "No," answered Mr. Henry, rising aloft in all his majesty, "*you dare not do it; in such a parricidal attempt, the steel would drop from your nerveless arm.*"

Proceeding, he asked "Whether the county of Charlotte would have any authority to dispute an obedience to the laws of Virginia;" and he pronounced Virginia to be to the Union what the county of Charlotte was to *her*. Having denied the right of a State to decide upon the constitutionality of federal laws, he added, that perhaps it might be necessary to say something of the laws in question. His private opinion was, that they were *good* and *proper*. But whatever might be their merits, it belonged to the people, who held the reins over the head of Congress, and to them alone, to say whether they were acceptable or otherwise to Virginians; and that this must be done by way of petition. That Congress were as much our representatives as the Assembly, and had as good a right to our confidence. He had seen, with regret, the unlimited power over the purse and sword consigned to the General Government; but that he had been overruled, and it was now necessary to submit to the constitutional exercise of that power. "If," said he, "I am asked what is to be done when a people feel themselves intolerably oppressed, my answer is ready—*overturn the Government*. But do not, I beseech you, carry matters to this length without provocation. Wait, at least, until *some* infringement is made upon your rights, and which cannot otherwise be redressed; for if ever you recur to another change, you may bid adieu forever to representative government. You can never exchange the present government but for a monarchy. If the administration have done wrong, let us all go wrong together rather than split into factions, which must destroy that *Union* upon which our existence hangs. Let us preserve our strength for the French, the English, the Germans, or whoever else shall dare to invade our territory, and not exhaust it in civil commotions and intestine wars."

When he concluded, his audience were deeply affected; it is said that they wept like children, so powerfully were they moved by the emphasis of his language, the tone of his voice, the commanding expression of his eye, the earnestness with which he declared his design to exert himself to allay the heart-burnings and jealousies which had been fomented in the State legislature, and the fervent manner in which he prayed that if he were deemed unworthy to effect it, that it might be reserved to some other and abler hand to extend this blessing over the community. As he concluded, he literally sunk into the arms of the tumultuous throng: at that moment John H. Rice exclaimed, " the sun has set in all his glory !"

Randolph rose to reply. For some moments he stood in silence, his lips quivering, his eye swimming in tears; at length he began a modest though beautiful apology for rising to address the people in opposition to the venerable father who had just taken his seat; it was an honest difference of opinion, and he hoped to be pardoned while he boldly and freely, as it became the occasion, expressed his sentiments on the great questions that so much divided and agitated the minds of the people.

" The gentleman tells you," said he, " that the late proceedings of the Virginia Assembly have filled him with apprehension and alarm. He seems to be impressed with the conviction, that the State has quitted the sphere in which she was placed by the Constitution; and in daring to pronounce on the validity of federal laws, has gone out of her jurisdiction in a manner not warranted by any authority. I am sorry the gentleman has been disturbed in his repose; still more grieved am I, that the particular occasion to which he alludes should have been the cause of his anxiety. I once cherished the hope that his alarms would have been awakened, had Virginia failed to exert herself in warding off the evils he so prophetically warned us of on another memorable occasion. Her supineness and inactivity, now that those awful squintings towards monarchy, so eloquently described by the gentleman, are fast growing into realities, I had hoped would have planted thorns in his pillow, and awakened him to a sense of the danger now threatening us, and the necessity of exerting once more his powerful faculties in warning the people, and rousing them from their fatal lethargy.

" Has the gentleman forgotten that we owe to him those obnoxious principles, as he now would have them, that guided the Legislature in its recent course? He is alarmed at the rapid growth of the seed he himself hath sowed—he seems to be disappointed that they fell, not by the wayside, but into vigorous and fruitful soil. He has conjured up spirits from the vasty deep, and growing alarmed at the potency of his own magic wand, he would say to them, Down, wantons! down!' but, like Banquo's ghost, I trust they will not down. But to drop metaphor—In the Virginia Convention, that was called to ratify the Constitution, this gentleman declared that the government delineated in that instrument was peculiar in its nature—partly national, partly federal. In this description he hit upon the true definition—there are certain powers of a national character that extend to the people and operate on them without regard to their division into States—these powers, acting alone, tend to consolidate the government into one head, and to obliterate State divisions and to destroy State authority; but there are other powers, many and important ones, that are purely federal in their nature—that look to the States, and recognize their existence as bodies politic, endowed with many of the most important attributes of sovereignty. These two opposing forces act as checks on each other, and keep the complicated system *in equilibrium.* They are like the centrifugal and centripetal forces in the law of gravitation, that serve to keep the spheres in their harmonious courses through the universe.

"Should the Federal Government, therefore, attempt to exercise powers that do not belong to it—and those that do belong to it are few, specified, well-defined—all others being reserved to the people and to the States—should it step beyond its province, and encroach on rights that have not been delegated, it is the duty of the States to interpose. There is no other power that can interpose. The counterweight, the opposing force of the State, is the only check to overaction known to the system.

"In questions of *meum et tuum,* where rights of property are concerned, and some other cases specified in the Constitution, I grant you that the Federal Judiciary may pronounce on the validity of the law. But in questions involving the right to power, whether this or that power has been delegated or reserved, they cannot and ought not to be the arbiter; that question has been left, as it always was, and always must be left, to be determined among sovereignties in the best way they can. Political wisdom has not yet discovered any infallible mathematical rule, by which to determine the assumptions of power between those who know no other law or limitation save that imposed on them by their own consent, and which they can abrogate at pleasure. Pray let me ask the gentleman—and no one knows better than himself—who ordained this Constitution? Who defined its powers, and said, thus far shalt thou go, but no farther? Was it not the people of the States in their sovereign capacity? Did they commit an act of suicide by so doing?—an act of self-annihilation? No, thank God, they did not; but are still alive, and, I trust, are becoming sensible of the importance of those rights reserved to them, and prohibited to that government which they ordained for their common defence. Shall the creature of the States be the sole judge of the legality or constitutionality of its own acts, in a question of power between them and the States? Shall they who assert a right, be the sole judges of their authority to claim and to exercise it? Does not all power seek to enlarge itself?—grow on that it feeds upon? Has not that been the history of all encroachment, all usurpation? If this Federal Government, in all its departments, then, is to be the sole judge of its own usurpations, neither the people nor the States, in a short time, will have any thing to contend for; this creature of their making will become their sovereign, and the only result of the labors of our revolutionary heroes, in which patriotic band this venerable gentleman was most conspicuous, will have been a change of our masters—New England for Old England—for which change I cannot find it in my heart to thank them.

"But the gentleman has taught me a very different lesson from that he is now disposed to enjoin on us. I fear that time has wrought its influence on him, as on all other men; and that age makes him willing to endure what in former years he would have spurned with indignation. I have learned my first lessons in his school. He is the high-priest from whom I received the little wisdom my poor abilities were able to carry away from the droppings of the political sanctuary. He was the inspired statesman that taught me to be jealous of power, to watch its encroachments, and to sound the alarm on the first movement of usurpation.

"Inspired by his eloquent appeals—encouraged by his example—alarmed by the rapid strides of Federal usurpation, of which he had warned them—the legislature of Virginia has nobly stepped forth in defence of the rights of the States, and interposed to arrest that en-croachment and usurpation of power that threaten the destruction of the Republic.

"And what is the subject of alarm? What are the laws they have dared to pronounce upon as unconstitutional and tyrannical? The first, is a law authorizing the President of the United States to order any alien he may judge dangerous, any unfortunate refugee that may happen to fall under his royal suspicion, forthwith to quit the coun-try. It is true that the law says he must have *reasonable* grounds to suspect. Who is to judge of that reason but himself? Who can look into his breast and say what motives have dominion there? 'Tis a mockery to give one man absolute power over the liberty of an-other, and *then* ask him, when the power is gone, and cannot be re-called, to exercise it reasonably! Power knows no other check but power. Let the poor patriot who may have fallen under the frowns of government, because he dared assert the rights of his countrymen, seek refuge on our shores of boasted liberty; the moment he touches the soil of freedom, hoping here to find a period to all his persecu-tions, he is greeted, not with the smiles of welcome, or the cheerful voice of freemen, but the stern demands of an officer of the law—the executor of a tyrant's will—who summons him to depart. What crime has he perpetrated? Vain inquiry! He is a *suspected* per-son. He is judged dangerous to the peace of the country—rebel-lious at home, he may be alike factious and seditious here. What remedy? What hope? He who condemns is judge—the sole judge in the first and the last resort. There is no appeal from his arbi-trary will. Who can escape the suspicion of a jealous and vindictive mind?

"The very men who fought your battles, who spent their fortunes, and shed their blood to win for you that independence that was once your boast, may be the first victims of this tyrannical law. Kosci-usko is now on your shores; though poor in purse and emaciated in body, from the many sacrifices he has made in your cause, he has yet a proud spirit that loves freedom, and will speak boldly of op-pression. Is not this enough to bring him under the frowns of power, and to cause the mandate to be issued, ordering him to de-part from the country? What may be true of one to whom we owe so much, has already been fulfilled in the person of many a patriot, scholar, and philosopher, whose only crime was, that of seeking refuge from oppression and wrong, on these shores of boasted freedom.

"And what is that other law that so fully meets the approbation of my venerable friend? It is a law that makes it an act of sedition, punishable by fine and imprisonment, to utter or write a sentiment that any prejudiced judge or juror may think proper to construe into disrespect to the President of the United States. Do you understand me? I dare proclaim to the people of Charlotte my opinion to be, that John Adams, so-called President, is a weak-minded man, vain, jealous, and vindictive; that influenced by evil passions and prejudices, and goaded on by wicked counsel, he has been striving to force the country into a war with our best friend and ally. I say that I dare repeat this before the people of Charlotte, and avow it as my opinion. But let me write it down, and print it as a warning to my countrymen. What then? *I subject myself to an indictment for sedition!* I make myself liable to be dragged away from my home and friends, and to be put on my trial in some distant Federal Court, before a judge who receives his appointment from the man that seeks my condemnation; and to be tried by a prejudiced jury, who have been gathered from remote parts of the country, strangers to me, and any thing but my peers; and have been packed by the minions of power for my destruction. Is the man dreaming! do you exclaim? Is this a fancy picture, he has drawn for our amusement? I am no fancy man, people of Charlotte! I speak the truth—I deal only in stern realities! There is such a law on your Statute Book in spite of your Constitution—in open contempt of those solemn guarantees that insure the freedom of speech and of the press to every American citizen. Not only is there such a statute, but, with shame be it spoken, even England blushes at your sedition law. Would that I could stop here, and say that, though it may be found enrolled among the the public archives, it is a dead letter. Alas! alas! not only does it exist, but at this hour is most rigidly enforced, not against the ordinary citizen only, but against men in official stations, even those who are clothed by the people with the sacred duties of their representatives—men, the sanctity of whose persons cannot be reached by any law known to a representative government, are hunted down, condemned, and incarcerated by this odious, tyrannical, and unconstitutional enactment. At this moment, while I am addressing you, men of Charlotte! with the free air of heaven fanning my locks—and God knows how long I shall be permitted to enjoy that blessing—a representative of the people of Vermont—Matthew Lyon his name—lies immured in a dungeon, not six feet square, where he has dragged out the miserable hours of a protracted winter, for daring to violate the royal maxim that the king can do no wrong. This was his only crime—he told his people, and caused it to be printed for their information, that the President, 'rejecting men of age, experience, wisdom, and independency of sentiment,' appointed those who had no other merit but devotion to their master; and he intimated that the 'President was fond of ridiculous pomp, idle parade, and selfish avarice.' I speak the language of the indictment. I give in technical and official words the high crime with which he was charged. He pleaded justification—I think the lawyers call it—and offered to prove the truth of his allegations. But the court would allow no time to procure witnesses or counsel; he was hurried into trial all unprepared; and this representative of the people, for speaking the truth of those in authority, was arraigned like a felon, condemned, fined, and imprisoned. These are the laws, the venerable gentlemen would have you believe, are not only sanctioned by the Constitution, but demanded by the necessity of the times—laws at which even monarchs blush—banishing from your shores the hapless victim that only sought refuge from oppression, and making craven, fawning spaniels, aye! dumb dogs, of your own people! He tells you, moreover, that if you do not agree with him in opinion—cannot consent that these vile enactments are either constitutional or necessary—your only remedy, your only hope of redress, is in petition.

" *Petition!* Whom are we to petition? But one solitary member from Virginia, whose name is doomed to everlasting infamy, dared to record his vote—dared to record, did I say? I beg pardon—but one who did not spurn from them this hideous offspring of a tyrant's lust. Whom, then, I repeat, are we to petition? those who are the projectors of these measures, who voted for them, and forced them upon you in spite of your will? Would not these men laugh at your petition, and, in the pride and insolence of new-born power, trample it under their feet with disdain? Shall we petition his majesty, who, by virtue of these very laws, holds your liberties in his sacred hands? I tell you he would spurn your petition from the foot of the throne, as those of your fathers, on a like occasion, were spurned from the throne of George the Third of England. From whose lips do we hear that word petition—an abject term, fit only for the use of subjects and of slaves? Can it be that *he* is now willing to petition and to supplicate his co-equals in a common confederacy, who proudly disdained entreaty and supplication to the greatest monarch on earth—whose fleets covered our seas, whose armies darkened our shores—sent over to bind and to rivet those chains that had been so long forging for our unfettered limbs! Has age so tamed his proud spirit that he will gently yield to a domestic usurper what he scorned to grant to a foreign master? I fear he has deceived himself, and would deceive you; let not his siren song of peace lull you into a fatal repose. For what is this large standing army quartered on the country? why those recruiting officers insulting every hamlet and village with their pride and insolence, and decoying the honest farmer from his labor, to become the idle, corrupt, and profligate drone of a military camp? Why this large naval establishment? Why such burthensome and odious taxes imposed on the industry of the country? Why those enormous loans at usurious interest in times of peace; and, above all, why those unconstitutional laws to banish innocence—to silence inquiry—stifle investigation, and to make dumb the complaining mouths of the people? Are these vast preparations in consequence of some imminent peril overhanging the country? Are we threatened with war? With whom? with France? France has showed that this wicked administration cannot *drive* her into a war with her ancient friend and ally. She has almost compelled them to keep a minister of peace within her borders, and offered them almost any terms of conciliation consistent with justice and dignity. Yet do you see any abatement in the warlike energies of the Government?

"For what, I ask, are these vast and hostile preparations? Let the late pretended whisky insurrection in the western counties of Pennsylvania answer the question. I am no alarmist; but I cannot close my eyes to the truth when I see it glaring before me. These "provisional" armies, as they have chosen to call them, are meant for you; they are intended, not to meet the troops of France, which they know will never insult the soil of this republic, but to awe you, the people, into submission, and to force upon you, by a display of military power, the destructive measures of this vaulting and ambitious administration. And yet the gentleman tells you we must wait until *some* infringement is made on our rights! Your Constitution broken, your citizens dragged to prison for daring to exercise the freedom of speech, armies levied, and you threatened with immediate invasion for your audacious interference with the business of the Federal Government; and still you are told to wait for *some infringement* of your rights! How long are we to wait? Till the chains are fastened upon us, and we can no longer help ourselves? But the gentleman says your course may lead to civil war, and where are your resources? I answer him in his own words, handed down by the tradition of the past generation, and engraven on the hearts of his grateful countrymen. I answer, in his own words: 'Shall we gather strength by irresolution and inaction? Shall we acquire the means of effectual resistance by lying supinely on our backs, and hugging the delusive phantom of hope, until our enemies shall have bound us hand and foot? Sir, we are not weak, if we make a proper use of those means which the God of nature hath placed in our power. The battle, sir, is not to the strong alone; it is to the vigilant, the active, the brave.'

"But we are not only to have an invading army marching into our borders, but the gentleman's vivid imagination has pictured Washington at the head of it, coming to inflict military chastisement on his native State; and who, exclaims he, would dare lift his hand against the father of his country? Sternly has he rebuked one of you for venturing, in the outburst of patriotic feeling, to declare that he would do it. I bow with as much respect as any man at the name of Washington. I have been taught to look upon it with a veneration little short of that of my Creator. But while I love Cæsar, I love Rome more. Should he, forgetful of the past, grown ambitious of power, and, seduced by the artful machinations of those who seek to use his great name in the subjugation of his country, lift a parricidal hand against the bosom of the State that gave him birth and crowned him with his glory, because she has dared to assert those rights that belong to her, not by the laws of nature, but those rights that have been reserved to her by this very Constitution that she partly ordained, and without which she must drag out an existence of helpless and hopeless imbecility, I trust there will be found many a Brutus to avenge her wrongs. I promise, for one, so help me God!—and it is in no boastful spirit I speak—that I will not be an idle spectator of the tyrannical and murderous tragedy, so long as I have an arm to wield a weapon, or a voice to cry shame! Shame on you for inflicting this deadly blow in the bosom of the mother that gave you existence, and cherished your fame as her own brightest jewel."

We do not pretend, reader, to give you the language of John Randolph on this occasion; nor are we certain even that the thoughts are his. We have nothing but the faint tradition of near fifty years to go upon; and happy are we if all our researches have enabled us to make even a tolerable approximation to what was said. He spoke for three hours; all that time the people, standing on their feet, hung with breathless silence on his lips. His youthful appearance, boyish tones, clear, distinct, thrilling utterance; his graceful action, bold expressions, fiery energy, and manly thoughts, struck them with astonishment. A bold genius and an orator of the first order suddenly burst upon them, and dazzled them with his power and brilliancy. A prophet was among them, and they knew it not. When he concluded, an old planter, turning to his neighbor, exclaimed; "He's no bug-eater now, I tell you." Dr. Hogue turned from the stand, and went away, repeating to himself these lines from the "Deserted Village:"

> " Amazed, the gazing rustics ranged around,
> And still they gazed, and still the wonder grew,
> That one small head could carry all he knew."

Mr. Henry, turning to some by-stander, said: "I haven't seen the little dog before, since he was at school; he was a great atheist then." He made no reply to the speech; but, approaching Mr. Randolph, he took him by the hand, and said: "Young man, you call me father; then, my son, I have somewhat to say unto thee (holding both his hands)—*keep justice, keep truth*, and you will live to think differently."

They dined together, and Randolph, ever after venerated the memory of his friend, who died in a few weeks from that day.

They were both elected in April; the one to Congress, the other to the State Legislature; and, doubtless, many of the good free-

holders of Charlotte voted for both.   Who can blame them?   Happy
people of Charlotte! it was your lot to behold the bright golden sunset of the great luminary whose meridian power melted away the
chains of British despotism and withered up the cankered heart of
disaffected Toryism; then, turning with tearful eyes from the last
rays of the sinking orb, to hail, dawning on the same horizon, another
sun, just springing, as it were, from the night of chaos, mounting
majestically into his destined sphere, and driving clouds and darkness
before his youthful beams.

CHAPTER XXII.

FRANCE AND THE ADMINISTRATION.

MR. ADAMS saved the country from a war with France, and a consequent alliance with Great Britain, and all the unimaginable events
that must have followed that connection; but in so doing he destroyed
his party, and defeated his own re-election.   No one, to our knowledge, has ever attributed these results to a foreseen and predeter-
mined self-sacrifice on his part for the good of the country.   Those
who were associated with him and knew him best attribute his course
to far other causes.   Before we proceed with our narrative, we will
give the reader a further insight into the character of this man, so
necessary to understand the complicated history of those times.   A
mere detail of facts, without a knowledge of the causes that produced
them, or the character and motives of the men that acted them, can
afford no instruction to the student of history.   Without some such
insight, the battle of the frogs or the wars of the giants would be
equally as instructive as the Punic Wars or the conflicts in the forum.

What we say of Mr. Adams is drawn from cotemporary history,
and in the language of those who were most intimately associated
him.   The reader is already aware of his course before and during
the negotiations for the treaty of Paris, in 1782, and Dr. Franklin's
opinion of his character.

General Hamilton, a very good judge, said of him while President,
and during the great events we are now discoursing of, and in explana-

tion of their causes, that he possessed patriotism and integrity, and even talents, of a certain kind; but that he did not possess the talents adapted to the administration of government, and that there were great and intrinsic defects in his character, which unfitted him for the office of Chief Magistrate. With all his virtues, he was tainted with a disgusting egotism, a distempered jealousy, and an ungovernable indiscretion of temper. When he and General Washington were run together as candidates for the presidential and vice-presidential office, it was thought all-important to secure the first office to General Washington (a majority at that time determining the question), by dropping a few votes from Mr. Adams. He complained of this as unfair treatment—said he ought to have been permitted to take an equal chance with General Washington. When, at a subsequent period, he and Mr. Pinckney were on the same ticket, it was thought, by the federal party, that the success of their cause ought not to be hazarded by dropping any of the votes; it was not a matter of such importance that Mr. Adams or Mr. Pinckney should be elected President, as that Mr. Jefferson should be defeated. He was enraged with all those who thought that Mr. Pinckney ought to have an equal chance with himself. To this circumstance, in a great measure, may be attributed the serious schism which, at a subsequent period, grew up in the federal party. Mr. Adams never could forgive the men who were engaged in the plan, though it embraced some of his most partial admirers. He discovered bitter animosity against several of them. His rage against General Hamilton was so vehement, that he could not restrain himself within the forms of civility or decorum, in the presence of that gentleman. His jealousy of the Pinckneys was notorious, and it dated as far back as the appointment of Mr. Thomas Pinckney, by Washington, as envoy to the Court of London. Mr. Adams desired the appointment for himself, notwithstanding the impropriety—he being the Vice-President—and next he desired it for his son-in-law. In the bitterness of disappointment, he played into the hands of the opposition party, and charged upon General Washington that the appointment had been made under British influence.

Soon after his own appointment of General Washington, in July, 1798, as Commander-in-Chief of all the armies of the United States, he became jealous of the overshadowing influence of that great character, and did all he could, consistently with his station, to thwart the plans, to delay and derange the measures, that Washington thought most essential to the service.

His conduct in the appointment of general officers, proved that he was fickle, inconsistent, and under the baneful influence of a distempered jealousy.

With the country in imminent danger of a war; with Washington and Hamilton and C. C. Pinckney at the head of her armies, it was natural that those who felt themselves responsible for the measures that had brought the nation into that predicament, should look to those great men as their guides, instead of the impulsive, aimless, and unsteady character, nominally at the head of affairs. Even his own cabinet had more frequent, intimate, and confidential communications, on all public affairs, with the head of the army than with himself. He did not fail to perceive this; and soon became enraged with his own counsellors. Not long afterwards, some of them were dismissed. A prominent charge against McHenry was, that the Secretary, in a report to the House of Representatives, had eulogized General Washington, and had attempted to eulogize General Hamilton, which was adduced as one proof of a combination, in which the Secretary was engaged, to depreciate and injure him, the President. Here, then, was the secret. His jealous and distempered fancy, stimulated by evil counsel, had conjured up a formidable conspiracy, in which his cabinet were implicated, the object of which was to depreciate and injure him, and to exalt Hamilton or Pinckney above him. To this cause may be attributed his extraordinary course in regard to French affairs; and those fatal aberrations, as they were called by his friends, that resulted in peace with the French nation, but in the destruction of himself and of his party.

We now proceed with the current of events, down to the meeting of Congress, in 1798.

As our object is not a history of the country, but only of those leading causes of history, a knowledge of which is essential to understand the position of political characters who figured at the time, we shall confine ourselves to a development of French affairs, because they absorbed all others, gave weight to the political atmosphere, and indicated, by the elevation or depression of the barometer, the advance or retrograde position of the two great parties that divided men and controlled the politics of the country.

The reader is already aware, that on the departure of Messrs. Pinckney and Marshall from Paris, in the spring of 1798, Mr. Gerry was induced to remain; but he obstinately persisted in refusing to enter into any negotiation. About the last of May, 1798, the X. Y. Z. dispatches, which had been published in America, found their way to the hands of the French Minister of Foreign Affairs, M. Talleyrand. He immediately inclosed the *very strange publica-tion*, as he called it, to Mr. Gerry, and added: "I cannot observe without surprise that intriguers have profited of the insulated con-dition in which the envoys of the United States have kept themselves to make proposals and hold conversations, the object of which was, evidently, to deceive you." He demanded the names of the parties implicated, and to be informed whether any of the citizens attached to his service, and authorized by him to see the envoys, told them a word which had the least relation to the disgusting proposition which was made by X. and Y., to give any sum whatever for corrupt distri-bution.

Mr. Gerry disclosed the names of the parties. Two of them, the most conspicuous characters, X. and Y., were foreigners, and unknown to the French Government; the third, Mr. Z., made himself known, and proved that the part he had acted was wholly honorable. Mr. Gerry added, further, that in regard to the citizens attached to the employments of M. Talleyrand, and authorized by him to see the en-voys on official communications, not a word had fallen from any of them which had the least relation to the proposition made by X. and Y. in their informal negotiations, to pay money for corrupt purposes.

It is not at all improbable that members of the Directory, whose term of office was exceedingly precarious, and even Talleyrand him-self, were not too virtuous to receive a douceur, or a bribe, to secure their influence in the negotiation of a treaty; but that they were, in a roundabout way, actually fishing for one on this occasion, depends solely on the statement of the two principal actors in the business, who, in a most remarkable degree, gained the confidence of the envoys, but who were, in fact, foreigners, unknown to the Government, and corrupt persons, who fled the country on the discovery of the plot. There is not one corroborating circumstance to strengthen their story.

Mr. Gerry admits that every member of the Government with whom they communicated acted with the utmost propriety; and that no corrupt proposition came either from them or M. Talleyrand.

Napoleon, in his Revelations from St. Helena, in giving a history of these transactions, says: "Certain intriguing agents, with which sort of instruments the office of foreign relations was at that period abundantly supplied, insinuated that the demand of a loan would be desisted from, upon the advance of twelve hundred thousand francs, to be divided between the Director Barras and the Minister Talleyrand." This whole narrative of Bonaparte, when carefully examined, is obviously drawn from public documents; just such materials as we have before us at this time. There is not the slightest evidence that he had any personal knowledge of the transactions, and that he knew from any other source than common report growing out of the publications of the day, that Barras, or Talleyrand, had, through intriguing agents, made an overture for a bribe.

Notwithstanding the publication of those X. Y. Z. dispatches, so questionable in their character and design, so well calculated to irritate, yet the French Government would not be excited into a feeling of hostility. "As to the French Government," says Talleyrand, on the 10th of June, "superior to all personalities, to all the manœuvres of its enemies, it perseveres in the intention of conciliating with sincerity all the differences which have happened between the two countries. I confirm it to you anew." He then proposes to proceed with Mr. Gerry on the business of negotiation, discards any further demand for a loan, and rests the whole negotiation on three simple propositions, which might have been speedily and satisfactorily adjusted; and he urged on Mr. Gerry to send home for authority to conclude the treaty, if he did not feel that he was already clothed with sufficient power for the purpose. But he strangely persisted in doing neither one thing nor another: he would not send home and ask *for instruments* necessary to the negotiation, nor for a successor to be put in his stead for that purpose, nor would he enter into a full description of all the points necessarily involved in a treaty, that he might lay before his Government the terms of one he had informally entered into, for their ratification or rejection. He had it in his power, by a firm and manly course of statesmanship, to throw upon the administration the responsibility of closing at once all subjects

:f difference with the French Republic, or by rejecting a favorable treaty, to involve the country in war with that formidable power. His only thought seems to have been to avoid doing any thing that might hurt the feelings of his late colleagues, and to devise means to get home. He never ceased begging Talleyrand to let him go home. Talleyrand never ceased begging him to stay, and to attend to the important and pressing affairs of his country. At length, finding Mr. Gerry wholly impracticable, he sent him his passports about the last of July, and added, " As long as I could flatter myself, sir, with fulfilling the wish of the Executive Directory, by endeavoring with you to establish the good understanding between the French Republic and the United States, I used my efforts, both in our conferences and in my correspondence with you, to smooth the paths, to establish the basis, to enter on the business, and to convince you of the utility of your presence in Paris. It is in your character of Envoy of the American Government I received you and wrote to you; it depended on yourself to be publicly received by the Executive Directory. . . . You cannot dissemble, that if nothing prevented you from pursuing with me the examining and reconciling of the grievances which divide the two countries, we should not long stand in need of any thing but the respective ratifications. . . . . When scarcely informed of the departure of Messrs. Pinckney and Marshall, I endeavored in every conference I afterwards had with you to demonstrate to you the urgency, the propriety, and the possibility of an active negotiation. I collected your ideas; they differed from my own—I endeavored to reconcile them. On the 18th June I transmitted to you a complete plan of the negotiations. On the 27th I sent you my first note for discussion upon one of the points of the treaty; you declined answering it. On the 6th of July I sent you two others. In vain I accompanied these documents with the most cordial invitation rapidly to run over with me this series of indispensable discussions upon all our grievances. You have not even given me an opportunity of proving what liberality the Executive Directory would use on the occasion. *You never wrote, in fact, but for your departure.*" In a postscript, dated three days later, and after receiving advices from America giving an account of the warlike acts of Congress, passed in May and June, M. Talleyrand adds: " It seems that, hurried beyond every limit, your Government no longer preserves appearances." . . . . . .

(He then cites the various acts that have been passed.) " The long-suffering of the Executive Directory," continues he, " is about to manifest itself in the most unquestionable manner. Perfidy will no longer be able to throw a veil over the pacific dispositions, which it has never ceased to manifest. It is at the very moment of this fresh provocation, which would appear to leave no honorable choice but war, that it confirms the assurances I have given you on its behalf. It is yet ready, it is as much disposed as ever, to terminate by a candid negotiation the differences which subsist between the two countries. Such is its repugnance to consider the United States as enemies, that notwithstanding their hostile demonstrations, it means to wait until it be irresistibly forced to it by real hostilities. Since you will depart, sir, hasten, at least, to transmit to your Government this solemn declaration."

Mr. Gerry did hasten to lay these declarations before his Government on the *first day of October*, and added, that *from the best information he could obtain relative to the disposition of the Executive Directory, they were very desirous for a reconciliation between the Republics.*

No sooner had Mr. Gerry left the shores of France, than M. Talleyrand opened a correspondence on American affairs with M. Pichon, Secretary of Legation of the French Republic, near the Batavian Republic, and requested that gentleman to give copies of the same to the American minister, Mr. Murray, doubtless with an expectation that they would be forwarded to the President of the United States. In his letter of August the 28th, just twenty days from the departure of Mr. Gerry, he says: " I see between France and the United States no clashing of interests, no motives of jealousy. Where is, therefore, the cause of the misunderstanding, which, if France did not show herself the wisest, would bring from this moment a great rupture between the two Republics? There are neither incompatible interests, nor projects of aggrandizement, which divide them. *Lately, distrust* has done all the mischief. The Government of the United States has believed that France wished to have revolutionized America; France has believed that the Government of the United States wished to throw itself into the arms of England. It is because acrimony, having mingled itself with distrust, neither side has taken true conciliatory means. It has been supposed, in the

United States, that the French Government temporized, in order to strike with greater safety. Hence followed a crowd of measures, each one more aggravating than the other. In France, it has been supposed that the Government of the United States wished only to support the appearances of negotiation. *Thence there was a certain insisting on pledges of good faith.* Let us substitute calmness to passions, confidence to suspicions, and we shall soon agree. I have made my efforts to wind up a negotiation, in this manner, with Mr. Gerry. My correspondence with him, until the day of his departure, is a curious monument of advances from me, and of evasions from him. I wished to encourage Mr. Gerry, by the marks of regard which his good intention deserved, though I cannot dissemble to myself that he had been wanting decision, at the moment when he might easily have settled every thing properly." In a word, he winds up with giving Mr. Murray, through M. Pichon, the most solemn assurances that a new plenipotentiary would be received without hesitation, and that an act of confidence towards them would encourage confidence on their part. This letter, so unequivocal in its nature, and another, of a like tenor, making more direct overtures, if possible, towards re-opening negotiations, must have reached the President before the meeting of Congress in December. The President had other unequivocal, though less direct, evidences of the pacific disposition of the French Directory. Dr. George Logan, a native of Pennsylvania, while in France, was introduced to the Director Merlin, and afterwards visited him on the footing of a private friend. On one of these occasions, Merlin informed him that France had not the least intention to interfere in the public affairs of the United States; that his country had acquired great reputation in having assisted America to become a free republic, and that they never would disgrace their own revolution by attempting the destruction of the United States. Dr. Logan returned home early in November, and hastened to communicate what he thought good news, to the Secretary of State. He was coldly received by Mr. Pickering, and informed that his news was of no importance. General Washington was at the seat of government about the time (Nov., 1798), arranging his military operations with Generals Hamilton, Pinckney, and the Secretary of War. Dr. Logan called on him. His reception was even more cold and repulsive than that of the Secretary.

When Logan repeated to him the conversation with Merlin, he replied, that it was very singular; that he, who could only be viewed as a private character, unarmed with proper powers, and presumptively unknown in France, could effect what three gentlemen of the first respectability in our country, specially charged under the authority of the Government, were unable to do. " *You*, sir," with some emphasis on the word, "were more fortunate than our envoys, for they would neither be received nor heard by M. Merlin, nor the Directory."

It is very evident that General Washington, at that time, was highly exasperated with France; that all his feelings were enlisted against her; and that, had he been at the head of affairs, it would have taken much more than Talleyrand's overtures to have induced him to recommence negotiations. Had Washington been President in 1798, or Hamilton, or Pinckney, or had Mr. Adams yielded more readily to the counsel of his cabinet, who were wholly under the influence of the Triumvirate, the United States would unquestionably have been involved in a war with the French Republic. But Mr. Adams, whether from the motives assigned, or from higher patriotic considerations, refused the dictation, and saved the country from so calamitous a war as that would have been with the French Republic. Just before the meeting of Congress, he arrived in Philadelphia, from his seat at Quincy. The tone of his mind seemed to have been raised, rather than depressed. It was suggested to him (by the *military conclave*—says Mr. Jefferson) that it might be expedient to insert in the speech to Congress, a sentiment of this import—that after the repeatedly rejected advances of this country, its dignity required that it should be left with France, in future, to make the first overture; that if, desirous of reconciliation, she should evince the disposition by sending a minister to this Government, he would be received with the respect due to his character, and treated with in the frankness of a sincere desire of accommodation.

The suggestion was received in a manner both indignant and intemperate. Mr. Adams declared as a sentiment, which he had adopted on mature reflection, *That if France should send a minister to-morrow, he would order him back the next day.*

So imprudent an idea was easily refuted. But yet, in less than forty-eight hours from this extraordinary sally, the mind of Mr.

Adams underwent a total revolution. He resolved not only to insert
in his speech the sentiment which had been proposed to him, but to
go farther, and to declare, that if France would give explicit assurances of receiving a minister from this country, with due respect,
he would send one.

In vain was this extension of the sentiment opposed by all his
ministers, as being equally incompatible with good policy and with
the dignity of the nation. He obstinately persisted, and the declaration was introduced. The reader may account for this change in
the mind of the President in two ways. In the first place, we may
presume that he knew nothing of the dispatches containing the correspondence of Mr. Gerry with M. Talleyrand, which might have
been received in his absence; but that on perusing the correspondence, he was forcibly struck with the fact that a reconciliation with
France depended solely on him. That correspondence presented the
business in this light: France says—Two of the ministers you sent
to treat with me are personally offensive, on account of their hostile
opinions and haughty demeanor, a sentiment, according to the laws
of nations, we have a right to express, without giving offence to you.
I early expressed a desire that those gentlemen would depart, and a
readiness to open negotiation with the third, who evinced better dispositions towards conciliation. I told him to send home for additional powers, if he doubted his authority to act alone, or to inform
his Government that another minister would be received to treat in
his stead, or to agree informally on the terms of a treaty, which he
might submit for consideration on his return to the United States.
But declining to act on the one or the other of these propositions,
and still insisting on his return home, I then told him distinctly to
say to his Government, France has no cause of quarrel with America,
does not desire war, and is ready to receive in good faith a minister
of peace, whenever one may be sent. Such was the attitude of the
subject exhibited by the dispatches of Mr. Gerry.

It was impossible for a President of the United States to understand them, and then to take upon himself the responsibility of rejecting those overtures of peace. In this way we may account for the
sudden change in the mind of Mr. Adams, and do credit to his firmness and patriotism. But is it reasonable to suppose that he was
ignorant of those dispatches, or their contents, till so late a period?

Mr. Gerry had arrived, and communicated them to the State Department on the first day of October. He himself was an intimate personal friend of the President, and lived in the same State and neighborhood. The most reasonable conclusion, therefore, is, that Mr.
Adams was well informed on the whole subject when he arrived in
Philadelpha, and that the change in his course was produced by the
motives assigned at the time—that is, a jealousy of Hamilton and
Pinckney, and a belief that a plot was on foot in which his cabinet
were implicated, to degrade and injure him, and to exalt the one or
the other of those military characters in his place.

But, notwithstanding this apparent change in his mind towards
the most pacific measures, he kept back from Congress those important dispatches of Mr. Gerry, and other information of a pacific kind,
till the 18th of January, 1799. They were then accompanied by an
elaborate report of the Secretary of State, in which he says the
points chiefly meriting attention are the attempts of the French Government; 1. To exculpate itself from the charge of corruption; 2.
To detach Mr. Gerry from his colleagues, and to inveigle him into a
separate negotiation; and 3. Its design, if the negotiation failed, and
a war should take place between the United States and France, to
throw the blame of the rupture on the United States. The Secretary labors to keep up the spirit of distrust towards France, and to prove
that all the overtures of her minister are insincere, merely intended
to deceive the United States, and to gain time. " Warmly professing its desire of reconciliation," says he in conclusion, " it gives no
evidence of its sincerity; but proofs, in abundance, demonstrate that
it is not sincere. From standing erect, and in that commanding attitude requiring implicit obedience, cowering, it renounces some of its
unfounded demands. But I hope we shall remember that *the tiger
crouches before he leaps upon his prey*." A very different temper this
from that of the President in his opening speech to Congress in December; nor does it show a very harmonious co-operation between
the Chief Magistrate and his ministers.

Just one month from the communication of the Secretary's report
to Congress—that is, on the 18th of February, the President nominated William Vans Murray as envoy to the French Republic. This
measure was taken without any previous consultation with his ministers. The nomination was, to each of them, even to the Secretary

of State, his constitutional counsellor in such affairs, the first notice
of the project. The nomination was accompanied with a letter of
Talleyrand to M. Pichon, dated 28th September, 1798; and the
second, of like tenor, giving assurances that a minister from the
United States would be received and accredited.

The precipitate nomination of Mr. Murray brought Mr. Adams
into an awkward predicament. He found it necessary to change his
plan in its progress, and, instead of one, to nominate three envoys,
and to superadd a promise, that, though appointed, they should not
leave the United States till further and more perfect assurances were
given by the French Government. This remodification of the measure was a virtual acknowledgment that it had been premature. It
argued either instability of views, or want of sufficient consideration
beforehand.

General Washington disapproved very highly of the measure.
He was immediately informed of it by the Secretary of State: and
in reply, said—"The unexpectedness of the event communicated
in your letter of the 21st ultimo did, as you may suppose, surprise me not a little. But far, very far indeed was this surprise
short of what I experienced the next day, when, by a very intelligent
gentleman, immediately from Philadelphia, I was informed that there
had been no *direct* overture from the Government of France to that
of the United States for a negotiation; on the contrary, that M. Talleyrand was playing the same loose and round-about game he had
attempted the year before with our wrongs; and which, as in that
case, might mean any thing or nothing, as would subserve his purpose
best."

The speculations of the Republicans on the other hand were to
the following effect. "I inform you," says Mr. Jefferson in a letter
to Madison, "of the nomination of Murray. There is evidence that
the letter of Talleyrand was known to one of the Secretaries, and
therefore probably to all; the nomination, however, is declared by
one of them to have been kept secret from them all. He added that
he was glad of it, as, had they been consulted, the advice would have
been against making the nomination. To the rest of the party, however, the whole was a secret till the nomination was announced.
Never did a party show a stronger mortification, and consequently,
that war had been their object. Dana declared in debate (as I have

from those who were present), that we had done every thing which
might provoke France to a war; that we had given her insults which
no nation ought to have borne; and yet she would not declare war
The conjecture as to the Executive is, that they received Talleyrand's
letter before or about the meeting of Congress: that not meaning to
meet the overture effectually, they kept it secret, and let all the war
measures go on; but that just before the separation of the Senate,
the President, not thinking he could justify the concealing such an
overture, nor indeed that it could be concealed, made a nomination,
hoping that his friends in the Senate would take on their own shoulders the odium of rejecting it; but they did not choose it. The
Hamiltonians would not, and the others could not, alone. The whole
artillery of the phalanx, therefore, was played secretly on the President, and he was obliged himself to take a step which should parry
the overture while it wears the face of acceding to it. (Mark that I
state this as conjecture; but founded on workings and indications
which have been under our eyes.) Yesterday, therefore. (25th Feb.),
he sent in a nomination of Oliver Ellsworth, Patrick Henry, and
William Vans Murray, Envoys Extraordinary and Ministers Plenipotentiary to the French Republic, but declaring the two former
should not leave this country, till they should receive from France
assurances that they should be received with the respect due by the
laws of nations to their character. This, if not impossible, must
keep off at least the day so hateful and so *fatal* to them, of reconciliation, and leave more time for new projects of provocation."

The truth is, the friends of the Government were not agreed as
to ulterior measures. Some were for immediate and unqualified war—
of this class were Hamilton and most of the military gentry—others
were for a more mitigated course: the dissolution of treaties, preparation of force by land and sea, partial hostilities of a defensive
tendency; leaving to France the option of seeking accommodation,
or proceeding to open war. As most of the responsibility rested
on members of Congress, this latter course was preferred by them,
and prevailed. Either course was consistent with itself and admitted of a steady line of policy. But the President, having no fixed
object, and governed by the impulse of the moment, came athwart all
their plans and destroyed them. Notwithstanding the modifications
of his embassy, it was very evident that most of the federal members

of both branches of Congress carried home with them a settled dislike to the measure. They regarded it as ill-timed, built upon too slight grounds, and, therefore, humiliating to the United States; as calculated to revive French principles, strengthen the party against Government, and produce changes in the sentiments and conduct of some of the European powers, that might materially affect the interests and growing commercial prospects of the United States.

Before the envoys departed, intelligence was received of a new revolution in the French Government, and the expulsion of two of the Directory. This was thought to be a valid motive for delay—at least till it could be known whether the new Directory would ratify the assurances of the old one. When the news of the revolution in the Directory arrived, Mr. Adams was at his seat in Massachusetts His ministers addressed to him a joint letter, communicating the intelligence, and submitting to his consideration, whether that event ought to suspend the projected mission. In a letter which he afterwards wrote from the same place, he directed the preparation of a draft of instructions for the envoys, and intimated that their departure would be suspended for some time.

Shortly after, about the middle of October 1799, he came to the seat of government, when he adjusted with his ministers the tenor of the instructions to be given; but observed a profound silence on the question whether it was expedient that the mission should proceed. The ministers expected a consultation on the great question, whether the mission to France would be suspended until the fate of its Government could be known. But they were disappointed. The President alone considered and decided. The morning after the instructions were settled, he signified to the Secretary of State that the envoys *were immediately to depart*.

Though uncommunicative to his constitutional advisers, he was very free in his conversations with the envoys as to his expectations in regard to their embassy. He told them that the French Government would not accept the terms, which they were instructed to propose; that they would speedily return; and that he should have to recommend to Congress a declaration of war. "But as to the French negotiation producing a war with England," said he, "if it did, England could not hurt us." "When," Mr. Ellsworth says, "Pickering recited this last idea to me and Mr. Wolcott, I had not patience to hear more. And yet the President has several times, in his letters to me, from Quincy, mentioned the vast importance of keeping on good terms with England."

The reader cannot be surprised that such a man should work the destruction of any party that regarded him as its head ; indeed that, with him, there was no such thing as party ; either he was elevated above ordinary mortals, and studied the good of the country alone, without regard to his own interests, or sunk below the level of common-trading politicians who care for neither measures nor men, only so far as they may conspire to their own personal elevation.

When the new Congress, of which John Randolph was a member, assembled at the Capitol in December, 1799, the federal party apparently compact, and with a majority of at least twenty in the House of Representatives, carried within it all the elements of dissolution. The death blow had been given by its own friends, and it required time only to discover the causes of its rapid decay. When the extraordinary events of which we have spoken were made known to Washington, on the 17th of November, 1799, but a few weeks before his death, he would answer nothing to them, but exclaimed, " *I have been stricken dumb!* I have, some time past," says he, " viewed the political concerns of the United States with an anxious and painful eye. They appear to me to be moving by hasty strides to a crisis; but in what it will result, that Being who sees, foresees, and directs all things, alone can tell. The vessel is afloat, or very nearly so, and considering myself as a passenger only, I shall trust to the mariners, whose duty it is to watch, to steer it into a safe port." Thou great and good man ! *the ship is afloat !* When first launched upon the deep, thine own seamanship guided the untried vessel o'er many a stormy billow, with Scylla and Charybdis on either hand ; thy wakeful eye didst steer right onward; but never was it permitted thee, thou good Palinurus, to see the ship *steered into a safe port !* From amidst thy fellow-passengers, all weeping and gazing in the heavens, thou wert borne aloft in a chariot of fire, and, by bands of celestial spirits heralded into realms of immortal glory. And now, the old Iron-sides having buffeted many a stormy sea, and riding gallantly with all her banners streaming, hails thee her first, her best, her greatest Captain !

CHAPTER XXIII.

SCENE IN THE PLAYHOUSE—STANDING ARMY.

ON the first day of January, *eighteen hundred*, Washington was dead; Bonaparte First Consul of France. Our envoys had been favorably received. Every prospect of a satisfactory adjustment of the differences between the two republics, and no further need for the large army which had been established, and the other vast and expensive military preparations that had been projected with so much vigor under the X. Y. Z. excitement. Accordingly, on the 7th of January, Mr. Nicholas, a leading member of the republican party, moved in the House a resolution to repeal the act passed the 16th of July, 1798, entitled "An act to augment the army of the United States." The debate lasted for several days, and was warm and animated. On the 10th the motion was lost by a vote of *sixty* to *thirty-nine*. It was a strict party vote, and showed a majority of *twenty-one* for the federalists. John Randolph, for the first time, participated in the debate this day. The part he performed will be given in his own words. "In the course of the debates upon the resolution of Mr. Nicholas, I took occasion to say that the people of the United States ought not to depend for their safety on the soldiers enlisted under the laws, the repeal of which was the object of the resolution, and casually, but justly, applied to them the epithet of *ragamuffins*. I also declared that standing, or mercenary armies, were inconsistent with the spirit of our Constitution, or the genius of a free people. General Lee, and others, dilated upon these terms. He affirmed the last to be misapplied, and defined the word *mercenary* so as to give it an application only to troops hired for the defence of a country *other than their own*. In reply, I contended that there was no etymology which would warrant his construction; that the term was derived from a Latin word which signified *wages*, and did not embrace, as he had declared my meaning would justify, the militia, which likewise receives pay when in actual service, but was exclusively appropriated to such men (whether foreigners, or otherwise) as made the art military a profession or trade, and was properly expressive of a *stand-*

ing army who served for *wages* and by contract, in contradistinction to a militia, or patriotic army, which was composed of all ranks of citizens, equally bound to fight the battles of their country, and in which each contributed his share to the public safety, and who received pay only when in actual service, to enable the poorer citizen to perform his military duty.

"In consequence of my application of these terms to the existing establishment—the first of which I confined to such recruits as had been picked up in my own country—a party of officers, the principal agents among whom were a Captain M'Knight and a Lieutenant Michael Reynolds, both belonging to the marine corps, being apprised that I was in the playhouse on Friday evening last (on which day the resolution was lost, about six o'clock), came into the box where I was, and commenced their operations by frequent allusions, *aimed at me*, to what was going on in the house. The play was The Stranger, and the after-piece Bluebeard. They asked one another if the soldiers on the stage did not act very well for mercenaries; said they supposed from their color (Turks) they were Virginians; squeezed into the seat with evident intention to incommode us, particularly myself; and when we were leaving the box, gave me a twitch by the coat; but upon the author being demanded, they had disappeared. On going down stairs, some of the gentlemen said they tried to push us all down in mass, and in the street they passed with a rude quickness, jostling one of the gentlemen, and striking another's foot. In their aim upon me they were disappointed. I regarded all they said with the most perfect nonchalance; was unmoved by their attempts to insult me, except when they offered personal violence; and in conformity to what I thought my duty, laid a written complaint before the President. To-day (Tuesday, the 14th) he sent it to the House with a letter, in which he lays it before us 'without any comment upon its style.' I must not omit telling you that my feelings were strongly excited. A motion was made to provide a committee of privileges, to whom it was to be referred. This I opposed, expressing my surprise that the letter had been laid before us, a measure which I had not contemplated when I wrote it; that I had addressed it to the authority whose particular duty it was to suppress such conduct in the military, and disclaimed all wish to throw myself upon the protection of himself or of that House; that the privileges of

Congress being expressly defined by the Constitution, I was unwilling to give my assent to any measure which might lead to enlarge them, and which, even if we had a right to adopt it, would hereafter be prostituted to nefarious designs. My objection was overruled, and a committee appointed of seven, on which the speaker had the uncommon goodness to nominate *three* republicans.

"Perhaps some misguided persons may be induced to depreciate the motives 'by which I have been actuated. I cannot help it. My business is to do what I conceive right, careless of the opinion of all. I was delighted to find my sentiments upon this subject coincided with those of Dr. Tucker; it is no bad criterion of the truth of any opinion that it meets his assent. I sometimes look back upon the principles which once governed my moral conduct with astonishment—how much to be regretted it is, that the painted phantom of honor should be dressed in such captivating colors as to suffer few of the nobler minds to escape her contagious embrace."

The letter addressed to the President, after stating the affair in the theatre, proceeds thus—"Having stated the fact, it would be derogatory to your character for me to point out the remedy. So far as they relate to this application addressed to you in a public capacity, they can only be supposed by you to be of a public nature. It is enough for me to state, that the independence of the legislature has been attacked, and the majesty of the people, of which you are the principal representative, insulted, and your authority contemned. In their name, I demand that a provision commensurate with the evil be made, and which will be calculated to deter others from any future attempt to introduce the reign of terror into our country. In addressing you in this plain language of man, I give you, sir, the best proof I can afford of the estimation in which I hold your office and your understanding; and I assure you with truth, that I am with respect, your fellow-citizen,

"JOHN RANDOLPH.

"Chamber H. Representatives Jan. 11,—24th Independence.

"To the President of the U. States."

The reader perceives here none of those courtly and unmeaning (if not worse) phrases that usually begin and end the epistles addressed to high functionaries by those who seek to gain their favor by obsequiousness and flattery—*To his Excellency, thè President of the United States—Your most obedient and humble servant*—none of that, but an unvarnished, straight-forward statement of facts; he tells the President that the independence of the legislature has been attacked, the majesty of the people insulted, and demands that he, their chief representative, shall make some provision adequate to prevent the reign of terror from being introduced into the country. The whole letter was conceived in a stern, independent, republican spirit, and ought not, we would suppose, to have given offence to any one who understood and duly appreciated the term *fellow-citizen.*

This letter the President thought proper on the 14th of the month to communicate to the House—" As the inclosed letter," says he, " from a member of your body, received by me on the night of Saturday the 11th inst., relates to the privileges of the House, which in my opinion ought to be inquired into by the House itself, *if any where.* I have thought proper to submit the whole letter and *its tendencies* to your consideration, without any other *comments on its matter and style.*" It is very plain what he and Pickering thought about both.

The committee appointed to take this matter of privilege into consideration, consisted of Messrs. Chauncey, Goodrich, Macon, Kittera, Jones, Sewell, Robert Williams, and Bayard—Mr. Macon was excused and Mr. Hanna appointed in his stead.

Messrs. Goodrich, Kittera, Sewell, and Bayard, constituting the majority of the committee, were the most distinguished and influential members of the federal party in the House.

On the 18th, Mr. Randolph addressed the following communication to the Chairman of the Committee:—" A mature consideration of the subject induces me to suspect, that a refusal on my part to communicate the information requested by you a few days ago, could only have originated in a false delicacy, under whose impulse I am determined never to act; I shall therefore proceed to state some instances of the misconduct of Capt. M'Knight and Lieut. Reynolds, on the night of Friday, the 10th instant.

" Exclusive of repeated assertions to what passed in the House of Representatives during the debate of the preceding day, and a frequent repetition of some words which fell from me during that discussion, in a manner so marked as to leave no doubt on *my* mind, or that of Messrs. Van Rensselaer, Christie, or Macon, of their intention to insult me personally ; finding me determined to take no notice of their *words*, they adopted a conduct which placed their designs beyond every possibility of doubt, and which they probably conceived to be calculated to *force* me into their measures. Mr. Christie had left his seat between me and the partition of the box; after which, Mr. Van Rensselaer, who sat on the other side of me, laid down, so as to occupy a more than ordinary portion of room, and occasioned my removal to a part of Mr. Christie's former seat, leaving a very small vacancy between myself and the partition. Into this Lieut. Reynolds *suddenly*, and without requesting or giving time for room to be made for him, dropped with such violence as to bring our hips into contact. The shock was sufficient to occasion a slight degree of pain on my part, and for which it is probable he would in some degree have apologized, had not the act been intentional. Just before I left the box, one of them, I believe M'Knight, gave me a sudden and violent pull by the cape of my coat. Upon my demanding who it was, (this was the first instance in which I noticed their proceedings,) no answer was given. I then added, that I had long perceived an intention to insult me, and that the person offering it was a puppy. No reply that I heard was made.

"It will be impossible for me, sir, to specify the various minute actions of these persons and their associates, which tended to the same point. Suffice it to say, that their whole deportment exhibited an insolence, and their every act betokened a bold defiance, which can nether be *defined* nor *mistaken*, and which, according to the generally received opinions of the world, not only would have justified, but demanded chastisement.

"Referring the committee to the numerous and authentic accounts of this transaction, which the gentlemen present are so well calculated to give, I remain with respect, sir,

"Your fellow-citizen,

"JOHN RANDOLPH."

Those gentlemen, Mr. Christie, Mr. Macon, Mr. Nicholson, and others, men of great respectability, and members of Congress, did confirm in every particular the above statement. There rested not the shadow of a doubt on their mind, that Reynolds and M'Knight intended to insult Mr. Randolph, and to inflict personal injury on him, for words spoken in debate.

The only testimony in opposition to those gentlemen of such high respectability, and Mr. Randolph's own statement, so detailed and explicit, was the declaration of those persons themselves. Their testimony is evidently an equivocation: they say they did not go to the theatre with the intention of insulting Mr. Randolph. "I did not know," says M'Knight, "Mr. Randolph was to be at the theatre, nor do I ever recollect seeing him previous to Friday evening; and, from his *youthful appearance and dress, I had no idea of his being a member of the House of Representatives.*" All this may be very true, and yet after reaching there, it is very evident they conceived the idea of insulting and injuring him.

The committee, after collecting all the evidence they could find material in the case, report the following resolutions :

Resolved, That this House entertains a respectful sense of the regard which the President of the United States has shown to its rights and privileges, in his message of the 14th instant, accompanied by a letter addressed to him by John Randolph, Jun., a member of this House.

Resolved, That in respect to the charge alleged by John Randolph, Jun., a member of this House, in his letter addressed to the President of the United States, on the eleventh instant, and by him submitted to the consideration of this House, that sufficient cause does not appear for the interposition of this House, on the ground of a breach of its privileges.

The first resolution was passed without a division. To the second, several amendments were offered, going to censure M'Knight and Reynolds, but were rejected. Then the resolution itself was rejected, by a majority of *twelve*, showing that even that House were not prepared to sacrifice their privileges, which had been so evidently and wantonly insulted and trampled on. The Speaker then ruled all further action on the subject out of order, and so shoved it aside.

We leave Mr. Randolph's friend and contemporary, William Thompson, to make his commentaries on these transactions, the more valuable as the spontaneous effusions of an ingenuous and noble mind:—" The committee," says he, " who sat to examine the charge against several minions of executive power, which, of all that can be

brought against men, was most serious, as being most destructive to
the liberties of America—the committee who were called on to say
whether the privileges of the House should be prostrated, as the privileges of the people have been—the committee who were called on to
decide whether a set of armed ruffians should surround the capitol,
and dictate our laws—this committee have determined, that although
there were *some circumstances* (language of the report) which deserved
censure, yet they were not of such a nature as to be considered a
breach of the privileges of the House. Admit the meaning which
they wish to give to *some circumstances*, I say, if there were any circumstance, no matter how trivial in its nature it may be, if on the
most rigid inquiry it can be found that a legislator is insulted for his
official conduct, that the man who insults offers an insult to the people; and that the men who do not, when called on, inflict all the
punishment their power licenses, is an enemy, are enemies to the
liberty of America. What, sir, will result from the decision of that
committee? The republicans are liable to daily and hourly insults—
the soldiers of Philadelphia are to be raised to a Pretorian band—
our measures are to be dictated by the willing foes of our liberty—
and virtuous opposition is to be silenced by the bayonet. Let me
not be told that these apprehensions are ridiculous; I say they are
grounded in the full conviction, that the military mob is supported by
the administration, and that administration will make great sacrifices
to their love of power. I say it is grounded on a conviction that this
army is not now kept up to secure us from invasion; but that it contemplates something, and I fear that something is injurious to my
country. That the insults you received were not offered to you as
an individual, is certain; for as an individual, separate from your
principles, I perceive they knew you not; it is certain, because your
words were quoted. Not content with debasing us in fact, they wish
to debase us even in appearance—*they cavil at your words.* Had
you addressed the President in courtly style, *they* would forgive the
contents of your letter; addressing him as you have done, we applaud
the conduct, and we rejoice there is one man left us whose principles
and whose manners stand uncorrupted in these corrupted times.
I say we, for I speak the language of many; I say we, for I
speak the language of your State. The persecutions of a faction
have made you more dear to us. Not that your merits are in-

creased by circumstances, but because this is a glaring instance amongst many, that men are persecuted as the organs of principles. This committee have done more, anxious that no opportunity should be lost to liquidate part of the great debt of adulation, they have interwoven a motion of thanks to the President for the respectful sense he has shown of their privileges. Whither does this lead? Is it not to be apprehended, that by this conduct your rights are to be changed into courtesy, that your rights are to hang on the nod of your President? Does this man deserve thanks for the compliance with his official duties? Does he deserve thanks for doing that for which he is paid by his country? The friends of America look at this affair with wonder and with horror. The timid part of the community say we will not send a man whose principles are obnoxious, for fear of consequences; the patriots of your State say we will send men who dare to speak the truth, no matter in whose ears it is grating. But it was disrespectful to call him fellow-citizen! Yes, he is not a fellow-citizen, because he is chief officer, he is alienated by promotion. There is more truth in his having been aliened than they would admit. I will forget for a moment that I am personally acquainted with you, and state, that you evinced in this affair an intrepid coolness, a firmness, and calmness, which must convince every man, not sworn to partiality, that every word of your evidence is most rigid truth. But your remark of mercenary and ragamuffin was galling to certain men in that House; your arguments throughout the whole were unanswerable; and your *naked* truths (for I will adopt your very appropriate expression) were dangerous to men who, unveiled, are damned."

This affair created, at the time, great excitement through the country. It was considered as but one of a series of events that had for their end the subjugation of the people to the will of the federal oligarchy. The enormous public debt, which was daily increasing by heavy loans at usurious interest, the funding system, the National Bank, the recently-created navy establishment, and large standing army without an enemy or the prospect of an enemy, the alien and the sedition laws in active operation, sparing neither station nor age, had given an alarming and a powerful centralizing action to the Government. And it was thought that the evil tendencies of all those measures were now consummated in the humiliation of the legislature to executive authority, and its tame submission to the arrogance of military pride. The trivial occurrence in the theatre, giving an opportunity to the President to display his petulant temper and his high sense of official consequence, and to the House of Representatives to manifest their subservient spirit, proved to be a very serious business. The people, more sagacious than they have credit for among some politicians, saw at once the tendency of these proceedings; and Randolph was hailed throughout the Union as the champion of the rights of the people. The very morning (15th January) his correspondence with the President appeared in the Philadelphia papers, and before any action thereon by the House, he received a communication professing to convey *the sentiments of a number of respectable citizens.* "It is our decided opinion," say they, "that the person of a delegate in Congress ought to be as sacred from public or private insult as the person of an ambassador to a foreign power. Should this flagrant violation of the privilege of a member of your House which has been offered to your person be *winked at*, may not enterprising men introduce parties into the House, which, by putting its members in bodily fear, will completely shackle the freedom of debate, and thereby injure the public good?" They then proceed to thank him for having the boldness *candidly to avow the real sentiments* of his heart, with a huge capital *R* and a tremendous underscoring of the word *real* in the original document, which is now before us. We might infer from this that such boldness was very unusual at that time. And indeed it was true. Madison had retired before the storm; so had Giles and the plain blunt-spoken Finlay, of Pennsylvania. Gallatin was still there; but he was not the man for the crisis; he was a foreigner, modest, plain in his elocution, and dealt more in facts and figures of arithmetic than those bold metaphors and figures of speech so essential to arouse and interest the people. The whole House might slumber under Gallatin's demonstrations, while one schrill echo of Randolph's voice would wake the seven sleepers. Matthew Lyon is seen among the silent voters; but three months' imprisonment last winter in a dungeon, not six feet square, under the sedition law, for daring to *publish* words in disparagement of the President, has cooled his Irish temper, and awed him into silence. This Harry Hotspur, therefore, or young cornet of horse, burst suddenly among them like a sky-rocket. His boldness, his eloquence, his youthful appearance, struck them with astonishment. But who can tell the effect of those *naked truths*, which fell like hot shot among the enemy, all intrenched and secure, as they supposed themselves, behind their formidable walls! John Thompson's prediction was fulfilled in the very outset of his career : *He will become an object of admiration and terror to the enemies of liberty!*

—————•♦•—————

CHAPTER XXIV.

MAKE TO YOURSELF AN IDOL, AND, IN SPITE OF THE DECALOGUE, WORSHIP IT.

DURING the winter and spring of 1800 he kept up a regular correspondence with his friend, William Thompson, who, the reader knows, had found a home and an asylum in his misfortunes under the hospitable roof of Bizarre. The soothing temper he manifests towards that unfortunate youth, the sound advice he gave him, so fraught with wisdom and a knowledge of human nature, and his judicious and well-timed encouragement, to arouse from his lethargy and become the man he was capable of being, present the character of John Randolph in a pleasing point of view, and explain in a measure those traits of mind and disposition, known only to a few, that made him such an object of devoted friendship on the part of those who were honored by his intimate regard.

John Randolph, jun to his friend and brother, William Thompson.

PHILADELPHIA, Dec. 31, 24th year.

" Your letter was peculiarly acceptable to me. It relieved me from considerable anxiety on account of your health, to the ill state of which I attributed that suspension of our correspondence, which has originated in the derangement of the post office department; it contained assurances of that regard of which I never entertained a doubt, but which, nevertheless, were extremely gratifying to me ; but above all it put my mind at ease upon a subject which has been productive of considerable concern. I mean your change of residence, which, as you will find by my last, I understood you had removed to Chinquepin Church—not knowing your reasons for leaving Bizarre, I could not combat. Great, however, was my surprise and pleasure to receive a letter from Judy (Mrs. Richard Randolph) and yourself; both of which relieved my anxiety upon this head. I am, moreover, charmed, my friend, that you are resolutely bent upon study, and have made some progress therein. Let me conjure you to adhere inflexibly to this rational pursuit. Your destiny is in your own hands. Regular employment is of all medicines the most effectual for a wounded mind. If the sympathy of a friend who loves you because you are amiable and unfortunate; because you are the representative of that person (John Thompson died January, 1799) who held the first place in his heart, and the first rank in the intellectual order; if my uniform friendship, my dear Thompson, could heal the wounds of your heart, never should it know a pang. Your situation is of all others the one most eminently calculated to repair, so far as it is possible, the ills which you have sustained. An amiable woman, who regards you as a brother, who shares your griefs, and will administer as far as she can to your consolation, who unites to talents of the first order a degree of cultivation uncommon in any country, but especially in ours—such a woman is under the same roof with you. Cultivate a familiarity with her; each day will give you new and unexpected proof of the strength of her mind, and the extent of her information. Books you have at command; your retirement is unbroken. Such a situation is, in my opinion, the best calculated for a young man (under any circumstances) who will study; or even for one who is determined to be indolent. Female society, in my eye, is an indispensable requisite in forming the manly character. That which is offered to you is not to be paralleled, perhaps, in the world. You call on me, my friend, for advice. You bid me regard your foibles with a lenient eye; you anticipate the joy which I shall derive from your success. I will not permit yself to doubt of it. You shall succeed—you must. You have it in your power. Exertion only is necessary. You owe it to the memory of our departed brother, to yourself, to me, to your country, to humanity! Apprised that you have foibles to eradicate, the work is more than half accomplished. I will point them out with a friendly yet lenient hand. You will not shrink from the probe, knowing that in communicating present pain your ultimate cure and safety is the object of the friendly operator. If I supposed myself capable of inflicting intentional and wanton pain upon your feelings, I should shrink with abhorrence from myself. In the course of my strictures I may, perhaps, appear abrupt. I am now pressed for time.

"Self-examination, when cool and impartial, is the best of all correctives. It is a general and trite observation that man knows his fellows better than himself. This is too true; but it depends upon every individual to exhibit, in himself, a refutation of this received maxim. Retirement and virtuous society fit the mind for this task.

" Among your foibles I have principally observed unsteadiness ; a precipitate decision, and the want of mature reflection, *generally*. It would be uncandid to determine your character by these traits, which originate, perhaps, or are at least heightened, by the uneasiness which preys upon your mind, which renders you more than usually restless. Endeavor, my friend, to act less upon momentary impulse; pause, reflect ; think much and speak little ; form a steadiness of demeanor, and having once resolved, persevere. Read, but do not devour, books. Compare your information ; digest it. In short, according to the old proverb, " Make haste slowly." There is one point upon which I must enjoin you to beware. You appeared restless, when I saw you, to change your property. Let things stand as they are a little. Facilis discensus, sed revocare gradum, hoc opus. (Excuse, I beseech you, this pitiful display of learning.)

" The Duc de la Rochefoucault—who, by the by, is a bad moral preceptor—has, among others, this very excellent maxim: ' We are never made so ridiculous by the qualities we possess, as by those which we affect to have.' I never knew a man who would not profit of this observation. To preserve your own esteem, merit it. I have no fear that you will ever render yourself unworthy of its greatest good. Yet, a man who is so unfortunate as to lose his own good opinion, is wrong to despair. It may be retrieved. He ought to set about it immediately, as the only reparation which he can make to himself or society. The ill opinion of mankind is often misplaced ; *but our own of ourselves never.*

" Pardon, my dear brother, this pedantic and didactic letter. Its sententiousness is intolerable, yet it was almost unavoidable. I had written till my fingers were cramped. The hour of closing the mail approached, and I was obliged to throw my sentiments into the offensive form of dogmas. That I, who abound in foibles, and, to speak truth, *vices*—that I should pretend to dogmatize, may appear to many arrogant indeed. Yet, let them recollect that we are all frail, and should sustain each other; and that the truth of a precept is not de termined by the practice of him who promulges it. Go on, my dear Thompson, and prosper. I regret that I am debarred the pleasure of sharing your literary labors, and of that interchange of sentiment which constitutes one of the chief sources of my enjoyment. To our amiable sister—for such she considers herself with respect to you—I commit you, confident that your own exertion, aided by her society, will form you such as your friend will rejoice to behold you. Write to him frequently I beseech you; cheer his solitary and miserab.e existence with the well known characters of friendship. Adieu, my dear brother."

William Thompson to John Randolph.

" Dear Jack,—I am not ceremonious. I feel a conviction that your silence does not proceed from a want of regard, but from a cause more important to the world, to yourself, and, if possible, more distressing to me than the loss of that place in your heart, on which depends my future prosperity. I had fondly hoped that the change of scene, and the novelty of business, would have dissipated that melancholy which overhung you. To see my friend return happy and well, was the only wish of my heart.

" To the man who is not devoted to unnatural dissipations, a great city has no charms: it awakens the most painful sensations in the breast of the philanthropist and patriot. It is disgusting to behold such a mass of vice, and all its attendant deformities, cherished in the bosom of an enlightened country. Prostitutions of body, and still greater prostitution of mind, excite our pity and hatred. The political life has not those attractions to the virtuous which it once had, and which it ought still to have in this country. The spirit of party has extinguished the spirit of liberty. The enlightened orator must be shocked at the willing stupidity of his auditors. Our exertions are vain and impotent. Every man is the avowed friend of a party. Converts to reason are not to be found; whilst converts to interest are innumerable.

" You know I promised not to visit Richmond. I have rigidly adhered to that. I felt a necessity of *cooling down.* I foreboded the acquirement of dissipated habits, which would haunt me unceasingly. I saw that the patronage of the virtuous would awaken an emulation in me to attain their perfection. I feel confident that if my friends bear a little longer with my foibles, they will be corrected. I look forward with honest pride to the day when I shall merit the regard—when, by my conduct and by my principles, I shall make some retribution for the exalted generosity which I have met with from your family. I am not made of such stern stuff as to resist singly ; but the idea of friendship will steel my heart against temptation. Since you left me, I have been generally at *home,* conscious how little I merit regard. That which I feel for your .amiable family may perhaps appear presumption, yet the thought of losing it is stinging. * * * To your sister, your most amiable sister, I try to render myself agreeable. There is a gentleness of manners, an uniformity of conduct, and a majesty of virtue, which seem to render admiration presumptuous."

John Randolph to his brother, William Thompson.

" Your letter, my dear Thompson, has communicated to my heart a satisfaction to which it has not been at all familiar. It has proved beyond dispute that the energies of your mind, however neglected by yourself, or relaxed by misfortune, have been suspended, but not impaired ; and that the strength of your understanding has not been unequal to the ordeal of misfortune, of which few are calculated to bear the test. Proceed, my friend, in the path in which you now move ; justify those lively hopes which I have never ceased to entertain, or to express, of your future attainments : in the words, although not in the sense of the poet, let me exhort you, ' carpe diem.' The past is not in our power to recall. The future we can neither foresee nor control. The present alone is at our disposal : on the use to which it is applied, depends the whole of what is estimable or amiable in human character."

Poor Thompson went to Petersburg about this time (February, or March, 1800), and got entangled in a way that most young men of his temper are apt to be. He shall tell the story in his own way. After getting back to Bizarre, in April, he thus writes :

" You will be surprised, dear brother, when you are informed, that my stay in Petersburg was protracted by a circumstance against which you warned me in a letter some time past. I allude to Mrs. B——. Nature has compensated for mental imperfection, by bodily perfection in that woman. And my attachment to her corroborates a heresy in love, that desire is a powerful ingredient. Her mind is not cultivated, her disposition is not calculated to make a man of my enthusiasm in regard *happy*. Fully aware of these circumstances, I cherished her name as dear. Thus situated, let me ask you a question. Had you been told—nay, had you known that this woman was the victim of infamous oppression—that these charms had been wrested from your possession by unfeeling relations (they were engaged when he went to Europe in 1798), that your name was dear, her husband's name odious—that on you she looked with tenderness, and on him with hatred, what line of conduct would you adopt? * * * I had resolved to shun her, and in truth did ; but that fate, which shows refinement in its policy, forced me to an interview. * * * * * * After several resolutions, some ridiculous (as is usual in such cases), and one which had near proved fatal, I fled to the asylum of the distressed (wisely thought of), to the spot where tender friendship forms a character exalted to a height, which makes the feebler of her sex look low indeed, would make me blush at my folly, and banish the idea of a baneful passion. I will not recapitulate the wrongs of fortune, but I fondly hope that they will plead in apology for the failings of your friend."

Now for the answer ; and let every young man, and young woman too, ponder well upon it.

" April 19, 24 year.—To-day I received your letter of the 12th. It has unravelled a mystery, for whose solution I have before searched in vain. That you should have been in Petersburg, sighing at the feet of the fair Mrs. B., is what I did not expect to learn, since I supposed you all the while in Sussex. I am now not at all surprised at your silence, during this period of amorous intoxication ; since nothing so completely unfits a man for intercourse with any other than the object of his infatuation.

" The answer to your questions is altogether easy. In the first place, it is not true, because it cannot be true, that this lady was compelled to the step which she has taken. What *force* could be brought to act upon her, which materials as hard as wax would not resist? The truth is, if ever she felt an attachment to you, she sacrificed it to avarice; not because money was the end, but the means, of gratification; her vanity, the ruling passion of every mind as imbecile as her own, delighted in the splendor which wealth alone could procure. At this time the same passion, which is one of the vilest modifications of self-love, would gratify itself with a little coquetry; and if your prudence has not exceeded that of the lady, it has gone, I fear, greater lengths than she at first apprehended. Nor have you, my friend, done this woman a good office, in rendering her discontented with her lot, by suffering her to persuade herself that she is in love with you, and that oppression alone has driven her to a detested union with a detestable brute, for such (on all hands, I believe, it is agreed) is Mr. B. Never did I see a woman apparently better pleased with her situation. She did not lose one pennyweight of her very comfortable quantity of flesh; and, however she *might have hesitated between* my friend and the cash, minus the possessor, had you been on the spot to contest your right to her very fair hand, yet W. T., on the other side of the Atlantic, or perhaps at the bottom of it, was no rival to the *solid* worth of her now cara sposa. Perhaps, in the first instance, she might have disliked the man, for good reasons; and in the second, for no reason at all, but because her relations were very anxious for the match; but be assured her imagination was not sufficiently lively to induce her to *shed one tear* on your account.

"You ask me, my friend, what conduct you ought to pursue; and you talk of revenge. B. has never injured you; he has acted like a fool, I grant, in marrying a woman whose only inducement to the match, he must be conscious, was his wealth; but he has committed no crime; at least he was unconscious of any. That the fellow should wear antlers, is no great matter of regret, because the os frontis is certainly substantial enough to bear their weight. Yet I do not wish them to be planted by you, *for your sake*. I will allow that this lady is as fair as she is *fat*—that she is a very inviting object; yet why should you prevent her leading a life of as much happiness as she is susceptible of—fruges consumere, &c. Has not her conduct in relation to *you* and to her husband been such as renders her unworthy of any man of worth? Has he not conferred on you a

benefit, by preventing the possibility of an alliance with a woman capable of carrying on a correspondence with any other than her husband; and can you, who enjoy the society of that pattern of female virtue, feel for this woman any sentiment but contempt? . . .
So far from injuring you, B. is the injured person, if at all. His impenetrable stupidity has alone shielded him from sensations not the most enviable, I imagine. Do not suppose from my style that I am unfeeling, or have too low an estimate of the sex; on the contrary, I am the warmest of their admirers. But silly and depraved women, and stupid, unprincipled men, are both objects of my pity and contempt. I wish you to form a just estimate of what is valuable in female character—then seek out a proper object and marry. Intrigue will blast your reputation, and, what is more to the purpose, your peace of mind; it will be a stumbling-block to you through life. An acquaintance with loose women has incapacitated you from forming a proper estimate of female worth. . . . .
I must congratulate you on your escape, and on your resolution to behold no more the fascinating object which has caused you so much uneasiness. I shall shortly have the pleasure of embracing you.

"P. S. My servant (Johnny?) has been packing up some effects, which I am about sending to Petersburg by water, and at every three words I have had a query to solve. This will account for my incoherence.

"P. S. (Characteristic, two postscripts.) I have been so hurried, as perhaps to betray myself into an inaccuracy of expression. But let me suggest two ideas to you. Has not your conduct been such as to injure a woman for whom you have felt and professed a regard? is it a liberal or disinterested passion (passion is never liberal or disinterested), which risks the reputation of the beloved object? Has not her conduct in admitting your attentions rendered her unworthy of any man but her present possessor? View this matter in its proper light and you will never think more of her. . . . . Success attend your study of law."

About the middle of May, Essex was dispatched with Jacobin and other horses, to meet his young master at the Bolling-green. He took along with him the following letter from William Thompson:

"What are my emotions, dearest brother, at seeing your horse thus far on his way to return you among us! How eagerly do I await the appointed day! Ryland (Randolph) has returned (some unsuccessful adventure), and another of the children of misfortune will seek refuge and consolation under this hospitable roof. He has promised me by letter to be with us in a day or two,—what pleasure do I anticipate in the society of our incomparable sister, in yours, in Ryland's! I wish I had the vanity to suppose I was worthy of it.

" We have been visited by the young ladies of Liberty Neck, and by its mentor, Major Scott. I had rather have his wisdom than Newton's or Locke's; for depend on it, he has dipped deep in the science of mind. According to the laws of gallantry, I should have escorted them to Amelia; but I am not fitted for society, and the continued round of company in the Neck is painful instead of pleasing.

" Our sister is now asleep; she would have written but for her being busy in finishing the children's clothes, and being obliged to write to Mrs. Harrison. When I came in last evening, I found her in the passage, a candle on the chair, sewing. I could hardly help exclaiming, what a pattern for her sex. The boys are well; they have both grown—the Saint particularly, whose activity will astonish you. Every body is cheerful—your arrival in anticipation is the cause. Farewell, dearest brother—hasten to join us.

" W. Thompson.

" Take care how you ride Jacobin, and if not for your own, at least for our sakes, run no risks by putting him in a carriage—we all dread the attempt."

He returned safely, to the joy of more people (ladies too?) than those at Bizarre. This delightful society was now complete; books, high discourse on philosophy, morals, government, the destiny of man—intermingled with the charming conversation and the music of elegant and accomplished women—exercise on the high-mettled steed, and frequent visits and dining parties at neighbors' houses, whose warm reception, bountiful hospitality, and unostentatious refinement of manner (universal with the gentlemen of the olden time), made the guest perfectly at home, and at ease in heart and in behavior. Such was the Old Dominion, half-a-century ago, such is she now in some degree; but, alas! the difference!

But poor Thompson, the hapless child of misfortune, was not long permitted to enjoy the sweets of this paradise. Some wicked and envious Mephistophiles looked in with his jealous eyes on the happy beings that composed it; and sought to blast it with his malicious tongue. It was rumored that Thompson staid at Bizarre for a selfish purpose; that, besides the convenience of the thing in his condition, his object was to win the affection of its fair mistress What if it were true? But this base world will allow nothing but a base motive for the most generous action. The insinuation was enough for the high-minded Thompson. He immediately left Bizarre, and wrote the following letter:—" The letter which I have transmitted by the same opportunity to that most amiable of women our sister, communicates intelligence of a report, the effects of which on my mind you will be fully aware of, from a former conversation on the subject. Would you suppose, my dearest brother, that the world would have dared to insinuate, that my object in remaining at Bizarre is to solicit the affections of our friend! Time, and the apprehension that I shall be intruded on, compel me to conciseness My abode will be Ryland's until I receive letters from you both. View the subject with impartiality—enter into my feelings, for you know my heart—tell me with candor whether I am not bound to leave the abode of innocence and friendship? Tell me whether refined friendship does not demand on my part a sacrifice of every prospect of happiness, to the amiable, to the benevolent and virtuous woman who is wronged from her generous sympathy to the hapless."

A most delicate task this imposed on a friend—particularly one holding the relation of Mr. Randolph to the lady in question. But see how nobly, how manfully he discharged the duty : " For the first time I perceive myself embarrassed how to comply with the requisition of friendship. But yesterday, and I should have been unable to comprehend the speculative possibility of that which to-day is reduced to practice. If I decline the task which you have allotted me, it is not because I am disposed to shrink from the sacred obligations which I owe to you. My silence is not the effect of unfeeling indifference, of timid indecision, or cautious reserve. It is the result of the firmest conviction that it is not for *me* to advise you in the present crisis. It is a task to which I am indeed unequal. Consult your own heart, it is *alone* capable of advising you. The truly fraternal regard which you feel for our most amiable sister, does not require to be admonished of the respect which is due to her feelings. You alone are a competent judge of that conduct which is best calculated not to wound her delicacy; and it is that alone which you are capable of pursuing. Whatever may be your determination, you will not be the less dear to me. That spirit of impertinent malice, which mankind seem determined to cherish at the expense of all that should constitute their enjoyment, may, indeed, intrude upon our arrangements and deprive me of your society; but it can never rob me of the pure attachment which I have conceived for you, and which can never cease to animate me. I hold this portion of good, at least, in contempt of an unfeeling and calumnious world—invulnerable to every shaft, it derides their impotent malice.

"Let me suggest to you to pursue that line of conduct which you shall be disposed to adopt, as if it were the result of your previous determination. Prosecute, therefore, your intended journey, and do not permit malicious curiosity to enjoy the wretched satisfaction of supposing that IT has the power of influencing your actions.

"I have perceived, with extreme pleasure, that your mind has for some time been rapidly regaining its pristine energy. Keep it, therefore, I beseech you, my friend, in constant exercise. Get up some object of pursuit. Make to yourself an image, and, in defiance of the decalogue, worship it. Whether it be excellence in medicine or law, or political eminence, determine not to relax your endeavors until you have attained it. You must not suffer your mind, whose activity must be employed, to prey upon *itself*. The greatest blessing which falls to the lot of man is thus converted into the deadliest curse. I need not admonish you to keep up the intercourse which subsists between us, and which nothing shall compel me to relinquish.

"I trust that I shall hear from you in the space of a week at farthest. Meanwhile rest assured of the undiminished affection of the firmest of your friends."

Poor Thompson! why could he not follow the advice so delicately given—pursue the line of conduct he had previously determined on—which was, doubtless, to stay at Bizarre—prosecute his journey, and then come back, without regard to the malicious surmises of a wicked world? He did not sacrifice his happiness to that amiable, benevolent and virtuous woman, as he supposed; she did not need it or require it—but to malicious curiosity. He had not strength of mind to resist the vague impression of the world's censure; and suffered the spirit of impertinent malice to enjoy the wretched satisfaction of supposing that *it* had the power of influencing his actions. He never came back to Bizarre as a home again—soon fell into his old habits—wandered over Canada a-foot, seeking rest but finding none—a wandering spirit that rapidly glided into irregular courses; the world, erewhile so bright and smooth, had suddenly become dark and slippery to him ; ne'er again could he find rest for the sole of his foot;—turned out from that paradise, a world of turbid waters was all his wearied eye could light upon. What further befell him shall be made known to the reader in the sequel.

CHAPTER XXV.

THE COURSE OF TRUE LOVE NEVER DID RUN SMOOTH.

THE reader is already aware that John Randolph was the centre of a very extensive correspondence with some of the first young men of the country—among others, Joseph Bryan, of Georgia. In the month of January, last winter (1800), Bryan informed him that he was about to embark soon for England, and wished his friend to procure certificates of citizenship for himself and companion from Mr. Jefferson ; and promised in his next to give the reason for quitting his native country—which accordingly he did in the following words : " I have in that time, my friend (since this time twelve months), been on the verge of becoming a member of the fraternity of Benedicts, as you humorously style married men. In short, I paid my addresses to an accomplished young woman, of both family and fortune, in Carolina—quarrelled with my father and mother because I would not relinquish the pursuit—followed her with every prospect of the desired success for eighteen months—went to her abode last Christmas, with the comfortable idea of marrying her on the commencement of the new year—and was discarded by her parents because mine would not consent to the match. There were one or two other trifling objections, such as—I was a ———, a man of no religion— a Georgian ; and would take their child where they might never see her face again, &c. All this you may think apocryphal—'tis true, upon my word. Yet 'my heart does not bleed at every pore from the bitterest of recollections ;' to be sure I was in a hell of a taking for two or three days. But I found that keeping myself employed, made it wear off to a miracle. So much for my love affairs. You may perhaps be a little surprised at my going to England ; 'twas a sudden resolution, I must confess; I'll tell you how it happened. While I was laboring under the horrors of my dismission, I swore to my little grisette, in order to melt her, that if she would not quit father and mother and run away with me, I would go off immediately and fight the Russians! She would not do that, so I am obliged by a point of honor to make the attempt, at least.

" If, after my arrival in England, I can conveniently get to France, I shall go there; if not, I shall spend the money I carry with me, and come home again.

" I don't know whether 'twill be proper to apply to Mr. Jefferson for the certificate I wrote to you for—my reasons were these : I knew that he was better known and better liked in France than any distinguished person in our country, therefore, a certificate from him would do me more service than from any other; besides, I don't like any of the Adamites well enough to receive a favor of that kind from their hands.

" I expect to sail from Savannah about the 20th instant (February, 1800) ; as soon as I arrive you will hear from me. One of my *principal reasons* for going to Europe, is to improve my health, which is very indifferent at this time."

So then it was your own pleasure and convenience at last, and not the sting of disappointed love, that drove you away to France ! The girls are very much deceived when they flatter themselves that men generally will do rash things for their sweet sakes; they may be in *a hell of a taking* for a time, but the fever soon wears off. Men are no better treated. This girl, in his absence, while he was fighting for liberty under the banners of France, did the very thing she refused to do with him—ran away and got married against the will of her parents.

But the answer to the first letter, and in anticipation of the one above : " Your letter of the 7th of last month was this moment put into my hands. Need I say that it distresses me beyond measure ? Ah, my friend, it is then too true ! My suspicions were but too well grounded ! The eagle-eye of friendship finds no difficulty in piercing the veil which shrouds you ; which, until now, I did not dare to lift. You have related nothing, yet I know every thing. This omission, for which you promise to atone in another letter, is but too well supplied by conjectures which cannot, I fear, deceive me.

" Bryan, my friend, you are about to render yourself, me, all who are interested in your happiness, wretched, perhaps, for ever. These are more numerous than you are at present willing to allow. At one stroke you are about to sever all those ties which bind you to the soil which gave you birth, to the tender connections of your childhood, to the most constant of friends—relations which give to existence its only value. Your sickly taste loathes that domestic happiness which is yet in store for you—perhaps you deny that it can have, for yourself, any existence ; you prefer to it, *trash* of foreign growth. You seek in vain, my friend, to fly from misery. It will accompany you—it will rankle in that heart in whose cruel wounds it rejoices to dwell. It is of no country, but *yourself*, and time alone can soothe its rage.

" Among the dangers you are about to encounter, I will not enumerate those of a personal nature ; not because they are in themselves contemptible, however they may be despised by yourself, but because in comparison to the gigantic mischiefs which you are about to court, they are indeed insignificant. I mean in respect to yourself—to your friends they are but too formidable. Recall then, I beseech you, your rash determination—pause, at least, upon the rash step which you meditate ! It is, however, the privilege of friendship *only* to *advise*. The certificates which you require, I will endeavor to procure time enough to accompany this letter. This is Saturday, and after the hour of doing business at the offices ; and to be valid they must issue from that of the Secretary of State. Be not impatient, they shall be forwarded by Tuesday's mail, *in any event ;* letters from Jefferson to some of his European friends shall follow them."

Thus we find this young man, not yet twenty-seven years of age,

the grave Mentor to his young friends. They confide to his friend·
ship, constant and pure, all their cares and troubles, and confidently
expect in return his sympathy, his advice, and the practical lessons of a sage wisdom. But was he without care? Had he no
troubles of his own to perplex his bosom? Had this young Mentor so soon fought the battle of life, and gained the victory? Was
his heart serene and lifted above the storm of passion that raged
around him? *I, too, am wretched!* " To the procuring and transmitting," continues he, " of these certificates of birth and citizenship,
I annex a condition of which I will not brook the refusal—a compliance is due to that attachment which has so long subsisted between
us; it is an exertion certainly not too great to be yielded to a friendship, whose constancy has been rarely equalled, but never surpassed.
Listen, therefore :

"I, too, am wretched; misery is not your exclusive charter. I
have for some months meditated a temporary relinquishment of my
country. The execution of this scheme has no connection with
yours. The motives which produced it originated in events which
happened before I took my seat in Congress, although I was then
ignorant of their existence; they were, indeed, prior to my election to
an office, of which nothing but a high sense of the obligations of public duty has prevented the resignation. A second election could not,
in that event, have been practicable, until the present session was
somewhat advanced. I determined, therefore, not to relinquish my
seat until its expiration; then to resign it, and bid adieu to my
native shores for a few years, at least. In this determination I still
remain. If, therefore, you refuse to rescind your hasty resolution,
I desire permission to be the companion of your voyage—to partake
your sorrows and to share with you my own—to be the friend of him
who is to accompany you, because he is *yours*. Yet, believe me, Joe,
and it is unnecessary to declare by what motives I am influenced to
the assertion, that I shall be glad to hear that I am to prosecute my
voyage alone—to be informed that you have receded from a project
which has not, like my own, been the fruit of deliberate resolve. I
had, indeed, hoped that the relation of your own domestic enjoyment
would have beguiled many a sad hour of my life. But, pardon me,
my dear fellow, I see my indiscretion. It shall not be repeated.

If, then, you persist in carrying into execution your plan, take a passage with your friend for New-York, or the Delaware, it is open ; meet me here about the middle of March—we rise in April—there is a resolution laid upon our table to adjourn on the first of the month ; it will certainly be carried; they even talk of substituting ' March.' We will then embark together for any part of the other continent that you may prefer; I am indifferent about places. But if I go alone, I shall take shipping for some English port, London or Liverpool. I wish I could join you in Savannah ; but it would be extremely inconvenient. I fear the climate ; a passage would be more uncertain too from thence, and the accommodations perhaps not so good. Yet I will even meet you there, or in Charleston, in case you are resolved to leave America, if I can have your company on no other terms. Write immediately and solve this business. I repeat, that it will be very inconvenient to take my passage from a southern port; it will likewise occasion delay. I shall have a voyage to make thither, and then to wait the sailing of a vessel ; whereas, if you meet me here, I can fix myself for any ship bound to Europe about the time of the rising of Congress; and in the great ports of New-York, Philadelphia, or Baltimore, we cannot fail to procure a speedy embarkation, and agreeable berths. Again I entreat you to write to me immediately upon the receipt of this : in expectation of the answer, I shall remain under no common anxiety until its arrival. Meantime, remember, my friend, that there is one person, at least, and he an unshaken friend, who is not insensible to your worth. Farewell, dear Joseph.

" P. S. I had like to have omitted enjoining you to preserve inviolable secrecy with respect to my designs. The reason I will detail to you at meeting. It is unnecessary to say that they are not such as I should be ashamed to avow ; yet I do not wish it to be known that I am about to leave the country until a week or ten days before my departure. Adieu !"

Bryan did not receive this letter before his embarkation. Had it come to hand in time, there can be no question that he would have gladly accepted the offer of his friend, and gone to Philadelphia and awaited the adjournment of Congress, that they might have the pleasure of a voyage together.

But it is certain Randolph did not go abroad at that time. Had his friend arrived in Philadelphia, in obedience to his wishes, he would unquestionably have strained a point, and, at all hazards, fulfilled an engagement he had so solemnly made. In that case, the events of history would have been changed. But he did not go; the reason why is unknown to us. It may have been pecuniary embarrassment. He was paying large instalments of the British debt about that time to Mr. Wickham. In 1824, writing to a friend from Paris, he says: " Here, then, am I, where I ought to have been thirty years ago, and where I would have been, had I not been plundered and oppressed."

But he did not escape from his sorrows at that time by flying across the sea. He staid at home to brood over them. *I, too, am wretched.*

" My character" (says he in a letter to a friend about this time August, 1800), "like many other sublunary things, hath lately undergone an almost total revolution." It seems that he had some special sorrow that weighed upon his heart, the cause of which originated before his election in April, 1799, but was unknown to him for some months afterwards. That it was of the same nature with that which drove one friend across the Atlantic and the other to Canada—that it was the malady of love which brought him into trouble, and that oppressed his soul, cannot be questioned.

Soon after he took his seat in Congress Thompson wrote to him, detailing the circumstances of a report which had been fabricated and secretly circulated to his injury, tracing it to its source, and proving it to be an idle tale without foundation, and confined to the knowledge of a few only. He then continues: "Repose on thy pillow and heed not the shafts that are thrown against you. The world has not injured me, and it has not despised you. Mrs. M. assured me that in your honor she placed the most implicit confidence. When you communicate with M——a, as probably you have already done, she will declare herself unaffected by this tale, which has disturbed your peace. I have spoken with candor, but I have spoken with truth. Demand the author, and if he be given up, you will find it a child. The time of telling it, the month of August.

" Alas, my brother, what are not you destined to suffer! What tremendous trials of fortitude have you not undergone! In the enthusiasm of friendship I look forward to your happiness, and each day brings to life some new pang which is unfeelingly inflicted. Let not this affair make too deep an impression on your

mind—command my services if they be required; for be assured
that the mind which personifies irregularity and want of system
in the affairs of the world, is nerved to act with dauntless energy
in the cause of my brother. Prudence, caution, all the requisites
of successful friendship, are at the command of him, who in the
walk of life is eccentric and unsteady."

About the time of the correspondence with Bryan, and his
determination to go abroad, Thompson again writes:—"I have
mingled with society; I have purposely spoken of you and Miss
W——d to ascertain precisely the public opinion; and I can
repeat with joy, that my brother has not been wronged by the
world. As to the idle suggestions of babbling men and women,
shall they be heaped together and transformed into most serious
charges, that even your confidence of yourself may be shaken if
possible, and thus your peace of mind be for ever blasted? Enough
on this subject. I have violated my common rule of conduct by
being aggressor on the topic."

On another occasion he says:—"In our lives, my brother, we
have seen two fine women (Mrs. Judith Randolph and Miss M——a
W—d); never extend your list; never trust your eyes, or your ears,
for they stand alone." And in his voluntary banishment from the
asylum of the wretched and unfortunate, when he deeply felt his
bereavement and forlorn condition, he thus writes: "M——a, the amiable, the good M——a, has honored me with a short letter; such
tokens of esteem, such evidences of generous pity, for a man cast on
the wide world unfriended and unprotected, create a gratitude not
to be expressed. It is not until we are humiliated by misfortune that
we feel these things, for in the height of worldly prosperity the wish
and the pursuit go hand in hand, and successive gratifications blunt
the sensibilities of our nature. Whilst we rejoice in a mortality as
the termination of lives mutually painful, in which we have been
called on to exercise a fortitude sufficient to overwhelm minds less
noble and less firm, in which every fair prospect has been blighted,
every brilliant expectation thwarted, and every tender emotion hate-
fully disappointed, let us linger out a remnant which cannot be long,
mutually cherishing and supporting each other on the tedious road.
My dear friend, let us not leave each other behind; for, alas! how
sterile and how barren would creation then be! United, we are

strong, but unsupported we could not stand against the increasing pressure of misfortune. Often do I exclaim, Would that you and I were cast on some desert island, there to live out the remainder of our days unpolluted by the communication with man. Separated from each other, our lips are sealed, for the expression of sentiments which exult and ennoble humanity. Even in the support of virtue, the cautious language of vice must be adopted ; even in the defence of truth we must descend to the artifice of error."

Here, reader, we let drop the curtain. Its thick folds of half a century are impervious to the light of mortal eyes; ask not a look beyond the mysterious veil. There are secrets we trust not to a friend, that we betray not to ourselves, and which none but the impious curiosity of a heartless world would ever dare to penetrate. Let the gross impulses, the base considerations of worldly gain, that constitute the ground and the motive of most human associations, suffice as fit subjects for your cold observation, your ridicule and contempt; but hold sacred, or look with awe, on that deep self-sacrificing passion, which, springing from the soul of man, is all-embracing in its love, fathomless, infinite, and divine. Enough to know, that in the bosom of this man there glowed the fires of such a love, that continued to burn through life, and were only extinguished amid the crumbling ruins of the altar by the damp dews that gathered over them in the dark valley and the shadow of death. He hath said : " *One* I loved better than my own soul, or him that created it." " My apathy is not natural, but superinduced. There *was* a volcano under my ice, but it is burnt out, and a face of desolation has come on, not to be rectified in ages, could my life be prolonged to a patriarchal longevity. The necessity *of loving and being beloved* was never felt by the imaginary beings of Rousseau and Byron's creation more imperiously than by myself. My heart was offered up with a devotion that knew no reserve. Long an object of proscription and treachery, I have at last (more mortifying to the pride of man) become one of utter indifference."

To you, reader, he is far from being an object of indifference, and we trust that before the end of these volumes he will be drawn to your heart by the cords of affection, and that his memory will ever hereafter awaken in your bosom those noblest emotions of sympathy and veneration.

CHAPTER XXVI.

PRESIDENTIAL ELECTION, 1800–1—MIDNIGHT JUDGES.

THE reader is already aware of the intense political excitement raging through the country at this time. The civil wars, and violent upturning of the whole social system in Europe, spread the contagion of their influence across the Atlantic. The efforts of the belligerent powers to draw the United States into the war, and the anxiety of leading politicians here at home to cast on their political adversaries the odium of their foreign associations—Anglo-mania and Gallo-mania—threw into the contest a bitterness and violence little short of actual civil commotion. The excited political campaign in the spring of 1799, was but a prelude to the more violent presidential election that was to take place in the autumn of 1800. The fate of the Republic depended on that election. Had the federalists succeeded, there can be no doubt that a degradation of the States and a concentration of all power in a splendid central empire, would have been the final result. Happily for the cause of human freedom, the election terminated in the triumph of the republican cause.

Thomas Jefferson and Aaron Burr being the candidates of the republicans, got seventy-three votes, John Adams sixty-five votes, Charles Cotesworth Pinckney sixty-four votes, and John Jay one vote. But a difficulty grew out of this result that could not have been anticipated. The Constitution, by an amendment made in consequence of this difficulty, now requires the electors to designate the person they vote for as president, and the person they vote for as vice-president; but at that time there was no means of discrimination; they voted for two persons, and the one getting the highest number of votes was declared to be elected president, and the person getting the next highest number of votes was declared to be elected vice-president. Mr. Jefferson and Mr. Burr had an equal number of votes; neither of them could be declared as being elected president; and the question had to be decided by the House of Representatives voting by States. So soon as this state of things was known, a high degree of uneasiness and alarm was excited in the minds of the republicans, lest the will of the people might be frustrated by intrigue and corruption. Mr. Jefferson charged the federalists with a design of preventing an election altogether. In a letter to Mr. Madison he says: "The federalists appear determined to prevent an election, and to pass a bill giving the government to Mr. Jay, reappointed chief justice, or to Marshall, as secretary of state." This would have been an act of revolution; and some of the more violent and unprincipled may have carried their designs thus far; but there can be no question that the aim of the party was to defeat Mr. Jefferson and to elect Burr. This was carrying their opposition to the will of the people very far. Aaron Burr never was thought of for president; not a single vote was cast for him with that view, and the mere accident of his having the same number of votes with the favorite of the people, brought his name into the House of Representatives; and yet the federalists determined to take advantage of this circumstance, and to elevate him to the presidency, in spite of the popular will. They justified themselves on the ground that the public will could only be expressed to them through the constitutional organs. There were two candidates, they said, for the office of president, who were presented to the House of Representatives with equal suffrages. The Constitution gave them the right, and made it their duty, to elect that one of the two whom they thought preferable. Neither of them was the man of their choice, but the Constitution confined their election to one of the two, and they gave their vote to the one they thought the greater and the better man. That vote they repeated, and in that vote they declared their determination to persist, had they not been driven from it by imperious necessity. The prospect ceased ·of the vote being effectual, and the alternative only remained of taking one man for president, or having no president at all. They chose, as they thought, the lesser evil. The republicans, on the other hand, condemned their course as factious and revolutionary; and, had they succeeded in electing Burr to the presidency, in all probability he would have been driven from his seat at the point of the bayonet. From all quarters the sound came up, "We will obey no other president but Mr. Jefferson." There are many interesting facts and important lessons connected with this election that come within the province of the general historian, but which we must pass over as inappropriate to this Biography. The part that John Randolph took in these affairs was that of a silent voter and watchful observer. He dispatched daily bulletins to his father-in-law, giving the result of each balloting as it took place. After the nineteenth ballot he writes: "No election will, in my opinion, take place." But on the 17th of February he writes: "On the thirty-sixth ballot there appeared, this day, ten States for Thomas Jefferson; four (New England) for A. Burr, and two blank ballots (Delaware and South Carolina). This was the second time that we balloted to-day. The four Burrites of Maryland put blanks into the box of that State; the vote was, therefore, unanimous. Mr. Morris, of Vermont, left his seat, and the result was, therefore, Jeffersonian. I need not add that Mr. J. was declared duly elected."

Mr. Randolph attributed this result to the patriotism of Alexander Hamilton. That gentleman was the influential and popular leader of the federal party, and when he saw the extremity to which things were likely to be driven by a longer persistence in their course, he advised his friends, rather than to produce a revolution in the government, or excite popular commotion, to give way and suffer Mr. Jefferson to be elected. Mr. Randolph often expressed the opinion, in after life, that we owed the safety of the Republic to Hamilton, and that his course on that trying occasion had elevated him very much in his estimation.

The federalists perpetrated another act during the session that excited a great deal of indignation. They so altered and enlarged the judiciary system as to require the appointment of a great many new judges. It was urged as an objection to the bill, that it was made by a party at the moment when they were sensible that their power was expiring and passing into other hands. They replied it was enough for them that the full and legitimate power existed. The remnant left them (the bill passed 15th February, 1801) was plenary and efficient—and it was their duty to employ it according to their judgments and consciences for the good of the country. They thought the bill a salutary measure, and there was no obligation upon them to leave it as a work for their successors. They had no hesitation in avowing that they had no confidence in the persons who were to follow them, and were, therefore, the more anxious to accomplish a work which they believed would contribute to the safety and stability of the government. It was further urged as an objection to the bill, that it was merely designed to create sinecures and retreats for broken-down political hacks—and to erect battlements and fortresses in which the discomfited leaders of federalism might rally their scattered forces for another contest. Mr. Jefferson said of this measure, "I dread this above all the measures meditated, because appointments in the nature of freehold render it difficult to undo what is done." Yet the next Congress did not hesitate to undo what was done. The first regular speech made by Mr. Randolph was on the proposition to repeal this law. It was in answer to Mr. Bayard, the leader and the ablest champion on the opposite side. This speech was published, many years ago, in a collection intended to be specimens of American eloquence; and notwithstanding he was so young a man, it will bear a comparison, in point of style and argument, with the very best that were delivered at that day. In justifying a repeal of the law, and thereby displacing judges, who by the Constitution hold their appointments during good behavior, Mr. Randolph argued—"I agree that the Constitution is a limited grant of power, and that none of its general phrases are to be construed into an extension of that grant. I am free to declare, that if the extent of this bill is to get rid of the judges, it is a perversion of your power to a base purpose; it is an unconstitutional act. If, on the contrary, it aims not at the displacing one set of men from whom you differ in political opinion, with a view to introduce others, but for the general good, by abolishing useless offices, it is a constitutional act. The *quo animo* determines the nature of this act, as it determines the innocence or guilt of other acts. But we are told that this is to declare the judiciary, which the Constitution has attempted to fortify against the other branches of government, dependent on the will of the legislature, whose discretion alone is to limit their encroachments. Whilst I contend that the legislature possesses this discretion, I am sensible of the delicacy with which it is to be used. It is like the power of impeachment, or the declaring of war, to be exercised under a high responsibility. But the power is denied—for, say they, its exercise will enable flagitious men to overturn the judiciary, in order to put their creatures into office, and to wreak their vengeance on those who have become obnoxious by their merit; and yet the gentleman expressly says, that arguments drawn from a supposition of extreme political depravity prove nothing; that every government presupposes a certain degree of honesty in its rulers, and that to argue from extreme cases is totally inadmissible. Nevertheless, the whole of his argument is founded on the supposition of a total want of principle in the legislature and executive."

While speaking on the subject of the judiciary in the Virginia Convention, nearly thirty years after this transaction, Mr. Randolph thus alludes to it: "At the very commencement of my public life, or nearly so, I was called to give a decision on the construction of that clause in the Federal Constitution which relates to the tenure of the judicial office; and I am happy to find that, after the lapse of thirty years, I remain precisely of the same opinion that I then held."

If a law should be passed *bona fide*, for the abolition of a court which was a nuisance, and ought to be abolished, he considered such a law as no infringement of judicial independence; but, if the law was enacted *mala fide*, and abolished a useful court, for the purpose of getting rid of the judge who presided in it, such a law was undoubtedly a violation of that independence; just as the killing of a man might be murder or not, according to the intention, the *quo animo* with which it was done. He said that it could not be necessary to recount to the gentleman who occupied the chair (Mr. Barbour) the history of the decision which was given in Congress, as to the true intent and meaning of this part of the Federal Constitution. Parties had never run higher than at the close of the administration of the elder Adams, and the commencement of that of Mr. Jefferson. After efforts the most unparalleled, Mr. Adams was ejected from power, and the downfall of the party attached to him was near at hand. After this decision by the American people, when they were compelled to perceive that the kingdom was passing from them, in the last agonies and throes of dissolution, they cast about them to make some provision for the broken-down hacks of the party; and at midnight, and after midnight, on the last day of Mr. Adams's administration, a batch of judges was created, and bequeathed as a legacy to those who followed.

The succeeding party on coming into power, found that they must consult the construction of the Constitution, to prevent the recurrence of such a practice; because, if the construction should be allowed under which this had been done, it would enable every political party, having three months notice of their departure from the helm of affairs, to provide for themselves and their adherents, by getting up a judiciary system, which would be irrevocable; a city of refuge where they would be safe from all approach of danger. To avoid such a result it became necessary to abolish the system, which was then believed to be injurious, and which experience has proved to be unnecessary. Mr. Randolph said, that he was one of those who voted for the decision which declared that the court might be abolished *bona fide*, and that the office of the judge should cease with it.

Shortly after these midnight appointments, Mr. Adams left the city, under the cover of darkness, that he might not witness, the next day, the inauguration of his successful rival. Many of his friends were deeply mortified at this undignified and unmanly retreat.

On reaching an inn beyond Baltimore, 'tis said (we speak on the authority of Mr. Randolph) that Mr. Adams, walking up to a portrait of Washington, and placing his finger on his lips, exclaimed, " If I had kept my lips as close as that man, I should now be the President of the United States."

It is very true, Mr. Adams had no judgment, no discretion. He possessed a brilliant imagination, a bold and an ardent temper, that made him the impassioned and powerful orator of the Revolution; but he could lay claim to few of those faculties that fit a man to conduct wisely and prudently the affairs of a great republic.

CHAPTER XXVII.

THE SEVENTH AND EIGHTH CONGRESSES.—CHAIRMAN OF THE COMMITTEE OF WAYS AND MEANS. — THE WORKING PERIOD.—THE YAZOO BUSINESS.

AT the opening of the first Congress under the new administration, in December, 1801, Mr. Randolph had the satisfaction of seeing his friend, Nathaniel Macon, elected Speaker of the House of Representatives. Mr. Randolph was placed at the head of the Committee of

Ways and Means. Some notion may be formed of the duties of this committee from the resolution calling for its appointment.

" *Resolved*, That a Standing Committee of Ways and Means be appointed, whose duty it shall be to take into consideration all such reports of the Treasury Department, and all such propositions relative to the revenue, as may be referred to them by the House; to inquire into the state of the public debt, of the revenue, and of the expenditures; and to report, from time to time, their opinion thereon."

The duties of this committee, as we may perceive, embraced a wide field of inquiry. The new administration had pledged itself to the people to place the " ship of state on its republican tack," and to furnish a model of a simple and economical government. All unnecessary offices and useless expenditures were to be abolished, the army and navy reduced, and the national debt was to be redeemed. All the necessary inquiries, investigations, reports, and bills, touching these important subjects, had to emanate from the Committee of Ways and Means. The chairman of that committee had to be brought in daily official communication with the executive departments; his relation towards them was of a most confidential character; and he was regarded as the leader of the friends of the administration in the representative department.

Mr. Randolph and the President were intimate friends; they were on terms of unreserved intercourse—personally and politically they cordially agreed, and heartily co-operated in accomplishing the great ends of the administration. In accordance with the recommendation of the President, Mr. Randolph introduced a proposition, " that a committee be appointed to inquire whether any, and what alterations can be made in the judiciary department of the United States, and to provide for securing the impartial selection of juries in the courts of the United States;" and also another resolution, to inquire what reductions could be made in the civil government of the United States. They were referred to a select committee, of which he was chairman. On the 4th of February, he reported a bill to repeal the laws of the last session with respect to the judiciary, and after undergoing considerable discussion in committee of the whole, it was finally passed by the House on the 3d March, 1802, by a large majority. Mr. Randolph's speech on this subject we have already alluded to in the preceding chapter. On the 20th January he introduced a resolution, directing the Secretary of the Treasury to lay before the House a list of the exports to the Mediterranean, distinguishing those of the growth of the United States. He also took part in the debate on the apportionment under the census of 1800. Mr. Randolph took a lively interest in this subject, and long foresaw the effect each succeeding census would have on the political power of his native State. He introduced on the 9th of June, a resolution to reduce the military establishment. Having been appointed chairman of the select committee to see what could be done to expedite the public printing, he reported a resolution to appoint a public printer; and to his exertions may be justly attributed an economical improvement in the printing of the House.

But one of the most important subjects to which Mr. Randolph turned his attention was the public debt. On the 9th of April, 1802, he reported a bill making provision for the redemption of the public debt of the United States. It provided that so much of the duties on merchandise and tonnage, &c., as will amount to an annual sum of seven millions three hundred thousand dollars, be yearly appropriated as a sinking fund; and said sums were declared to be vested in Commissioners of the Sinking Fund, to be applied by them to the payment of interest and charges, and to the redemption of the principal of the public debt. After this appropriation he kept a watchful eye on its faithful disbursement. The subject was frequently before the Committee of Ways and Means, and the conduct and management of the commissioners minutely criticised.

The chief subject that attracted the attention of Congress during the next session, which began in December, 1802, was the navigation of the Mississippi and the cession of Louisiana to France. In the preceding October, the Governor of New Orleans, Don Morales, had issued a proclamation, excluding that port as a dépôt for our commerce, a privilege we had a right to enjoy under our treaty with Spain. This conduct on the part of the Spanish authorities had created great excitement in the western country. In addition to this, it was rumored abroad that Louisiana had been transferred to the dominion of the all-powerful and all-grasping French Republic, now under the sway of the ambitious Bonaparte. These important facts, together with the private information he had obtained on the subject, were deemed by the President as being worthy of a secret and confidential communication to Congress, which was made the 22d of December. Additional information was communicated on the 31st, and on the 5th of January Mr. Griswold moved that the President be requested to lay before the House copies of such official documents as have been received by the Government, announcing the cession of Louisiana to France, together with a report explaining the stipulations, circumstances, and conditions, under which that province is to be delivered up. Those private messages, which called forth this resolution, had, on motion of Mr. Randolph, been referred to a committee, and had been under consideration in the House with closed doors. He now moved to refer Mr. Griswold's resolution to a Committee of the Whole on the state of the Union. The motion, after some discussion, was carried, and the House went into committee. Mr. Randolph observed that he had in his hand certain resolutions connected with the message, relative to the late proceedings at New Orleans, the discussion of which had been ordered to be conducted with closed doors. He asked the decision of the question, whether, previously to offering his resolutions, the doors ought not to be closed. Much opposition was made to this motion. Mr. Griswold's resolution, it was said, was one for information, and ought to be discussed with open doors. Mr. Randolph observed, that he had already more than once stated his objections to discuss this subject in public. He had observations, which, he had said, must be made in secret. " The gentleman from Connecticut says he is willing the resolution should be fully discussed, and therefore concludes that it must not be referred to a select committee, as he is pleased to term it, where alone, as we contend, and have informed him, the discussion can take place. Sir, this may be logic, but it is new to me. A message from the President relative to New Orleans has been referred to a certain committee, and we propose to refer the resolution to the same committee. Gentlemen exclaim that this is denying them information. Does it follow of necessity that we deny the information because we choose to consider the subject with closed doors ? Cannot the resolution be as fully discussed in private as in public ? Do all the reasoning faculties of the House cease to exist the moment the doors are closed ? Cannot the eloquence of the gentleman be exerted unless when addressed to the ladies who do us the honor of attending in this hall ?" Mr. Randolph's motion prevailed. The House

was cleared, and he offered, with closed doors, the following resolu
tion, to which he had alluded in debate; "Resolved—That this House
receive, with great sensibility, the information of a disposition in certain officers of the Spanish Government at New Orleans to obstruct
the navigation of the river Mississippi, as secured to the United States
by the most solemn stipulations. That, adhering to the humane and
wise policy which ought ever to characterize a free people, and by
which the United States have always professed to be governed, willing, at the same time, to ascribe this breach of compact to the unauthorized misconduct of certain individuals, rather than to a want of
good faith on the part of his Catholic Majesty, and relying with perfect confidence on the vigilance and wisdom of the Executive, they
will wait the issue of such measures as that department of the Government shall have pursued for asserting the rights and vindicating the
injuries of the United States; holding it to be their duty, at the same
time, to express their unalterable determination to maintain the boundaries and the rights of navigation and commerce through the river
Mississippi, as established by existing treaties."

One of the measures of the Executive to which Mr. Randolph
alludes, was a pending negotiation for the purchase of Louisiana.
Mr. Livingston, our minister at Paris, had received ample instructions on this subject, and, about this time, Mr. Monroe had been
dispatched as envoy extraordinary, to aid him in the negotiation.
The proposition happened to have been made at a most fortunate
juncture of affairs, when Bonaparte was preparing for a war with
England. He wished to keep on good terms with the United States—
feared that the British navy might wrest his newly acquired province
from him during the coming war, and was much in need of money.
These considerations induced him to listen favorably to the proposition of the United States to purchase Louisiana for a large sum of
money.

Mr. Livingston conducted the business with great ability, and
when Mr. Monroe arrived, he had but little more to do than sign the
articles of the treaty. Bonaparte, in a very short time, repented of
this measure. He saw the great blunder he had committed in parting with a country so large, so rich, and so important, in a political
and commercial point of view; and would have availed himself of
any pretext to break the treaty, and take back the province. The

President was apprised of all these facts, and warned by our min-isters, that if there should be the slightest delay in the ratification, and in the provisions to be made by Congress to pay the instal-ments of the purchase, we should lose it altogether. The treaty was signed at Paris, the 30th of April, 1803. So soon as it reached the United States, the President, by proclamation, called Congress on the first Monday in October, to take measures to carry it into effect.

In all his efforts to bring this business to a successful issue, the President received the hearty co-operation of the leader of the House of Representatives. Mr. Randolph's quick and comprehensive mind saw, at a glance, the importance of the crisis, and, is chairman of the Committee of Ways and Means, his aid was most prompt and efficient in getting over the difficulty. By the 10th of November, a bill had been passed, and approved by the President, creating certificates of stock in favor of the French Republic, for the sum of eleven mil-lions two hundred and fifty thousand dollars, bearing an interest of six per centum per annum, from the time when possession of Louisiana shall have been obtained, in conformity with the treaty of the thir-tieth day of April, one thousand eight hundred and three, between the United States of America and the French Republic. Possession was given the 20th of December following; and all the measures adopted by Congress in regard to the newly acquired territory, were either matured by the Committee of Ways and Means, of which Mr. Randolph was chairman, or by some select committee, appointed at his instance. Few men did more than he to secure the purchase of Louisiana, when once made, and then to provide for it a good and efficient government. Next to the Declaration of Independence, and the adoption of the present Constitution, the acquisition of Louisiana has had more influence than any other thing on the destiny of the United States.

Mr. Jefferson was a strict constructionist, and held that no pow-ers should be exercised but those specifically granted. The Consti-tution contemplates no territory beyond that in possession of the Con-federacy or of the States at the time of its adoption. The purchase of foreign territory was a thing not dreamed of by its framers, nor is there any clause authorizing such a measure. Mr. Jefferson was fully aware of this; but he considered that there was such an imperi-

ous necessity in this case, requiring such immediate action—now or
never—that he would be justified in making the acquisition, and procuring a sanction of it afterwards, by an amendment of the Constitution. "The Constitution has made no provision for our holding
foreign territory," says he, "still less for incorporating foreign nations
into our Union. The Executive, in seizing the fugitive occurrence,
which so much advances the good of their country, have done an act beyond the Constitution. The legislature, in casting behind them metaphysical subtleties, and risking themselves like faithful servants, must
ratify and pay for it, and throw themselves on their country, for doing for them, unauthorized, what we know they would have done for
themselves, had they been in a situation to do it. But we shall not
be disavowed by the nation, and their act of indemnity will confirm and not weaken the Constitution, by more strongly marking out
its lines."

But unfortunately this act of indemnity was never performed—
the amendment of the Constitution was never made. What was an
exception, justified only by necessity, has now become a precedent;
and nearly all the difficulties that threaten a dissolution of the
Union, growing out of the slavery question, and the acquisition of
new territory, have been occasioned by that fatal omission. Had the
Constitution been amended, as contemplated, by first sanctioning
that which had been admitted as a violation of it, and then by
defining minutely the powers to be exercised in future by Congress,
the present embarrassments of the country could never have happened. We see also in this transaction the insufficiency of a paper
constitution to resist the current of the popular will—unless there be
power to restrain power, nothing else can withstand it—the plea of
necessity has been urged by Congress for nearly every unconstitutional
act they have perpetrated.

The next subject of importance to which Mr. Randolph's attention was turned, was the impeachment and trial of Judge Chase.
On Thursday the 5th of January, 1804, he moved that a committee
be appointed to inquire into the official conduct of Samuel Chase,
one of the associate justices of the Supreme Court of the United
States, and report their opinion whether the said Samuel Chase had
so acted in his judicial capacity as to require the interposition of the
constitutional power of the House. The committee reported seven

articles of impeachment drafted by their chairman, and detailing charges of misconduct on the part of the judge in the trial of John Fries, for high treason, in levying war against the United States during the Whisky Insurrection in Pennsylvania; and also in the trial of Thomas Cooper and James Callender, for sedition or libel against the President.

This trial was a very important one, as Judge Chase had been one of those high-handed federalists, who not only approved the Alien and Sedition Laws, but had transcended all bounds in his eagerness to enforce them.

For want of time the subject was postponed to the next session. On the 30th November, 1804, the articles of impeachment were again reported, and Mr. Randolph was appointed chief manager to conduct the trial before the Senate. The proceedings were very tedious—many witnesses were examined—and many arguments during the progress of the examination were delivered on both sides. Mr. Randolph conducted the cause on the part of the prosecution with the skill of a practised attorney. He opened the case on the part of the House, the 14th February, 1805, in a speech of one hour and a half. Though it is out of the line of his usual forensic efforts, it will well repay a perusal. As two-thirds of the senators present were required to concur in sustaining an impeachment, and as only a majority concurred in sustaining some of the articles, Judge Chase was acquitted.

There was scarcely any subject of importance before Congress at this period that did not attract the personal attention of Mr. Randolph. Not content with the laborious duties of the Finance Committee, furnishing work enough for any ordinary mind, we find him on innumerable select committees, embracing the widest range of investigation on all subjects of legislation. Nothing escaped his vigilant eye—nothing too laborious for him to undertake. These four years, from the opening of Mr. Jefferson's administration to the 4th of March, 1805, the close of the eighth Congress, were indeed his working days. He was abstemious in his habits, unceasing in his labors, unremitting in his attention to public duties.

No man had ever risen so rapidly, or attained a higher degree of eminence and influence; his career was brilliant and successful. The President in the executive department, and he as the leader of the legislative, had done all that was expected of them in the great work of reforming the government, and bringing it back to its original simplicity. Many years afterwards he recurred to this period with just pride. " Sir, (said he in a speech on retrenchment, in 1828,) I have never seen but one administration, which seriously, and in good faith, was disposed to give up its patronage, and was willing to go farther than Congress, or even the people themselves, so far as Congress represents their feelings, desired—and that was the first administration of Thomas Jefferson. He, sir, was the only man I ever knew or heard of, who really, truly, and honestly, not only said " *nolo episcopari*," but actually refused the mitre. It was a part of my duty, and one of the most pleasant parts of public duty that I ever performed, under his recommendation—not because he recommended it, thank God !—to move, in this House, to relieve the public at once from the whole burden of that system of internal taxation, the practical effect of which was, whatever might have been its object, to produce patronage rather than revenue. He, too, had really at heart, and showed it by his conduct, the reduction of the national debt ; and that in the only mode by which it can ever be reduced, by lessening the expenses of the Government till they are below its receipts."——" Never was there an administration," says he, " more brilliant than that of Mr. Jefferson, up to this period. We were indeed in the full tide of successful experiment ! Taxes repealed ; the public debt amply provided for, both principal and interest ; sinecures abolished ; Louisiana acquired ; public confidence unbounded."

None deserved more than himself a large portion of that unbounded public confidence, which attached to the administration— and he was, indeed, looked to from all quarters as the fearless champion of truth and justice. But no man ever drank of the cup of life unmingled with bitter waters. The mean and the envious had grown jealous of his greatness, and were seeking by low and cunning arts to destroy his influence, and to withdraw from him the confidence of the people. It was a trait of his character never to abandon principle for policy ; never to relinquish a favorite measure how-ever hopeless of success ; never to quit his books and his study for idle conversation ; never to permit a vulgar familiarity for the sake of gaining popularity with those who were to vote on his measures.

Hence, they began to speak of him as a person possessing proud and haughty manners ; and as a leader, having failed to harmonize the republican members of Congress. " Great God !" exclaims Thompson, " to think that measures of the highest import to our country are opposed, because their advocate does not make a bow in the right way ! This is the fact : I have taken the liberty of asking, what your manner has to do with your public character—whether there are laws penal against study, reading, and devotion to the welfare of your country." But the cause of offence lay not in his reserved and retiring deportment—his proud and haughty manners—it was found in that keen sense of injustice and wrong that made him detect baseness and corruption in their most secret hiding-places, and in that manly independent spirit that made him fearless in dragging out the perpetrators into the light of day, and drawing on them the scorn and indignation of the world. Mr. Randolph was one that never could tolerate corruption in public men. There were many of that class—or many that he suspected to be of that class—connected with the administration. He was unsparing in his denunciations of them. This was the cause of the growing discontent, and the desire to throw him off as a leader.

His patriotic endeavors to overturn that colossus of turpitude, the Yazoo speculation, was the cause of the hostility which soon manifested itself against him in the ranks of the administration. Unfortunately, too many were interested in upholding this gigantic robbery. The reader has already been made acquainted with its character; by a reference to chapter thirteen of this volume, he will see something of its history. Randolph was in Georgia at the time of the perpetration of this villany, and participated in the shame and mortification of his friends at seeing persons, reputed religious and respectable, effecting a public robbery, by bribing the legislators of the State, and reducing them to the horrors of treachery and perjury. A more detestable, impudent, and dangerous villany is not to be found on record. Notwithstanding the notoriety of these transactions in the State of Georgia—the law was not only pronounced unconstitutional, fraudulent and void, was not only repealed, but it was burnt by the common hangman, and the record of it expunged from the statute book—notwithstanding these facts, known to all men, a company of individuals in other States purchased up

this fraudulent title and presented their petition to Congress, asking
remuneration for the land, which in the mean time had been transferred by Georgia to the United States.

In the "Articles of Agreement and Cession" between Georgia
and the United States, is a proviso that the United States may dis
pose of, or appropriate a portion of the said lands, not exceeding
five millions of acres, or the proceeds of the five millions of acres, or
any part thereof, for the purpose of satisfying, quieting, or compensating for any claims, other than those recognized in the articles of
agreement, which may be made to the said lands. It was under this
provision, that the New England and Mississippi Land Company,
who in the mean time had purchased the spurious title of the original grantees of a corrupt legislature, petitioned Congress to satisfy
their claim by a fair purchase or commutation. In the session of
1802-3, this subject was first brought to the attention of the legislature. Mr. Madison and Mr. Gallatin, members of the President's
cabinet, and Mr. Levi Lincoln, were appointed commissioners to
investigate this subject. They made an elaborate report, and concluded with a proposition, that so much of the five millions of acres
as shall remain after having satisfied the claims of settlers and
others, not recognized by the agreement with Georgia, which shall
be confirmed by the United States, be appropriated for the purpose
of satisfying and quieting the claims of the persons who derive their
titles from an Act of the State of Georgia, passed on the 7th day of
January, 1795. Thus we see that the leading members of the administration were pledged to the justice of this claim, and the propriety of some compensation on the part of the United States.

Gideon Granger, the Postmaster General, was at the head of
the New England and Mississippi Land Company, and was its agent
to prosecute the claim before Congress. He wrote an extended and
elaborate argument to prove that the Company were innocent purchasers without notice; and indeed he undertook to cast censure on
the people of Georgia for repudiating and repealing the act of a
bribed legislature, and to charge that State and the United States
with injustice in appropriating to themselves lands which had
been legally sold by the State and purchased by his Company. Not
only, therefore, was the cabinet of the President committed as to
the justice of this claim; but one of its most active and influential
members was deeply interested personally in its success.

Mr. Randolph opposed it, however, from the beginning: he knew its origin, its history; and no consideration of prudence or policy could induce him for a moment to tolerate the monstrous iniquity.

On the 25th of January, 1805, a resolution was introduced into the House, that three commisssioners be appointed to receive propositions of compromise and settlement from the several companies or persons holding claims to lands within the present limits of the Mississippi Territory, in such manner as in their opinion shall conduce to the interests of the United States, provided such settlement shall not exceed the limit prescribed by the convention with the State of Georgia. This resolution was introduced by a few remarks from Mr. Dana, chairman of the Committee of Claims.

Mr. Randolph then rose:—"Perhaps," said he, "it may be supposed from the course which this business has taken, that the adversaries of the present measure indulge the expectation of being able to come forward at a future day—not to this House, for that hope was desperate, but to the public—with a more matured opposition than it is in their power now to make. But past experience has shown to them that this is one of those subjects which pollution has sanctified, that the hallowed mysteries of corruption are not to be profaned by the eye of public curiosity. No, sir, the orgies of Yazoo speculation are not to be laid open to the public gaze. None but the initiated are permitted to behold the monstrous sacrifice of the best interest of the nation on the altar of corruption. When this abomination is to be practised, we go into conclave. Do we apply to the press, that potent engine, the dread of tyrants and of villains, but the shield of freedom and of worth? No, sir, the press is gagged. On this subject we have a virtual sedition law; not with a specious title, but irresistible in its operations, which goes directly to its object. This demon of speculation has wrested from the nation at one sweep, their best, their only defence, and has closed the avenue of information. But a day of retribution may yet come. If their rights are to be bartered away, and their property squandered, the people must not, they shall not be kept in ignorance by whom it is done. We have often heard of party spirit, of caucuses, as they are termed, to settle legislative questions, but never have I seen that spirit so visible as at present. The out-door intrigue is too palpable to be disguised. When it was proposed to abolish the judiciary system, reared in the last moments of an expiring administration, the detested offspring of a midnight hour; when the question of repeal was before the House; it could not be taken until midnight in the third or fourth week of the discussion. When the great and good man who now fills, and who (whatever may be the wishes of our opponents) I hope and trust will long fill the executive chair, not less to his own honor than to the happiness of his fellow-citizens—when he recommended the repeal of the internal taxes, delay succeeded delay, till patience itself was worn threadbare. But now, when public plunder is the order of the day, how are we treated? Driven into a committee of the whole, and out again in a breath by an inflexible majority, exulting in their strength, a decision must be had immediately. The advocates for the proposed measure feel that it will not bear scrutiny. Hence this precipitancy. They wince from the touch of examination, and are willing to hurry through a painful and disgraceful discussion. As if animated by one spirit, they perform all their evolutions with the most exact discipline, and march in firm phalanx directly up to their object. Is it that men combined together to effect some evil purpose, acting on previous pledge to each other, are even more in unison than those who, seeking only to discover truth, obey the impulse of that conscience which God has placed in their bosom? Such men will not stand compromited. They will not stifle the suggestions of their own minds, and sacrifice their private opinions to the attainment of some nefarious object.

" The memorialists plead ignorance of that fraud by which the act from which their present title was derived, was passed. As it has been a pretext for exciting the compassion of the legislature, I wish to examine the ground upon which this allegation rests. When the act of stupendous villany was passed, in 1795, attempting under the form and semblance of law to rob unborn millions of their birthright and inheritance, and to convey to a band of unprincipled and flagitious men, a territory more extensive, more fertile than any State in the Union, it caused a sensation scarcely less violent than that caused by the passage of the Stamp Act, or the shutting up of the port of Boston: with this difference, that when the Port Bill of Boston passed, her Southern brethren did not take advantage of the forms of law, by which a corrupt legislature attempted to defraud her of the bounties of nature; they did not speculate on the wrongs of their insulted countrymen. * * * * * Sanction this claim, derived from the act of 1795, and what, in effect, do you declare? You record a solemn acknowledgment that Congress has unfairly and dishonestly obtained from Georgia a grant of land to which that State had no title, having previously sold it to others for a valuable consideration, of which transaction Congress was at the time fully apprised. The agents of this Mississippi Land Company set out with an attempt to prove that they are entitled to the whole fifty millions of acres of laid, under the act of 1795; and thus they make their plea to be admitted to a proportional share of five. If they really believed what they say, would they be willing to commute a good legal or equitable claim for one-tenth of its value! * * * * We are told that we stand pledged, and that an appropriation for British grants, not granted by Spain especially, was made for the especial benefit of a particular class of claimants, branded too by the deepest odium, who dare talk to us of the public faith, and appeal to the national honor! * * * * The right of the State of Georgia to sell is denied by your own statute book. So far from being able to transfer to others the right to extinguish the Indian title to land, she has not been able to exercise it for her own benefit. It is only through the agency of the United States that she can obtain the extinguishment of the Indian title to the sale of land within her limits; much less could she delegate it to a few Yazoo men. * * * * * The present case presents a monstrous anomaly, to which the ordinary and narrow maxims of municipal jurisprudence cannot be applied. It is from great first principles, to which the patriots of Georgia so gloriously appealed, that we must look for aid in such extremity. Extreme cases, like this, call for extreme remedies. They bid defiance to palliatives, and it is only by the knife, or the actual cautery, that you can expect relief. There is no cure short of extirpation. Attorneys and judges do not decide the fate of empires. * * * * * The Government of the United States, on a former occasion, did not, indeed, act in this firm and decided manner. But those were hard, unconstitutional times, that never ought to be drawn into precedent. The first year I had the honor of a seat in this House, an act was passed somewhat of a similar nature to the one now proposed. I allude to the case of the Connecticut Reserve, by which the nation was swindled out of three or four millions of acres, which, like other bad titles, had fallen into

the hands of innocent purchasers. When I advert to the applicants
by whom we were then beset, I find among them one of the persons
who styled themselves the Agents of the New England Mississippi
Land Company, who seems to have an unfortunate knack of buying
bad titles. His gigantic grasp embraces with one hand the shores of
Lake Erie, and with the other stretches to the Bay of Mobile. Millions of acres are easily digested by such stomachs. Goaded by avarice, they buy only to sell, and sell only to buy. The retail trade of
fraud and imposture yields too small and slow a profit to gratify their
cupidity. They buy and sell corruption in the gross, and a few millions of acres, more or less, is hardly felt in the account. The
deeper the play, the greater their zest in the game; and the stake
which is set upon the throw is nothing less than the patrimony of the
people. Mr. Speaker, when I see the agency which is employed on
this occasion, I must own that it fills me with apprehension and
alarm. The same agent is at the head of an executive department of
our Government, and inferior to none in the influence attached to it.
* * * * This officer presents himself at your bar, at once a party and
an advocate. Sir, when I see such a tremendous influence brought
to bear upon us, I do confess it strikes me with consternation and
despair. Are the heads of executive departments, with the influence and patronage attached to them, to extort from us now, what we
refused at the last session of Congress? * * * * * I will pin myself upon this text, and preach upon it as long as I have life. If no
other reason could be adduced, but for a regard for our own fame—if
it were only to rescue ourselves from this foul imputation—this weak
and dishonorable compromise ought to receive a prompt and decisive
rejection. Is the voice of patriotism lulled to rest, that we no longer
hear the cry against an overbearing majority, determined to put
down the Constitution, and deaf to every proposition of compromise?
Such were the dire forebodings to which we have been compelled
heretofore to listen. But if the enmity of such men be formidable,
their friendship is deadly destruction, their touch deadly pollution!
What is the spirit against which we now struggle—which we have
vainly endeavored to stifle? A monster generated by fraud, nursed
in corruption, that in grim silence awaits its prey. It is the spirit
of Federalism."

*   *   *   *   *   *   *

It may readily be conceived what effect this and similar speeches which had been delivered, whenever the subject was presented, would have on the members of the republican party who were interested, for themselves or their friends, in the Yazoo speculation. An intrigue was set on foot to supplant Mr. Randolph. It was determined that he should be put down. The Postmaster General openly declared that he or Randolph—one must fall. This expression was understood as intimating an intention to call him out. Some one observed that Randolph would not be backward in answering to a call of that kind. He replied, not in that way—"*I mean, as a public man—as a political character.*" After the adjournment of Congress, March, 1805, he made a tour of the New England States, for the purpose of organizing a party to *pull down* Randolph. Some of the republican members from that quarter gave countenance to the plan, and Mr. Barnabas Bidwell was put forward as their file-leader. These men insinuated themselves into favor, and assumed to be the exclusive friends of the President; but they were charged, many of them, with being in league with Burr, and having no other design but to embarrass the Executive, and to force the President into a sanction of their views. "If some members of Congress," says a leading journal of that day, "are to be *bribed with post-office contracts* to obtain their votes for a nefarious speculation, on one hand; and if a member of Congress, superior to all corruption, and all pollution or dishonor, is to be *pulled down;* and the offices of Government are to be employed to such ends; it is vain to pretend that republican government can stand, if such corruption and such corrupt men are suffered to retain all the power, which they prostitute; and if men of virtue, honor. talents and integrity, are to be made victims of intrigue, bottomed on such corruption."

CHAPTER XXVIII.

FRIENDSHIP.

WE have seen what an immense task, and what a weight of responsibility, devolved on Mr. Randolph for the last four years. He found time, nevertheless, to keep up an extensive correspondence with his friends. He had now added to the list his two half-brothers and their sister, who were just growing up. His sentiments in regard to the conduct of a family towards those " worthy lads," who just begin to feel the pride and self-importance of budding manhood, are so true and so worthy of imitation, that we give them to the reader.— " Give to dear Beverly," says he, " my warmest love. Let me, my dear sister, caution you (and be not offended at it) respecting that worthy lad. Treat him with a marked attention. I know you love him tenderly—he is deserving of it. Display that affection by a manner the most *considerate* and *kind*. Cherish him; for he is a jewel above price. Beverly is now of an age to receive from every body the treatment due to a *man*—a young one, I grant—and to a *gentleman*. No consideration should dispense with this conduct on any part. It does not imply *formality*, but *respect*—not coldness, but kind attention. These, I pronounce, are *essentially requisite*, and in a *greater degree* than usual, to the development of his amiable character."

But poor Thompson continued, by his erratic ways, to keep alive the anxious solicitude of his friend. That brilliant, though wayward genius, had fallen into desperate courses. Calumny, acting on a morbid sensibility, had banished him from that home where alone he could find sympathy and encouragement. Misfortune had so perverted his feelings, as to make him, in the spirit of misanthropy, shun the observation of those that once knew and respected him, and to seek oblivion and forgetfulness in the haunts of low dissipation. Now was the time to test true friendship. The cold world would pass him by with averted look, and protest they never knew him; the friend would take him by the hand, and gently and affectionately draw him back to the paths of virtue. Randolph professed to be his friend—how nobly did he redeem that pledge! In the following letter, he speaks to him in plainness and in truth. But whilst he does not spare his erring friend, his censure is accompanied with such a tone of delicacy and affection, as to melt the most obdurate heart, and kindle emotions of reformation in the most desperate outcast.

" Whatever may be the motives," says he, " which have determined you to renounce all intercourse with me, it becomes me, perhaps, to respect them; yet to be deterred from my present purpose by punctilio would evince a coldness of temper which I trust does not belong to me, and would, at the same time, convict me to myself of the most pitiful insincerity, in professing for you a regard which has never been inferior to my professions, and which is not in any circumstance entirely to destroy. To tell you that during the last three months I have observed your progress through life with uninterrupted and increasing anxiety, would be to give you a faint idea of what has passed in my mind. The mortification which I have experienced on hearing you spoken of in terms of frigid and scanty approbation, can only be exceeded by that which I have felt on the silent embarrassment which my inquiries have occasioned those who were unwilling to wound your character or my feelings. You know me too well, William, to suppose that my inquiries have been directed by the miserable spirit which seeks to exalt itself on the depression of others. They have, on the contrary, been very few, and made with the most guarded circumspection. To say the truth, I have never felt myself equal to the task of hearing the recital of details which were too often within my reach, and which not unfrequently courted my attention. They have always received from me the most decisive repulse. My own pride would never bear the humiliation of permitting any one to witness the mortification which I felt. After all this preamble, let me endeavor to effect the purpose of this address. Let me beg of you to ask yourself what are your present pursuits, and how far congenial to your feelings or character. I have not, I cannot, so far have mistaken you ; you cannot so successfully have deceived yourself. Yours is not the mind which can derive any real or lasting gratification from the pursuits or the attainments of a grovelling ambition. These may afford a temporary and imperfect relief from that voice which tells you who you are, and what is expected from you. The world is well disposed to forgive the aberrations of youthful indiscretion from the straight road of prudence ; but there is a point beyond which its temper can no longer be played upon. After a certain degree of resistance, it becomes more prone to asperity than it had ever been to indulgence. But grant that its good nature were unlimited, you are not the character who can be content to hold by so humiliating a tenure that which you can and ought to demand of right. Can you be content to repose on the courtesy of mankind for that respect which you may challenge as your due, and which may be enforced when withheld? Can you quit the high ground and imposing attitude of self-esteem to solicit the precarious bounty of a contemptuous and contemptible world? I can scarcely forgive myself for dwelling so long on so invidious a theme. I have long meditated to address you on this subject. One of the dissuasives from the plan is now removed. Let me again conjure you to ask yourself seriously, What are your present objects of pursuit? How far any laudable acquirement can be attained by a town residence, particularly in a tavern? Whether such a life be compatible with the maintenance of that respectability of character which is necessary to give us value in the eyes of others or of ourselves? And let me conjure you to dissolve by a single exertion the spell which now enchains you. The only tie which could have bound you is no more. Town fetters are but those of habit, and that of but short standing. Were it confirmed, there would indeed be but little hope, and this letter would never have been penned. As it would be improper to urge the dissolution of your present plan of life without pointing out some alternative, I recommend a residence of twelve or eighteen months with Taylor, and a serious application, before it be too late, to that profession which will be a friend to you when the sunshine insects who have laughed with you in your prosperity shall have passed away with the genial season which gave them birth. The hour is fast approaching, be assured, when it will be in vain to attempt the acquirement of professional knowledge. Too well I know that readiness of apprehension and sprightliness of imagination will not make amends for application. The latter serves but to light up our ignorance.

"There is one topic on which I cannot trust even my pen. Did I not believe that this letter would occasion you pain, it certainly never had been written. Yet to write it with that view would be a purpose truly diabolical. You are a physician; you probe not the wounds of the dead. Yet 'tis to heal, and not to agonize, that you insert your instrument into the living body. Whatever may be the effect of this attempt—whatever may be the disposition which it creates in you, I shall never, while you live, cease to feel an interest in your fate. Every one here remembers you with undiminished affection. If I judge from myself, you are more than ever interesting to them, and whenever, if ever, you revisit Bizarre, you will recognize in every member of the family your unchanged friends.

"Adieu,

"J. R., Jr."

This last and noble effort to redeem a fallen friend was not in vain. The advice was followed. Thompson spent a few months with Creed Taylor, in the neighborhood of Bizarre; he then went to Richmond and read law, in the office of George Hay, Esq., a distinguished lawyer and politician of that day. From this time, with few exceptions, his letters are more cheerful, and replete with sallies of his fine genius; he communicates much instructive and amusing information about the proceedings of the legislature, and the leading characters of Richmond; and never failed to give vent to those deep feelings of gratitude that swelled in his bosom, towards one who had been to him a brother indeed, in his hour of degradation and misfortune.

Having obtained a competent knowledge of his profession, Mr. Randolph procured for him an office in the newly acquired territory of Louisiana—encouraged him to break off from his old associations, and to seek his fortune anew, in a land of strangers. In the spring of 1804, he married a virtuous and accomplished wife, and set out on his journey to the far west, with all those bright prospects that his ardent imagination knew so well how to picture before him. This is the last letter ever addressed to him by his friend:

BIZARRE, 13 May, 1804.

" When I requested you to inquire at the post-office at Abington for a letter from me, it did not occur to me by how circuitous a route my communication must travel before it could reach that place. To guard against accidents, therefore, I have directed it to be forwarded to Nashville, in case you should have left Abington before its arrival there. We have been every day suggesting to ourselves the inconvenience to which you must have been exposed by the bad weather which we have invariably experienced ever since your departure, and regretting that the situation of your affairs would not permit you to continue with us until a change took place. You, however, my good friend, have embarked upon too serious a voyage to take into consideration a little rough weather upon the passage. The wish which I feel to add my mite to the counsels through which alone it can prove prosperous, is repressed by the reflection, that your success depends upon the *discovery* of no *new principle* of human affairs, but upon the *application* of such as are familiar to all, and which none know better how to estimate than yourself. Decision, firmness, independence, which equally scorns to yield our own rights as to detract from those of others, are the only guides to the esteem of the world, or of ourselves. A reliance upon our resources for all things, but especially for relief against that arch fiend the tædium vitæ, can alone guard us against a state of dependence and contempt. But I am growing sententious, and, of course, pedantic. Judy joins me in every good wish to yourself and Mrs. Thompson. Permit me to add that there is one being in the world who will ever be ready to receive you with open arms, whatsoever may be the fate of the laudable endeavors which you are now making.

" Yours, truly,

" JOHN RANDOLPH.

" WM. THOMPSON."

Poor Thompson did not live to test the strength of his redeemed virtue, and to make a new application of those principles that he had learned in the school of adversity so well how to estimate. He died by the way-side, and all the renewed hopes of himself and of his friend, were swallowed up in the oblivious night of death. On the back of the copy of the foregoing letter, which is written in Mr. Randolph's own handwriting, is found the following endorsement: " W. T., May 13, 1804. Alas!" What more could he write as an epitaph on the lonely tomb of this wandering, ill-starred young man? Alas! alas! was all that could be said of the misfortunes and the untimely end of poor William Thompson.

Joseph Bryan, in the meantime, had returned from his travels; the joyous, free-hearted Bryan had ceased "fighting the Russians," recrossed the broad Atlantic main, and from his sea-girt isle was inditing letters to his friend, describing the cities he had seen, the men and their manners—if not with the depth of observation of the wise Ulysses, at least with as much pleasure and freedom of narration. He urged his old companion to visit once more his friends in Georgia: " You are the popular man here," says he, " the federalists to the contrary notwithstanding." But Randolph, ever seeking to make his friends useful to themselves and to their country, turned the thoughts of this volatile young man to a higher aim.

On his solicitation, Bryan became a candidate for Congress; was defeated; renewed the attempt, and was successful. He stood by the side of his gallant friend and fought manfully that Medusa head of fraud, the Yazoo speculation, whenever it reared its horrid front upon the floor of Congress. He had been to Bizarre, and formed an acquaintance with the charming society there, of which he ever afterwards spoke in terms of the highest admiration; he had hunted, fished, flown kites, and played marbles with "the boys;" but above all, his wild fancy had been caught at last, and, like the fly in the spider's web, he was entangled in the inextricable meshes of all-conquering love. Miss Delia Foreman, daughter of General Foreman, of the Eastern Shore of Maryland, intimate friends of Mr. Randolph, was the charming object of attraction. The summer recess of 1804 was spent in Georgia, but the island in the sea, with all its means of pleasure, had lost its charm, and he was about to desert it, and to go in search of the fair nymph whose dwelling looked out on the broad waters of the Chesapeake.

On the 8th of September, 1804, from Bizarre his friend writes to him: "Should this find you at Wilmington, which I heartily wish it may not, I trust, my dear Bryan, that you will derive the most satisfactory information from the inclosed respecting your fair tyrant. To *me* the Major says not a word on the subject of his daughter, but I infer from a variety of circumstances that she is about this time on a visit to her aunt, Mrs. Van Bibber, in Gloucester, about eighty miles from Richmond; I hope, therefore, very soon to see you in Virginia.

"I have nothing worth relating, except that Mrs. Randolph was almost as much disappointed as myself when our messenger arrived last night from the post-office without a letter from you. How easy would it be, once a week, to say 'I am at such a place, in such health, and to-morrow shall go to ————.' These little bulletins of your well-being and motions would be a thousand times more interesting to me than those of his Britannic Majesty's health, or his Corsican Highness's expeditions. Let me beg of you to make dispatch.

"Yours as ever,

"JOHN RANDOLPH."

After the adjournment of Congress, March, 1805, Bryan hastened on to Chestertown to be married. On the 8th of March he writes from th : place: "You will hardly believe me when I tell you, that my tyrants have had the unparalleled barbarity to postpone my marriage until the 25th of this month. Sumptuousness, pomp, parade, &c., must be observed in giving away a jewel worth more than the kingdoms of this world.—I rather suspect I shall be myself the most awkward and ungraceful movable used on the occasion: curse it, I hate to be exhibited; and nothing but the possession of the jewel itself would induce me to run the gauntlet of felicitation I shall receive from the whole file of collaterals.————Lovely as her person is, I prize her heart more. Jack! what have I done to induce the good God to favor me so highly? Sinner that I am, I deserve not the smallest of his gifts, and behold I am treated more kindly than even Abraham, who saw God face to face, and was called his friend; he, poor fellow, had to put up with his sister Sarah, who, beside other exceptionable qualities, was cursed with a bad temper; while I, having sought among the beauties of the earth, have found and obtained the loveliest and best, which I am willing to prove against all comers on foot or on horseback, in the tented field with sword and spear, or on the roaring ocean at the cannon's mouth. If you will come and see us (on their island in the sea), my Delia will make one of her best puddings for your entertainment. In the course of a year or two you may expect to see your friend *Brain* metamorphosed into a gentleman of high polish, able to make as spruce a bow, and to hand a lady to her carriage with all the graces of an Adonis. Adieu! may heaven prosper and bless you."

In the course of a year or two, alas! he *was* metamorphosed; the beautiful Delia also faded away; and their two little boys were left orphans! John Randolph showed his attachment to the father by his devotion to the sons; they were raised partly in his own house, and educated at his expense. The oldest and the namesake, John Randolph Bryan, many years after this period, when he grew up to manhood, married Miss Elizabeth Coulter, the niece of Mr. Randolph; "my charming niece," as he used to call her, and the daughter of his beloved and only sister. Mr. Bryan and his accomplished wife now live in Gloucester county, Virginia, on the Bay Shore. A bountiful soil blesses them with its abundant fruits; and the tide, that daily flows at their feet, wafts to their door the rich treasures of the sea. May they long live to enjoy in their "happy nook" the blessings of a peaceful home; and to dispense that elegant hospitality, so rare now, but, at the time their father first visited Bizarre, so common in the Old Dominion.

The causes of this great change, or at least some of them, we are now about to investigate. John Randolph has said that " The embargo, like Achilles' wrath, was the source of our Iliad of woes!"

———•••———

CHAPTER XXIX.

NINTH CONGRESS.—FOREIGN RELATIONS.—DIFFICULTIES WITH FRANCE AND SPAIN.

NEVER had an administration a more difficult task to perform than *hat of Mr. Jefferson at this time. Ever since the French revolution there had been a constant warfare, with short breathing intervals, between France and England. The hostility of their political principles, added to old national antipathies, now made it a war of extermination. These great belligerent powers strove to involve the United States in the controversy. But our policy was neutrality : General Washington early announced this course, and his firm hand steadily pursued it so long as he grasped the helm of affairs. Mr. Adams was not so successful—his English predilections swerved him from the straight path of neutrality, and involved his administration in a " quasi war" with France. Mr. Jefferson had hitherto been eminently successful in all his domestic and foreign policy. But now, in 1805, he seemed to be involved in almost inextricable difficulties. Our embarrassments with Spain, France, and England, had grown so complicated and critical, that it seemed impossible to escape without war, or national disgrace. The purchase of Louisiana removed a present peril, but brought with it a train of difficulties. Bonaparte made the sale just before his meditated rupture of the treaty of Amiens, and at a time when he feared the province would be wrested from him by the superior maritime power of England. But he soon repented of his bargain, and sought every opportunity to regain his lost empire beyond the Atlantic. Spain, but three years before, had made an exchange of it with France, and had not surrendered possession. She was much displeased at the transfer made by the First Consul, and between them they embarrassed the United States as much as they could, and threw every obstacle in the way of a full and peaceable possession of the new territory. England still retained much of her old grudge towards the United States as revolted provinces—looked with a jealous eye on their growing commerce, their rising greatness—and sought every opportunity to clip the wing of the aspiring eagle. Entertaining these feelings towards the peaceful and neutral govern ment beyond the Atlantic, these two great powers were involved in a war of life and death between themselves; all Europe was in battalion, every engine of destruction was brought to play; like the Titans of old, they tore up mountains, islands, whole continents, and hurled them at each other; the globe itself seemed as though it might tumble into ruins beneath their giant warfare. What chance had the commerce or the neutral rights of the United States to be respected in such a strife? The President, in his opening message, the 3d of December, 1805, describes in glowing terms the destructive course of the great belligerents towards his own country. Again, on the 6th of December, three days after the opening of Congress, he sent a special message on the subject of Spanish aggressions; they seemed to be first and most urgent. The depredations, he said, which had been committed on the commerce of the United States during a preceding war, by persons under the authority of Spain, had been adjusted by a convention; so also the spoliations committed by Spanish subjects and carried into ports of Spain; it had been likewise agreed that those committed by French subjects and carried into Spanish ports should remain for further discussion. Before this convention was returned to Spain with our ratification, the transfer of Louisiana by France to the United States took place, an event as unexpected as disagreeable to Spain. From that moment she seemed to change her conduct and dispositions towards us; it was first manifested by her protest against the right of France to alienate Louisiana to us, which, however, was soon retracted, and the right confirmed. Her high offence was manifested at the act of Congress establishing a collection district on the Mobile, although by an authentic declaration, immediately made, it was expressly confirmed to our acknowledged limits; and she now refused to ratify the convention signed by her own minister under the eye of his sovereign, unless we would consent to alterations of its terms, which would have affected our claims against her for spoliations by French subjects carried into Spanish ports.

To obtain justice, as well as to restore friendship, the President thought proper to send Mr. Monroe on a special mission to Spain. " After nearly five months of fruitless endeavors," says the message, " to bring them to some definite and satisfactory result, our ministers ended the conferences without having been able to obtain indemnity for spoliations of any description, or any satisfaction as to the boundaries of Louisiana, other than a declaration that we had no right eastward of the Iberville ; and that our line to the west was one, which would have left us but a string of land on that bank of the Mississippi. Our injured citizens were thus left without any prospect of retribution from the wrong-doer, and as to boundary, each party was to take its own course. That which they have chosen to pursue will appear from the documents now communicated. They authorize the inference, that it is their intention to advance on our possessions until they *shall be repressed by an opposing force.*"

The message then speaks of the conduct of France in regard to the misunderstanding between the United States and Spain. " She was prompt and decided in her declarations, that her demands on Spain for French spoliations carried into Spanish ports, were included in the settlement between the United States and France. She took at once the ground, that she had acquired no right from Spain, and had meant to deliver us none, eastward of the Iberville."

In conclusion, the President says: " The present crisis in Europe is favorable for pressing a settlement, and not a moment should be lost in availing ourselves of it. Should it pass unimproved, our situation would become much more difficult. Formal war is not necessary ; it is not probable it will follow ; but the protection of our citizens, *the spirit and honor of our country require, that force should be interposed to a certain degree ;* it will probably contribute to advance the object of peace. But the course to be pursued will require the *command of means,* which it belongs to Congress exclusively, to deny or to yield. To them I communicate every fact material for their information, and the documents necessary to enable them to judge for themselves. To their wisdom, then, I look for the course I am to pursue, and will pursue with sincere zeal that which they shall approve."

The President recommends no definite plan of action—leaves every thing to the discretion of Congress; but it is obvious that he expected them to appropriate means to raise an army of some sort, to repel the invasions of Spain, and to protect the persons and the property of our citizens in the disputed territory.

This message was secret and confidential: all propositions in regard to it were discussed in conclave. The debate is said to have taken a very wide range, and was very animated. On that occasion, John Randolph is said to have delivered the ablest and most eloquent speech ever heard on the floor of Congress. When this message was read in the House of Representatives, it was referred to a select committee, of which Mr. Randolph was chairman. He immediately waited on the President, and informed him of the direction which had been given to the message. We have his authority for saying, that he then learned, not without surprise, *that an appropriation of two millions was wanted to purchase Florida!* He told the President that he would never agree to such a measure, because the money had not been asked for in the message; that he would not consent to shift to his own shoulders, or those of the House, the proper responsibility of the Executive. If the money had been explicitly demanded, he should have been averse to granting it, because, after a total failure of every attempt at negotiation, such a step would disgrace us for ever; because France would never withhold her ill offices, when, by their interposition, she could extort money from us; that it was equally to the interest of the United States, to accommodate the matter by an exchange of territory;—(to this mode of settlement the President seemed much opposed)—that the nations of Europe, like the Barbary powers, would hereafter refuse to look on the credentials of our ministers, without a previous *douceur.*

The committee met on the 7th of December. One of its members (Bidwell of Massachusetts) *construed* the message into a requisition of money for *foreign intercourse.* To draw such a conclusion, it is plain he must have had some other key of interpretation than that of the words in which the message was expressed. He proposed a grant to that effect, which was overruled. On the 14th of December, the chairman was obliged to go to Baltimore, and did not return till the 21st of the month. During this interval, the dispatches from Mr. Monroe, of the 18th and 25th of October, bearing on the subject of Spanish aggressions, were received by Government, but never submitted to the committee. Previous to the chairman's departure for Baltimore, he had occasion to call on the Secretary of State (Madison) to obtain a passport for his nephew, Saint George Randolph, whom he was about sending to Braidwood's and Sicard's schools, near London and Paris. Mr. Madison took this opportunity to enter into an explanation of the policy about to be pursued in regard to Spanish aggression. He concluded his remarks with the declaration, *that France would not permit Spain to adjust her differences with us; that France wanted money, and that we must give it to her, or have a Spanish and French war!*

It will be remembered that this declaration was made to one who was reputed to be the leader of the House of Representatives, and who was chairman of the Committee of Ways and Means. The appropriation here intimated would have to be recommended by that committee, and explained and defended before the House by its chairman. It is not surprising that a man of Mr. Randolph's high sense of honor and of personal dignity; and, above all, that one who had so nice a perception of the rights of the representative, and of the delicate relation existing between him and the Executive, which admitted not of the slightest approach towards influence or dictation, should have fired with indignation at a proposition which seemed to make him and the House of Representatives a mere tool of the Executive, to do that for them which they dare not avow before the world.

When this declaration was made, so different from the sentiments expressed by the President's public and secret messages, and so humiliating to the pride and honor of the country, Mr. Randolph abruptly left the presence of the Secretary with this remarkable exclamation, " Good morning, sir! I see I am not calculated for a politician !"

Mr. Randolph returned from Baltimore, the 21st of December, and convened the committee. As they were assembling, the Secretary of the Treasury (Gallatin) called him aside, and put into his hands a paper headed, " Provision for the purchase of Florida."

Mr. Randolph declared he would not vote a shilling; and expressed himself disgusted with the whole of this proceeding, which he could not but consider as highly disingenuous—the most scrupu-

lous care, he said, had been taken to cover the reputation of the administration, while Congress were expected to act as though they
had no character to lose; whilst the official language of the Executive
was consistent and dignified, Congress was *privately* required to take
upon itself the odium of shrinking from the national honor and
national defence, and of delivering the public purse to the first cut-
throat that demanded it. From the official communication, from the
face of the record, it would appear that the Executive had discharged
his duty in recommending manly and vigorous measures, which he had
been obliged to abandon, and had been compelled, *by Congress*, to pursue an opposite course; when, in fact, Congress had been acting all the
while at Executive instigation. Mr. Randolph further observed, that
he did not understand this *double* set of opinions and principles; the
one *ostensible*, to go upon the journals and before the *public;* the other,
the *efficient* and real motives to action; that he held true wisdom and
cunning to be utterly incompatible in the conduct of great affairs; that
he had strong objections to the measure itself; but in the shape in which
it was presented, his repugnance to it was insuperable. In a subsequent conversation with the President himself, in which those objections were recapitulated, he declared that he too had a character to
support and principles to maintain, and avowed his determined opposition to the whole scheme.

On the 3d of January, 1806, Mr. Randolph made a report, under the
instructions of the committee, which seems to be fully responsive to
the views of the President, as expressed in both his messages. "The
committee have beheld," says the report, "with just indignation, the
hostile spirit manifested by the court of Madrid towards the government of the United States, in withholding the ratification of its convention with us, although signed by its own minister, under the eye
of his sovereign unless with alteration of its terms, affecting claims
of the United States which, by the express conditions of the instrument itself, were reserved for future discussion; in piratical depredations upon our fair commerce; in obstructing the navigation of
the Mobile; in refusing to come to any fair and amicable adjustment
of the boundaries of Louisiana; and in a daring violation, by persons acting under the authority of Spain, and, no doubt, apprised of
her sentiments and views, of our undisputed limits, which she had solemnly recognized by treaty.

" To a government having interests distinct from those of its people, and disregarding its welfare, here is ample cause for a declaration of war, on the part of the United States, and such—did they obey the impulse of their feelings alone—is the course which the committee would not hesitate to recommend. But, to a government identified with its citizens, too far removed from the powerful nations of the earth for its safety to be endangered by their hostility, peace must always be desirable, so long as it is compatible with the honor and interest of the community. Whilst the United States continue burdened with a debt which annually absorbs two-thirds of their revenue, and duties upon imports constitute the only resource from which that revenue can be raised, without resorting to systems ;f taxation not more ruinous and oppressive than they are uncertain and precarious—the best interests of the United States cry aloud for peace. When that debt shall have been discharged, and the resources of the nation thereby liberated, then may we rationally expect to raise, even in time of war, the supplies which our frugal institutions require, without recurring to the hateful and destructive expedient of loans; then, *and not till then*, may we bid defiance to the world. The present moment is peculiarly auspicious for the great and desirable work. Now, *if ever*, the national debt is to be paid, by such financial arrangements as will accelerate its extinguishment, by reaping the rich harvest of neutrality, and thus providing for that diminution of revenue which experience teaches to expect on the general pacification of Europe. And the committee indulge a hope, that in the changed aspect of affairs in that quarter, Spain will find motives for a just fulfilment of her stipulations with us, and an amicable settlement of limits, upon terms not more beneficial to the United States than advantageous to herself; securing to her an ample barrier on the side of Mexico, and to us the countries watered by the Mississippi, and to the eastward of it. But whilst the committee perceive, in the general uproar of Europe, a state of things peculiarly favorable to the peaceable pursuit of our best interests, they are neither insensible to the indignity which has been offered on the part of Spain, nor unwilling to repel similar outrages. On the subject of self-defence, when the territory of the United States is insulted, there can be but one opinion, whatever differences may exist on the question whether that protection, which a vessel finds in our harbors, shall be extended

to her by the nation in the Indian or Chinese seas. Under this impression the committee submit the following resolution : That such
number of troops (not exceeding ——) as the President of the United States shall deem sufficient to protect the southern frontier of the
United States from Spanish inroad and insult, and to chastise the
same, be immediately raised."

Mr. Randolph explained, that the peculiar situation of the frontier
at that time insulted, had alone induced the committee to recommend
the raising of regular troops.   It was too remote from the population
of the country for the militia to act, in repelling and chastising Spanish incursion.   New Orleans and its dependencies were separated by
a vast extent of wilderness from the settlements of the United States ;
filled with disloyal and turbulent people, alien to our institutions,
language, and manners, and disaffected toward our government.   Little reliance could be placed upon them ; and it was plain that if " it
was the intention of Spain to advance on our possessions until she
should be repulsed by an opposing force," that force must be a regular army, unless we were disposed to abandon all the country south
of Tennessee ; that if the " protection of our citizens and the spirit
and the honor of our country required that force should be interposed," nothing remained but for the legislature to grant the only
practicable means, or to shrink from the most sacred of all its duties,
to abandon the soil and its inhabitants to the tender mercy of hostile
invaders.

Such were the proposition and the views of the committee, in ex
act correspondence, as they conceived, with the wishes of the President as expressed in his public and secret message.

Yet the report of the committee, moderate as it might seem, was
deemed of too strong a character by the House.   It was rejected. A
proposition, the avowed object of which was, to enable the President
to open a negotiation for Florida, was moved as a substitute, by Mr.
Bidwell of Massachusetts.   Mr. Randolph moved that the sum to
be appropriated should be confined to that object ; which was agreed
to.   But afterwards, when the bill was formally brought in, this specific appropriation was rescinded by the House, and the money left
at the entire discretion of the Executive, to be used " toward any extraordinary expense which might be incurred in the intercourse between the United States and foreign nations."

Mr. Randolph also moved to limit the amount which the Government might stipulate to pay for the territory in question; upon the ground that if Congress were disposed to acquire Florida by purchase, they should fix the extent to which they were willing to go, and thereby furnish our ministers with a safeguard against the rapacity of France; that there was no probability of our obtaining the country for less, but every reason to believe that without such a precaution on our part, she would extort more. This motion was overruled.

When the bill came under discussion, various objections were urged against it by the same gentleman; among others, that it was in direct opposition to the views of the Executive, as expressed in the President's official communication (it was on this occasion that General Varnum declared the measure to be consonant to the secret wishes of the Executive); that it was a prostration of the national honor at the feet of our adversary; that a concession so humiliating would paralyze our efforts against Great Britain, in case the negotion then pending between that government and ours, should prove abortive; that a partial appropriation towards the purchase of Florida, without limiting the President to some specific amount, would give a previous sanction to any expense which he might incur for that object, and which Congress would stand pledged to make good; that if the Executive, acting entirely upon its own responsibility, and exercising its acknowledged constitutional powers, should negotiate for the purchase of Florida, the House of Representatives would, in that case, be left free to ratify or annul the contract; but that the course which was proposed to be pursued (and which eventually was pursued) would reduce the discretion of the legislature to a mere shadow; that at the ensuing session Congress would find itself, in relation to this subject, a deliberative body but in *name;* that it could not, without a manifest dereliction of its own principles, and, perhaps, without a violation of public faith, refuse to sanction any treaty entered into by the Executive, under the auspices of the legislature, and with powers so unlimited; that, however great his confidence in the Chief Magistrate, he would never consent to give any President so dangerous a proof of it; and that he never would preclude himself, by any previous sanction, from the unbiassed exercise of his judgment on measures which were thereafter to come before him; that the House had no official recommendation for the step which they proposed to take; on the contrary, it was in direct opposition to the sentiments as expressed in the confidential message; and that the responsibility would be exclusively their own; that if he thought proper to ask for an appropriation for the object (the purchase of Florida), the responsibility of the measure would rest on him; but when the legislature undertook to prescribe the course which he should pursue, and which he had pledged himself to pursue, the case was entirely changed; that the House could have no channel through which it could be made acquainted with the opinions of the Executive, but such as was official, responsible, and known to the Constitution; and that it was a prostitution of its high and solemn functions, to act upon an unconstitutional suggestion of the private wishes of the Executive, irresponsibly announced by an irresponsible individual, and in direct hostility to his avowed opinions.

It will be remembered that these proceedings and discussions took place in conclave, on the President's confidential message. Mr. Randolph's course was so grossly misrepresented, and his motives so basely calumniated, that, at a subsequent period of the session, he moved the House to take off the injunction of secrecy from the President's communication, that the world might see what the Executive had really required at the hands of the legislature, and how far they had complied with his publicly expressed wishes, in the report and resolution of the committee.

The secret journal of the House had been published; but, for some reason unaccountable to us, the message, which was the foundation of the whole proceeding, and without which the journal was wholly unintelligible, had been withheld from the public. Mr. Randolph's motion was, to publish the message and the documents—he was willing to abide the decision of an impartial judgment on the perusal. This motion gave rise to much debate and angry recrimination. Mr. Randolph said:

"It is not my wish, Mr. Speaker, to trespass on the patience of the House. But I think it necessary to explain what I am sure the House has not well understood; for my positions have been grossly perverted, whether intentionally or not I will not undertake to say. Gentlemen opposed to us act a very strange and inconsistent part.

They will not give credit to a private individual as to a conversation had with him. I only stated that conversation as a reason for saying I had withdrawn my confidence. And will gentlemen say I am bound, when evidence has come to my private knowledge which is sufficient to damn any man, to legislate on a principle of confidence? When I find misrepresentations made to the public, and insinuations of the most despicable kind on this floor, I come out, and call on any man to deny what I have stated. They cannot—they dare not. For I take it for granted no man will declare in the face of the nation a wilful falsehood. But while gentlemen will not give credit to what has fallen from one individual, they have no hesitation in giving credit to an individual member for the whole course of the Government.

"In my opinion it is of the first importance that the message should be published, from a material fact which took place in this House. A member in his place told you, that the course recommended by a particular individual was consonant with the secret wishes of the Executive. I did then reprehend that language as the most unconstitutional and reprehensible ever uttered on this floor. I did believe that the people of the United States possessed as free a Constitution as the British people, and I had hoped freer; and I knew that such language had in the British Parliament been considered as reprehensible, and had brought forward a vote of indignation in that body. I allude to the case, where the King's name was used for the purpose of throwing out Mr. Fox's India bill. I then reprobated this back-stair influence, this double dealing, the sending one message for the journals and newspapers, and another in whispers to this House. I shall always reprobate such language, and consider it unworthy of any man holding a seat in this House. I had before always flattered myself, that it would be a thousand years hence before our institutions would have given birth to these Charles Jenkinson's in politics. I did not expect them at this time of day, and I now declare it important, in my opinion, that the message should be published, that the public may be enabled to compare the official with the unofficial message which decided the vote.

"There is another reason for its publication. The gentleman from Pennsylvania has said there is no mention of France on the journals; and that we have no cause of complaint against France

I wish the publication of the message to prove what causes of com
plaint we have against France. Let men of sense take a view of all
the papers, and I am willing to abide the issue. It is said France
has done us no injury—that the bubble is burst. We are told that
this is a plain answer to all the speeches made on this floor. Permit
me to say, the gentleman (Mr. Epps) has given a plain answer to all
the speeches delivered on this floor; it was impossible to have given
a plainer answer to them. He says, I will vote with you, but I will
make a speech against you. Permit me to say, this is the first time I
would not rather have had his vote than his speech. After this
speech there can be no doubt as to the issue of the question. I will
go further, after the adjournment on Saturday there could be no
doubt. Saturday, it seems, is an unfortunate day, on which no expedition is to be undertaken, no forlorn hope conducted.

"The same gentleman has said that we pursued precisely the
same course in 1803 as in 1806, and for obtaining the same object.
He says the same course is now pursued, and yet he says he will not
undertake to say the cases are not dissimilar; put this and that
together, and what do you make of it? The cases are decidedly dissimilar. In 1803 there was no existing misunderstanding between
the American and French governments with regard to our differences
with Spain. Those differences have started up like a mushroom in
the night. We made an appropriation to purchase the Floridas—
to buy them—from whom? From their rightful owner. The circumstances would have been similar, if the United States had given
money to France to compel Spain to form a treaty with us; then the
national honor would have received a deadly wound. But there was
nothing of this sort in the formation of the treaty then made. Spain,
under the operation of causes in which we had no agency, transferred
Louisiana to France, and France transferred it to us. But this is
not now the case. We are told that Spain is no longer an independent power, but is under the control of France. What follows? That
France is an aggressor on us, which proves every thing I have
alleged.

"There is another thing to be observed. The public have been
given to understand, that two millions have been appropriated for
the purchase of the Floridas. This is not so. The appropriation is
only towards doing something; but what that is, is not defined by law.

Now if in 1803 we appropriated two millions for the purchase of the Floridas, and did not get them, what security is there now that by making an appropriation in the same language, we shall obtain them? Although the persons making the appropriation are not the same identical beings, those applying the sum appropriated are. I do not believe that we shall get the Floridas. In this I may be mistaken: I hope I shall be; for after having descended to prostitute the national character, let us at least receive the wages of iniquity.

"But gentlemen inquire, will you become the guardians of Spain? This is a mistake which has run through every attempt at argument I have heard. We never professed to be the guardians of Spain. We profess to be the guardians of our own honor. We care not for France trampling on Spain. Let her pick her pockets, for what we care; but if we instigate her to it, it is no longer a mere question between France and Spain, but a question in which our own honor is engaged, which is at once mortgaged and gone.

"Until the gentleman from Virginia got up, I confess that, what with my exhausted state, the badness of the air, and the tenuity of the arguments of gentlemen, so excessively light that they at once vanished into thin air, that I had not a word to say; for it is not to be supposed that I intended to reply to any thing offered by the gentleman behind me. If I am to fall, let me fall in the face of day, and not be betrayed by a kiss,—I mean no profane allusion. I shall do my duty as an honest man. I came here prepared to co-operate with the government in all its measures. I told them so. But I soon found there was no choice left, and that to co-operate in them would be to destroy the national character. I found I might co-operate, or be an honest man; I have therefore opposed, and will oppose them. Is there an honest man disposed to be the go-between, to carry down secret messages to this House? No. It is because men of character cannot be found to do this business, that agents must be got to carry things into effect, which men of uncompromited character will not soil their fingers, or sully their characters with.

"One word on the subject of voting on unofficial notice, on the representations of individuals, in the place of communications officially received from the officers of the executive department. I have always considered the Executive, in this country, as atanding in the same relation to the two Houses, that the minister or administration bore to the legislature under governments similar to our own. I have always considered that the responsibility for public measures, rested more particularly on them. For those measures they are answerable to the people—and to me it has been a subject of peculiar regret (I do not speak of the general character of the Constitution) that they have not a seat on this floor. For whatever may be supposed to be my feelings, as to the members of the administration, I am ashamed when I see their fame and character committed to such hands as we are in the daily habit of witnessing. If their measures are susceptible of justification, I should like to have a justification at their own hands, instead of hearing Yazoo men defend them. Much less did I expect, on such an occasion, to hear a Yazoo man, assigning his motives for a vote, on a totally different subject, and this in justification of a man with whom he is connected by ties of consanguinity. This reminds me of the intention imputed to me, to bring forward an impeachment against a great officer of state. This, however, is so far from being the truth, that I appeal to those who heard me, whether I did not declare that I washed my hands of impeachments—that I was done with them. No, I will neither directly, nor indirectly, have any thing to do with them. But I will in all questions that shall come before this House, discuss the public character and conduct of any public agents from a secretary to a constable : and I will continue to do it, until it shall be admitted by the Constitution that the king can do no wrong. I say I wish the heads of departments had seats on this floor. Were this the case, to one of them I would immediately propound this question : Did you, or did you not, in your capacity of a public functionary, tell me, in my capacity of a public functionary, that France would not suffer Spain to settle her differences with us, that she wanted money, that we must give her money, or take a Spanish or French war ? And did not I answer, that I was neither for a war with Spain or France, but in favor of defending my country ? I would put that question to him. I would put this question to another head of department : Was, or was not, an application made to you for money, to be conveyed to Europe to carry on any species of diplomatic negotiation there ? I would listen to his answer, and if he put his hand on his heart, and like a man of honor said no, I would believe him, though it would require a great stretch of credulity. I would

call into my aid faith, not reason, and believe when I was not con
vinced. I would then turn to the first magistrate of the nation and
say: Did you not buy Louisiana of France? Has France acted in
that transaction in a bona fide manner? Has she delivered into your
possession the country you believed you had bought from her? Has
she not equivocated, prevaricated, and played off Spain against you,
with a view of extorting money? I will answer for the reply. There
cannot be the smallest doubt about it. I will put the whole business
on this issue. All the difficulty has arisen from that quarter.

"Yes, the bubble has burst! It is immaterial to us, whether you
publish the President's message or not. But it is material to others
that you should; and let me add, the public will not rest satisfied
with the conduct of those, who profess to wish it published, while
they vote against the publication. The public will not confide in
such professions. Gentlemen may show their bunch of rods, may
treat them as children, and offer them sugar-plums; but all will not
avail them, so long as they refuse to call for the dispatches of our
ministers, and other documents, which if published would fix a stain
upon some men in the government, and high in office, which all the
waters in the ocean would not wash out. Gentlemen may talk about
our changing and chopping about, and all that. What is the fact?
We are what we profess to be—not courtiers, but republicans, acting
on the broad principles we have heretofore professed—applying the
same scale with which we measured John Adams to the present administration. Do gentlemen flinch from this and pretend to be republicans? They cannot be republicans, unless they agree that it
shall be measured to them as they measured to others. But we are
perhaps to be told, that we all have become federalists—or that the
federalists have become good republicans. This, however, is a charge
which, I am convinced, the federalists will not be more anxious to
repel than we to be exonerated from. No, they will never become
good republicans. They never did, they never will act with us.
What has happened? they are in opposition from system, and we
quo ad hoc, as to this particular measure. Like men who have
roughed it together, there is a kind of fellow-feeling between us.
There is no doubt of it. But as to political principle, we are as
much as ever opposed. There is a most excellent alkali by which
to test our principles. The Yazoo business is the beginning and the

end, the alpha and omega of our alphabet. With that our differences began, and with that they will end ; and I pray to God that
the liberties of the people may not also end with them.

"When the veracity of a man is called in question it is a serious
business. The gentleman from Massachusetts has appealed to the
House for the correctness of his statement. I, too, appeal to the
House whether this was not his expression, when he undertook to
explain away what he had said, for he did not deny it: "That he
would vouch that such were the secret wishes of the President;" and
whether I did not observe that his attempt to explain was like Judge
Chase attempting to draw back a prejudicated opinion in the case of
Fries ; that he might take back the words, but not the effect they
had made on the Assembly ; that the Constitution knows only of two
ways by which the Executive could influence the Legislature : the
one by a recommendation of such measures as he deemed expedient ;
the other, by a negative on our bills ; and that the moment it was
attempted to influence the House by whispers and private messages
its independence was gone. I stated the proneness of legislative
bodies to be governed by Executive influence, and, in illustration,
referred to the Senate, who, from its association with the Executive
and the length of time for which its members hold their seats, was
necessarily made up of gaping expectants of office, and there can be
no doubt of the fact. It must be so from the nature of things. Now,
if it be necessary, let the House appoint a Committee of Inquiry to
ascertain what the gentleman from Massachusetts did say, and let
us see who can adduce the most witnesses and swear the hardest.
No, the gentleman from Massachusetts had on that occasion so different a countenance, dress and address, that I could not now recognize him for the same man. He seemed thunderstruck and to be in
a state of stupefaction at his indiscretion. He appeared humbled
in the presence of those who heard what he had said, and beheld his
countenance. His words were these, my life on it: 'I will vouch
that such are the secret wishes of the President, or the Executive,'
I do not know which."

CHAPTER XXX.

DIFFICULTIES WITH GREAT BRITAIN.

THE aggressions of Great Britain on the persons, the property, and the rights of American citizens began at an early period, and were still continued with increased aggravation. It was high time for some firm stand to be taken in regard to them. The peace, prosperity, and honor of the country demanded an effectual system of measures to arrest them. Officers of the British navy had long been in the habit of boarding American vessels, dragging seamen thence, and forcing them into their own service under the pretext that they were British subjects. The law of England did not recognize the right of expatriation. The sovereign claimed the services of all his subjects in time of war, and impressed them wherever they could be found. The similarity of language, of person, and of habits, made it difficult to distinguish an American from an English sailor. Many of the latter had taken refuge from their own hard naval service in the profitable commercial marine of the United States. In re-capturing their own subjects, they not unfrequently dragged American citizens from their homes. They were charged with not being very scrupulous in this regard. Not less than three thousand American sailors, it was said, had been forced to serve in the British navy. The government of the United States denied the right of Great Britain to impress seamen on board any of their vessels on the high seas, or within their own jurisdiction. They contended that a neutral flag on the high seas was a safeguard to those sailing under it. They were sustained in this doctrine by the law of nations.

Although Great Britain had not adopted in the same latitude with most other nations the immunities of a neutral flag, yet she did not deny the general freedom of the high seas, and of neutral vessels navigating them, with such exceptions only as are annexed to it by the law of nations. The exceptions are objects commonly denominated contraband of war; that is, enemies serving in the war, articles going into a blockaded port, and enemy's property of every kind. But nowhere, it was contended, could an exception to the freedom of the seas and of neutral flags be found that justified the taking away of *any person, not an enemy in military service, found on board a neutral vessel.*

The right of impressment, growing out of their different interpretation of the law of nations, was one, and the gravest, of the subjects of dispute between the two nations. The other was in regard to the carrying trade. The question commonly presented itself in this form: Was that commerce allowable in time of war which was prohibited in time of peace? Great Britain, by her powerful marine, had swept the ocean nearly of the whole of the vessels of her enemies. In consequence of this, the produce of the colonies of France, Spain, and Holland, was imported into the mother countries by neutral ships; in fact, it was almost wholly transported in American bottoms. The restrictive colonial system of these powers did not suffer this transportation by foreigners in times of peace; but the necessities arising from a calamitous naval war induced them to lay their ports open by a forced liberality to this general commerce. French, Spanish, and Dutch property in American bottoms now became neutralized, and was protected, as some contended, by the American flag. But the property was still enemy's property, and fell within the exception of the law of nations. The French navy had been totally annihilated; in consequence, the products of her colonies had to lie rotting on their wharfs, for want of transportation, while the mother country was suffering both from the want of the products and of the revenue arising from the sale and consumption of them. These were the evils intended to be inflicted by a naval victory, in order to force her to an honorable peace. But the United States came in with their ships, and relieved France of these evils, by becoming carriers between her and her colonies.

Can that be a *neutral* commerce which robs one of the belligerent parties of all the advantages of a victory, and relieves the other from nearly all the evils of a defeat? It can hardly seem possible at this day that any one could have contended for such a doctrine; yet Mr. Madison maintained that the contrary principle, denying the neutral character of such a commerce, *was of modern date*—that it was avowed by no other nation than Great Britain, and that it was assumed by her, under the auspices of a maritime ascendency, which rendered such a principle subservient to her particular interests.

This doctrine, however, contended for by a nation that had the power to maintain it, was gotten over by subterfuge and evasion. We will illustrate the manner by an example. A French subject purchases a cargo of coffee at Guadaloupe, intending it for the market of Nantes : to ship it in a vessel belonging to any one of the nations belligerent with England, was absolutely throwing it away ; but the ordinary device of sending it under the cover of an American flag is resorted to ; the American refuses to carry it directly for the harbor of Nantes, alleging, that if he is captured by an English cruiser, a condemnation must follow such an attempt at an immediate commerce between the mother country and her colony. False owners are created for the ship's cargo, in the character of Americans. The vessel instead of sailing for Nantes, makes for New York, and in due time arrives there ; bonds for the payment of duties are given, and the cargo is landed. The vessel loads again with the same coffee ; the debentures of the custom-house are produced ; the bonds for duties are cancelled, and she now makes her way boldly for Nantes, as a neutral ship, not to be molested. The entire trade of the French, Spanish and Dutch colonies was conducted in American vessels, in this indirect way. A most profitable business it was surely, but it is shocking to contemplate the influence on the moral character of those engaged in it. All this chicanery and duplicity were often forced through by absolute perjury—*always* by a prostration of honorable delicacy.

The British Courts of Admiralty allowed this indirect trade through a neutral port, where there was proof of an actual change of ownership. Whenever the neutral party could show that he had *purchased* the property, he was suffered to pass unmolested ; but such a *bona fide* purchase rarely took place ; and enemy's property was covered up and protected by neutral names, under false pretences. *Such was the carrying trade.*

These two—the impressment of seamen and the carrying trade—constituted the main difficulties existing between the United States and Great Britain ; all others grew out of them, and would necessarily cease on a satisfactory adjustment of those leading subjects of complaint.

These questions were involved in much obscurity. Much might be said on both sides. Each nation had just cause of complaint against the other. Here was a fair field for negotiation and compromise. But we can now perceive the secret motives that would incessantly throw obstacles in the way of a satisfactory arrangement of these difficulties. There was the old grudge against England, cherished in the prejudices of the people; the jealousy of her superior naval power on that element where we were as much at home as she was; the spirit of rivalry that stimulated our merchants to share with her the commerce of the world; the barren results of any settlement of difficulties with her during the wars in Europe—it might secure peace, but could bring no profit. On the other hand, there were the old partialities for our ancient ally; the fraternizing spirit between the two Republics; the enthusiasm enkindled in a martial people, by the daring exploits and brilliant successes of Napoleon; the secret consciousness that his irresistible power would always be interposed between them and any hostile movements of England; the lucrative commerce, and the absolute monopoly of the carrying trade between France, Spain, Holland, and their dependencies, and which must cease on a compromise with England;—add to these causes, that went home to the prejudices and the interests of the people, the all-controlling influence of party spirit—which had long since attached to the friends of England the epithet of monarchists and tories, and to the friends of France that of republicans and friends of the people—and we cannot fail to perceive that every agency which was calculated to give direction to public opinion would bend it against any adjustment of British difficulties during the continuance of the wars in Europe.

The subjects of difference were ably discussed by the Secretary of State in his instructions to our minister at the Court of St. James; but when the President thought proper to bring the matter before Congress, and to call on them for action, he had no plan to propose. He did not recommend, as the Constitution required, any specific mode of adjustment. He left the Legislature to grope their way in the dark, and to adopt such measures as they might think proper, without any previous participation on his part in the responsibility.

Various crude and illy-digested schemes were offered in the House and in the Senate. They all seemed to contemplate coercing England into measures by operating on her commerce. Gregg's resolution—the one principally discussed in the House—went so far as to prohibit all intercourse between the two nations, until England would consent to settle the subjects of dispute between them on fair terms. This professed to be a peace measure, but it was actual war in disguise. Many of its friends discussed it as a war measure. Mr. Randolph so regarded it. " I am not surprised," said he, " to hear this resolution discussed by its friends as a war measure. They say, it is true, that it is not a war measure ; but they defend it on principles that would justify none but war measures, and seemed pleased with the idea that it may prove the forerunner of war. If war is necessary, if we have reached this point, let us have war. But while I have life, I will never consent to these incipient war measures, which in their commencement breathe nothing but peace, though they plunge us at last into war. * * * * * What is the question in dispute? The carrying trade. What part of it? The fair, the honest, and the useful trade, that is engaged in carrying our own productions to foreign markets and bringing back their productions in exchange? No, sir; it is that carrying trade which covers enemy's property, and carries the coffee, the sugar, and other West India products to the mother country. No, sir; if this great agricultural nation is to be governed by Salem and Boston, New York and Philadelphia, and Baltimore, and Norfolk, and Charleston, let gentlemen come out and say so ; and let a committee of public safety be appointed from these towns to carry on the government. I, for one, will not mortgage my property and my liberty to carry on this trade. The nation said so seven years ago ; I said so then, I say so now ; it is not for the honest carrying trade of America, but for this mushroom, this fungus of war, for a trade, which as soon as the nations of Europe are at peace will no longer exist—it is for this that the spirit of avaricious traffic would plunge us into war. I am forcibly struck on this occasion by the recollection of a remark, made by one of the ablest, if not the honestest, ministers England ever produced; I mean Sir Robert Walpole; who said that the country gentlemen (poor, meek souls!) came up every year to be sheared, that they laid mute and patient whilst their fleeces were taking off, but if he touched a single bristle of the commercial interest the whole stye was in an uproar. It was, indeed, shearing the hog—great cry and little wool.

" What is the fact? Whilst we boast of our honor on this floor, our name has become a by-word among the nations. Europe, and

Paris especially, swarms with pseudo-Americans, with Anglo and Gallo Americans, and American French and English, who have amassed immense fortunes by trading in the neutral character—by setting it up to auction, and selling it to the best bidder. Men of this description—striplings, without connections or character—have been known to buy rich vessels and their cargoes, in Amsterdam and Antwerp, and trade with them under the American name to the Indies. Neutral character has constituted one of the best remittances for colonial produce, or the goods which purchase it; and the trade in this commodity of neutrality has produced a most lucrative branch of traffic. This it is that has sunk and degraded the American name abroad, and subjected the fair trader to vexatious seizure and detention.

"But yet, sir, I have a more cogent reason against going to war, for the honor of the flag in the narrow seas, or any other maritime punctilio. It springs from my attachment to the principles of the Government under which I live. I declare, in the face of day, that this Government was not instituted for the purposes of offensive war. No; it was framed (to use its own language) for the common defence and general welfare, which are inconsistent with offensive war. I call that offensive war, which goes out of our jurisdiction and limits, for the attainment or protection of objects not within those limits and that jurisdiction. As in 1798, I was opposed to this species of warfare, because I believed it would raze the Constitution to its very foundation—so in 1806, am I opposed to it, and on the same grounds. No sooner do you put the Constitution to this use—to a test which it is by no means calculated to endure, than its incompetency to such purposes becomes manifest and apparent to all. I fear, if you go into a foreign war, for a circuitous, unfair foreign trade, you will come out without your Constitution. Have you not contractors enough in this House? or do you want to be overrun and devoured by commissaries, and all the vermin of contract? I fear, sir, that what are called the energy men, will rise up again—men who will burn the parchment. We shall be told that our Government is too free, or, as they would say, weak and inefficient—much virtue, sir, in terms; that we must give the President power to call forth the resources of the nation—that is, to filch the last shilling from our pockets, or to drain the last drop of blood from our veins. I am against giving this power to any man, be he who he may. The American people must either withhold this power, or resign their liberties. There is no other alternative. Nothing but the most imperious necessity will justify such a grant; and is there a powerful enemy at our door? You may begin with a First Consul. From that chrysalis state he soon becomes an emperor. You have your choice. It depends upon your election whether you will be a free, happy, and united people at home, or the light of your executive majesty shall beam across the Atlantic, in one general blaze of the public liberty.

"But, sir, it seems that we, who are opposed to this resolution, are men of no nerve—who trembled in the days of the British treaty—cowards, I suppose, in the reign of terror. Is this true? Hunt up the journals—let our actions tell. We pursue our old, unshaken course. We care not for the nations of Europe, but make foreign relations bend to our political principles, and serve our country's interests. We have no wish to see another Actium, or Pharsalia, or the lieutenants of a modern Alexander playing at piquet, or all-fours, for the empire of the world. 'Tis poor comfort to us to be told that France has too decided a taste for luxurious things to meddle with us; that Egypt is her object, or the coast of Barbary, and, at the worst, we shall be the last devoured. We are enamored with neither nation. We would play their own game upon them—use them for our interest and convenience. But, with all my abhorrence of the British Government, I should not hesitate between Westminster Hall and a Middlesex jury, on the one hand, and the wood of Vincennes and a file of grenadiers, on the other. That jury trial which walked with Horne Tooke, and Hardy through the flames of ministerial persecution, is, I confess, more to my taste than the trial of the Duke d'Enghein."

But we must forbear any further quotations from Mr. Randolph's speeches against Gregg's resolutions. There were two of them, delivered on the 5th and 6th of March. They were not merely eloquent and forcible in their expression, but display a comprehensive knowledge of our foreign relations, and a deep insight into the motives of men who foment discord between nations that should be at peace with each other. They are patriotic in their tone, and show a warm devotion to the Constitution and the Union, and a profound comprehension of those principles which alone can preserve them in their integrity.   While we forbear further quotation, we feel constrained to give the substance of Mr. Randolph's views on the questions therein discussed.

This was an important crisis, not only in his own history, but in that of the country.   This was the beginning of a series of measures that separated Mr. Randolph' from his old political associations, and that finally involved the country in a disastrous war.   The party heats and animosities that rankled in the bosoms of men at that day have all died away.   Let impartial history speak the truth, and do justice to one whose name has long been calumniated.   We shall give facts as they are condensed from his own speeches, and leave the world to judge how far he acted as a zealous patriot, an honest man, and an enlightened statesman.

It was notorious, says Mr. Randolph, that in regard to the course to be pursued towards Great Britain, no opinion was expressed by the members of the Cabinet, in their collective or individual capacities.   On the contrary, the President frequently declared, without reserve, that he had no opinion on the subject.   Similar declarations were made by other influential and leading persons presiding over the executive departments—and it is a fact, that no consultation was held between them, from the meeting of Congress, on the 3d of December, till some time in the month of March.   This want of concert and decision in the administration, might easily have been inferred (even if there were no other proof of it) from the various, discordant, and undigested projects which were brought forward in the legislature, and to this want of system must be referred much of the mischief which then resulted from this subject, as well as the embarrassment which afterwards ensued.

Mr. Randolph was of opinion that the impressment of our seamen furnished just cause for indignant resentment on our part; but he saw no reason for pushing that matter to extremity at that time, which had not existed in as full force, for the last five years, or even twelve years.   Our government, in consideration of the great number of British seamen in our employment, and of the identity of language and manners between that class of their subjects, and the same description of our citizens, but above all, from motives of sound policy (too obvious to need recapitulation), had hitherto deemed it expedient to temporize on this interesting and delicate topic—he could see no just ground, at present, for departing from this system—more especially pending an actual negotiation between the two governments, on the point in dispute. He was of opinion that nothing should be left undone to accommodate our differences amicably, and that no step should be taken which might interrupt or defeat such a settlement—that even if we should resort to war, it must eventuate in a treaty of peace, by which the points in controversy would be adjusted, or left *in statu quo ante bellum*—and that after incurring the incalculable mischiefs of war, the derangement of our finances and the augmentation of the public debt, to an extent which could not now be foreseen; to say nothing of its baneful effects upon our political institutions, and of the danger which must accrue from throwing our weight, at this juncture, into the preponderating scale of Europe; there was no prospect that we should obtain better terms at any future pacification, than were attainable at present—at any rate, he was disposed to give fair play to a fair experiment at negotiation. But if any active measures were to be taken against Great Britain, they should be of the most efficient and decisive nature. He deprecated half measures, as the most injurious to ourselves which could be adopted.

Whilst the Bill was yet under discussion, the news of the death of Mr. Pitt, and of the consequent change of ministry, reached the United States. No circumstance could have afforded a fairer or more honorable pretext, or a more powerful motive, for suspending our measures against Great Britain, than this. The late Premier was known to be decidedly hostile to the institutions, the interests, and the very people, of America.

No administration, not even that of Lord North himself, had been or could be more inimical to the United States, than that of Mr. Pitt. His power, moreover, was connected with, and depended upon, the continuation and duration of the war. He was succeeded by Mr. Fox, unquestionably the most liberal and enlightened statesman of Europe; the man above all others, beyond the Atlantic, the best affected towards the principles of our government, and the illustrious character by whom it was administered.

Never did a fairer occasion present itself to any nation for changing, without any imputation of versatility, or any loss of honor, the course which they had chosen to prescribe to themselves. The ex-

citement of public sentiment, and the measures consequent upon that
excitement, might, fairly and honorably, have been referred to the
known character of the late Premier, the pupil of Dundas, and the
disciple of Charles Jenkinson; and the United States might have
awaited, in a dignified and imposing inactivity, the manifestation of
a different sentiment by the new ministry. But the new leaders of
the House of Representatives were men who soared above, or skim-
med below, all considerations of time, place, and circumstance—they
gloried in their ignorance of men and things in Europe, and boasted
that their policy should not be modified by any change in the aspect
of affairs at home, or abroad—and in the pursuit of an abstract metaphysical *ignis fatuus*, they did not hesitate to embark the best interests of the Union.

Against these measures, Mr. Randolph further objected, that during the "*five months which our ministers had spent in fruitless discussion at Madrid*," it had entered into the head of nobody to suggest any proposition of a coercive nature in relation to Spain, and
that, even after the total failure of that negotiation, no such measure
had been proposed—that Great Britain had indeed impressed our
seamen, and advanced certain injurious principles of national law,
which, if carried into their full extent, would materially affect our
commerce; but that Spain, after having refused to make good her
solemn stipulations to compensate us for former spoliations committed on our commerce, had "*renewed the same practices during the
present war.*" She had not, it was true, impressed our seamen, but
her cruisers had "*plundered and sunk our vessels, and maltreated
and abandoned their crews in open boats, or on desert shores, without
food or covering.*" Her Courts of Admiralty had, indeed, advanced
no "new principles of the law of nations," but they had confiscated
our ships and cargoes, without the pretext of principles of any sort,
new or old. She had, moreover, insulted our territory, violated the
property and the persons of our citizens, within our acknowledged
limits, and insolently rejected every overture to accommodation.
With Spain, all our attempts to negotiate had failed—with Great
Britain, we had a negotiation actually pending, and which the dispatches of our minister at the Court of London gave us every reason to suppose would have a prosperous issue—and even admitting,
for the sake of argument, that our vote of money to purchase Flori-

da was, in itself, no derogation from the national honor, inasmuch as we proposed to receive a fair equivalent for it, yet, having refused to take any coercive measures for the unparalleled indignities of Spain, who had peremptorily rejected all our propositions for pacific accommodation, how could we, with any face of impartiality towards the belligerent powers, assume this elevated tone towards Great Britain? Mr. Randolph further declared, that the proposed measure was, in itself, inefficient to every valuable purpose—that its sole operation would be to pique the pride and rouse the resentment of our adversary, and whilst it indicated a strong spirit of hostility on our part, would afford her a fair opening to strike the first effectual blow—that it was indeed showing our teeth, without, at the same time, daring to bite—that Great Britain would have, until the next session of Congress, ample time to devise means for annoying us in the most effective manner, and that, meanwhile, she might withdraw her property from our grasp, and guard every valuable point from our attack.   He conjured the House not to suffer themselves, from the honest prejudices of the revolution, from their ancient partiality to France, and their well-grounded antipathy to England, to be legislated into a war, which would involve the best interests of their country.

Another strong objection to the non-importation bill arose from its bearing the aspect (especially when taken in conjunction with our recent conduct towards Spain and France) of a disposition on our part to aid the views of the French governement in cramping the navigation and destroying the manufactures of Great Britain. This constituted one principal source of animosity between those rival nations, and the American government could perhaps take no step which would so strongly excite the resentment of the British ministry.   The prompt and decisive conduct of that government towards Prussia, so soon as she manifested a disposition to come into the views of France on this subject, forms the best commentary upon this opinion, and the sudden change in the tone of Mr. Fox towards the United States is no bad criterion of its truth.

When Mr. Randolph declared, that if any coercive measures were to be pursued towards Great Britain they should be of the most energetic stamp, and mentioned an embargo as that which he deemed the most efficient in the outset, he was asked by some " why he did not move such a proposition?" and they declared at the same time, that if he would bring forward the measure, they would support it. To this he answered: That he wished to try the fair experiment of negotiation in the first instance—that he deemed it impolitic, pending that negotiation, to take any step that might defeat it—and that it was astonishing to him, that gentlemen who had remained entirely passive under the aggressions of Spain, who had refused even to concur in measures of self-defence against her inroads—made too after a peremptory rejection of every overture to accommodation, should advocate an opposite course towards another power, with whom we were at that moment actually treating.

Mr. Randolph's powerful opposition was so far successful as to defeat Gregg's resolution, which contemplated a total suspension of commercial intercourse between the two countries. Another was introduced, prohibiting only certain enumerated articles of British manufacture, and passed by a large majority. *Eighty-seven* republicans voted for these restrictive measures, while only *eleven* republicans and the whole body of federalists, being but *four and twenty* in all voted against them.

The Act passed by Congress, it was said by the friends of it, was the first leading step in a system of measures well calculated to awaken England from her delusive dreams; and that it was expressly adopted as a measure equally fitted for producing a change in her conduct, or for standing as a part of our permanent commercial regulations. Here the reader will observe was the beginning of those measures, which if not designedly, indirectly fostered the manufactures of the country (by prohibiting importation) at the expense of its agriculture and commerce.

How far this non-importation scheme of the Legislature was likely to influence the minds of the British Cabinet, may be seen from the following extract taken from an essay styled "Observations on Randolph's Speech," and written by the most eminent British writer of the day, in immediate connection too with the ministry, and well possessed of their views—no less a personage than the author of "War in Disguise," a book that took all Mr. Madison's learning and ability to give a plausible answer to. The áuthor is expressly recommending to the British minister, to send an envoy to the American Government to treat for an adjustment of differences. He concludes thus: "The only objection I can possibly imagine to arise against this expedient is, from the passing of the limited non importation bill, the fate of which is yet unknown, and which is represented as containing a clause, making its operation depend either on the fiat of the executive government, or on that of its minister in this country ; or, as other accounts intimate, on the bare event of our refusing immediate compliance with the demands of the American government.

" Now such a bill either has, or has not been passed by the Congress. In the latter case, the difficulty will not arise; but in the former, I hesitate not to say, that it makes your compliance, consistently with any regard to the dignity and honor of this great nation, absolutely impossible.

" What ! Is a rod to be put into the hands of a foreign minister, to whip us into submission ; and are we broadly and coarsely to sell our maritime rights, for the sake of passing off a little haberdashery along with them !

" Are we to make a lumping pennyworth to the buyers of our leather wares, our felt and tin wares, and the other commodities enumerated in this insolent bill, by tossing our honor, our justice, and our courage also into the parcel ! ! I would not consent to disparage even the quality of our manufactures, much less of our public morals, by so shameful a bargain.

" No, sir ! if Mr. Monroe is indeed instructed and empowered to treat with us in this humiliating style of huckstering diplomacy, a new reason arises for delay, and for treating beyond the Atlantic.

" Let the threatened prohibition take place. Our hats, our shoes, and our tea kettles, must find some other market for a few months ; unless the American merchants should be impatient enough to import them by smuggling, into that country, in the mean time ; which, I doubt not, they will, in a more than usual abundance. Perhaps when our minister arrives, the advanced price of British goods, and the loss of the duties upon them, may form an argument of some weight in our favor."

CHAPTER XXXI

CLOSING SCENE.

In looking over the House of Representatives of the ninth Congress, who had devolved on them the important duty of giving the first impulse and direction to the policy of the country in regard to foreign nations, at this critical period, when the powers of Europe, not content with destroying one another, seemed to be aiming at the commercial and political annihilation of this transatlantic republic also, we are struck with the very common and unimportant characters of which it was composed. There were, doubtless, some modest and retiring men, of sound judgment, who were content to give their vote in silence, and to pass their opinions on men and things around them without giving the world the benefit of their wisdom. But all those who were most prominent in the lead of affairs, were without reputation, without political experience or information, the mere hacks of a party, possessing none of the qualities of head or heart that constitute the statesman, filled at the same time with all the narrow conceptions and the intolerance of political bigotry. The reputation of not one has survived the age in which he lived. The world is none the wiser for what they have said or done. Their names, with all their acts, have gone down to oblivion. Such men require a head to think for them; without knowledge, or independence of character, they needed a leader to guide and to instruct them in their duty. Coming into office under the auspices of Mr. Jefferson, his opinion was law to their understanding, his will the harmonizing agent to all their actions. The true character of the representative office, and the delicate relationship existing between that and the Executive, was beyond their conception; and they made a boast and a virtue of their unbounded confidence in the source of all power and patronage. In the hands of a virtuous President, these men were the confiding representatives without question to approve his measures; in the hands of a corrupt and ambitious aspirant, they would have been the subtle tools to enregister his edicts of usurpation or oppression. Fortunately for the country, Mr. Jefferson was a pure patriot and an honest man ; he seemed to have no other wish but the good of his country. And, perhaps, it was a consciousness of this fact that made his followers place such implicit reliance on the propriety and the wisdom of whatever he did. What is blind fidelity to the leader of an opposition, will soon be converted into corrupt adulation to the bountiful dispenser of all honors and rewards. An honest coincidence of opinion will be the source of allegiance in the one case ; but a base affinity for the loaves and fishes will be the means of cohesion in the other. Corruption follows power ; and the rapacious and the profligate, like sharks in the sea, are sure to swim in the wake of the rich freighted argosy of state.

The proceedings of Congress, in regard to our foreign relations, furnish a fruitful commentary on the facility with which men will surrender their opinions and their consciences into the keeping of a popular leader; and the readiness with which bodies of men, in a corporate capacity, will do an act that would disgrace an individual of common respectability. As to these foreign affairs, so complicated and so critical, the President had no plan to propose. On this subject, above all others, he had a right to give a direction to the acts of the legislature ; the treaty-making power belonged to him and to the Senate. He did not comply with the Constitution; he informed them of the facts in his possession, but did not recommend what should be done. He had no well-digested plan, on which he was willing to stake his reputation as a statesman ; but he stimulated the legislature, by an expression of his secret wishes, to do those things which he was not willing to assume the responsibility of recommending. This was certainly degrading the representative body to a menial purpose. But they were wholly unconscious of the part they were made to act; and when the proud and independent spirit of their leader rose in rebellion, they sought to hunt him down like some wild beast that had broken into the quiet close of a browsing herd. But in justice to these men, it must be conceded, that it was not so much the acts of Mr. Randolph on the Spanish question that offended them, as the bitter and sarcastic words used by him on all occasions towards some of those who professed to belong to the same party, and claimed to be his political friends. It is true. he did not mince his words, and in the heat of debate, he spoke the plain truth in strongest terms. There was no diplomatic ambiguity about him;

and often his blunt directness of expression gave offence where it was not intended. But possessing, as he did, a keen insight into the motives of men; having a high sense of the dignity and purity of the representative character, and a strong disgust for selfishness and grovelling meanness in those who should be patterns of truth and nobleness, he was unsparing in his denunciations of men who, under the guise of republicanism, had crept into official places for no other purpose but to rob the treasury. And it must be confessed that there were not a few of this class to be found in all the departments of government. The Yazoo speculation, Proteus-like, had assumed every shape by which it could glide into the councils of the nation, and find favor in the eyes of the people; it was the dry-rot of the body politic, that secretly consumed the very joints of its massive timbers. A member of the President's cabinet, as we already know, was the Hercules on whose shoulders was upreared this vast fabric of speculation; the boundless patronage of his office was prostituted to his purposes; and he insolently boasted of the means that he used and the triumph he anticipated over the public virtue. There were many post-office contractors in the House of Representatives; the evil had grown to such an extent that Randolph moved an amendment to the Constitution, prohibiting all contractors from holding a seat on the floor of Congress. "I have said, and I repeat it," said Mr. Randolph, "that the aspect in which this thing presents itself, would alone determine me to resist it. (The Yazoo petitioners.) In one of the petitioners I behold an executive officer, who receives and distributes a yearly revenue of three hundred thousand dollars, yielding scarcely any net profit to the government—a patronage limited only by the extent of our country. Is this right? Is it even decent? Shall political power be made the engine of private interest? Shall such a suspicion tarnish your proceedings? How would you receive a petition from a President of the United States, if such a case can be supposed possible? Sir, I wish to see the same purity pervading every subordinate branch of administration, which I am persuaded exists in its great departments. Shall persons holding appointments under the great and good man who presides over our counsels, draw on the rich fund of his well-earned reputation, to eke out their flimsy and scanty pretensions? Is the relation in which they stand to him to be made the cloak and cover of their dark designs? To the gentleman from New-York, who takes fire at every insinuation against his friend, I have only to observe on this subject, that what I dare say, I dare to justify. To the House I will relate an incident how far I have lightly conceived or expressed an opinion to the prejudice of any man. I owe an apology to my informant for making public what he certainly did not authorize me to reveal. There is no reparation which can be offered by one gentleman and accepted by another that I shall not be ready to make him, but I feel myself already justified to him, since he sees the circumstances under which I act. A few evenings since a profitable contract for carrying the mail was offered to a friend of mine, who is a member of this House. You must know, sir, the person so often alluded to, maintains a jackal; fed not, as you would suppose, upon the offal of contract, but with the fairest pieces in the shambles; and at night, when honest men are abed, does this obscene animal prowl through the streets of this vast and desolate city, seeking whom he may tamper with. Well, sir, when this worthy plenipotentiary had made his proposal in due form, the independent man to whom it was addressed, saw at once its drift. 'Tell your principal,' said he, 'that I will take his contract, but I shall vote against the Yazoo claim, notwithstanding.' Next day he was told that there had been some misunderstanding of the business, that he could not have the contract, as it was previously bespoken by another.

"Sir, I well recollect, when first I had the honor of a seat in this House, we were then members of a small minority—a poor forlorn hope—that this very petitioner appeared at Philadelphia on behalf of another great land company on Lake Erie. He then told us, as an inducement to vote for the Connecticut reserve (as it was called), that if that measure failed, it would ruin the republicans and the cause in that State. You, sir, cannot have forgotten the reply he received: 'That we did not understand the republicanism that was to be paid for; that we feared it was not of the right sort, but spurious.' And having maintained our principles through the ordeal of that day, shall we now abandon them to act with the men and upon the measures which we then abjured? Shall we now condescend to means which we disdained to use in the most desperate crisis of our political fortunes? This is indeed the age of monstrous coalitions; and this corruption has the qualities of connecting the most inveterate enemies, personal as well as political. It has united in close concert those, of whom it has been said, not in the figurative language of prophecy, but in the sober narrative of history, 'I have bruised thy head and thou hast bruised my heel.' Such is the description of persons who would present to the President of the United States an act, to which, when he puts his hand, he signs a libel on his whole political life. But he will never tarnish the unsullied lustre of his fame; he will never sanction the monstrous position (for such it is, dress it up as you will), that a legislator may sell his vote, and a right which cannot be divested will pass under such sale. Establish this doctrine, and there is an end of representative government; from that moment republicanism receives its death-blow.

"The feeble cry of Virginian influence and ambitious leaders, is attempted to be raised. If such insinuations were worthy of a reply, I might appeal to you, Mr. Speaker, for the fact, that no man in this House (yourself perhaps excepted) is oftener in a minority than I am. If by a leader be meant one who speaks his opinion frankly and boldly—who claims something of that independence, of which the gentleman from New-York so loudly vaunts—who will not connive at public robbery, be the robbers who they may,—then the imputation may be just; such is the nature of my ambition: but in the common acceptation of words, nothing can be more false. In the coarse but strong language of the proverb, ''tis the still sow that sucks the draff.'

"No, sir, we are not the leaders. *There* they sit! and well they know it, forcing down our throats the most obnoxious measures. Gentlemen may be silent, but they shall be dragged into public view. If they direct our public counsels, at least let them answer for the result. We will not be responsible for their measures. If we do not hold the reins, we will not be accountable for the accidents which may befall the carriage.

"But, sir, I am a denunciator! Of whom? Of the gentlemen on my left? Not at all; but of those men and their principles whom the people themselves have denounced; on whom they have burnt their indelible curse, deep and lasting as the lightning from heaven.

"Mr. Speaker, I had hoped that we should not be content to live upon the principal of our popularity, that we should go on to deserve the public confidence, and the disapprobation of the gentleman over the way; but if every thing is to be reversed—if official influence is to become the handmaid of private interest—if the old system is to be revived with the old men, or any that can be picked up,—I may deplore the defection, but never will cease to stigmatize it. Never shall I hesitate between any minority, far less that in which I find myself, and such a majority as is opposed to us. I took my degrees, sir, in this House in a minority, much smaller, indeed, but of the same stamp: a minority, whose very act bore the test of rigorous principle, and with them to the last I will exclaim, *Fiat justitia ruat cœlum.*"

It is too plainly to be perceived, that a man of this bold, fearless, and independent character, was not to be tolerated by those who, in their connection with the government, had far other objects in view than pure principle or patriotism; or even by those honest plodding men, whose blundering mediocrity was awed and overshadowed by his superior genius. He must be put down; the *fiat*, we know, had already gone forth. Whole States had been traversed last summer to organize an opposition to him; he must be silenced, or driven into the ranks of the federalists, and then nobody will believe what he says. The plot was now ripe for execution: like Cæsar, he was to fall on the floor of the Senate by the hands of his treacherous friends. The evening of the 21st of April, on the final adjournment of the House, was selected as the time—that parting hour, usually given up to hilarity, to friendship, and an oblivious forgetfulness of all past animosities, was chosen as the fit occasion to stab to the heart one who should have been their pride and their ornament—one, whose only crime was, not that of having conspired against the liberties of his country, but that of having spoken the truth, and maintained right. Alas! for the virtue and the liberties of mankind. This has most usually been the crime they have ignorantly pursued and punished. Corruption opens a path where truth finds an impassable barrier.

As the shades of night were gathering over the legislative hall, while the dim light of the taper served only to make darkness visible, the conspirators, each with his part well conned and prepared, commenced the assault on their unsuspecting victim, who sat as a confiding friend in their midst.

Mr. William Findley, a member from Pennsylvania, rose and ad-

dressed the House, without provocation, in a strain of gross and inde
cent personal abuse of Mr. Randolph, charging him with having
designs to pull down the present administration.   It was plainly to
be perceived, from the language and manner of Findley, that he was
at this time very much intoxicated with strong drink; and many of
the members then present declared the same opinion.   Mr. Findley
was so outrageously indecent in his language, that he was repeatedly
called to order; but, without regarding the call, he continued to
speak in the same strain, until the House was thrown into a state of
confusion, perhaps never before witnessed.

As soon as Findley sat down, John Randolph rose, and without
taking particular notice of the conduct of the unfortunate old man,
observed, in a manner the most mild, dignified and conciliatory, that
" he had hoped, however we might have differed in opinion on the various subjects discussed this session, we should, on the eve of separation, have forgiven and forgotten any asperities and political animosities that had occurred during the session; and that we should have
parted like men and friends.   He had hoped the harmony of that
House would not have been disturbed in the last moments of the session, either by those who had been habitual declaimers, or by those
who had *kept the noiseless tenor of their way;* that contumely and
personal hatred would have been banished from these walls, and that
we should at least have separated in good humor."   These remarks
produced a gleam of pleasure on the countenance of almost every person present.   The language he used and the sentiments he expressed
were so mild and conciliatory, that Mr. Randolph's friends were particularly delighted.   Although there was nothing in his language or
manner that would justify in the smallest degree an idea that he intended to make any particular or personal allusion, yet the attention
of every member then present was immediately directed to Mr.
Thomas Mann Randolph, the President's *son-in-law,* who, under the
impression that John Randolph had made some allusion to him
(which no person present but himself could have supposed), rose, and
in a manner indicative of rage and defiance, vociferated:

" Mr. Speaker, I rise to reply to the gentleman from Virginia.   I
will not pretend to vie with him in point of talent or of eloquence:
.in these he is far, very far, my superior.   This is not the first time
that gentleman has availed himself of the sanction and the presence

of this assembly, to apply his personal allusions to me, and to make use of language and conduct here, which he would not do out of this House.

" But, sir, I will tell that gentleman, that however he may be my superior in talents and eloquence, in patriotism I am his superior; yes, sir, his superior. Last year, sir, that gentleman commenced florist, and dealt in flowers and gardening; I saw him with his spade and pitchfork, and rake and manure, cultivating his flower-garden. This, sir, was on the *Yazoo question;* and then I perceived the gentleman launch forth to sea, without compass or rudder, his masts broken, his sails tattered and torn, and his vessel in a leaky condition; and, when I saw that, sir, I thought it high time to quit him, and look out for the land. The gentleman can talk and boast of the arguments of lead, and powder, and steel; with these arguments, sir, I am as expert as himself, and as willing as he may be to use them."

Mr. Thomas Mann Randolph possessed as quick and as fiery a temper as his kinsman; but it is impossible to conceive any motive for the anger, rage, and threatening denunciation exhibited on this occasion, unless it was premeditated, and the deliberate part of a concerted scheme to immolate John Randolph on the altar of party intolerance, for having dared to differ from them as to what they chose to assume and hold forth as the wishes of the Executive. This gentleman had taken no part in the previous debate, and it is impossible that any allusion could have been made to him. As he progressed, towering in rage, astonishment and regret were exhibited in the looks and expressions of the members. This speech had the most strange and alarming effect. The atmosphere seemed to be surcharged with electric fire, and another spark would blow it into a flame.

Coming from the quarter it did, and under existing circumstances, this denunciation excited in the minds of a great part of those present, sentiments of the most serious nature. Where this thing might end, they could not conjecture, but felt the most anxious apprehension. That Randolph was to be denounced on this occasion by all the self-anointed priests of the true faith, and to be cast out of the synagogue, cannot be questioned. The moment Thomas Mann took his seat, he was followed by James Sloan, of New Jersey, who *read* a speech of about two sheets, closely written, and then delivered it over into the hands of the printer, who was present to receive it, and to publish it. Randolph had not been sparing in his ridicule of the crude conceptions of this man, put forth in a series of resolutions on the great and grave questions about which the administration itself had no settled opinion. He called the nostrums of this man *"Sloan's mint-drops."* Now was the time for revenge—when the whole pack was in full cry, and the noble stag at bay, he could slyly thrust his fangs into his side with impunity. But Randolph did not wait to hear this well-studied lecture, which for false assertions, low scurrility, and personal abuse, cannot be surpassed. If he heard it at all, it fell senseless on his ears. He was after other game. A few minutes after T. M. Randolph closed his remarks, John Randolph left his seat, and desired Mr. Garnett to make a formal application to know whether the remarks that had fallen from that gentleman were addressed to him, and unless he disavowed any such intention, to demand a meeting. Mr. Garnett seemed deeply concerned at this request, and endeavored to dissuade his friend from the step. Randolph replied, that his resolution was irrevocably taken; that, perhaps, on the whole, he had cause to be obliged to Mr. Thomas Mann Randolph; that he had long been a target for every worthless scoundrel in that House to aim his shafts at; and that Mr. T. M. Randolph, by this unprovoked and studied outrage, had given him an opportunity to answer them all, in the person of an adversary who would not disgrace his contest, and under circumstances in which no possible blame could attach to him. Mr. T. M. Randolph replied to Mr. Garnett, that unless he had supposed some of Mr. John Randolph's expressions pointed particularly at him, he should have thought himself highly culpable in saying what he had; but believing that they were intended for him, he felt himself called upon to say something.

Having acknowledged that his observations were levelled at Mr. John Randolph, he was told that that gentleman expected to meet him. He replied that he was ready to do so; but that if Mr. John Randolph would only say that he meant no allusion to him, there was no apology which a man of honor could or ought to make, which he would not be ready to offer. When Mr. Garnett delivered this message, Mr. John Randolph observed 'that the course which Mr. T. M. Randolph had chosen to pursue precluded any sort of declaration or acknowledgment on his part; that Mr. T. M. R. must make reparation commensurate with the injury aimed at his feelings, or meet him, and give him satisfaction. Mr. Garnett immediately apprised the gentleman of these conditions, and requested that he would choose some friend with whom he might have farther conversation on the subject. Mr. Coles was called in; after a short consultation aside with his friend, he rejoined Mr. Garnett, and said: All that Mr. T. M. R. desired was an assurance that none of Mr. J. R.'s remarks were intended for him, and that he would be willing (in that case) to make any apology a man of honor could offer. Mr. Garnett replied, that there was no doubt on his mind, or, he believed, of any other spectator, that Mr. T. M. R. had entirely misconceived Mr. J. R.'s expressions; but that, after what had passed, Mr. J. R. would make no statement whatever; and if Mr. T. M. R. could not reconcile it to himself to make a suitable apology, Mr. J. R. would expect Mr. T. M. R. to meet him either that night (which he preferred) or in the morning. Mr. Coles said he was too much engaged in the public business at that time to see his friend, but would do it as soon as he could, and let Mr. Garnett know the result. Mr. Garnett returned with this statement to Mr. John Randolph, who was in a remote room of the Capitol, and then took his seat in the House. In a few minutes afterwards, Mr. Thomas Mann Randolph rose in his place, and said that he had been assured, by several of those who sat near him, that he had acted in what he had before said under a misapprehension of Mr. John Randolph's remarks, which none of them understood as having been intended for him; that under this misapprehension he had acted; it was the sole cause of his saying what he had said; and that he was then persuaded by the assurance of his friends of his mistake. He regretted very much what he had said, for he had no disposition to wound any gentleman's feelings who did not intend to wound his.

Mr. Garnett immediately went to Mr. John Randolph, and stated that Mr. T. M. R. had made such an apology in the House as Mr. Garnett conceived, and as every member said who mentioned the subject in his hearing (which several did) was proper for Mr. T. M. R. to make and for Mr. J. R. to receive.

Mr. Randolph then requested his friend to say to Mr. Coles that he received the apology of Mr. T. M. Randolph, and had no further commands for that gentleman, which Mr. Garnett did just as the House was breaking up; and thus the business terminated.

CHAPTER XXXII.

AARON BURR.

MISFORTUNES, 'tis said, come not alone; it proved so with Mr. Randolph on this occasion. In his retirement at Bizarre, after the stormy session just passed, and other occurrences of a domestic nature, his reflections could not have been of the most pleasant kind. However conscious of rectitude, the prospect before him must have been cheerless indeed. For four years he had been the popular leader of a triumphant party, who were successfully carrying into operation those great measures of reform that would bring back the Federal Government to the few simple and general subjects of legislation for which alone it was designed. Never had a young man risen so rapidly or so high in the public estimation. He was the idol of his party; his eloquence and his practical wisdom were extolled on every hand; and it seemed that there was no station or honor in the gift of the people that he was not destined to attain. But now the scene was changed. For having ventured to suggest a plan of action different from that which *seemed* to be favored by the Executive, he was denounced by his old friends, his motives calumniated, and he was charged with a design of pulling down the present administration. How bitter must have been his feelings, at the reflection that the highest stretch of patriotism, which could cause a sacrifice of all the bright prospects before him for the sake of doing his duty, should meet with such a reward. But it has always been so. In popular governments, the intolerant spirit of a triumphant majority will allow no deviation from that standard of orthodoxy which it has set up for itself. Freedom of opinion is professed, but you exercise it at the peril of being banished from the society of those who hold the reins and prescribe the course that ought to be pursued. There are so many interested in degrading a popular and leading man in a political party, that it is almost impossible for him ever to retrieve the first false step. It matters not how pure his motives, or how far it may be from his intention to separate from his party friends, yet there are always enough, from interested motives, to take advantage of the slightest deviation from the standard of the majority, to denounce him as a deserter, and to drive him into the opposition. Politicians, generally, are a heartless and selfish race of men. There are many honorable exceptions; but for the most part, their own aggrandizement is the end of their patriotism; and they always look with secret satisfaction on the disappointment or the fall of one whose superior talents overshadowed their own self-importance, or whose stern virtues and integrity stood in the way of the accomplishment of their selfish ends.

Mr. Randolph never deviated from those principles he professed, while in a minority; his party, in many instances, had departed from them; he undertook the ungracious task of holding up to view their own dereliction. Sovereign majorities, as well as sovereign princes, do not like to hear their own infallibility brought in question—especially will they not tolerate it in one who is a subject of their power. Mr. Randolph had no faith in the Cabinet, while he retained the utmost confidence in the Chief Magistrate. He knew that corruption had crept into the legislature, through the Post Office department and the Yazoo speculation, and that, as a body, they had surrendered their independence into the hands of the Executive. His great crime was that of maintaining the independence of the legislature, as a co-ordinate department of government. Let posterity judge how far he should be condemned for such an offence.

During the excited and sleepless hours of the past session, Mr. Randolph was assailed by his old hereditary disease, in its most aggravated form—he was prostrate on his bed for many weeks, racked with the most excruciating torture. With repeated accumulation of mental distress, and even of mental agony, caused by domestic occurrences, the diseases of the body seemed to keep pace with them, and to produce a degree of suffering such as no mortal man ever endured before. With heroic fortitude, he suppressed his feelings, and the world, while they condemned his outbursts of passion, never knew the real cause of his eccentricities. With a pride and a haughty reserve rarely equalled, he shut himself up from common observation, and was content to be the subject of misrepresentation and of malicious calumny, without condescending to explanation or reply. To a few only did he unbosom himself, and expose the wounds of body and of soul, which he carried, with increased aggravation, to the grave.

Hereafter, the reader will have an opportunity of reading his confessions, poured into the bosom of his most intimate friend, and to weep over the many sufferings he endured, in what he chose to call his "most unprosperous life."

But there was one occurrence, which took place in the month of March, that affected Mr. Randolph more than all things else. The reader is already aware of the great attachment he had formed, many years ago, to a young lady of remarkable beauty, virtues, and accomplishments—*one I loved more than my own soul, or the God that made it.* Many untoward events had prevented their union, and made it impossible—yet he vainly cherished the hope that their love, sublimated into a pure, Platonic affection, might last to the end of life—idle expectation, that no other human being could have indulged. There was no reason in the indulgence of such a wish ; but love is blind, tyrannical, and has no reason. The lady thought proper to unite her fortunes with one in whose society she might hope to live a more happy life, than in that of her present most devoted but unfortunate lover. This event, which took place in the midst of the excited debates of Congress, and at a moment when his friends were deserting him on every hand, struck deep into the heart of Mr. Randolph—he never recovered from it—it had a visible influence on the whole of his after life. His love, now purified of all earthly desire, became a genuine worship—the image of the beloved object, mirrored in the distance, hovered over his path, like some angelic being, whose celestial smiles shed benignest influence on his heart, where all else had grown cold and desolate. Long years afterwards, when the body was locked in the fitful embraces of a feverish sleep, and the soul wandering in dreams, that once loved name has been heard to escape from his lips, in a tone that evinced how deeply the love of the being who bore it had been engraven on the inmost sanctuary of his heart. But why do we call up these things ? Reader ! there was a tragedy in the life of this man, more thrilling than romance. But this is a subject not for us to deal with ; we promised not to touch it more ; let it go down to the oblivion of the grave, and there sleep with those who, in life, endured its agonies. We ask pardon for having glanced at it here, and for the last time, because it is impossible to form a correct estimate of the man, without some knowledge of this occurrence, which constituted one of the most important events of his life. Let the skeptical look into his own heart, and see whether he is capable of elevating his affections above a mere sensual appetite. If not, then he is no fit judge of that man, whose exalted passion, rising above all earthly desire, knows no other bounds but the infinite longing of an immortal soul.

Let us now proceed with our narrative.

Notwithstanding the harsh and unfriendly manner in which he had been treated, Mr. Randolph returned to Washington in December, with every disposition to harmonize and co-operate with the republican party. His difference from them last session, was on a question of mere expediency—the propriety of which time alone could prove. Unless they intended to abandon, in the conduct of affairs, all the principles they professed while in a minority, it was impossible for him to co-operate with any other body of men. However much he might be irritated in his feelings towards certain individuals, he did not allow that circumstance so far to influence his judgment as to cause him to vote for or against a measure merely to be in opposition to them. Accordingly we find him, on most occasions, working in harmony with the friends of the administration; and there seems to have been a good feeling restored between him and some of the leading members. It is true, there was no important question on which there was likely to be a diversity of sentiment. The non-importation law, by the terms of its enactment, was not to go into operation till the last of November; and now that the time had arrived, it was proposed, on the part of its friends, to postpone it to a still later period. It was alleged that the British commissioners desired not a repeal, but a postponement merely, while negotiations were pending between the two countries. Of course Mr. Randolph readily united with them in this measure; and it is not surprising that he took occasion to intimate that, in his judgment, time had proved the impolicy and inefficiency of the original enactment. But the only question of any importance to which their attention was called, during the last session of the *ninth* Congress, was the conspiracy of Aaron Burr. After his bitter disappointments, both on the national theatre and in New-York, his adopted State—after the sudden and irretrievable fall of this ambitious man, and when the cold eye of neglect had chilled, like a frost, the last spark of patriotism in the breast of this legalized murderer, he had gone into the great Mississippi Valley, in search of some adventure adequate to his genius and his ambition. Here, indeed, was a vast field for enterprise—abundant material for any undertaking that might require perseverance, privation, and heroic daring—there was also a little discontent in the popular mind, in some parts of the West, which might have inspired a less sanguine man than Aaron Burr with hopes of tampering with their patriotism.

Soon rumors came that this man was planning and organizing some vast expedition, the precise object of which was the subject only of conjecture. Whether it was his design to make war on the Spanish province of Mexico, or whether, in co-operation with Spain, he was aiding her in the long cherished scheme of separating the western country from the United States, none could tell; but all agreed that the genius and the resources of the chief director of the enterprise were adequate to any desperate adventure, whether of foreign aggression or domestic treason.

The Executive was soon apprised of the state of things, and were endeavoring to get all the information they could in regard to the matter. But the newspapers were so full of rumors and statements, implicating the Spanish Government as the prime mover of this conspiracy, that Mr. Randolph, after having waited five or six weeks for official intelligence, at length moved a resolution to call on the President for information. We give his speech entire on this occasion, as it shows his views of the Spanish question twelve months after his separation from the administration on that subject.

" In the President's Message," said Mr. Randolph, " at the commencement of the session, he announced to us as follows :

"' Having received information, that in another part of the United States a great number of private individuals were combining together, arming and organizing themselves, contrary to law, to carry on a military expedition against the territories of Spain, I thought it necessary, by proclamation, as well as by special orders, to take measures for preventing and suppressing this enterprise, for seizing the vessels, arms, and other means provided for it, and for arresting and bringing to justice its authors and abettors.'

" So long," said Mr. Randolph, " as the illegal movements of these persons were supposed to be directed against a foreign nation, although the interest of the United States, and their honor too, required that prompt and decisive measures should be taken for suppressing their designs, yet I believe there is no gentleman in this House but will agree with me in the opinion that the United States, and this House in particular, could not feel so deep and lively an interest against a conspiracy of that kind as against one for the subversion of the Union, and perhaps of the liberties of those who compose it. I have waited with anxious solicitude for some information in relation to this subject, that might be depended upon—for some official information. I contented myself for a long time with the belief, inasmuch as no information had been given to the House, that there were imperious reasons connected with the public welfare which forbade a disclosure; but the aspect which affairs have taken on the Mississippi is such, that I can no longer reconcile it to my sense of duty, as the independent representative of an independent people, to rest satisfied in that state of supineness and apathy in which the House has been satisfied to remain for the six or seven weeks past. Sir, from the information I have been able to collect—and it is such that I am obliged to place great if not implicit reliance on it—it does appear to me, that if the government of Spain is in any wise connected in these measures, it is concerned not as the defendant, but as the plaintiff—as the aggressing party, and not as the party on whom the aggression is made. So long as I was induced to believe, that by withholding correct information from the Legislature the substantial interests of the nation would be more essentially subserved than by laying it before them, so long, though not without reluctance, I acquiesced in its being withheld. But from the hostile appearances on the Mississippi, it seems to me that the state of things is such as requires the most prompt and efficacious measures for securing the Union. The bubble is said to have burst, and there no longer remains any reason why the information in the possession of the Executive ought to be withheld. But to guard against all possible objection, I have endeavored so to frame the motion as to do away with any objection arising from this consideration. It does appear—from the newspapers it is true, but under a much higher sanction than is generally attached to information received through such a channel—it does appear in evidence, under the sanction of an examination before the legislature of Kentucky, that ever since the peace of 1783, Spain has incessantly labored to detach the western people from the Union; that subsequently to the peace of San Lorenzo she has carried on intrigues, and in the most faithless manner withheld acceding to its stipulations, in order to excite a spirit in the western country subversive of the Union; that she subsequently made a proposition of the most flagitious kind to several leading characters in Kentucky, and as I believe elsewhere. It seems, indeed, that she has never lost sight of this object; and I believe she never will lose sight of it so long as she shall find materials to work upon, or a shadow of hope that she will succeed. It appears to me that she has found those materials; that they are of the most dangerous nature; that they are now in operation; and that, perhaps, at this moment, while I am addressing you, at least for a time, the fate of the Western country may have been decided.

"Sir, this subject offers strong arguments, in addition to the numerous reasons offered at the present session of Congress, to justify the policy avowed by certain gentlemen during the last session, so highly condemned; and if I am correctly informed, the other branch of the Legislature are now acting on that policy so condemned and despised.

"We have had a bill before us authorizing the President to accept volunteers. A member of the committee with whom this bill originated, and with whom I have the pleasure of concurring, intimately connected and domesticated with the Secretary of War, did make a proposition before that committee, substantially the same with that rejected the last session—to augment the military forces to meet the pressing exigencies of the times; and which I presume must have had the sanction of that officer. Is there a man in this House who at this day doubts, that if the Government—I mean the Executive and Legislature—had taken a manly and decisive attitude towards Spain, and instead of pen, ink, and paper, had given men and arms—is there a man who disbelieves that not only Spain would have been overawed, but that those domestic traitors also would have been intimidated and overawed, whose plans threaten to be so dangerous? Would any man have dreamed of descending the Mississippi at the head of an unprincipled banditti, if New Orleans had been fortified, and strong fortifications erected in its neighborhood? What did we then hear? Money! dollars and cents! Is there not now every reason to believe, especially when we consider the superintendence under which the expenses are incurred, that the saving of the campaign on the Sabine, and the saving of the costly measures taken by the commander-in-chief on his own responsibility, would have been equal to the expense of raising and maintaining for one year the additional forces proposed at the last session to be raised. There can be no doubt, but that on the principle of economy, without taking into view the effect on the Union, the United States would have been gainers. A spectator, not in the habit of reading our public prints, or of conversing with individuals out of doors, but who should draw his ideas of the situation of the country from the proceedings of this House during the present session, would be led to infer that there never existed in any nation a greater degree of peace, tranquillity, or union, at home or abroad, than in the United States at this time; and yet, what is the fact? That the United States are not only threatened with external war, but with conspiracies and treasons, the more alarming from their not being defined. And yet we sit, and adjourn; adjourn, and sit; take things as schoolboys, do as we are bid, and ask no questions. I cannot reconcile this line of conduct to my ideas of the duty of a member on this floor. Yes, the youngest member of the federal family has been found to be the first to ward off the impending danger, while the eldest members are sleeping, snoring, and dozing over their liberties at home.

Under this view of the subject, I beg leave to offer the following resolution:

"Resolved—That the President of the United States be and he is hereby requested to lay before this House any information in possession of the Executive, except such as he may deem the public welfare to require not to be disclosed, touching any illegal combination of private individuals against the peace and safety of the Union, or any military expedition planned by such individuals against the territories of any power in amity with the United States; together with the measures which the Executive has pursued and *proposes to take* for suppressing or defeating the same."

The resolution was carried by a large majority. As more authentic news came of the designs and actual movements of the conspirators, the country became still more alarmed; every one of discernment saw the danger of this enterprise; they knew the combustible materials that artful intriguer had to work upon, and could readily perceive how he might take advantage of the unfriendly relations existing between the United States and Spain, and by the secret aid, if not the open co-operation of that discontented power, effect a dismemberment of the Union.

The Senate, in their alarm, went so far as to suspend the " Habeas Corpus Act," which is never resorted to except in extreme cases of danger to the peace and integrity of the country. This act of suspension was arrested in the House. Mr. Randolph was most active and efficient in his opposition : he denounced it as unnecessary, oppressive, and tyrannical. Most fortunately it was rejected by the House, and can never be set up as a precedent.

Aaron Burr, it is well known, was arrested in Alabama, and brought to trial in Virginia, on the ground that he had levied his forces and commenced his treasonable acts within the borders of that State. The trial took place in the city of Richmond, in the month of May, 1807 ; it excited a great deal of interest, and brought together many of the most distinguished men of the Union. John Randolph was foreman of the grand jury that brought in a true bill against Aaron Burr of high treason against his country. It is not our purpose to go into the details of this trial, or the incidents of the conspiracy : they belong to the general historian, and must form an interesting and important chapter in the history of those critical and eventful times.

During his sojourn in Richmond on this occasion, Mr. Randolph formed many new and valuable acquaintances. Mr. Wirt was at this time collecting materials for his Life of Patrick Henry. He was conversing one day on that subject in a company of gentlemen, when Mr. Tazewell, who was present, said to him : " Mr. Wirt, you should, by all means, see John Randolph on that subject ; he knows more of Patrick Henry than any other man now living." Mr. Wirt confessed that he was not personally acquainted with that gentleman. The difficulty was, how to bring them together ; for Tazewell said it would not do to make a formal introduction, and say, " This is Mr. Wirt, sir, who is desirous of obtaining from you some materials for his Life of Henry. In that case Randolph would not open his lips. However," said he, " I will contrive a meeting." In a few days Mr. Wirt was invited to Tazewell's room, where he found Randolph and other gentlemen assembled. Very soon, in the course of conversa tion, as if by accident, the name of Patrick Henry was mentioned. Randolph immediately caught up the theme, and delighted the company with a graphic account of his personal appearance, his habits, and his eloquence. He frequently rose from his seat, and repeated passages from the speeches, and imitated the peculiar style and fervid manner of the renowned orator. Wirt was so much pleased, that when he retired he wrote a note to Mr. Randolph, thanking him for the rich treat he had given him, and begging that he would put down in writing the substance of what he had said. Randolph now saw the trick that was played upon him. He immediately went to his friend Tazewell, and chided him soundly for having made an exhibition of him in that way. Tazewell turned it off as a pleasant joke; nevertheless, the biographer of Patrick Henry never got from that quarter any additional materials for the subject of his memoir. It was on this occasion also that Mr. Randolph first made the acquaintance of Dr. John Brockenbrough, who from that time to the day of his death was the most intimate friend of his bosom—the friend to whom he daily unfolded without reserve or fear of exposure the inmost thoughts and feelings of his heart. The doctor was a member of the grand jury, and the acquaintance commenced in a way peculiar to John Randolph. "I did not seek his acquaintance," says the doctor, "because it had been impressed on my mind that he was a man of a wayward and irritable temper; but as he knew that I had been a school-fellow of his brothers, Richard and Theodoric (while he was in Bermuda for the benefit of his health) he very courteously made advances to me to converse about his brothers, to whom he had been much devoted, and ever afterwards I found him a steady and confiding friend. He frequently passed much of his time at my house, and was the most agreeable and interesting inmate you can imagine. No little personal attention was ever lost on him, and he rendered himself peculiarly a favorite with my wife by his conversation on belles-lettres, in which he was so well versed; and he read (in which he excelled) to her very many of the choice passages of Milton and Shakspeare. Mr. Randolph also had another remarkable quality, irritable and sensitive as he was; *when alone* with a friend he would not only bear with patience, but would invite a full expression of his friend's opinion on his conduct, or acts and sentiments, on any subject, either private or public."

CHAPTER XXXIII.

EMBARGO—THE ILIAD OF ALL OUR WOES.

By Jay's treaty of 1794, our difficulties with Great Britain, though not settled, were quieted for the time being; while in consequence of the same cause we were nearly involved in an open rupture with France.

The change of administration and the convention with France in 1800 restored a more friendly feeling between the two republics—and the purchase of Louisiana in 1803 was accomplished with more ease than Mr. Jefferson himself could have expected. Our commerce for the first four years of the new administration was exceedingly prosperous—and the management of our domestic affairs was conducted on strictly republican principles. Had peace continued in Europe during the remainder of his term, Mr. Jefferson's would have been a most brilliant and successful career. But after the rupture of the treaty of Amiens and the renewal of hostilities between the great belligerent powers, an unfavorable change took place in our foreign relations.

By a series of extraordinary victories, Great Britain had annihilated the combined fleets of France, Spain and Holland, and made herself undisputed mistress of the sea. The trade between these countries and their colonies, their navies being destroyed, was now for the first time opened to foreign bottoms. The United States were the only people that could avail themselves of this advantage. Their commercial marine in consequence was greatly enlarged, and commerce itself was more than ever expanded and prosperous.

But England soon perceived that so long as this kind of traffic was permitted she would derive no advantage from her naval victories. She commenced a series of measures to put an end to it.

Bonaparte, in the mean time, having elevated himself to the imperial throne of France, had conquered nearly all Europe, driven the Russian bear back into his polar regions, and was now seriously contemplating the destruction of England as the only barrier in the way of universal conquest. But sad experience had taught him that the only way in which he could reach that sea-girt empire was through her manufactures and commerce. His restrictive system on the continent was designed to sap and undermine these two sources of English wealth and power. In their gigantic efforts to destroy each other, these great belligerents paid no respect to neutral rights or to the laws of nations—might became right, and Robin Hood's law of the strongest was the only available rule. Whatever could affect the other injuriously was unhesitatingly adopted without regard to the effect it might have on the rights of neutral parties. They even resolved there should be no neutrals in the contest; and as the United States were the only independent power left, this warfare on their commerce was intended to force them into the controversy on the one side or the other.

The first act of hostility was commenced by Great Britain on the 16th May, 1806: the British government, by an order of the King in council, decreed that all the rivers and ports from Brest to the Elbe (being about a thousand miles of sea-coast) should be considered in a state of blockade. Where a port is actually blockaded by an adequate force, any vessel attempting to enter is liable to be captured by the besieging squadron, and to be condemned as lawful prize. But where no fleet was stationed on the prohibited coast, and the blockade merely consisted in a decree of the government, all vessels laden or sailing for the ports decreed to be in a state of siege, were liable to be captured and condemned wherever found. This was regarded as a gross violation of neutral rights; and on the 21st November, Bonaparte commenced his acts of retaliation. After charging England with disregarding the law of nations and the rights of neutrality, and with declaring places in a state of blockade before which she had not a ship, he declared all the British Isles in a state of blockade, and prohibited all trade and commerce with them. He provided also in the decree (Berlin decree) for the capture and condemnation of English produce and manufactures, and prohibited all neutral ships coming direct from England or the English colonies, or having been there, from entering the ports of France.

By this decree all commerce between England and the continent and between the United States and England was intended to be cut off. Any neutral vessel (and there were none but those belonging to citizens of the United States) sailing for England, or from an English port to the continent, was subject to capture and condemnation. The French minister, in consequence of a remonstrance on the part of the United States, gave it as his opinion, that the decree of blockade would be so qualified by the existing treaty as not to operate on American commerce. Not much respect, however, was paid to this opinion by French cruisers; and in September 1807 the decree was ordered to be fully enforced against all neutrals.

In the mean time a negotiation was going on between the com missioners of England and the United States. On the 30th of December, 1806, a treaty was signed settling amicably, if not satisfactorily, all the difficulties between the two nations. But Bonaparte's Berlin decree having come to their knowledge, the British commissioners, in a note delivered by order of the King, declared to the American commissioners, that if France should execute that decree, and the United States acquiesce in it, the British government would hold themselves discharged from the treaty and issue retaliatory orders against neutral commerce with France. Had the treaty been ratified on that condition, it would have pledged the United States to such a co-operation with Great Britain against France, as must have ended in hostilities with the one and alliance with the other. This was the object of England—but Mr. Jefferson was determined if possible to continue in his position of neutrality. The treaty was received before the adjournment of Congress, the 4th March, 1807; but he boldly suppressed it, and would not even submit it to the Senate for their consideration. He remembered too well the effect of Jay's treaty on the public mind to venture one himself. A total surrender of all her claims by Great Britain at that time would not have been acceptable, because it would have forced the United States into an alliance with England, contrary to the popular sentiment, which was decidedly in favor of the French cause. In times of peace that treaty would have been favorably received, but under existing circumstances, the President had no intention of suffering himself to be *treaty-foundered* as his predecessors had been. Mr. Monroe, the principal negotiator, was much offended at the rejection or rather unceremonious suppression of his treaty; he had hoped to gain much credit by this act of pacification.

In the mean time the affair of the Chesapeake took place, which greatly inflamed the public mind. A British squadron it seems was lying near the mouth of Hampton Roads, in Lynnhaven Bay; several sailors deserted and took refuge on board the American frigate Chesapeake, then in the port of Norfolk, fitting out for sea, the sailors were demanded, but were refused to be given up on the ground that they were American citizens. As the Chesapeake, on her destined voyage, passed out of the Capes, she was followed by a British vessel detached from the squadron for that purpose; so soon as the Chesapeake got out of neutral waters into the ocean, she was fired upon, her hull and rigging were much injured and several persons were killed; she was boarded, the sailors recaptured, and some of them were put to death. This gross outrage, though unauthorized and disavowed by the government, had an unhappy effect on the public mind in the United States. A spirit of revenge seized the people; and although England sent over a special minister to settle the difficulty, a slight punctilio in the forms and etiquette of diplomacy was seized upon as a pretext to prevent any advancements or explanations on the part of the British envoy.

Such was the situation of affairs, when, on the 11th of November, 1807, before the Berlin decree had been enforced against American vessels, and while the government had reason to hope it would not be enforced, Great Britain executed her threat intimated at the signing of the treaty. By an order in council (with a preamble, charging France with a want of respect to the laws of nations and rights of neutrality), it was decreed that all the ports and places of France and her allies, or any other country at war with his majesty, and all other ports and places in Europe from which, although not at war with his majesty, the British flag is excluded, and all ports and places in the colonies belonging to his majesty's enemies, shall from henceforth be subject to the same restrictions, in point of trade and navigation, (with certain exceptions,) as if the same were actually blockaded by his majesty's naval forces, in the most strict and vigorous manner.

By these acts of England and France, professing to be acts of retaliation, and not at all in a spirit of hostility to the United States, the neutral commerce of America was entirely destroyed. Not a vessel could sail to Europe or to England, to the vast colonial regions of North and South America, and the East and West Indies, without being subject to capture and condemnation. The trade of the whole world, in fact, was interdicted, and could not be carried on without the risk of forfeiture. Both belligerents, however, had distinctly intimated that if the United States would side with them, every advantage should be given to their commerce. But this is what they did not intend to do; they did not mean to surrender all the advantages they had hitherto enjoyed from their neutral position, if it could be avoided. To side with England was war with France—with France was war with England. Mr. Jefferson was not prepared for either alternative. What was to be done? Commerce, left thus exposed, must be ground into powder between the upper and nether millstone, and be scattered as chaff before the winds of heaven. The President advised a dignified retirement from the ocean, until the storm should have passed over. For the first time since our difficulties with foreign nations, he took the responsibility of advising a definite course of action. In a secret message to Congress, about the 19th of December, 1807, he recommended that an embargo should be laid on all American vessels. In a few days a bill to that effect was passed into a law: all American vessels were prohibited, under high penalties, from sailing to foreign ports, or from port to port within the United States, without license.

The measure of an embargo was at first advocated by Mr. Randolph. He introduced the resolution, in accordance with the President's message; but the bill which was finally adopted, originated in the Senate; it contained provisions that he could not approve, and he opposed it on its passage. This is given as an instance of Mr. Randolph's fickleness and want of object in his parliamentary course. The debates were conducted in secret—in fact, the bill was hurried through the forms of legislation, with scarcely any debate. We do not know, therefore, what was said on the occasion, and are left to infer the grounds of Mr. Randolph's opposition to the bill, from his general views on the subject of an embargo. He approved of such a step in the beginning, as a war measure. An embargo of sixty or ninety days, collecting and protecting all our resources, followed by a declaration of war, at the end of that period, against that one of the belligerents whose restrictive course manifested the strongest spirit of hostility, would have fulfilled Mr. Randolph's idea of such a measure. But such was not the intention of the friends of the administration, in passing the act now under consideration. It was designed as a measure to be permanent for an indefinite period. France and England were told that it was not conceived in a spirit of hostility to them, but was merely intended as a *municipal regulation*. The truth was, however, and they did not fail to perceive it, that the whole object of withdrawing our commerce from the ocean, was to operate on those two nations. It was intended to starve France and her dependencies, and to break England, unless they would abandon their absurd pretensions over the rights of neutral nations. But when this happy result would take place, it was impossible to tell. For a measure of this kind to come home to the bosom and the business of a great nation, must necessarily take a very long time. Indeed, it was reasonable to suppose that the desired object never could be accomplished in that way. The resources of England and of France were too great and too varied, to be seriously affected by a suspension of even the whole of American commerce. The event proved what, it would seem, a little forethought ought to have anticipated. After the embargo had been in operation for twelve months, those two nations were no nearer being forced into terms than they were at first; while their spirit of hostility was greatly exasperated.

But what effect did the measure have on affairs at home—on the character of our own people? Here, it was disastrous in the extreme. An embargo is the most heroic remedy that can be applied to state diseases. It must soon run its course, and kill or cure in a short time. It is like one holding his breath to rush through flame or mephitic gas: the suspension may be endured for a short time, but the lungs at length must be inflated, even at the hazard of suffocation. Commerce is the breath that fills the lungs of a nation, and a total suspension of it is like taking away vital air from the human system; convulsions or death must soon follow. By the embargo, the farmer, the merchant, the mechanic, the capitalist, the ship-owner, the sailor, and the day-laborer, found themselves suddenly arrested in their daily business. Crops were left to rot in the warehouses; ships in the docks; capital was compelled to seek new channels for investment, while labor was driven to every shift to keep from starvation.

Sailors, seeing the uncertain continuation of this state of things, flocked in great numbers to the British navy. That service which, in former years, they most dreaded, necessity now compelled them to seek with avidity. Smuggling was extensively carried on through the whole extent of our wide-spread borders; the revenue was greatly reduced; and the morals of the people were corrupted by the vast temptations held out to evade the laws. It is difficult to tell on what classes of the community this disastrous measure did not operate. On the planting and shipping interest, perhaps, it was most serious. On the one, it was more immediate, on the other, more permanent, in its evil consequences.

In cities and commercial regions, capital and labor are easily diverted from one employment to another. That which to-day is profitably engaged in commerce, may to-morrow, if an inducement offers, be as readily turned into successful manufactures. Not so with the labor and capital employed in agriculture; here the change must be slow. But with the capital and the *kind* of labor employed in the tobacco and cotton planting of the South, no change, to any perceptible degree, was possible. The Southern people, being wholly agricultural, could live a few years without the sale of their crops; but the Northern people, being mainly dependent on their labor and commerce, could not exist with an embargo of long duration. Hence we find a patient endurance of its evils on the part of the South, while a spirit of insurrection pervaded the people of the North. In this restless condition, much of their capital and labor were permanently directed to manufactures. The bounties offered by a total prohibition of foreign articles, stimulated this branch of business in a remarkable degree; and when the embargo, non-intercourse, and war ceased to operate as a bounty, they have had to be sustained by heavy duties imposed on foreign commerce, at the expense of the planting interest of the South, which is mainly dependent on a foreign market for the sale of its commodities. Every dollar taken from commerce, and invested in manufactures, was turning the current from a friendly into a hostile channel, to that kind of agriculture which was dependent on foreign trade for its prosperity. The immediate effect of the embargo was, to starve New England. Its more permanent consequence has been, to build it up at the expense of the planting interest of the South. New England has now two sources of wealth, in her manufactures and commerce; while the South have still the only one of planting tobacco and cotton on exhausted lands, and with a reduced market for the sale of her commodities.

It was impossible for Mr. Randolph to advocate such a measure. He could not foresee all the evils it might entail on his country; but his practical wisdom, aided by his deep interest in the welfare of his constituents, taught him that no good could come out of an embargo reduced to a system, and made a part of the municipal regulations of the Government. As the first step towards an immediate preparation for war, he could approve the act; but as a scheme destined to act on foreign countries, while it was wasting the resources of Government, and consuming the substance of the people at home, it met his decided disapprobation.

Twelve months had now rolled around, and all parties had become of his opinion. No impression abroad. Nothing but disaster at home. The legislature of Massachusetts pronounced it an unconstitutional act. They were not far from the truth. For a short period, and as a war measure, an embargo would be constitutional; but the embargo acts adopted from time to time by Congress, and persisted in for more than a year, were very far from being clearly constitutional. Massachusetts pronounced them not only unconstitutional, but unjust and oppressive.

In 1799, when Virginia interposed her State authority, and declared the alien and sedition laws unconstitutional, Massachusetts then said, that the Supreme Court was alone competent to pronounce on the constitutionality of a federal law. But she now saw the error and the evil consequences of such a doctrine. The Supreme Court had declared the embargo acts to be constitutional; while a sovereign State, crushed and ruined by the burdens they imposed, saw those enactments in a very different light. Was she to be silent, and bear the evils inflicted by those laws, merely because the courts had pronounced in their favor? By no means. She was one of the sovereign parties who had ordained the Constitution as a common government, endowing it with certain general powers for that purpose; and surely, from the very nature of things, she had a right to say whether this or that law transcended those delegated powers or not.

Whether Massachusetts strictly followed the doctrine of State rights, as laid down by Mason, Jefferson, and Madison, we pretend not to say; but we do say, that she had a right to interpose her authority, to pronounce the embargo laws unconstitutional, to show

their injustice and oppression, and to demand their repeal by instructions to her own senators and representatives. Massachusetts did
interpose; pronounced her repugnance to the law; and her will was
respected.

Mr. Jefferson might have taken a very different course from the
one pursued by him. He might have said, This disaffection is only
found among the federalists; they despise State rights, and have
only resorted to them on this occasion to abuse them; the people of
Massachusetts are favorable to my administration, and to the obnoxious law; my popularity and influence are unbounded in other
sections of the Union; by persevering a little longer, we shall accomplish all that was designed by the embargo; I will therefore disregard the clamors of these people, and persist in enforcing the law,
even should it drive them to extremity. But Mr. Jefferson did not
reason in this way. He saw that a sovereign State, through her
regular legislative forms, had pronounced against the law; it was not
for him to scrutinize, the character and composition of that legislature; it was enough for him to know, that a State had solemnly declared the law unconstitutional, unjust, and oppressive. When, in
addition, he was told by a distinguished statesman from Massachusetts, that a longer persistence might endanger the integrity of the
Union, he unhesitatingly acquiesced in a repeal of the most important
and favored measure of his administration.

What might have been the consequences if Massachusetts had
been driven to extremities, we will not conjecture—we do not reason
from extreme cases. All we have to say is, that so long as the States
have the independence to maintain those rights guaranteed to them
by the Constitution, and that so long as there is patriotism and
virtue in the administration of the Federal Government, there will
never be the necessity of driving the States into those extreme
measures of secession or nullification.

CHAPTER XXXIV

GUNBOATS.

THE question may be asked here, Why did Mr. Jefferson make so little preparation for a war which, sooner or later, seemed to be inevitable ? To understand his policy, we must first know the political principles that governed his conduct. He came into power as the leader of the republican State-Rights party. During the first four years of his administration, he applied the few simple and abstemious doctrines of that party most successfully in the management of our domestic affairs. But now a new and untried scene was opened before him. Never were the embarrassments of any government in regard to foreign powers more intricate and perplexing; and, to increase his difficulties, he had to deal with the most powerful nations on earth, who, in their hostility to each other, paid no respect to the laws of nations or the rights of neutrality. The Constitution was ordained mainly for the purpose of regulating commerce, foreign and domestic, and establishing a common rule of action in our intercourse with other countries. While the States at home preserved their political existence, retained much of their original sovereignty, were distinct, variant, and even hostile in some of their domestic interests, to the world abroad they presented but one front. At home each pursued its own policy, developed its own internal resources, and was unconscious of the existence of a common government, save in the negative blessing that it bestowed upon them of peace with each other and with the world. They literally fulfilled the spirit of their national motto, *E pluribus unum*—at home many, abroad one. It is obvious that peace must be an essential element in the successful operation of such a complicated system of government. War of whatever kind, especially an aggressive war, whether by land or sea, must destroy its equilibrium, and precipitate all its movements on the common centre, which, by an intense over-action, must finally absorb all countervailing influences. Mr. Jefferson was thoroughly penetrated with the true spirit of our Constitution ; so was John Randolph. These profound statesmen thought alike on that subject : they differed as to certain measures of policy, but not at all in their principles. They both sought the peace of the country, not only as the best condition for developing its resources, but as an essential means for preserving the purity of its institutions. Neither could look with complacency on a standing army or a large naval establishment. They did not even consider them as essential in the present emergency, more imminent, perhaps, than any that could possibly occur at a future period.

Negotiation having failed, and both belligerents still continuing to plunder our commerce, Mr. Jefferson recommended, as the only remedy, a total abandonment of the ocean. Mr. Randolph's advice was to arm the merchant marine, and let them go forth and defend themselves in the highways of a lawful commerce. As the means of home defence, Jefferson recommended the construction and equipment of gunboats, in numbers sufficient to protect the harbors and seaports from sudden invasion. Randolph advised to arm the militia, put a weapon in the hands of every yeoman of the land, and furnish the towns and seaports with a heavy train of artillery for their defence.

In all this we perceive but one object—a defence of the natal soil (*natale solum*) by the people themselves, and a total abstinence from all aggression. " Pour out your blood," said these wise statesmen to the people ; " pour out your blood in defence of your borders ; but shed not a drop beyond." Happy for the country could this advice have always been followed ! As Randolph foresaw and predicted, we came out of the war with Great Britain without a constitution ; mainly to his exertions in after years are we indebted for its restoration. The late war with Mexico has engendered a spirit of aggression and of conquest among the people, and has taught the ambitious, aspiring men of the country, that military fame achieved in an hour is worth more than the solid reputation of a statesman acquired by long years of labor and self-sacrifice. Where these things are to end it does not require much sagacity to foresee. Let the people take warning in time, and give heed to the counsel of their wisest statesmen ; let them dismiss their army and their navy, relieve the country of those burthensome and 'dangerous accompaniments of a military government, and trust to negotiation, justice, and their own energies and resources for defence. What was visionary and impracticable in the warlike days of Jefferson, is now wholly reasonable and proper. What gunboats could not do, steam vessels can fully accomplish. For defence there is no need of a navy; for aggressive war, we trust the day may never come when it shall be called into requisition.

There was one subject on which Randolph and Jefferson differed so essentially that it would seem to indicate a more radical divergency of principles than we are willing to admit existed between them. They both sincerely labored to preserve a strict neutrality between the great belligerents of Europe; but when driven to extremity, and forced to choose between the one and the other, Jefferson would have selected France as a friend, whilst Randolph would have chosen England. In the days of John Adams these predilections would have marked their political characters as being essentially different on all the great principles of government. But Randolph contended that since that day circumstances had greatly altered. France was then a free republic, fighting for the liberties of Europe, while England was in coalition with the old monarchies to destroy them. France was now a military despotism, grasping at the empire of the world, while England was the only barrier in the way of universal conquest. To suffer old partialities and prejudices to influence their conduct in such a state of affairs, he thought, was the height of folly and madness. He had no greater friendship for England and her institutions than before; but she had become essential for his own protection, and he was willing to use her for that purpose. These views seem not only to be plausible, but just. A practical statesman, at that time, looking at events as they transpired around him, and gazing on the rapid strides of Napoleon towards universal conquest, would have coincided with Mr. Randolph—have exclaimed with him that it was poor consolation to reflect that we were to be the last to be devoured, and have taken refuge behind the floating batteries of England as the last retreat to the expiring liberties of the world. But Thomas Jefferson did not view the subject in this practical way: he was the profound philosopher that looked at political causes and consequences in their radical and essential relations to each other, and the bold pioneer that dared to sacrifice what seemed to be the present interest to the future and more permanent welfare of his country.

In his judgment the great causes that produced the marvellous events then daily transpiring on the theatre of Europe, had not changed; it was still the spirit of democracy contending against the old feudal aristocracy, which had so long oppressed and enslaved the nations. The crusade of Bonaparte, aside from his own personal ambition, had no other end but the overthrow of those rotten dynasties that sat like a leaden weight on the hearts of the people; and a revival of those old memories of privileges and franchises that lay buried and forgotten beneath the rubbish and worthless trivialities of a profligate court and a heartless monarchy.

To repress the numerous factions that were tearing her vitals within, and to beat back the myrmidons of power that assailed her from without, it was necessary that France should concentrate all her energies in the hands of a military despot. The times called for a dictator. But Napoleon himself was a phenomenon that must soon pass away; his long existence was incompatible with the just order of things; his downfall must be followed by a restoration of the Bourbons, or by a revival of the Republic, chastened and purified by the ordeal through which she had passed. Bonaparte saw to the root of the matter when he said, that in a few years Europe must be Republican or Cossack. Jefferson perceived and acted on this profound principle long before Bonaparte gave utterance to it. He knew well that England was the same now that she was in the days of the coalition; her allies were gone, because the arms of France and the insurrection of their own subjects had overturned their power; the *French evil* had spread over Europe, and her battle was still against that; the right of the people to pull down and to build up dynasties —the doctrine that governments belong to the people and not the people to governments, and that they can alter or abolish them at pleasure, were principles that she fought against and labored to repress and to destroy. Had she succeeded in overturning the power of Napoleon, she would have forced on the nations of Europe, by virtue of her cherished doctrine of legitimacy, the worst of all governments—a restoration of the old monarchies claiming to rule, not by the will of the people, but by the divine right of kings. It was not in the nature of Thomas Jefferson to aid in the remotest degree in the accomplishment of such an end. Besides all this, he knew there was no sympathy between the democracy of America and the aristocracy of England; the one was progressive, the other conservative;

the one readily embraced every measure that tended to elevate and to improve the masses of mankind, the other repressed every proposition that contemplated a change in the present order of things; the one held that government must spring from the will of the people, and is but an agent in the hands of their representatives for the good of the whole; the other that all wealth and power belong to the few, and government but an instrument to preserve and perpetuate their authority. Any coalition or union between elements so repugnant would have produced evil rather than good; it would have shed a malign influence on the one hand, while on the other the contact would have been regarded as a vile contamination. Jefferson was the embodiment of American democracy; the masses of the people felt that he gave form and expression to the great sentiments that lay confused and voiceless in their own bosoms, and they knew that he would be faithful in following the impulses of that mighty concentration of a people's will in his own person: hence his influence over the public mind—his almost despotic sway over the legislation of the country. In 1806, a subservient legislature, in obedience to his secret wishes, voted him money without restriction to negotiate with Spain and France, when his public messages declared that negotiation was at an end, and breathed the strongest spirit of resistance. In 1807 his commissioners, his favorite negotiator, Monroe, being one of them, had made a treaty with England, as favorable as could be expected at that time, but he put it in his pocket and refused to submit it to the consideration of that branch of the government which had a right and might have advised its ratification. When Great Britain sent a special envoy to make reparation for the unauthorized attack on the Chesapeake, he stood on an untenable point of etiquette, refused to receive or even to hear any propositions on that subject, and suffered the public mind to be inflamed by an unnecessary delay of adjustment. Before he had any official information of the orders in council, issued in retaliation to the Berlin decree, on the mere authority of newspaper reports, he sent a secret message to Congress advising an embargo: in silence and in haste his will was obeyed— a sudden pause was given to business—at his command the people stood still, and let fall from their hands the implements of trade and the means of their subsistence. This measure, whether so intended or not, coincided with the views of Napoleon: while it could affect

France but slightly, it formed an essential part of that great continental system that had for its object the subjugation of England by a destruction of her commerce and manufactures.

Bonaparte approved, and the indomitable Saxon spirit of England refused to yield: the dire recoil was most severely felt at home, but the patriotism of the people increased with the disasters inflicted upon them; and they continued to follow their bold leader with a fortitude and intrepidity that would have persevered to the bitter end, had he not said, enough! and acquiesced in the repeal of his favorite measure. Jefferson stood to the people of America as Napoleon to the people of France—he embodied the will of a free and enlightened republic, devoted to the arts of peace, and governed by laws and a written constitution; Napoleon was the dread symbol of a wild democracy, sprung from the bosom of a volcano, chaotic in all its fiery elements, and armed with firebrands to burn up the dross and stubble of the worn-out and rotten monarchies that surrounded it; both were invincible, so long as they continued to stand in the focus, and to reflect the mighty energies that were concentrated in their own person.

We say, then, that the policy of Jefferson, viewed by a practical statesman, would seem to be unwise. It inflicted many evils on the country at the time, and entailed a lasting injury on the planting interests of the South: but it saved the principles of democracy; and it saved the country, if not from an actual participation in the Congress of Vienna, saved them from a humiliating acquiescence in the holy alliance of despots, confederated under a solemn oath to smother and extinguish every sentiment of liberty that might dare to breathe its existence in the bosoms of their oppressed and degraded subjects.

CHAPTER XXXV.

JAMES MADISON—PRESIDENTIAL ELECTION.

MR. RANDOLPH was opposed to the elevation of James Madison to the presidency. His objections extended back to an early period in the political history of that gentleman. As we have said, the country is indebted to the efforts of Mr. Madison for their present Constitution. His great labors and untiring zeal, both in the Federal convention that framed it, and the Virginia convention that ratified it, overcame every obstacle, and finally presented to the people a form of government to strengthen and consolidate their union. But the happy blending of national and federal features in the constitution, whereby the States have preserved their independence, and much of their sovereignty, was not the conception of Mr. Madison. He thought the States ought not to be entirely obliterated; but until the plan of George Mason was developed, he did not understand how their existence could be made compatible with a common central government, operating alike on all the people. He did not cordially acquiesce in the States-rights doctrine ingrafted on the Constitution. In all the debates in both conventions, he is generally found opposed to the views of Mr. Mason. And it was charged against him, that in the essays which he wrote, in conjunction with Jay and Hamilton, with the view of recommending the Constitution to the people, he advocated, with as much earnestness as those avowed centralists, a strong consolidated government. When party excitement grew very violent, in the times of the whisky insurrection, and of Jay's treaty, when Randolph was driven, in disgrace, from the Cabinet, and Monroe recalled, under sentiments of strong displeasure, Mr. Madison was charged with having abandoned his post on the floor of Congress, and seeking ease and personal safety in retirement. In the Virginia legislature it was said he opposed the general ticket system, which was adopted with the view of casting the whole vote of the State in favor of Mr. Jefferson, at the approaching election, and without which he would have been defeated. But the weightiest charge of all was that preferred by John Randolph, on the floor of Congress. The reader is already familiar with that subject. Randolph declared that the Secretary of State, in a conversation with him, expressed his willingness to buy peace with Spain, by paying tribute to France; and he averred that, on the expression of such pusillanimous sentiments, his confidence, which at no time was very great, had entirely vanished. Mr. Madison, it was also said, was a mere closet philosopher—an able logician, but a weak and timid statesman. The times required a man of nerve and energy. James Monroe was held up by his friends, as combining, more than any other man, all the qualities needed for the present exigency. A number of the republican members of Congress met together in caucus, and nominated Mr. Madison for the presidency. John Randolph and some sixteen or seventeen others, denounced this nomination, and protested against the right of members of Congress to make it. They said that such a plan had been resorted to on a former occasion, in order to concentrate the votes of the republican party on one candidate, to prevent their defeat by the federalists; but there was no necessity for that concert of action now; the federalists, as a party, had been annihilated, had no intention of bringing out a candidate ; and that whoever was elected must be a republican. They contended. therefore, that each should have a fair field, and that no advantage should be given to either by a resort to party machinery. Shortly after this, Mr. Monroe was nominated by a convention in Virginia, called together from the different counties of the State. Thus we see two candidates from the same state, for the highest office within the gift of the people ; both professed the same political principles, each had high claims to the confidence and support of their country, and each was put forward and sustained by a fraction of the same party. We may well imagine the heart-burnings and the angry feelings excited by such a contest. The ablest men in the State employed their talents in writing for the newspapers. Their essays, for the most part, were elaborate, well written, and not unfrequently filled with wit, ridicule, irony, and the bitterest sarcasm, and too frequently did they descend to the most direct and pointed personalities. Mr. Madison was the candidate of the administration—Monroe of the *Tirtium Quids*, as they were called. John Randolph was the master-spirit ʼof this third party. He of course came in for his full share of abuse. Even ridicule and doggerel rhyme were resorted to as the means of bringing his name into disrepute.

> " Thou art a pretty little speaker, John—
> Though some there are who think you've spoke too long;
> And even call, sweet sir, your tongue a bell,
> That ding-dong, dong-ding, tolls away !
> Yet mind not what such ' ragamuffins' say,
> Roar still 'gainst ' back-stairs influence,' I pray,
> And lash ' the pages of the water-closet' well ;
> To ' dust and ashes' pray thee grind 'em,
> Though I'm told 'twould puzzle you to find 'em.

"But John, like water, thou must find thy ' level,'
   Those horn-book politicians are the devil,
   Some how or other they've so pleased the nation;
   For spite of ' cobweb theories' and ' sharks,'
   Russels, Garnetts, Clays and Clarks,
   ' Strait-jackets,' ' water gruel,' and ' depletion,'
   Yes, yes, in spite of all those *curious things*,
   The name of each with glory around us rings,
   Whilst *thou* of even patriotism doubted,
   Art on all hands detested—laughed at—' scouted,'
   Nay, many think (though this perhaps is scandal,)
   That soon you'll nothing be but plain Jack R——dal."

Many a volley was aimed at his head, and many a valiant pen
was wielded in his defence.   He sometimes descended into the lists
himself, and under a borrowed name hurled his polished and effective
shafts against the exposed and vulnerable points of his adversaries.
Many of the most distingushed men of the State were on his side of
the question ; indeed, it may be said that most of the young men of
talents and independence of character were his admirers and followers.   But it soon became manifest that Mr. Monroe would get no
support out of the State of Virginia, and that the contest would be
between Mr. Madison and DeWitt Clinton, of New-York.   Many of
the best friends of Mr. Monroe were unwilling to contribute to the
election of Clinton, by a loss of the State of Virginia to his opponent;
they therefore determined, however reluctantly, to cast their votes for
Mr. Madison ; so that when the election came on, the vote for Monroe was very thin.   It would seem that the Tirtium Quids, with all
their genius, eloquence, and fine writing, had made no impression on
the people.   We can well conceive how this exposure of their weakness operated on the nerves of those politicians who love always to
be found on the side of the majority.   One by one they began to re-
cant their heresies, and to fall into the ranks of the administration.
Mr. Monroe became a candidate for the legislature in the county of
Albemarle : he was interrogated on the subject, and professed him
self friendly to the new dynasty ; was elected; appointed Governor
of the State ; and in due time was placed by Mr. Madison in his
Cabinet.
    Very soon Randolph was left with only a few personal and devo-
ted friends to stand by him.   Those who valued consistency more

than office, and who regarded it as an act of dishonor to abandon a friend in his hour of need, still adhered to him; but the majority of politicians, who look only to the loaves and fishes, had no hesitation in making their escape from what they conceived to be a falling house. This "ratting," as he called it, Mr. Randolph never forgot nor forgave. His pride was cut to the quick; his disgust was unbounded; and to the events of this period may be traced much of that bitterness of feeling which he manifested towards certain individuals in after life. Never did he suffer an occasion to pass that he did not make them feel, by some cutting allusion, his deep indignation. This seemed to the world a wanton indulgence of a vile, cruel, and sarcastic temper: but the parties themselves understood and keenly felt the meaning of his allusions; and well did they repay his disgust and contempt, by a most cordial hatred.

"Why have you not gone to Philadelphia?" says one of his flatterers, writing to him about this time—" every one there whose attention could confer either pleasure or honor was prepared for your reception. The learning, the genius, and the eloquence of the city, with all its train of social manners, wit, beauty, gayety and innocence, were prepared to spread for you a rich and varied feast of enjoyment. You have ceased to be the head of a great triumphant party, but, rely upon it, you are at the head of the taste, feeling and honor of the nation."

Yet this man in a few years glided into the ranks of the administration—became the secret reviler of one on whom he had bestowed the grossest adulation : and finally supported all the Federal measures of Monroe and John Quincy Adams ; bank, tariff, internal improvements, and whatever else that tended to produce a strong, magnificent, corrupt, and consolidated government. It is not surprising that a man of Mr. Randolph's temper, exasperated as it had been by so many instances of the same kind, could not look with complacency on such characters ; but he visited as a crime on the head of the offender that which he should have forgiven as a weakness of our common nature. He understood mankind too well not to have known the certain consequences of defeat; the abdicating Emperor at Fontainebleau, when abandoned by all those whom he had made marshals and princes, might have told him that misfortune is like a nipping frost, that scatters the leaves and the blossoms, and leaves bare the naked limbs to battle alone with the rude blasts of winter.

The following extract taken from an unpublished essay, dated August 31, 1808, will throw much light on the excited and angry nature of the controversy carried on at that time between the followers of John Randolph and the adherents of Mr. Madison :

"I addressed you formerly with a view to the approaching presidential election ; but before I could recover from the repulse which I met in my first attempt to approach the people, it was already too late. Every man had already chosen his part in that drama—many were already in imagination tricked out in the robes of office in which they were to assist at the installation of Mr. Madison ; and, so far as it could depend upon the votes of Virginia, that election was already decided. The partisans of government have ceased to bestow their attention upon this subject, and have already turned it to another. I mean the election of a representative from the counties of Cumberland, &c. The stormy rage of the presidential contest has been no sooner hushed, than both the Argus and the Enquirer have, at once, turned their batteries against the gentleman who at present represents that district. Writers, scarcely worthy to be noticed, and whom it would be a disgrace to answer, have hastened to engage in the meritorious service of removing the only eye that watches over the administration. Looking forward to the election of Mr. Madison, they no doubt anticipate much from this attempting to destroy the man, before whom, in spite of all the pomp of office, he would be compelled to feel the intrinsic littleness of his character. Unworthy as their childish arguments and groundless assertions are of the poor respect of refutation and contradiction, they at least remind us of the proverbial truth, 'that straws show the course of the wind;' and if I mistake them not, it is not the only occasion on which they have displayed the properties of the weathercock. Though their arguments prove nothing, their attempts at argument prove much. They show the real offence of Mr. R., they show the real causes of the clamor which is raised against him. It is the usual fate of fools and knaves that the weapons which they pretend to wield, recoil upon their own heads. These men have endeavored to detract from the merit of Mr. R., but they have exposed their own weakness ; they have evinced the irreconcileable malignity of themselves and their party towards him, at the same time that they have stated objections, which, if true and well founded, as they are false and groundless, would be utterly inadequate to the production of such an effect; and they compel us to believe that there is some other secret cause or motive for their antipathy to that gentleman, which is not revealed, only because it will not bear the light. Mr. R's constituents have been much at a loss to know wherefore the whole force of the government has been exerted to provide them a representative, some worthy associate of John Love and John Dawson. They feel indeed the importance of his past services, and they see in them some evidence of abilities not to be despised. They perceive also that he differs from the administration on some points. They are even told by the newspapers that he is opposed to them on all, but at the same time they are assured, that he stands alone in this opposition, without a party, even without personal friends, and that there is more to pity in his infatuation than to dread from this hostility. Why then all this struggle, this ceaseless anxiety? and (to use a quotation of your own Mr. Ritchie,) this 'ocean into tempest wrought to drown a fly?' Is the spirit of federalism then extinct; is that monster no more, that nothing remains but to turn the whole force of the administration to the destruction of such an insect, as they would represent Mr. Randolph? This surely is not the case. The federal representation of Connecticut yet remains entire. Its banners are yet displayed, and those who yesterday deserted, are, to-day, returning to them. The mighty State of Massachusetts, which of late the administration so proudly numbered among their supporters, has already repented of her conversion ; while the Vermontese are newly baptized to the federal faith in the blood of their countrymen. Perhaps indeed they balance all this with the conversion of Mr. J. Q. Adams, and by the same political arithmetic, which teaches them that the downfall of Mr. Randolph is of more importance than the defeat of the federalists, they think the acquisition of this gentleman an ample compensation for the loss of two entire States. No doubt indeed they augur well from it, no doubt they regard it as an all-sufficient evidence of Mr. Adams's conviction of the stability of their power. Ten years ago they would have told you that this gentleman knew, as well as any one, who kept the key of the exchequer, and it would be strange indeed, if, when his father held it so long, he had not found out the value of the coin. They perhaps remember too, that about that time he was talked of as the contemplated successor to the crown of these realms, and they possibly regard his accession to their party as an implied relinquishment of his title, in favor of the hopeful progeny of our modern Livia. I would warn them, however, not to build too much upon that. They should rather infer from the example of Spain, that the minority of the imperial nephew of his majesty, the emperor and king, may be terminated by an invitation to Bayonne.

"But it cannot be that the administration, and the friends of the administration, think that there is less to be feared from the federal party than there was three years ago. How then does it happen that the necessity of putting down this great and growing evil is forgotten in the struggle to remove that gentleman from the confidence of his constituents? They tell us indeed, themselves, that the republican cause has nothing to fear from Mr. R., and they say true, sir. They know that the republican cause has nothing to fear from him; but they feel at the same time, that the pretended supporters of that cause have every thing to fear from him. They see in him the only man on the floor of Congress who has the sagacity to detect and the spirit to expose their unconstitutional practices and their nefarious designs, and they wish his ruin, for the same reason that rogues wish the absence of the sun. How else can their conduct be explained? At a time when the shattered forces of the federalists are again assembling, when they are even enjoying a partial triumph, the Government are seen endeavoring to drive from their ranks the most distinguished and formidable adversary to that cause. No, sir; they love not the light, because their deeds are evil. And do those who urge this clamor against Mr. R. suppose that the people are blind to the real cause of it, that they form no judgment of the motives and characters of the men who seek his ruin, by the means they use for that purpose? No; they know that dirty tools are used for dirty work, and that he who employs them in that way cannot have clean hands. What can they think when they see his private letters betrayed, and his unguarded moments of gayety and conviviality watched and exposed? Shall they be told that these are private occurrences? No, sir. Mr. G. will not do even an act of treachery for nothing.

Indeed, some of the partisans of Mr. Madison have not scrupled to declare, that they consider his election as of little more importance than the defeat of Mr. R. Can the people be at a loss to understand wherefore? As long as the views of Mr. Madison are constitutional, and his conduct honorable, he can have nothing to fear from Mr. R. In questions of mere policy, the weight of Executive patronage will always preponderate, and, in questions of right, always powerful, becomes invincible when supported by the name and authority of a President. It is not until he transcends the limits of the Constitution that any opposition can be formidable. If such be their projected course—if the system of standing armies and navies, of treason bills and habeas corpus acts, of unauthorized expenditures, and splendid impunity to favored traitors and felons, with the practice of buying peace, and giving to the President the powers of Congress—are still to be persisted in, let them beware of Mr. R. Already has he declaimed against these practices, and he has not been heard; but they know that the slumbers of the people are not to last for ever, and they look forward with the apprehensions of a sinner, trembling in the midst of his guilt, to the day when the vengeance of a deluded nation shall be roused; and at the sound of his voice, as at that of the last trump, they shall call upon the mountains to cover them. I have no doubt that those who made this avowal have somewhat transcended their orders. Their instinctive sagacity leads them to the game which their master is in pursuit of; but in the eagerness of their zeal, they have flushed it too soon. They are at this moment trembling in the expectation of being corrected for the blunder; but they are not so true spaniels as I take them to be, if they will not consent to have their ears pulled for the mistake, provided they be fed for their activity."

CHAPTER XXXVI.

WAR WITH ENGLAND.

THE great event of Mr. Madison's administration was the war with England. For a long time, the grounds of complaint against that Government were, the carrying trade and the impressment of seamen. Since 1806, another and more serious difficulty, if possible, had been thrown in the way of an amicable arrangement between the two countries. By the Berlin decree and its supplements, France interdicted all trade between the United States and Great Britain and her dependencies. By her orders in council, professing to be in retaliation of the Berlin decree, Great Britain interdicted all trade between the United States and France, and her allies and their dependencies, which embraced nearly all Europe and the civilized world. These edicts did not affect the carrying trade merely, which was of very doubtful justice, but they destroyed all commerce whatever.

By the British orders in council, American citizens were not allowed to carry the products of their own country, in their own ships, to a country hostile to England, and to bring back, in exchange, the commodities of that country, without first paying tribute in a British port, and obtaining license for that purpose. This extraordinary assumption of power was acknowledged to be contrary to the law of nations and the rights of neutrality; but it was justified on the ground of necessity. *Lex talionis* was the only plea. To bring about a sense of justice in the great belligerents, and a repeal of their unwarrantable edicts, the embargo law was enacted; but that proved to be a two-edged sword, more deeply wounding our own sides than those of the parties it was designed to effect. It was repealed, and a non-importation act, as to England and France, substituted in its place. This proving ineffectual, also, the olive branch was at length held out, with these words: "That if Great Britain or France (Act of May ' 1810,) should cease to violate the neutral commerce of the United States, which fact the President should declare by proclamation, and the other should not, within three months thereafter, revoke or modify its edicts in like manner, that then certain sections in a former act, interdicting the commercial intercourse between the United States and Great Britain and France, and their dependencies, should, from and after the expiration of three months from the date of the proclamation, be revived, and have full force against the former, its colonies, and dependencies, and against all articles the growth, produce, or manufacture of the same." France acceded to this proposition. On the 5th of August, 1810, the minister of foreign affairs addressed a note to the minister plenipotentiary of the United States at Paris, informing him that the decrees of Berlin and Milan were revoked—the revocation to take effect on the first of November following; that the measure had been taken by his Government, in confidence that the British Government would revoke its orders, and renounce its new principles of blockade, or that the United States would cause their rights to be respected. The means by which the United States should cause their right to be respected, in case Great Britain should not revoke her edicts, it was understood, consisted merely in the enforcement of the non-importation act against that nation.

Great Britain declined to revoke her edicts; insisted that those of France had not been revoked, and complained that the United States had done injustice, by carring into effect the non-importation act against her.

Great Britain contended that, in the French decrees, it was expressly avowed, that the principles on which they were founded, and the provisions contained in them, were wholly new, unprecedented, and in direct contradiction to all ideas of justice, and the principles and usages of civilized nations. The French Government did not pretend to say that any one of the regulations contained in those decrees was a regulation which France had ever been in the previous practice of. They were, consequently, to be considered, and were indeed allowed by France herself to be, all of them, parts of a new system of warfare, unauthorized by the established law of nations. It was in this light in which France herself had placed her decrees, that Great Britain was obliged to consider them.

The submission of neutrals to any regulation made by France, authorized by the law of nations, and practised in former wars, would never be complained of by Great Britain; but the regulations of the Berlin and Milan decrees did, and were declared to violate the laws of nations and the rights of neutrals, for the purpose of attacking, through them, the resources of Great Britain. The ruler of France had drawn no distinction between any of them, nor had he declared the cessation of any one of them.

Not until the French decrees, therefore, it was contended by the British minister, shall be effectually repealed, and thereby neutral commerce be restored to the situation in which it stood previously to their promulgation, can his royal highness conceive himself justified, consistently with what he owes to the safety and honor of Great

Britain, in foregoing the just measures of retaliation which his majesty, in his defence, was necessitated to adopt against them.

The Berlin and Milan decrees prohibited every thing that was the manufacture or product of Great Britain from being imported to the Continent, under any pretence whatever, whether owned by British subjects, or owned and transported by neutrals. This latter part of the decrees was in violation of the rights of neutrality. They also, at the same time, prohibited all trade, on the part of neutrals, with the British dominions. This portion was now repealed, so far as it affected the United States. They were allowed to trade with Great Britain and her dependencies, but were not permitted to carry to the Continent any goods that were the manufacture or produce of Great Britain, though they might have been purchased, and were actually owned by American citizens. Great Britain insisted that she could not repeal her orders in council, so long as the United States suffered this infraction of their rights of neutrality. On the other hand, it was contended that Great Britain had pledged herself to repeal the orders in council whenever the decrees were revoked. The decrees, it was said, were now revoked as it regarded the United States; but Britain, in violation of her pledge, persisted in refusing to repeal her orders. The whole question, then, was narrowed down to this: Had the Berlin and Milan decrees been revoked, in the sense it was understood by the parties, at the time of the pledge? Great Britain said they had not. The United States said they had been revoked, according to the understanding.

In this attitude matters stood, when Congress, on the 4th of November, 1811, was called together by proclamation of the President. "At the close of the last session of Congress," says the message, "it was hoped that the successive confirmations of the extinction of the French decrees, so far as they violated our neutral commerce, would have induced the government of Great Britain to repeal its orders in council, and thereby authorize the removal of the existing obstructions to her commerce with the United States. Instead of this reasonable step towards satisfaction and friendship between the two nations, the orders were, at a moment when least to have been expected, put into more rigorous execution; and it was communicated, through the British envoy just arrived, that whilst the revocation of the edicts of France, as officially made known to the British Government, was denied to have taken place, it was an indispensable con dition of the repeal of the British orders that commerce should be restored to a footing that would admit the manufactures and pro- ductions of Great Britain, when owned by neutrals, into markets shut against them by her enemy—the United States being given to understand that, in the mean time, a continuation of the non-importa- tion act would lead to measures of retaliation. * * * * * *

" With the evidence of hostile inflexibility, in trampling on our rights, which no independent nation can reliquish, Congress will feel the duty of putting the United States into an armor and an attitude demanded by the crisis, and corresponding with the national spirit and expectations."

The subject was referred to a committee, who, in a report, reviewed the grounds of complaint, and concluded with offering a series of reso- lutions, the object of which was, to put the United States imme- diately "into an armor and attitude demanded by the crisis." The friends of the administration admitted that they urged the resolu- tions as an immediate preparation for war. That war was inevitable, and would be declared so soon as the nation was put into a posture of defence. It was also said in debate that one of the objects, and a necessary result of the war, would be the conquest of Canada.

On the 10th day of December, Mr. Randolph made one of his most powerful and eloquent speeches in opposition to these war mea- sures. As the speech is to be found in most of the collections of American eloquence that have been published from time to time, we must content ourselves with an extract here and there, barely suffi- cient to explain in his own words the grounds of opposition.

" It is a question," said Mr. Randolph, " as it has been presented to the House, of *peace* or *war*. In that light it has been regarded; in no other light can I consider it, after declarations made by mem- bers of the Committee of Foreign Relations. Without intending any disrespect to the chair, I must be permitted to say, that if the deci- sion yesterday was correct, ' that it was not in order to advance any arguments against the resolution, drawn from topics before other committees of the House,' the whole debate—nay, the report itself on which we are acting—is disorderly, since the increase of the mili- tary force is a subject at this time in agitation by the select com- mittee raised on that branch of the President's message. But it is impossible that the discussion of a question, broad as the wide ocean, of our foreign concerns, involving every consideration of interest, of right, of happiness, and of safety at home; touching in every point all that is dear to freemen—'their lives, their fortunes, and their sacred honor;' can be tied down by the narrow rules of technical routine. The Committee of Foreign Relations has indeed decided that the subject of arming the militia (which I pressed upon them as indispensable to the public safety) does not come within the scope of their authority. On what ground, I have been, and still am, unable to see. They have felt themselves authorized (when the subject was before another committee) to recommend the raising of standing armies, with a view (as has been declared) of immediate war—a war not of defence, but of conquest, of aggrandizement, of ambition—a war foreign to the interests of this country, to the interests of humanity itself.

"I know not how gentlemen calling themselves republicans can advocate such a war. What was their doctrine in 1798-9, when the command of the army, that highest of all possible trusts in any government, be the form what it may, was reposed in the bosom of the Father of his country! the sanctuary of a nation's love!— the only hope that never came in vain? When other worthies of the revolution, Hamilton, Pinckney, and the younger Washington, men of tried patriotism, of approved conduct and valor, of untarnished honor, held subordinate command under him? Republicans were then unwilling to trust a standing army even to his hands, who had given proof that he was above all human temptation. Where now is the revolutionary hero to whom you are about to confide this sacred trust? To whom will you confide the charge of leading the flower of your youth to the heights of Abraham? Will you find him in the person of an acquitted felon? What! *Then* you were unwilling to vote an army, when such men as have been named held high command! When Washington himself was at the head, did you *then* show such reluctance, feel such scruple? And are you now nothing loth, fearless of every consequence? Will you say that your provocations were less then than now, when your direct commerce was interdicted, your ambassadors hooted with derision from the French court, tribute demanded, actual war waged upon you? Those who opposed the army then were indeed denounced as the partisans of France, as the same men—some of them at least—are now held up as the advocates of England; those firm and unde-viating republicans, who then dared, and now dare, to cling to the ark of the Constitution, to defend it even at the expense of their fame, rather than surrender themselves to the wild projects of mad ambi-tion. There is a fatality, sir, attending plenitude of power. Soon or late some mania seizes upon its possessors; they fall from the dizzy height, through the giddiness of their own heads. Like a vast estate, heaped up by the labor and industry of one man, which seldom sur-vives the third generation. Power gained by patient assiduity, by a faithful and regular discharge of its attendant duties, soon gets above its own origin. Intoxicated with their own greatness, the federal party fell. Will not the same causes produce the same effects now as then? Sir, you may raise this army, you may build up this vast structure of patronage, this mighty apparatus of favoritism; but ' lay not the flattering unction to your souls,' you will never live to enjoy the succession: you sign your political death warrant. * * * *

" This war of conquest, a war for the acquisition of territory and subjects, is to be a new commentary on the doctrine that republics are destitute of ambition; they are addicted to peace, wedded to the happiness and safety of the great body of their people. But it seems this is to be a holiday campaign; there is to be no expense of blood or treasure on our part; Canada is to conquer herself; she is to be subdued by the principles of fraternity. The people of that country are first to be seduced from their allegiance, and converted into trai-tors, as preparatory to the making them good citizens. Although I must acknowledge that some of our flaming patriots were thus man-ufactured, I do not think the process would hold good with a whole community. It is a dangerous experiment. We are to succeed in the French mode—by the system of fraternization. All is French! But how dreadfully it might be retorted on the southern and western slaveholding States. I detest this subornation of treason. No: if we must have them, let them fall by the valor of our arms; by fair, legitimate conquest; not become the victims of treacherous seduction.

" I am not surprised at the war-spirit which is manifesting itself in gentlemen from the South. In the year 1805–6, in a struggle for the carrying trade of belligerent colonial produce, this country was most unwisely brought into collision with the great powers of Europe.

By a series of most impolitic and ruinous measures, utterly incomprehensible to every rational, sober-minded man, the Southern planters, by their own votes, succeeded in knocking down the price of cotton to seven cents, and of tobacco (a few choice crops excepted) to nothing, and in raising the price of blankets (of which a few would not be amiss in a Canadian campaign), coarse woollens, and every article of first necessity, three or four hundred per cent. And now that by our own acts we have brought ourselves into this unprecedented condition, we must get out of it in any way but by an acknowledgment of our own want of wisdom and forecast. But is war the true remedy? Who will profit by it? Speculators; a few lucky merchants, who draw prizes in the lottery; commissaries and contractors. Who must suffer by it? The people. It is their blood, their taxes, that must flow to support it.

"But gentlemen avowed that they would not go to war for the carrying trade; that is, for any other but the direct export and import trade—that which carries our native products abroad, and brings back the return cargo; and yet they stickle for our commercial rights, and will go to war for them! I wish to know, in point of principle, what difference gentlemen can point out between the abandonment of this or of that maritime right? Do gentlemen assume the lofty port and tone of chivalrous redressers of maritime wrongs, and declare their readiness to surrender every other maritime right, provided they may remain unmolested in the exercise of the humble privilege of carrying their own produce abroad, and bringing back a return cargo? Do you make this declaration to the enemy at the outset? Do you state the minimum with which you will be contented, and put it in her power to close with your proposals at her option? give her the basis of a treaty ruinous and disgraceful beyond example and expression? and this too after having turned up your noses in disdain at the treaties of Mr. Jay and Mr. Monroe? Will you say to England, '*End the war when you please; give us the direct trade in our own produce, we are content?*' But what will the merchants of Salem, and Boston, and New York, and Philadelphia, and Baltimore—the men of Marblehead and Cape Cod, say to this? Will they join in a war professing to have for its object what they would consider, and justly too. as the sacrifice of their maritime rights, yet affecting to be a war for the *protection of commerce?*

"I am gratified to find gentlemen acknowledging the demoralizing and destructive consequences of the non-importation law; confessing the truth of all that its opponents foretold when enacted; and will you plunge yourselves in war, because you have passed a foolish and ruinous law, and are ashamed to repeal it? 'But our good friend, the French Emperor, stands in the way of its repeal,' and, as we cannot go too far in making sacrifices to him, who has given such demonstration of his *love for the Americans*, we must, in point of fact, become parties to this war. 'Who can be so cruel as to refuse him this favor?' My imagination shrinks from the miseries of such connection. I call upon the House to reflect whether they are not about to abandon all reclamation for the unparalleled outrages, 'insults and injuries' of the French Government; to give up our claim for plundered millions, and ask what reparation or atonement we can expect to obtain in hours of future dalliance, after we shall have made a tender of our persons to this great deflowerer of the virginity of republics. We have, by our own wise (I will not say *wise-acre*) measures, so increased the trade of Montreal and Quebec, that at last we begin to cast a wistful eye at Canada. Having done so much towards its improvement, by the exercise of our 'restrictive energies,' we begin to think the laborer is worthy of his hire, and to put in claim for our portion. Suppose it ours, are we any nearer our point? As his minister said to the King of Epirus, 'May we not as well take our bottle of wine before as after this exploit?' Go! march to Canada! Leave the broad bosom of the Chesapeake, and her hundred tributary rivers, the whole line of sea-coast, from Machias to St. Mary's, unprotected: you have taken Quebec—have you *conquered England?* Will you seek for the deep foundations of her power in the frozen deserts of Labrador?

'Her march is on the mountain wave,
Her home is on the deep!'

Will you call upon her to leave your ports and harbors untouched, only just till you can return from Canada to defend them? The coast is to be left defenceless, whilst men of the interior are revelling in conquest and spoil. But grant for a moment, for mere argument's sake, that in Canada you touched the sinews of her strength, instead of removing a clog upon her resources—an incumbrance, but one, which, from a spirit of honor, she will vigorously defend. In what situation would you then place some of the best men of the nation? As Chatham and Burke, and the whole band of her patriots prayed for her defeat in 1776, so must some of the truest friends of the country deprecate the success of our arms against the only power that holds in check the arch enemy of mankind.

" Our people will not submit to be taxed for this war of conquest and dominion. The government of the United States was not calculated to wage *offensive foreign war ;* it was instituted for the common defence and general welfare; and whosoever will embark it in a war of offence, will put it to a test which it is by no means calculated to endure. Make it out that Great Britain did instigate the Indians on a late occasion, and I am ready for battle, but not for dominion. I am unwilling, however, under present circumstances, to take Canada at the risk of the Constitution ; to embark in a common cause with France, and be dragged at the wheels of the car of some Burr or Bonaparte. For a gentleman from Tennessee, or Genesee, or lake Champlain, there may be some prospect of advantage. Their hemp would bear a great price by the exclusion of foreign supply. In that, too, the great importers were deeply interested. The upper country on the Hudson and the lakes, would be enriched by the supplies for the troops, which they alone could furnish. They would have the exclusive market; to say nothing of the increased preponderance from the acquisition of Canada, and that section of the Union, which the southern and western States had already felt so severely in the apportionment bill."

Mr. Randolph dwelt on the danger arising from the black population. He said he would touch this subject as tenderly as possible ; it was with reluctance that he touched it at all ; but in cases of great emergency the state physician must not be deterred by a sickly, hysterical humanity, from probing the wound of his patient; he must not be withheld by a fastidious and mistaken humanity from representing his true situation to his friends, or even to the sick man himself, where the occasion called for it. " What, sir, is the situation of the slaveholding States ? During the war of the Revolution, so fixed were their habits of subordination, that while the whole country was overrun by the enemy, who invited them to desert, no fear was ever entertained of an insurrection of the slaves. During a war of seven years, with our country in possession of the enemy, no such danger was ever apprehended. But should we therefore be unobservant spectators of the progress of society within the last twenty years? of the silent but powerful change wrought by time and chance upon its composition and temper? When the fountains of the great deep of abomination were broken up, even the poor slaves escaped not the general deluge. The French revolution polluted even them. Nay, there were not wanting men in that House—witness their legislative *Legendre*, the butcher who once held a seat there—to preach upon that floor, these imprescriptable rights to a crowded audience of blacks in the galleries; teaching them that they are equal to their masters; in other words, advising them to cut their throats. Similar doctrines are disseminated by pedlars from New England, and elsewhere, throughout the Southern country; and masters have been found so infatuated, as by their lives and conversation, by a general contempt of order, morality and religion, unthinkingly to cherish those seeds of self-destruction to them and their families. What is the consequence? Within the last ten years, repeated alarms of insurrection among the slaves; some of them awful indeed. From the spreading of this infernal doctrine, the whole Southern country has been thrown into a state of insecurity. Men dead to the operation of moral causes, have taken away from the poor slave his habits of loyalty and obedience to his master, which lightened his servitude by a double operation—beguiling his own cares, and disarming his master's suspicions and severity; and now, like true empirics in politics, you are called upon to trust to the mere physical strength of the fetter which holds him in bondage. You have deprived him of all moral restraint; you have tempted him to eat of the tree of knowledge, just enough to perfect him in wickedness; you have opened his eyes to his nakedness; you have armed his nature against the hand that has fed, that has clothed him, that has cherished him in sickness; that hand which, before he became a pupil of your school, he had been accustomed to press with respectful affection. You have done all this, and then, show him the gibbet and the wheel, as incentives to a sullen, repugnant obedience. God forbid, sir, that the southern States should ever see an enemy on their shores, with these infernal principles of French fraternity in the van. While talking of taking Canada, some of us are shuddering for our own safety at home. I speak from facts when I say, that the night-bell never tolls for fire in Richmond, that the mother does not hug the infant more closely to her bosom. I have been a witness of some of the alarms in the capital of Virginia."

Mr. Randolph then proceeded to notice the unjust and illiberal imputation of *British attachments*, against certain characters in this country; sometimes insinuated in the House, but openly avowed out of it. " Against whom are these charges brought? Against men who in the war of the Revolution were in the councils of the nation, or fighting the battles of your country. And *by whom* are they made? By *runaways*, chiefly *from the British dominions*, since the breaking out of the French troubles. It is insufferable! It cannot be borne! It must, and ought, with severity, to be put down in this House, and out of it, to meet the *lie direct*. We have no fellow-feeling for the suffering and oppressed Spaniards! Yet even *them* we do not reprobate. Strange! that we should have no objection to any other people or government, civilized or savage, in the whole world. The great autocrat of all the Russias receives the homage of our high consideration; the Dey of Algiers, and his divan of pirates, are very civil, good sort of people, with whom we find no difficulty in maintaining the relations of peace and amity; 'Turks, Jews, and Infidels;' *Melimelli*, or the *Little Turtle*; barbarians and savages, of every clime and color, are welcome to our arms; with chiefs of banditti, negro or mulatto, we can *treat* and can *trade*—name, however, but England, and all our antipathies are up in arms against her. Against whom? Against those whose blood runs in our own veins; in common with whom we can claim Shakspeare, and Newton, and Chatham for our countrymen; whose form of government is the freest on earth, our own only excepted; from whom every valuable principle of our own institutions has been borrowed—representation, jury trial, voting the supplies, writs of habeas corpus—our whole civil and criminal jurisprudence; against our *fellow-protestants*, identified in blood, in language, in religion with ourselves. In what school did the worthies of our land, the Washingtons, Henrys, Hancocks, Franklins, Rutleges, of America, learn those principles of civil liberty which were so nobly asserted by their wisdom and valor? And American resistance to British usurpation had not been more warmly cherished by these great men and their compatriots; not more by Washington.

Hancock, and Henry, than by Chatham, and his illustrious associates in the British Parliament. It ought to be remembered, too, that the *heart* of the *English people* was with us. It was a selfish and corrupt ministry, and their servile tools, to whom *we* were not more opposed than they were. I trust that none such may ever exist among us ; for *tools* will never be wanted to subserve the purposes, however ruinous or wicked, of kings and ministers of state.

"But the outrages and injuries of England. Bred up in the principles of the Revolution, I can never palliate, much less defend them. I well remember flying with my mother, and her new-born child, from Arnold and Philips ; and they had been driven by Tarleton, and other British pandours, from pillar to post, while her husband was fighting the battles of his country. The impression is indelible on my memory ; and yet (like my worthy old neighbor, who added seven buckshot to every cartridge at the battle of Guilford, and drew a fine sight at his man) I must be content to be called a tory by a patriot of the last importation. Let us not get rid of one evil, supposing it possible, at the expense of a greater. Suppose France in possession of the British naval power—and to her the trident must pass should England be unable to wield it—what would be your condition ? What would be the situation of your seaports and their seafaring inhabitants ? Ask Hamburg, Lubec—ask *Savannah ?* What ! sir, when their privateers are pent up in our harbors by the British bull-dogs ; when they receive at our hands every rite of hospitality, from which their enemy is excluded ; when they capture within our waters, interdicted to British armed ships, American vessels ; when such is their deportment toward you, under such circumstances, what could you expect if they were the uncontrolled lords of the ocean ? Had those privateers at Savannah borne British commissions, or had your shipments of cotton, tobacco, ashes, and what not, to London and Liverpool been confiscated, and the proceeds poured into the English exchequer, my life upon it ! you would never have listened to any miserable wire-drawn distinctions between 'orders and decrees affecting our neutral rights,' and 'municipal decrees,' confiscating in mass your whole property. You would have had instant war ! The whole land would have blazed out in war.

"And shall republicans become the instruments of him who has effaced the title of Attila to the 'SCOURGE OF GOD !' Yet, even

Attila, in the falling fortunes of civilization, had, no doubt, his advocates, his tools, his minions, his parasites, in the very countries that he overran—sons of that soil whereon his horse had trod, where grass could never after grow.   If perfectly fresh," Mr. Randolph said, "instead of being as I am—my memory clouded, my intellect stupefied, my strength and spirits exhausted—I could not give utterance to that strong detestation which I feel toward (above all other works of the creation) such characters as Zingis, Tamerlane, Kouli Khan, or Bonaparte.   My instincts involuntarily revolt at their bare idea—malefactors of the human race, who ground down man to a mere machine of their impious and bloody ambition.   Yet, under all the accumulated wrongs, and insults, and robberies of the last of these chieftains, are we not, in point of fact, about to become a party to his views, a partner in his wars ?

"I beseech the House, before they run their heads against this post, Quebec, to count the cost.   My word for it, Virginia planters will not be taxed to support such a war ; a war which must aggravate their present distresses ; in which they have not the remotest interest.   Where is the Montgomery, or even the Arnold, or the Burr, who is to march to the Point Levi?

"I call upon those professing to be republicans, to make good the promises held out by their republican predecessors when they came into power; promises, which for years afterwards, they honestly, faithfully fulfilled.   We vaunted of paying off the national debt, of retrenching useless establishments; and yet have now become as infatuated with standing armies, loans, taxes, navies and war, as ever were the Essex junto.   What republicanism is this?"

Mr. Randolph resolutely and earnestly combated every measure that had a tendency to widen the breach between the United States and Great Britain, and to precipitate them into a war.

On the 1st of April, 1812, the President sent in a secret message, recommending an immediate embargo.   The Committee of Foreign Relations, in anticipation of the message, had a bill already prepared: it was read the first and second time, reported to the Committee of the Whole, referred back to the House, and immediately put on its passage.   Some member wished to know whether it was to be considered as a peace measure, or a precursor to war.

Mr. Grundy, a member of the committee, replied that he understood it as a war measure; and it is meant, said he, that it shall lead directly to it.

Mr. Clay (the Speaker) warmly expressed his satisfaction and full approbation of the message, and the proposition before the House.

Mr. Randolph then rose: " I am so impressed," said he, " with the importance of the subject and the solemnity of the occasion, that I cannot be silent. Sir, we are now in conclave; the eyes of the surrounding world are not upon us: we are shut up here from the light of heaven, but the eyes of God are upon us. He knows the spirit of our minds. Shall we deliberate upon this subject with the spirit of sobriety and candor, or with that spirit which has too often characterized our discussions upon occasions like the present? We ought to realize that we are in the presence of that God who knows our thoughts and motives, and to whom we must hereafter render an account for the deeds done in the body. I hope, sir, the spirit of party, and every improper passion, will be exorcised, that our hearts may be as pure and clean as fall to the lot of human nature.

" I am confident in the declaration, Mr. Chairman, that this is not a measure of the Executive; but that it is engendered by an extensive excitement upon the Executive— * * * *

" I will appeal to the sobriety and reflection of the House, and ask, what *new* cause of war for the last twelve months? What *new* cause of embargo within that period? The affair of the Chesapeake is settled.—No new principles of blockade interpolated into the laws of nations. I suppose every man of candor and sober reflection will ask why we did not go to war twelve months ago? Or will it be said we ought to make up, by our promptness now, for our slowness then? Or will it be said, that if the wheat for which we have received two dollars a bushel had been rotting in our barns, we should have been happier and richer. What would the planter say, if you were to ask him which he would prefer,—the honorable, chivalrous course advocated by the Speaker, with the consequences which must attend it, the sheriff at his back, and the excise collector pressing him? He would laugh in your face. It is not generally wise to dive into futurity; but it is wise to profit by experience, although it may be unpleasant. I feel much concerned to have the bill on the table for one hour."

But he was not allowed that privilege. The bill was immediately

hurried through the forms of legislation, and became a law in a short
time after the President's message that recommended it had been
read.

On the 29th of May, 1812, having learned that a proposition
would certainly be made in a few days to declare war, he rose and
stated that he had a motion to make. He then commenced a speech,
involving generally the present state of our relations with France
and Great Britain. After he had spoken for some time, a question
of order was raised, and it was decided by the Speaker that the gentleman ought, previous to debating so much at large, to submit his
motion to the House.

"After some desultory debate, and decisions on points of order, Mr.
Randolph submitted the following proposition : " *That under present
circumstances, it is inexpedient to resort to a war with Great
Britain.*"

The question being taken, that the House do now proceed to the
consideration of the said resolution, it was by a large majority decided in the negative. By this most unparliamentary proceeding, as
he thought, the subject was taken from before the House, and Mr.
Randolph was deprived of an opportunity, if not denied the right, of
addressing them on the momentous questions involved in his resolution. Next day he addressed the following letter to his constituents:

*To the Freeholders of Charlotte, Prince Edward, Buckingham, and
Cumberland.*

FELLOW-CITIZENS,—I dedicate to you the following fragment.
That it appears in its present mutilated shape, is to be ascribed to
the successful usurpation which has reduced the freedom of speech
in one branch of the American Congress to an empty name. It is
now established, *for the first time, and in the person of your representative,* that the House may and will refuse to hear a member in his
place, or even to receive a motion from him, upon the most momentous subject that can be presented for legislative decision. A similar motion was brought forward by the republican minority in the
year 1798, before these modern inventions for stifling the freedom of
debate were discovered. It was discussed as a matter of *right,* until
it was abandoned by the mover, in consequence of additional information (the correspondence of our envoy at Paris) laid before Con-

gress by the President. In "the reign of terror," the father of the sedition law had not the hardihood to proscribe liberty of speech, much less the right of free debate on the floor of Congress. This invasion of the public liberties was reserved for self-styled republicans, who hold your understandings in such contempt, as to flatter themselves that you will overlook their every outrage upon the great first principles of free government, in consideration of their professions of tender regard for the privileges of the people. It is for you to decide whether they have undervalued your intelligence and spirit, or whether they have formed a just estimate of your character. You do not require to be told that the violation of the rights of him whom you have deputed to represent you is an invasion of the rights of every man of you, of every individual in society. If this abuse be suffered to pass unredressed—and the people alone are competent to apply the remedy—we must bid adieu to a free form of government for ever.

Having learned from various sources that a declaration of war would be attempted on Monday next, *with closed doors,* I deemed it my duty to endeavor, by an exercise of my constitutional functions, to arrest this heaviest of all calamities, and avert it from our happy country. I accordingly made the effort of which I now give you the result, and of the success of which you will have already been informed before these pages can reach you. I pretend only to give you the substance of my unfinished argument. The glowing words, the language of the heart, have passed away with the occasion that called them forth. They are no longer under my control. My design is simply to submit to you the views which have induced me to consider a war with England, under existing circumstances, as comporting neither with the *interest* nor the *honor* of the American people; but as an idolatrous sacrifice of both, on the altar of *French rapacity, perfidy and ambition.*

France has for years past offered us terms of undefined commercial arrangement, as the price of a war with England, which hitherto we have not wanted firmness and virtue to reject. That price is now to be paid. We are tired of holding out; and, following the example of continental Europe, entangled in the artifices, or awed by the power of the destroyer of mankind, we are prepared to become instrumental to his projects of universal dominion. *Before these pages meet your eye, the last republic of the earth will have enlisted under the banners of the tyrant and become a party to his cause.* The blood of the American freemen must flow to cement his power, to aid in stifling the last struggles of afflicted and persecuted man, to deliver up into his hands the patriots of Spain and Portugal, to establish his empire over the ocean and over the land that gave our fathers birth—to forge our own chains! And yet, my friends, we are told, as we were told in the days of Mr. Adams, *"the finger of heaven points to war."* Yes, the finger of heaven *does* point to war! It points to war, as it points to the mansions of eternal misery and torture—as a flaming beacon warning us of that vortex which we may not approach but with certain destruction. It points to desolated Europe, and warns us of the chastisement of those nations who have offended against the justice, and almost beyond the mercy, of heaven. It announces the wrath to come upon those who, ungrateful for the bounty of Providence, not satisfied with the peace, liberty, security and plenty at home, fly, as it were, into the face of the Most High, and tempt his forbearance.

To you, *in this place,* I can speak with freedom; and it becomes me to do so ; nor shall I be deterred by the cavils and the sneers of those who hold as "foolishness" all that savors not of worldly wisdom, from expressing fully and freely those sentiments which it has pleased God, in his mercy, to engrave on my heart.

These are no ordinary times ; the state of the world is unexampled; the war of the present day is not like that of our revolution, or any which preceded it, at least in modern times. It is a war against the liberties and the happiness of mankind; it is a war in which the whole human race are the victims, to gratify the pride and lust of power of a single individual. I beseech you, put it to your own bosoms, how far it becomes you as freemen, as Christians, to give your aid and sanction to this impious and bloody war against your brethren of the human family. To such among you, if any such there be, who are insensible to motives not more dignified and manly than they are intrinsically wise, I would make a different appeal. I adjure you by the regard you have for your own safety and property, for the liberty and inheritance of your children—by all that you hold dear and sacred—to interpose your constitutional powers to save your country and yourselves from the calamity, the issue of which it is not given to human foresight to divine.

Ask yourselves if you are willing to become the virtual allies of Bonaparte? Are you willing, for the sake of annexing Canada to the Northern States, to submit to that overgrowing system of taxation which sends the European laborer supperless to bed, to maintain, by the sweat of your brow, armies at whose hands you are to receive a future master? Suppose Canada ours; is there any one among you who would ever be, in any respect, the better for it?—the richer, the freer, the happier, the more secure? And is it for a boon like this that you would join in the warfare against the liberties of man in the other hemisphere, and put your own in jeopardy? Or is it for the *nominal* privilege of a licensed trade with France that you would abandon your lucrative commerce with Great Britain, Spain and Portugal, and their Asiatic, African, and American dependencies; in a word, with every region of those vast continents?—that commerce which gives vent to your tobacco, grain, flour, cotton ; in short, to all your native products, which are denied a market in France? There are not wanting men so weak as to suppose that their approbation of warlike measures is a proof of personal gallantry, and that opposition to them indicates a want of that spirit which becomes a friend of his country ; as if it required more courage and patriotism to join in the acclamation of the day, than steadily to oppose one's self to the mad infatuation to which every people and all governments have, at some time or other, given way. Let the history of Phocion, of Agis, and of the De Witts, answer this question.

My friends, do you expect to find those who are now loudest in the clamor for war, foremost in the ranks of battle? Or, is the honor of this nation indissolubly connected with the political reputation of a few individuals, who tell you *they* have gone too far to recede, and that you must pay, with *your ruin*, the price of their *consistency?*

My friends, I have discharged my duty towards you, lamely and inadequately, I know, but to the best of my poor ability. The destiny of the American people is in their own hands. The net is spread for their destruction. You are enveloped in the toils of French duplicity, and if—which may Heaven in its mercy forbid—you and your posterity are to become hewers of wood and drawers of water to the modern Pharoah, it shall not be for the want of my best exertions to rescue you from the cruel and abject bondage. This sin, at least, shall not rest upon my soul.

JOHN RANDOLPH OF ROANOKE.

May 30th, 1812.

———•◦•———

CHAPTER XXXVII.

CLAY—CALHOUN.

ON the 18th of June, 1812, an act was approved by the President declaring that a state of war existed between the United States and Great Britain. It forms no part of the plan of this biography to enter into the details of the war. From them the student of history can derive but little information as to the causes of the growth, development and decay of nations. But there is an inquiry that might properly be made here, immediately bearing on this great subject, and deeply affecting the public conduct of John Randolph at the same time : *might not this war have been avoided?* might not the nation have saved the blood and treasure wasted in its prosecution, and escaped the evil consequences, both moral and political, that followed in its train? John Randolph declared that it might have been done; his whole opposition was based on the conviction that there was no need for such an extreme measure. "We can escape this conflict, said he, with honor—it is our duty to wait." No new cause of war had arisen—there would have been as much reason for the step in the June preceding as there was at the time of the declaration. The reader is already aware of the grounds of complaint against Great Britain ; he must be satisfied also that there was at least some color of reason for the course which she declared she was compelled to pursue towards neutrals, in order to save her own existence in the general wreck of European nations.

As to the impressment of seamen, she only claimed the right to search for British subjects on board of American merchant vessels; yet it was one, arising from the common origin of the two nations, most difficult to be enforced, liable to be abused, and was greatly abused by proud and insolent naval officers. But because there was right and reason on both sides, this was not between rational people a subject of war, but of adjustment and compromise, and in truth it was adjusted to the satisfaction of Mr. Monroe and Mr. Pinckney in the treaty of December, 1806; but the President, as we know, put that treaty in his pocket, and refused to submit it to the consideration of the Senate.

As to the denial of our right to the *carrying trade*, and the question of *constructive blockade*, which had been so much discussed, and were charged as interpolations by Great Britain into the law of nations, they were now swallowed up by the orders in council. The reader is informed of the exact posture of that question on the 4th of November, 1811, when Congress was first assembled. It was narrowed down to this: Britain declared, that, notwithstanding the revocation of the French decrees so far as they affected the United States, she could not repeal her orders until the United States should procure a further modification so as to allow goods of British origin owned by American citizens to be carried to France and other parts of the continent. As the matter stood they were only restored to half their rights as a neutral power. By the law of nations, enemy's goods not contraband of war, purchased and owned by neutrals, are lawful subjects of trade; but there lay the rub; in the exercise or non-exercise of this right was involved the commercial jealousy and rivalry of the two nations. The United States did not want a restoration of their rights, because if British goods under cover of the American flag could be carried to the continent, it would at once open a vast and profitable outlet to the manufactures and other products of England, now locked up in·their warehouses, and would cut off that monopoly enjoyed by the citizens of the United States in consequence of the prohibition laid on all articles of English origin. It was not then a question of principle, but one of pure commercial rivalry.

England urged on the United States that she should demand a restoration of all her rights as a neutral nation; the United States replied that they had been restored as far as they required, and insisted that England should comply with her pledges, and proceed *pari passu* with France in the repeal of her orders in council. The true motives for the persistence of both in their demands, were very perceptible, but by neither were avowed. Here then was the whole question, and on this issue the Congress of the United States resolved to go to war.

But in the position assumed by the British ministry, which was certainly plausible, if not just, they were not sustained by the nation. The clamors of the commercial and manufacturing interests were heard in Parliament and by the Royal cabinet. There was a powerful and influential party, with Canning at their head that demanded a repeal of the orders in council; the ministry were dissolved, and a commission given by the prince regent to one of the opposition party to form a cabinet friendly to American interests. Owing to the discordant elements of the opposition itself, and not to any difficulty on this question, the new organization did not take place at that time, but these circumstances manifested the temper of the nation, and showed plainly that the obnoxious measures of government must soon be condemned and repealed. These facts were known to the Congress of the United States before the declaration of war, and they must have convinced any reasonable and candid mind that a favorable change in the posture of affairs was to be expected at no distant period. And in fact on the 23d day of June, just five days after the declaration of war, it was ordered and declared by the prince regent, in council, "that the order in council, bearing date the 7th of January, 1807, and the order in council bearing date the 26th of April, 1809, be revoked, so far as may regard American vessels and their cargoes, being American property, from the first day of August next."

The embargo that was laid preparatory to war, commenced the 4th of April, and was to last ninety days—until the 4th of July. No one expected war to be declared before that period. Mr. Madison, it was well known, wished the embargo to be extended to four months; that is, to the 4th of August. A motion was actually made in the House to this effect, but was rejected. He said, that if at the end of four months no favorable news came from abroad, he would then be ready to recommend a declaration of war. By the 4th of August, news came of the repeal of the orders in council! Had his inclinations then been followed, the nation might have been saved from all the disastrous consequences of the precipitate action of Congress.

Mr. Madison, indeed, was not favorable to the embargo—it was

forced upon him. " I am confident in the declaration," said Mr.
Randolph, in conclave, " that this is not a measure of the executive,
but that it is engendered by an extensive excitement upon the executive." The relation of the two great departments of government
had entirely changed from what it was in the days of Mr. Jefferson ;
then the commanding power of a great mind and a determined will
gave direction to all the measures of the legislature, but now the
master-spirits that controlled affairs were to be found on the floor of
Congress. The Speaker of the House of Representatives, and the
leading member of the Committee of Foreign Affairs, from their
position, if they had talents, were most likely to exert a large influence over the proceedings of the House. The persons occupying
those stations were Henry Clay and John C. Calhoun. They were
both possessed of great minds, endowed with extraordinary powers of
eloquence, were young, ardent, ambitious, and for the first time members of the popular branch of the national legislature. In the excited state of the country, a better field could not have been found for
the display of their talents. The deep enthusiasm of their souls,
the chief element of their greatness, enlivened by a brilliant imagination in the one, and tempered by large faculties of reason in the
other, gave such a strength and boldness to their thoughts, that they
imparted confidence to the timid, clearness to the obscure, and infused
a portion of their own zeal into more phlegmatic natures,—none could
escape the contagion of their influence.

A few months after the opening of Congress, Mr. Randolph,
while speaking of these new lights of the administration, said to a
friend, " They have entered this House with their eye on the Presidency, and mark my words, sir, we shall have war before the end of
the session !" Aside from the aspiration of a noble mind to tread
some brilliant and high career, we do not believe they had any selfish
end in view. Cold and calculating natures only influence others by
motives akin to their own. Neither calculation nor logic, but the
sympathizing impulses of a great soul, can deeply move the masses
of mankind. A magnanimous spirit, animated with the inspiring
breath of a whole people, may go forth with the confidence of a
Moses, feeling that the voice of the people is the voice of God. But
not always are the acts even of a great nation the result of divine
inspiration. Sometimes they are influenced from the opposite quar-

ter of the spiritual world, and partake more of the demoniac than the godlike.

The mere abstract question of international law involved between Great Britain and the United States, if left to a court of admiralty and a jury composed of citizens of the world, might have been decided against them. But neither courts nor attorneys can decide the fate of empires.

The democracy of America, which constituted the great mass of the people of America, were thoroughly anti-British; a common origin and a common tongue served only as points of contrast. There was a deep-rooted antipathy between them and the proud, pampered aristocracy of England. Their sympathies were all on the side of France and her struggles for liberty; even Bonaparte came in for a share of their regard. His boldness, his humble origin, his brilliant success, shed such a halo of glory around his brow as to obscure the darker features of his tyrannical nature. Then there were the old memories of Bunker's Hill, Monmouth, La Fayette, Rochambeau, and Yorktown—these household themes were familiar to every domestic fireside. Add the long catalogue of modern grievances—the plunder of our commerce, the capture of our seamen, the insults to our national flag, the insolence, and proud, contemptuous bearing of British officers even in our own ports—this is too much! we will not endure it! We will fight rather than suffer their aristocratic insolence any longer—" Free trade and sailors' rights! God and Liberty!" We will fight for these, come what will of it! We will teach these insulting English better manners, or blow them to the devil!

Such was the universal sentiment throughout the vast regions of the south and west. Their newspapers and their popular orators (who was not an orator in those excited times?) proclaimed *Free trade and sailors' rights!* Without a sailor or a ship on the sea, the fiery multitude echoed back, *Free trade and sailors' rights!* This comprehensive phrase served the same turn now, that *millions for defence, not a cent for tribute*, had served on a former occasion. A deep sense of indignation and wrong, vaguely shadowed forth in that expression "*free trade and sailors' rights*," pervaded the whole country. It was vain to argue with people in such a temper; he who had the folly to attempt it would imagine that he could arrest the bellowing thunder storm on the point of a bodkin. Henry Clay and John C. Calhoun were the representatives of these excited elements on the floor of Congress; it was in their power to temper these impetuous energies, and to have served as conductors to the surcharged electric fires that threatened momentary explosion; but they were too full themselves of the same fiery impulses to repress them in others; they boldly marched forward; and knowing and feeling that the people were pressing close behind them, plunged the nation headlong into a ruinous war—we do not mean ruinous in a military sense—no one ever doubted that our people, sooner or later, would be triumphant in every conflict, by land and by sea. The energies and the courage of a free people are irrepressible and unconquerable—we mean disastrous in the sense predicted by John Randolph; disastrous to the Constitution and to the principles of the people.

Two of the avowed objects of this war were, the conquest of Canada, and the plunder of the high seas; ends that fostered a spirit of aggression and of retaliation unbecoming the character of our country or of its peaceful institutions. We say nothing of the disturbance of that balance of power between the States and the Federal Government so necessary for their just and harmonious action, which was the necessary consequence of the enormous patronage and excessive energy of the executive in the time of a foreign war. Exhausted of its resources by a long series of restrictive measures, the nation commenced hostilities with borrowed money; a large national debt was accumulated; a depreciated, ruinous, demoralizing paper currency deluged the whole land, and a hot-bed system of domestic manufactures were stimulated into existence, at the expense of agriculture and commerce, which were the natural sources of wealth and prosperity to a new, wide-spread, and sparsely populated country.

The proclamation of peace found the people burdened with a national debt, ruined by a depreciated currency, corrupted, as far as they could be corrupted, by all the demoralizing influences which for years had been working on their integrity; and incumbered with innumerable domestic manufactures, which, like Jonah's gourd, had sprung up in a night, and could not bear the rude shocks of foreign competition produced by returning commerce.

Those who brought on and sustained the war were necessarily expected to find a remedy for the evils that followed in its train. The same master-spirits who conducted the war, controlled the course of legislation for years after the restoration of peace. They recommended a National Bank as the agent for managing and liquidating the national debt, and as the means of restoring and regulating the currency; they advocated the imposition of heavy duties on the importation of foreign goods, as the means of producing a revenue to pay the national debt, and also as a protection to those infant manufactures, which, since the death of their nurses and foster-mother, non-intercourse, embargo, and war, would be left entirely exposed to the crushing weight of maturer rivals; and as these enormous duties were likely soon to furnish means to pay off the national debt and to take away the pretext for imposing them, a convenient sinking fund was found in a system of internal improvements by the Federal Government. These were the remedies furnished by the advocates of the war to cure the evils it had produced. And how do we find them? just such as the federalists would have recommended—gross violations of the Constitution, that nothing but the most imperious necessity could tolerate, are established into precedents and made part of a regular system of legislation—vile excrescences, that like a cancer had eaten into the heart of the body politic, and defaced the fair features of the Constitution, are hailed as the beautiful outgrowth of her vital functions.

By some righteous retribution of Providence both these great men —for truly great they were—have been punished for their sins in precipitating a war that might have been retarded, and perhaps honorably avoided, and for violating the Constitution to find a remedy for its evils. If Randolph's supposition be true, they both failed of their end. The reason is very plain—they ceased to embody the sentiment and to reflect the will of the great body of the democracy, when they began to undermine the Constitution to find a remedy for evils they had inflicted on the country, and became the advocates of special interests, monopolies, and a moneyed aristocracy. Mr. Clay, with a zeal and perseverance worthy of a better cause, labored all his days to force his miscalled American System as a permanent institution on the country: but the people were against him, and not one of his measures can now be found on the statute book.

Mr. Calhoun, when too late, saw and acknowledged the error of his ways, and in a desperate effort to retrieve his own section of the country from the evil consequences of his own measures, well nigh involved the whole in civil war and ruin.

But, for the time being, they rode triumphantly on the full tide of popularity, while Randolph, who foresaw and warned them of the consequences of their rash measures, was driven into retirement. All the powers of two administrations and the political presses in their employment, the government at Washington, and the government at home in his native State, were employed to crush and destroy him. John W. Eppes, the most distinguished and experienced leader of the administration party, was induced to make his residence in the county of Buckingham, that Randolph might have the most able and formidable opposition the country could afford. These two men, who had been friends and companions in their youth, and rival leaders on the floor of Congress, met for the first time, in 1811, as candidates for the suffrages of the same people. But the long services of their old servant were triumphant on this occasion. Again they met, in the spring of 1813; times had changed; the country was involved in war, and all its resources were pledged to a successful issue; redoubled efforts must now be made to drive him from the councils of the nation, who had opposed its measures, and foreboded nothing but evil as their consequence. Never was a political canvass conducted with more animation. In Buckingham, Mr. Randolph was threatened with personal violence if he attempted to address the people. Some of the older and more prudent persons advised him to retire, and not appear in public. " You know very little of me," said he, " or you would not give such advice." He was a man incapable of fear. Soon proclamation was made that Mr. Randolph would address the people. A dense throng gathered around; he mounted the hustings; on the outskirts there hung a lowering and sullen crowd that evidently meditated insult or violence on the first opportunity; he commenced: "I understand that I am to be insulted to-day if I attempt to address the people—that a mob is prepared to lay their rude hands upon me and drag me from these hustings, for daring to exercise the rights of a freeman." Then fixing his keen eye on the malcontents, and stretching out and slowly waving his long fore-finger towards them, he continued : " My Bible teaches me that the fear of God is the beginning of wisdom, but that the fear of man is the consummation of folly." He then turned to the people, and went on with his discourse. No one dared to disturb him—his spell was upon them—like the Ancient Mariner, " he held them with his glittering eye," and made them listen against their will to the story of their country's wrongs, and to feel that deep wounds had been inflicted in the sides of her constitution by those that now sought his political destruction, if not his life.

Mr. Randolph made extraordinary exertions during this canvass; he felt that something more than his own success or his own reputation were staked on the issue, and never was he more powerful, more commanding, more overwhelming in his eloquence.

In his favorite county of Prince Edward, where the people loved him like a brother, he surpassed even himself. A young man, who was a student in a neighboring college, declares that he stood on his feet for three hours unconscious of the flight of time—that he never heard such burning words fall from the lips of man, and was borne along on the tide of his impassioned eloquence like a feather on the bosom of a cataract. When he had ceased—when his voice was no longer heard, and his form had disappeared in the throng, no one moved—the people stood still as though they had been shocked by a stroke of lightning—their fixed eyes and pallid cheeks resembled marble statues, or petrified Roman citizens in the forum of Pompeii or Herculaneum.

But it was all in vain; the overwhelming pressure from without was more than even Charlotte District could withstand; and their favorite son was compelled to retire for a short time, while the storm of war was passing over the land, and to seek repose in the shades of Roanoke. How magnanimously he bore this defeat shall be made known in the following chapters.

END OF VOL. I.

LIFE OF JOHN RANDOLPH.

VOL. II.

JOHN RANDOLPH IN ENGLAND.

THE LIFE

OF

JOHN RANDOLPH

OF ROANOKE.

BY

HUGH A. GARLAND.

VOL. II.

TWELFTH EDITION.

CONTENTS OF VOL. II.

CONTENTS.

CHAPTER I.

WE have now to view Mr. Randolph in a new aspect. After an active, uninterrupted, and eventful career of fourteen years in the public service, in one of the most remarkable epochs of human history, we have now to follow him into retirement. The triumph of his enemies at the recent election had no power to shake the firmness of his purpose, or to disturb the serenity of his mind. "It relieves me from an odious thraldom," says he, "and, I assure you, my dear sir, I have thought and yet think, much more of the charming Mrs. G. than of the election. The low and base arts to which my adversaries have resorted, have not raised them or sunk me in my own estimation."

At home he lived in the utmost seclusion and solitude. Up to 1810 he made Bizarre his principal place of residence. Here he enjoyed the best of female society, for which no man had a higher relish—found employment in the education of his young nephews, the future heirs of his name and fortune, and on whom he doted with the fondness of a father; and solace for his leisure hours in a large miscellaneous library, and the society and conversation of old neighbors and well-tried friends. In 1810 he removed to Roanoke, his estate in Charlotte county, on the Roanoke river, some thirty-five or forty miles south of Bizarre " *a savage solitude,*" says he, " *into which I have been driven to seek shelter.*" Shortly before the recent election, on Sunday, March 21, 1813, the house at Bizarre took fire—the family were at church—very little saved. "I lost," says he, "a valuable collection of books. In it was a whole body of infidelity. the Encyclopedia of Diderot and D'Alembert. Voltaire's works, seventy volumes, Rousseau, thirteen quartos, Hume, &c., &c." By this calamity, if calamity it may be called (some of his friends congratulated him on the event), he was deprived of the chief source of pleasure and amusement in his *comfortless home*. The only companion of his solitude was Theodore Bland Dudley, a young relation he had taken to live with him in 1800. He educated this young man with much care and at great expense. He manifested towards him the solicitude and affection of a fond father—his letters are models of parental instruction. Dudley had recently graduated in medicine at Philadelphia, and returned to console the solitary hours of his best and most constant friend. "Consider yourself," said Randolph to him, "as not less entitled to command here, than if you were the child of my loins, as you are the son of my affections." Apart from the society of this young man, which he valued above all price, his only real enjoyment was in the correspondence of some two or three of his most intimate friends, to whom he unbosomed himself with a fulness and a freedom that showed in a remarkable degree the strength and constancy of his attachment, and the unbounded confidence he had in the fidelity and integrity of those men. To none did he speak or write more unreservedly than to Dr. John Brockenbrough, the President of the Bank of Virginia. No wonder, for his *superior* is not to be found—a man of rare talents, varied learning, large experience in the business of life, refined manners, delicate sensibility, a perfect gentleman and a faithful friend. "Cherish the acquaintance of that man," he exhorts Dudley; "he is not as other men are." In writing to this gentleman he says: "Your two letters, the last of which I received this evening by my servant, have given me a degree of satisfaction that I find it difficult to express. Let me beg a continuance of these marks of your remembrance and friendship. At all times they would be highly acceptable; but in my present isolated state—a state of almost total dereliction—they are beyond price. I should have thanked you for your letter by the post, through the same channel, but I was induced from its contents to suppose that you would have left Richmond before my answer could reach it; and I wish that you had, because I *may* be debarred the pleasure of seeing you and Mrs. B. at my lonely and (as it will probably appear to you both) savage habitation. It is therefore that this letter is written. You will not wonder, when you see how I live, at my reluctance to leave you, and I was going to say my other *friends* in Richmond. It is indeed a life of seclusion that I live here, unchequered by a single ray of enjoyment. I try to forget myself in books; but that 'pliability of man's spirit' which yields him up to the illusions of the ideal world, is gone from me for ever. The mind stiffened by age and habit refuses to change its career. It spurns the speculative notions which hard experience has exploded; it looks with contempt or pity, in sorrow or in anger, upon the visionary plans of the youthful and sanguine. My dear sir, 'there is another and a better world,' and to it alone can we look without a certainty of disappointment, for consolation, for mercy, for justice." On another occasion he says : " I passed but an indifferent night, occasioned, in a great measure, by the regret I feel at leaving such friends as yourself and Mrs. Brockenbrough, and at the prospect of passing my time in that utter solitude of my comfortless habitation, where I have prepared for myself, by my own folly, many causes of uneasiness. If I had followed old Polonius's advice, and been 'to mine own self true,' I might have escaped the lot which seems to be in reserve for me."

To another friend, Francis S. Key, of Washington City, he writes more cheerfully. His letters to that gentleman about this time were very frequent and copious; they show more fully the workings of his mind. We shall draw largely on the correspondence for the instruction of the reader.

In one of his letters he gives a description of his habitation, the log cabins, and the boundless primeval forest by which they were surrounded. In reply, Key says, " I could not help smiling at the painting you have given me of Roanoke—*laudat diversa sequentes.* To me it seemed just such a shelter as I should wish to creep under,

> " A boundless contiguity of shade,
> Where rumor of oppression and deceit
> Might never reach me more."

In reference to the recent election he thus writes ·

ROANOKE, May 10, 1813.

DEAR FRANK :—For so, without ceremony, permit me to call you. Among the few causes that I find for regret at my dismissal from public life, there is none in comparison with the reflection that it has separated me—perhaps for ever—from some who have a strong hold on my esteem and on my affections. It would indeed have been gratifying to me to see once more yourself, Mr. Meade, Ridgely, and some few others; and the thought that this may never be, is the only one that infuses any thing of bitterness into what may be termed my disappointment, if a man can be said to be disappointed when things happen according to his expectations; on every other account, I have cause of self-congratulation at being disenthralled from a servitude at once irksome and degrading. The grapes are *not* sour —you know the manner in which you always combated my wish to retire. Although I have not, like you, the spirit of a martyr, yet I could not but allow great force to your representations. To say the truth, a mere sense of duty alone might have been insufficient to restrain me from indulging the very strong inclination which I have felt for many years to return to private life. It is now gratified in a way that takes from me every shadow of blame. No man can reproach me with the desertion of my friends, or the abandonment of my post in a time of danger and of trial. " I have fought the good fight, I have kept the faith." I owe the public nothing; my friends, indeed, are entitled to every thing at my hands; but I have received my discharge, not indeed *honestam dimissionem*, but passable enough, as times go, when delicacy is not over fastidious. I am again free, as it respects the public at least, and have but one more victory to achieve, to be so in the true sense of the word. Like yourself and Mr. Meade, I cannot be contented with endeavoring to do good for goodness' sake, or rather for the sake of the Author of all goodness. In spite of me, I cannot help feeling something very like contempt for my poor foolish fellow-mortals, and would often consign them to Bonaparte in this world, and the devil, his master, in the next; but these are but temporary fits of misanthropy, which soon give way to better and juster feelings.

When I came away I left at Crawford's a number of books, letters, papers, &c., in (and out of) an open trunk; also a gun, flask, shot-belt, &c. Pray take them in charge for me, for although one-half of them are of no consequence, the *rest* are; and you may justly ask why I have been so careless respecting them?—because I am the most lazy and careless man on earth (La Bruyere's absent man is nothing to me), and because I am in love. Pray give the letters special protection.

To the same.

ROANOKE, May 22, 1813.

MY DEAR FRIEND —Your letter being addressed to Farmville, did not reach me until yesterday, when my nephew brought it up. *Charlotte Court House* is my post-office. By my last you will perccive that I have anticipated your kind office in regard to my books and papers at Crawford's: pray give them protection "until the Chesapeake shall be fit for service." It is, I think, nearly eight years since I ventured to play upon those words in a report of the Secretary of the Navy. I have read your letter again and again, and cannot express to you how much pleasure the perusal has given me.

I had taken so strong a disgust against public business, conducted as it has been for years past, that I doubt my fitness for the situation from which I have been dismissed. The House of R. was as odious to me as ever school-room was to a truant boy. To be under the dominion of such wretches as (with a few exceptions) composed the majority, was intolerably irksome to my feelings; and although my present situation is far from enviable, I feel the value of the exchange. To-day, for the first time, we have warm weather; and as I enjoy the breeze in my cool cabin, where there is scarce a fly to be seen, I think with loathing of that "compound of villanous smells" which at all times inhale through the H. of R., but which in a summer session are absolutely pestilential. Many of those, too, whose society lessened the labors of our vocation are gone; Bleecker, Elliott, Quincy, Baker, and (since) Bayard; so that I should find myself in Congress among enemies or strangers. Breckenridge, Stanford, and Ridgely, and Lloyd in the Senate, are left; and I am glad that they are not in a minority so forlorn as the last. They have my best wishes—all the aid that I shall ever give to the public cause. The great master of political philosophy has said that "mankind has no title to demand that we should serve them in spite of themselves." It is not upon this plea, however, that I shall stand aloof from the bedside of my delirious country. My course is run. I acquiesce in the decision that has been passed against me, and seek neither for appeal nor new trial.

I shall not go northward until towards the autumn, when I must visit Philadelphia. My late friend Clay's youngest son will return with me; and that journey over, I shall probably never cross James River again.

You are mistaken in supposing that "we Virginians like the war better the nearer it approaches us;" so far from it, there is a great change in the temper of this State, and even in this district, paradoxical as it may seem, against the war. More than half of those who voted against me, were persuaded that I was the *cause* of the war; that the Government wished for peace (e. g. the Russian Embassy), but that I thwarted them in every thing, and that without unanimity amongst ourselves, peace could not be obtained. If you are acquainted with Daschoff, tell him that the Russian mediation was (strange as it may appear) made the instrument of my ejection. It gave a temporary popularity to the ministry—the people believing that peace was their object. Its effect on the elections generally has been very great. Some were made to believe that the British fleet in the Chesapeake was to aid my election.

My kinsman, Dudley—now M. D.—is with me, and his society serves to cheer the solitude in which I am plunged. He desires to be remembered to you. Present my best love to Mrs. Key and the little folks. When you see the family at Blenheim, present me to them—also to Mr. Stone—and believe me, always, dear sir, and most affectionately,

Yours

John Randolph of Roanoke.

To the Same.

May 23d, 1813.

Your letter of the 14th was received to-day—many thanks for it. By the same mail, Mr. Quincy sent me a copy of his speech of the 30th of last month. It is a composition of much ability and depth of thought; but it indicates a spirit and a temper to the North which is more a subject of regret than of surprise. The grievances of Lord North's administration were but as a feather in the scale, when compared with those inflicted by Jefferson and Madison.

I fervently hope that we may meet again. I do not wish you so ill as to see you banished to this Sinope; and yet to see you here would give me exceeding great pleasure. Every blessing attend you.

Francis Scott Key, Esq.

John Randolph to Dr. John Brockenbrough.

Roanoke, June 2d, 1813.

I did not receive your letter of the 26th until last evening, and then I was obliged for it to my good old neighbor, Colonel Morton, who never omits an occasion of doing a favor, however small. The gentleman by whom you wrote is very shy of me; nor can I blame him for it. No man likes to feel the embarrassment which a consciousness of having done wrong to another is sure to inspire, and which the sight of the object towards whom the wrong has been done never fails to excite, in the most lively and painful degree.

My neighbor, Colonel C——k, who goes down to Petersburg and Richmond to-morrow, enables me (after a fashion) to answer your question, "How and where I shall pass the summer months?" To which I can only reply—*as it pleases God!* If I go to any watering-place, it will be to our hot springs, for the purpose of stewing the rheumatism out of my carcase, if it be practicable.

It would have been peculiarly gratifying to me to have been with you when Leigh, Garnett, W. Meade, and, I must add, M——, were in Richmond. If we exclude every "party-man, and man of ambition," from our church, I fear we shall have as thin a congregation as Dean Swift had, when he addressed his clerk, "Dearly beloved Roger!" What I like M—— for, is neither his courtesy, nor his intelligence, but a certain warm-heartedness, which is now-a-days the rarest of human qualities. His manner I think peculiarly unfortunate. There is an ostentation of ornament (which school-boys lay aside when they reach the senior class), and a labored infelicity of expression, that is hateful to one's feelings. We are in terror for the speaker. But this fault he has already in some degree corrected; and by the time he is as old as you or I, it will have worn off. I was greatly revolted by it on our first acquaintance, and even now, am occasionally offended; but the zeal with which he devotes himself to the service of his friends and of his country, makes amends for all. It is sometimes a bustling activity, of little import to its *object*, but which is to be valued in reference to its motive.

I am not surprised at what you tell me of our friend. We live in fearful times, and it is a perilous adventure that he is about to undertake. In a few years more, those of us who are alive will have to move off to *Kaintuck*, or the *Mississippi*, where corn can be had for sixpence a bushel, and pork for a penny a pound. I do not wonder at the rage for emigration. What do the bulk of the people get here, that they cannot have for one-fifth of the labor in the western country? Surely that must be the Yahoo's paradise, where he can get dead drunk for the hundredth part of a dollar.

What you tell me of Milnor is quite unexpected. He was one of the last men whom I should have expected to take orders; not so much on account of his quitting a lucrative profession, as from his fondness for gay life. I am not sure that it is the safest path. The responsibility is awful—it is tremendous.

Thanks for your intelligence respecting my poor sister. If human skill could save her, Dr. Robinson would do it; but there is nothing left, except to smooth her path to that dwelling whither we must all soon follow her. I can give Mrs. B. no comfort on the subject of her son. For my part, it requires an effort to take an interest in any thing; and it seems to me strange that there should be found inducements strong enough to carry on the business of the world. I believe you have given the true solution of this problem, by way of corollary from another, when you pronounce that free-will and necessity are much the same. I used formerly to puzzle myself, as abler men have puzzled others, by speculations on this opprobrium of philosophy. If you have not untied the Gordian knot, you have cut it, which is the approved *methodus medendi* of this disease.

Write to me when you can do no better. Worse you cannot do for yourself, nor better for me. You can't imagine what an epoch in my present life a letter from you constitutes. If I did not know that you could find nothing here beyond the satisfaction of mere animal necessity, I should entreat Mrs. B. and yourself to visit my solitary habitation. May every blessing attend you both.

Yours, unchangeably,
JOHN RANDOLPH OF ROANOKE.

John Randolph to Francis S. Key.

ROANOKE, July 17th, 1813

DEAR FRANK,—I rode twenty miles this morning, in the hope of receiving letters from some of those few persons who honor me with their regard. Nor have I been disappointed. Your letter, and one from Dr. B., had arrived a few moments before me. I received the pamphlets through friend Stanford, who has too much on his hands to think of me every post; and I am not at all obliged to the gentleman who detained them on their passage, and who annotated one of them, I suppose for my edification. It is certainly not all *emendation*, for this critical labor.

I heartily wish that I were qualified in any shape to advise you on the subject of a new calling in life. Were I Premier, I should certainly translate you to the see of Canterbury; and if I were not too conscious of my utter incompetency, I should like to take a professorship in some college where you were principal; for, like you, "*my occupation* (tobacco-making) *is also gone.*" Some sort of employment is absolutely necessary to keep me from expiring with ennui. I "see no reviews," nor any thing else of that description. My time passes in uniform monotony. For weeks together I never see a new face; and, to tell you the truth, I am so much of Captain Gulliver's way of thinking respecting my fellow-Yahoos, (a few excepted, whose souls must have transmigrated from the generous Houyhnhnms,) that I have as much of their company as is agreeable to me, and I suspect that they are pretty much of my opinion; that I am not only ennuyé myself, but the cause of ennui in others. In fact, this business of living is, like Mr. Barlow's reclamations on the French Government, *dull work;* and I possess so little of pagan philosophy, or of Christian patience, as frequently to be driven to the brink of despair. "The uses of this world have long seemed to me stale, flat, and unprofitable;" but I have worried along, like a worn-out horse in a mail coach, by dint of habit and whipcord, and shall at last die in the traces, running the same dull stage, day after day.

When you see Ridgely, commend me to him and his amiable wife. I am really glad to hear that he is quietly at home, instead of scampering along the bay shore, or inditing dispatches. Our upper country has slid down upon the lower. Nearly half our people are below the falls. Both my brothers are gone; but I must refer you to a late letter to Stanford, for the state of affairs hereabouts. Henry Tucker is in Richmond; Beverly at Norfolk; whence, if he return, he will win his life with the odds against him.

I am much pleased with Mr. Gaston's speech on Webster's motion. Chief Justice Marshall had taught me to think highly of his abilities; and my expectations, although raised, have not been disappointed.

I have seen the scotched *tail* of Mr. Secretary M——'s report to his master, which drags its wounded length along most awkwardly. I should like to hear what Mons. Serrurier would say. Mr. Russell and the Duke of Bassano are, it seems, confronted across the Atlantic. I should be glad to have his Imperial and Royal Majesty's Envoy called into court, and examined touching Mr. M——'s declaration. * * *

Nicholson has luckily shifted his quarters, from an exposed to a very safe position, where he may reflect undisturbed on the train of measures which have issued in the present unparalleled state of things. With me, he condemned them at the beginning, but gradually coincided with the views of the administration. He may live to see the time when he will wish that he had steadily opposed himself to them. I would not give the reflection that, under every circumstance of discouragement, I never faltered or wavered in my opposition to them, to be president for life. Nearly eight years ago the *real views and true character* of the Executive were disclosed to me, and I made up my mind as to the course which my duty called upon me to follow. I predicted the result which has ensued. The length of time and vast efforts which were required to hunt me down, convince me that the cordial co-operation of a few friends would have saved the Republic. Sallust, I think, says, speaking of the exploits of Rome, 'Egregiam virtutem paucorum civium cuncta patiavisse;' and if those who ought to have put their shoulders to the work, had not made a vain parade of disinterestedness in returning to private life, all might have been saved. But the delicacy and timidity of some, and the versatility of others, insured the triumph of the court and the ruin of the country. I know not how I got upon this subject. It is a most unprofitable one.

Farewell, my good friend, and believe me, in truth

Yours,

JOHN RANDOLPH OF ROANOKE.

Have you met with a queer book,* by a Mr. James Fishback, of Lexington, Kentucky? He very politely sent me a copy, and accompanied it with a letter, in which, like the rest of his brethren, he flatters himself that his book will be generally read, and (of course) productive of great benefit. It is a most curious work for a lawyer (a Kentucky lawyer I mean), for such it seems he is, and brother-in-law to Mr. Pope, late of the Senate. I have dipped into it here and there, and whatever may be the skill displayed in its execution, the object I think is a good one. The man has thought much—but I doubt if clearly. Like many other writers in the same walk of composition, he appears not always to affix a precise meaning to his terms.

Sunday. Post in—not a line or newspaper from Washington.

Francis S. Key to J. Randolph.

GEORGETOWN, August 30, 1813.

MY DEAR FRIEND— * * * As you appeared to be tired of the country, I thought it likely you would have begun before now your journey to Cambridge, and hoped to have seen you as you passed. I have less regard for those Eastern people now than I used to have, and should care less about seeing them or their country. I cannot help suspecting them of selfish views, and that, if they can collect strength enough, they will separate. Their policy has certainly been a crooked one. The Quarterly Reviewers say well that the expedient of driving the administration into the war for the purpose of making them unpopular was " dangerous and doubtful." They might have added that it was dishonest. Certainly, the sort of opposition they are making now is one from which nothing good can be expected.

There was old ———, the other day, while I was at Frederickstown, travelling out of his road, and giving up his passage in the stage, and then travelling post to overtake it, and all to eat a dinner given by some of Mr. ———'s tools, apparently to him, but in fact to give eclat to his " distinguished young friend," and help on his intrigues. I believe this old man is honest, but can he be so vain as to run panting after praise in this way? or is he told and does he believe that people are to be driven from their opinions and made to fall into the ranks behind him and Mr. ——— and his Boston party, whenever he chooses to show himself?

I suppose Stanford told you that I was half inclined to turn politician. I did feel something like it—but the fit is over. I shall, I hope, stay quietly here, and mind my business as long as it lasts. I

* The title of the work is " The Philosophy of the Human Mind in respect to Religion."

have troubled myself enough with thinking what I should do—so I shall try to prepare myself for whatever may appear plainly to be my duty. That I must make some change, if the war lasts much longer (as I think it will), is very probable; but whether it shall be for a station civil, military, or clerical, I will not yet determine. To be serious, I believe that a man who does not follow his own inclina-tions, and choose his own ways, but is willing to do whatever may be appointed for him, will have his path of life chosen for him and shown to him, and I trust this is not enthusiasm.

Our friend Ridgely has really turned politician. He is a candi-date for the Maryland Legislature, and it is thought will be elected. I hardly know whether to wish he may succeed or not. He has some good, and, indeed, most excellent qualities for such a place, but he wants others, and will have few, if any, worthy of his confidence, to join him in a stand against the folly and wickedness of both parties. His situation will be peculiarly difficult and disagreeable, requiring great prudence and self-command. I know some of the men he will have to deal with, who are as cunning as he is unsuspicious.

Lloyd was here the other day. I was sorry I was out of town, as I should have liked to have seen him. He told Mrs. Key he believed you had given him up, and complained that you never wrote to him. She told him you almost always inquired of him in your letters to me, and mentioned what you said in your last about your observation in Congress, at which he laughed. I make great allowances for Lloyd's wrongheadedness. The federalists flattered and supported him—he was moderating in his opinions, but did not abandon his party—he still called himself a democrat—this affronted them, and at the next session they all voted against him. This conduct was calculated to convince him that their former support was an artifice, that they wished to dupe him, and expected their favors had bought him off from his party. At the same time the federal newspapers opened their abuse upon him, which was gross, false, and abominable.

Now, when all this is considered, I think he cannot yet be thought incorrigible. He has had no chance of judging coolly and dispassion-ately. I am convinced, though (N.'s) influence with him is great, it would never (but for these things) have been sufficient to keep him among the supporters of such a party. A man could not long be so blind to his own interest, and that of the country, but by his passions and prejudices being continually excited.

Randolph to Key.

ROANOKE, Sept. 12, 1813

DEAR FRANK—I had almost begun to fear that you had forgotten me, but this morning's mail brought me yours of the 30th of August.

Our post-office establishment is under shameful mismanagement. To-day I received a letter from Boston, post-marked Aug. 22d, and last week I got one from the same place marked Aug. 23d. I still keep up an intercourse, you see, with the head-quarters of good principles—for although I do not dabble in politics, " I have more regard for these Eastern people *now* than I used to have." Of the policy of driving the administration into war, I have the same opinion that you quote from the Quarterly Review. It was a crooked scheme, and has met its merited fate. But, my dear friend, great allowance is to be made for men under the *regime* of Clay, Grundy & Co.; and besides a few individuals only are answerable for the consequences of this tortuous policy. The great bulk of the Eastern States are guiltless of the sin. When I consider how much more these people have borne from the pettifoggers of the West, than they would submit to from Lord North; and reflect that there is no common tie of interest or of feeling between them and their upstart oppressors, I cannot pronounce them (in this instance at least) to be selfish. Indeed, I should not like them less if they were so—I am becoming selfish myself (when too late), and bitterly regret that I did not practise upon this principle many years ago. On this scheme I have abandoned politics for ever—and for the same reason should be sorry to see you, or our noble, spirited friend, Sterritt Ridgely, engaged in their pursuit. I have more faith in free will than you seem to express—for I believe we have it all in our power to choose wisely if we would. As to Ridgely, he is utterly unfit for public life. Do you ask why? You have partly answered the question. He is too honest, too unsuspicious, too deficient in *cunning.* I would as soon recommend such a man to a hazard-table and a gang of sharpers, as to a seat in any deliberative assembly in America.

Our quondam friend Lloyd—for "quondam friends are no rarity with me"—I made this answer at the ordinary at our court, to a gentleman who had returned from Rappahannock, and told me that he had seen some of my quondam friends. It was casually uttered, but I soon saw how deep it was felt by a person at table, whom I had not before observed. To return to Lloyd. He cannot, with any show of justice, complain of "my giving *him* up." The saddle is on the other horse. He is a spoiled child of fortune, and testy old bachelors make a poor hand of humoring spoiled children. Lloyd required to be flattered, and I would not perform the service. I would hold no man's regard by a base tenure. I see that Ridgely stands committed to abide the issue of an election. I am sorry for it for his own sake, and yet more on account of Mrs. R. Electioneering is upon no very pleasant footing any where; but with you, when the "*base proletarian rout*" are admitted to vote, it must be peculiarly irksome and repugnant to the feelings of a gentleman.

I am highly pleased with the XIVth number of the Quarterly Review, particularly the article on the subject of the poor laws; and that on the literature of France during the past century. Alas! for Walter Scott! These learned reviewers cannot prevail upon me to "revive the opinion" which the first reading (or attempt at reading) Rokeby produced. It is beneath criticism.

My will, but *not* my poverty, consents to my eastern tour. Our blessed rulers have nearly ruined me, and should the war be protracted much longer, I must go into some business, if there be any for which I am fit. My body is wholly worn out, and the intellectual part much shattered. Were I to follow the dictates of prudence, I should convert my estate into money, and move northwardly. Whether I shall have firmness and vigor enough to execute such a scheme, remains to be seen. My bodily infirmities are great and rapidly increasing, so that it will be impossible for me to sustain existence here when deprived of field exercises. I write now under the pressure of severe headache. You are not my physician, yet I cannot omit telling you that I am afflicted with a strange anomalous disease. It is of the heart; the most violent palpitations, succeeded by a total suspension of its functions for some seconds: and then, after several sudden spasmodic actions, the pulse becomes very slow, languid, and weak. When the fit is on, it may be seen through my dress across the room. It was this demon that put it out of my head to suggest to you the practical wisdom of damping the opposition to the government at this time. Of the print in question, I think nearly as you do; but it has done a deal of good with some mischief, and perhaps in the attempt to do more. How was the last administration overthrown, do you suppose? By rejecting proffered service from any quarter? Had the Aurora no agency, think you, in the work? "Homo sum:" man must work with mortal means. Not choosing to use such, I am idle. When administration call to their aid the refuse of New England in the persons of the ――― ――― ――― ――― and opposition reject the aid, or stand aloof from such high-minded, honorable men as S―――, K―――, G―――, Q―――, L―――, O―――, L―――, P―――, what can be expected but defeat? It is as if in the Southern States the assistance of the whites should be rejected against an adversary that embodied the negroes on his side. Be assured that nothing can be done with effect, without union among the parts, however heterogeneous, that compose the opposition. They have time enough to differ among themselves after they shall have put down the common foe; and if they must quarrel, I would advise them to adjourn the debate to that distant day.

I wish I could say something of my future movements. I look forward without hope. Clouds and darkness hang upon my prospects; and should my feeble frame hang together a few years longer the time may arrive when my best friends, as well as myself, may pray that a close be put to the same.

My best respects and regards to Mrs. Key, and love to the young folks. I fear I shall live to see you a grandfather. Farewell.

J. R. OF ROANOKE.

To the same.

ROANOKE, Sept. 26, 1813.

DEAR FRANK.—You owe the trouble of this letter to another which I threw upon your shoulders some time ago. As the shooting season approaches, I am reminded of my favorite gun, &c., in George-town. 'Tis true I have a couple of very capital pieces here, but neither of them as light and handy as that I left at Cranford's, and I fear it may be injured or destroyed by *rust—verbum sat.*

We have to-day the account of Perry's success on Lake Erie, which will add another year to the life of the war. Have you seen Woodfall's Junius ? The private correspondence has rsised the cha-racter of this mysterious being very much in my estimation. If you will pardon the *apparent* vanity of the declaration, it has reminded me frequently of myself. I hope he will never be discovered. I feel persuaded that he was an honest man and a sincere patriot, which heretofore I was inclined to doubt. We have been flooded. This river has not been so high since August, 1795. A vast deal of corn is destroyed. I fear I have lost 500 barrels, and eighty odd stacks of oats.

In tenderness to you, I have said nothing of Rokeby. Alas ! "good Earl *Walter dead and gone !*" God bless you !

J. R.

Best love to Mrs. Key, and Ridgley, when you see him.

John Randolph to Dr. John Brockenbrough

ROANOKE, Oct. 4, 1813

MY DEAR FRIEND :—By this time I trust you have returned to Richmond for the winter. It has been a grievous separation from you that I have endured for the last two months. In this period I have experienced some heavy afflictions, of which no doubt common fame has apprised you, and others that she knows not of. Let us not talk, and, if possible, not think of them. I hope that Mrs. B. has derived every possible advantage from her late excursion. As-sure her from me, that she has no friend who is more sincerely inter-ested in her temporal and eternal happiness than myself. Absorbed as I may be supposed to be with my own misfortunes, I live only for my friends. They are few, but they are precious beyond all human estimation. Write to me I beg of you; the very sight of your hand-writing gives a new impulse to my jaded spirits. I would write, but I cannot. I sometimes selfishly wish that you could conceive of my feelings. It is not the least painful of my thoughts that I am per-petually destined to be away from the sympathy of my friends, whilst I am deprived of every thing but affection towards them.

Yours truly,

John Ranlolph of Roanoke.

Mr. Randolph filed away his etters with great care. He in-dorsed on them the name of the author, the date, the time it was received and answered; and if the letter contained any subject of special interest, it was in like manner noted. On the following let-ter was indorsed " *Party Spirit;*" the words were underscored, and in addition was the figure of a hand, with the index finger pointing to them.

F. S. Key to John Randolph.

Georgetown, Oct. 5, 1813.

My dear Sir :—I was thinking of your gun a few days before I received your letter, and determined to rub off some of your rust, and try if I could kill Mrs. Key a bird or two. She has just given me another son, and of course deserves this piece of courtesy. As to amusement in shooting, I have lost it all, though once as ardent a sportsman as yourself. I am pleased to find that you are anticipat-ing such pleasures, as I therefore hope that the complaint you men-tioned in your former letter has left you. Exercise will no doubt tend to relieve you.

I have never read the private correspondence of Junius. I have a late edition, and will see if it contains it. I was always against Junius, having sided with Dr. Johnson and his opponents. There was, I know, great prejudice, and perhaps nothing else in this, but since the prejudice has worn away I have had no time to read so long a book. The article you speak of in the Quarterly Review (on the Poor Laws) I admire, and assent to more cordially than any thing on the subject I ever saw. It excited my interest greatly. What sound and able men are engaged in that work! I know none who are offering so much good to their country and the world, and I will not suffer myself to believe that it is thrown away. As to their rivals, the Edinburgh Reviews, I believe we should differ in opinion. I consider them as masked infidels and Jacobins; and if I had time, and it was worth while. I think I could prove it upon them. I would refer to the review of the life of Dr. Beatty, and of Cœlebs, and a few others, to prove that either knowingly, or ignorantly (I have hardly charity enough to believe the latter), they have misrepresented and attacked Christianity. Were you not pleased with the spirited defence against them which the Quarterly reviewers have made for Montgomery ? As to Walter Scott, I have always thought he was sinking in every successive work. He is sometimes himself again in " Marmion" and the " Lady of the Lake ;" but when I read these. and thought of the " Lay of the Last Minstrel," it always seemed to me that " hushed was the harp—the minstrel gone." I believe I am singular in this preference, and it may be that I was so " spell-bound" by " the witch notes" of the first, that I could never listen to the others. But does it not appear that to produce one transcend-ently fine epic poem is as much as has ever fallen to the life of one man ? There seems to be a law of the Muses for it. I was always provoked with him for writing more than his first. The top of Par-nassus is a point, and there he was, and should have been content. There was no room to saunter about on it; if he moved, he must descend ; and so it has turned out, and he is now (as the Edinburgh reviewers say of poor Montgomery) " wandering about on the lower slopes" of it.

I have not seen nor heard of Ridgley since his political campaign commenced. It closed yesterday, and we have not yet heard how he has fared. There is a report in town of the federalists having suc-ceeded in Frederick, which I expected would be the case from P——'s having had the folly and meanness to go all over the county making speeches. Ridgley's election is more doubtful, as the ad-ministration are very strong in his county. If he is elected, you will write to him, but don't discourage him too much. If he can command his temper, and be tolerably prudent, I think he may do some good. If cunning is necessary, he is indeed in a desperate case. I cannot think that the duty of an honest man when he con-sents to become a politician, is so difficult and hopeless as you seem to consider it. He will often, it is true, be wrong, but this may enable him to correct his errors. He will often have to submit to disappointments, but they may make him better and wiser. If he pursues his course conscientiously, guarding against his own am-bition, and exercising patience and forbearance towards others, he will generally succeed better than the most artful intriguer ; and the worst that can happen is, that in bad and distempered times he may be released from his obligations. [Meant to be a picture of Ran-dolph himself.—*Editor*.] Nor even then is there an end of his use-fulness ; for, besides many things that he may yet do for the common good, the public disorder may pass away, and when the people are sobered by suffering, they will remember who would have saved them from it ; and his consequence and ability to serve them will be incalculably increased, and their confidence in him unbounded. " Egregia virtus paucorum." I have forgotten your quotation from Sallust —you can supply it. It struck me forcibly, and I believe it admirably suited to these times; and that if this " egregia virtus" can be found among even a few of our politicians, who can be pressed and kept in the public service, we may be safe.

The opposition making to the administration may succeed (though I do not think it can) ; but if it did I should hope but little from it ; and that, because it is the opposition of a party. If it is the honestest party, it would be beaten again immediately ; for of two contending factions, the worst must be, generally, successful. This is just as plain to me as that of two gamesters; he who cheats most will commonly win the game. We should therefore, I think, burn the cards, or give up the game of party, and then, I believe, the knaves might be made the losers. " Keep up party and party spirit" should be (if they have any sense) the first and great commandment of the administration to its followers. Let P—— & Co. keep up a constant volley of the most irritating provocations against every one who does not belong to their party, and the weakest friend of the administration will fall into the ranks against them, and follow wherever they are ordered.

Suppose some ruinous and abominable measure, such as a French alliance, is proposed by the government; will the scolding of the federalists in Congress gain any of the well-meaning but mistaken and prejudiced friends of the administration, and induce them to oppose it ? Will not such persons, on the contrary, be driven to consider it a party question, and the clamor and opposition of these persons, as a matter of course ? Will men listen to reasonings against it, judge of it impartially, and see its enormity, who are blinded by party spirit ? But let such men as Cheves or Lowndes, men who are not party men or who will leave their party when they think them wrong; let them try if conciliation, and a plain and temperate exposure of the measure will not be effectual ; and it is certainly reasonable to expect it would. I am, besides, inclined to think that the worst men of a party will be uppermost in it ; and if so, there would, perhaps, be no great gain from a change. If every man would set himself to work to abate, as far as possible, this party spirit ; if the people could be once brought to require from every candidate a solemn declaration, that he would act constitutionally according to his own judgment, upon every measure proposed, without considering what party advocated or opposed it (and I cannot think that such a ground would be unpopular), its effects would be, at least, greatly diminished. This course might not, it is possible, succeed in ordinary times, and when this spirit is so universally diffused and inflamed; but we are approaching to extraordinary times, when serious national affliction will appease this spirit, and give the people leisure and temper to reflect. Something too might then be done towards promoting a reformation of habits and morals, without which nothing of any lasting advantage can be expected. Could such an administration as this preserve its power, if party spirit was even considerably lessened? And is this too much to expect? If so, there is nothing, I think, to be done but to submit to the punishment that Providence will bring upon us, and to hope that that will cure us. I am, you will think, full of this subject.

Farewell. Yours,

F. S. KEY.

Randolph to Key.

ROANOKE, October 17, 1813.

DEAR FRANK—Never was letter more welcome than that which I just now received from you, and which I must thank you for on the day set apart for letter-writing in the city of O., or defer it for another week. Alas! so far from taking the field against the poor partridges, I can hardly hobble about my own cabin. It pleased God on Tuesday last to deprive me of the use of my limbs. This visitation was attended with acute pain, reminding me most forcibly of my situation at your uncle's nearly six years ago.

By the papers, I see that our friend Ridgely has not succeeded in his election. I am gratified, however, to find that he was at the head of the ticket on which his name stood. Lloyd, I perceive, has carried his point in Talbot. I have a great mind to publish your letter. If any thing could do good, that, I am certain, would open the eyes of many, as many, at least, as would read it. But I have no faith, and cannot be saved. I look to the sands of Brandenburgh and the mountains of Bohemia with a *faint* hope of deliverance. You can expect nothing but groans and sighs from a poor devil, racked by rheumatism and tortured by a thousand plagues. I can barely summon heart enough to congratulate you and Mrs. K. (to whom give my best love) on the late happy event in your family. I shall be proud if my gun can furnish a piece of game for her. When I get better you shall hear from me at full. When you see Ridgely present me most affectionately to him and his truly excellent wife. I cannot be *glad* of his defeat, since it seems that the complexion of your legislature depended upon success there or in some county on the eastern shore; but I am convinced that it is best for him and his; and I am inclined to think no worse for the country. How can a foolish spendthrift young man be prevented from ruining himself? How can you appoint a guardian to a people bent on self-destruction? The state of society is radically vicious. It is there, if at all, that the remedy should be applied.

I will give you an instance. One of my overseers had acted in the most scandalous and indeed dishonest manner. Of course he had to decamp. Two gentlemen, in the most friendly manner, cautioned me against a contest at law with *an overseer*. No matter what the merits of the case, the employer must be cast. If I had been in Turkey, and this fellow a Janizary, they could not have thought the case more desperate, *and I know that they were right*.

We agree entirely in opinion respecting the Review, and nearly so on the subject of the rival journal. I wish I could get them more regularly, for in my condition any thing of that kind is a treasure. Under any other circumstances I should be ashamed of returning you this meagre epistle, in reply to your rich and copious letter.

Yours entirely,
JOHN RANDOLPH OF ROANOKE.

Key to Randolyh.

GEORGETOWN, November 27, 1813.

MY DEAR FRIEND—* * * I have heard indirectly that your are still sick. I hope this attack will not be such an one as you had at my uncle's. Pain and sickness are sad companions any where, but particularly in the country. It is hard to feel them and think them the trifles that (compared to other things) they certainly are. He alone who sends them can give us *strength and faith* to bear them as we ought. I wish you every relief, but above all, *this*. Let me hear from you as often as you can. Your letters may be short, but I shall not find them "meagre." * * * Maryland is in great agitation about the Alleghany election. The returned members will take their seats, and when they have elected the Governor and Council, then their right to their seats will be tried. This piece of jockeyship will degrade and ruin the party for ever. Perhaps it is well it should be so; the more each party disgraces itself the better.

I agree exactly with you, that " the state of society is radically vicious," and that it is there that the remedy is to be applied. Put down party spirit; stop the corruption of party elections; legislate not for the next election, but for the next century; build Lancaster schools in every hundred, and repair our ruined churches; let every country gentleman of worth become a justice of the peace, and show his neighbors what a blessing a benevolent, religious man is; and let the retired patriot, who can do nothing else, give his country his prayers, and often in his meditations " think on her who thinks not for herself"—"egregia virtus paucorum," &c. I often think of your apt quotation. I believe, nay, I am sure, that such a course, if honestly attempted, would succeed and save us. God bless you.

Your friend,

F. S. KEY.

Randolph to Key.

RICHMOND, Dec. 15, 1813.

DEAR FRANK:—I thank you very sincerely for your kind letter, which has been forwarded to me at this place (where I have been upwards of a month), and also for your remembrance of my request about the pamphlets, which I received yesterday. I wish, if any opportunity offers (I mean a good one), you would send me "War in Disguise;" it is bound up with the "Dangers of the Country," and some other pamphlets; and I pray you take care of my favorite fowling-piece. My fears are not from the *use* of it, but from *rust*.

You see what great objects fill my mind when the day "is big with the fate" of the whole race of man For my part, my fears of the power and arts of France, almost overpower the exercise of my judgment. I can see no cause why the world should not be punished now as in the days of Cæsar or Nebuchadnezzar; nor why Bonaparte may not be as good an instrument as either of those tyrants. Endeavoring to turn away my mind from such contemplations, I *try* to submit myself to him whose chastisement is love.

"Put down party spirit !" Put a little *fresh salt* on the sparrow's tail, and you will infallibly catch him. You will put down party spirit when you put down whisky-drinking, and that will be when the Greek calends come. I agree with you perfectly on the subject of the poor, unoffending Canadians. To us they are innocent; and in the eye of Heaven we must appear like so many descendants of Cain, seeking to imbrue our hands in our brothers' blood ! Suppose England to lose Canada, she gets in exchange for it our whole navigation. We were her great and only commercial rival. We possessed a tonnage, six years ago, greater than that of Great Britain at the accession of the present king. Greater than any other nation, except our parent state, ever owned. Our ships are short-lived, our seamen must have employment; all the foreign seamen, and many of the native, will seek the Russian, or some other neutral service. We may establish manufactures; but what of that? Those of England want no vent here. Moreover, she well knows that although peace may be restored, it will be a peace of double duties and restrictions, a "war in disguise " In short, I can see no motive in a wise English administration for putting an end to the war. My only trust is in their folly. Lord Castlereagh is not much better than his countryman, with the last syllable of his name, whom you met in the street.

Peace or *war*, the ruin of this country is inevitable ; *we* cannot have manufactures on a great scale.   Already our specie is drawn off to pay for domestic manufactures from the middle and eastern States. All the loans, &c., are spent in New-York ; and whilst she and Pennsylvania and New England are thriving in the most wonderful manner, with us the straw (near market) of a crop of wheat is worth more than the grain ; and we are feeding our horses and oxen with superfine flour, although the crop of Indian corn is superabundant— the flour being the cheaper of the two.

I heard of our friend, Sterrett Ridgley, by a gentleman who saw him at the races.   I cannot regret that he is not compelled to mingle in the throng at Annapolis.   Sallust, in that quotation of mine to which you so frequently refer, speaking of the exploits of the Roman people (surpassed by the Greeks in eloquence and learning, and by the Gauls in military prowess), declares it to be his opinion, after long and attentive study and observations, that " Egregiam virtutem paucorum civium cuncta patiavisse."   He goes on to add (I wish I had the book before me), " Sed post quam luxu atque desidio civitas corrupta est, rursus Respublica magnitudine sua, vitia sustentabat." In like manner, we have seen modern France, by the very force of magnitude and number, support the unutterable vices of her rulers, and bear down all before her.   As we cannot be saved by the extraordinary virtue of a few, so neither can we rely upon the height of our power to sustain the incapacity and corruption of our rulers, and of the great mass of our people.

As to Lancaster schools, I am for the *thing*, the *substance*, but not the name.   It is stolen by a fellow whom I detest.   I hope you have abolished his cruel and stupid punishments in your Georgetown Institution.   An article in the Quarterly Review (I think No. XI.), satisfied me that Lancaster was an impostor, and a hard-hearted wretch.   There is a late review on " National Education " (in No. XV. I believe), which pleased me very much   My best wishes attend all who are dear to you.   I hear that your poor protegée, Miss A. B., has sealed her final ruin.

Adieu, and believe me, always, most cordially, yours,
JOHN RANDOLPH OF ROANOKE.

Tuesday, Dec. 15, 1813.   Wednesday.

P. S. Have you read Lord Byron's Giaour? I have been delighted with it.   He *is* a poet, as was emphatically said of our P. Henry, " *He is* an orator !"   I have also been much pleased with Horace in London, and the Intercepted Twopenny Post.

Key to Randolph.

GEORGETOWN, January 20, 1814.

My DEAR FRIEND,— * * * I have no news that I think would interest you. Cheves is said to have been made Speaker, against the wishes of the administration party, who were very active for Grundy. I cannot help thinking his election a favorable circumstance.

I can hear nothing of the book you mention (English) from any one but Swift, who says he heard it spoken of in New-York as an ingenious performance. I would read it, and give you my opinion of it, if I came across it, provided it was not too long. I don't believe there are any new objections to be discovered to the truth of Christianity, though there may be some art in presenting old ones in a new dress. My faith has been greatly confirmed by the infidel writers I have read ; and I think such would be the effect upon any one who has examined the evidences. Our Church recommends their perusal to students of divinity, which shows she is not afraid of them. Men may argue ingeniously against our faith—as indeed they may against any thing—but what can they say in defence of their own ? I would carry the war into their own territories. I would ask them what they believed. If they said they believed any thing, I think that thing might be shown to be more full of difficulties, and liable to infinitely greater objections than the system they opposed, and they more credulous and unreasonable for believing it. If they said they believed nothing, you could not, to be sure, have any thing further to say to them. In that case they would be insane, or, at best, illy qualified to teach others what they ought to believe or disbelieve.

I can never doubt (for we have the word of God for it, and it is so plainly a consequence of his goodness) that all who inquire, with that sincerity and earnestness which so awful a subject requires, will find the truth—" Seek, and ye shall find." Did you ever read " Grotius de Veritate ?" I should like to see an infidel attempt an answer to that book. * * *.

Randolph to Key.

RICHMOND, February 17, 1814.

DEAR FRANK :—You plead want of time, and I may, with equal truth declare, that I have nothing worth twelve and half cents— which, I believe, is the postage from here to the city of O. Indeed I have been living myself in " a world without souls," until my heart is " as dry as a chip," and as cold as a dog's nose." Do not suppose, however, that the *Jew book* has made any impression upon me; as I cannot see how the human mind, unassisted by the light of Christianity, can stop half-way at deism, instead of travelling the whole length to which fair deduction would lead it, to frozen, cheerless atheism; so it appears to me most wonderful, that any man, believing in the *Old* Testament, can reject the *New;* and it is perhaps not the least conclusive of the proofs of the authenticity of the latter, that the Jews, admitting as it were the premises, should blindly reject the inevitable conclusion.

Have you read the work of Paley, reviewed in a late Edinburgh? "The Lord deliver me from Archdeacon Paley!" I am persuaded that, with the best intentions, this man has done infinite—rather great mischief to the cause he espouses. You are rich in having Swift and Meade with you. I am glad that the Colonel (what is his Christian name?) has escaped the recoil of our own measures. Bid him and W—— accept my best wishes. Poor W——! what a situation his imprudence has reduced him to! I have thought a hundred times of the meeting and parting, when he returns to his prison-house, between him and his family; and I bless God that I have been the probable means of saving Charles and Mrs. Ridgely from a like pang. Why do you say nothing of Charles Sterrett Ridgely? It is the more necessary, since he has given up writing to me. My warmest wishes attend him and all at Oakland! Remember me, also, to Blenheim and the Woodyard.

We are all in a bustle here with the news from Europe. For my part, I hope that Blunderbuss Castlereagh may succeed in preventing a peace "which shall confirm to the French Empire an extent of territory France under her kings never knew." If they permit him to retain the low countries and Piedmont, they will act like the sapient commissioner appointed to examine the vaults of the Parliament House, on the alarm of the gunpowder-plot, who reported, "that he had discovered seventy-five barrels of gunpowder concealed under faggots; that he had caused fifty to be removed, and *hoped the other twenty-five would do no harm.*"

I see the Federal Republican, on the authority of the Evening Post, has accused me of being "an obvious imitator of Lord Chatham." Let them bepraise their favorites as much as they please, and at my expense, too, provided they do not class me with the servile herd of imitators whom I despise and shun. No man is more sensible than I am of the distance between myself and Lord Chatham; but I would scorn to imitate even him. My powers, such as they are, have not been improved by culture. The first time that I ever dreamed of speaking in public, was on the eve of my election in March, 1799, when I opposed myself (fearful odds!) to Patrick Henry. My manner is spontaneous, flowing, like my matter, from the impulse of the moment; and when I do not feel strongly, I cannot speak to any purpose. These fits are independent of my volition. The best speech that I ever made, was about the third or fourth, on the subject of the Connecticut Reserve, 1800. During the last four or five years, I have perceived a sensible decline in my powers—which I estimate with as much impartiality as you would; in a word, as if they had belonged to another. I am not better persuaded of the loss of my grinders, or of the wrinkles in my face—and care as much for the one as the other. Any other man but yourself (or perhaps Meade) would take this long paragraph as proof that I am insincere, or self-deceived. To tell you the truth, I am sensible of the gross injustice that has been done me in the paragraph in question. I had as lief be accused of any crime, not forbidden by the decalogue, as of *imitation*. If these critics choose to say that I have neglected, or thrown away, or buried my talent, I will acquiesce in the censure; but amongst the herd of imitators I will not be ranked, because I feel that I could not descend to imitate any human being. But I have long ago learned—

Malignum spurnere vulgus.

Best wishes to Mrs. Key and the little ones. If Meade be with you, I salute him.

Yours, truly,
JOHN RANDOLPH OF ROANOKE.

Francis Scott Key, Esq.

I have been delighted with the Posthumus Works of Burke—the father of political wisdom—and have revelled in literary sweets: Horace in London; Rejected Adresses; Twopenny-post Bag; The Giaour, and the critique upon it in the Edinburgh Review. Many articles in that journal, and in the Quarterly, have amused and instructed me. I know you do not like the Scotch fraternity of critics; neither do I; but *fas est ab hoste docere*. What a picture of French society does the review of Grimm unfold! There are some deep reflections in that article, which I suppose comes from the pen of Dugald Stewart. It is eminently favorable to the cause of morality.

Our great folks at Cr. treat us little folks in Virginia very much as great folks are wont to treat little ones, viz., with sovereign neglect.

Randolph to Key.

RICHMOND, March 2, 1814.

DEAR SIR,—Your letter found me in bed, harassed and afflicted with gouty affection of the alimentary canal. It was, I believe, the best medicine that could have been administered to me, but, aided by an anniversary discourse, which Joe Lewis was considerate enough to send me, and which came also in the nick of time, the effect was wonderful. I am half disposed to be angry with you for passing over the said discourse as if it never had existed, and especially for leaving me to the charity of Joe Lewis, but for whose contribution I might have been deprived of the pleasure of seeing it at all ; for you need not flatter yourself that the newspapers generally will republish it. Now, by way of penance for this misplaced modesty, I do enjoin upon you to thank the aforesaid Joe in my name for his most obliging attention ; one that has given me a pleasure that I shall not offend you in attempting to express.

You are right, my friend, but who will follow you ? Who will abandon the *expedient* to adopt the counsels of self-denial, of mortification, of duty ? For my part, much as I abhor the factious motive and manner of the opposition prints, and many of its leaders, if I could find as many men of my way of thinking as drubbed the French at Agincourt, I would throw off the yoke, or perish in the attempt.

Louisiana is not my country. I respect as much the opinions of the people of London as of the Western States. After these avowals you will *not* " be glad" I fear " to see my *nil admirari*." My father left, for some reason of his own, this old family adage, and adopted *fari quæ gentiat* for his motto. But although I have returned to the old family maxim, I cannot shake off the habit which I acquired during thirty years' practice of speaking my mind *sometimes.* Nevertheless, I am persuaded that if we could all read your discourse, it would produce a most happy and beneficial effect on all ranks of the people. But the people will not hear, cannot read, and if they could, cannot understand, until the paroxysm of drunkenness is over. Wanting your faith I cannot repress *my* forebodings. They weigh me down and immerse body and soul. I never stood more in need of your society. In this world without souls every body is taken up with " the one thing needful"—what that is you must not consult St. Paul but the Jewish doctors, to discover.

I was struck with the review of Grimm, and with the hypothesis of the reviewer, on the tendency of a certain state of society to deaden the feelings, ossify the heart, and sharpen the sense of ridicule. Yes, in spite of its being *French verse*, I was pleased with the tribute of Voltaire to the power of that God, whom he never knew. I have been looking over the four first numbers of the Edinburgh Review, and was struck with the change of principle.

In answer to the foregoing letter Mr. Key writes :

" I have not yet seen the Giaour, but have looked over the Bride of Abydos. It has some fine passages in it, but it is too full of those crooked-named out-of-the-way East Indian things. I have long ago. however, resolved that there shall be no such poet as Walter Scott as long as he lives, and I can admire nobody that pretends to rival him.

" I should like to have the first numbers of the Edinburgh Review. I remember very well the great and shameful change of principle it has undergone. It is to be regretted that it is so popular a work in this country. How came the re-publishers by their recommendations of it ? I see you are among them—with some good company, and some rather bad. Is it not desirable that there should be a good American Literary Review ? One inculcating the sound principles of the quarterly reviewers, and exposing our book-makers, would perhaps improve both our taste and habits. Have you seen an article in Bronson's select reviews on American song-writing ? I do not know who the author is, but I think he could conduct such a work with much spirit. I have seldom, I think, seen a better piece of criticism."

In reply, Randolph says :

" I *do* think a review on the plan you mention would be highly beneficial, and if I was fit for any thing I should like to engage in a work of the sort. But fourteen years of congressional life have rendered me good for nothing. It may be an excuse for idleness, for this devil attacks me in every shape. But it seems to me, to work any material change in the state of things, we must begin (as some logicians lay their premises) a great way off. I mean with the children ; the old folks have taken their *ply*, and will neither bend nor break.

" ' How came the Edinburgh Review by my recommendation ?' Because the re-publishers applied for it by letter ; and when I gave it I had not gotten sight of the cloven foot ; I had seen, however, some puerile abuse of myself in that journal ; but this and much more would have been amply atoned for by very many masterly articles, if they had not betrayed a want of reverence for religion, and a hankering after France. Nevertheless, some of the late numbers in a great measure redeem their former sins. The truth is that men of diffrent principles, political as well as religious, write for that journal, and it may be always quoted against itself. There are some noble specimens of the art of criticism in the two last numbers that I have seen.

" I cannot yield the precedence of Lord Byron to Walter Scott. I admit your objection to the ' crooked-named out-of-the-way Turkish things.' But this must be pardoned in a traveller, who has explored the woods that wave o'er Delphi's steep, and swam across the Hellespont. No poet in our language (the exception is unnecessary), Shakspeare and Milton apart, has the same power over my feelings as Byron. He is, like Scott, *careless*, and indulges himself in great license; but he does not, like your favorite, write by the piece. I am persuaded that his fragments are thrown out by the true spirit of inspiration, and that he never goads his pen to work. When you have read the Giaour, the first, I think, of his poems, I am persuaded that you will change your opinion of this singular author, and yet more singular man. His feelings are too strong to endure the privation of religious sentiment. His time is not yet come, but he cannot continue to exist in the chill and gloom of skepticism.

"Meade is daily expected here. There is a general wish that he should preach the first sermon in the Monumental Church.

" What an occasion for a man who would not sink under it! He might do a great deal of good were he to yield to the desire of the congregation, and establish himself amongst them; but where is the field in which he would not do good?

" I have not seen the article you mention in Bronson's Select Review. In its new form I think that a respectable and useful publication. To be sure, it is made of scissors; but it is so far beyond the Port-Folio as to be comparatively good. The last is the most contemptible thing that ever imposed on the public in the shape of a magazine—and that is going very far. When your letter and W——'s P. S. arrived, I was in all the horrors of what is vulgarly called *Blue Devils ;* nor am I yet wholly recovered. I could not, however, resist the inclination to make my acknowledgments for your kindness."

Randolph to Key.

RICHMOND, May 7th, 1814.

MY DEAR FRIEND—Mr. Meade tells me that he expects to see you in a few days. I cannot let him depart without some token of my remembrance. He goes away early on Monday morning, so that, to guard against failure, I write to-day. He has made an engagement to preach in Hanover, thirty-five miles off, on Monday evening. No man can respect or admire his zeal in the sacred cause to which he has devoted himself, more than I do—but I fear he will wear himself out, and that the sum of his usefulness will, on the whole, be diminished, unless he will consent to spare himself. His health and strength are evidently impaired since I saw him last. I fear for his breast. I must refer you to him for what occurs here, except the eagerness of all classes and ranks of people to hear him. No man can be more generally revered than he is.

As to the review, I am out of the question on that and every other subject requiring any species of exertion. I said truly when I told you that congressional life had destroyed me—*fruges con sumere*—this is all that I am fit for; and such is my infirmity of body that I make a very poor hand even at that—notwithstanding I am one of those who (as the French say) *sum nè pour la digestion.*

Since the hot weather set in, I have been in a state of collapse, and am as feeble as an infant—with all this I am tortured with rheumatism, or gout, a wretched cripple, and my mind is yet more weak and diseased than my body. I hardly know myself, so irresolute and timid have I become. In short, I hope that there is not another creature in the world as unhappy as myself. This I can say to *you.* To the world I endeavor to put on a different countenance, and hold a bolder language ; but it is sheer hypocrisy, assumed to guard against the *pity* of mankind.

Mr. Meade will preach to-morrow in the new church. He is anxious on account of a silly piece, which that prince of coxcombs ———— has stuck into his paper. He has had no time for preparation on so useful a subject, and is uneasy that the public expectation has been led to it. Indeed who could treat it as it deserves ? certainly no man whom I ever heard. Remember me kindly to Mrs. Key and all friends, amongst whom I must particularly mention West and Sterrett Ridgely.

Most sincerely yours,

JOHN RANDOLPH OF ROANOKE.

I left the letter open that I might say a word about my friend's discourse. He explained in a few satisfactory and appropriate words why he should not touch upon a subject which many of his hearers had been led to expect he would treat (the burning of the theatre on whose site the new church was erected), and then gave us a most excellent sermon on the pleasure of the true Christian's life. A prayer which he introduced into this discourse, that the heart, *even if it were but one,* of the unconverted might be touched, was most affecting.

He preaches this afternoon at the Capitol, on the subject of the Bible Societies.

Sunday, 2 o'clock, P. M.

— • • —

CHAPTER II.

ANCESTRAL PRIDE—ST. GEORGE—MADNESS.

JOHN RANDOLPH had a morbid sensibility on the subject of his family and his property. He belonged to one of the oldest, most numerous, and wealthy families in Virginia—he cherished his family pride, and valued hereditary fortune far beyond its pecuniary worth. A money-loving, or a money-making spirit constituted no part of his character. His feelings and opinions on these subjects were purely English ; the proud, yet munificent and accomplished Baron of some time-honored castle with its thousand acres, and its villages of grateful and happy tenants, handed down from sire to son, with all the associations of pride and affection clustering around its walls and its forests, consti-tuted his *beau ideal* (not without reason) of the perfect gentleman. Such, in no small degree, were the characters that composed the old Virginia aristocracy. Randolph loved their memory—formed him-self on their model—despised the law that sapped the foundation of their greatness—and still hoped to preserve, in his own name and family, some specimen that might be worthy of a comparison with those *noble* men of the olden time.

He cherished the memory of his father with an increasing fond-ness to the day of his death. He always kept his father's miniature hung up before him in his chamber, or about his person, when long abroad from home. Last November, when on his way to Richmond, where he expected to be detained a few weeks only, he wrote back to Dudley, " be so *good* as to send me my father's picture and three lockets—they are in my writing-table drawer." He was now the only son, St. George and Tudor the sons of Richard, the only other de-scendants of that father whose memory he dwelt on so fondly. His had been an " unprosperous life," and was now, as he thought, rapidly drawing to a close. St. George was deaf and dumb—" the most pitiable of the step-sons of nature." Tudor was all that was left, the pride and hope of the family. These subjects caused him unceasing anxiety. The intensity of his feelings cannot be understood, nor justly appreciated by the *novi homines* of modern times. They amounted almost to a monomania—they furnish a solution of many of the apparent inconsistencies of his after life, and was the imme-diate cause of a rupture between himself and his step-father, whom, up to a very recent period, he had loved and venerated with the affec-tion and pride of a son. The efforts of mutual friends to heal this unfortunate breach between father and son, was the principal cause of his long delay in Richmond during the past winter and spring. Writing to Dudley in January, he says, " I have been detained here by a very unpleasant piece of business"—and again in February, " I

have been, indeed, very much disturbed of late, by an occurrence as
unexpected as it is distressing ; and, perhaps, I tinge other objects
with the hue of the medium through which I observe them."

The first cause of this misunderstanding with his step-father is
very characteristic of the man, and illustrates the feeling of family
pride that burned so intensely in his breast. The subject of conversation was the passing of the Banister estate from an infant of
that family, to a brother of the half blood of the Shippen family.
Mr. Randolph said that occurrence gave rise to the alteration
of the law of descents, and placed it on its present footing: he also
expressed in strong terms his disapprobation of the justice or
policy of such a law. Judge Tucker replied: "Why, Jack, you
ought not to be against that law, for you know if you were to die
without issue, you would wish your half brothers to have your estate."
"I'll be damned, sir, if I do know it," said Randolph, in great excitement; and from that day ceased with his good and venerable step-
father all friendly intercourse. This occasion gave rise to many
cruel and unjust suspicions. Once brought to suspect a selfish motive in him he had so much venerated, he began to look back with a
jealous eye on all his past transactions, and "trifles light as air"
became "confirmations strong as holy writ."

In 1810–11 he called in an attorney and proposed instituting suit.
He stated that Judge Tucker had never, in fact, settled his accounts
as his guardian—that he had taken the accounts stated upon trust—
that Judge Tucker had contrived. fraudulently he thought, to appropriate to himself certain slaves, which had been given to his mother
by her father, Colonel Bland, upon her marriage with his father,
John Randolph the elder, which his father had held thenceforth till
the day of his death, and which were mentioned as a part of his
estate. He stated all the circumstances of the case; and admitted
that the question of his father's right to the slaves depended on the
construction and effect of the statute of Virginia of 1758, making
parole gifts of slaves void. He stated the facts and the law on which
he rested his claim to the slaves with as much precision as counsel could have stated them in a bill in Chancery; he was perfectly
acquainted with the statute on the subject, and the decisions of the
Court of Appeals upon it. His counsel dissuaded him from his purpose of bringing suit; but he often afterwards recurred to the subject,

and never seems to have been wholly reconciled. The old man, how-ever, was unconscious of having given him any cause of offence. He sent a mutual friend to see Mr. Randolph soon after his arrival in Richmond : " Do me the favor," says he, " to go and see Mr. Ran-dolph, and ask him if he ever received a letter from me on the sub-ject of the misunderstanding between himself and his brother Bev-erly, and whether he ever answered it? Then ask him what has alienated him from one, whom for more than thirty years he has known as a father ?"

Randolph replied to the messenger, after a frown, that he had received the letter alluded to, and had not answered it ; and after a long pause said he had imposed it as a law on himself on this subject, not to converse about it.

The cause of this alienation of mind we have seen. His morbid sensibility on these subjects was now in a new and unexpected form to be sorely tried ; his family pride to be deeply mortified, and his fond hopes of its future continuance and of its future distinction to be blasted forever.

He thus writes to Mr. Key :

ROANOKE, June 3, 1814.

DEAR FRANK—My departure from Richmond was as sudden as the occasion was mournful and distressing. My eldest nephew, St. George, in consequence of an unsuccessful attachment to Miss ————, the daughter of a worthy neighbor of his mother, had become unsettled in his intellects, and on my arrival at Farmville I found him a frantic maniac. I have brought him up here, and Dr. Dudley, a friend and treasure to me above all price, assists me in the manage-ment of him We have no hopes of his restoration.

I would congratulate you on the late most important occurrences in Europe ; but I cannot write. Let me hear from you, I pray. Commend me to Mrs. Key, and West, and Ridgely, and all who care to inquire after me.

Yours ever,
JOHN RANDOLPH OF ROANOKE.

Randolph to Key.

ROANOKE, July 14, 1814.

DEAR FRANK—I have but half a sheet of paper left, and it is too late to send to the Court House (thirteen miles) for more. But with this half sheet and half a drop of ink diluted to a penful, I hope to make out something like a letter.

It is not the young man you saw in Georgetown, just before the declaration of war, whose unhappy condition I described; *he* is yet at Cambridge: the patient is his elder brother, just entering his twenty-third year, and has been deaf and dumb from his cradle.

This is the principal cause of his present situation: He has made several attempts to marry, and brooding over the cause of his failure has reduced him to his present state. He has become manageable with little trouble. His memory for words, persons, and events is unimpaired, but he cannot *combine*. He has dwelt a great deal on the terrors of future punishment also, and often mentioned the devil, but that was subsequent to his total derangement. His mind runs on it only as on other subjects of primary interest.

I saw some account of your campaigns in the newspapers. Wadsworth's letter is a curiosity—an honest account from a military commander. Your labors, my good friend, are drawing to a close. Rely upon it, we have peace forthwith. The points in "contestation," our rulers say, are removed by the peace in Europe, and will not be "touched" (another favorite phrase) in the treaty of peace. They might as well say they were removed by our declaration of war, if they were *neutral* rights, for that they contended for. Poor devils, what a figure they do cut! Yet they will look as consequential as ever, and even carry the people with them.

Have you read the Corsair? or have you lost all relish for such productions? I think his lordship is falling into the errors ascribed by him to Walter Scott. There is, however, some exquisite poetry. I have been trying to forget my wretched situation in the perusal of Burke. I have read his matchless diatribe on the attack of D. of B. and L. of L.—his letters on the regicide peace, and indeed the whole of the fifth volume, New-York edition. How much it is to be regretted that he did not live to publish his abridgment of English History I have also run over the Reflections, and the Appeal from the New to the Old Whigs. O that he could have seen this day! You say nothing of Bonaparte. How I long for half an hour's chat with you on the subject of these late surprising and providential events.

Present me affectionately to Mrs. Key and your little one, and remember me kindly to West and Ridgely, when you see them. If Lord Byron's Ode to Bonaparte is in Georgetown, pray send me a copy by post. Dudley returns your greeting. He is to me a treasure above all price. Exclusive of his excellent temper, alacrity, and intelligence, he is a most skilful physician. I should sink without his support. I thank God that he has raised up to me such an help.

Adieu, my dear sir. I am in truth, yours,

JOHN RANDOLPH OF ROANOKE.

I came down here yesterday with my poor nephew, who seems incurably alienated from his mother. I shall return in a few days.

Randolph to Brockenbrough.

Roanoke, July 15, 1814.

I had begun to fear that my long visitation of last winter and spring, had put you so much out of the habit of writing to me, that you would never resume it. But your letter of the 6th (just received) encourages me to hope that I shall hear from you as formerly. It was a sensible relief to me. But I will say nothing about my situation.

Poor St. George continues quite irrational. He is however very little mischievous, and governed pretty easily. His memory of persons, things, words, and events, is not at all impaired ; but he has no power of combination, and is entirely incoherent. His going to the Springs is out of the question, and mine, I fear, equally so, although my rheumatism requires the warm bath. By this time you are on your way thither. Except that it is too *cold*, the weather could not have been finer.

What a climate we live under !

As to peace, I have not a doubt that we shall have it forthwith. Our folks are prepared to say that the pacification of Europe has swept away the *matters in contestation*, as M——, the Secretary of State, has it. All that we see in the Government prints is to reconcile us the better to the terms which they must receive from the enemy. From the time of his flight from Egypt, my opinion of the character of Bonaparte has never changed, except for the worse. I have considered him from that date a coward, and ascribed his success to the deity he worships, Fortune. His insolence and rashness have met their just reward. Had he found an efficient government in France, on his abandonment of his brave companions in arms in Egypt, and returned to Paris, he would have been cashiered for ruining the best appointed armament that ever left an European port. But all was confusion and anarchy at Paris, and instead of a coup de fusil, he was rewarded with a sceptre. He succeeded in throwing the blame of Aboukir on poor Brueys. He could safely talk of " his orders to the Admiral," after L'Orient had blown up. His Russian and German campaign is another such commentary on his character ; it is all of a piece.

If the allies adhere to their treaty of Chaumont, the peace of Europe will be preserved ; but in France, I think, the seeds of disorder must abound. Instead of the triple aristocracy of the Noblesse, the Church, and the Parliaments, I see nothing but janissaries, and a divan of ruffians—Algiers on a great scale. Moral causes I see none ; and I am well persuaded that these are not created in a day. Matters of inveterate opinion, when once rooted up, are *dead*, never to revive ; *other* opinions must succeed them. But I am prosing—

uttering a string of common-place that every one can write, and no one can deny. But you brought it on yourself. You expected that I would say something, and I resolved to try. I can bear witness to the fact of Mrs. Brockenbrough's prediction respecting Bonaparte's retirement. I wish I were permitted to name five ladies who should constitute the Cabinet of this country; our affairs would be conducted in another guess manner. This reminds me of Mrs. G., of whom I have at last heard. Mr. G. wrote me late in February, from London. They were going to Bath, and "if circumstances on the continent would permit, meant to take a tour through France." How well-timed their trip to Europe has been.

I am here completely *hors du monde*. My neighbor, ——, with whom I have made a violent effort to establish an intercourse, has been here *twice, by invitation*—W. Leigh, as often, on his way to court; and on Saturday, I was agreeably surprised, by stumbling on Frank Gilmer, who was wandering to and fro in the woods, seeking my cabin. He left on Tuesday for his brother's in Henry. Except my standing dish, you have my whole society for *nine weeks*. On the terms by which I hold it, life is a curse, from which I would willingly escape, *if I knew where to fly*. I have lost my relish for reading; indeed, I could not devour even the Corsair with the zest that Lord Byron's pen generally inspires. It is very inferior to the Giaour, or the Bride. The character of Conrad is unnatural. Blessed with his mistress, he had no motive for desperation.

My plantation affairs, always irksome, are now revolting. I have lost three-fourths of the finest and largest crop I ever had.

My best respects and regard to Mrs. B.

I am, as ever, yours,

JOHN RANDOLPH OF ROANOKE

Dr. Dudley is (as you may suppose) a treasure to me above all price. Without him, what should I do? He desires his respects to you both.

As to an English Constitution for France, they will have one when they all speak the English language, and not before. Have you read Morris's oration on the 29th of June? His description of Bonaparte, "taking money for his crown," is very fine. It is a picture. I see him. There are some cuts in the same page that our fulminating statesmen will not like.

Sunday the 17th.—I am compelled to be at Prince Edward Court to-morrow, and the weather is so intolerably hot, that I shall go a part of the way this afternoon, and put my letter in the Farmville post-office, whence it will go direct to Richmond, instead of waiting five days on the road. Our crops, lately drowned, are now burning up. I begin to feel the effects of the fresh in my *health* as well as my purse. Dudley and myself both have experienced the ill consequences of our daily visits to the low grounds. The negroes, however, continue healthy. Out of more than two hundred, not a patient since I came home.

Who is it that says "il-y-a tant de plaisir à bavarder avec un ami!" Perhaps you will reply that the pleasure is not so great *ctre bavardí*.

Randolph to Key.

ROANOKE, July 31, 1814.

Affliction has assailed me in a new shape. My younger nephew whom you saw in G. Town two years ago has fallen, I fear, into a confirmed pulmonary consumption. He was the pride, the sole hope of our family. How shall I announce to his wretched mother that the last stay of her widowed life is falling? Give me some comfort, my good friend, I beseech you. He is now travelling by slow journeys home. What a scene awaits him there! His birth-place in ashes, his mother worn to a skeleton with disease and grief, his brother cut off from all that distinguishes man to his advantage from the brute beast. I do assure you that my own reason has staggered under this cruel blow. I know, or rather have a confused conception of what I ought to do, and sometimes strive, not altogether ineffectually I hope, to do it; but again all is chaos and misery. My faculties are benumbed; I feel suffocated; let me hear from you, I pray.

Yours, in truth,

J. R.

St. George, my elder nephew, is calm and governable, but entirely irrational. Commend me to Mrs. Key, and to Ridgely and West. Since writing the above my whole crop (tobacco and corn) is destroyed by a fresh, the greatest that has been known within twenty years. I fear a famine next summer; for this country, if we had the means of buying, is out of the way of a supply, except by distant land-carriage, and the harvests of Rappahannock, &c., cannot be brought up to Richmond by water. The poor slaves I fear will suffer dreadfully.

Randolph to Brockenbrough.

ROANOKE, Aug. 1, 1814.

You find in me, I fear, not merely an unprofitable but a troublesome correspondent; all my conversation is on paper. I have no one to converse with, for I have hardly seen Dudley since my return from Farmville, and I try to forget myself, or to obtain some relief from my own thoughts, by pouring them out on one who has heretofore lent to me perhaps too partial an ear. I have lived to feel that there are "many things worse than poverty or death," those bugbears that terrify the great children of the world, and sometimes drive them to eternal ruin. It requires, however, firmer nerves than mine to contemplate, without shrinking, even in prospect, the calamities which await this unhappy district of country—famine and all its concomitant horrors of disease and misery. To add to the picture, a late requisition of militia for Norfolk carries dismay and grief into the bosoms of many families in this country; and to have a just conception of the scene, it is necessary to be on the spot. This is our court day, when the conscripts are to report themselves, and I purposely abstain from the sight of wretchednes that I cannot relieve. I have indeed enough of it at home. The river did not abate in its rise until last night at sunset. It has, after twenty-four hours, just retired within its banks. The ruin is tremendous. The granary of this part of the State is rifled of its stores. Where then are the former furnishers of the great support of life to look for a supply? With a family of more than two hundred mouths looking up to me for food, I feel an awful charge on my hands. It is easy to rid myself of the burthen if I could shut my heart to the cry of humanity and the voice of duty. But in these poor slaves I have found my best and most faithful friends; and I feel that it would be more difficult to abandon them to the cruel fate to which our laws would consign them, than to suffer with them.

Among other of his tracts, I have been reading to-day Burke on the Policy of the Allies. If the book is within your reach, pray give it a perusal. It has a strong bearing on the present circumstances of France. A thousand conceptions have arisen in my mind on that subject and on the actual condition of our country, which I regret it has not been in my power to commit to paper; but these bubbles of the imagination have vanished: I could not embody them in the happy moment of projection. You see that I speak the language of an *adept*, although hardly out of my noviciate.

CHAPTER III.

MILITARY CAMPAIGN.

Some time in the month of July, 1814, Cochrane made his appearance in the Chesapeake. This appearance of a formidable enemy within their own borders, spread consternation among the unprotected people along the shores. Many depredations and outrages were committed at Hampton, Havre de Grace, and other exposed places. Finally an army was landed and marched across the country towards Washington City. They were met by a body of raw militia and a few marines, at Bladensburg, where was fought, or rather was run, the celebrated races of Bladensburg. Washington fell into the hands of the enemy, and the archives and public buildings were destroyed. On the news of this disaster, Randolph hastened to the scene of action, prepared, if occasion required, to lend his aid in defending the shores of Virginia.

The following letter, addressed to Dr. Dudley, will show how the military spirit had come over him :

CAMP FAIRFIELD, September 2, 1814.

MY DEAR THEODORE—You may be surprised at not hearing from me. But, first, I lost my horses ; secondly, I got a violent bilious complaint, not cholera, but cousin-german to it ; thirdly, I heard the news of Washington, and, without delay, proceeded hither. I am now under orders to proceed to the brick house, forty-two miles on York road, just below the confluence of Pamunkey and Mattapony. Should you come down, report yourself to the surgeon-general, Dr. Jones, of Nottoway. But first come to camp, and see Watkins Leigh, the governor's aid.

But his military career was very brief. Finding that the enemy meditated an attack on Baltimore, and that all danger of an immediate invasion of the shores of Virginia had passed by, he hastened back to Richmond. On the 8th of September, he writes to Mr. Key from that city :

" I have been here ten days, including four spent in reconnoitering the lower country between York and James River, from the confluence of Mattapony and Pamunkey to the mouth of Chickahomany. You will readily conceive my anxiety on the subject of my friends at Blenheim, the Woodyard, and Alexandria. Thank God ! Georgetown is safe. I was in terror for you and yours. Pray, let me hear from you. Tell me something of Sterrett Ridgely, and remember me to him and all who care to remember me. I have witnessed a sad spectacle in my late ride ; but I do not wish to depress your spirits. Dudley is at home with St. George. Poor Tudor is ill, very ill, at Mr. Morris's, near New-York.

Mr. Randolph remained in Richmond about a month. Hearing still more unfavorable tidings of his nephew, he set out about the 9th of October on a journey to Morrisania, the family residence of

Governeur Morris, Esq., near the city of New-York. On the 13th, he writes from Baltimore to Dudley:

"I have been detained here since Monday, by the consequences of an accident that befel me at Port Conway (opposite Port Royal), on Monday morning. At three o'clock, I was roused to set out in the stage. Mistaking, in the dark, a very steep staircase for a passage, at the end of which I expected to find the descent,—walking boldly on, I fell from the top to the bottom, and was taken up senseless. My left shoulder and elbow were severely hurt; also the right ankle. My hat saved my head, which was bruised, but not cut. Nevertheless, I persevered, got to Georgetown, and the next day came to this place, where I have been compelled to remain in great pain."

October 23d, 1814, he writes from Morrisania:

"After various accidents, one of which had nearly put an end to my unprosperous life, and confined me nearly a week on the road, I reached this place yesterday. Tudor is better; I have hopes of him, if we can get him to Virginia in his present plight."

November 17th, he again writes to Dr. Dudley:

"On returning from Morrisania, on Sunday, the 24th of October, the driver overturned me in Cortlandt-street, by driving over a pile of stones, &c., before a new house, unfinished, which nuisance extended more than half way across a narrow street. I am very seriously injured. The patella is, in itself, unhurt; but the ligaments are very much wrenched, so that a tight bandage alone enables me to hobble from one room to another with the help of a stick. I hope to be able to bear the motion of a carriage by the last of this week. I shall then go to Philadelphia, and hope to see you by the first of next month; assuredly (God willing) before Christmas. I am a poor miserable cripple, and you are my only support."

He arrived in Philadelphia about the first of December, and remained in that city the greater part of the winter, the weather being too inclement for him to travel. His time was most agreeably spent in the society of some of his old and most valued friends. Mrs. Clay, the widow of his late much lamented friend, Joseph Clay; Dr. Chapman, Mr. Parish, and others. The son of Mr. Clay, who bore his name, John Randolph Clay, he took to Virginia with him, defrayed the expenses of his education for a number of years, and watched over him with the care and anxiety of a father.

On his arrival in Richmond, he thus writes to Mr. Key:

RICHMOND, March 9, 1815.

DEAR FRANK:—I have lately got out of the habit of writing to my friends, even to you—you to whom I am so much indebted.

Such is the consequence of that state of mind under which I have unhappily labored for a long, long time past—the victim of ennui, indolence, and despair. I am not even as thankful as I ought to be for the great blessing lately vouchsafed us, at the moment when the wits of our rulers had become inextricably puzzled, and all their expedients to raise men or money had failed. Well, here is a peace at last; and a peace, if I may judge of the stagnation here, very like a war: but this topic has become stale and threadbare.

I found my poor boy here worse than I left him four months before, and daily declining. I must try to send him to the Mediterranean coast of Europe, although with little hope. Sometimes I think he had better give up his innocent life in the arms of his poor mother, instead of perishing (as I fear will be his lot should he cross the Atlantic) among strangers in a foreign land! Yet, again, what boots it *where* we die.

What are you going to do—have you given up the editorial scheme? Do you really think that the mere restoration of peace has anticipated all your schemes to be of service to this poor country? Are the present men and measures riveted upon the nation, at least for our lifetime? I think so, and therefore I wish to keep out of the vortex " betwixt vexed Scylla and the hoarse Calabrian shore;" not to tread that " huge Serbonian bog, where armies whole (of politicians) have sunk."

Do not think this a *nolo episcopari*, because of a certain letter that you may have seen. Times have changed since that letter was written, and *nos mutamus in illis*. If I can compass it, I will go with my poor sick boy, and sit by him and *comfort* him as well as I can.

On his return home, Mr. Randolph was urged by his old friends to become a candidate for Congress in the approaching elections; they assailed him on all hands, entreated him, followed him with solicitations that brooked no denial. Many who had deserted him on a former occasion wished for an opportunity to retrieve themselves, and to show their high appreciation of a man whom, in the hour of excitement and party blindness, they had been induced to abandon. The communication of the determination of his friends to support him at the ensuing election brought out a swarm of detractors, whom he was urged to answer. He steadily refused. "It is too late," says he, "in the day to vindicate my public character before a people whom I represented fourteen years, and whom, if they do not now know me, never will. I therefore abstain from all places of public resort, as well from inclination as principle." He entered the field with his old competitor, Mr. Epps, and was triumphantly elected. Writing to Mr. Key on the 25th of April, he says : " You will have heard of my re-election ; an event which has given me no pleasure, except so far as it has been gratifying to my friends. It is a station as unfit for me as I am for it. For a long time my mind has refused to travel in that track. I cannot force myself to think on the subject of my public affairs. I am engrossed by reflections of a very different, and far more important nature. I am 'a stricken deer,' and feel disposed to ' leave the hind.' The hand of calamity has pressed sorely upon me ; I do not repine at it. On the contrary, I return thanks for the (apparent) evil as well as good, which He who knows what is best for me has appointed for my portion in this life. May it have the effect of drawing me close unto Him, without whose gracious mercy I feel that I am a lost, undone creature."

Mr. Key expressed himself sincerely gratified at the triumph of his friend : " Such an one," says he, " has not to my knowledge ever fallen to the lot of any man. It does equal honor to the electors and the elected." Mr. Key delicately suggested to him that there is a virtue, the most difficult, but the most noble, which he was now called upon to practise ; it was to show the meekness and moderation of true magnanimity after so signal a victory. " Excuse me," says he, " for thinking of reminding you of this. It springs from a heart, among whose warmest wishes it is, that you should exhibit every grace and dignity of which this poor frail nature of ours is capable."

Randolph, in reply, says : " You will have perceived I hope, my good friend, from my letter by Dr. ——, that I have felt no disposition to indulge in an unbecoming triumph on the event of the late election in this district. I do assure you with the utmost sincerity, that, so far as I am personally concerned, I cannot but regret the partiality of my friends, who insisted on holding me up on this occasion. I am engrossed by sentiments of a far different character, and I look forward to the future in this world, to say nothing of the next, with anticipations that forbid any idle expression of exultation. On the contrary, my sensations are such as become a dependent creature, whose only hope for salvation rests upon the free grace of Him to whom we must look for peace in this world, as well as in the world to come. I cannot give expression to the feelings which fill my mind, and by which it is overcome; I struggle even with the difficulty of repressing them on occasions, and before persons, where the only effect would be to cover me with ridicule."

———•◦•———

CHAPTER IV.

NEW ENGLAND.

THE subjects of difficulty between the United States and Great Britain affected the interests of the New England States more than any other section of the Union. It was their seamen that were captured, their carrying trade that was interdicted by maritime adjudications, their shipping and commerce that were crippled and destroyed by the orders in council. The Southern States, being wholly given to planting and other agricultural pursuits, were only affected by the temporary suspension of a market for the sale of their products. Both, however, united in their petitions and remonstrances to Congress, and in demands for a redress of their grievances. But when the measures adopted for this purpose began to operate, it was found by the New England States that the remedy was more burthensome and destructive than the evils complained of. An American seaman was occasionally captured, but as a compensation hundreds of British sailors fled to our more lucrative and agreeable service. Much too frequently, it is true, an American vessel and her cargo were condemned by a British court of admiralty, yet many escaped and pursued a successful and profitable voyage; but the embargo drove every seaman from the service, and by one fell blow put an end to all commerce. Before this fatal expedient there was hazard in every enterprise, but there was hope to cheer on the adventurers; now even hope was extinguished, and the means of winning a precarious subsistence from the perilous deep were wrested from them. These were the feelings and opinions in New England. Massachusetts interposed her authority; pronounced the law unconstitutional and oppressive, and declared, that unless some speedy remedy were applied, necessity, the law of self-preservation that rises above all other law, would impel her to some ulterior and more decisive course. To the honor of Mr. Jefferson be it said, he yielded to the necessity of the case, and consented to a repeal of the embargo laws. Up to this period there was nothing but what was highly creditable to both parties. But Mr. Jefferson had gone into retirement, and other councils ruled the destiny of the nation. Measure after measure was adopted, embarrassing and ruinous to the interests of New England, until finally the whole nation was plunged in war. All its armies and military resources were transported to the frontiers of Canada, and pledged to a war of aggression and conquest, while the Atlantic borders were left exposed to the ravages of the enemy. Napoleon had been conquered by the frosts of Russia, and was an exile on the shores of Elba. England had redoubled her energies and made the war a vindictive punishment of the people for the sins of their government—rapine, brutality, and murder followed in the train of her armies, and their approach was more to be dreaded by the helpless and the innocent, than the invasion of the traitorous Arnold. In this state of affairs Massachusetts again interposed; but times had changed; the country was involved in war, and whether right or wrong, she required all good citizens to help to bring it to a successful end. New England at this crisis was charged—at least Massachusetts, Rhode Island, and Connecticut were charged—with the design of seeking a separate peace with Great Britain, and placing themselves in a position of neutrality during the further progress of the war, if indeed they did not cherish the ulterior purpose of a complete and final separation from the other States of the Union.

Whether this accusation be true or not, forms no part of our inquiry. We would fain hope—indeed we have good reason to believe that it was untrue—and that it formed a part of those party tactics which are too often resorted to to bring odium on political opponents, by misrepresenting their designs and their motives. The accusation, however, was made at the time by the minority of the Massachusetts Legislature that opposed the election of delegates to the Hartford Convention.

At this dark and melancholy period, when a vindictive foreign war was ravaging our coasts, and disrupture and civil war were threatened within, Mr. Randolph was called upon to interpose his good offices in behalf of his country. He was told that his voice would be heard in New England, and that his admonitions would receive their just consideration. He did not hesitate to give them—in the midst of pain, disease, domestic affliction, and mental suffering, he addressed to the people of New England, through one of her distinguished Senators, the following letter. Let it be read with attention; it does honor to the head and to the heart of the man that penned it. The reader cannot fail to be animated by the patriotism that glowed in his bosom, and to be cheered by the high appreciation he placed on the value of the Union, not as an end to be maintained at all hazards, but as a means to secure the peace and the happiness of the whole country. Let it not be said, after a perusal of this letter, that Mr. Randolph entertained unfounded and unreasonable prejudices against the people of New England. He cherished no such feelings. When New England became the advocate of a system of protection that proved to be as ruinous to the interests of his people as the embargo had been to them, he did not complain and declare in his peculiar and emphatic way, that nothing manufactured north of Mason and Dixon's line should ever enter into his house; but he never ceased to cherish towards the people of New England the profoundest sentiments of respect and regard.

PHILADELPHIA, Dec. 15, 1814.

DEAR SIR,—You will doubtless be surprised, but (I trust) not offended at the receipt of this letter. Of the motives which dictate it I shall forbear to speak: let them be gathered from its context. But should you ascribe my selection of you as the object of its address to any other cause than respect for your character and confidence in your love of country, you will have done much injustice to me; but more to yourself.

At Washington, I learned the result of the dispatches brought by the John Adams (a name of evil omen), and there rumors were afloat, which have since gathered strength, of a disposition in Massachusetts, and indeed throughout New England, to follow the example of Nantucket, and declare for a neutrality in the present contest with Great Britain. I will not believe it. What! Boston, the cradle of American independence, to whose aid Virginia stept forth unsolicited, when the whole vengeance of the British ministry was wreaked on that devoted town. Boston! now to desert us, in our utmost need, to give up her old ally to ravage, at the price of her own impunity from the common enemy?—I cannot, will not believe it. The men, if any such there be among you, who venture to insinuate such an intent by the darkest inuendo, do they claim to be the disciples of Washington? They are of the school of Arnold. I am not insensible to the vexations and oppressions, with which you have been harassed, with little intermission, since the memorable embargo of 1807. These I am disposed, as you well know, neither to excuse, nor to extenuate. Perhaps I may be reminded of an authority, to which I always delight to refer, " *Segnius irritant animos, &c.*," but let me tell such gentlemen, that our sufferings under political quacks of our own calling in, are not matter of *hearsay.* It is true they are considered by the unhappy, misguided patient, as evidence of the potency and consequently (according to his system of logic) of the efficacy of the medicine, as well as the inveteracy of the disease. It is not less true that this last has become, from preposterous treatment, in the highest degree alarming. The patient himself begins to suspect something of the sort, and the doctors trembling, each for his own character, are quarrelling and calling hard names among themselves. But they have reduced us to such a condition, that nothing short of the knife will now do. "We must *fight,* Mr. Speaker!" said Patrick Henry in 1775, when his sagacious mind saw there was nothing else left for us but manly resistance or slavish submission; and his tongue dared to utter what his heart suggested. How much greater the necessity now, when our country is regarded not as a property to be recovered, and therefore spared, so far as is compatible with the end in view; but as an object of vengeance, of desolation.

You know my sentiments of the men at the head of our affairs, and of the general course of administration during the last eight years. You know also that the relation, in which I stand towards them, is one of my own deliberate choice; sanctioned not more by my judgment than by my feelings. You, who have seen men (in the ranks, when I commanded in chief in the House of Representatives, and others, at that time too green to be on the political muster roll —whose names had never been pronounced out of their own parish) raised to the highest offices; you who are thoroughly acquainted with the whole progress of my separation from the party with which I was once connected in conduct, do not require to be told, that "there was a time in which I stood in such favor in the closet, that there must have been something extravagantly unreasonable in my wishes, if they might not ALL have been gratified." But I must acknowledge that you have seen instances of apostasy among your quondam political associates, as well as my own, that might almost justify a suspicion, that I too, tired of holding out, may wish to make my peace with the administration, by adding one more item " to the long catalogue of venality from Esau to the present day." Should such a shade of suspicion pass across your mind, I can readily excuse it, in consideration of the common frailty of our nature, from which I claim no peculiar exemption, and the transcendent wickedness of the times we live in; but you will have given me credit for a talent which I do not possess. I am master of no such ambidexterity; and were I to attempt this game, which it is only for adepts (not novices) to play! I am thoroughly conscious, that like other bungling rogues, I should at once expose my knavery and miss my object —not that our political church refuses to open her arms to the vilest of heretics and sinners who can seal their abjuration of their old faith by the prosecution of the brethren with whom they held and professed it: but I know that my nerves are of too weak a fibre to hear the question ordinary and extraordinary from our political inquisitors. I can sustain with composure and even with indifference the rancorous hatred of the numerous enemies, whom it has been my lot to make in the course of my unprosperous life—but I have not yet steeled myself to endure the contemptuous pity of those noble and high-minded men, whom I glory to call my friends, and I am on too bad terms with the world, to encounter my own self-disrespect.

You may however very naturally ask, why I have chosen you for the object of this address? Why I have not rather selected some one of those political friends, whom I have yet found "faithful among the faithless," as the vehicle of my opinions? It is because the avenue to the public ear is shut against me in Virginia, and I have been flattered to believe that the sound of my voice may reach New England. Nay, that it would be heard there, not without attention and respect. With us the press is under a virtual *imprimatur*, and it would be more easy, at this time, to force into circulation the treasury notes, than opinions militating against the administration, through the press in Virginia. We were indeed beginning to open our eyes in spite of the opiate with which we were drugged by the newspapers, and th' busy hum of the insects that bask in the sunshine of court patronage, when certain events occurred, the most favorable that could have happened for our rulers; whose "luck," verifying the proverb, is in the inverse ratio of their wisdom; or, perhaps I ought to say, who have the cunning to take advantage of glaring acts of indiscretion, in their adversaries at home and abroad, as these may affect the public mind; and such have never failed to come to their relief, when otherwise their case would have been hopeless. I give you the most serious assurance, that nothing less than the shameful conduct of the enemy and the complexion of certain occurrences to the eastward could have sustained Mr. Madison after the disgraceful affair at Washington. The public indignation would have overwhelmed, in one common ruin, himself and his hireling newspapers. The artillery of the press, so long the instrument of our subjugation, would, as at Paris, have been turned against the destroyer of his country: when we are told that old England says he "shall," and New England that he "must," retire from office, as the price of peace with the one, and of union with the other, we have too much English blood in our veins to submit to this dictation, or to any thing in the form of a threat. Neither of these people know any thing of us. The ignorance of her foreign agents, not only of the country to which they are sent, but even of their own, has exposed England to general derision. She will learn, when it is too late, that we are a high-minded people, attached to our liberty and our country, because it is free, in a degree inferior to no people under the sun. She will discover that " our trade would have been worth more than our spoil," and that she has made deadly enemies of a whole people, who, in spite of her and of the world, of the sneers of her sophists, or of the force of her arms, are destined to become, within the present session, a mighty nation. It belongs to New England to say, whether she will constitute a portion, an important and highly respectable portion of this nation, or whether she will dwindle into that state of insignificant, nominal independence, which is the precarious curse of the minor kingdoms of Europe. A separation made in the fulness of time, the effect of amicable arrangements, may prove mutually beneficial to both parties : such would have been the effect of American independence, if the British ministry could have listened to any suggestion but that of their own impotent rage : but a settled hostility embittered by the keenest recollections, must be the result of a disunion between you and us, under the present circumstances. I have sometimes wished that Mr. Madison (who endeavored to thwart the wise and benevolent policy of General Washington " to regard the English like other nations, as enemies in war, in peace friends,") had succeeded in embroiling us with the Court of St. James, twenty years sooner. We should in that case, have had the father of his country to conduct the war and to make the peace ; and that peace would have endured beyond the lifetime of the authors of their country's calamity and disgrace. But I must leave past recollections. The present and the immediate future claim our attention.

It may be said, that in time of peace, the people of every portion of our confederacy find themselves too happy to think of division ; that the sufferings of a war, like this, are requisite, to rouse them to the necessary exertion : war is incident to all governments ; and wars I very much fear will be wickedly declared, and weakly waged, even by the New England confederacy, as they have been by every government (not even excepting the Roman republic), of which we have any knowledge ; and it does appear to me no slight presumption that the evil has not yet reached the point of amputation, when peace alone will render us the happiest (as we are the freest) people under the sun ; at least too happy to think of dissolving the Union, which, as it carried us through the war of our revolution, will, I trust, bear us triumphant through that in which we have been plunged, by the incapacity and corruption of men, neither willing to maintain the relations of peace, nor able to conduct the operations of war. Should I, unhappily, be mistaken in this expectation, let us see what are to be the consequences of the separation, not to us, but to yourselves. An exclusion of your tonnage and manufactures from our ports and harbors. It will be our policy to encourage our own, or even those of Europe in preference to yours; a policy more obvious than that which induced us of the South, to consent to discriminating duties in favor of American tonnage, in the infancy of this government. It is unnecessary to say, to you, that I embrace the duties on imports, as well as the tonnage duty, when I allude to the encouragement of American shipping. It will always be our policy to prevent your obtaining a naval superiority, and consequently to cut you off entirely from our carrying trade. The same plain interest will cause us to prefer any manufactures to your own. The intercourse with the rest of the world, that exchanges our surplus for theirs, will be the nursery of our seamen. In the middle States you will find rivals, not very heartily indisposed to shut out the competition of your shipping. In the same section of country and in the boundless West, you will find jealous competitors of your mechanics—you will be left to settle, as you can, with England, the question of boundary on the side of New Brunswick, and unless you can bring New-York to a state of utter blindness, as to her own interests, that great, thriving, and most populous member of the southern confederacy will present a hostile frontier to the only States of the union of Hartford, that can be estimated as of any efficiency. Should that respectable city be chosen as the seat of the Eastern Congress, that body will sit within two days' march of the most populous county of New-York (Duchess), of itself almost equal to some of the New England States. I speak not in derision, but in soberness and sadness of heart. Rather let me say, that like a thorough-bred diplomatist, I try to suppress every thing like feeling, and treat this question as a dry matter of calculation; well knowing, at the same time, that in this, as in every question of vital interest, " our passions instruct our reason." The same high authority has told us that jacobinism is of no country, that it is a sect found in all. Now, as our jacobins in Virginia would be very glad to hear of the bombardment of Boston, so, I very much fear, your jacobins would not be very sorry to hear of a servile insurrection in Virginia. But such I trust is the general feeling in neither country, otherwise I should at once agree that union, like the marriages of Mezentius, was the worst that could befall us. For, with every other man of common sense, I have always regarded union as the means of liberty and safety; in other words of happiness, and not as an end, to which these are to be sacrificed. Neither, at the same time, are means so precious, so efficient (in proper hands) of these desirable objects, to be thrown, rashly aside, because, in the hands of bad men, they have been made the instrument almost of our undoing.

You in New England (it is unnecessary I hope to specify when I *do not* address myself personally to yourself) are very wide of the mark, if you suppose we to the south do not suffer at least as much as yourselves, from the incapacity of our rulers to conduct the defence of the country. Do you ask why we do not change those rulers? I reply, because we are a people, like your own Connecticut, of steady habits. Our confidence once given is not hastily withdrawn. Let those who will, abuse the fickleness of the people; I shall say such is not the character of the people of Virginia. They may be deceived, but they are honest. Taking advantage of their honest prejudices, the growth of our revolution, fostered not more by Mr. Jefferson than by the injuries and (what is harder to be borne) the insults of the British ministry since the peace of 1783, a combination of artful men, has, with the aid of the press, and the possession of the machinery of government (a powerful engine in any hands) led them to the brink of ruin. I can never bring myself to believe, that the whole mass of the landed proprietors in any country, but especially such a country as Virginia, can seriously plot its ruin. Our government is in the hands of the landed proprietors only. The very men of whom you complain, have left nothing undone that *they* dared to do, in order to destroy it. Foreign influence is unknown among us. What we feel of it is through the medium of the General Government, which acted on, itself, by foreign renegadoes, serves as a conductor, between them and us, of this pernicious influence. I know of no foreigner who has been, or is, in any respectable office in the gift of the people, or in the government of Virginia. No member of either House of Congress, no leading member of our Assembly, no judge of our Supreme Courts: of the newspapers printed in the State, as far as my knowledge extends, without discrimination of party, they are conducted by native Virginians. Like yourselves, we are an unmixed people. I know the prejudice that exists against us, nor do I wonder at it, considering the gross ignorance on the subject that prevails north of Maryland, and even in many parts of that neighboring State.

What member of the confederacy has sacrificed more on the altar of public good than Virginia? Whence did the General Government derive its lands beyond the Ohio, then and now almost the only source of revenue? From our grant,—a grant so curiously worded, and by our present Palinurus too, as to except ourselves, by its limitations, from the common benefit.

By its conditions it was forbidden ground to us, and thereby the foundati n was laid of incurable animosity and division between the States on each side of that great natural boundary, the river Ohio. Not only their masters, but the very slaves themselves, for whose benefit this regulation was made, were sacrificed by it. Dispersion is to them a bettering of their present condition, and of their chance for emancipation. It is only when this can be done without danger and without ruinous individual loss that it will be done at all. But what is common sense to a political Quixote?

That country was ours by a double title, by charter and by ¬on-quest. George Rogers Clark, the American Hannibal, at the head of the State troops, by the reduction of Post Vincennes, obtained the lakes for our northern boundary at the peace of Paris. The march of that great man and his brave companions in arms across the d¡owned lands of the Wabash, does not shrink from a compari-son with the passage of the Thrasimene marsh. Without meaning any thing like an invidious distinction, I have not heard of any ces-sion from Massachusetts of her vast wilds ; and Connecticut has had the address, out of our grant to the *firm*, to obtain, on her own pri-vate account, some millions of acres : whilst we, yes we, I blush to say it, have descended to beg for a pittance, out of the property once our own, for the brave men by whose valor it had been won, and whom heedless profusion had disabled us to recompense. We met the just fate of the prodigal. We were spurned from the door, where once we were master, with derision and scorn ; and yet we hear of undue Virginian influence. This fund yielded the Gov-ernment, when I had connection with it, from half a million to eight hundred thousand dollars, annually. It would have preserved us from the imposition of State taxes, founded schools, built bridges and made roads and canals throughout Virginia. It was squandered away in a single donative at the instance of Mr. Madison. For the sake of concord with our neighbors, by the same generous but mis-guided policy, we ceded to Pennsylvania Fort Pitt, a most important commercial and military position, and a vast domain around it, as much Virginia as the city of Richmond and the county of Henrico. To Kentucky, the eldest daughter of the Union, the Virginia of the west, we have yielded on a question of boundary, from a similar con-sideration. Actuated by the same magnanimous spirit at the in-stance of other States (with the exception of New-York, North Ca-rolina, and Rhode Island), we accepted, in 1783, the present Consti-tution. It was repugnant to our judgment, and fraught, as we feared, with danger to our liberties. The awful voice of our ablest and soundest statesmen, of Patrick Henry, and of George Mason, never before or since disregarded, warned us of the consequences. Neither was their counsel entirely unheeded, for it led to important subse-quent amendments of that instrument. I have always believed this disinterested spirit, so often manifested by us, to be one of the chief causes of the influence which we have exercised over the other States. Eight States having made that Constitution their own, we submitted to the yoke for the sake of union. Our attachment to the Union is not an empty profession. It is demonstrated by our practice at home. No sooner was the Convention of 1788 dissolved, than the feuds of federalism and anti-federalism disappeared. I speak of their effects on our councils. For the sake of union, we submitted to the lowest state of degradation; the administration of John Adams. The name of this man calls up contempt and derision, wheresoever it is pronounced. To the fantastic vanity of this political Malvolio may be distinctly traced our present unhappy condition. I will not be so ungenerous as to remind you that this personage (of whom and his addresses, and his answers, I defy you to think without a bitter smile) was not a Virginian, but I must in justice to ourselves, insist in making him a set-off against Mr. Madison. They are of such equal weight, that the trembling balance reminds us of that passage of Pope, where Jove "weighs the beau's wits agains the lady's hair.

> "The doubtful beam long nods from side to side,
>   At length the wits mount up, the hairs subside."

Intoxicated not more by the fulsome adulation with which he was plied, than by the fumes of his own vanity, this poor old gentleman saw a visionary coronet suspended over his brow, and an air-drawn sceptre "the handle towards his hand," which attempting to clutch, he lost his balance, and disappeared never to rise again. He it was, who "enacting" Nat. Lee's Alexander, raved about the people of Virginia as "a faction to be humbled in dust and ashes," when the sackcloth already was prepared for his own back.

But I am spinning out this letter to too great a length. What is your object—PEACE? Can this be attained on any terms, whilst England sees a prospect of disuniting that confederacy, which has already given so deep a blow to her maritime pride, and threatens at no very distant day to dispute with her the empire of the ocean? The wound which our gallant tars have inflicted on her tenderest point, has maddened her to rage. Cursed as we are with a weak and wicked administration, she can no longer despise us. Already she begins to hate us ; and she seeks to glut a revenge as impotent as it is rancorous, by inroads that would have disgraced the buccaneers, and bulletins that would only not disgrace the sovereign of Elba. She already is compelled to confess in her heart, what her lips deny, that if English bull-dogs and game-cocks degenerate on our soil, English MEN do not :—and should (which God forbid) our brethren of the East desert us in this contest for all that is precious to man, we will maintain it, so long as our proud and insulting foe shall refuse to accede to equitable terms of peace. The Government will then pass into proper hands—the talents of the country will be called forth, and the schemes of moon-struck philosophers and their disciples pass away and " leave not a rack behind."

You know how steady and persevering I endeavored, for eight years, to counteract the artful and insidious plans of our rulers to embroil us with the country of our ancestors, and the odium which I have thereby drawn upon myself. Believing it to be my duty to soften, as much as possible, the asperities which subsisted between the two countries, and which were leading to a ruinous war, I put to hazard, nay, exposed to almost certain destruction, an influence such as no man, perhaps, in this country, at the same age, had ever before attained. (The popularity that dreads exposure is too delicate for public service. It is a bastard species: the true sort will stand the hardest frosts. Is it my fault (as Mr. Burke complained of the crowned heads of Europe) that England will no longer suffer me to find palliatives for her conduct? No man admired more than I did her magnanimous stand against the tyrant, before whom all the rest of Christendom at one time bowed: No man, not even her own Wilberforce and Perceval, put up more sincere prayers for her deliverance. In the remotest isle of Australasia, my sympathy would have been enlisted, in such a contest, for the descendants of Alfred and Bacon, and Shakspeare, and Milton, and Locke, on whom I love to look back as my illustrious countrymen—in any contest I should have taken side with liberty; but on this depended (as I believed and do still believe) all that made my own country dear in my sight. It is past—and unmindful of the mercy of that protecting Providence which has carried her through the valley of the shadow of death, England " feels power and forgets right." I am not one of the whining set of people who cry out against mine adversary for the force of his blow. England has, unquestionably, as good a right to conquer us, as we have to conquer Canada; the same right that we have to conquer England, and with about as good prospect of success. But let not her orators declaim against the enormity of French principles, when she permits herself to arm and discipline our slaves, and to lead them into the field against their masters, in the hope of exciting by the example a general insurrection, and thus render Virginia another St. Domingo. And does she talk of jacobinism ! What is this but jacobinism ? and of the vilest stamp ? Is this the country that has abolished the slave trade? that has made that infamous, inhuman traffic a felony ? that feeds with the bread of life all who hunger after it, and even those who, but for her, would never have known their perishing condition ? Drunk with the cup of the abominations of Moloch, they have been roused from the sleep of death, like some benighted traveller perishing in the snows, and warmed into life by the beams of the only true religion. Is this the country of Wilber force and Howard? It is;—but, like my own, my native land, it has fallen into the hands of evil men, who pour out its treasure and its blood at the shrine of their own guilty ambition. And this impious sacrifice they celebrate amidst the applauses of the deluded people, and even of the victims themselves.

There is a proneness in mankind to throw the blame of their sufferings on any one but themselves. In this manner, Virginia is regarded by some of her sister States; not adverting to the fact, that all (Connecticut and Delaware excepted) are responsible for the measures that have involved us in our present difficulties. Did we partition your State into those unequal and monstrous districts which have given birth to a new word in your language, of uncouth sound, calling up the most odious associations. Did we elect the jacobins whom you sent to both Houses of Congress—the Bidwells, and Gannetts, and Skinners,—to spur on the more moderate men from Virginia to excesses which they reluctantly gave into at the time, and have since been ashamed of? Who hurried the bill suspending the privilege of the writ of HABEAS CORPUS through a trembling servile Senate, in consequence, as he did not blush to state, of a *verbal* communication from the President? A Senator from Massachusetts, and professor in her venerable university. In short, have not your first statesmen (such I believe was the reputation of the gentleman in question at the time), your richest merchants, and the majority of your delegation in Congress vied in support of the men and the measures that have led to our present suffering and humiliated condition?

If you wished to separate yourselves from us, you had ample provocation in time of peace, in an embargo the most unconstitutional and oppressive; an engine of tyranny, fraud, and favoritism. Then was the time to resist (we did not desert England in a time of war), but you were then under the dominion of a faction among yourselves, yet a formidable minority, exhibiting no signs of diminution; and it is not the least of my apprehensions, from certain proceedings to the eastward, that they may be made the means of consigning you again, and for ever, to the same low, insolent domination. The reaction of your jacobins upon us (for although we have some in Virginia, they are few and insignificant) through the men at Washington, ("who must conciliate good republicans,") is dreadful. Pause, I beseech you, pause! You tread on the brink of destruction. Of all the Atlantic States you have the least cause to complain. Your manufactures, and the trade which the enemy has allowed you, have drained us of our last dollar. How then can we carry on the war? With men and steel—stout hearts, and willing hands—and these from the days of Darius and Xerxes, in defence of the household gods of freedom, have proved a match for gold. Can they not now encounter paper? We shall suffer much from this contest, it will cut deep;

but dismissing its authors from our confidence and councils for ever, (I speak of a few leaders and their immediate tools, not of the deluded, as well in as out of authority,) we shall pass, if it be the good pleasure of Him whose curses are tempered with mercies, through an agony and a bloody sweat, to peace and salvation; to that peace which is only to be found in a reconciliation with Him. " Atheists and madmen *have* been our lawgivers," and when I think on our past conduct I shudder at the chastisement that may await us. How has not Europe suffered for her sins! Will England not consider, that. like the man who but yesterday bestrode the narrow world, she is but an instrument in his hands, who breaketh the weapons of his chastisement, when the measure of his people's punishment is full?

When I exhort to further patience—to resort to constitutional means of redress only, I know that there is such a thing as tyranny as well as oppression; and that there is no government, however restricted in its power, that may not, by abuse, under pretext of exercise of its constitutional authority, drive its unhappy subjects to desperation. Our situation is indeed awful. The members of the Union in juxtaposition—held together by no common authority to which men can look up with confidence and respect. Smitten by the charms of Upper Canada, our President has abandoned the several States to shift for themselves as they can.—Congress is *felo de se.* In practice there is found little difference between a government of requisitions on the States, which these disregard, or a government of requisitions on the people, which the governors are afraid to make until the public faith is irretrievably ruined. Congress seemed barred by their own favorite act of limitations, from raising supplies; prescription runs against them. But let us not despair of the commonwealth. Some master-spirit may be kindled by the collision of the times, who will breathe his own soul into the councils and armies of the republic; and here indeed is our chiefest danger. The man who is credulous enough to believe that a constitution, with the skeleton of an establishment of 10,000 men, not 2,000 strong, (such was our army three years ago,) is the same as with an army of 60,000 men, may be a very amiable neighbor, but is utterly unfit for a statesman. Already our government is in fact changed. We are become a military people, of whom more than of any other it might have been said *fortunatos sua si bona norint.* If under such circumstances you ask me what you are to do, should a conscription of the model of Bonaparte be attempted? I will refer you to its reputed projector, Colonel Monroe. Ask him what he would have done, whilst governor of Virginia, and preparing to resist Federal usurpation, had such an attempt been made by Mr. Adams and his ministers; especially in 1800 He *can* give the answer.

But when you complain of the representation of three-fifths of our slaves, I reply that it is one of the articles of that compact, which you submitted to us for acceptance, and to which we reluctantly acceded. Our Constitution is an affair of compromise between the States, and this is the master-key which unlocks all its difficulties. If any of the parties to the compact are dissatisfied with their share of influence, it is an affair of amicable discussion, in the mode pointed out by the constitution itself, but no cause for dissolving the confederacy. And when I read and hear the vile stuff against my country printed and uttered on this subject, by fire-brands, who ought to be quenched for ever, I would remind, not these editors of journals and declaimers at clubs, but their deluded followers, that every word of these libels on the planters of Virginia, is as applicable to the father of his country as to any one among us; that in the same sense we are "slaveholders," and "negro drivers," and "dealers in human flesh," (I must be pardoned for culling a few of their rhetorical flowers,) so was *he*, and whilst they upbraid Virginia with her Jeffersons and her Madisons, they will not always remember to forget that to Virginia they were indebted for a Washington.

I am, with the highest respect and regard, dear sir, your obedient servant,

JOHN RANDOLPH OF ROANOKE.

------ • • • ------

CHAPTER V.

RELIGION.

THE reader is already aware, from many expressions let fall from the pen of Mr. Randolph, that he is deeply engaged in the great subject of religion; his necessary duties give way, and are postponed to this all-engrossing question.

In childhood and early youth, he was trained by a devoted and pious mother, in the doctrines and the practices of the Christian church. The impressions of those early lessons, though a long time disregarded, were never entirely effaced from his memory; and the hallowed associations that clustered around the name of his adored and sainted mother, the fond remembrances of childhood and innocence, never failed to awaken the deepest emotions in his affectionate and sympathetic heart. Yet he lived for many years in open derision and mockery of that religion whose holy and divine precepts he could not efface from his mind. Coming into life at an epoch when French philosophy had not only overturned the monarchies of Europe, but had undermined and destroyed the foundation of all morals and religion, his ardent soul, like thousands of the best spirits of the age, caught the contagion of its influence. threw off all religious restraint, as the highest proof of freedom, and became, if not a mocker, at least a cold despiser of the religion of numility and self-sacrifice. But the despotism under which France had been made to groan, in consequence of her atheistic madness; the desolation that had swept over Europe; the deep calamities brought on his own country by war and restrictions; the many misfortunes and afflictions that in thick succession had befallen himself and his ill-fated family; his entire separation from all political associations and party excitements, and the profound solitude, for the most part, in which he lived, all conspired to bring back his mind to its early associations. As " the stricken deer," to which he likened himself, faint, and panting in the hot chase, seeks the fresh fountains and cooling shades of its native valley, so he, faint and heart-stricken at the desolations of an irreligious age, and athirst for the pure waters of life, sought consolation in that religion which his mother, on bended knee, with his little hands in hers uplifted to heaven, had taught him in his infancy.

He read the Old and New Testament, with the aid of good commentators, with care and diligence. The best authors were at his command—" old standard authors" constituted his daily food, though sometimes, in humility, he would complain that they were " too solid for his weak stomach." It is a great mistake to take Mr. Randolph at his word, and suppose him to be an ignorant man. " I am an ignorant man, I am an ignorant man," is the mortifying yet too deeply conscious sentiment of every man of an all-grasping genius like his; but no man was more thoroughly imbued than he with the rich lore of old English learning, or more deeply penetrated with the manly and martyr-like spirit of that religion which triumphed over the faggot and the dungeon. Being a man of the highest order of poetic genius himself, he sought only the society of kindred spirits. Milton and Cowper, and the old English divines, now obsolete and forgotten, were his daily and nightly companions. He was also most fortunate in his living associates. No man had better or more faithful friends

His country or age can furnish no nobler specimens of a high Chris
tian virtue than the *three* friends with whom Mr. Randolph alone
conversed on "free-will, fate and philosophy," and to whose opinions
he bowed with the profoundest respect and reverence.   The first to
whom we allude is the present Bishop Meade, of Virginia, a gentleman, a scholar, and a Christian.   The reader is already aware of the
high regard Mr. Randolph had for that pious and venerable man.
The second person was the late Dr. Moses Hogue, president of
Hampden Sydney College.   Mr. Randolph, for many years, lived
in the immediate neighborhood of the college ; and the society of
its venerable head, the chief ornament of the institution, was
always sought by him with avidity.   "I consider Dr. Hogue," says
he, " as the ablest and most interesting speaker that I ever heard,
in the pulpit or out of it ; and the most perfect pattern of a Christian
teacher that I ever saw.   His life affords an example of the great
truths of the doctrine that he dispenses to his flock ; and if he has a
fault (which, being mortal, I suppose he cannot be free from) I have
never heard it pointed out."   Nothing can be added to this picture.
Francis Scott Key, Esq., late of Washington City, is the other person to whom we have made allusion.   The reader has already perceived the great intimacy existing between these two friends.   They
were kindred spirits.   "Frank Key," though an eminent and successful advocate, was a poet of a high order of genius.   "The Star-
spangled Banner," written while he was detained on board the British fleet, an anxious spectator of the bombardment of Fort M‘Henry
and the assault on Baltimore, thrills the heart of every American
who hears its patriotic strains, and has become one of our most popular national songs.   He was a pure spirit ; the friend that knew him
best and valued him most, thus speaks of him : " He perseveres in
pressing on toward the goal, and his whole life is spent in endeavors
to do good for his unhappy fellow-men.   The result is that he enjoys
a tranquillity of mind, a sunshine of the soul, that all the Alexanders
of the earth can neither confer nor take away."

Dr. Brockenbrough had hitherto, for the most part, been in the
same category with himself, somewhat skeptical ; hence, in their relations, Randolph rather assumed the province of a teacher than
scholar, on the subject of morals and religion.   Writing to that gentleman from Buckingham Court House, the 29th May, 1815, he says :

"I got here to-day. To-morrow we are to begin our inquisition. [A contested election.] This business does not suit me at all. My thoughts are running in a far different channel. I never feel so free from uneasiness as when I am reading the Testament, or hearing some able preacher. This great concern presses me by day and by night, almost to the engrossing of my thoughts. It is first in my mind when I wake, and the last when I go to sleep. I think it becomes daily more clear to me. All other things are as nothing when put in comparison with it. You have had a great comfort in the presence of Mr. Meade. I, too, am not without some consolation; for I have received a letter from Frank Key, that I would not exchange for the largest bundle of bank notes that you ever signed. Hear him. 'I cannot describe to you the gratification your letter has given me. The sentiments they express, I thank God I am no stranger to; and they have been made to lead me, through much anxiety and distress, to a state of peace and happiness—as far above what I have deserved, as below what I yet hope, even in this life, to attain. May you soon, my friend. experience the most delightful of all sensations, that springs from a well grounded hope of reconciliation with God! You are in the right track. [God grant it may be so!] God is leading you. Your sentiments show the divinity that stirs within you. That we have ruined ourselves—that an everlasting life is before us—that we are about (how soon we know not) to enter upon it, under the sentence of Almighty condemnation —and that we can do nothing to save ourselves from this misery; these convictions are the genuine work of the Spirit; other foundation can no man lay! They lead us to a Saviour who gives us all we want—pardon, peace, and holiness. They do not bid us first to become righteous, and then come to him; but they bring us to him as we are—as sinners to be pardoned for our sins, and cleansed from all our iniquities. This is the true doctrine of our Church, and the plain meaning of the Gospel; and indeed it seems to me, notwithstanding some peculiarities (about which there has been much useless disputation), that in these essential points almost all sects agree.' "

Writing to Mr. Key himself, from the same place, two days after the above, he says:

"I cannot refrain from unburthening some of my thoughts to you. I carry your last letter (of the 11th) constantly in my pocket, reading it frequently, and praying God that your charitable anticipations respecting me may be realized. After all, is there not selfishness at the bottom of that yearning of my heart to believe? Can that faith, setting aside its imperfection, be acceptable in the sight of God, to which the unhappy sinner is first moved by the sense of self-preservation ?

" I am brought on here by this contested election ; but my mind is not at all in the thing.

" Indeed I must tell you what gives me great uneasiness ; that, instead of being stimulated to the discharge of my duties, I am daily becoming more indifferent to them, and, consequently, more negligent. I see many whose minds are apparently little occupied on the subject that employs me, with whom I think I should be glad to exchange conditions ; for surely, when they discharge conscientiousiy their part in life, without the same high motive that I feel, how culpable am I, being negligent ! For a long time the thoughts that now occupy me, came and went out of my mind. Sometimes they were banished by business ; at others, by pleasure. But heavy afflictions fell upon me. They came more frequently, and staid longer—pressing upon me, until, at last, I never went asleep nor awoke but they were last and first in my recollection. Oftentimes have they awakened me, until, at length, I cannot, if I would, detach myself from them. Mixing in the business of the world I find highly injurious to me. I cannot repress the feelings which the conduct of our fellow-men too often excites ; yet I hate nobody, and I have endeavored to forgive all who have done me an injury, as I have asked forgiveness of those whom I may have wronged, in thought or deed. If I could have my way, I would retire to some retreat, far from the strife of the world, and pass the remnant of my days in meditation and prayer ; and yet this would be a life of ignoble security. But, my good friend, I am not qualified (as yet, at least,) to bear the heat of the battle. I seek for rest—for peace. I have read much of the New Testament lately. Some of the texts are full of consolation ; others inspire dread. The Epistles of Paul I cannot, for the most part, comprehend ; with the assistance of Mr. Locke's paraphrase, I hope to accomplish it. My good friend, you will bear with this egotism ; for I seek from you instruction on a subject, in comparison with which all others sink into insignificance. I have had a strong desire to go to the Lord's Supper ; but I was deterred by a sense of my unworthiness ; and, only yesterday, reading the denunciation against those who received unworthily, I thought it would never be in my power to present myself at the altar. I was present when Mr. Hogue invited to the table, and I would have given all I was worth to have been able to approach it. There is no minister of our church in these parts. I therefore go to the Presbyterians, who are the most learned and regular ; but having been born in the Church of England, I do not mean to renounce it. On the contrary, I feel a comfort in repeating the Liturgy, that I would not be deprived of for worlds. Is it not for the want of some such service that Socinian-

ism has crept into the eastern congregations? How could any So-
cinian repeat the Apostle's Creed, or read the Liturgy? I begin to
think, with you, about those people. You remember the opinions
you expressed to me last winter concerning them. Among the causes
of uneasiness which have laid hold upon me lately, is a strong anxiety
for the welfare of those whom I love, and whom I see walking in
darkness. But there is one source of affliction, the last and deepest,
which I must reserve till we meet, if I can prevail upon myself to
communicate it even then. It was laid open by one of those wonderful coincidences, which men call chance, but which manifest the hand
of God. It has lacerated my heart, and taken from it its last hope
in this world. Ought I not to bless God for the evil (as it seems in my
sight) as well as the good? Is it not the greatest of blessings, if it be
made the means of drawing me unto him? Do I know what to ask
at his hands? Is he not the judge of what is good for me? If it
be his pleasure that I perish, am I not conscious that the sentence is
just?

"Implicitly, then, will I throw myself upon his mercy; 'Not my
will, but thine be done;' 'Lord be merciful to me a sinner;' 'Help,
Lord, or I perish.' And now, my friend, if, after these glimpses of
the light, I should shut mine eyes and harden my heart, which now
is as melted wax; if I should be enticed back to the 'herd,' and lose
all recollection of my wounds, how much deeper my guilt than his
whose heart has never been touched by the sense of his perishing, undone condition. This has rushed upon my mind when I have thought
of partaking of the Lord's supper. After binding myself by that sacred rite, should passion overcome me, should I be induced to forget
in some unhappy hour that holy obligation, I shudder to think of it.
There are two ways only which I am of opinion that I may be serviceable to mankind. One of these is teaching children; and I have
some thoughts of establishing a school. Then, again, it comes into
my head that I am borne away by a transient enthusiasm; or that I
may be reduced to the condition of some unhappy fanatics who mistake the perversion of their intellects for the conversion of their
hearts. Pray for me."

On another occasion, writing to Mr. Key, he says:

"I took up yesterday a work, which I never met with before, the
'Christian Observer.' In a critique of Scott, vol. XII., upon the
Bishop of Lincoln's 'Refutation of Calvinism,' it is stated that no man
is converted to the truth of Christianity without the self-experience of a
miracle. Such is the substance. He must be sensible of the working
of a miracle in his own person. Now, my good friend, I have never
experienced any thing like this. I have been sensible, and am
always, of the proneness to sin in my nature. I have grieved un-
feignedly for my manifold transgressions. I have thrown myself

upon the mercy of my Redeemer, conscious of my own utter inability to conceive one good thought, or do one good act without his
gracious aid.   But I have felt nothing like what Scott requires.
Indeed, my good friend, I sometimes dread that I am in a far worse
condition than those who never heard the Word of God, or, who
having heard, reject it—if any condition can be worse than the last.
When I am with Mr. Hogue I am at ease.   He makes every thing
plain to me.   But when I hear others I am disturbed.   Indeed, my
doubts and misgivings do not desert me always in his presence.   I
wish I could see you, and converse with you.   To you I have no
scruple in writing in this style; but to any other I feel repugnant
to communicate.   I fear that I mistake a sense of my sins for true
repentance, and that I sometimes presume upon the mercy of God.
Again, it appears incredible that one so contrite as I sometimes
know myself to be, should be rejected entirely by infinite mercy.
Write to me upon this topic—not my own state—but give me your
ideas generally on salvation; or direct me to some publication that
puts it in the clearest light.   I have carefully read the gospels, but
cannot always comprehend."

Writing to Dr. Brockenbrough, from Roanoke, the 4th of July,
1815, he says:

" It was to me a subject of deep regret that I was obliged to
leave town before Mr. Meade's arrival.   I promised myself much
comfort and improvement from his conversation.   My dear sir, there
is, or there is not, another and a better world.   If there is, as we
all believe, what is it but madness to be absorbed in the cares of
a clay-built hovel, held at will, unmindful of the rich inheritance
of an imperishable palace, of which we are immortal heirs ?   We acknowledge these things with our lips, but not with our hearts ; we
lack faith.

" We would serve God provided we may serve mammon at the
same time.   For my part, could I be brought to believe that this
life must be the end of my being, I should be disposed to get rid of
it as an incumbrance.   If what is to come be any thing like what is
passed, it would be wise to abandon the hulk to the underwriters, the
worms.   I am more and more convinced that, with a few exceptions,
this world of ours is a vast mad-house.   The only men I ever knew
well, ever approached closely, whom I did not discover to be unhappy,
are sincere believers of the Gospel, and conform their lives, as far as
the nature of man can permit, to its precepts.   There are only *three*
of them."   [Meade, Hogue, Key ?]   "And yet, ambition, and avarice, and pleasure, as it is called, have their temples crowded with
votaries, whose own experience has proved to them the insufficiency
and emptiness of their pursuits, and who obstinately turn away from

the only waters that can slake their dying thirst and heal their diseases.

"One word on the subject of your own state of mind. I am well acquainted with it—too well. Like you, I have not reached that lively faith which some more favored persons enjoy. But I am persuaded that it can and will be attained by all who are conscious of the depravity of our nature, of their own manifold departures from the laws of God, and sins against their own conscience; and who are sincerely desirous to accept of pardon on the terms held out in the Gospel. Without puzzling ourselves, therefore, with subtle disquisitions, let us ask, are we conscious of the necessity of pardon? are we willing to submit to the terms offered to us—to consider ' Christianity as a scheme imperfectly understood, planned by Infinite Wisdom, and canvassed by finite comprehensions'—to ask of our Heavenly Father that faith and that strength which by our own unassisted efforts we can never attain? To me it would be a stronger objection to Christianity did it contain nothing which baffled my comprehension, than its most difficult doctrines. What professor ever delivered a lecture that his scholars were not at a loss to comprehend some parts of it? But that is no objection to the doctrine. But the teacher here is God! I may deceive myself, but I hope that I have made some progress, so small indeed that I may be ashamed of it, in this necessary work, even since I saw you. I am no disciple of Calvin or Wesley, but I feel the necessity of a changed nature; of a new life; of an altered heart. I feel my stubborn and rebellious nature to be softened, and that it is essential to my comfort here, as well as to my future welfare, to cultivate and cherish feelings of good will towards all mankind; to strive against envy, malice, and all uncharitableness. I think I have succeeded in forgiving all my enemies. There is not a human being that I would hurt if it were in my power; not even Bonaparte."

Mr. Randolph was now destined to receive the severest stroke of misfortune that had befallen him since the death of his brother Richard. It seems that his ill-fated family were destined to fall one by one, and to leave him the sole and forlorn wreck of an ancient house, whose name and fortunes he had so fondly cherished. Tudor, *the last hope*, had been sent abroad this spring (1815) in search of health. He had scarcely reached Cheltenham, England, when he fell into the arms of death. In a letter from Dr. Brockenbrough, Mr. Randolph received the first tidings of this melancholy event. He was dumb—he opened not his mouth. "Your kind and considerate letter," says he, "contained the first intelligence of an event which I have long expected, yet dreaded to hear. I can make nc comment upon it. To attempt to describe the situation of my mind would be vain, even if it were practicable. May God bless you : to him alone I look for comfort on this side the grave; there alone, if at all, I shall find it."

Many said his mind was unsettled; that this dark destiny drove reason from her throne, and made him mad. In the vulgar estimation of a cold and selfish world he was purely mad. The cries of a deep and earnest soul are a mockery to the vain and unfeeling multitude. David had many sons: Randolph this only hope, *the child of his affections.* Yet when Absalom was slain, " the king was much moved, and went up to the chamber over the gate, and wept; and as he wept, thus he said, ' O my son Absalom—my son, my son Absalom! would God I had died for thee, O Absalom, my son, my son!'"

CHAPTER VI.

POLITICAL REFLECTIONS—CONGRESS—BANK CHARTER.

IN the midst of all his domestic afflictions, bodily ailments, and mental anxiety, Mr. Randolph never lost sight of public affairs. " As to politics," says he, " I am sick of them, and have resolved to wash my hands of them as soon as possible." The thought of mingling again in the strife of party politics was loathing to him ; but he could not banish from his mind the intimate knowledge of political events, their causes and consequences, which he possessed in so eminent a degree ; nor could he prevent the natural affinity for those great moral and political principles and agencies, which are for ever moving and moulding the social and political institutions of mankind. He was a statesman by nature—nascitur non fit—a born statesman. His observations, however trivial or brief, have a pith and meaning beyond the sagest reflections of most other men.

Many of his reflections rise to the dignity of political aphorisms, and are worthy to be ranked with the profound maxims of the great master of political philosophy. Last May, after Bonaparte had escaped from Elba, marched in triumph to Paris, and driven the frighted Bourbon once more from his throne, Mr. Randolph thus discourses on the affairs of Europe:

" On the late events in Europe, which baffle all calculation, I have looked with an eye not very different from yours." [Addressed to Mr. Key.]   " The Bourbons refused to abolish the slave trade. Bonaparte, from temporal views, no doubt, has made it the first act after his restoration! Here is food for solemn meditation. The situation of England is, according to my conception of things, more awful than ever. A sated libertine at the head of the government; a profligate debauchee her prime minister. When I think on Wilberforce and his worthy compeers, I cannot despair. Ten such would have saved Sodom. But what a frightful mass of wickedness does that country, as well as our own, present! Both rescued, by the most providential interference of Heaven, from ruin. But what do we see? Humble and hearty thanks for unmerited mercy? Self-abasement, penitence for past offences, and earnest rosolutions for future amendment, through divine assistance? I can recognize none of these. Even in myself how faint are these feelings, compared with my consciousness of their necessity! England, I sometimes think, stands on the verge of some mighty convulsion. The corruption of her government and her principal men, the discontents of her needy and profligate lower orders, the acts of her Cobbetts and Burdetts, all seem to threaten the overthrow of her establishment, in Church and State. Jacobinism has, I believe, a stronger hold in that country than in any other in Europe. But the foolishness of human wisdom, nothing daunted by repeated overthrows of all its speculations and the confusion of its plans, yet aspires to grasp and to control the designs of the Almighty."

But the period had come for John Randolph to appear again on the public stage. The times had been truly eventful. The cycle of five and twenty years, in which the spirit of human liberty fought for her existence, had rolled round and come to a close. Born of the divine love shed forth in the gospel of Jesus Christ, bursting up in radiant majesty from the crumbling ruins of an effete feudalism, the cheerful voice of the Spirit of Liberty was first heard in the National Assembly of France, speaking in the accents of hope and of joy to the down-trodden millions of the earth. But, alas! in the wanton excess of an untried freedom, she quickly ran into a wild fanaticism, and swept the good as well as the evil into one common ruin. Seeking to break the oppressor's rod, and to tear down his towers and his dungeons of cruelty, she condemned time-honored virtue to the same indiscriminate death with hoary-headed vice, and pointed her finger of contempt and mockery at venerated wisdom no less than at cant and hypocrisy. This mad Spirit, lovely even in her madness, though mangled by the guillotine, and suffocated in the dungeons of the Conciergerie, rose triumphant, swept like an angel of destruction over the hills of Ardenne, the plains of Lombardy, and called down from the Pyramids of Egypt the witness of ages on the heroic deeds of her sons amid the desert sands of Africa. But wearied with excess, and hunted down, like Acteon, by the blood-hounds that had been nurtured in her own bosom, she at length fell beneath the iron heel of an imperial despotism, and was finally crushed and stifled in the blood of Waterloo. In the death agonies of Waterloo, freedom expired; a leaden peace was restored to Europe, and a new lease of thirty years for their dominions and their thrones, was vouchsafed to monarchs. Peace also, about the same time, was restored to our own borders, and with it came temptations to seduce the watchful guardian from his vigilant protection of the Constitution, and dangers more threatening than war to the liberties of the country. Pressed by a common necessity, bearing a heavy burthen of taxes, and confronting on every hand the external foes of their country, the mass of the people had but one object, were impelled by one sentiment—a speedy and successful termination of hostilities. That accomplished, each individual plunged into his own chosen field of enterprise, eagerly bent on his own aggrandizement, while the government was left, unrestrained and unobserved, to pursue its course in repairing the damages brought on the country by that most unprofitable of all work, the struggle to see how much harm each can do to the other. The obstructions of embargo and non-intercourse, followed by the destructive operations of a maritime war, had brought in their train a series of evil consequences. The republican party, as we already know, advocated those measures. Without stopping to inquire whether right or wrong, the task devolved on them, being still in the ascendent, to remedy the evils they must have foreseen and anticipated. "The embargo," said Mr. Randolph long ago, "was the Iliad of all our woes." The republicans were placed in a most difficult and critical position.

Those young and ardent spirits who urged on the war, and conducted it to a successful termination, were well suited for a time of excitement and destruction; but when the period arrived for healing and building up, graver counsel would have been more desirable. It required the utmost prudence and delicacy to restore the Constitution to its normal state, and to adjust the various and conflicting interests of the country in the well-poised scale of a wise abstinence and justice. Unfortunately, the republican party adopted those measures of relief which were most fatal to their principles. They who had come into power on the overthrow of the doctrines of Hamilton, were now, under the plea of necessity, about to outstrip the great federal leader himself in the adoption and advocacy of those temporizing and unconstitutional expedients they had so loudly condemned. " Until the present session," says Mr. Randolph, " I had not a conception of the extent of the change wrought in the sentiments of the people of this country by the war. I now see men trained in the school of the opposition to the administration of John Adams, who, down to June, 1812, were stanch sticklers for the Constitution, abjure all their former principles, and declare for expediency against right." " We have been told, sir," said Mr. Randolph at a later period, " that the framers of the Constitution foresaw the rising sun of some new sects, which were to construe the powers of the government differently from their intention ; and therefore the clause granting a general power to make all laws that might be necessary and proper to carry the granted powers into effect, was inserted in the Constitution. Yes, such a sect did arise some twenty years ago ; and, unfortunately, I had the honor to be a member of that church. From the commencement of the government to this day, differences have arisen between the two great parties in this nation ; one consisting of the disciples of Mr. Hamilton, the Secretary of the Treasury ; and another party, who believed that in their construction of the Constitution, those to whom they opposed themselves exceeded the just limits of its legitimate authority; and I pray gentlemen to take into their most serious consideration the fact, that on this very question of construction, this sect, which the framers of the Constitution foresaw might arise, did arise in their might, and put down the construction of the Constitution according to the Hamiltonian version. But, did we at that day dream that a new sect would arise after them, which would as far transcend Alexander Hamilton and his disciples as they outwent Thomas Jefferson, James Madison and John Taylor, of Caroline? This is the deplorable fact. Such is now the actual state of things in this land; and it is not a subject so much of demonstration as it is self-evident; it speaks to the senses, so that every one may understand it."

The first of that series of measures which gave birth to this new sect of politicians, and brought about the state of things so much deplored by Mr. Randolph, was the Bank. Charter, passed at this session of Congress.

The first incorporation of a bank, in 1791, was opposed by Thomas Jefferson and the republican party, as being an unwarranted assumption of power, nowhere granted in the Constitution. Consequently, when the charter of the old bank expired in 1811, they refused to renew it on the same ground. Henry Clay, then a senator from Kentucky, argued the question at great length: "This vagrant power," says he, "to erect a bank, after having wandered throughout the whole Constitution in quest of some congenial spot whereon to fasten, has been at length located, by the gentleman from Georgia, on that provision which authorizes Congress to lay and collect taxes. In 1791 the power is referred to one part of the instrument; in 1811, to another. Sometimes it is alleged to be deducible from the power to regulate commerce. Hard pressed here, it disappears, and shows itself under the grant to coin money. The sagacious Secretary of the Treasury, in 1791, pursued the wisest course. He has taken shelter behind general high-sounding and imposing terms. He has declared in the preamble to the act establishing the bank that it will be very *conducive* to the successful *conducting* of the national *finances;* will *tend* to give *facility* to the obtaining of loans ; and will be productive of considerable advantage *to trade* and *industry* in general. No allusion is made to the collection of taxes. What is the nature of this government? It is emphatically federal, vested with an aggregate of specified powers for general purposes, conceded by existing sovereignties, who have themselves retained what is not so conceded. It is said that there are cases in which it must act on implied powers. This is not controverted, but the implication must be necessary, and obviously flow from the enumerated power with which it is allied. The power to charter companies is not specified in the grant, and, I contend, is of a nature not transferable by mere implication. It is one of the most exalted attributes of sovereignty. In the exercise of this gigantic power, we have seen an East India Company created, which has carried dismay, desolation and death, throughout one of the largest portions of the habitable globe; a company which is, in itself, a sovereignty, which has subverted empires, and set up new dynasties, and has not only made war, but war against its legitimate sovereign! Under the influence of this power, we have seen arise a South Sea Company and a Mississippi Company, that distracted and convulsed all Europe, and menaced a total overthrow of all credit and confidence, and universal bankruptcy. Is it to be imagined that a power so vast would have been left by the wisdom of the Constitution to doubtful inference?"

Such was the forcible reasoning that induced the republicans in 1811 to refuse to recharter the bank or to incorporate another similar institution. They stood by the Constitution. But now, in 1816, every thing was changed; and what seemed unconstitutional before had become clearly necessary and proper, and therefore constitutional. Mr. Clay, who had become their leader and exponent, undertakes to justify his change of position: "The consideration," says he, "upon which I acted in 1811 was, that as the power to create a corporation, such as was proposed to be continued, was not specifically granted in the Constitution, and did not then appear to me to be necessary to carry into effect any of the powers which were specifically granted, Congress was not authorized to continue the bank. The Constitution contains powers delegated and prohibitory; powers expressed and constructive. It vests in Congress all powers *necessary* to give effect to the enumerated powers; all that may be necessary to put in motion and activity the machine of government which it constructs. The powers that may be so necessary are deducible by construction; they are not defined in the Constitution; they are, from their nature, undefinable. When the question is in relation to one of these powers, the point of inquiry should be, is its exertion necessary to carry into effect any of the enumerated powers and objects of the General Government? With regard to the *degree* of necessity, various rules have been at different times laid down; but, perhaps, at last, there is no other than a sound and honest judgment exercised, under the checks and control which belong to the Constitution and the people.

" The constructive powers being auxiliary to the specifically granted powers, and depending for their sanction and existence upon a necessity to give effect to the latter—which necessity is to be sought for and ascertained by a sound and honest discretion—it is manifest that this necessity may not be perceived, at one time, under one state of things, when it is perceived, at another time, under a different state of things. The Constitution, it is true, never changes; it is always the same; but the force of circumstances and the lights of experience may evolve, to the fallible persons charged with its administration, the fitness and necessity of a particular exercise of constructive power to-day, which they did not see at a former period." Mr. Clay then goes on to state facts which, in his judgment, rendered a bank in 1811 unnecessary. There were other means of conducting the fiscal affairs of the Government; "They," says he, "superseded the necessity of a national institution." But how stood the case in 1816, when he was called upon again to examine the power of the General Government to incorporate a national bank? A total change of circumstances was presented; events of the utmost magnitude had intervened. These events made a bank, in the opinion of Mr. Clay, necessary and proper, as an implied power, and therefore constitutional. But Mr. Clay does not do full justice to his position in 1811. He then declared that *the power to charter companies is not specified in the grant, and is of a nature not transferable by mere implication. It is one of the most exalted attributes of sovereignty.* It is inconceivable how a man, holding these opinions, could suffer any possible circumstances that might arise, to influence and change his position.

Yet Mr. Clay did shift his ground entirely, and contend, that although the power to charter companies was not specified in the grant, and was one of the most exalted attributes of sovereignty, still it was a constructive power necessary and proper to carry into effect those specifically granted, and therefore to be implied as a consequent and appendage to them. *The force of circumstances* may evolve to the fallible persons, charged with the administration of the government, the *fitness and necessity* of a particular exercise of *constructive power* to-day, which they did not see at a former period. And the *degree of necessity* which renders such *constructive power constitutional* is made to depend on the sound and honest judgment of those in authority. Men who wish to exercise a doubtful power, not specified in the grant, may themselves create the circumstances that shall render its exercise, in their estimation, necessary and proper. Instead of looking to the charter to see whether the power is granted, they have only to consider the *force of circumstances* urging on them, and to consult their own judgments (fallible persons) as to the *degree of necessity* which justifies the assumption of an undelegated authority. This is a virtual surrender of the Constitution. By such a law of interpretation, the jurisdiction of the Federal Government is made unlimited, and, instead of possessing delegated, specifically defined, and limited powers, it becomes a magnificent, all-absorbing, all-governing empire, with unrestrained and unlimited authority.

But Mr. Clay did not stand alone in this abandonment of the Constitution. He was followed by a decided majority of the republican party in Congress, and by all the executive authorities, with the President at their head. At first, there were some constitutional scruples manifested by the members of the House of Representatives. Men could not be brought to believe the difficulties in question, if they existed at all, were such as to require the House to sacrifice principle at the shrine of necessity. On the 10th of January, 1814, Mr. Eppes, from the Committee of Ways and Means, reported that the power to create corporations within the territorial limits of the States, without the consent of the States, is neither one of the powers delegated by the Constitution of the United States, or essentially necessary for carrying into effect any delegated power.

Mr. Calhoun, of South Carolina, moved that the Committee of the Whole be discharged from the consideration of this report, which was agreed to, and offered, as a substitute, a resolution that the Committee of Ways and Means be instructed to inquire into the expediency of establishing a national bank, *to be located in the District of Columbia.* In this way they thought to get around the constitutional question. But men soon came to see the alarming consequences of an interpretation which permitted Congress, in the District, to do the most unconstitutional acts, merely because they possessed exclusive jurisdiction.

At length, all these subterfuges were abandoned; and on the 8th of January, 1816, an ominous day for the bank, Mr. Calhoun reported "A bill to incorporate the subscribers to the Bank of the

United States." In his opening argument, he undertook to show the necessity that urged to the adoption of the measure now proposed. " We have," says he, " in lieu of gold and silver, a paper medium, un-equally but generally depreciated, which affects the trade and indus-try of the nation: which paralyzes the national arm ; which sullies the faith, both public and private, of the United States—a paper no longer resting on gold and silver as its basis. We have, indeed, laws regulating the currency of foreign coin, but they are, under pre-sent circumstances, a mockery of legislation, because there is no coin in circulation. The right of making money—an attribute of sove-reign power, a sacred and important right—was exercised by two hundred and sixty banks, scattered over every part of the United States; not responsible to any power whatever for their issues of paper. The next and great inquiry was," he said, " how this evil was to be remedied ? Restore," said he, " these institutions to their original use; cause them to give up this usurped power ; cause them to return to their legitimate office of places of discount and deposit; let them be no longer mere paper machines ; restore the state of things which existed anterior to 1813, which was consistent with the just policy and interests of the country; cause them to fulfil their contracts; to respect their broken faith ; resolve that every where there shall be an uniform value to the national currency; your constitutional control will then prevail." A National Bank, he argued, was the specific to cure all these evils.

Mr. Randolph, who made his appearance in the House for the first time about the period that Mr. Calhoun introduced his bill, took occasion to say, that he had listened to the honorable gentleman with pleasure. He was glad to see a cause so important in hands so able. He promised the honorable gentleman, though he might not agree with his mode of remedying the evil, he would go with him in the application of any adequate remedy to an evil which he regarded as most enormous.

Mr. Randolph said he rose to ask two questions—one of the gen-tleman from South Carolina, and the other of the gentleman from Maryland :—first, how the paper to be created by this bank' will cor-rect the vitiated state of our currency? and, secondly, how bank notes can answer the purpose of a circulating medium better than treasury notes? Though no stickler for treasury notes, Mr. Randolph intimated his opinion that they were, in time of peace, a better substitute for gold and silver than any paper he had yet heard submitted. He added some incidental observations, and concluded by saying, that he was sorry to see the apathy, the listlessness on this subject; on a question, which, if it passed, would, perhaps, be the most important decided since the establishment of the Constitution; and that though he agreed fully as to the extent of the existing evil, the *remedy* had been totally mistaken.

During the progress of the bill through the House, a motion was made to strike out that part which authorizes the Government to subscribe a certain portion of the stock. Mr. Randolph said he should vote for this motion, because one of his chief objections (one of them, he repeated) was the concern which it was proposed to give to the United States in the bank. He referred to the sale, by the Secretary of the Treasury, some years ago, of the shares belonging to the Bank of the United States, and stated the reasons of his approving that step; but, he added, that it was a strong argument against the feature of the bank bill now under consideration, that whenever there should be in this country a necessitous and profligate administration of the Government, that bank stock would be laid hold of by the first Squanderfield at the head of the Treasury, as the means of filling its empty coffers. But, if there was no objection to this feature stronger than that it would afford provision for the first rainy day, it might not be considered so very important. He argued, however, that it was eternally true, that nothing but the precious metals, or paper bottomed on them, could answer as the currency of any nation or age, notwithstanding the fanciful theories that great payments could only be made by credits and paper. How, he asked on this point, were the mighty armies of the ancient world paid off? Certainly not in paper or bank credits. He expressed his fears, lest gentlemen had got some of their ideas on these subjects from the wretched pamphlets under which the British and American press had groaned, on the subject of a circulating medium. He said he had once himself turned projector, and sketched the plan of a bank, of which it was a feature, that the Government should have a concern in it; but he became convinced of the fallacy of his views—he found his project would not answer. His objections to the agency of the Government in a bank was, therefore, he said, of no recent date, but one long formed—the objection was vital; that it would be an engine of irresistible power in the hands of any administration; that it would be in politics and finance, what the celebrated proposition of Archimedes was in physics—a place, the fulcrum; from which, at the will of the Executive, the whole nation could be hurled to destruction, or managed in any way, at his will and pleasure.

This bill, in the view of Mr. Randolph, presented two distinct questions: the one frigidly and rigorously a mere matter of calculalation; the other, involving some very important political considerations.

In regard to the present depreciation of paper, he did not agree with those who thought the establishment of a National Bank would aid in the reformation of it. If he were to go into the causes which produced the present state of things, he said, he should never end. As to the share the banks themselves had in producing it, he regarded the dividends they had made since its commencement as conclusive proof.

"The present time, sir," continued Mr. Randolph, "is, in my view, one of the most diastrous ever witnessed in the republic, and this bill proves it. The proposal to establish this great bank is but resorting to a crutch, and, so far as I understand it, it is a broken one; it will tend, instead of remedying the evil, to aggravate it. The evil of the times is a spirit engendered in this republic, fatal to republican principles—fatal to republican virtue: a spirit to live by any means but those of honest industry; a spirit of profusion: in other words, the spirit of Catiline himself—*alieni avidus sui profusus*—a spirit of expediency, not only in public but in private life: the system of Didler in the farce—living any way and well; wearing an expensive coat, and drinking the finest wines, at any body's expense. This bank, I imagine, sir, (I am far from ascribing to the gentleman from South Carolina any such views,) is, to a certain extent, a modification of the same system. Connected, as it is to be, with the Government, whenever it goes into operation, a scene will be exhibited on the great theatre of the United States, at which I shudder. If we mean to transmit our institutions unimpaired to posterity; if some, now living, wish to continue to live under the same institutions by which they are now ruled—and with all its evils, real or imaginary, I presume no man will question that we live under the easiest government on the globe—we must put bounds to the spirit which seeks wealth by every path but the plain and regular path of honest industry and honest fame.

Let us not disguise the fact, sir, we think we are living in the better times of the Republic. We deceive ourselves; we are almost in the days of Sylla and Marius : yes, we have almost got down to the time of Jugurtha. It is unpleasant to put one's self in array against a great leading interest in a community, be they a knot of land speculators, paper jobbers, or what not ; but, sir, every man you meet in this House or out of it, with some rare exceptions, which only serve to prove the rule, is either a stockholder, president, cashier, clerk, or doorkeeper, runner, engraver, paper-maker, or mechanic, in some way or other, to a bank. The gentleman from Pennsylvania may dismiss his fears for the banks, with their one hundred and seventy millions of paper, on eighty-two millions of capital. However great the evil of their conduct may be, who is to bell the cat ? who is to take the bull by the horns ? You might as well attack Gibraltar with a pocket pistol as to attempt to punish them. There are very few who dare speak truth to this mammoth. The banks are so linked together with the business of the world, that there are very few men exempt from their influence. The true secret is, the banks are creditors as well as debtors ; and if they were merely debtors to us for the paper in our pockets, they would soon, like Morris and Nicholson, go to jail (figuratively speaking) for having issued more paper than they were able to pay when presented to them. A man has their note for fifty dollars, perhaps, in his pocket, for which he wants fifty Spanish milled dollars ; but they have his note for five thousand in their possession, and laugh at his demand. We are tied hand and foot, sir, and bound to conciliate this great mammoth, which is set up to worship in this Christian land : we are bound to propitiate it. Thus whilst our government denounces hierarchy ; will permit no privileged order for conducting the services of the only true God; whilst it denounces nobility—has a privileged order of new men grown up, the pressure of whose foot, sir, I feel at this moment on my neck. If any thing could reconcile me to this monstrous alliance between the bank and the government, if the object could be attained of compelling the banks to fulfil their engagements, I could almost find it in my heart to go with the gentleman in voting for it.

" The stuff uttered on all hands, and absolutely got by rote by the haberdashers' boys behind the counters in the shops, that the paper now in circulation will buy any thing you want as well as gold and silver, is answered by saying that you want to buy silver with it. The present mode of banking, sir, goes to demoralize society ; it is as much swindling to issue notes with the intent not to pay, as it is burglary to break open a house. If they are unable to pay, the banks are bankrupts ; if able to pay and will not, they are fraudulent bankrupts. But a man might as well go to Constantinople to preach Christianity, as to get up here and preach against the banks. To pass this bill would be like getting rid of the rats by setting fire to the house. Whether any other remedy can be devised, I will not now undertake to pronounce. The banks have lost all shame, and exemplify a beautiful and very just observation of one of the finest writers, that men banded together in a common cause, will collectively do that at which every individual of the combination would spurn. This observation has been applied to the enormities committed and connived at by the British East India Company; and will equally appply to the modern system of banking, and still more to the spirit of party.

" As to establishing this bank to prevent a variation in the rate of exchange of bank paper, you might as well expect it to prevent the variations of the wind; you might as well pass an act of Congress (for which, if it would be of any good, I should certainly vote) to prevent the northwest wind from blowing in our teeth as we go from the House to our lodgings.

"But, sir, I will conclude by pledging myself to agree to any adequate means to cure the great evil, that are consistent with the administration of the government, in such a manner as to conduce to the happiness of the people and the reformation of the public morals."

Mr. Randolph combated the bill in all its stages, moved amendments with a view of abridging and restraining the powers of the corporation, and, finally, on the 5th of April, 1816, when the bill was sent back from the Senate with sundry amendments for the concurrence of the House, he moved, for the purpose of destroying the bill, that the whole subject be indefinitely postponed; and supported his motion by adverting to the small number of members present, and the impropriety of passing, by a screwed up, strained, and costive majority, so important a measure, at the end of a session, when the members were worn down and exhausted by a daily and long attention to business; a measure which, in time of war, and of great public emergency, could not be forced through the House; a measure so deeply involving the future welfare, and which was to give a color and character to the future destiny of this country; a measure which, if it and another (the tariff) should pass into laws, the present session would be looked back to as the most disastrous since the commencement of the republic; and which, much as he deprecated war, he would prefer war itself to either of them. Mr. Randolph then proceeded to argue against the bill as unconstitutional, inexpedient, and dangerous. His constitutional objections, he said, were borne out by the decision of Congress in refusing to renew the charter of the old bank, which decision was grounded on the want of constitutional power. He adverted, also, in support of his opinion, to the instructions from the legislatures of Virginia and Kentucky to their senators to vote against the old bank; which instructions were given on the ground of that institution being unconstitutional. " I declare to you, sir," said Mr. Randolph, " that I am the holder of no stock whatever, except live stock, and had determined never to own any —but, if this bill passes, I will not only be a stockholder to the utmost of my power, but will advise every man, over whom I have any influence, to do the same, because it is the creation of a great privileged order of the most hateful kind to my feelings, and because I would rather be the master than the slave. If I must have a master, let him be one with epaulettes—something that I can fear and respect, something that I can look up to—but not a master with a quill behind his ear."

After finally passing through both Houses, the bank bill was presented to Mr. Madison; he signed it, and it became a law. Mr. Madison, it is well known, was hitherto opposed to the incorporation of a National Bank on constitutional grounds. His Report in 1799– 1800, to the Virginia legislature on the general powers of the Federal Government, is conclusive and unanswerable on that subject. But on the present occasion he waived the question of the constitutional authority of the legislature to establish an incorporated bank, as being precluded, in his judgment, by repeated recognitions, under varied circumstances, of the validity of such an institution in acts of the legislative, executive, and judicial branches of the government, accompanied by indications, in different modes, of a concurrence of the general will of the nation.

Mr. Clay and his compeers surrendered the Constitution on the plea of necessity—*the force of circumstances*—Mr. Madison on the score of *precedent*—repeated recognitions of the validity of such an institution ! Well might the patriot weep over this last, fatal act of a great and a good man ! Well might he bemoan the imbecility of human nature, when he beheld the same hand that constructed the immortal argument by which the Constitution is made to rest on its true and lasting basis, in old age destroy the glorious work of its meridian power.

Randolph did not scruple to charge this act to the weakness of old age. Some years after this event, and when the bank was in full career, fulfilling all his predictions, hear what he says :—

" I am sorry to say, because I should be the last man in the world to disturb the repose of a venerable man, to whom I wish a quiet end of his honorable life, that all the difficulties under which we have labored, and now labor, on this subject (Tariff and Internal Improvement by the General Government), have grown out of a fatal admission, by one of the late Presidents of the United States, an admission which runs counter to the tenor of his whole political life, and is expressly contradicted by one of the most luminous and able state papers that ever was written, the offspring of his pen—an admission which gave a sanction to the principle, that this government had the power to charter the present colossal Bank of the United States. Sir," said Mr. Randolph, " that act, and one other, which I will not name, bring forcibly home to my mind a train of melancholy reflections on the miserable state of our mortal being.

'In life's last scenes, what prodigies arise !
Fears of the brave and follies of the wise.
From Marlborough's eyes the streams of dotage flow ;
And Swift expires a driv'ler and a show.'

" Such is the state of the case, sir. It is miserable to think of it—and we have nothing left to us but to weep over it."

And again, on the same occasion, in 1824—

" But the gentleman from New-York, and some others who have spoken on this occasion, say, What ! shall we be startled by a shadow ? Shall we recoil from taking a power clearly within (what ?) our reach ? Shall we not clutch the sceptre—the air-drawn sceptre that invites our hand, because of the fears and alarms of the gentleman from Virginia ?

" Sir, if I cannot give reason to the committee, they shall at least have authority. *Thomas Jefferson*, then in the vigor of his intellect, was one of the persons who denied the existence of such powers—*James Madison* was another. He, in that masterly and unrivalled report in the legislature of Virginia, which is worthy to be the text-book of every American statesman, has settled this question. For me to attempt to add any thing to the arguments of that paper, would be to attempt to gild refined gold—to paint the lily—to throw a perfume on the violet—to smooth the ice—or add another hue unto the rainbow—in every aspect of it, wasteful and ridiculous excess. Neither will I hold up my farthing rush-light to the blaze of that meridian sun. But, sir, I cannot but deplore—my heart aches when I think of it—that the hand which erected that monument of political wisdom, should have signed the act to incorporate the present Bank of the United States."

CHAPTER VII.

HOME—SOLITUDE.

MR. RANDOLPH was not less strenuous in his opposition to the "revenue bill," or *tariff measure*, of this eventful session; but we pass that, for the present, until it comes up again in a more aggravated form. Death, it seems, had made his friends the chosen mark for his fatal weapons. Mrs. Judith Randolph died in March, at the house of her friend—a great and a good man—Dr. John H. Rice, of Richmond. She doubtless died of a broken heart. Bereft of every comfort, life had no charms for her, and she sought death as a blessing. Her friends and Mr. Randolph's friends followed her mortal remains in sad procession to Tuckahoe—the family seat of her ancestors—some miles above Richmond, on James River, where they rest in peace beneath the shadow of those venerable oaks that witnessed the sweet gambols of her joyous and innocent childhood.

No sooner was this sad bereavement communicated to Mr. Randolph, than he was called to the bedside of a dying friend—an old and tried friend—a companion who had stood by him through evil as well as good report, as he fought like a bold champion for the Constitution and the rights of the people. "Yesterday (April 11th) we buried poor Stanford. I staid by his bedside the night before he died. Jupiter was worn down by nursing him, and is still feeling the effects of it. He returned home on Sunday morning, and has been sick ever since. My own health is not much better, and my spirits worse. Poor Stanford! he is not the least regretted of those who have been taken from me within the past year."

In addition to his present family—Dr. Dudley and young Clay—Mr. Randolph took upon himself the charge and the responsibility of two other orphan boys. "I have just returned from Baltimore, where I went to meet the sons of my deceased friend Bryan, consigned to my care. They are fine boys, but have been much neglected. I propose to place them at Prince Edward College, under the care of Dr. Hogue, after they shall have undergone some preparatory tuition at Mr. Lacy's school."

These acts speak for themselves. By these, and such as these, that crowd his whole life, let him be judged. Here is one the world have agreed to condemn as a misanthrope—a hater of his fellow-man. It is certain he did not seek to be known of men. Few could understand ("My mother—she understood me!"), few could appreciate him.

While apparently absorbed in the business of legislation, *the great question* was still uppermost in his thoughts. Before leaving Washington for his solitary home, he sought an interview with his trusty friend, "Frank Key," and rode over to Georgetown (May 7th, 1816,) for that purpose. But failing to meet with him. he went into Semmes's Hotel, and wrote him the following letter :

" Hearing, at Davis's, yesterday, that you were seen in Georgetown the evening before, I came here in the expectation of the pleasure of seeing you; but my intelligence proved to be like the greater part that happens under that name in this poor, foolish world of ours. I had also another motive. I wished to give Wood an opportunity to finish the picture. I called last evening, but he was gone to Mt. Vernon. I shall drive by his apartment, and give him the last sitting this morning. It is a soothing reflection to me, that your children, long after I am dead and gone, may look upon their sometime father's friend, of whose features they will have perhaps retained some faint recollection. Let me remind you that, although I am childless, I cannot forego my claim to the return picture, on which I set a very high value.

"Your absence from home is a sore disappointment to me. I wanted to have talked with you. unreservedly, on subjects of the highest interest. I wanted your advice as a friend, on the course of my future life. Hitherto it has been almost without plan or system— the sport of what we call chance.

"About a year ago, I got a scheme into my head, which I have more than once hinted to you; but I fear my capacity to carry it into execution.

" There is, however, another cause of uneasiness, about which I could have wished to confer freely with you. It has cost me many a pang, within a few months past especially. In the most important of human concerns I have made no advancement; on the contrary (as is always the case when we do not advance), I have fallen back. My mind is filled with misgivings and doubts and perplexities that leave me no repose. Of the necessity for forgiveness I have the strongest conviction ; but I cannot receive any assurance that it has been accorded to me. In short, I am in the worst conceivable situation as its respects my internal peace and future welfare. I want aid; and the company and conversation of such a friend as yourself might assist in dispelling, for a time, at least, the gloom that depresses me. I have humbly sought comfort where alone it is effectually to be obtained, but without success. To you and Mr. Meade I can venture to write in this style, without disguising the secret workings of my heart. I wish I could always be in reach of you. The solitude of my own dwelling is appalling to me. Write to me, and direct to Richmond."

To this Mr. Key replied:

"As we could not confer upon the subjects you mention, we must postpone them till we meet again, or manage them in writing; just as you please. In either way you will have much to excuse in me; but I trust you will find within yourself a counsellor and comforter who will guide you 'into all peace.' Desperate indeed would be our case, if we had nothing better to lead us than our own wisdom and strength or the experience of our friends. If, notwithstanding all your doubts and misgivings, you are sincerely and earnestly desirous to know the truth, and resolved to obey it, cost what it may, you have the promise of God that it shall be revealed to you. If you are convinced you are a sinner, that Christ alone can save you from the sentence of condemnation incurred by your sins, and from the dominion of them; if you make an entire and unconditional surrender of yourself to his service, renouncing that of the world and of yourself; if you thus humbly and faithfully come to him, 'he will in no wise cast you out.'

"You can do much for the cause of religion, whatever plan of life you may adopt; you can resolutely and thoroughly bear your testimony in its favor. You can adorn its doctrines, and so preach them most powerfully by a good life. You can be seen resisting and overcoming, in the strength of God, the powerful and uncommon temptations that oppose you; and your light can, and, I trust, will shine far and brightly around you. Do not be disheartened by the difficulties you may feel; they are experienced by all, and grace and strength to overcome them are offered to all. The change from darkness to light, from death to life, is the result of no single effort, but of constant and persevering, and, often, painful striving. How can it be otherwise when we think of what that change is? It finds us 'dead in trespasses and sins,' 'having our conversation in the flesh,' 'fulfilling the desires of the flesh and of the mind,' 'children of wrath,' 'without Christ,' 'strangers to the covenant of promise,' 'having no hope, and without God in the world;' and it makes us 'nigh by the blood of Christ;' 'no more foreigners and strangers, but fellow-citizens with the saints and of the household of God;' 'justified by faith, and having peace with God, through our Lord Jesus

Christ.' .May you experience this change, my dear friend, in all its blessedness."

Randolph thus replied:

" ROANOKE, June 16, 1816.

" Owing to the incorrigible negligence of the postmaster at Richmond, I did not get your letter of the 22d of last month until this morning. I had felt some surprise at not hearing from you, and the delay of your letter served but to enhance its value. I read it this morning in bed, and derived great consolation from the frame of mind to which it disposed me. My time has been a wretched one since I saw you—dreary and desponding. I heard Mr. Hogue yesterday; and during a short conversation, riding from church, he told me that he believed that there were times and seasons when all of us were overcome by such feelings in spite of our best efforts against them; efforts which, however, we ought by no means to relax, since they tended both to mitigate the degree and shorten the period of our sufferings. My own case (every body, no doubt, thinks the same) appears to be peculiarly miserable. To me the world is a vast desert, and there is no merit in renouncing it, since there is no difficulty. There never was a time when it was so utterly destitute of allurement for me. The difficulty with me is to find some motive to action—something to break the sluggish tenor of my life. I look back upon the havoc of the past year as upon a bloody field of battle, where my friends have perished. I look out towards the world, and find a wilderness, peopled indeed, but not with flesh and blood—with monsters tearing one another to pieces for money or power, or some other vile lust. Among them will be found, with here and there an exception, the professors of the religion of meekness and love, itself too often made the bone of contention and faction. Is it not strange that a being so situated should find difficulty in renouncing himself, the dominion of his own bad passions? To such an one another and a better world is a necessary refuge, and yet he cannot embrace it.

" My dear friend, it is very unreasonable that I should throw the burthen of my black and dismal thoughts upon you; but they so weigh me down that I cannot escape from them; and when I can speak without restraint, they will have vent."

Mr. Randolph spent the summer at home entirely alone. Dr. Dudley's health required a visit to the Virginia Springs, where he remained during the season. The boys were at school. With the exception of a short visit to Richmond, he did not leave his own plantation. His time was consumed in silence and in solitude. There can be no question that this entire abstinence from human society—the cheerful face of man and woman—the morning salutation and the evening converse with friends loving and beloved—had **a** pernicious influence on his health, his mind, and his temper.

No man enjoyed with a higher relish the intellectual and polished society of those friends, men and women, whom he had endeared to him by the strongest ties of affection, no man felt more keenly its absence. Yet it seems to have been his lot to live in solitude; so few understood him!

On the 25th of October he thus writes to Mr. Key:

"If your life is so unsatisfactory to you, what must that of others be to them? For my part, if there breathes a creature more empty of enjoyment than myself, I sincerely pity him. My opinions seem daily to become more unsettled, and the awful mystery which shrouds the future alone renders the present tolerable. The darkness of my hours, so far from having passed away, has thickened into the deepest gloom. I try not to think, by moulding my mind upon the thoughts of others; but to little purpose. Have you ever read Zimmerman on Solitude? I do not mean the popular cheap book under that title, but another, in which solitude is considered with respect to its dangerous *influence* upon the mind and the heart. I have been greatly pleased with it for a few hours. It is a mirror that reflects the deformity of the human mind to whomsoever will look into it.

"Dudley is with me. He returned about a month ago from our Springs, and I think he has benefited by the waters. He returns your salutation most cordially. We have been lounging a la Virginianne, at the house of a friend, about a day and a half's ride off. In a few days I shall return to the same neighborhood, not in pussuit of pleasure, but pursued by ennui."

———• • •———

CHAPTER VIII.

DYING, SIR—DYING.

THE session of Congress which terminated the 4th of March, 1817, presents nothing of much public interest. The most remarkable act of the session is the compensation law, as it was called, by which members voted themselves a fixed salary for their services, instead of the usual per diem allowance.

Mr. Randolph's half brother, Henry St. George Tucker, was **a** member of this Congress. On his way to Washington he was upset in the stage—had his shoulder dislocated, and in other respects was much injured. So soon as the news of this accident reached him, Mr. Randolph hastened to the bedside of his brother, and on his return to Washington wrote the following letter :

" I have been very unwell since I left you, but not in consequence of my journey to your bedside. On the contrary I believe I am the better for it in every respect. A wide gulf has divided us, of time and place and circumstance. Our lot has been different, very different indeed. I am ' the last of the family '—of my family at least— and I am content that in my person it should become extinct. In the rapid progress of time and of events, it will quickly disappear from the eye of observation, and whatsoever of applause or disgrace it may have acquired in the eyes of man, will weigh but little in the estimation of Him by whose doom the everlasting misery or happiness of our condition is to be irrevocably fixed. ' We are indeed clay in the potter's hands.' "

Mr. Randolph's health during this winter was wretched in the extreme ; more especially towards the close. The reader is already aware of his determination " to wash his hands of politics "—he had announced to his friends that he would not be a candidate again for Congress. On Saturday night, February 8th, he wrote to Dr. Dudley—

" Your letter of the 2d was put into my hands this morning, just as I was about to make my last dying speech." The next Tuesday he says—" I scribbled a few lines to you on Saturday evening last, at which time I was laboring under the effects of fresh cold, taken in going to and coming from the House, where I delivered my valedictory. It was nearer being, than I then imagined, a valedictory to this world. That night, and the next day and night, I hung suspended between two worlds, and had a much nearer glimpse than I have ever yet taken of the other.

" That I have written this letter with effort will be apparent from the face of it. I am not ashamed to confess that it has cost me some bitter tears—but they are not the tears of remorse. They flow from the workings of a heart known only to Him unto whom the prayers and the groans of the miserable ascend. I feel that in this world I am alone—that all my efforts (ill-judged and misdirected I am willing to allow they must have been) have proved abortive. What remains of my life must be spent in a cold and heartless intercourse with mankind, compared with which the solitude of Robinson Crusoe was bliss. I have no longer a friend. Do not take this unkindly, for it is not meant so. On this subject, as well as on some others, per

haps, I have been an enthusiast—but I know neither how to conciliate the love nor to command the esteem of mankind; and like the
officious ass in the fable, must bear the blows inflicted on my presumption. May God bless you, my brother. You have found the
peace of this world. May you find that of the world to come, which
passeth all understanding. If it be his good pleasure, we may meet
again; if not in this life, in life everlasting, where all misunderstanding and misinterpretation shall be at an end; and the present delusions of self appear in their proper and vile deformity, and the busy
cares and sorrows which now agitate and distress us seem more trivial
than the tears of infancy—succeeded, not by transient, but everlasting sunshine of the heart. Amen, and so let it be.

JOHN RANDOLPH OF ROANOKE.

Jan. 21, 1817. Tuesday.

Sunday morning.—I have been reading Lear these two days, and
incline to prefer it to all Shakspeare's plays. In that and Timon only,
it has been said, the bard was in earnest. Read both—the first especially.

Tuesday, Feb. 18th.—" I had hardly finished my last letter (Sunday the 16th) to you, when I was seized by spasms that threatened
soon to terminate all my earthly cares; although the two nights since
have been passed almost entirely without sleep, I am much better."

Sunday, February 23d.—" The worst night that I have had since
my indisposition commenced. It was, I believe, a case of *croup*, combined with the affection of the liver and the lungs. Nor was it un-
like tetanus, since the muscles of the neck and back were rigid, and
the jaw locked. I never expected, when the clock struck two, to
hear the bell again; fortunately, as I found myself going, I dispatched
a servant (about one) to the apothecary for an ounce of laudanum.
Some of this poured down my throat, through my teeth, restored me
to something like life. I was quite delirious, but had method in my
madness; for they tell me I ordered Juba to load my gun and to
shoot the first "doctor" that should enter the room; adding, they are
only mustard seed, and will serve just to sting him. Last night I
was again very sick; but the anodyne relieved me. I am now persuaded that I might have saved myself a great deal of suffering by
the moderate use of opium. This day week, when racked with cramps
and spasms, my "doctors" (I had two) prescribed (or rather, administered) half a glass of Madeira. Half a drop of rain water would
have been as efficient. On Tuesday, Wednesday, and Thursday, I
attended the House; brought out the first day by the explosion of
the motion to repeal the internal taxes; and the following days by
some other circumstances that I will not now relate. Knocked up
completely by the exertion, instead of recalling my physicians, I took
my own case boldly in hand; took one and a half grains of calomel;

on Tuesday night and yesterday using mercurial friction. The liver is again performing its functions, and I am, this evening, decidedly better than I have been since the first attack, which I may date from my fall at Mr. T.'s, on Tuesday, the 21st of January. From that period, the operations of the liver have been irregular and disturbed. I conceive the lungs to be affected by sympathy, with the other viscus. I have taken from five to ten grains of the hypercarbonated natron every day, most generally five grains, in a tablespoonful of new milk, sometimes repeating the dose at night. My drink has been slippery elm tea and lemonade. Appetite for acids very strong. Severe pains in the fasciæ of the legs and the tendons, just above the outer ankle bone; also, knees, &c. I have taken, from the first, a pill of one and a half grains of calomel about two, sometimes three times a week; and several doses of Cheltenham salts. I have used the volatile liniment for my throat and limbs; also, gargles of sage tea. borax, &c.

Mrs. John M., Mrs. B., and Mrs. F. K., have been very kind in sending me jellies, lemons, &c., &c. Thomas M. N. has been extremely attentive and obliging. Mr. K. of New York, Mr. Chief Justice, Mr. H. of Maryland, Mr. M. of South Carolina, Mr. B. of Georgetown, (I need not name Frank Key,) M. (no longer Abbé) C. de S., and D., have been very kind in their attentions. Mr. M. sent me some *old*, choice Madeira, and his man cook to dress my rice (a mystery not understood any where on this side of Cape Fear river), sending also the rice to be dressed; and Mr. Chief Justice came to assist me in drawing up my will—which I had strangely and *criminally* neglected for some time past, and of which neglect I was more strangely admonished in a dream."

About this time, says Mr. Wm. H. Roane, who was a member of Congress from Virginia during the session of 1816–17, " I remember that one morning Mr. Lewis came into the House of Representatives and addressed Mr. Tyler and myself, who were the youngest members from Virginia, and said we must go to Georgetown to Mr. Randolph. We asked for what; he said that Mr. Randolph had told him that he was determined not to be buried as beau Dawson had been, at the public expense, and he had selected us young bloods to come to him and take charge of his funeral. We went over immediately. When we entered Mr. Randolph's apartments he was in his morning gown. He rose and shook us by the hand. On our inquiries after his health, he said, ' Dying! dying! dying! in a dreadful state.' He inquired what was going on in Congress. We told him that the galleries were filling with people of the District, and that there was considerable excitement on the re-chartering of the batch of banks in the District. He then broke off and commenced upon another subject, and pronounced a glowing eulogium upon the character and talents of Patrick Henry. After sitting for some time, and nothing being said on the business on which we had been sent to him, we rose and took our leave. When we got to the door, I said, 'I wish, Mr. Randolph, you could be in the House to-day.' He shook his head—'Dying, sir, dying!' When we had got back to the 'House of Representatives, Mr. Lewis came in and asked how we had found Mr. Randolph. We laughed and said as well as usual—that we had spent a very pleasant morning with him, and been much amused by his conversation. Scarcely a moment after, Mr. Lewis exclaimed, 'There he is!' and there to be sure he was. He had entered by another door, having arrived at the Capitol almost as soon as we did. In a few moments he rose and commenced a speech, the first sentence of which I can repeat verbatim.—'Mr. Speaker,' said he, 'this is Shrove Tuesday. Many a gallant cock has died in the pit on this day, and I have come to die in the pit also.' He then went on with his speech, and after a short time turned and addressed the crowd of 'hungry expectants,' as he called them—tellers, clerks, and porters in the gallery."

Mr. Randolph left Washington the day after Mr. Monroe's inauguration. "No mitigation of my cruel symptoms took place until the third day of my journey, when I threw physic to the dogs, and instead of opium, tincture of columbo, hypercarbonate of soda, &c., &c., I drank, in defiance of my physician's prescription, copiously of cold spring water, and ate plentifully of ice. Since that change of regimen my strength has increased astonishingly, and I have even gained some flesh, or rather, skin. The first day, Wednesday the 5th, I could travel no farther than Alexandria. At Dumfries, where I lay, but slept not, on Thursday night, I had nearly given up the ghost. At a spring, five miles on this side, after crossing Chappawamsick, I took, upon an empty and sick stomach, upwards of a pint of living water, unmixed with Madeira, which I have not tasted since. It was the first thing that I had taken into my stomach since the first of February that did not produce nausea. It acted like a charm, and enabled me to get on to B.'s that night, where I procured ice. I also devoured with impunity a large pippin (forbidden fruit to me). Next day I got to the Oaks, forty-two miles. Here I was more unwell than the night before. On Sunday morning I reached my friends, Messrs. A. & Co., to breakfast, at half past eight."

On the road between the Bolling Green and Fredericksburg, he came up with the stage with Mr. Roane and other members of Congress on their homeward journey. As he drew up his phaeton along side the stage, Mr. Roane called out, " How are you, Mr. Randolph?" " Dying, sir, dying !" and then dashed off and out travelled the stage.

He was, indeed, much nearer dying than his friends imagined. Shortly after his arrival in Richmond he was taken very ill, and lay for many weeks utterly prostrate and helpless at the house of Mr. Cunningham, in that city. In after years he often recurred to this period as the time of his greatest prostration. March 3d, 1824, he says, " You have no idea how very feeble I am. I crawled yesterday to P. Thompson's bookseller's shop, butcould not get back afoot. The vis vitæ has not been lower with me since the spring of 1817. How well I recollect this very day of that year !"

CHAPTER IX.

CONVERSION.

For a long time the state of Mr. Randolph's health was such that he confined himself entirely at home, and even ceased correspondence with his friends, which at all times constituted his principal source of enjoyment. His first attempt was the following letter addressed to his friend Key:

ROANOKE, Feb. 9, 1818.

DEAR FRANK : A long while ago I wrote to you in reply to the only letter that I have received for many, many months. I know that you have something better to do than to be scribbling to me ; but I beg you to take my case into your special consideration. I am as much out of the world as if I were in Kamtschatka or Juan Fernandez—without a single neighbor, confined by my infirmities often to the house, and disabled by them from attending to my affairs, which might give me amusement and employment at the same time.

The state of manners around me cannot be paralleled, I believe, on the face of the earth—all engaged with unremitting devotion in the worship of

> " The least erected spirit
> That fell from heaven."

This pursuit I know to be general throughout the land, and, indeed, I fear throughout the world; but elsewhere it is tempered by the spirit of society, and even by a love of ostentation or of pleasure. Here it reigns undivided. There is no intercourse but of business; and a man who will ride more miles for a shilling than a post-boy, will hardly go one to visit a sick neighbor. * * * * I am afraid you will consider the foregoing as no proof of what I am about to add; but let me assure you that there is nothing personal between these " poor rich men" and me ; on the contrary, I feel toward them only pity and good will, and let no occasion pass without manifesting the latter disposition.

I think that the state of solitude and dereliction in which I am placed, has not been without some good effect in giving me better views than I have had of the most important of all subjects; and I would not exchange it, comfortless as it is, for the heartless intercourse of the world. I know that " if a man says he loves God, and hates his brother, he is a liar;" but I do not hate my brethren of the human family. I fear, however, that I cannot love them as I ought. But God, I hope and trust, will in his good time put better dispositions into my heart. There are few of them, I am persuaded, more undeserving of love than I am.

March 2. Every day brings with it new evidences of my weakness and utter inability, of myself, to do any good thing, or even to conceive a single good thought. With the unhappy father in the Gospel, I cry out, " Lord ! I believe, help thou mine unbelief." When I think of the goodness, and wisdom, and power of God, I seem, in my own eyes, a devil in all but strength. I say this to you, who will not ascribe it to affected humility. Sometimes I have better views, but again I am weighed down to the very earth, or lost in a labyrinth of doubts and perplexities. The hardness of my own heart grieves and astonishes me. Then, again, I settle down in a state of coldness and indifference, which is worse than all. But the quivering of our frail flesh, often the effect of physical causes, cannot detract from the mercy of our Creator, and to him I commit myself. " Thy will be done !"

M—— does not " give me all the news," nor, indeed, any for a long time past. At the commencement of the session of Congress, he wrote pretty frequently, and through him I heard of you. It would delight me very much to spend a few weeks with you. I would even try to be an usher in your school. [Mr. Key was teaching his own children.] At least, I could teach the younger children to read. Give my love to them all, and to their mother. 1 had a sister once, and I never think of her without being reminded of Mrs. Key.

I have not read Cunningham's poem. Is it the author of " The Velvet Cushion ?" I have lately met with an entertaining work from the pen of an English Jacobin, Hazlitt's Character of Shakspeare ; and have tried to read Coleridge's Literary Life. There are fine passages, but his mysticism is too deep for me. I have seen, too, a romance, called the Life of Patrick Henry—a wretched piece of fustian.

I have not turned entirely a savage, although a man of the woods, and almost wild. Bodily motion seems to be some relief to mental uneasiness, and I was delighted yesterday morning to hear that the snipes are come. On this subject of mental malady, it appears that madness is almost epidemic among us. Many cases have appeared in Petersburg and elsewhere. In this county we had a preacher of the Methodist sect (not itinerant), a man of excellent character and very good sense. He was generally esteemed, and although quite poor, by the aid of a notable wife lived neatly and comfortably. Last winter the clerk of our county died, and this preacher, by diligent canvass, got the place by one vote, in a court of more than twenty magistrates. From the time that he commenced his canvass his manners changed. A still further change was perceptible after he got the office; and ·a few weeks ago he got quite insane. His friends set off with him on a journey to Georgia. But the first night he gave them the slip, and is supposed to have drowned himself. I heard yesterday that a party were out seeking for him. He had taken laudanum for the purpose of suicide, but his stomach would not retain it. Some ascribe his malady to remorse, others to the effects of sudden prosperity. This county seems to labor under a judgment. It has been conspicuous for the order and morality of the inhabitants ; and such is the general character, I hope, yet. But within two or three years past it has been the theatre of crimes of the deepest atrocity. Within a few months there have occurred two instances of depravity, the most shocking that can be conceived. But I am giving you a county history, instead of a letter. Farewell, my dear friend ; while I have life I am yours.

RICHMOND, April 29, 1818.

DEAR FRANK—On my arrival here the day before yesterday, I found the picture and the picture-frame which poor L. left for me.

Wood has again failed, but not so entirely as at first. It is you in some of your humors, but neither your serious nor more cheerful face. It shall hang, however, near my bed, and I hope will prove a benefit as well as a pleasure to me. My love to Mrs. Key. I hope she has presented you with a better likeness of yourself than any painter can draw. If I could envy you, I should covet one of your boys, and. perhaps, one of your girls too, if I were not so old.

I have "read Manfred," and was overpowered by the intense misery of the writer. Unless he shall seek refuge above, where alone it is to be found, it is to be feared madness, perhaps suicide, is his portion. It created in me the strongest interest for the unhappy author, and I actually projected writing him a letter, such a one as could have displeased no man, and might, perhaps, have done good. The air of presumption which such a step might carry with it made me drop the "notion."

I have long been satisfied in my own mind respecting the princi ples, political, moral, and religious, of the journal you mention. I suspect Franklin's were not very different. I am gratified, however, at this castigation of that caricature of a caricature, Phillips. He "out-Currans" Curran.

I do not take, but shall order the Christian Observer. I have seen many of the numbers, and found them admirable.

"Fare thee well, and if for ever,
Still for ever fare thee well."

I regret the stifling of your poetical bantling. Can't you send me some of the "disjecta membra?" There is no need of a bottle of spirits of wine to preserve them in apothecary fashion. On reaching this place, I found my poor nephew, who has been a tenant of the mansion that inspired your muse. Sir P. Francis is not Junius, the reviewer to the contrary notwithstanding.

On his return from Richmond, Mr. Randolph sank down into the deepest melancholy ; some even allege that it amounted to an aberration of mind—to positive delirium The reader is aware that for years previous to this time, the deepest gloom, lasting many days in succession, overshadowed his mind, evincing the existence of some corroding care, for which he neither sought, nor would receive, any sympathy.

The subject of religion had become the all-absorbing theme of his meditations. God, freedom, and immortality ; sin, death, and the grave ; Christ, redemption, and free grace, are "high matters," well calculated, at any time, to disturb the strongest intellect.

But when we come to consider the solitude in which he lived, the emaciated condition of his delicate frame, worn down by long and torturing disease, the irritable state of his nervous system—"he was almost like a man without a skin"—the constant and sleepless excitement of his mental faculties and of his brilliant imagination induced by this morbid irritability ; when we throw ourselves into his condition, and conceive of the crowd of burning thoughts that pressed upon his mind, pass in melancholy review the many friends that had been torn from him by the hand of death, the many who had forgotten him and forsaken him as a fallen man, no longer serviceable to them; call to remembrance that his own father's house was desolate, St. George in the mad-house, himself, like Logan, alone in his cabin, without a drop of his father's blood save that which coursed in his own well-nigh exhausted veins; and, above all, when we call to remembrance his first, his youthful, and his only love, which is said to have greatly revived in his mind at this time with the painful yet hallowed associations that clustered around its cherished memory, who can wonder that a man, with the temperament of John Randolph, under these circumstances should fling away all restraint, and should cry aloud in the anguish of his soul, and should so act and speak as to excite the astonishment of those around, and induce them to believe that he was a madman ! In a similar situation David was a madman; Byron was a madman; Rousseau—all high-souled, deep-feeling men of genius, in the eye of the world were madmen.

Dr. Dudley says, that for many weeks his conduct towards himself, who was the only inmate of his household, had been marked by contumelious indignities, which required almost heroic patience to endure, even when aided by a warm and affectionate devotion, and an anxious wish to alleviate the agonies of such a mind. All hope of attaining this end, he says, finally failed, and he announced to Mr. Randolph his determination no longer to remain with him. Mr. Randolph then addressed him the following letter, so full of affection and tenderness, that it shows his best friends did not understand him, and that in his dark days of horror, when caprice and petulance marked his conduct, they did him a cruel injustice by supposing that the harsh expression or extravagant conduct, forced out by the anguish of his soul, was really intended as a premeditated injury to their feelings.

"August, 1818.

"I consider myself under obligations to you that I can never repay. I have considered you as a blessing sent to me by Providence, in my old age, to repay the desertion of my other friends and nearer connections. It is in your power (if you please) to repay me all the debt of gratitude that you insist upon being due to me; although I consider myself, in a pecuniary point of view, largely a gainer by our connection. But if you are unwilling to do so, I must be content to give up my last stay upon earth; for I shall, in that case, send the boys to their parents. Without you, I cannot live here at all, and will not. What it is that has changed your manner towards me, I cannot discover. I have ascribed it to the disease (hypochondriasis) by which you are afflicted, and which affects the mind and temper, as well as the animal faculties. In your principles, I have as unbounded confidence as I have in those of any man on earth. Your disinterestedness, integrity, and truth, would extort my esteem and respect, even if I were disposed to withhold them. I love you as my own son—would to God you were! I see, I think, into your heart—mine is open before you, if you will look into it. Nothing could ever eradicate this affection. which surpasses that of any other person (as I believe) on earth. Your parents have other children—I have only you. But I see you wearing out your time and wasting away in this desert, where you have no society such as your time of life, habits, and taste require. I have looked at you often engaged in contributing to my advantage and comfort. with tears in my eyes, and thought I was selfish and cruel in sacrificing you to my interest. I am going from home; will you take care of my affairs until I return? I ask it as a favor. It is possible that we may not meet again; but, if I get more seriously sick at the springs than I am now, I will send for you, unless you will go with me to the White Sulphur Springs. Wherever I am. my heart will love you as long as it beats. From your boyhood I have not been lavish of reproof upon you. Recollect my past life."

Mr. Randolph set out on his journey to the Springs—spent some days in Lynchburg—went as far as Bottetourt County—ascended the Peaks of Otter, the highest point of the Blue Ridge Mountains in Virginia—and then returned home to Roanoke. There seems to have been a total change in his mind about this time. From the deepest gloom and despondency, he seems to have attained clearness and satisfaction on the subject of religion. He said they wanted him to go to the Springs, but he had found a spring here, on this hill (Roanoke), more efficacious—a well—a fountain of living waters. He thus writes to Mr. Key:

ROANOKE, Sept. 7, 1818.

Congratulate me, dear Frank—wish me joy you need not; give it you cannot—I am at last reconciled to my God, and have assurance of his pardon, through faith in Christ, against which the very gates of hell cannot prevail. Fear hath been driven out by perfect love. I *now know* that *you know* how I feel; and within a month, for the first time I understand your feelings and character, and that of every *real* Christian Love to Mrs. Key and your brood.

I am not now afraid of being "righteous overmuch," or of "Methodistical notions."

Thine, in Truth,
J. R. OF R.

Let Meade know the glad tidings, and let him, if he has kept it read and preserve my letter to him from Richmond years ago.

He thus writes to Dr. Brockenbrough:

September 25.

MY GOOD FRIEND,—I am sorry that Quashee should intrude upon you unreasonably. The old man, I suppose, knows the pleasure I take in your letters, and therefore feels anxious to procure his master the gratification. I cannot, however, express sorrow— for I do not feel it—at the impression which you tell me my last letter made upon you. May it lead to the same happy consequences that I have experienced—which I now feel—in that sunshine of the heart, which the peace of God, that passeth all understanding, alone can bestow!

Your imputing such sentiments to a heated imagination does not surprise me, who have been bred in the school of Hobbs and Bayle, and Shaftesbury and Bolingbroke, and Hume and Voltaire and Gibbon; who have cultivated the skeptical philosophy from my vainglorious boyhood—I might almost say childhood—and who have felt all that unutterable disgust which hypocrisy and cant and fanaticism never fail to excite in men of education and refinement, superadded to our natural repugnance to Christianity. I am not, even now, insensible to this impression; but as the excesses of her friends (real or pretended) can never alienate the votary of liberty from a free form of government, and enlist him under the banners of despotism, so neither can the cant of fanaticism, or hypocrisy, or of both (for so far from being incompatible, they are generally found united in the same character—may God in his mercy preserve and defend us from both) disgust the pious with true religion.

Mine has been no sudden change of opinion. I can refer to a record, showing, on my part, a desire of more than nine years' standing, to partake of the sacrament of the Lord's Supper; although, for two-and-twenty years preceding, my feet had never crossed the threshold of the house of prayer. This desire I was restrained from indulging, by the fear of eating and drinking unrighteously. And although that fear hath been cast out by perfect love, I have never yet gone to the altar, neither have I been present at the performance of divine service, unless indeed I may so call my reading the liturgy of our church, and some chapters of the Bible to my poor negroes on Sundays. Such passages as I think require it, and which I feel competent to explain, I comment upon—enforcing as far as possible, and dwelling upon, those texts especially that enjoin the indispensable accompaniment of a good life as the touchstone of the true faith. The Sermon from the Mount, and the Evangelists generally; the Epistle of Paul to the Ephesians, chap. vi.; the General Epistle of James, and the First Epistle of John; these are my chief texts.

The consummation of my *conversion*—I use the word in its strictest sense—is owing to a variety of causes, but chiefly to the conviction, unwillingly forced upon me, that the very few friends which an unprosperous life (the fruit of an ungovernable temper) had left me were daily losing their hold upon me, in a firmer grasp of ambition, avarice, or sensuality. I am not sure that, to complete the anti-climax, avarice should not have been last; for although, in some of its effects, debauchery be more disgusting than avarice, yet, as it regards the unhappy victim, this last is more to be dreaded. Dissipation, as well as power or prosperity, hardens the heart; but avarice deadens it to every feeling but the thirst for riches. Avarice alone could have produced the slave-trade; avarice alone can drive, as it does drive, this infernal traffic, and the wretched victims of it, like so many post-horses, whipped to death in a mail-coach. Ambition has its reward in the pride, pomp, and circumstance of glorious war; but where are the trophies of avarice?—the handcuff, the manacle, and the blood-stained cowhide? What man is worse received in society for being a hard master? Every day brings to light some H——e or H——ns in our own boasted land of liberty! Who denies the hand of a sister or daughter to such monsters? Nay, they have even appeared in "the abused shape of the vilest of women." I say nothing of India, or Amboyna, of Cortez or Pizarro.

When I was last in your town I was inexpressibly shocked (and perhaps I am partly indebted to the circumstance for accelerating my emancipation) to hear, on the threshold of the temple of the least erect of all the spirits that fell from heaven, these words spoken, by a man second to none in this nation in learning or abilities; one, too, whom I had, not long before, seen at the table of our Lord and Saviour: " I do not want the Holy Ghost (I shudder while I write), or any other spirit in me. If these doctrines are true (St. Paul's), there was no need for Wesley and Whitfield to have separated from the church. The Methodists are right, and the church wrong. I want to see the old church," &c. &c.: that is, such as this diocese was under Bishop *Terrick*, when wine-bibbing and buck-parsons were sent out to preach "a dry clatter of morality," and not the word of God, for 16,000 lbs. of tobacco. When I speak of morality it is not as condemning it; religion includes it, but much more. Day is now breaking and I shall extinguish my candles, which are better than no light; or if I do not, in the presence of the powerful king of day they will be noticed only by the dirt and ill savor that betray all human contrivances, the taint of humanity. Morality is to the Gospel not even as a farthing rushlight to the blessed sun.

By the way, this term Methodist in religion is of vast compass and effect, like tory in politics, or aristocrate in Paris, " with the lamp-post for its second," some five or six-and-twenty years ago.

Dr. Hoge? "a Methodist parson." Frank Key? "a fanatic," (I heard him called so not ten days ago,) "a Methodistical, whining, &c., &c." Wilberforce? "a Methodist." Mrs. Hannah More? "ditto." It ought never to be forgotten, that real converts to Christianity on opposite sides of the globe agree at the same moment to the same facts. Thus Dr. Hoge and Mr. Key, although strangers, understand perfectly what each other feels and believes.

If I were to show a MS. in some unknown tongue to half a dozen persons, strangers to each other and natives of different countries, and they should all give me the same translation, could I doubt their acquaintance with the strange language? On the contrary, can I, who am but a smatterer in Greek, believe an interpreter who pretends to a knowledge of that tongue, and yet cannot tell the meaning of τυπτω?

I now read with relish and understand St. Paul's epistles, which not long since I could not comprehend, even with the help of Mr. Locke's paraphrase. Taking up, a few days ago, at an "ordinary," the life of John Bunyan, which I had never before read, I find an exact coincidence in our feelings and opinions on this head, as well as others.

Very early in life I imbibed an absurd prejudice in favor of Mahomedanism and its votaries. The crescent had a talismanic effect on my imagination, and I rejoiced in all its triumphs over the cross (which I despised) as I mourned over its defeats; and Mahomet II. himself did not more exult than I did, when the crescent was planted on the dome of St. Sophia. and the cathedral of the Constantines was converted into a Turkish mosque. To this very day I feel the effects of Peter Randolph's Zanga on a temper naturally impatient of injury, but insatiably vindictive under insult.

On the night that I wrote last to you I scribbled a pack of nonsense to Rootes, which serves only to show the lightness of my heart. About the same time, in reply to a question from a friend. I made the following remarks, which, as I was weak from long vigilance, I requested him to write down, that I might, when at leisure, copy it into my diary. From it you will gather pretty accurately the state of my mind.

I have been up long before day, and write with pain, from a sense

of duty to you and Mrs. B., in whose welfare I take the most earnest concern. You have my prayers: give me yours, I pray you.
Adieu!

JOHN RANDOLPH OF ROANOKE.

I was on the top of the pinnacle of Otter this day fortnight: a little above the earth, but how far beneath heaven!

" NOTE.—It is my business to avoid giving offence to the world, especially in all matters merely indifferent. I shall therefore stick to my old uniform, blue and buff, unless God sees fit to change it for black. I must be as attentive to my dress, and to household affairs, as far as cleanliness and comfort are concerned, as ever, and indeed more so. Let us take care to drive none away from God by dressing religion in the garb of fanaticism. Let us exhibit her as she is, equally removed from superstition and lukewarmness. But we must take care, that while we avoid one extreme we fall not into the other; no matter which. I was born and baptized in the Church of England. If I attend the Convention at Charlottesville, which I rather doubt, I shall oppose myself then and always to every attempt at encroachment on the part of the church, the clergy especially, on the rights of conscience. I attribute, in a very great degree, my long estrangement from God to my abhorrence of prelatical pride and puritanical preciseness; to ecclesiastical tyranny, whether Roman Catholic or Protestant; whether of Henry V. or Henry VIII; of Mary or Elizabeth; of John Knox or Archbishop Laud; of the Cameronians of Scotland, the Jacobins of France, or the Protestants of Ireland. Should I fail to attend, it will arise from a repugnance to submit the religion, or church, any more than the liberty of my country, to foreign influence. When I speak of my country, I mean the Commonwealth of Virginia. I was born in allegiance to George III.; the Bishop of London (*Terrick!*) was my diocesan. My ancestors threw off the oppressive yoke of the mother country, but they never made me subject to *New* England in matters spiritual or temporal; neither do I mean to become so, voluntarily."

Mr. Key, on getting the news of his friend's conversion, responded in this wise:—

" I do, indeed, my dear friend, rejoice with you—I have long wished, and often believed with confidence, that you would experience what God has now blessed you with. I need not tell you (if I could) of its value, for I trust you feel it to be 'unspeakable.' May the grace that has brought you from 'darkness to light,' from 'death to life,' keep you forever!

" Nor do I rejoice merely on your own account or mine. The

wonders that God is every where doing show us that these are no ordinary times. and justify us in hoping and expecting for greater mani-
festations of his power and goodness.   You stand on an eminence—
'let your light shine' brightly, that all may see it—steadily, that they
may know whence it comes, and 'glorify your Father which is in
heaven.'

   "Write to me often and particularly; 'out of the abundance of the
heart the mouth speaketh;' and may I always hear that you are following the guidance of that blessed Spirit that will 'lead you into all
truth,' leaning on that Almighty arm that has been extended to deliver
you, trusting only in the only Saviour, and 'going on' in your way to
him 'rejoicing.'

CHAPTER X.

IDIOSYNCRACIES.

A quick, intuitive understanding, a vivid imagination, an irritable
temper, superadded to an extremely delicate and diseased constitution, produced a complicated character in John Randolph, that rendered him remarkably sensitive to outward influences.   He was,
indeed, a creature of impulse, influenced for the time being by the circumstances by which he was surrounded.   Things that could produce
no impression on men of less delicate sensibility, would affect him
most seriously.   An east wind, that could produce no impression on
the cold, phlegmatic temperament of Dr. Johnson, operated on the
nerves of John Randolph like a sirocco of the desert.   He was generally disposed to look on the dark side of the picture, to imagine the
worst, and suffer intensely from an anticipation of what might never
happen

   So long as he lived in solitude, unaffected by the influences of the
busy world, his mind dwelt for the most part on religious subjects;
but when again thrown into the excited arena of political strife, he perceived so clearly, by a sort of intuition as it were, the lowest intrigues
of party politicians, felt so intensely the meanness and baseness of
their trafficking purposes, that he was often betrayed into a harshness
of expression and an extravagance of behavior, that might lead one
unacquainted with his peculiar temperament to suppose that he was

a man of a vindictive and unfeeling temper that delighted in the torture of others, while he was himself uninfluenced by a moral or religious restraint of any kind. No man was more conscious than he of this peculiarity of his nature, or more deeply deplored its consequences. The reader will perceive, through all his correspondence, that he did not conceal from his friends these deformities of character, and that he never relaxed in earnest efforts—however useless they may have proved—to overcome and to correct the unfortunate deficiencies of his nature.

During the present year (1819) there was a general pecuniary embarrassment and distress in the country. Mr. Randolph lost a large sum of money deposited in the hands of a mercantile firm in Richmond. He is said to have been deeply affected by this occurrence, and, as might have been expected, spoke in harsh terms of the delinquent merchants

Frequent allusion is made to the subject in the following correspondence, though religion is the principal theme.

RICHMOND, May 3, 1819.—Sunday.

DEAR FRANK :—It is so long since I heard from you that I almost begin to think that you have struck me out of your books. I had, however, the gratification to hear of you through Mr. Meade, whom I had not the good fortune to see as he passed through this town, having left it on the day of his arrival. You have no conception of the gloom and distress that pervade this place. There has been nothing like it since 1785, when, from the same causes (paper money and a general peace) there was a general depression of every thing. It seems to me, my dear friend, that in the present instance we are punished in the offending member, if I may so express myself. We have been the devoted worshippers of mammon, and in our darling wealth we are made to suffer. May it be the means of opening our eyes to the folly and sinfulness of our past conduct, and of inducing us to lay up treasure where moth corrupteth not and thieves do not break in and steal.

Very contrary to my judgment, and yet more against my feelings, I am again a public man. The application was made in a way that I could not with propriety resist. I was called upon (among other considerations) to "redeem a pledge" and to prevent a contest for the Representation of the District. My views upon the subject of public affairs, as well as other matters, are far other than they have been. I now see in its full deformity the wickedness of Party Spirit, of which I was so long a votary, and I look forward to the next winter with no other pleasant anticipation but that of seeing you.

Poor H——n! He is gone, I see, to his account. I heard with much gratification that he had been long engaged in serious preparation for this awful change. How poor and pitiful now seem all the angry and malevolent feelings of which he was the author or the object! My dear Frank, what is there in this world to satisfy the cravings of an immortal nature? I declare to you that the business and pleasures of it seem to me as of no more consequence than the game of push-pin that occupies the little negroes at the corner of the street.

Do not misunderstand me, my dear friend. My life (I am ashamed to confess it) does not correspond with my belief. I have made a vile return for the goodness which has been manifested towards me—but I still cling to the cross of my Redeemer, and with God's aid firmly resolve to lead a life less unworthy of one who calls himself the humble follower of Jesus Christ. I am here on a business of much consequence to me. It is to draw, if I can, a sum of money from the hands of a merchant which has been appropriated to an object which I have long had at heart. I have some fears of losing it; but if I do, I have the fullest confidence that I *ought ;* and must devise some other provision against the *daily nightmare* that has so long oppressed me. You will be at no loss to conjecture the subject.

Since I saw you, I have become more infirm and more indolent than ever. This last is my besetting sin. My spirits often desert me, and indeed it is no matter of wonder; for a more forlorn and destitute creature can hardly be found. I have outlived my relations and friends, except a few who are far away.

On the subject of his return to Congress, Key replies:—

"You know my opinion about public life—that a man has no more right to decline it than to seek it. I do not know, perhaps, all its dangers, but I have no doubt they are great. But whatever they be, the grace of God is sufficient for them, and he who enters upon them with a sole view to his glory, and depends entirely on his grace, will find 'crooked things made straight,' and the mountains made plains before him. Certainly in such a state, a man who lives 'by faith and not by sight' can evidently serve the cause of religion, and I trust and pray that thus your light may shine.

"You will indeed be set 'on a hill.' Innumerable eyes will be fastened on you. The men of the world will look for something with which they may reproach you, and your faith; while 'the blessed company of all faithful people' will look to see if they may 'take knowledge of you. that you have been with Christ'—may they have to thank God always for you!"

" You have no idea what an interest is excited in your behalf among religious persons. I believe that many a fervent prayer is offered up for you by people who never saw your face."

To whom thus Randolph :—

"Your letter has produced a strange and indescribable feeling. That I, who have long been an object of malevolence or indifference to most of them that know me, should receive the prayers of strangers! May God bless all such charitable souls. Perhaps if we were together I could explain the state of my feelings—on paper I find it out of my power to do so. When I think on Mr. Hoge, our friend Meade and some others, I am almost driven to despair. To divest ourselves of our human feelings, is, I know, impossible—neither have I ever supposed it otherwise. But there are times when they quite overcome me, and when the chaos of my mind can be compared with nothing but the state that poor Cowper was in before he found peace, or rather after the death of Mrs. Erwin. But at my gloomiest moments, when I think how much less I suffer than I have deserved—when I remember that ' he who bore in heaven the second name had not on earth whereon to lay his head,' and that he died the death of the Cross—when I think how far my ingratitude to God transcends all other human ingratitude—the treachery and unthankfulness of mankind vanish before these considerations, and I cry out, ' not my will but thy will be done.' But although I can suffer, I cannot do ; and my life is running off in indolent speculations upon my duty, instead of being devoted to its performance. Amidst all these lamentable failures, however, I hold fast my resolution, with his gracious assistance, to put my whole trust in God, to pour out my whole soul in fervent prayer ; and in his good time he may increase my strength to wrestle with the temptations that beset me. By the late bankruptcies I am reduced from ease and independence to debt and straitened circumstances. I have endavored in vain to sell a part of my property at a reduced price, to meet my engagements.

" I had not heard of M——'s death. May our latter end be like his. Indeed I am here entirely removed from the converse of my species. I know not what is doing in the world ; but even in this retreat the groans of the children of mammon sometimes break upon my ear. If I cannot arrange my affairs I fear I must resign my seat. I say " I fear," because I would avoid all appearance of fickleness and caprice. What you tell me ought to nerve my resolution. Alas ! it is in the persons of her friends and from their hands that religion receives her deadliest wounds. God grant that I may always bear this in mind, and that this consideration may deter me from much evil, and spur me on to do good."

August 8th, 1819.—" You have formed too favorable an opinion of my state, which too often reminds me of the seed that 'fell upon stony places.' This is not said out of any affected humility, far worse than the highest presumption, but from a comparison of the *fruit* with what the tree ought to bear.

"Can there be faith even as a grain of mustard seed when such is the life? It has pleased God to visit us with the most destructive drought in the memory of any living man. Great apprehensions are entertained of famine, but I trust that he who feedeth the young ravens will not suffer us to starve. Indeed, so far from being over-careful and troubled about the things of this world, I am culpably remiss respecting them, and this indolent supineness had led to more than one evil consequence. I am worn out, body and mind, and the least exertion, corporeal or intellectual, exhausts me entirely. Even the writing of this letter will be sensibly felt. Whilst you and others of my friends are bearing the heat and burthen of the day, I am languishing in inglorious indolence.

"I am more than satiated with the world. It is to me a fearful prison-house of guilt and misery. I fear that my feelings towards it are not always sufficiently charitable; but an eternity here would be punishment enough for the worst offenders. Towards the meeting of Congress I look forward with no agreeable anticipations. I am sensible of a great decline of my faculties, not the less injurious from being premature. In short, I have lost all hope of public service, and whithersoever I direct my eyes a dark cloud seems to impend. This gloom is not constitutional. It is the result of sad experience of myself as well as others. I would not have you think that it is accompanied by a spirit of repining; far from it. I adore the goodness and the wisdom of God, and submit myself to his mercy most implicitly, acknowledging that if he were to deal with me according to my deserts 'I could not abide it.' My own short-comings are the sources of my regrets, 'and why call ye me Lord, Lord, and do not the things that I say?' This, my dear friend, troubles me by day and by night. 'Tis not what others do, but what I do, or omit, that annoys me.

"Cases of insanity and suicide (although not so numerous as might have been expected, judging from the effects of the South Sea and Mississippi bubbles) have not been unfrequent in this quarter. As many as three ministers of the gospel, and several other devout professors, have ended their lives by their own hands. I wish you had been a little more explicit on the Baltimore matters. There are many individuals there that I personally wish well to, and would be glad to hear that they had escaped the general contamination."

"I am sorry," says Key in response, "to observe your desponding feelings; you must fight your way through them. 'Heaviness may endure for a night, but joy cometh in the morning.' The Christian must always lament his remaining corruptions, and that the fruits of his faith correspond so little with what he intends and desires. But that he brings forth *any* fruit is matter of rejoicing, for it is the work of grace ; and he has cause to be thankful for this very desire to do better—and he has the consolation of a clear promise from God that he will not leave his work undone, but that this grace shall make him 'abound more and more in every good word and work.'

" In the seasons of despondency which I have felt, great relief has been afforded to my mind by the Psalms. I often come to passages that seem to be spoken right at me, and joy and peace were 'shed abroad in my heart.' I think they would be blessed in the same way to you. Have you read Miss Taylor's Poems ? You may see them reviewed in the Christian Observer. I send you a Magazine that is published here, which I hope will be faithfully conducted.

" I would tell you more of these Baltimore troubles and abominations, but I really know very little about them. I understand the grand jury, at their late court, have found indictments against many of them."

To which Randolph replied, August 22d :

" Your letter of the 16th has just arrived to cheer my solitude. Acceptable as it is, it would not have been so promptly acknowledged but for what you say about the Psalms. Once, of all the books of Holy Writ, they were my especial aversion ; but, thanks be to God ! they have long constituted a favorite portion of that treasure of wisdom. As you say, many passages seem written 'right at me.' It is there that I find my sin and sorrows depicted by a fellow-sinner and fellow-sufferer ; and there too I find consolation. I chiefly read the version in the Book of Common Prayer, and mine is scored and marked from one end to the other. ' Why art thou so heavy, O my soul? and why art thou so disquieted within me ? O put thy trust in God, for I will yet give him thanks, which is the help of my countenance and my God. "

After making inquiries about many of his old friends, some of whom, he feared, had gone by the board in the general wreck, he thus continues :

" I do assure you that I sometimes look back upon old times until it seems a dream ; but it is a dream that often draws tears in my eyes.

" Miss Key (your uncle Philip's daughter) is, I presume, unmarried ; for there was nobody in the district deserving of her, when I knew it, and she has too much good sense to throw herself away on flimsy members of Congress or diplomatic adventurers. I often think of the pain I suffered at her father's, more than eleven years ago; of the kindness and attention I then received. Cripple as I then thought myself, I had no forecast that in so short a time I should be almost superannuated. My sight is nearly gone, and my memory of recent events no better. When you see or hear from Mr. Meade, mention me in the warmest terms of regard and respect. * * * * In your next I expect a dish of chit-chat. P. S. I wish the first leisure half hour you light upon you would take up your pen and tell me all about it. 'About what?' Why, every thing and every body. There's that fine fellow, D. M——y, whom you have not once named; nor J. C——n, whom, for the life of me, I can hear nothing about—whether he has gone to pieces in the general wreck? I speak of his fortune, for my confidence in his principles is unshaken. Then there is your friend Mr. T.

"You see, Frank, that I am, indeed, growing old, and, like other dotards, delight in garrulity and gossip. To tell you the truth, I stay here, and look at the trees until I almost *conceit* myself a dryad; at least you perceive I am no grammarian."

To Dr. Brockenbrough he speaks more unreservedly on all subjects than to any other man. Take the following letters, written about the same time as those addressed to Mr. Key:

"I was very glad to learn from Quashee that you were well enough to walk the streets when he was in Richmond. I make it almost a matter of conscience, notwithstanding, to *bore* you with my letters; but I must beg you to take into consideration that I am cut off from all intercourse with the rest of the world, and unable to obtain the slightest information of what is passing in it. It would be a charity to drop me a line now and then. I have hardly seen a white face since I got home, until last evening, when Colonel C. showed me a letter from T. asking a discharge from him and his brother and son-in-law. If I had had any expectations from that quarter, this letter would have put an end to them. T. and M. will receive no release from me. I will not persecute them; but their conduct deserves no indulgence. I had intended to have been in Richmond ten days ago, but my health is so deplorably bad that I cannot venture to leave my own house even for a day; and it is well for me. Here, then, I must live, and here I must die, 'a lone and banished man;' and what banishment can be worse than his who is ashamed to show his face to society? I nerve myself up to bear it as I would to undergo a surgical operation; but the cases are widely different. The one must soon end in a cure, or in death; but every succeeding day brings no relief, but utter aggravation of wretchedness, to the other. These days, however, God be praised! must have an end.

"An Enquirer fell into my hands yesterday. What a contrast between the universal cry of the country and the testimony of our gracious sovereign to our great and increasing prosperity! You have them in the same columns. It will make a figure in Europe. Baltimore seems to have suffered not less than Richmond. Pray let me know if S. and B. have failed; and, if you can, the cause of J. S. leaving the Bank of Baltimore.

"My best respects to Mrs. B. These glaring long days make me think of her. I lie in bed as long as I can to shorten them, and keep my room darkened. Perhaps a strait waistcoat would not be amiss. Have E. and A. stopped? Farewell. If we ever meet again, it must be here. Should I ever get in reach of a ship bound to any foreign land, I will endeavor to lose sight of this for ever."

To the same:

"I have long been indebted to you for your letter by Mr. Watkins, which reminded me of those which I used to receive from you some years ago, when I was not so entirely unable as I am now to make a suitable return to my correspondents. I feel most seriously this incapacity and deplore it, but for the life of me I cannot rouse myself to take an interest in the affairs of this 'trumpery world' as 'the antiquary' calls it, and with a curious felicity of expression; for it is upon a larger scale what a strolling play-house is upon a smaller, all outside show and tinsel, and frippery, and wretchedness. There are to be sure a few, a very few, who are what they seem to be. But this ought to concern me personally as little as any one; for I have no intercourse with those around me. I often mount my horse and sit upon him ten or fifteen minutes, wishing to go somewhere but not knowing where to ride, for I would escape any where from the incubus that weighs me down, body and soul; but the fiend follows me 'ex croupa.' You can have no conception of the intenseness of this wretchedness, which in its effect on my mind I can compare to nothing but that of a lump of ice on the pulse of the wrist, which I have tried when a boy. And why do I obtrude all this upon you? Because from the fulness of the heart the mouth speaketh. I can be and am silent for days and weeks together, except on indifferent subjects; but if I address myself to a friend, the misery that preys upon me will not be suppressed. The strongest considerations of duty are barely sufficient to prevent me from absconding to some distant country, where I might live and die unknown. There is a selfishness in our occupations and pursuits, after the first gloss of youth has worn off, that hardens us against our fellow-men. This I _now_ know to be the necessary consequence of our nature, but it is not therefore the less revolting I had hoped to divert the gloom that overhangs me by writing this letter at the instigation of old Quashee, but I struggle against it in vain. Is it not Dr. Johnson who says that to attempt 'to think it down is madness?'"

" Your brother William and myself hit upon the same 4th of July toast with some variation; mine was ' State Rights, *de mortuis nil nisi bonum.*' It will hardly appear in the newspapers. I agree with you on the subject of the Bankrupt Law, with some shades of difference. I would not have the General Government touch the subject at all. But some mode I think ought to be devised for setting aside the present shameful practices: robbing one man to pay another, &c.

After a good deal about the pecuniary embarrassment of the times, and many friends who were involved in the catastrophe, the letter thus concludes:

" My best regards to Mrs. B. Tell her I have read nothing for six weeks, being ' high gravel blind,' and having nothing to ʻead but old standard authors, who are too solid for my weak stomach and this hot weather. Adieu!

Yours truly,

J. R. OF ROANOKE.

A worn-out man and pen.

———•••———

CHAPTER XI.

CONGRESS — POLITICAL PARTIES.

AFTER Mr. Randolph had been in Washington some two or three weeks, he thus gives the result of his observations to a friend, under date of the 21st of December, 1819.— " Here I find myself *isolé*, almost as entirely as at Roanoke, for the quiet of which (although I left it without a desire ever to see it again) I have sometimes panted; or rather, to escape from the scenes around me. Once the object of proscription, I am become one of indifference to all around me; and in this respect I am in no wise worse off than the rest; for, from all that I can see and learn, there are no two persons here that care a single straw for one another. My reception is best by the old jacobins *enragés;* next, by the federalists, who have abjured their heresies and reconciled themselves to the true Catholic Church; worst of all, by the old minority men, white washed into courtiers."

When Mr. Randolph returned to Congress in 1819, the relation of political parties had been entirely changed. The restoration of

peace put an end to all the questions which had hitherto divided them. With the exception of the bank—whose chartered existence commenced in 1791, and closed in 1811—all the great subjects discussed in the halls of legislation and by the press, grew out of our relations with foreign countries. Washington had scarcely taken in hand the reins of government when the French revolution burst forth, and disturbed the repose of Europe. The Republican tendencies of the French people, notwithstanding their bloody extravagancies, found at all times in the United-States a strong and sympathizing party. On the other hand, there was a powerful party that deprecated French influence, and sympathized with England in her efforts to repress those revolutionary tendencies. All those who were opposed to a strong centralizing government, and favored the independence of the States so far as consisted with the strict limitations of the Constitution, leaned to the French side of the question. Those of the contrary opinions took the opposite. As the destructive war between those great belligerent powers waxed hotter and hotter, its exciting and maddening influences were more deeply felt by the sympathizing parties here. Each accused the other of wishing to involve the country in the war on the side of their respective friends. Anglomania, Gallomania, raged like an epidemic through the land, and every subject discussed partook of its influence—the Indian Wars, Whisky Insurrection, Gennet's reception, Jay's treaty, and the depredations on our commerce.

As those who were opposed to French influence were in the ascendent, they pushed their measures to an open rupture with France, and, as a means of repressing the further progress of her revolutionary doctrines, enacted those harsh and unconstitutional remedies called the Alien and Sedition Laws, which were the immediate cause of their overthrow.

The resolutions of the legislatures of Virginia and of Kentucky, growing out of the above laws, and the exposition of those resolutions by Mr. Madison, in his report to the Virginia legislature in 1800, constitute the doctrine and political faith, so far as they go, of the republican party that came into power under the auspices of Mr. Jefferson.

But no sooner was Mr. Jefferson installed in office, than he was called on to encounter the same difficulties which had so much embarrassed his predecessors in their intercourse with foreign powers. The federal party, now in the minority, and much weakened by their late overthrow, opposed all his measures, and wielded his own arguments against him.   They had contended that the Constitution justified any measure that tended to promote "the public good and general welfare."   This broad doctrine was denied by the republican party, and was totally annihilated by Mr. Madison's report.   But the first important measure of Mr. Jefferson involved a contradiction of his doctrines.   We were in danger of a rupture with Spain and France, on account of the navigation of the Mississippi.   To put an end to these difficulties, Louisiana was purchased.   Mr. Jefferson said there was no constitutional authority for the act, that it could only be justified from the necessity of the case, and that the people must sanction it by an express provision in the Constitution.   Then followed the embargo law, which the federalists in like manner opposed on the ground of its unconstitutionality.   They contended that it was the result of "the public good and general welfare" construction, so much and so successfully condemned by the party now in power.   Then followed other restrictive measures, and finally the war with Great Britain, all of which were opposed, as we already know, by the federalists, as parts of the same erroneous and destructive and unconstitutional policy.   These divisions and difficulties, growing out of our foreign relations, were finally healed and put to rest by the termination of the war.   Former asperities were smothered down, old animosities forgotten, and the exciting cause of party heats was burnt out and extinguished in the general pacification of the world.   New questions, arising for the first time since the organization of the government, had now to be discussed and solved.   The functions of the government, as restrained and directed by the limitations of the Constitution, had to be exercised on a class of cases entirely different from those which had hitherto tested their capacity.

Under the monopolizing influence of the embargo, non-intercourse, and war measures of the last eight or nine years, a great manufacturing interest had been stimulated into being.   During this long period of stagnation to commerce and agriculture, much capital was withdrawn from them and vested in manufactures.   This great interest was likely to be seriously affected by the restoration of peace and of reciprocal commerce with other manufacturing nations.

During the long continental wars, when the omnipotent British fleet drove the commerce of all the belligerent powers from the ocean, our merchantmen, under the protection of the neutral flag of their country, gathered a rich harvest in the carrying trade. They had now to be reduced to the bounds of a legitimate commerce, and subjected to the eager rivalry of other more powerful and commercial States.

By the acquisition of Louisiana, a vast dominion had been added to our territories, and our population was rapidly spreading over that immense and fertile region. The means of internal communication became questions of serious consideration. The resources of the country lay dormant in their primeval state, like a vast weltering chaos, waiting for some brooding spirit to breathe life and form into its teeming elements. The South American provinces catching the spirit of freedom from our example, had thrown off the yoke of the mother country, and were looking to us for countenance, and stretching forth the hand for aid in their arduous struggle for independence.

These were the great themes that filled the public mind at the coming in of Mr. Monroe's administration and during its continuance. It was called the period of good feeling. The Federal party entirely disappeared, and its members were received into the ranks of their old opponents. But many respectable men among them, not disposed to abandon principles which they had honestly adopted, retired to private life. The rhetorical phrase of Mr. Jefferson, in his inaugural address, was made to have a practical meaning. The popular word was, "We are all Federalists, all Republicans." The existence of a distinct Federal party, or a distinct Republican party, was denied, and the leading politicians cultivated with great assiduity, the favor and support of all men, without regard to former distinctions, counting them as brothers of the same republican family.

This new state of things was made the theme of congratulation to the country by the newspaper writers and the fourth of July orators of the time. " I come not here to burn the torch of Alecto," says one of the latter; "to me there is no lustre in its fires, nor cheering warmth in its blaze. Let us rather offer and mingle our congratulations, that those unhappy differences which alienated one portion of our community from the rest, are at an end ; and that a vast fund of the genius and worth of our country has been restored to its service, to give new vigor to its career of power and prosperity To this blessed consummation the administration of our venerable Monroe has been a powerful auxiliary. The delusions of past years have rolled away, and the mists that once hovered over forms of now unshaded brightness, are dissipated for ever. We can now all meet and exchange our admiration and love in generous confraternity of feeling, whether we speak of our Jefferson or our Adams, our Madison or our Hamilton, our Pinckney or our Monroe; the associations of patriotism are awakened, and we forget the distance in the political zodiac which once separated these illustrious luminaries, in the full tide of glory they are pouring on the brightest pages of our history."

This amalgamation of all parties was a dangerous experiment on the health and soundness of the Republic. Over action was the necessary consequence of the destruction of all the countervailing influences of the system; and the generation of some latent chronic disease, which in after time must seriously affect the constitution of the body politic. The French government, the laborious work of a thousand years, was destroyed in a single night, by the sacrifice of all the orders of their distinctive privileges and opposing influences on what they fondly deemed to be the altar of patriotism. The floodgates were now opened; and from this single blunder there followed a series of frightful consequences, which history in the course of half a century has not been able to understand nor to portray.

It is lamentable to see a country cut up into factions, following this or that great leader with a blind, undoubting hero-worship; it is contemptible to see it divided into parties, whose sole end is the spoils of victory; such an one is nigh its end: but, on the other hand, it is equally true, that no government can be conducted by the people and for the benefit of the people, without a rigid adherence to certain fixed principles, which must be the test of parties, and of men and of their measures. These principles once determined, they must be inexorable in their application, and compel all men either to come up to their standard, or to declare against it; their criterion of political faith must be the same as that of Christian faith laid down by Christ himself—*they who are not for us are against us.* Men may betray, principles never can. Oppression is the invariable consequence of misplaced confidence in treacherous man; never is it the result of the working of a sound, just, and well-tried principle.

If the proposition be true, that ours is a government peculiar in its nature, unknown in former times, or to other nations, then the political doctrines arising from a contemplation of its structure and the principles by which it is to be conducted, should be peculiar also: the analogies of history, and the examples of other states, should serve rather as beacons of warning than as precedents to be followed. If it be true, that ours is a government of delegated authority, arising out of the constitutional compact of sovereign and independent States, which delegated powers are specified and strictly limited, while all others are reserved to the States, or to the people of the States; then there must grow out of this peculiar and jealous relation of the States and the people of the States to each ьther and to the government they have mutually drawn over them for their common protection, certain political principles as essential for the sound and healthy action of the complicated system as vital air is to the human body.

The same wise abstinence that influenced the structure should control the action of this governmental machinery. It would seem that the first inquiry a prudent statesman should propound to himself would be this—is the power delegated? Does the charter specify the grant? If not, is it a necessary inference as the means of carrying into effect a power granted? If it be neither the one nor the other, but is in itself a distinct and substantive power, he should say to himself, this power ought not to be exercised, however expedient or necessary it may seem to me at this time; to place it among the delegated powers by construction, is to construe away the Constitution—my example will be made a precedent for still bolder construction, until there shall be nothing left to the States or to the people; and this well balanced republic of confederated States shall sink down into a consolidated and despotic empire. These reflections seem not to have influenced the statesmen of Mr. Monroe's administration. The new and brilliant career that lay before them kindled their imaginations; and each, like an Olympian courser, eagerly pressed forward to take the lead in every enterprise. In projecting schemes to develope and to direct the resources and the domestic concerns of the people, they seemed to vie with each other in giving to the limitations of the Constitution the utmost latitude of interpretation. Nor is it at all surprising, when we consider the materials of which the government was composed. The minority men of embargo times had been *whitewashed into courtiers*, with their old leader (Monroe) at the head of the government, who, to obtain that station, was accused of sacrificing every principle he ever professed. The Federalists (latitudinarians in principle), who had *abjured their heresies*, and *reconciled themselves to the true catholic church*, constituted the body of voters in the two Houses of Congress; while their parliamentary leaders were the same intrepid young men, who entering into public life in times of war, when boldness was the first requisite in a statesman, kept up the same ardent career in peace, and mounted first the one and then the other hobby, on which they hoped to ride into popular favor. The only men left behind in this wild race, were the few *Jacobins* of the Adams and Jefferson times, who looked with astonishment and rage (enragès) on the adroit and unexpected manner in which the reins of government had been slipped from the hands of the true Republicans.

"The spirit of profession and devotion to the court has increased beyond my most sanguine anticipations," says John Randolph in a letter to Dr. Brockenbrough, dated December 30th, 1819. "The die is cast. The Emperor is master of the Senate, and through that body commands the life and property of every man in the *Republic!* The person who fills the office seems to be almost without a friend. Not so the office itself."

------ • • ------

CHAPTER XII.

MISSOURI QUESTION.

THE great subject not only of discussion, but of deep and fearful agitation in Congress to its close, on the 3d of March, 1821, and among the people, was the Missouri Question, or the question of slavery in its political influence on the legislation of the country. This subject, together with the question of right to the waste lands lying within the jurisdiction of some of the larger States, constituted the chief obstacle in the way of a cordial and harmonious union of the States, even in the time of their utmost peril, when they were contending for their independence. When the States were called upon to contribute their portion of men and money to conduct the war on the issue of which depended their existence, the question was, In what ratio shall they contribute? After trying the valuation of landed property, with its improvements, they abandoned it, and adopted the ratio of population as the best evidence of ability to contribute, and as the most practicable plan ; and it was agreed that in determining the amount of population in each State, *five slaves* should be counted as equal to *three* free men. Thus the slavery question was settled for the time.

When the Articles of Confederation were proposed to the States for adoption, some of them, enough to defeat the measure, refused to come into the Confederation, unless the *waste lands* were admitted and received as common property ; especially after the treaty of peace in 1783, and the boundaries of the United States were defined, they contended that all the waste, or *back lands* within those boundaries, having been bought with the common blood and treasure of all, was the joint property of all the States. It was maintained by the States on the other hand, that the land lay within their chartered limits, and rightfully belonged to them. This subject was a serious obstacle in the way of a more permanent union. At length it was agreed to propose to the States to grant, in a spirit of harmony and concession, all their rights to the Confederation. New-York set the example, and made a concession of all her rights west of her present boundary ; though her title was regarded as of no value. South Carolina followed next; she also had little or nothing to concede. Then came Virginia : her title to lands lying northwest of the Ohio, and extending to the Lakes and the Mississippi, was for a long time disputed, but after a jealous and thorough investigation, it was finally given up and conceded that her title was valid. On the 1st of March, 1784, a deed was executed by Virginia, granting this immense domain to the Confederation—on the condition that the territory so ceded shall be laid out and formed into States, and that the States so formed shall be distinct republican States, and admitted members of the Federal

Union, having the same rights of sovereignty, freedom, and independence, as the other States.

Immediately on the reception of this grant, Congress, on the 23d of April, 1784, passed a resolution extending its jurisdiction over the newly acquired territory, and projected a plan of government for the new States that might grow up therein, according to the conditions of the grant. It was admitted that Congress had no authority under Articles of Confederation for the measures adopted; the plea of necessity alone was urged in their justification. Congress resolved that the settlers shall, either on their own petition or on the order of Congress, receive authority from them, for their *free males* of full age, to meet together, for the purpose of establishing a temporary government, to adopt the constitution and laws of any one of the original States, subject to alteration by their ordinary legislature; and to erect counties or other divisions, for the election of members of their legislature. They further resolved, that when any such State shall have acquired twenty thousand *free* inhabitants, on giving due proof thereof to Congress, they shall receive from them authority to call a convention of representatives to establish a permanent constitution and government for themselves. Provided, that both the temporary and permanent governments be established on the principle that they shall for ever remain a part of the Confederacy of the United States of America, and be subject to the articles of confederation.

These articles, together with others, prescribing the mode of self-government to be pursued by the new States, as they shall from time to time be carved out of the recently acquired territory, Congress resolved shall be formed into a *charter of compact;* and shall stand as fundamental constitutions between the thirteen original States, and each of the several States now newly described, *unalterable* from and after the sale of any part of the territory of such State but by the joint consent of the United States in Congress assembled, and of the particular State within which such alteration is proposed to be made. Notwithstanding the unalterable nature of this charter of compact, Congress did, by an Ordinance of the 13th of July, 1787, materially modify the same, and introduced a new article, by which it was ordained that " there shall be neither slavery nor involuntary servitude in the territory, otherwise than in the punishment of crimes, whereof the party shall have been duly convicted." Thus we per ceive that, prior to the adoption of the present Constitution, which was some months after the above ordinance, the whole of the Northwestern Territory had been provided with a government.

No other lands were ceded to the Confederation, or were expected to be. The jurisdiction of Virginia extended over the District of Kentucky to the borders of the Mississippi. So did the jurisdiction of North Carolina extend over Tennessee, and of Georgia over the whole country now embraced within the limits of Alabama and Mississippi. Massachusetts did not surrender her jurisdiction over the District of Maine; Vermont was a sovereign State, though not in the Confederation, disputing her independence with New-York on the one hand, and New Hampshire on the other.

Thus it appears that at the time of the adoption of the present Constitution, every foot of land embraced within the borders of the United States under the treaty of independence in 1783, was embraced within the jurisdiction of some one of the States, or the Congress of the United States *under* the *charter of compact* of the 23d April, 1784; amended and enlarged by the Ordinance of the 13th July, 1787. The framers of the Constitution, therefore, in contemplation of the facts before them, had only to introduce an article binding the new government to fulfil the contracts of the old one, and an article authorizing Congress to dispose of, and make all needful rules and regulations, respecting the territory or other property belonging to the United States. Such articles were introduced, and they were sufficient for the purpose.

A proposition was made in the Convention to authorize Congress " to institute temporary governments for the new States" *arising within the unappropriated lands of the United States.* But this was unnecessary, because the object contemplated had already been accomplished by the charter of compact and the ordinance, and the article in the Constitution requiring a fulfilment of those contracts. As to lands within tne jurisdiction of the States ; Georgia for example, however much Congress might claim the right to them as common property, they never disputed the jurisdiction of the State. Those wise men, therefore, declined acting on the proposition, they never granted an unnecessary power.

The slave-question was equally well and wisely settled by the provisions of the Constitution. The same rule which had been adopted under the Confederation as the ratio of contribution, was made the basis of representation and taxation. Representatives and direct taxes were apportioned among the several States according to their respective numbers; and to determine the number, *five slaves* were to be counted as equal to *three free men*. The Slave-States, by this rule, lost in representation, but they gained whenever the government resorted to direct taxation; that being very seldom, the general result has been a loss to the slave-holding States. But they cannot complain, it was a rule insisted on by themselves when, under the Confederation, it was only the basis of contribution of men and money. They said that *two-fifths* of the slaves, the old and the young, were a burthen to their owners and ought not to be taxed; this was considered reasonable, and they were exempted.

By an article in the Constitution, the importation of slaves was permitted for twenty years: that is, the slave-trade was tolerated for that length of time; and by another provision, owners of slaves were protected in their rights whenever they escaped into States where involuntary servitude was not allowed by law. It is obvious, that every other question which could arise touching the subject of slavery was of a local and domestic nature, and was reserved to the States or to the people.

Thus did the framers of our Constitution, clearly perceiving and appreciating the delicacy of the subject, wisely provide for the difficulties which had so much embarrassed the States and the Confederation in regard to the public lands and the subject of slavery. Their measures were complete and exhaustive of the subject, so far as the existing limits of the United States were concerned. They did not contemplate an extension of the Union beyond its present boundaries. The serious difficulties that now so much threaten the integrity of the republic, have grown out of the purchase and acquisition of foreign territory. It is true the Constitution provides for the admission of new States; but the States contemplated were those expected to grow up within the existing borders of the Union—Maine, Vermont, the North Western States, Kentucky, Tennessee, Mississippi, and Alabama. None others were anticipated. That the vast dominions of the King of Spain, extending from the borders of the Mississippi to the Pacific Ocean, would ever become a portion of the territories of the United States, was a thing our forefathers never dreamed of, much less provided for in that Constitution they had so cautiously limited and guarded in all its parts, as a fit government for their posterity.

The acquisition of Louisiana was without constitutional authority. Mr. Jefferson, who made the purchase, admitted it to be so. He wished a ratification of the act by the people; but that was never done. It would be dangerous to take their silent acquiescence as evidence of approval. The amendment of the Constitution, which Mr. Jefferson desired, by the insertion of an *ex post facto* clause, pardoning its infraction under the pressure of an imperious necessity, was never attempted. The deed stands now as it did then—a naked usurpation of power, sanctioned only by the silent acquiescence of the people. We do not wish to be understood as condemning it. The evils which must necessarily have flowed from the continuance of Louisiana in the hands of a foreign and hostile power, are much greater, as we conceive, than those which *ought* to result as a necessary consequence of its annexation to the Union. But this does not alter the fact in regard to it—that it was acquired without authority, and that there has been no amendment of the Constitution ratifying the deed.

It is said, however, that under the war and treaty-making power, Congress may acquire foreign territory ; under the same authority by which it is obtained, it may be held and governed—conquered by the sword, it may be held and governed by the sword. This doctrine, whether derived from the war or treaty-making power, leads to the consequence that Congress may acquire foreign territory, and hold it and govern it as a province—as England governed the old thirteen provinces, as she now governs Canada and the East Indies ! This is a startling conclusion ; but it is the inevitable consequence of the premises ; grant the one, and you are forced to admit the other. But Congress, having acquired the territory, must govern it in the *spirit of the Constitution.* This is a total surrender of the doctrine of strict construction, which requires a distinct grant for the exercise of every substantive power by Congress, as the governing of a territory, making and unmaking laws for it, must be admitted to be. In the spirit of the Constitution ! What that may be is a matter of opinion. A States-rights man holds one opinion on that subject ; a Consolidationist or Federalist holds another ; and it is left to a majority of Congress for the time being to say what is legislation in the spirit of the Constitution. These are the absurd and dangerous conclusions of a false doctrine, and we are now reaping the consequences. Better admit honestly and candidly with Mr. Jefferson, that the first acquisition was without constitutional authority, and, of consequence, that all the subsequent acts in regard to it must partake of the same character. The truth is, that nearly all the legislation of Congress for the last half century, on the subject of territories, can be sustained by their own examples and precedents alone, and not by any grant of power in the Constitution.

When Missouri presented herself for admission into the Union, a proposition was made in Congress to amend her constitution, by inserting the clause, that " all children of slaves, born within the said State after the admission thereof into the Union, shall be free, but may be held to service until the age of twenty-five years ; and the further introduction of slavery, or involuntary servitude, is prohibited, except for the punishment of crimes, whereof the party shall have been duly convicted." This proposition came too late. Missouri was now an independent State, made so by the permission and by the authority of Congress ; she could not be thrown back by the will of Congress into the colonial state. Her internal and domestic affairs were under her absolute control ; and the only inquiry left to Congress was, to determine whether her Constitution was republican, and whether, as a new State, she shall be admitted into the Union. The attempted restriction on her domestic policy was a monstrous proposition that no other Congress, save such an one as we have described in the preceding chapter, could have entertained. Men having a just conception of the limitations of the Constitution and of the rights of the States, would have perceived that the internal affairs of a State were wholly beyond the jurisdiction of a government, whose powers were specially and strictly limited to a few general subjects common to all States.

But as it regards the Territory beyond the limits of the State of Missouri, wholly a different question was presented—here was a fair subject of compromise. Congress had no right to legislate, we are told, on the subject of slavery in that Territory—what right had they to legislate on any subject ? What right had they in the first instance to acquire possession of foreign territory ? Under the treaty·

making power, it is answered. Then under the treaty-making power it must be governed as a necessary inference, or implication. The proposition to confer on Congress the power to make a temporary government for territories was distinctly rejected by the framers of the Constitution. Any specific grant to that effect is not pretended. Congress has the right to make treaties—this confers on them the power to purchase by treaty and to take possession of foreign territory—having a right to acquire by treaty, the *necessary inference* is that they have the right to make laws and to govern the territory or the province acquired—this is the line of argument. Now all *implied powers* have no other limitation on them, but the will of those who make the implication—let the Protective Tariff, the system of Internal Improvements by the General Government, and the Bank, serve as examples and illustrations of this truth. When you go beyond the specific grants and resort to implication for such a distinct, substantive and important power as the one under consideration, then all the limitations in the Constitution are of no avail. Take either alternative, therefore, that Congress had no constitutional authority either to purchase or to govern foreign territory—or that, under the treaty-making power, they had the right to acquire and to govern, then there is no limitation on the *exercise* of the power, *usurped or implied*, save that imposed by themselves. The examples and precedents set by their predecessors constitute their only guide. The spirit of the Constitution as manifested in these authorities must be their only rule of action. It was precisely in accordance with the history of past legislation that the Missouri compromise was accomplished. It seems to have grown up as a tacit, though well understood agreement, that North of a certain line involuntary servitude should not exist, and South of it slavery should be tolerated. The compromise ordinance of 1787 originated in this feeling.

Repeated attempts at an early day were made in Indiana and Illinois to suspend the article of the Ordinance prohibiting slavery beyond the Ohio—but they were always opposed and defeated by Southern men. On the contrary, when the provisions of the Ordinance were extended to Southern territory, the article on the subject of slavery was striken out. Thus there grew up from the nature of the case, and under the force of circumstances, a sort of common law understanding, that all North of a certain line, restrictions on the subject of slavery should be enforced, and South of it, they should be removed. When, therefore, the question was raised in regard to newly acquired foreign territory, the same rule was enforced. It was imposed by a combined northern majority on the South who, without a dissenting voice, steadily opposed it. This geographical majority ingrafted on the Missouri bill a provision—" that in all that territory ceded by France to the United States, under the name of Louisiana, which lies north of thirty-six degrees and thirty minutes north latitude, not included within the limits of the State contemplated by this act, slavery and involuntary servitude, otherwise than in the punishment of crimes, whereof the parties shall have been duly convicted, shall be and is hereby for ever prohibited." Thus we see that the line was extended and definitely laid down by northern men. The whole South voted against it under the impression that Congress had no right to legislate on the subject; but we have seen their error in supposing that there were any constitutional provisions on the subject at all—and that, whether as usurped or implied power, there was no other limitation on it, save that of precedent and authority. And it was precisely in accordance with precedent and authority, and the common sentiment silently grown up among the States, that this line was laid down and extended. The northern men took on themselves the fearful responsibility of acting alone in this business. They dictated the line and said by that we will stand. All subsequent legislation has been based on the faith of this pledge. Iowa has been admitted as a State into the Union—Minnesota and Oregon organized as Territories on its faith. And can any reasonable man see why this line should not as well extend to the Pacific ocean, as to the Rocky Mountains? to the territories recently acquired of Mexico, as well as to those which in 1803 were purchased of France? There is no constitutional authority for the acquisition or the government of either as territory or a province—the necessity of the case in the first instance, and the subsequent *practice* of the government, can alone be adduced as justification and authority.

The same rules, precedents, and examples, apply as well in the one case as in the other. And above all, that overwhelming sentiment of justice, that spirit of concession and compromise, which presided over the birth and infancy of the Constitution, and preserved it from destruction when well-nigh torn asunder by the Missouri convulsion, urge on us now with tenfold force, at a moment when all the nations of the earth are torn up from their deep foundations—and this blessed Constitution stands as the only sheltering rock in whose broad shadow, far stretching over the dark waters, their scattered fragments may come together and be re-formed.. If the sentiment of brotherly forbearance, if a generous pride in the glory and prosperity of our common country do not prevail at this crisis, we shall then hang our heads in sorrow, mourn over the departed spirit of our fathers, and look with fearful forebodings on that dark demon, that has come to usurp its place—the mad spirit of fanaticism, engendered in ambition and fostered by the lust of plunder and dominion.

CHAPTER XIII.

COMPROMISE BILL SMUGGLED THROUGH THE HOUSE.

Mr. Randolph's opposition to the Missouri Bill, with the obnoxious clause in it prohibiting slavery beyond a certain line, was very decided. In common with the southern members, he regarded the whole proceeding as unconstitutional—destructive of the vital interests of the South—a dangerous precedent, that might be used for still greater encroachments hereafter—and would listen to no compromise on the subject. One night, when the House was engaged in debating the great question, and there seemed but a faint prospect of its adjustment, Mr. Randolph, it is said, accosted Mr. Clay, the Speaker of the House, who, for a moment, was absent from the chair, and said to him, " Mr. Speaker, I wish you would quit the chair, and leave the House ; I will follow you to Kentucky, or any where else." Mr. Randolph was told, in reply, that his proposition was a very serious one ; and that if he would meet Mr. Clay the next morning, in the Speaker's room, the latter would converse with him fully on the whole subject. The interview accordingly took place, and the parties had a long conversation, relating, principally, to the propriety of a compromise. Mr. Randolph was decidedly opposed to any compromise, and Mr. Clay was in favor of acceding to one, if it could be done without any sacrifice of principle. After the termination of this interview, they never exchanged salutations, or spoke to each other again, during the session. We do not vouch for the truth of this statement; but it is very certain, that Mr. Randolph spoke in no measured terms of the course of the Speaker of the House (Mr. Clay) on the subject of the compromise, and charged him with taking advantage of his office, and conniving, if not actually aiding, in smuggling the bill through the House, contrary to the rules of proceeding, thereby depriving him and other members of their constitutional right to a final vote, on a motion for reconsideration, which the Speaker knew Mr. Randolph was about to make.

His own account of that transaction is so graphic, so characteristic of the man, that we here give it to the reader entire.

" On the night that that bill had its last vote in the House, my colleague, W. S. Archer, was a new member. I declared, publicly and openly, that in case that bill should pass, with the amendment then proposed, unless another amendment should succeed—which did not succeed—I declared, conditionally, that I should move for a reconsideration of the vote. Myself and my colleague, who, with another gentleman, whom I shall not refer to, though near me (Mr. Macon), were the only persons whom I have heard of, belonging to the Southern interest, who determined to have no compromise at all on this subject. They determined to cavil on the *ninetieth* part of a hair, in a matter of sheer right, touching the dearest interests, the life-blood of the Southern States. The House was exhausted ; a gentleman fainted in front of the chair, and tumbled on the ground. In this state of things, my colleague asked whether it would not do as well to put off the motion till to-morrow (for he was in ill health and much fatigued) ? I said I could not agree to that, till I had taken the opinion of the court, in the last resort. After that question had eventuated, as I foresaw it might, I rose in my place, and asked of the Speaker whether it was in order to move a reconsideration of the vote. He said that it was. Sir, I am stating facts of more importance to the civil history of this country than the battle which took place not far from this. He said it was. I then asked him (to relieve my colleague, who had just taken his seat for the first time that session), whether it would be in order to move the reconsideration of the vote, on the next day ? He said something to this effect : Surely the gentleman knows the rules of the House too well not to know that it will be in order at any time during the sitting, to-morrow or the next day. I replied, I thought I did ; but I wanted to make assurance doubly sure, to have the opinion of the tribunal, in the last resort. I then agreed—to accommodate my colleague, in the state of exhaustion in which the House then was—I agreed to suspend my motion for a reconsideration, and we adjourned. The next morning, before either House met, I learned—no matter how— no matter from whom, or for what consideration—that it was in contemplation that this clock (Senate chamber), which is hardly ever in order, and the clock in the other House, which is not in a better condition, should somehow disagree; that the Speaker should not take his seat in the House till the President had taken his seat nere; and then, that when I went into the House to make my motion, I was to be told that the Chair regretted very much that the clerk had gone off with the bill; that it was not in their possession, and the case was irreparable; and yet I recollect very well, when we applied to the Secretary of State for a parchment roll of an act which had not been duly enrolled, two sections were left out by the carelessness of the clerks and of the committee of enrollment. That act was, by the House of Representatives, in which it originated, procured from the archives of the Department of State, and put on the statute books, as it passed—not as it was on the roll—and enrolled anew. It was the act for the relief of the captors of the Mirboha and Missonda. As soon as I understood this, sir, I went to the Speaker myself, and told him that I must have my vote for reconsideration that day.

"I can only say that I inferred—not from what he *told* me—that my information was correct. I came off immediately to this House (Senate.) It wanted about twenty minutes of the time when the Senate was to meet. I saw that most respectable man whom we have just lost, and begged to speak with him in private. We retired to a committee room, and to prevent intrusion we locked the door. I told him of the conspiracy laid to defeat me of my constitutional right to move a reconsideration, (though I think it a dangerous rule, and always voted against its being put on the rules at all, believing that, to prevent tampering and collusion, the vote to reconsider ought to be taken instantly, yet, sir, as it was then, I had a right to make the motion.) I told this gentleman that he might, by taking the chair of the Senate sooner than the true time, lend himself unconsciously to this conspiracy against my constitutional rights as a member of the other House from the State of Virginia. I spoke, sir, to a man of honor and a gentleman, and it is unnecessary to say that he did not take the chair till the proper hour arrived. As soon as that hour arrived, we left the committee room together. I went on to the House of Representatives, and found them in session, and the clerk reading the journal, meanwhile there had been runners through the long passage, which was then made of plank, I think, between the two Houses, hunting for Mr. Gaillard. Where is he? He is not to be found. The House of Representatives having organized itself,

when I came in from the door of the Senate, I found the clerk read
ing the journal; the moment after he had finished it I made the motion, and was seconded by my colleague, Mr. Archer, to whom I could
appeal—not that my testimony wants evidence. I should like to see
the man who would question it on a matter of fact. This fact is well
remembered; a lady would as soon forget her wedding day as I forget
this. The motion to reconsider was opposed; it was a debateable
question, and the Speaker stated something this way—'that it was
not for him to give any orders; the Clerk knew his duty.' The Clerk
went more than once—my impression is, that he went more than
twice. I could take my oath, and so, I believe, could Mr. Archer,
that he made two efforts, and came back under my eye, like a mouse
under the eye of a cat, with the engrossed bill in his hand. His
bread was at stake. At last he, with that pace, and countenance, and
manner, which only conscious guilt can inspire, went off, his poverty,
not his will consenting; and before the debate was finished, back he
comes with the bill, from the Senate, which had then become a law,
before it was decided whether they would reconsider it at my motion or not, which motion nailed the bill to the table until it should
have been disposed of. Notorious as these facts are, so anxious was
one side of that House to cover up their defection; such was the anxiety of the other to get Missouri in on any conditions, that this thing
was hushed up, just as the suspension of the *Habeas Corpus* was
hushed up.

"The bill was passed through the forms of law. Missouri was admitted into the Union contrary to the Constitution, as much so as if
I had voted the other way in the first instance, and the Speaker had
ordered the Clerk to put my name with the *ayes* in the journal when
I had voted *no*—because, sir, agreeably to the Constitution of the
United States every member has a right to his vote, under the forms
of the House, whether these forms are wise or foolish; and my colleague and myself were ousted out of our right to reconsider, for
which I would not have taken all the land within the State of Missouri."

Mr. Randolph was greatly excited during the agitation of the
Missouri question; he did not sleep of nights; and his energetic,
quick temper, exasperated by the scenes around him, inflamed by
long watching and anxiety, gave a peculiar force and piquancy to all
he said. His indignation was particularly levelled at Mr. Clay, not
that he had any personal dislike to that gentleman, apart from his
political course, but as he was the leader of the spurious Republican
party then in the ascendent, Mr. Randolph thought him entitled to
the animadversions that were aimed at the party itself, particularly

as he was not only their leader, but their chief spokesman, setting forth on all occasions, and embellishing their doctrines by his copious and ornate style of oratory.

Old minority men, *turned courtiers, and whitewashed Federalists*, composed the self-styled Republican party, when in truth they did not possess the first principle—the doctrine of State rights, that should characterize a party bearing that title. Mr. Clay's course on the bank in 1811, and again in 1816, his course on internal improvements, and his conduct in regard to " the compromise," as it was understood by all strict constructionists, eminently fitted him for the leadership of such a mongrel party ; and surely he was not spared in the animadversions of those who perceived the old leaven of Federalism penetrating the whole mass under the shallow disguise of a new name.

In the following strictures Mr. Randolph is particularly pointed and severe.

" The anniversary of Washington's birth-day (says he, in a letter to Dr. Brockenbrough, Feb. 23d, 1820) will be a memorable day in the history of my life, if indeed any history shall be attached to it. Yesterday, I spoke four hours and a half to as attentive an audience as ever listened to a public speaker. Every eye was riveted upon me, save one, and that was sedulously and affectedly turned away. The ears, however, were drinking up the words as those of the royal Dane imbibed " the juice of cursed heberon," though not, like his, unconscious of the leprous distilment ; as I could plainly perceive by the play of the muscles of the face, and the coming and going of the color, and the petty agitation of the whole man, like the affected fidget and flirt of the fan whereby a veteran coquette endeavors to hide her chagrin from the spectators of her mortification.

" This person was no other than Mr. Speaker himself, the only man in the House to whose attention I had a right. He left the chair, called *Cobb* to it, paced the lobby at the back of it in great agitation, resumed, read MSS., newspapers, printed documents on the table (i. e. affected to read them), beckoned the attendants, took snuff, looked at his shoe-buckles, at his ruffles, towards the other side of the House—every where but at me. I had mentioned to him as delicately as I could, that being unable to catch his eye, I had been obliged (against my will, and what I thought the rule of order and decorum in debate) to look elsewhere for support. This *apology* I expected would call him to a sense of what was due to himself and his station, as well as to me ; but it had none effect. At last, when you might have heard a pin drop upon the carpet, he beckoned one of the attendants and began whispering to the lad (I believe to fetch his snuff-box). 'Fooled to the top of my bent,' I 'checked in mid volley,' and said : ' The rules of this House, sir, require, and properly require, every member when he speaks to address himself respectfully to Mr. Speaker; to that rule, which would seem to imply a correlative duty of respectful attention on the part of the Chair, I always adhere; never seeking for attention in the countenances of the members, much less of the spectators and auditors in the lobby or the gallery: as, however, I find the Chair resolutely bent on not attending to me, I shall take my seat:' which I did accordingly. The chastisement was so deserved, so studiously provoked, that it was not in my nature to forego inflicting it. Like 'Worcester's rebellion, *it lay in my way and I found it.*'

" He replied in a subdued tone of voice, and with a manner quite changed from his usual petulance and arrogance (for it is generally one or t'other, sometimes both), ' that he had paid all possible attention,' &c., which was not true, in fact: for from the time that i entered upon the subject of his conduct in relation to the bank in 1811 (renewal of old charter), and in 1816 (the new bank), and on internal improvements, &c. (quoting his words in his last·speech, that ' this was a limited, *cautiously restricted* government'), and held up the ' Compromise' in its true colors, he never once glanced his eye upon me but to withdraw it, as if he had seen a basilisk.

" Some of the pretenders to the throne, if not the present incumbent, will hold me from that day forth in cherished remembrance. I have not yet done, however, with the pope or the pretenders, their name is legion.

" My dear friend, I have been up since three o'clock; as soon as I could see to write I began this letter, if it deserve the name of one. I have received my death-wound on Tuesday, the 1st, and Wednesday, the 2d of February. Had I not spoken on the last of these days, I might have weathered this point and clawed off of death's lee shore. My disease is assuming a hectic type. I believe the lungs are affected symptomatically, through sympathy with the liver, at least I hope so. Yet why hope when the vulture daily whets his beak for a repast upon my ever-growing liver, and his talons are fixed in my very vitals? I am done with public life, as soon as the business of Congress will permit me to leave it; at any rate, immediately after the adjournment I shall travel—perhaps take a sea voyage, not to get rid of duns (although the wolf will be at my door in the shape of the man I bought that land of), but to take the only chance of prolonging a life, that I trust is *now* not altogether useless.

" Remember me kindly to all friends; respectfully to Mr. Roane. Tell him that I have fulfilled his injunction, and I trust proved myself ' a zealous, and consistent, and (I wish I could add) *able*

defender of State Rights.' I have yet to settle with the Supreme
Court ——

"'I am hurt—a plague of *both the Houses*—I am sped! 'Tis not
so deep as a well, nor so wide as a church door, but 'twill serve : ask
for me to-morrow, and you shall find me a grave man.'"

The foregoing, and other letters that followed close upon it in
quick succession, show the diseased condition of body, and the excited
and feverish state of mind under which Mr. Randolph was laboring
at this time.

Thursday morning, 5 o'clock, Feb. 24, 1820.

"I have been up since half past three. My sensations are indescribable. The night before last I had a return of the spasms. At
present I am free from pain ; but what I feel is worse than pain, unless in its most acute form, and even then I think I ccnld better bear
it. Whatever it be, something is passing in the nobler viscera of no
ordinary character. They have got a Missouri question there, that
threatens a divulsion of soul from body. Nausea in its worst form
(sea sickness) is not equal to what I feel. I have it slightly, accompanied with a sinking of the spirits, a soul-sickness, a sensation
as if I should swoon away instantly ; meantime, diarrhœa is not idle,
from twenty to fifty calls in the four and twenty hours. Every thing
I eat (only milk and crackers, heated over again in the oven) passes
unchanged. So did gruel when I took some well boiled and gelatinous.

"You will not see my name on the yeas and nays yesterday on the
Senate's bill. I could not remain in the house, the air of which is
unchanged for weeks. It smells like a badly kept comodité, (shouldn't
there be two m's in that word ?) and even worse, for you have in addition to ordure and urine all the exhalations that overpowered Matt.
Bramble at a fashionable squeeze, and stale tobacco smoke into the
bargain ; cigars are smoked in the ante-room. The avenues to our
hall are narrow, mean, dark and dangerous, and when you pass the
first portal, you are assailed by a compound of villanous smells, which
is only a little more diluted when you emerge into light, or rather
darkness visible through cross lights that torture the eye.

"My faithful Juba is sick, very sick, and four nights ago I heard
him in his sleep cry out 'I wish I and master *was* at home.' These
Yankees have almost reconciled me to negro slavery. They have
produced a revulsion even on my mind, what then must the effect be
on those who had no scruples on the subject. I am persuaded that
the cause of humanity to these unfortunates has been put back a
century, certainly a generation, by the unprincipled conduct of ambitious men, availing themselves of a good as well as of a fanatical
spirit in the nation.

"Tell Mrs. Brockenbrough that Mr. Meade makes anxious inquiries about the state of her mind on the subject of religious opinions. He and Frank Key are with us on the question. Frank has just returned from Frederick, where he was summoned a fortnight ago to attend a (supposed) dying father. The old gentleman is recovering slowly. What must it have been to have his bedside attended by such a son! He is indeed as near perfection as our poor nature can go, although he would be shocked to hear it said. Severe to himself, considerate and indulgent to others, speaking ill of none. Day is breaking; good morning."

"J. R. of R. to J. B., a letter, like Mrs. Rowe's, from the dead to the living.

Saturday, Feb. 26, 1820.

"Hear all ye nations! Last evening the late J. R. of R. who is 'stone dead (the major) precisely', went to Mrs. F——h's 'con-sort'—said dead man being like any other great personage deceased, tired of 'toujours perdrix.' (N. B.: the plural of this French noun-substantive is *perdros*, according to Mr. Speaker Clay, who has been to Paris, aye, and to Ghent too; and ought surely to know.) Why shouldn't dead men enjoy a little variety as well as folks that talk in their sleep in Congress?—and there were 'lots of *them*' there — (see Tom Crib). The French lady proved to be a noun-adjective, as old Lilly hath it, she 'could not stand by herself' (or would not) for after some execrable *airs*, at the beginning of the third (not the third by at least thirty—it is Dogberry who, after 'sixthly and lastly' brings in 'thirdly') she enacted something like a fit, and threw herself into the arms of a gentleman (not a false concord I hope—I trust it was her husband), whereupon the 'dead man' not the 'master of the rolls' (he deals only in crackers) 'opened wide his mouth' and called a coach and threw himself into it and drove home, not *sham-sick*. I was heartily glad of our early dismission, and after an almost sleepless night, *me voici*, at my daily occupation, by day-break, boring you.

"I learn from a very direct source, that this lady was an obscure girl, whom Mrs. B——ll 'patronized' and placed at Mad. Rivaldi's boarding-school; where the protegée was shown off to the glory of the patroness, and sung at Mad. R——'s concerts and married one of the teachers, and in short, has been used to exhibition and *dis-play* from the egg-shell. I felt very much ashamed of being there, not because the room was mean and badly lighted, and dirty, and the company ill dressed, but because I saw, for the first time, an American woman singing for hire. I would import our actors, singers, tumblers and jack-puddings, if we must have such cattle, from Europe. Hyde de Neuville, a Frenchman, agreed with me, 'that although the lady was universally admitted to be *very amiable*, it was a danger-ous example.' At first (*on dit*) she was unaffected and sang naturally, and, I am told, agreeably enough, but now she is a bundle of 'affectations' (as Sir Hugh hath it), and reminds me of the little screech 'owels' as they say on 'the south side.' Her voice is not bad, but she is utterly destitute of a single particle of taste or judgment. Were she a lady and I in her company, my politeness should never induce me to punish myself by asking her to sing.

"A member from Virginia, whose avoirdupois entitles him to weight, as well as his being a sort of commis to the P., told me yesterday, 'that the tale in circulation of the P. having written a letter to Mr. Roane, declaring his disapprobation of the compromise, was an idle scandal, for that he had seen the letter (or rather that it had been read to him) and there was no such sentiment expressed in it.' Hem! Pretty good! Don't you think so?

"When Mrs. F. was 'screeching,' I was strongly reminded of two lines of a mock Methodist hymn, that poor John Hollingsworth used to sing, when we were graceless youths at college—

> "'O! that I, like Madame French,
> Could raise my 'vice' on high,
> Thy name should last like oaken bench,
> To parpetui-ty.'

"The same 'two single gentlemen rolled into one,' told me that M——e expressed a desire to maintain the relations of peace and amity and social intercourse, with me; that he did not stand upon etiquette; did not require any gentleman to pay him the respect of a call in the first instance; gave examples to that effect, some of which I know to be true (N. B. election coming on), and that he should have sent his invitations to me as well as to the rest, but that he thought they would not be acceptable—that I had repelled, &c., &c., &c.

"Whereupon I said that I had not seen said great man but once (Friday, the 11th, riding by, after Mr. King's speech in the Senate) since the Georgetown sheep-shearing, in the spring of 1812. That I had called more than once that spring, on him and Madame, and not at home was the invariable reply; that he had invited Garnett, as it were out of my own apartment that year, to dine with General Moreau, Lewis and Stanford, the only M. C.'s that lodged there besides myself, and omitted to ask me, who had a great desire to see Moreau; that I lacqueyed the heels of no great man; that I had a very good dinner at home, which I could not eat, although served at an hour that I was used to; and that I was very well, as I was, &c. Hodijah Meade writes Archer that I am becoming popular, even in Amelia. Perhaps the great man has heard something to this effect.

"Write me volumes—all your news, chat, &c. Yesterday we 'settled the chat,' not by the rules of 'the Finish' (see Tom Crib), but of the House of Commons, actually coughing, and scraping, and 'question' questioning some brave fellows that made a stout resistance to be heard, but were outnumbered. I was not party to the outrage—did not cough nor cry, but I heard the speaker's voice above the rest. G. T. spoke the last—promised us novelty at least, borrowed largely from Pinkney, P. Barbour, and your humble servant, during three quarters of an hour that I listened to him, when I left him, I believe, without a single auditor except Mr. Chairman C——b! as very a Johnny Raw' as ever entered a ring. See again my standard authority, Tom Crib."

CHAPTER XIV.

"I NOW GO FOR BLOOD"—MADNESS.

IMMEDIATELY on the settlement of that exciting subject—the Missouri question—followed the death of Commodore Decatur, who fell in a duel the 20th March, 1820, with Commodore Barron. This sad event produced a shock throughout the community. The gallant seaman lived in the hearts of his countrymen. His untimely end shrouded the country in mourning. The occasion, the manner, and the place—not on the proud deck, in face of the enemies of his country, added poignancy to their grief. None felt more deeply on the occasion than John Randolph. They were friends, and they were kindred spirits. To lose so noble a soul from among the few whose love he cherished, under such painful circumstances, and at a time when the country could illy spare so gallant a heart, was more than his weak frame could endure. Worn out with excessive watching and anxiety on the momentous question which had well nigh torn the Union asunder, emaciated with disease bodily and mental, that for years had known no intermission, with the keen sensibility of a woman, delicate as a sensitive plant, this last calamity proved too rude an assault on the nicely balanced, mysteriously wrought machinery of mind, which went whirling and dashing in mad disorder, and defying for a time the controlling influence of the master's will.

His conduct on the occasion of the funeral of Commodore Decatur is said to have been very extravagant. The cold and heartless world, that is unconscious of any thing else but a selfish motive, and the ignorant multitude that followed the funeral pageant, with gaping mouth, agreed on a common explanation of his extravagance by proclaiming " *the man is mad !*"

That he might have been greatly excited in manner and conversation, and that he was wholly indifferent as to what other people might say or think of him, is highly probable. All his friends agree that his mind, from the cause above alluded to, had been wrought up to the highest pitch of fervor, and that, like a highly-charged electric battery, it threw off brilliant and fiery sparks that scorched and burnt the uncautious person who had the temerity to approach too near.

This highly charged electric state of mind—it can be likened to nothing else—lasted through the spring. Mr. Anderson, the Cashier of the United States Branch Bank, in Richmond, says that about the 20th of April, 1820, Mr. Randolph came into the Bank and asked for writing materials to write a check. He dipped his pen in the ink, and finding that it was black, asked for red ink, saying, "I now go for blood." He filled the check up, and asked Mr. Anderson to write his name to it. Mr. Anderson refused to write his name; and after importuning that gentleman for some time, he called for black ink, and signed John Randolph, of Roanoke, ⋈ his mark. He then called for the porter, and sent the check to Mr. Taylor's, to pay an account. " One day I was passing along the street," says Mr. Anderson, " when Mr. Randolph hailed me in a louder voice than usual. The first question he asked me was, whether I knew of a good ship in the James River, in which he could get a passage for England. He said he had been sick of a remittent and intermittent fever for forty days, and his physician said he must go to England. I told him there were no ships here fit for his accommodation, and that he had better go to New-York, and sail from that port. ' Do you think,' said he, ' I would give my money to those who are ready to make my negroes cut my throat ?—if I cannot go to England from a Southern port I will not go at all.' I then endeavored to think of the best course for him to take, and told him there was a ship in the river. He asked the name of the ship. I told him it was the ' Henry Clay.' He threw up his arms and exclaimed ' Henry Clay ! no, sir ! I will never step on the planks of a ship of that name.' He then appointed to meet me at the bank at 9 o'clock. He came at the hour, drew several checks, exhausted his funds in the bank, and asked me for a settlement of his account, saying he had no longer any confidence in the State banks, and not much in the Bank of the United States; and that he would draw all his funds out of the bank, and put them in English guineas—that there was no danger of them."

Mr. Randolph spent the summer, as usual, in retirement at Roan oke—his excitement gradually wore away, and on the return of au tumn he was himself again. "I saw him in the autumn of the same year, 1820, says a friend—he was then as perfectly in possession of his understanding as I ever saw him or any other man." He return ed to Washington about the latter part of November, and thus writes to his friend Brockenbrough:

WASHINGTON, Nov. 26, 1820.

Dr. Dudley informs me that you have been sick of the prevailing Catarrh. If it has treated you as roughly as it has me, you have found it to be no trifling complaint. By this time, I trust you are as free from it as I have always found you to be from other *undue* in fluences. My infirmities of body and mind, have nearly obliged me to lay aside the use of the pen. I cannot see to make or mend one, and am wholly at the mercy of our stationers, whose pens, like Peter Pindar's razors, are "made to sell," and whose interest it is that fifty bad pens should supply the place of one good one. Indeed I have little use for the instrument—the receipt of a letter being a rare event in my annals. I ought, perhaps, to take somewhat unkindly, the withdrawal of my old correspondents from an intercourse so bene ficial on my side, but I do not. A commerce in which the advanta ges are all on one side will never be prosecuted long—what then must be the case with a trade in which (as at present throughout the com mercial world), both parties are losers.

The situation of public affairs, and of my own more especially, disturb my daily and nightly thoughts. I believe I must even make up my mind to "overdraw," or to be "an unfortunate man." Can you put me in no way to become a successful rogue to an amount that may throw an air of dignity over the transaction, and divert the at tention of the gaping spectators from the enormity of the offence, to that of the sum?

As to affairs here, I know nothing of them. They are carried on by a correspondence between Heads of Houses—I do not mean in the University sense of the term—but boarding-houses, who have an understanding with some Patron in the Ministry, to whom they "re port themselves," and from whom they "receive orders" from time to time.

I dined yesterday with the S. of the T., and, although as far as I was concerned, the party was a very pleasant one, I can conceive of nothing, in the general, more insipid than these Ministerial dinners. You are invited at *five*. The usage is to be there 15 or 20 minutes after the time. Dinner never served until six; and a little after *seven* coffee closes the entertainment, without the least opportunity for conversation. Quant a moi, I was placed at his S——ship's left hand, and he did me the honor to address his conversation almost exclusively to me. Now you know that as 'attentions' constitute the great charm of manners, so are they more peculiarly acceptable to them that are least accustomed to them—such as antiquated belles, discarded statesmen, and bankrupts of all sorts—whether in person or in character.

" Nothing can be more dreary than the life we lead here. 'Tis something like being on board ship, but not so various. We stupidly doze over our sea-coal fires in our respective messes, and may truly be said to hibernate at Washington."

CHAPTER XV.

MISSOURI QUESTION.—ACT THE SECOND.

SHORTLY after the opening of the session, this exciting subject again came up in a most unexpected form. Missouri under the "compromise act" of March the 6th, 1820, had adopted a constitution with a clause declaring that *free negroes and mulattoes should not emigrate into the State.* It was contended that free negroes and mulattoes were citizens of the State of their residence ; and as such, under the Constitution, had a right to remove to Missouri or any other State in the Union, and there enjoy all the privileges and immunities of other citizens of the United States emigrating to the same place ; and, therefore, that the clause in the constitution of Missouri, above alluded to, was repugnant to the constitution of the United States, and she ought not to be admitted into the Union. On the other hand it was maintained that the African race, whether bond or free, were not parties to our political institutions; that therefore, free negroes and mulattoes were not citizens, within the meaning of the constitution of the United States; and that even if the constitution of Missouri *were* repugnant to that of the United States, the latter was paramount, and would overrule the conflicting provision of the power without the interference of Congress.

Notwithstanding the reasonableness of this view of the subject, a stern and inflexible majority, the same as at the last session, repelled every proposition, in every form, which aimed at the reception of the offending State. Scarcely a day elapsed that did not bring up the question in some shape or other. The presidential election had taken place in November preceding; it became the duty of the President of the Senate, in presence of the other House, to count the votes of the States. The Senate being present, and their President having counted the votes of all the other States, opened the package containing the vote of the State of Missouri, and handed it to the tellers to be counted. Mr. Livermore, of New Hampshire, objected, because Missouri was not a State of this Union. The Senate then withdrew. In the House the following resolution was then submitted: "Resolved—That Missouri is one of the States of this Union, and her vote ought to be received and counted." An animated debate ensued, in which Mr. Randolph largely participated. We shall only bring together here, under one view, what he said on the constitutional question involved in the controversy. No man had a clearer perception of the meaning and spirit of that sacred instrument, more highly valued it as a government when properly administered, or did more, as the reader will see in the sequel, to restore it to its proper interpretation.

Mr. Randolph said—" He could not recognize in this House, or the other, singly or conjointly, the power to decide on the *votes of any State*. Suppose you strike out Missouri and insert South Carolina, which has also a provision in its Constitution repugnant to the Constitution of the United States; or Virginia, or Massachusetts, which had a test, he believed, in its Constitution; was there any less power to decide on their votes than on those of Missouri? He maintained that the electoral college was as independent of Congress as Congress was of them; and we have no right to judge of their proceedings. He would rather see an interregnum, or have no votes counted, than see a principle adopted which went to the very foundation on which the presidential office rested. Suppose a case in which some gentlemen of one House or the other should choose to object to the vote of some State, and say that if it be thus, such a person is elected; if it be otherwise, another person is elected; did any body ever see the absurdity of such a proposition? He deemed the course pursued erroneous, and in a vital part, on the ascertainment of the person who had been elected by the people Chief Magistrate of the United States, the most important office under the Constitution. * * * * She has now presented herself (Missouri) for the first time in a visible and tangible shape; she comes into this House, not *in formâ pauperis*, but claiming to be one of the co-sovereignty of this confederated government, and presents to you her vote, by receiving or rejecting which the election of your Chief Magistrate will be lawful or unlawful. He did not mean by the vote of Missouri, but by the votes of all the States.

"Now comes the question, whether we will not merely repel her, but repel her with scorn and contumely. *Cui bono?* she might add, *quo warranto?* He should like to hear from the gentleman from New Hampshire (Mr. Livermore) where this House gets its authority. He should like to hear some of the learned (or unlearned) sages of the land, with which this House, as well as all our legislative bodies, abounds, show their authority for refusing to receive the votes of the State of Missouri. He went back to first principles. The electoral colleges are as independent of this House as we are of them. They had as good a right to pronounce on their qualifications as this House has of its members. Your office in regard to the electoral votes, is merely ministerial—to count the votes—and you undertake *to reject votes!* To what will this lead ? * * * * The wisest men may make Constitutions on paper, as they please. What was the theory of this Constitution ? It is that this House, except upon a certain contingency, has nothing to do with the appointment of President and Vice-President of the United States, and by States only can it act on this subject, unless it transcend the limits of the Constitution. What was to be the practice of the Constitution as now proposed ? That an informal meeting of this and the other House is to usurp the initiative, the nominative power, with regard to the two first officers of the government; that they are to wrest from the people their indefeasible right of telling us whom they wish to exercise the functions of government, in despite and contempt of their decision. Is there to be no limit to the power of Congress ? no mound or barrier to stay their usurpation ? Why were the electoral bodies established? The Constitution has wisely provided that they shall assemble, each by itself, and not by one great assembly. By this means, assuredly, that system of intrigue which was matured into a science, or rather into an art here, was guarded against. But he ventured to say, the electoral college of this much despised Missouri, acting conformably to law and to the genius and nature of our institutions, if it were composed of but one man, was as independent of this House as the House was of it. * * * * * Let me tell my friend before me (Mr. Archer), we have not the power which he thinks we pos-

sess, and if there be a *casus omissus* in the Constitution, I want
to know where we are to supply the defect. You may keep Missouri
out of the Union by violence, but here the issue is joined, and
she comes forward in the persons of her electors, instead of representative, and she was thus presented in a shape as unquestionable as that of New-York or Pennsylvania, or the proudest and
oldest State in the Union. Will you deny them admission? Will
you thrust her electors, and hers only, from this hall? I made no
objection to the vote of New Hampshire; I had as good a right to
object to the vote of New Hampshire, as the gentleman from New
Hampshire had to object to the vote of Missouri. The electors of
Missouri were as much the *hominus probi et legales* as those of New
Hampshire. This was no skirmish, as the gentleman from Virginia
had called it. This was the battle where Greek meets Greek. Let
us buckle on our armor, let us put aside all this flummery, these
metaphysical distinctions, these unprofitable drawings of distinctions without differences; let us say now, as we have on another occasion (the election of Jefferson and Burr in 1801), 'we will assert,
maintain, and vindicate our rights, or put to every hazard, what you
pretend to hold in such high estimation.' "

These arguments, which clearly prove the false and absurd and
dangerous position assumed by the House on the Missouri question,
were of none avail. And yet a simple truism—a mere nullity in fact,
in the shape of a compromise resolution, had the effect of magic in healing all the differences that had arisen between the respective parties.
Another sad example of the blindness and obstinacy of men, when
passion assumes sway of their cooler judgment.

Mr. Randolph participated in the debate on other subjects during
this session of Congress.

"Yesterday," says, he in a letter dated January 5th, 1821, "we
had a triumph over the 'veteran Swiss of State' and the S. of W. on
the appropriation to cover Indian arrearages. He (C——n) is politically dead. L——s, towards the close of the debate, ' put in' and
imputed want of economy to the Committee of Ways and Means
when I was a member. This gave me an opportunity to contrast the
military expenditure of 1803–4–5 of 800,000—800,000, and 700,000,
respectively with the modern practice. In 1804 we took possession
of New Orleans (an event utterly unlooked for) without incurring
one farthing of additional expense. Mr. L——s looked very foolish,
and uglier than usual. Mr. M. of S. C. (the successor of Mr.
C——n's man Friday) made several attempts, I was told, to get
the floor, in his patron's defence, but his timidity prevented success.
* * * * You will see a most villainous report of yesterday's proceed-

ings, in the court paper. The r——l pretends he can't hear me. There was not a man in the House that did not hear me. It is a usual massacre. Pray ask Ritchie not to publish it. I will correct it for his paper, and send it on, that the people of Virginia at least may be undeceived. I am made to talk nonsense, such as 'kissing of hands' for 'imposition of hands.' There is a studied and designed suppression of what passed."

Besides Mr. Randolph, Nathaniel Macon, of North Carolina, and Spencer Roane, Chief Justice of Virginia, were the most conspicuous State-rights men in that time of amalgamation and confusion of all parties. They were ever consistent and uniform in their adherence to the principles of the strict construction school, and always urgent for those measures of economy and that course of " wise and masterly inactivity," which must ever characterize a party based on such principles. Of the former of those gentlemen Mr. Randolph was the mess-mate while in Congress, and on terms of unreserved daily intercourse; with Judge Roane he did not pretend to stand on a footing of intimacy; but he respected his virtues, his talents, his long services, and had begun to look to him as a fit person to be selected by " all the honest men" as a candidate for the presidency.

" With the exception of my old friend, Mr. Macon," says he to Dr. Brockenbrough, " you are the only person with whom I hold any intercourse, except of that heartless sort which prevails in what is called the world. Your letters, therefore, are as much missed by me as would be an only member of one's family who should disappear at breakfast and leave one to a solitary and cheerless meal. So much of your penultimate as relates to Mr. M—— I shall take the liberty to communicate to one of the N. C. delegation. I am truly concerned at your anticipations respecting Mr. Roane's health. I earnestly hope that your presage may prove fallacious, although, when I reflect on your skill and intimate knowledge of the man, I feel very apprehensive of its truth.

" I began Fabricius, but was obliged to drop it. He sets out with a string of truisms conveyed in the style of a schoolboy's theme. Mercy upon us! What has become of the intellect and taste of our country? Your *secret* is as safe with me as in your own breast; but rely upon it, if either of the personages you mention should present any thing fit to be offered to the H. of D. it will be ascribed to some other hand, and, if it smack of the old school, to the pen of Mr. Roane. I differ from you about 'his being a Virginian;' not that I doubt the fact. But take my word for it, he is becoming every day more and more known out of the State, and occupies a large space in the public eye. I think he can be elected easily against any one yet talked of."

" I read Mr. Roane's letter," says he on another occasion, " with the attention that it deserves. Every thing from his pen on the subject of our laws and institutions excites a profound interest. I was highly gratified at the manner in which it was spoken of in my hearing by one of the best and ablest men in our House. It is indeed high time that the hucksters and money-changers should be cast out of the Temple of justice. The tone of this communication belongs to another age; but for the date, who could suppose it to have been written in this our day of almost universal political corruption? I did not read the report on the lottery case. The print of the Enquirer is too much for my eyes; and, besides, I want no argument to satisfy me that the powers which Congress may exercise, where they possess exclusive jurisdiction, may not be extended to places where they possess solely a limited and concurrent jurisdiction. The very statement of the question settles it, and every additional word is but an incumbrance of help."

In the same letter he says:

" If I possessed a talent that I once thought I had, I would try to give you a picture of Washington. The state of things is the strangest imaginable; but I am like a speechless person who has the clearest conception of what he would say, but whose organs refuse to perform their office. There is one striking fact that one can't help seeing at the first glance—that there is no faith among men; the state of political confidence may be compared to that of the commercial world within the last two or three years. * * * * * Our State politics, like those of the General Government, are a conundrum to me, and I leave the unriddling of them to the ingenious writers who construct and solve enigmas and charades for the magazines. * * * *

" I have been trying to read Southey's Life of Wesley for some days. Upon the whole, I find it a heavy work, although there are some very striking passages, and it abounds in curious information. From 279 to 285 inclusive of volume the second is very fine. Yesterday I was to have dined with Frank Key, but was not well enough to go. He called here the day before, and we had much talk together. He perseveres in pressing on towards the goal, and his whole life is spent in endeavoring to do good for his unhappy fellow-men. The result is, that he enjoys a tranquillity of mind, a sunshine of the soul, that all the Alexanders of the earth can neither confer nor take away. This is a state to which I can never attain. I have made up my mind to suffer like a man condemned to the wheel or the stake. Strange as you may think it, I could submit without a murmur to pass the rest of my life ' on some high lonely tower, where I might outwatch the bear with thrice great Hermes,' and exchange the enjoyments of society for an exemption from the plagues of life. These press me down to the very earth ; and to rid myself of them, I would gladly purchase an annuity and crawl into some hole, where I might commune with myself and be still."

"THURSDAY, March 1, 1821.

" I am in luck this morning. Johnny has brought me a letter from you instead of returning from the Post-office empty handed as usual. It gives me great satisfaction to find that the good people of my district are not dissatisfied with my course this winter.

" Last night there was, as I am informed by the gentlemen of our club, a most disgraceful scene in the H. of R. on the Bankrupt bill, which, by virtue of the previous question, will be forced through the House without being committed, or even once read ! except by its title—a bill of 65 sections !

" The bankrupt land speculators and broken merchants are, like ' the sons of Zeruiah, too strong for us.' So you see our coronation will be graced by a general jail delivery.

" Mrs. Brockenbrough's rheumatism, which is an opprobrium of medicine, gives me real concern. I sympathize with her in the literal sense of the term.

" My pains are aggravated by having neither society nor books to relieve my ennui.

" ' You mention whatever comes into your head'—To be sure you ought. It is the charm of a letter.

" The gentlemen you mention are right in their 'attentions' to Miss ——. I consider the society of such a woman as the best possible school for a young man, and solace for an old one.

I have not read Col. Taylor's book, but I heartily agree with Mr. Jefferson that ' the Judiciary gravitates towards consolidation.' I consider this district to be the πουστω and the Supreme Court to be the lever of the political Archimedes. I do not know whether you can make out my Greek character.

" I give you joy that this is the last epistle that you will be plagued with from me from this place."

CHAPTER XVI.

" BE NOT SOLITARY ; BE NOT IDLE." HIS WILL—SLAVES.

MR. RANDOLPH's solitary residence at Roanoke had become more and more intolerable to him. " The boys" were off at school. Dr. Dudley, at his solicitation, had moved to Richmond, and he was like the "Ancient Mariner" on the wide sea—"alone—alone—all—all alone!"

"You do not overrate the solitariness," says he, " of the life I lead here. It is dreary beyond conception, except by the actual sufferer. I can only acquiesce in it, as the lot in which I have been cast by the good providence of God, and endeavor to bear it, and the daily increasing infirmities, which threaten total helplessness, as well as I may. 'Many long weeks have passed since you heard from me'—and why should I write? To say that I have made another notch in my tally? or to enter upon the monstrous list of grievances, mental and bodily, which egotism itself could scarcely bear to relate, and none other to listen to. You say truly: 'there is no substitute' for what you name, 'that can fill the heart.' The better conviction has long ago rushed upon my own, and arrested its functions. Not that it is without its paroxysms, which, I thank heaven, itself alone is conscious of. Perhaps I am wrong to indulge in this vein ; but I must write thus or not at all. No punishment, except remorse, can exceed the misery I feel. My heart swells to bursting, at past recollections; and as the present is without enjoyment, so is the future without hope; so far at least, as respects this world.

"Here I am yearning after the society of some one who is not merely indifferent to me, and condemned, day after day, to a solitude like Robinson Crusoe's. But each day brings my captivity and ex ile nearer to their end."

To Dr. Brockenbrough, June 12th, he says:—"This letter is written as children whistle in the dark, to keep themselves from being afraid. I dare not look upon that 'blank and waste of the heart' within. Dreary, desolate, dismal—there is no word in our language, or any other, that can express the misery of my life. I drag on like a tired captive at the end of a slave-chain in an African Coffle. I go because I must. But this is worse than the sick man's tale."

From this solitude he sent forth lessons that should be graven on the heart of every young man. His own sad experience adds weight to his precepts. Out of the deep anguish of his heart poured forth the words of wisdom. His admonitions give a sure guide to the bewildered mind, and cheering hope to the depressed spirit. No young man can give heed to them and follow them, without finding to his joy that he has hit upon the true and only path of success in human life—he will find that activity, cheerful activity, in some useful calling in daily intercourse with his fellow man, is the business, the solace, and the charm of existence.

"The true cure for maladies like yours, " says he to Dr. Dudley,

who had written in a desponding tone, " is employment. ' Be not solitary ; be not idle !' was all that Burton could advise. Rely upon it,
life was not given us to be spent in dreams and reverie, but for active, useful exertion; exertion that turns to some account to ourselves or to others—not laborious idleness—(I say nothing about religion, which is between the heart and its Creator.) This preaching
is, I know, foolish enough; but let it pass. We have all two educa-
tions ; one we have given to us—the other we give ourselves; and
after a certain time of life, when the character has taken its *ply*, it is
idle to attempt to change it.

"If I did not think it would aggravate your symptoms, I would
press you to come here. In the sedulous study and practice of your
profession I hope you will find a palliative, if not a complete cure,
for your moral disease. Yours is the age of exertion—the prime and
vigor of life. But I have 'fallen into the sear and yellow leaf: and that
which should accompany old age, as honor, love, obedience, troops of
friends, (' *Regan*—What need *one* ?') I must not look to have; but,
in their stead ————.'

" Rely upon it, you are entirely mistaken in your estimate of the
world. Bad as it is, mankind are not quite so silly as you suppose.
Look around you, and see who are held in the highest esteem. I will
name one—Mr. Chief Justice. It is not the ' rogue' who gains the
good opinion of his own sex, or of the other. It is the man, who by
the exercise of the faculties which nature and education have given
him, asserts his place among his fellows; and, whilst useful to all
around him, establishes his claim to their respect, as an equal and
independent member of society. He may have every other good
quality under heaven; but, wanting this, a man becomes an object
of pity to the good, and of contempt to the vile. Look at Mr. Leigh,
his brother William, Mr. Wickham, Dr. Brockenbrough, &c., &c.,
and compare them with the drones which society is impatient to
shake from its lap.

" One of the best and wisest men I ever knew has often said to
me, that a decayed family could never recover its loss of rank in the
world, until the members of it left off talking and dwelling upon its
former opulence. This remark, founded in a long and close observation of mankind, I have seen verified, in numerous instances, in my
own connections; who, to use the words of my oracle, ' will never
thrive, until they can become " poor folks:"' he added, ' they may
make some struggles, and with apparent success, to recover lost
ground; they may, and sometimes do, get half way up again; but
they are sure to fall back; unless, reconciling themselves to circumstances, they become in form, as well as in fact, poor folks.'

" The blind pursuit of wealth, for the sake of hoarding, is a species
of insanity. There are spirits, and not the least worthy, who, con

tent with an humble mediocrity, leave the field of wealth and ambition open to more active, perhaps more guilty, competitors. Nothing
can be more respectable than the independence that grows out of
self-denial. The man who, by abridging his wants, can find time to
devote to the cultivation of his mind, or the aid of his fellow-crea-
tures, is a being far above the plodding sons of industry and gain.
His is a spirit of the noblest order. But what shall we say to the
drone, whom society is eager 'to shake from her encumbered lap?'—
who lounges from place to place, and spends more time in 'Adoniz-
ing' his person, even in a morning, than would serve to earn his
breakfast?—who is curious in his living, a connoisseur in wines, fastidious in his cookery; but who never knew the luxury of earning a
single meal? Such a creature, 'sponging' from house to house, and
always on the borrow, may yet be found in Virginia. One more
generation will, I trust, put an end to them; and their posterity, if
they have any, must work or steal *directly*.

"Men are like nations: one founds a family, the other an empire;
both destined, sooner or later, to decay. This is the way in which
ability manifests itself. They who belong to a higher order, like
Newton, and Milton, and Shakspeare, leave an imperishable name.
I have no quarrel with such as are content with their original obscurity, vegetate on from father to son; 'whose ignoble blood has crept
through *clodpoles* ever since the flood;" but I cannot respect them.
He who contentedly eats the bread of idleness and dependence is
beneath contempt.

"*Noscitur è socio.* 'Tell me your company and I will tell you
what you are.' But there is another description of persons, of far
inferior turpitude, against all connection with whom, of whatsoever
degree, I would seriously warn you. This consists of men of broken
fortunes, and all who are *loose* on the subject of pecuniary engagements. Time was, when I was fool enough to believe that a man
might be negligent of such obligations, and yet a very good fellow,
&c.; but long experience has convinced me that he who is lax in this
respect is utterly unworthy of trust in any other. He might do an
occasional act of kindness (or what is falsely called generosity) when
it lay in his way, and so may a prostitute, or a highwayman; but he
would plunge his nearest friends and dearest connections, the wife
of his bosom, and the children of his loins, into misery and want,
rather than forego the momentary gratification of appetite, vanity, or
laziness. I have come to this conclusion slowly and painfully, but
certainly. Of the Shylocks, and the smooth-visaged men of the
world, I think as I believe you do. Certainly, if I were to seek for
the hardest of hearts, the most obdurate, unrelenting, and cruel, I
should find them among the most selfish of mankind. And who are
the most selfish? The usurer, the courtier, and above all, the spend-

thrift. Try them once as creditors, and you will find, that even the Shylocks, we wot of, are not harder.

" You know my opinion of female society. Without it, we should degenerate into brutes. This observation applies with tenfold force to young men, and those who are in the prime of manhood ; for, after a certain time of life, the literary man may make a shift (a poor one, I grant) to do without the society of ladies. To a young man, nothing is so important as a spirit of devotion (next to his Creator) to some virtuous and amiable woman, whose image may occupy his heart, and guard it from the pollution which besets it on all sides. Neverthe- less, I trust that your fondness for the company of 'adies may not rob you of the time which ought to be devoted to reading and meditating on your profession ; and, above all, that it may not acquire for you the reputation of *dangler*—in itself bordering on the contemptible, and seriously detrimental to *your* professional character. A cautious old Squaretoes, who might have no objection to employing such a one at the bar, would, perhaps, be shy of introducing him as a practitioner in his family, in case he should have a pretty daughter, or niece, or sister ; although all experience shows, that of all male animals, the dangler is the most harmless to the ladies, who quickly learn, with the intuitive sagacity of the sex, to make a convenience of him, while he serves for a butt, also.

" Rely upon it, that to love a woman as ' a mistress,' although a delicious delirium—an intoxication far surpassing that of Cham- pagne—is altogether unessential, nay, *pernicious*, in the choice of a wife ; which a man ought to set about in his sober senses, choosing her, as Mrs. Primrose did her wedding-gown, for qualities that ' wear well.' I am well persuaded that few love-matches are happy ones. One thing, at least, is true, that if matrimony has its cares, celibacy has no pleasures. A Newton, or a mere scholar, may find employment in study ; a man of literary taste can receive, in books, a powerful auxiliary ; but a man must have a bosom friend, and children around him, to cherish and support the dreariness of old age."

Just as he was about to leave home for Washington, the first of December, 1821, while his horses were at the door, and he booted and spurred, and Johnny and his travelling companion, Richard Randolph, impatiently waiting for him in the cold, Mr. Randolph sat down and wrote his will—*the will* which, after a long contest, was finally established as his last will and testament.

In May, 1819, he wrote a will, and deposited it with Dr. Brocken- brough, to the following effect :

" I give to my slaves their freedom, to which my conscience tells me they are justly entitled. It has a long time been a matter of the deepest regret to me, that the circumstances under which I inherited them, and the obstacles thrown in the way by the laws of the land, have prevented my emancipating them in my lifetime, which it is my full intention to do, in case I can accomplish it.

"All the rest and residue of my estate (with the exceptions hereafter made), whether real or personal, I bequeath to William Leigh, Esquire, of Halifax, attorney at law, to the Rev. Wm. Meade, of Frederick, and to Francis Scott Key, Esqr., of Georgetown, District of Columbia, in trust, for the following uses and purposes, viz: 1st. To provide one or more tracts of land in any of the States or Territories, not exceeding in the whole four thousand acres, nor less than two thousand acres, to be partitioned and apportioned by them, in such manner as to them may seem best, among the said slaves. 2d. To pay the expense of their removal, and of furnishing them with necessary cabins, clothes, and utensils." Then follow other provisions. The will of 1821 is substantially the same as the above. The first *item* is: "I give and bequeath to all my slaves their freedom, heartily regretting that I have ever been the owner of one. 2. I give to my executor a sum not exceeding eight thousand dollars, or so much thereof as may be necessary, to transport and settle said slaves to and in some other State or Territory of the United States, giving to all above the age of forty not less than ten acres of land each."

He then makes a special annuity to his "old and faithful servants, Essex and his wife Hetty"—the same allowance to his "woman-servant, Nancy"—to Juba (alias Jupiter)—to Queen—and to Johnny, his body-servant.

In the codicil of 1826, he says: "I do hereby confirm the bequests to or for the benefit of each and every of my slaves, whether by name or otherwise."

In 1828, "Being in great extremity, but in my perfect senses," says he, "I write this codicil to my will in the possession of my friend, William Leigh, of Halifax, Esquire, to declare that that will is my sole last will and testament; and that if any other be found of subsequent date, whether will or codicil, I do hereby revoke the same."

In a codicil of 1831, Mr. Randolph says: "On the eve of embarking for the United States (he was then in London), considering my feeble health, to say nothing of the dangers of the seas, I add this codicil to my last will and testament and codicils thereto, affirming them all, except so far as they may be inconsistent with the following disposition of my estate." The third item of disposition is this: "I have upwards of two thousand pounds sterling in the hands of Baring Brothers & Co., of London, and upwards of one thousand pounds, like money, in the hands of Gowan and Marx. This money I leave to my executor, Wm. Leigh, as a fund for carrying into execution my will respecting my slaves; and, in addition to the provision which I have made for my faithful servant John, sometimes called John White, I charge my whole estate with an annuity to him, during his life, of fifty dollars, and as the only favor I ever asked of any government, I do entreat the Assembly of Virginia to permit the said John and his family to remain in Virginia."

And finally, in his dying hour, he gathered witnesses around him, and when the spirit was trembling to escape from the frail tenement that bound it, summoned all his energies in one last moment, and confirmed, in the most solemn form, before God and those witnesses, all the dispositions he had made in his will, in regard to his slaves. "More especially," said he, "in regard to this man!" bringing down his hand with force and energy on the shoulder of John, who stood weeping beside the couch of his expiring master and greatest benefactor.

Let the reader pause and reflect on these things; here are deeds, not promises—facts that speak for themselves; they need no addition, no embellishment. Here is a man who made no pretensions to philanthropy—despised the pretence of it. The hypocritical cant, for ever prating about it, pouring forth its cheap abundance of words, but which, unaccompanied with substantial works of true charity, are as sounding brass and a tinkling cymbal. Here is a man who cavilled for the nineteenth part of a hair in a matter of sheer right—who would admit no compromise in the Missouri question, and was ready to put every thing to hazard in vindication of the rights of the South. "I now," says he, on that occasion, "appeal to this nation, whether this pretended sympathy for the rights of a few free negroes is to supersede the rights of the free white population, of ten times their whole number." These words were uttered in February, 1821. In December following the same man *made free*, and provided for the comfortable maintenance of three hundred negro slaves Is there a man of

that majority that voted against him, with all their *professed* sympathy, who would have done likewise ?   And how completely has been
fulfilled the prophecy of Mr. Randolph, uttered on the occasion of
the Missouri agitation—" I am persuaded that the cause of humanity
to these unfortunates, has been put back a century—*certainly a generation*—by the unprincipled conduct of ambitious men, availing themselves of a good as well as of a fanatical spirit, in the nation."

There can be no doubt, that if the agitation of this slavery question had not been commenced and fermented by men who had no possible connection with it, and who, from the nature of the case, could
have no other motive but political ambition and a spirit of aggression ;
had that subject been left as we found it, under the compromises of
the Constitution, and the laws of God and conscience, aided by an enlightened understanding of their true interests—been left to work their
silent, yet irresistible influences on the minds of men, there can be
no doubt that thousands would have followed the example of John
Randolph, in Virginia, Maryland, Kentucky, and Missouri, and that
long ere this, measures would have been adopted for the final, though
gradual, extinguishment of slavery within their borders ; as it is, that
event has again been put off for another generation.

------------ • • • ------------

CHAPTER XVII.

LOG-BOOK AND LETTERS.

" As one of the very few persons in the world (Dr. Brokenbrough)
who really care whether I sink or swim, I am induced to send you
the following extract from my log-book ; relying on your partiality to
excuse the egotism ; and if you experience but the tenth part of the
pleasure I felt on reading your account of your November jaunt, I
shall be much gratified, as well as yourself :—

" 1821, December 10th, Monday, half-past 11, A. M.   Left Richmond.   Four miles beyond the oaks met Mrs. T——b and poor Mrs.
R——h.   Reached Underwood half-an-hour by run, and pushed on
to Sutter's, where I arrived quarter past five.   Very comfortable quarters.   Road heavy.

" 11th, Tuesday.   Breakfasted at eight A. M., and reached Batta-
der by quarter past twelve.   Fed my horses and arrived at Freder-

icksburg half-past three. Road heavy. Mansfield lane almost impassable. Excellent fare at Gray's, and the finest oysters I have seen
for this ten year.

" 12th, Wednesday. Hard frost. Left Fredericksburg at nine,
A. M. Reached Stafford, C. H., at half-past eleven, Dumfries at five
minutes past three, P. M., and Occoguon at half-past five. I made
no stop except to breathe the horses, from Dumfries to Neabsco, sixty-
five minutes three and a half miles. The five miles beyond Dumfries
employed nearly two hours. Roads indescribable.

" 13th, Thursday. Snow; part heavy rain. Waited until meridian, when, foreseeing that if the roads froze in their then state, they
would be impassable; and that the waters between me and Alexandria would be out perhaps for several days, I set out in the height of
the storm, and through a torrent of mud, and water, and sloughs of
all degrees of viscidity, I got to Alexandria before five, where a fine
canvas-back, and divers other good things, set my blood into circulation.

" 14th, Friday. Bitter cold. Reached Washington half-past
eleven. House does not sit to-day. Funeral. No southern mail.
Waters out.

" 15th. Very cold. No southern mail. Waters out. Just beyond
Pohick I met a man driving a double chair.

" J. R.—' Pray, sir, can I ford Accotink?'

" Traveller.—' If you drive brisk perhaps you may.'

" J. R.—' Did you cross it, sir?'

" T.—' Yes; but it is rising very fast.'

" As I pressed my little mare on, or rather as she pushed on after
comrade and Johnny, I thought of Sir Arthur and Miss Wardour,
of the old Gabertunzie, as, in breathless anxiety, they turned the
head-land, and found the water-mark under water. Pohick, a most
dangerous ford at all times, from the nature of the bend of the stream,
which is what is called a kettle-bottom, was behind me, and no retreat
and no house better than old Lear's hovel, except the church, where
were no materials for a fire. When I reached Accotink, the sand-
bank in the middle of the stream was uncovered; but for near a mile
I was up to the saddle-skirts. A great price, my good sir, for the
privilege of franking a letter, and the honor of being overlooked by
the great men, new as well as old.

" Just at the bridge over Hunting Creek, beyond Alexandria, I
met the mail cart and its solitary driver. The fog was Cimmerian.

" J. R.—' How far do you go to-night, friend?'

" D.—' To Stafford Court-house, sir. Can I ford the Accotink?'

" J. R.—' I think you may; but it will be impossible before mid
night: I am really sorry for you.'

" D.—' God bless your honor.'

"I am satisfied this poor fellow encounters every night dangers and sufferings in comparison with which those of our heroes are flea bites.

"Friday morning. Your letter of the 25th (Christmas day) did not reach me until this morning. I have been long mourning over the decline of our old Christmas sports and pastimes, which have given way to a spirit of sullen fanaticism on the one hand, or affected fashionable refinement on the other, which thinly veils the selfishness and inhospitality it is designed to cover. Your own letter may be cited as a proof that I am no grumbler (in this instance at least) at the times, although friend Lancaster, after puffing me in his way, was moved by the spirit (when I would not subscribe to his books) to say that the character I disclaimed in the H. of R. was the one that fitted me. 'Difficilis, querulus, laudatur temporis acti.' You date on Christmas day; you do not make the least mention of the season, into such 'desuetude' has the commemoration of the nativity of the great Redeemer fallen. On the eve of that day P——a gave a grand diplomatic dinner, at which Messrs. les Envoyès enragès were present, but held no intercourse. At this dinner J. Q. A. (the cub is a greater bear than the old one) gave this toast, rising from his chair at the time: 'Alexander the Great, Emperor of all the Russias, and the Cross.' Cross vs. Crescent, I presume; and no doubt M. P——a wrote to his court, announcing 'the disposition of this government towards Russia.' He is a wretched ass (this P.), who is writing a book on America, and whom every body quizzes. Some very laughable instances of this have been related to me. Travelling through Ohio, he was as much scandalized as John Wesley by the want of a commodité, and took the host to task about it. The fellow gravely assured him that were he to erect such a temple to a heathen and obscure deity, the people would rise in arms and burn it to the ground; and this mystification completely took, and was clapped down in P——'s notes. I expect to see it under the head of state of religion.

"To return. The next day the parties were reconciled, and all is hushed up. Yesterday, I had the honor of a visit from M. l'Envoyè de sa Majestè très Chretienne and the Secretary of Legation. This great honor and distinction (for such the folks here deem it) I suspect I owe to the exercise of a quality for which I have not, I fear, been greatly distinguished; I mean discretion; for, although I was present, I refused to be a referee, when applied to from various quarters, on the subject of the quarrel. I did not hesitate to say that certain very offensive words imputed to de N. were *not* uttered by him; but I declined giving any account of the matter, except to my old friend, Mr. Macon, and one other person, forbidding the mentioning of my name under the strongest sanctions.

"On reading over the above, I perceive that it is 'horribly

stuffed' with scraps of French. This apparent affectation (for it is only apparent) is owing to a silly falling in with the fashion in this place, where the commonest English word or phrase is generally rendered in (not always good) French.

"I showed your letter to my most discreet friend, Mr. Macon. He concurs with me that the first part (relative to the chair) of what you heard is pretty much 'all my eye, Betty;' but will not agree as to the remainder, which I class under the same head. Else how comes the greatest latitudinarian in our State, and a professed one too, who acknowledges no 'law,' but his favorite one of circumstances, a bank man, or any thing you please, to have received greater and more numerous marks of the favor of the Legislature of Virginia (recent ones too) than any citizen in it, the three last Presidents excepted? I detest mock-modesty, and will not deny that if I had the disposition, and could undergo the labor, (neither of which is the case,) I might acquire a certain degree of influence in the House, chiefly confined, however, to the small minority of old-fashioned Republicans. As to the first station, there was a time in which I might not have disgraced it, for I had quickness and a perfect knowledge of our rules and orders, with a competent acquaintance with parliamentary law in general. But since the dictatorship of Mr. C—y, 'on a changè tout cela' (French again), and I am now almost as raw as our newest recruits. *Then*, too, I had habits of application to business; but, my good friend, while I am running on (Alnaschar-like), I protest I believe the thought entered no head but Mr. S——'s (to whom, of course, I am much obliged for his good opinion); for no suggestion of the sort ever occurred to me until I read it under your hand.

"My days of business, of active employment, are over. My judgment, I believe, has not deserted me, and when it does, as old George Mason said, I shall be the last person in the world to find it out: my principles I am *sure* have not; and if, which God forbid, they should, I shall be the first person to find it out. Till that shall happen, I will be 'the warder on the lonely hill.'

"Why cannot all the honest men (not poor Burr's sort) unite in a man for the presidency who possesses: 1. Integrity, 2. firmness, 3. great political experience, 4. sound judgment and strong common sense, 5. ardent love of country and of its institutions and their spirit, 6. unshaken political consistency in the worst of times, 7. manners (if not courtly) correct. I could name such a man.

"Apropos to Burr. I have been reflecting this morning on the fate of some of the most active and influential (pardon the slang) of them that contributed to effectuate the change in 1800–1. Burr stands foremost; Ned. Livingston; W. C. N.! though last, not least. It is mournful to think on I might mention a good many more who played an under part in the drama, such as Duane, Merriwether, Jones, &c., &c."

In the appropriation bill for the ensuing year, there was a large undefined appropriation for the Indian Department asked for by the Secretary of War, and was understood to be intended to cover up a deficiency of the past year. Mr. Randolph, the 4th of January, 1822, moved a re-commitment of the bill.

" Unreasonable jealousy of the Executive Government," said he, " often led to the opposite extreme—a blind confidence in the governing power. From this jealousy and confidence he felt himself free. He believed that this House also was as free from unreasonable jealousy as any reasonable body ought to be. In fact, jealousy in public life was like that same 'green-eyed monster' in the domestic circle, which poisoned the source of all social happiness. It was extraordinary, and yet apparent, that the case had occurred in which confidence had lost its true character, and taken another, which he would not name in this House. It was remarkable, as well on the other side of the Atlantic as this, that a general suspicion had gone abroad, that the department which emphatically holds the purse-strings of the nation, was more remiss than any other in guarding against the expenditure of its subordinate agents. If it should be generally and unanswerably understood, that the body whose duty it was to guard the public treasure from wasteful expenditure, had abandoned their trust to a blind confidence in the dispensers of public patronage, they must immediately and justly lose all the confidence of the community. He had heard yesterday, with astonishment, a proposition to surrender inquiry to a confidence in the integrity and ability in the officer who had made the requisition. When this House should be disposed to become a mere chamber in which to register the edicts, not of the President, but of the heads of departments it would be unimportant whether the members of this House professed to represent 35,000 freemen, or collectively the single borough of Sarum. This proceeding was to him unprecedented. * * * * He would give to the Government his confidence when it was necessary, and he would not give it to the Government, nor to any man further than that, unless to his bosom friend. But there was a wide difference between voting for an advance for the service of the current year, and voting for the same sum to cover a deficiency of the past year, under cover of an advance for the present year."

The same day, January 4th, before making the above speech, he thus writes to Dr. Brockenbrough:

" A question will come on to-day respecting an appropriation, ostensibly in advance (or ' on account,' as trading folks say) of the military expenditures of the current year, but *really* to cover a deficiency (or excess of expenditure) for the last year. The sum is only $100,000; yet, my word for it! this honest gentleman (who had kept him up half a night to win back a few dollars) will vote it without the least scruple, at the nod of an executive officer. In short, the greater part of us view with equal eye

> 'The public million and the private groat.'

"The 'arguments' yesterday, when the question was pending, were 'Having the fullest confidence in the head of the war department;' 'can any gentleman believe or suppose that the Secretary of War could ask an improper appropriation,' &c., &c., all to the same tune; and although Tracey, of New-York, and Trimble, of Kentucky, distinctly opposed the imposition, that old sinner, —— of ' *Marland*,' by sheer force of lungs, induced some right well-meaning people to think the objections (which they did not understand, nor the answer neither) satisfactorily repelled. Even L——s, with whom I dined, agreed that the thing was wrong; said he had told S. S. it ought to be in a separate grant, expressive of its true character; but that S. said ' he did not like to trust it,' and so thrust it in the partial appropriation bill for 1822, where he hoped, no doubt, it would pass unobserved.

"By the way, I believe I wrote that C——n had ' accepted.' He and L. are, I think, shot dead by their want of *retenue*. More French, and I am not sure that it is good French.

"On the day of your ' debauch,' I dined with Van Buren and the whole New-York delegation in both Houses, with the V. P. at their head. Although it no doubt had a meaning like ' the shake of the head' in the ' Critic,' I did not *exactly* find it out, but I believe I was not far off the true construction. Many here think that neither C——n, nor C——s, nor C——y will be ' run'—that this is but a ruse de guerre to weaken C——d and of course strengthen the Eastern and Northern interest.

"Since I came to the House, Baldwin, speaking of the present candidate, said to me—" The people ought to put down (I trust they will) every man who has put himself forward at this premature time.' I left my letter open for what I might hear, and I have heard nothing else."

" *Washington*, *Jan.* 13, 1822.—My good friend—I had taken it for granted that you were gone. Orpheus like, to fetch your wife from the infernal regions, or at least through infernal ways, when I received, this morning, your welcome letter of Friday (the 11th). The truth is, I am disappointed by the Enquirer, and so you may tell him. Although it is not very desirable to be studiously misrepresented and caricatured to the rest of the States, yet I was fain to content myself with standing (substantially at least, if not in form) on my own title, with the good people of poor old Virginia (God help her) through the medium of the Enquirer. When any of the courtiers are to speak, G——s takes his seat in his box, and makes the best report he can: e. g. McD——'s speech, which is greatly softened in point of arrogance, and which is much improved by the total omission of the suicidal declaration towards its close, that the money was wanting ' to pay vouched accounts then lying on the Secretary of War's table.' When one of the country party speak, the duty is devolved upon an incapable deputy; but mere incapacity will not account for such manifest and repeated perversions. Take the following as some among the most glaring in the last report of a speech which satisfied many others much more than it did its author. (Here follow numerous corrections of the report alluded to.)

" The words for which I was called to order by S., are not those stated in the report. Those words were subsequently used—1 said not one syllable about the soldiers ' dealing in perfumery.' What the creature means I can't even divine. In short, it may be considered as the greatest outrage of the sort ever committed."

" *Tuesday, Jan.* 15, 1822.—I wrote you a letter the day before yesterday, in a character that might have passed for Sir Anthony Scrabblestone's. You no doubt remember that old acquaintance of our reverend friend the holy Clerk of Copmanhurst, and are full as well acquainted with his handwriting as that pious anchorite was with his person. However, I have (in addition to the apology that my implements are furnished by contract) the further justification of my Lord Arlington's high authority.

Did you preserve the Baltimore paper that contained No. 18, of ' a Native Virginian?' Nos. 19 and 20 have since been sent me. They are well written, and unanswered, if not unanswerable. Had they appeared in a paper of general circulation, and one that possessed any share of public confidence, they would, I think, have produced some effect, if indeed the public be not dead to all sensation.

" There is a young man here by the name of Chiles, making reports of our proceedings for the ' Boston Daily Advertiser.' Mr. Mills of the Senate (from Massachusetts) gave me *his* report of the *doings* of Friday, the 4th instant—with the help of such a report as that, I could have given Mr. Ritchie what I said almost verbatim. But the truth is, that after the occasion passes away, I can seldom recall what I said until I am put in mind, by what I did not say, or by some catch-word; at the same time, I have given Mr. Ritchie the substance, and, where any particular word or incident occurred, the very language that I used. I am determined, hereafter, to wait for Chiles's report from Boston, and with a slight alteration, when necessary, I will send it to the Enquirer. The N. I. does not *condense* as he pretends. Of all the speeches made on the subject, it was the longest and the most audible. In the report it is one of the shortest, and yet stuffed with expletives not used by me, as well as perversions of meaning. There is no mistaking this, when continually occurring.

" The discussion of the M. A. bill has done me no service."

" *Jan.* ¡8, 1822.—I'm afraid you think me such a tiresome egotist that you are fain to drop my correspondence. To say the truth, I am vexed at being made to talk such nonsense, and bad English into the bargain—' proven' cum multis aliis ejusdem farinae, familiar enough, indeed, to congressional ears, but which never escaped from my lips.

" There is a very impudent letter in Walsh, which I half suspect he wrote to himself—' hungry mouths to stop, and dogs not above eating dirty pudding'—must sound peculiarly offensive in his ears, since he could not even get the run of the kitchen when he was here in 1816–17. At that time he had the effrontery to tell me to my face, that he had no doubt I was far more eloquent than Patrick Henry. The Intelligencer puts words into my mouth that I never uttered, and these furnish the basis of Mr. W.'s comments, with those great critics and annotators—for ' debate,' read ' detail ' (which I said neither health nor inclination allowed me to enter into), and what becomes of the comment? Of one thing I am *sure*, that the House is not yet becoming tired of me ; and I shall take especial care that it do not."

" *Jan.* 19.—My avocations are such, that my time, like my money, runs away in driblets, without producing an ' *effeck.*' I have more than once thought of using my pen in some other way besides scribbling to you; but. some how or other, I can find none so pleasant, and *time* is always wanting. I have read nothing, but have been very much in company. Like the long waists of our mothers, I really believe I am growing, if not generally, at least somewhat, in fashion. But I hope I am not so old a fool as to presume upon this ; for of all fools, an old one is the least tolerable.

" Like most *parvenus*, the man you mention is a sorry blackguard, in dress, manners, figure (a complete paddy), countenance, and principle. I *could* have given him ' such a sackful of sair bones,' that he could have borne the marks to his grave. But I purposely abstained from the slightest notice of him. It is not the least of our success against temptation, to suppress the overwhelming retort, and, just as it rises to the tongue, to give a good gulp and swallow it."

" *Feb.* 1.—You will see a correction of Gales's in yesterday's Intelligencer. He has restored the words that I used, almost verbatim. They were these : ' Transubstantiation, I was going to say ; but I would not, from respect to a numerous and most respectable class of persons; but *would say*, as any in priestcraft, kingcraft, or another craft which (as great as is the Diana of the Ephesians!) I would not name.' Yet I have received an indignant remonstrance from a Roman Catholic of Washington City, 'on my invective against that sect,' of which you may see some notice in to-morrow's *Moniteur*.

Administration is sunk into much contempt with our House, and the other too. They hail from 'four corners.' Instead of Dana's 'triangular war.' we have a quadrangular one. They must dissolve in their own imbecility. By the way, I want my 'native Virginian,' when you are done with him.

"I trust the Virginian Government will not be weak enough to dismiss the "*claim*" of Kentucky. I suspect it was got up to defray C——s' electioneering campaign for the winter."

"*Feb.* 7.—I am at last gratified by a letter from you. To say the truth, I had rather, much rather, that the thing had not appeared; but as to 'being affronted' at it, that was out of the question. Indeed, if I do not egregiously deceive myself, a great change has been wrought in my character. I am become quiet and sedate—torpid, if you will—but much less disposed to take or give offence than I once was. This remark is made, not in reference to the little incident above alluded to, but in that vein of egotism to which I am too prone.

"You do right in endeavoring to reconcile L. and T.; but in the course of my observation, I cannot recall a single instance of cordiality between *reconciled friends*. Poor human nature! The view which I am compelled to take of it every day, augments my pity for it. We dare not trust ourselves with the truth. It is too terrible. Hence the whole world is in masquerade. 'Words were invented,' said Talleyrand, 'to conceal our thoughts.' Hence, a conventional language, in which it is understood that things are never to be called by their right names, and which at last ceases to answer its original design, except with the vulgar great and small.

"I must be a very uncommon personage to 'astonish all the world' with what *I do not do*. Since I am not able to astonish them with my exploits, it is very good in them to be negatively charged on my account. I heartily wish that I had never given them any other cause of wonder.

"Poor T. T——r! I know his disease. It has been killing me inch-meal, a long, long while. Give him my best regards. It is a dreadful thing to find out, as he has done, too late, what stuff the world is made of; to have an illusion dispelled that made life agreeable to us. Did you ever read ' Cobbett's Sermons,' or his ' Cottage Economy?' If not, pray do. They are written with great originality and power, and I heartily wish they were in the hands of all who can read.

"There has been a great deal of stuff uttered in our House for the last two or three days. It has degenerated into a mere bear garden; and, really, when I see strangers on the platform, I feel ashamed of belonging to the body. I have been a good deal pressed to join the squabble; for it don't deserve the name of debate; but I have refrained, if the expression can be applied, where, instead of desire, one feels only disgust. I have not yet seen the Chief Justice, although we have exchanged visits. I am glad to hear that you intend to ' write again soon.' If you knew the feeling I have when a letter from you is brought in, you would shower them down like snow. My health and spirits are incurably bad. If I can raise the money, I mean to dissipate my chagrin and ennui in some foreign land. Incessant change of place, and absence of all occupation, seem indispensable to my tolerable existence. I am become almost reconciled to pain; but there is a sensation of another sort that is worse than death. Familiar as I am to it, it serves but to increase its misery. At this moment, I am obliged to relinquish my pen from the combined effects of bodily disease and mental distress. Adieu.

"J. R. OF R."

CHAPTER XVIII.

THE APPORTIONMENT BILL.

"GOVERNMENT, to be safe and to be free, must consist of Representatives having a common interest and a common feeling with the represented."—JOHN RANDOLPH.

THE great business of the session was the apportionment of representatives among the States, according to the new census. It seems to have been the policy of Congress, as the population increased, to increase the ratio of representation from decade to decade, so as to keep down the numbers of the House of Representatives. This subject was one of exciting interest to all parties. None felt more deeply than Mr. Randolph, not only the importance of the principles involved but the serious influence the new apportionment was likely to have on the relative weight and standing of the old Commonwealth which he had been so proud to represent for so many years, as the Empire State. "Yesterday I rose, (says he, the 7th of February, the day the question was taken) at 3, and to-day at 2, A. M. I cannot sleep.

Two bottles of champagne, or a dozen of gas, could not have excited me like this apportionment bill."

A variety of propositions were made to fix the ratio, ranging from 35,000 to 75,000. The committee reported 40,000. Mr. Tucker, of Virginia, proposed 38,000. By the ratio of the committee, Virginia would lose one member, and fall below New-York and Pennsylvania. By the ratio of Mr. Tucker she would retain her present delegation in Congress. Mr. Randolph was in favor of the latter proposition. But his arguments reach far beyond the particular interest his own State had in the question. They are profound and statesmanlike—are worthy of our most serious consideration—and the principle they evolve should be made a cardinal doctine in the creed of those who hold that the responsibility of the representative—the independence and sovereignty of the States, and the cautious action of the Federal Government on the subjects strictly limited to it, are the only sound rules for interpreting the Constitution. The danger is in having too small a representation. No country was ever ruined by the expense of its legislation; better pay an army of legislators than an army of soldiers.

"I cannot enter into the reasoning," said Mr. Randolph, "which goes to show that two hundred members, or this ratio of 42,000, or what not, is to serve some great political purpose, whilst one member more or less, or 1000 in the ratio, more or less, would produce a calamitous effect. To such prescience which could discover such important effects from such causes he had no claim ; but this he would say, it was made an objection to the Constitution by some of the greatest men this country ever produced, and perhaps as great as it ever would produce. It was, in itself, a vital objection to George Mason's putting his hand to the Constitution, that the representation in Congress was limited not to exceed one member for every 30,000 souls, whilst on the other hand, a most unbounded discussion was given over the increase of the ratio. It was an objection to the Constitution, on the part of some of the wisest men this country ever produced. It was an objection on the part of Patrick Henry, whose doubts, I need not ask you, Mr. Speaker, to recur to. I fear you have been too familiar with them in the shape of verified predictions, whose doubts experience has proved to be prophetic. On a question of this sort, shall we be told of the expense of compensating a few additional members of this body ? He knew we had, in a civil point of view, perhaps the most expensive government under the sun. We had, taking one gentleman's declaration, an army of legislators. There was a time, and he wished he might live to see it again, when the legislators of the country

outnumbered the rank and file of the army, and the officers to boot.
I wish I may see it again. Did any man ever hear of a country ruined by the expense of its legislation? Yes, as the sheep are ruined
by so much as is required for the nourishment of the dogs. As to
the civil list, to pay a host of legislators, is it this pay that has run
up the national debt? Is it their pay that produces defalcations of
the revenue? Did mortal man ever hear of a country that was ruined by the expense of its civil list, and more especially by the legislative branch of it? We must take a number that is convenient for
business, and at the same time sufficiently great to represent the interests of this great empire. This empire, he was obliged to say,
for the term republic had gone out of fashion. He would warn, not
this House, for they stood in no need of it, but the good, easy, susceptible people of this country, against the empiricism in politics,
against the delusion that because a government is representative,
equally representative, if you will, it must therefore be free. Government, to be safe and to be free, must consist of representatives having
a common interest and common feeling with the represented.

When I hear of settlements at the Council Bluffs, and of bills for
taking possession of the mouth of the Columbia River, I turn, not a
deaf ear, but an ear of a different sort to the sad vaticination of
what is to happen in the length of time: believing, as I do, that
no government extending from the Atlantic to the Pacific can be fit
to govern me, or those whom I represent. There is death in the pot,
compound it how you will. No such government can exist, because it
must want the common feeling and common interest with the governed, which is indispensable to its existence. * * * * The first House
of Representatives consisted of but sixty-five members. Mr. Randolph said he well remembered that House. He saw it often, and
that very fact was, he said, to him a serious objection to so smal. a
representation on this floor. The truth is, said he, we came out of
the old Constitution in a chrysalis state, under unhappy auspices.
The members of the body that framed the Constitution were second
to none in respectability. But they had been so long without power,
they had so long seen the evils of a government without power, that
it begot in them a general disposition to have king Stork substituted
for king Log. They organized a Congress to consist of a small number of members, and what was the consequence? Every one in the
slightest degree conversant with the subject must know, that on the
first step in any government depends, in a great degree, the character and complexion of that government. What, I repeat, was the
consequence of the then limited number of the representative body?
Many, very many, indeed all that could be called fundamental laws,
were passed by a majority. which, in the aggregate, hardly exceeded in
number the committee which was the other day appointed to bring in

the bill now on your table ; and thereby, said he, hangs (not a tale, but) very serious ones, which it is improper to open here and now. Among the other blessings which we have received from past legislation, we should not have been sitting at this place if there had been a different representation.   Those who administered the government were in a hurry to go into the business of legislation before they were ready—and here I must advert to what had been said with regard to the redundance of debate.   For my part, said he, I wish we could have done nothing but talk, unless, indeed, we had gone to sleep for many years past ; and coinciding in the sentiment which had fallen from the gentlemen from New-York, give me fifty speeches. I care not how dull or how stupid, rather than one law on the statute book ; and if I could once see a Congress meet and adjourn without passing any act whatever, I should hail it as one of the most acceptable omens.   * * * * The case of a State wisely governed by its legislature, that of Connecticut, for example," he argued, "would be preposterously applied to this government, representing as it does more than a million of square miles, and more than twenty millions of people, for such ere long would be the amount of our population. To say that 200 shall be the amount of our representation, and then to proportion that number among the States, would be putting the cart before the horse, or making a suit of clothes for a man and then taking his measure.   The number of representatives ought to be sufficient to enable the constituent to maintain with the representative that relation without which representative government was as great a cheat as transubstantiation—he was going to say—but would not, from respect to a numerous and most respectable class of persons, but he *would say*, as any priest-craft, king-craft, or another craft, which (as great is the Diana of the Ephesians !) he would not name. When I hear it proposed elsewhere to limit the numbers of the representatives of the people on this floor, I feel disposed to return the answer of Agesilaus when the Spartans were asked for their arms—' come and take them !'—It appeared to be the opinion of some gentlemen, who seemed to think that He who made the world should have consulted them about it, that our population would go on increasing, till it exceeded the limits of the theory of our representative government.   He rememberered a case in which it had been seriously proposed, and by a learned gentleman too, that inasmuch as one of his brethren was increasing his property in a certain ratio, in the course of time it would amount, by progressive increase, to the value of the whole world, and this man would thus become master of the world.   These calculations would serve as charades, conundrums, and such matters, calculated to amuse the respectable class (much interested in such matters) of old maids and old bachelors, of which Mr. R. said he was a most unfortunate member.   To this objection, that the number of the House would soon become

too great, to this bugbear it was sufficient to reply, that when the
case occurred it would be time to provide for it. We will not take
the physic before we are sick, remembering the old Italian epitaph,
' I was well, I would be better, I took physic, and here I am.' * * * *
He was in favor of making the House as numerous as the Constitution would permit, always keeping within such a number as would
not be inconvenient to the House for the transaction of business.
For, in that respect, the legislature of a little Greek or Swiss republic might be as numerous as that of the Kingdom of Great Britain.
The only limit was, the capacity to do business in one chamber; and
it was desirable to have as great a number as would keep on this side
of a mob.

" One of the most profound female writers of the present age—
and, perhaps, he might amend by striking out the word female—had
pointed out the superiority of the legislative body of England over
that of France. from the circumstance that, of the British Parliament, no man is permitted to read a speech, but is obliged to pronounce it extempore; while in the French Legislative Assembly, the
rage for making speeches was excited by the usage, that any member
who could manufacture one, or get some one else to do it for him,
ascended the tribune, and delivered, and afterwards published it;
and hence their notion, that an assembly of more than one hundred,
if composed of Newtons, might be called a mob. The practice in
England naturally forced out the abilities of the house. The speaker
was obliged to draw on his own intellectual resources, and upon those
talents with which heaven had endowed him. Talents descend from
heaven; they are the gift of God; no patent of nobility can confer
them; and he who had the right, beyond a monarch's power to grant,
did conduct the public affairs of the country. By the contrary practice, according to Madame De Staël, the French nation was cheated,
and men passed for more than they were worth. * * * * A gentleman from Georgia had feared a large ratio would introduce an oligarchy. But it would be recollected that our government, in its
head, was monarchical. It was useless to quarrel about words, for
such is the fact; and, as some writers say, not the best form of monarchy, the elective; but on this he would express no opinion. There
was another body that was oligarchical—the Senate, and an oligarchy of the worst, for the representatives of the State sovereignties
were not revocable by them. What would become of the House of
Representatives if the whole rays of Executive influence were to be
concentrated upon it? It would be consumed, or, like a diamond
under a lens, would evaporate. Nevertheless, there were dull speeches
delivered in the Houses of Parliament, as well as here. Witness
those of Mr. Fuller, or of Mr. Drake. This was one of those cases
in which the maxim *de mortuis nil nisi bonum* did not hold. He
complained of the growth of the contingent expenses of the House,

which had been incurred for the accommodation of the members, in a profusion of stationery, easy arm-chairs, and a mass of printed documents that nobody reads! These accommodations, like those at Banks, did no good to those who made use of them. He believed that an increased ratio would be one of the means of getting rid of these incumbrances."

These observations are worthy of most serious consideration. In the opinion of Mr. Randolph, an enlargement of the numbers of the House of Representatives would, in the end, produce an economy of expenditure for their own accommodation, would reduce the chances of executive influence, give a more immediate and responsible representation to the people, enlarge the field of political interest in the country, by bringing the representative and the represented more closely together, would lessen the propensity, and take away the facilities for sectional combinations and partial and unconstitutional legislation, more effectually call forth the real talent and patriotism of the House, and add to the weight and respectability of the States, which are the only opposing forces and counterweights to the strong centripetal tendencies of the Federal Government. These are results greatly to be desired. The wisest men foresaw the dangers of too small a representation. It was a serious objection to the Constitution. We have felt the evil consequences in more ways than one. Let the evil be remedied: reduce the army; reduce the navy; they have almost become useless in our vastly-extended territory and commanding position. Build no more fortifications; build no more ships but steam-ships, and make them useful as mail-carriers and explorers of unknown regions. Abolish the land system (which is expensive), and sell out to the States the public lands within their respective borders. Collect no more revenue than is needed for an economical administration of the government. Increase the representatives of the people in Congress; let them avoid all doubtful questions; confine themselves to the few subjects of a common interest, specifically delegated, and proceed on the maxim, that a "wise and masterly inactivity" in the science of legislation, as well as in the practice of the healing art, is the truest evidence of wisdom and prudence When these things are done, then the great danger so much apprehended by our fathers need no longer to be the cause of uneasiness to their children, and we may go on adding State after State until our Federative Union shall overspread the whole continent. The truth is, the addition of States from different sections of widely-diversified and opposing interests has done more than any thing else to bring back the action of the government to its legitimate sphere, by diminishing the chances and the desire of sectional combinations.

Mr. Randolph's efforts were all in vain. The ratio was fixed at 40,000 On the 6th of February, by means of the previous question, the bill was carried by a vote of nearly two to one, and Virginia, henceforth, had to take her rank, in numerical strength at least, as a second or third-rate State. Mr. Randolph spoke most feelingly on the occasion.

" I confess," said he, " that I have (and I am not ashamed to own it) an hereditary attachment to the State that gave me birth. I shall act upon it as long as I act upon this floor, or any where else. I shall feel it when I am no longer capable of acting any where. But I beg gentlemen to bear in mind, if we feel the throes and agonies which they impute to us at the sight of our departing power, there is something in fallen greatness, though it be in the person of a despot— something to enlist the passions and feelings of men, even against their reason. Bonaparte himself believed he had those who sympathized with him. But if such be our condition—if we are really so extremely sensitive on this subject—do not gentlemen recollect the application of another received maxim in regard to sudden, I will not say upstart, elevation, that some who are once set on horseback, know not, nor care not, which way they ride? I am a man of peace. With Bishop Hall, I take no shame to myself for making overtures of pacification, when I have unwittingly offended. But, sir, I cannot permit, whatever liberties may be taken with me, I cannot permit any that may be taken with the State of Virginia to pass unnoticed on this floor. I hope the notice which I shall always take of them will be such as not only becomes a member of this House, but the dignity of that ancient State."

While the star of Virginia was in the ascendant, and her dominion was acknowledged by all, her course was one of self-sacrifice. A royal domain she surrendered as a peace-offering to the Confederation ; she exhausted her own resources to fill the common treasury ; ever careful of the rights of others, she neglected her own, and studied more the common welfare than her private interest. No statute can rise up and condemn her as mean or selfish, unjust or wasteful.

Let those who are now in the ascendant go and do likewise ; above all, let them take care that the maxim given by Mr. Randolph as a warning, prove not prophetic—" that some who" (by sudden elevation) "are once set on horseback, know not, nor care not, which way they ride."

Next day after the passage of the bill, Mr. Randolph thus writes to his friend Brockenbrough.

Washington, Thursday, 4 o'clock P. M., Feb. 7, 1822.

From Dudley's letter, written the day after the event, I had anticipated the cause of my not having heard from you within the week. My good friend, "neither can I write," but for a different reason. I am now down, *abraded*, by long-continued stretch of mind and feeling. We may now cry out "Ichabod," for our glory is departed. I made last night my final effort to retrieve our fortunes, and the Virginia delegation (to do them justice, sensible when too late of their error) did what they could to second me. I do them this justice with pleasure, if there was one I did not note the exception. Had they supported me from the first, we could have carried 38,000 or 38,500. S——e of W——e got alarmed at my earnest deprecation of the conduct of the majority, of which he was one, and came to me repeatedly, and tried to retrace his steps. So did some others (i. e. "try back"), but the mischief had gone too far to be remedied. Our fathers have eaten grapes, and my teeth, at least, are set on edge. I am sensible that I have spoken too much, and perhaps my friends at a distance may think me more faulty in this respect than they would do, had they been on the spot—for since my first (also unpublished) opposition to the "Yazoo" bill, I have never spoken with such effect upon the House, as on Saturday last: and I am certain by their profound attention last night, that I lost nothing even with them that divided against me, at least the far greater part of them. If in this I shall find by the representation of others that my self-love has deceived me, I will be more than ever on my guard against that desperately wicked and most deceitful of all things, my own heart. I pray you, therefore, not to have the fear of the Archbishop of Grenada before your eyes, but tell me truly, if I am mistaken. This you can readily learn through Mr. Ritchie, to whom please show this letter, or through some of our assembly men, or others, who have correspondents here. I do not want to know the source whence your information comes; nor yet am I setting a clap-trap, vain as I am (for vanity I know is imputed to me by my enemies, and I fear (as has been said) that they come nearer the truth of one's character than our friends do), and sweet as applause is, (Dr. South says of the seekers of praise, that they search for what "flashes for a moment in the face like lightning, and perhaps says he, it hurts the man.") I fish for no opinion on the character of my endeavors to render public service, except as regards their too frequent repetition; it is rather to obtain the means of hereafter avoiding censure that this request is made.

CHAPTER XIX.

PINCKNEY, MARSHALL, TAZEWELL—DEPARTURE FOR EUROPE.

MONDAY, the 25th of February, Mr. Randolph prematurely announced the death of William Pinckney, a Senator from Maryland, and a distinguished jurist and orator. He had obtained the information from one of the Judges of the Supreme Court, who came in while the House was in session, and gave the information to Mr. Randolph as coming from a gentleman of the bar, who told him he had seen the corpse. Mr. Randolph immediately rose and pronounced the following eulogy, which, considering that it was sudden and ex temporaneous, is unsurpassed in eloquence:

He arose to announce to the House the death of a man who filled the first place, in public estimation, in the first profession in that estimation, in this or any other country :—

"We have been talking," says he, "of General Jackson, and a greater man than he is not here, but gone for ever! I allude, sir, to the boast of Maryland and the pride of the United States—the pride of us all, and particularly the pride and ornament of that profession of which you, Mr. Speaker (Stephenson), are a member, and an eminent one. He was a man with whom I lived when a member of this House, and a new one too ; and ever since he left it for the other—I speak it with pride—in habits not merely negatively friendly, but of kindliness and cordiality. The last time I saw him was on Saturday, the last Saturday but one, in the pride of life and full possession and vigor of all his faculties, in that lobby. He is now gone to his account (for as the tree falls so it must lie), where we must all go—where I must soon go, and by the same road, too—the course of nature ; and where all of us, put off the evil day as long as we may, must also soon go. For what is the past but a span ; and which of us can look forward to as many years as we have lived ? The last act of intercourse between us was an act, the recollection of which I would not be without for all the offices that all the men of the United States have filled or ever shall fill. He had, indeed, his faults, his foibles ; I should rather say sins. Who is without them ? Let such, such only, cast the first stone. And these foibles, if you will, which every body could see, because every body is clear-sighted with regard to the faults and foibles of others, he, I have no doubt, would have been the first to acknowledge, on a proper representation of them. Every thing now is hidden from us—not, God forbid, that utter darkness rests upon the grave, which, hideous as it is, is lighted, cheered, and warmed with light from heaven; not the impious fire fabled to be stolen from heaven by the heathen, but by the Spirit of the living God, whom we all profess to worship, and whom I hope we shall spend the remainder of the day in worshipping; not with mouth honor, but in our hearts, in spirit and in truth; that it may not be said of us also, ' This people draweth nigh unto me with their lips, but their heart is far from me.' Yes, it is just so; he is gone. I will not say that our loss is irreparable, because such a man as has existed may exist again. There has been a Homer, there has been a Shakspeare, there has been a Milton, there has been a Newton. There may be another Pinckney, but there is none now. And it was to announce this event that I have risen. I am almost inclined to believe in presentiments. I have been all along, as well assured of the fatal termination of that disease with which he was afflicted as I am now; and I have dragged my weary limbs before sunrise, to the door of his sick chamber (for I would not intrude on the sacred grief of the family), almost every morning since his illness. From the first, I had almost no hope."

In these early and pious visitations to the sick chamber of virtue and genius, he was frequently accompanied by the Chief Justice. What a beautiful and touching tribute to the memory of Pinckney, that the greatest orator and statesman, and the greatest jurist of his age, should watch with so much interest and tenderness, the last expiring breath of him who in life had rivalled the one in eloquence and the other in profound learning.

Though premature, the event of Mr. Pinckney's death soon followed the announcement.

" Mr. Pinckney (says Randolph to a friend) breathed his last about 12 o'clock (midnight). The void cannot be filled. I have not slept, on an average, two hours, for the last six days. I have been at his lodgings, more than half a mile west of mine, every day, by sunrise—often before—and this morning before daybreak. I heard from him last night at ten, and sat up (which I have not done before for six weeks) until the very hour that he expired. He died literally in harness. To his exertions in the Dudley cause, and his hard training to meet Tazewell in the cochineal case, as 'tis called, may be fairly ascribed his death. The void will never be filled that he has left Tazewell is second to no man that ever breathed; but he has taken almost as much pains to hide his light under a bushel as P. did to set his on a hill.   He and the Great Lord Chief are in that *par-nobile;* but Tazewell, in point of reputation, is far beyond both Pinckney and Marshall."

Saturday, March 9th, Mr. Randolph made a speech of two hours, against the Bankrupt bill. Finding by a vote, to strike out the enacting clauses, that the bill would pass by a large majority, and that being the only remaining subject of importance before the House, he obtained leave of absence on Monday, the 11th, and set out for New-York, to embark on board the packet ship Amity, for Liverpool.

From "on board the steamboat Nautilus, under weigh to the Amity, Saturday, March 16, 1822," he addressed a letter to his constituents :—

"*My friends*, for such indeed you have proved yourselves to be, through good and through evil report, I throw myself on your indulgence, to which I have never yet appealed in vain. It is now just five years since the state of my health reluctantly compelled me to resist your solicitations (backed by my own wishes) to offer my services to your suffrages. The recurrence of a similar calamity obliges me to retire, for a while, from the field of duty.

"Should the mild climate of France and the change of air restore my health, you will again find me a candidate for your independent suffrages at the next election (1823).

"I have an especial desire to be in that Congress, which will decide (probably by indirection) the character of the executive government of the Confederation for, at least, four years—perhaps for ever; since now, for the first time since the institution of this government, we have presented to the people the army candidate for the presidency, in the person of him who, judging from present appearance, will receive the support of the Bank of the United States also. This is an union of the purse and sword, with a vengeance—one which even the sagacity of Patrick Henry never anticipated, in this shape at least. Let the people look to it, or they are lost for ever. They will fall into that gulf, which, under the artificial, military, and paper systems of Europe, divides Dives from Lazarus, and grows daily and hourly broader, deeper, and more appalling. To this state of things we are rapidly approaching, under an administration, the head of which sits an *incubus* upon the State, while the lieutenants of this new Mayor of the palace are already contending for the succession; and their retainers and adherents are with difficulty kept from coming to blows, even on the floor of Congress. We are arrived at that pitch of degeneracy when the mere lust of power, the retention of place and patronage, can prevail, not only over every consideration of public duty, but stifle the suggestions of personal honor, which even the ministers of the decayed governments of Europe have not yet learned entirely to disregard."

From the same steamboat, Nautilus, he addressed the following note to Dr. Brockenbrough.

"As I stepped into the Nautilus, a large packet from Washington, among which was yours inclosing ' Uncle Nat's' letter, was put into my hands.

" The ' Native of Virginia' is indiscreet in covering too much ground.   He ought to have darned and patched old Tom's Mantle, and fought behind it as a Telemonian shield.

" Add to my P. S. in the address to my constituents, that letters, via New-York, to the care of the P. Master, will reach me.   My address is, care of John & Wm. Gilliatt, London, until further notice. I am nearing the Amity.   Farewell! farewell!"

———•••———

CHAPTER XX.

THE VOYAGE.

AFTER the Amity had gotten fairly under way, and the passengers somewhat acquainted with each other, they sought, by various amusements, to relieve the tedium of their voyage.   Whist was a favorite game on board; and here Mr. Randolph soon proved his superiority as a player.   It became a contest each night, who should have him as a partner, and finally they took turns.

I observed, one morning, says Mr. Jacob Harvey, of New-York, to whom we are indebted for the incidents of this voyage, that Mr. Randolph was examining a very large box of books, containing enough to keep him busy reading during a voyage round the world.   I asked him why he had brought so many with him?   "I want to have them bound in England, sir," replied he.   "Bound in England!" exclaimed I, laughing, "why did you not send them to New-York or Boston, where you can get them done cheaper?"

"What, sir," replied he sharply, "patronize some of our Yankee taskmasters; those patriotic gentry, who have caused such a heavy duty to be imposed upon foreign books?   Never, sir, never; I will neither wear what they make, nor eat what they raise, so long as my tobacco crop will enable me to get supplies from *old* England ; and I shall employ John Bull to bind my books, until the time arrives when they can be properly done *South of Mason and Dixon's line !*" He was kind enough to offer me the use of them, saying : " Take my advice, and don't read any of the novels ; and when you get home, sir, tell your father that *I* recommended abstinence from novel reading and *whisky punch*. Depend upon it, sir, they are both equally injurious to the *brain !*"

His favorite author was Milton, and he frequently gave us readings from " Paradise Lost," stopping occasionally to point out the beauties of the poem. Young, Thomson, Johnson, and Southey, did not please his taste ; they were, he said, " too artificial." But his classification of modern poems was very original.

" Sir, I place first on this list, Tom Crib's Memorial to Congress, for its great wit and satire ; next, the Two Penny Post Boy, for similar excellencies ; and third, Childe Harold's Pilgrimage, for every variety of sentiment, well expressed. But, sir (no offence to Ireland), I can't go Moore's songs ; they are too sentimental by half ; all ideal and above nature."

Turning over his books one day, I was surprised to find a copy of " Fanny," Mr. Halleck's very clever satirical poem, which had been recently published. " I am glad," said I, " that you do not proscribe *Yankee* poetry as well as *Yankee* codfish."

" O no, sir," replied he, "I always admire talent, no matter where it comes from ; and I consider this little work as the best specimen of American poetry that we have yet seen. I am proud of it, sir ; and I mean to take it to London with me, and to present it to that lady whose talents and conversation I shall most admire."

I may mention here, although somewhat out of place, that when we met in London in June following, I suddenly recollected the circumstance, and said to him : " By the way, Mr. Randolph, to whom did you present ' Fanny ?' "

" To your countrywoman, Miss Edgeworth, sir : she has no competitor in my estimation. She fairly won the book, sir."

He proposed, one fine morning, to read Fanny to me aloud, and on deck, where we were enjoying a fine breeze and noonday sun. It was the most amusing " reading" I ever listened to. The *notes* were much longer than the poem ; for, whenever he came to a well-known

name, up went his spectacles and down went the book, and he branch
ed off into some anecdote of the person or of his family. Thus we
"progressed" slowly from page to page, and it actually consumed
three mornings before we reached—

> " And music ceases when it rains
>   In Scudder's balcony."

I was one morning looking over his books for my own amusement,
and observed that several of the prettiest editions were marked
" This for Miss ——"

" How is this?" said I; " some fair lady seems to have enchained
you."

" Ah," replied he, " if you only knew her, the sweetest girl in the
' Ancient Dominion,' and a particular favorite of mine, sir; I shall
have all these books beautifully bound in London, sir, fit to grace
her centre-table on my return."

I took up one of them, a volume of old plays, and after reading
a few pages, exclaimed: " Surely you have not read these plays
lately, Mr. Randolph, or you would not present *this* book to Miss
——; it is too lascivious for her eyes."

He immediately ran his eye over the page; then took the book
out of my hands, and immediately indorsed on the back " not fit for
Bet." Then, turning to me, he said with warmth:

" You have done me an infinite service, sir. I would not for
worlds do aught to sully the purity of that girl's mind. I *had* forgotten those plays, sir, or they would not have found a place in my
box. I abominate as much as you do, sir, that vile style of writing
which is intended to lessen our abhorrence of vice, and throw ridicule on virtuous conduct. You have given me the hint, sir. Come,
assist me in looking over *all* these books, lest some other black sheep
may have found its way into the flock."

We accordingly went through the whole box, but found no other
volume deserving of condemnation, much to Randolph's satisfaction.
He then presented me with several books, as keepsakes; and he
wanted to add several more, but I had to decline positively. His
generosity knew no bounds; and had I been avaricious of mental
food, I might have become possessed of half his travelling library.

On the 5th of April, we landed about noon. The wind had

changed since Randolph predicted that we would strike ' *Sligo Head*,' and we first saw the high mountains of Donegal. The atmosphere was beautifully clear, and we ran along the coast near enough to see the houses, &c. Towards night Randolph said to me:

" Well, sir, I *now* believe the anecdote related by Arthur Young. In his notes on Ireland he says, that one day a farmer took his son, a young boy, some distance from home, in the county Meath. They came to a tree; the boy was astonished, stopped, and asked, ' Father, what is that?' never having seen one before. Here have we been sailing along the Irish coast for a whole day, and not a single *tree* have I yet seen !"

It was too true. Barren are the mountains of Donegal, no trees are to be seen; and it is no wonder that an American should be struck with astonishment, just arriving from his own well-wooded shores.

The moon was shining brightly when we came up with the island of " Rathlin," or " Raghery;" but the tide ran so strongly against us we passed it very slowly, notwithstanding we had a stiff breeze in our favor. As Mr. Randolph gazed upon its rugged shore, he said :

" *That* island I have wished much to see, sir. I suppose that you are aware that its inhabitants are a most peculiar race. They look down with contempt upon the ' *Continent*,' as they call Ireland (only three miles distant); and the greatest curse known to them is, ' May Ireland be your latter end.' They have their own laws and usages; intermarrying among themselves; pay great deference to their landlord and priest; *smuggle* a little for an *honest* livelihood; and the severest punishment practised among them is, *banishment* to *Ireland !*"

Next day we ran down the Channel, passing and meeting hundreds of vessels, from the stately Indiaman to the small fishing-smack. The American vessels were easily discovered from the British, by their *white* canvas, bright sides, and sharp bows. It was a very exciting scene, and Randolph was in fine spirits. The sight of Old England brought back the " olden time" to his memory, and he shed tears of delight.

" Thank God," exclaimed he, " that I have lived to behold the land of Shakspeare, of Milton, of my forefathers ! May her greatness increase through all time !"

It was past eleven o'clock at night when we reached the dock, and we remained on board till next morning. Before parting, Randolph said to me, " I do not wish you to tell any one that I am here. I do not covet any attentions, at present, sir. I have come to England *to see, and not to be seen ; to hear, and not to be heard.* I don't want to be made a lion of, sir. *You* understand me. I have formed a friendship for you, which I hope will be continued, sir ; and when you come to London, you must instantly inform me of your arrival ; *there* is my address, sir. God bless you ; and remember you tell your father *not to give you whisky punch or novels.*"

LONDON, May 27th, 1822.   Monday.

MY DEAR BET: On Saturday I had the pleasure to receive your letter of the 10th of last month ; and a great one it was ; for, altho' I took somewhat of a French leave of you, I do assure you, my dear, that " my thoughts, too, were with you on the ocean." Among my treasures I brought a packet, containing all the letters I have ever received from you ; and the reading over these, and talking of you to a young Irish gentleman, whose acquaintance I happened to make on board the steamboat, was the chief solace of my voyage. It was a short one, although a part of it was somewhat boisterous, and the press of sail carried by our ships (the packets more especially), when those of other nations are under reefed and double-reefed topsails, exposes them to greater danger, while it shortens their voyage ; and yet, such is the skill of our seamen, that insurance is no higher upon our bottoms than upon European ones. Indeed, our voyages reminded me of our tobacco crop. You see I can't " sink the tailor." The vessel is out so short a time that she avoids many dangers to which dull sailers are exposed.

We made the coast of Ireland at noon on Good Friday, and at twelve on the following night we were safe in the Regent's Dock, in Liverpool. When you consider that we had to come the North Passage (that is, between the coast of Ireland and Scotland), and crooked as our path was, to go out of our way to Holyhead for a pilot, it was an astonishing run. The first land we made in Ireland was Runardallah (liquid *n,* as in Spanish), or the Bloody Foreland, bearing on our lee (starboard), bore S. S. E. 6 leagues—an ominous name. Falconer's beautiful poem, The Shipwreck, will render you mistress of the sea-phrases. The coast of Donegal, far as the eye can reach, is lonely, desolate, and naked ; not a tree to be seen, and a single Martello tower the only evidence that it was the dwelling-place of man Not even a sail was in sight ; and I felt a sensation of sadness and desolation, for we seemed more forsaken and abandoned than when surrounded only by the world of waters. This is the coast to which our honest American (naturalized) merchants smuggle tobacco, when piracy under Arligan colors or the slave-trade is dull. Tory island rises like the ruins of some gigantic castle, out of the sea. I presume that it is basaltic, like the Giant's Causeway, of which we could not get a distinct view; but Fairhead amply compensated us. I must not forget, however, the beautiful revolving light of Ennistra Hull, which at regular intervals of time broke upon us like a brilliant meteor, and then died away; while that on the Mull of Contire (mistaken by our captain, who had never gone the North Passage before, for Rachlin, or Rahery, as the Irish call it) was barely visible. It is a fixed light, and a very bad one. After passing Fairhead, I "turned in," and was called up at dawn to see Ailsa Craig, which our captain maintained would be too far distant to be seen in our course, while I as stoutly declared we must see it if we had light. And here, by the way, my dear, I found my knowledge of geography always gave me the advantage over my companions, and rendered every object doubly interesting. The Irish Channel swarmed with shipping, and as we "neared" the Isle of Man, and her Calf, I looked out for Dirck Hatteraick and his lugger. We hugged the Irish shore—Port Patrick, a nice little white town on our right; but the green hills of Erin were as "brown as a berry." When we came in sight of the entrance into Strangford Lock, I longed to go ashore and see Mrs. Cunningham, at Dundrum. Tell this to my friend Ed. C., and give my love to Mrs. Ariana, and the whole firm. Holyhead is a fine object; so is the Isle of Anglesea. At the first glance I recognized the Parry's Mine mountain, with Lord Grosvenor's copper treasures; and Gray's Bard rushed into my mind at the sight of the Carnarvonshire hills, with Snowdon overtopping them all—still, not a tree to be seen. The fields of Man are divided by stone "march-dykes," and the houses are without shade, or shelter from the bleak easterly winds. The floating light off Hoyle-sands, which we passed with the speed of a racehorse—a strong current and stiff breeze in our favor—was a most striking object. One view of it represented a clergyman preaching by candlelight, the centre light being the head; and the two others gave a lively picture of impassioned gesture of the arms, as they were tossed up and down.

Although our pilot, and the captain too, declared the thing to be impossible, we did get "round the rock," and passing a forest of masts in the Mersey, were safely moored at quarter-past twelve. in the dock, where ships are put away under lock and key, like books in a book-case.

After a very sound and refreshing sleep, I rose and went ashore, in search of breakfast—for not a spark of fire, not even a candle or lamp, can be brought into the dock, on any pretext whatsoever. At the landward gate I stopped, expecting to be searched, but the guard did not even make his appearance; so on I passed with little Jem, a wicked dog of a cabin-boy, carrying my bundle, to the King's Arms, in Castle street; but I had hardly commenced my breakfast, when the femme d'affaires, in the person of a strapping Welsh wench, who had tried before to put me up two pair of stairs, entered the room, and with well dissembled dismay " begged my pardon, but the room was engaged (it was the best in the house) for the Lord Bishop of the Isle of Man, and the—the—the Dean of—of Canterbury." Here again my knowledge of England, to say nothing of innkeepers, stood me in good stead. I coolly replied that they would hardly arrive before I had finished breakfast, and requested to see her master or mistress, as the case might be. " Mrs. Jones was sick," but her niece would wait on me. She came in the person of a pretty young married woman; and now the tale varied to " the room being engaged for a family daily expected." " The name ?" " The name had not been given—was very sorry for the mistake," &c. " Mistakes, madam, must be rectified; as soon as this nameless family arrives, I will make my bow and give up the parlor." " Very handsome, and very genteel, and a thousand thanks"—and a courtesy at every word. Next day, the arrival of a regiment from Ireland unlocked the whole mystery. The room was wanted for the officers. And here, my dear, I am sorry to say that, except by cross-examination, I have not obtained a word of truth from any of the lower orders in this country. I think that in this respect, as well as in honesty, our slaves greatly excel them. In urbanity they are also far superior. Now, don't you tell this to any body—not even to your father—but keep the fact to yourself, for a reason that I will communicate to you when I see you; and a very important one it is.

After receiving every civility from the collector, Mr. Swainson, and from my countrymen, Mr. James King, Mr. Maury, and Mr. Haggerty, and seeing the docks, and the Islington market, I was impatient to leave Liverpool, which bears the impress of trade upon it, and is, of course, as dull as dull can be. The market is of new erection, and I believe altogether unique—far surpassing even that of Philadelphia, not only in the arrangement (which is that of a square, roofed, well lighted, and unencumbered with carts, and unannoyed by a public street on each side of it), but in the variety and delicacy of its provisions. Here, for the first time, I saw a turbot, and Mr. King bought half a one for our dinner, for which he paid half a guinea. The variety and profesion of the vegetables, and the neat, rosy-cheeked " Lancashire witches," that sprinkled them with water to keep them fresh, who were critically clean in their dress and persons, was a most delightful spectacle. Whatever you buy is taken home for you by women whose vocation it is; and Mr. King's house is two miles off, at the beautiful village of Everton, commanding a fine view of the Mersey and the opposite coast of Cheshire. For a full account of Liverpool, see its "Picture," at Roanoke, where you will find, if you have them not, the other books referred to in this letter, and I shall write, by this packet, to Leigh, to send them to you. The packets sail with the punctuality of stage-coaches, and arrive almost as regularly. The Albion formed the first and most melancholly exception. We were long kept in painful suspense respecting the names of the passengers. I was afraid that my unfortunate friend Tubœuf was one of the "five Frenchmen." The Mr. Clark, and lady, I take for granted is an old acquaintance, George Clark, of Albany, son of a former royal governor of New-York, and a man of very large estate, returning with his wife to England, after fifteen or twenty years' absence. Dupont may be another very old acquaintance, whom I knew thirty-four years ago in New-York, and saw in Charleston in 1796, and a few months ago in Washington. His name is Victor Dupont, son of D—— de Nemours, and brother of Irenè D. They have a large powder and woollen manufactory on the Brandywine, in Delaware. Tubœuf, I see, had not left the U. S. Both he and Dupont told me they were about to cross the Atlantic. The history of the former is the "romance of real life." In education and feeling, he is more than half a Virginian. His father was killed by the Indians when he was a child, and he knows the rifle, hunting-shirt, and moccasons. His father was the friend of my near and dear relative, Jack Banister, of Battersea. When Tubœuf l'ainè arrived at City Point he found his young friend had been dead several years. This connection determined him to Virginia, and he went out to the Holston country, where he was killed, and where the son lived until manhood. But I shall never get off from Liverpool.

On Wednesday morning, April 10th, I set out alone, in a post-chaise; and now you must take an extract from my "log-book."

Verdure beautiful; moss on youngest trees shows dampness of climate. Dr. Solomon and Gilead House. The Doctor dead, but quackery is immortal. Highfield, the seat of Mrs. Parke, on the right; very fine object. Around Liverpool, in their fine pastures, I saw the most wretched looking horses, and even cows—not a good horse in the town. To Prescot, with a fine view of Knowsley Park, and a glimpse of the house. Legs of Man, (the arms of the Isle of Man are three legs, and the Stanleys, Earls of Derby, were lords of Man, as Shakspeare will tell you, Hen. VI.) The park-keeper in the kitchen—send for him and talk about the horses; all in training on Delamere forest, except old Milo and one other. The Earl and Countess in town, (this always means London κατεξοχην. Mr. G. will decipher and translate my Greek for you.) So is Lord Stanley, the Earl's eldest son, who represents the county in Parliament. Cross the Sankey canal, the first executed in England. Soon after, **pass**

under the Bridgewater canal. To Warrington, Nag's Head , cross
the Mersey, and enter Cheshire. At High Leigh, West Hall, Eger-
ton Leigh, Esq., (the road-book falsely places this seat beyond Knutsford), and High Leigh (or East) Hall, Geo. Leigh, Esq. See Debrett's
Baronetage. At Mere, which, as the name imports, is a beautiful
sheet of natural water, too small to be dignified with the name of
lake, but large enough to be quite rough with the wind, I came to
the first descent that could be called a hill; for although hills and
mountains too were in sight all around me, the roads are conducted
on a level. On the right is Mere Hall, Peter L. Brooke, Esq., a fine
seat. I ought to mention that all the seats are embosomed in fine
woods. There were some noble pines at High Leigh, which a Virginian overseer would soon have down for tobacco sticks. The houses
of the poorest people are adorned with honeysuckles, and have flower
pots in the windows, with geraniums, &c. Dear Mrs. Bell, I thought
of her at every step; and, by the way, Mr. G. writes that she was in
Richmond on the 26th, and well, although he does not say a word of
a certain E. T. C., or, indeed, any body else but the Brockenbro's,
and to them he allows not quite a line. His letter of a page and a
half is most provokingly concise. What there is of it is horribly
stuffed with epithets of war, and what not, about " Fox, and Burke,
and Pitt, and Brutus, and Cassius, and Junius, and Rome ;" descending by regular anti-climax to " Russia, and Poletica, and Adams."
Pray tell him from me, that I could hardly have expected much
worse even from Mr. Walsh, if I had the misfortune to be afflicted
with his correspondence. And I had rather have heard of old Aggy
than all those fine ancients and would-be-fine moderns. Now, this from
Frank G., who can write so well, and so much to the purpose, is too
bad. I assure you, reading the result of the election of Ned Mayo, in
Henrico, was more interesting.

Before reaching Knutsford, I travelled along the huge, high wall
of Tatton Park, twelve miles in circumference. It extends to the
very town. Dine at Knutsford, and drive into the park ; superb domain ; fine sheet of water on the right, with a view of the Lancashire
hills, about Worsley. For the sixth time to-day it snowed. Returned, and struck off from the London road, to Northwich, to see
the mines of fossil salt.

On the right of Northwich is the seat, and a very fine one it is,
of Sir John Stanley, who married the eldest daughter of Gibbon's
friend, Lord Sheffield. I felt when I saw him at Chester, as if he
was an old acquaintance. He was foreman of the grand jury, and
had his hands full of business, for there were seventy felons against
whom bills were preferred. I breakfasted at a small inn, at Sandy-
way head, having passed through a road of heavy and deep sand,
with considerable hills. But before reaching S. H., I made the

postillion drive through Vale Royal Park, the proprietor of which, Thomas Cholmondeley, Esq., is one of the new coronation peers, by the title of Lord Delamere. With the names and proprietors of all these places I was as familiarly acquainted as if I had lived all my life in the palatinate. Nothing can be more beautiful than these parks. Here I saw that *rara avis* (rare bird) the black swan, in company with white ones. I drove about two miles and a half before I reached the house, when I caused the postillion to return. There was no fear of disturbing the family, although his lordship had returned from town the day preceding, for it was only six o'clock, and the great in England seldom leave their beds before noon. The whole establishment, although not so great as Tatton, is princely. I told the keepers of the lodges, who were very grateful for their shillings, to tell Lord D., if he asked, that a foreign gentleman travelling for his health had taken the liberty to drive through his beautiful grounds. Over Delamere forest, a rough, barren tract, for eight miles. Very likely government have inclosed and planted it, for the "forest" contained not a tree or shrub; and individuals also have done much in this way. At present the trees are almost knee high. At Kelsah we leave the forest and emerge into the rich pastures and meadows of Cheshire. To Chester—the Albion hotel; drive to Eaton Hall, Lord Grosvenor's; return—dine; misconduct of innkeeper, who put me into his own filthy bed-chamber; (town full, it being assize time). Remove to the Royal hotel; visit the cathedral, "and let my due feet never fail to walk the studious cloisters pale," &c. At every turn since I came from Liverpool, I have been breaking out into quotations from Milton and Shakspeare. Bad Latin in a bishop; epitaph; and worse scholars in the Royal School. None of the boys could give the Latin of their coronation banner, and I offered half a guinea to him who would complete the following lines: "Vir bonus est quis? Qui consulta patruum, qui,"—and translate them. Only one boy could supply "leges juraque servat," and he began "Vir bonus est quis"—"He is a good man"—so I took up my half guinea and walked out, thinking of Mr. Brougham and his bill. To the Castle—here two boys arraigned for robbery.

Saturday—through Eaton Park; see the horses and grounds, and pheasants, and hares, and deer, and stables—in comparison with which last, the finest house I ever saw in America is a mere hovel. (I except the public buildings at Washington, and the Bank of Pennsylvania.) To *Wrexham*, in Wales, which principality I entered six miles from Chester. Near W., on the left, is a magnificent entrance into Acton Park, Sir Foster Cunliffe's, with greyhounds, in stone, on the gates. Cross the Dee, to Overton, eight miles. The beauty of this country throws all that I have seen before or since into the shade. Nothing can be imagined finer. The village of Overton is a perfect paradise, and the vale of Dee is more like fairy-land than real earth and water. Mr. Price's seat, at Bryxypys, surpasses all I have seen yet. To *Ellesmere*—Bridgewater arms. The Earl of B. has a great estate here. The mere very beautiful. Dine, and go on to Shrewsbury. Country changes, and becomes comparatively ugly. To the Lion inn, at Shrewsbury. Sunday—drive through a lovely country, to Battlefield church, five miles, on the very site of the battle ground where Harry Percy's spur became cold; mound of the slain. Parish clerk and wife true English cottagers. Sunday school of clean, fine children. Rev. Mr. Williams, of Battlefield, preaches to a congregation of rustics a truly evangelical sermon. Church perfectly clean; rush mats to kneel on. How different from Chester cathedral. Only equipage a single "taxed cart." Mr. Williams preached at Effington in the evening. Returned the same road to Shrewsbury; ascended Lord Hill's column—most heavenly view. Remember that I am now on the Severn, and turn to Gray's Letters. Leave the Lion, and my friend Bourne, the head waiter, and the truly respectable landlady, with regret I hope on all sides, and go on, with sleek, fine horses, and clean chaise, and obliging driver, to Ironbridge, thirteen miles, where I changed chaise and horses, and crossing the Severn a second time, over the bridge of one arch, ascended a mountainous hill on the other side, through Madely market. These are the greatest iron works (Colebrooke Dale) in England. To Bridgeworth, seven miles, to sup and sleep. This town pleases me more than any I have seen before or since. It is old, clean, pleasant, romantic, with no commercial, manufacturing, or fashionable *taint* about it. Cheltenham sickened me of the last.

Monday, 15th—wound round the high hill of red stone; stopped; ascended to the ruin of the castle and the church; ludicrous epitaph; returned to the chaise, and completed our descent to the Severn, "the very principal light and capital feature of my journey," which I again crossed. Stopped at a small house of call to beg an idle pin. Old man and wife show me their cows; their tenderness to the motherless lamb, and pity of me. Their gratitude to their cow, which, said the dame, "when my house was burnt, maintained our whole family, old and unsightly as she looks, but making me   pounds of butter a week." Cætera desunt.

Monday, past 12, May 27, 1822.

My dear Bet,—When, a few minutes ago, I wrote "cetera desunt," as I folded my letter which young Mr. Hammond waited to the last minute to take to Liverpool, I did not know that the beginning, as well as the conclusion, was wanting. I now inclose it to Mr. H., with a request that he will put the two under one cover, and address it to your father—as he promised to do with the first—for it was to avoid exposing your name to strangers, that I got him to take the letter. He carries a map of the city, in which the new improvements are laid down; with this, and the Ambulator, and the Pictures of London (all at Roanoke), and Smith's English Atlas (also there), you can travel with me without once mistaking your way, and, I hope, pleasantly, as well as easily.

I left the old farmer (Evans) and his dame (for he has a small farm under Mr. Whittemore, member for the borough of Bridgenorth), as well as his ale-house. I left the old couple fondling their lamb, and caressing it and their kine—one a Hereford red, with a fine calf, which they had been debating about selling to the butcher; but at last their affections got the better of their poverty, and the old man concluded, by saying, it would be a pity to kill the poor thing, and he would e'en keep it for the mother's sake. Although I stopped for a pin to fasten up the envious curtain behind the chaise, yet I asked for a draught of milk, warm from the favorite cow, which was given to me in a clean porringer, with a face of as true benevolence as I ever saw. On taking leave, I asked to contribute towards the rebuilding of the burnt house, telling them it was the custom in the country I came from. But the old man, with a face of great surprise, said, " I was kindly welcome to the milk; it was a thing of nothing;" and they both rejected the money (only two half-crowns), until I told them they must oblige me by accepting it, or I should be ashamed of having such a trifle returned. Whereupon the gude man said he would give the postillion with the return chaise a skinful of his best ale, when he came back; and the dame, ascribing her good fortune to the mercy shown to the calf, promised, at my request, to remember me, in her prayers, as the sick stranger to whom she had ministered; and I left them, with feelings of deep respect for their honest poverty and kind-heartedness. Mr. Whittemore is a great proprietor here. His great house, on the right, is under repair, and he occupies a " cottage" in the village; about such a house as Mr. Wickham's. His poor tenant at Quat is the third instance I have met with of a person refusing money here. The first was the parish-clerk, at Battlefield; the next, Bourne, the head-waiter at the Lion; a thing hardly credible in England, where the rapacity of this class, in particular, is proverbial; for—asking Mr. Wickham's pardon for making free with his person, as well as his house—you meet with as well dressed persons as himself who will make you a low bow for sixpence; aye, and beg for it, to boot. I thought a thousand times of Mr. Wickham's speech. Plunder is the order of the day. Shopkeepers, tradesmen, but, above all, innkeepers, waiters, postillions. ostlers, and chambermaids, fleece you without mercy; all is venal. Pray remember the boots ! Something for the waiter, sir !—and this at a coffee-house where you have only stepped in to take a glass of negus, after a play, and have paid a double price for it. You can't get a reply to the plainest question without paying for it, unless you go into a shop; and to speak to one whom you don't know, is received with an air as if you had clapped a pistol to his breast.

But I should do the greatest injustice were I not to say, that the higher ranks—a few despicable and despised fashionables excepted—are as unpretending and plain as our old-fashioned Virginian gentlemen, whom they greatly resemble. This class of men is now nearly extinct, to my great grief, and the shame and loss of our country. They are as distinct from the present race in their manners, dress, principles, and every thing but anatomical structure, as an eagle is from a pig, or a wild turkey from a turkey-buzzard. The English gentleman is not graceful, not affable, but plain, sincere, kind, without one particle of pretension in dress, manner, or any thing else.

At Kidderminster, I breakfasted (15 miles), and saw the carpet manufactory, and bought four hearth rugs. I also visited the old church, as was my custom, and copied an epitaph, not on the rich and great, but a poor sergeant, erected by his colonel; I mean the monument was, not the epitaph. We entered Worcestershire some miles before we reached Kidderminster. It is perhaps the finest county in the kingdom, take it for all and all. Among the seats between Kidderminster and Worcester, are Halleburg; the Bp. of W.'s, where the pigs (hogs, we should call them,) were in the beautiful grounds; Waverley House, Mrs. Orange, a rich widow lady, with an only daughter, unmarried—this is one of the prettiest and finest places I have seen; Sir John Fleming Leicester's, between Knutsford and Northwich (which I just remember to have omitted), is another very capital place; and I am sure I have not mentioned a thousand superior to any thing we have. But the air of comfort and fatness since we left Lancashire, is very refreshing. The houses are old and weather-stained, but clean to fastidiousness; some of framework, filled in with brick; the timbers black, and the brick-work overcast with lime, and white as this paper; casement-lights, leaden sashes, &c. Ombresley Court, Lady Downshire's, which is the ancient seat of the Sandys family, is a fine place. She is a Sandys, and Baroness S. in her own right. I thought of Walpole and Pulteney, and her progenitor who sunk into a peerage.

At Worcester, in driving into the Hop Pole Inn yard, the postillion had nearly killed a poor girl, with a child in her arms. She was thrown down, but, God be praised! neither were hurt. I would not endure what I felt while the suspense lasted for any consideration. Town full. Quarter sessions. Cleanest and prettiest town (a city) that I have yet seen. Determined to remain, and see the cathedral; but next morning I determined otherwise.

Giving up, for the present, my pilgrimage to Cheltenham, I set out on the top of the coach, paying 12 shillings for my fare to London, and through the Vale of Evesham, and an enchanting country through Pershire, Bengeworth, Morton, Broadway (where is a tremendous hill, commanding the whole vale and the Malvern Hills), Morton, Woodstock, Oxford, a city of palaces.

And here, my dear Bet, I must again abruptly close this long-winded epistle, with assurances of my exalted regard.

J. R. OF R.

I broke open this letter myself.

CHAPTER XXI.

INCIDENTS IN ENGLAND.

IN the month of June, says Mr. Harvey, I went over to London, accompanied by my father, who had been summoned to attend a committee of the House of Commons, to give evidence in a case of some importance. I had prepared my father for an introduction to my most eccentric friend, and yet, when I did introduce him, he could scarcely refrain from smiling. "Sir," said Mr. Randolph, "I am proud to make the acquaintance of the son of that man who received the thanks of Congress for his kindness to my poor countrymen. *Your* son, my young friend here, sir, tells me he has delivered my letter, and I hope you will soon receive the books from my bookseller in Washington. Keep them as a momento of my friendship, sir." My father thanked him warmly for his kindness, and we entered into a general conversation. Suddenly Randolph rose from his chair, and, in his most imposing manner, thus addressed him : " Mr. H——, two days ago I saw the greatest curiosity in London ; aye, and in England, too, sir—compared to which, Westminster Abbey, the Tower, Somerset House, the British Museum, nay Parliament itself, sink into utter insignificance ! I have seen, sir, Elizabeth Fry, of Newgate, and I have witnessed there, sir, miraculous effects of true Christianity upon the most depraved of human beings—*bad women*, sir, who are worse, if possible, than the devil himself ! and yet the wretched outcasts have been tamed and subdued by the *Christian eloquence* of Mrs. Fry! I have seen them weep repentant tears whilst she addressed them. I have heard their groans of despair, sir! Nothing but *religion* can effect this *miracle*, sir; for what *can* be a greater *miracle* than the conversion of a degraded, sinful woman, taken from the very dregs of society! Oh! sir, it was a sight worthy the attention of angels! *You* must, also, see this wonder, sir; and, by the way, *this* is one of her visiting days—let us go at once; we shall just be in time. She has given me permission to bring any of my friends with me. I shall introduce you, sir, with great pleasure." We immediately ordered a coach, and drove to Mrs. Fry's house, but found, to our no small disappointment, that she was not in town that day.

It was my good fortune, afterwards, to become acquainted with Mrs. Fry, and to spend a day or two at her country-seat, near London, and I need scarcely add, that my admiration of her character was, if possible, increased by this introduction into her social circle. In the course of conversation, I said to Miss Fry, "Pray tell me in what way you became acquainted with my eccentric friend Randolph?" "Why," replied she, "in rather an *eccentric* way. One day my mother was in town, getting ready to go to Newgate, when a stranger was announced. A tall, thin gentleman, with long hair, and very strangely dressed, entered the parlor, walked deliberately up to my mother, who rose to receive him, and held out his hand, saying, in the sweet tone of a lady's voice, 'I feel I have some right to introduce myself to Elizabeth Fry, as I am the friend of her friend, Jessy Kersey, of Philadelphia, (a celebrated preacher in the Society of Friends). I am John Randolph, of Roanoke, State of Virginia; the fellow countryman of Washington.' My mother, who had heard a great deal of him from different persons, gave him a cordial reception; and was so extremely pleased with his most original conversation, she not only took him with her to Newgate, but invited him to come and see us. We have since seen him several times, and have been highly delighted with him. Last week some strangers were to dine with us, and my mother invited him to be of the number. In writing the note of invitation, I apologized to him for naming so unfashionably early an hour as *four o'clock*, knowing that at the *west end* he never dined before *eight*. His reply was quite characteristic, and made us all laugh heartily. Here it is: 'Mr. Randolph regrets that a prior engagement will deprive him of the pleasure of dining with Mrs. Fry on Thursday next.   No apology, however, was necessary for the *early* hour named in her note, as it is *two hours later* than Mr. R. is accustomed to dine in Virginia; and he has not yet been long enough in London to learn how to turn day into night, and vice versa.' "

I told Randolph, next day, that I had seen his note.   " Well, sir," said he, " and was I not right to be candid?   Mrs. Fry is a most sensible woman, sir, and she shows her good taste by opposing the foolish customs of the aristocracy; and I wanted her to know that I agreed with her, sir.   I can go all but the late dinners; they are killing me, sir; and I must quickly run away from London, or *cut* my noble acquaintances."

Before my arrival in London, Lord L——, meeting Randolph one night, under the gallery of the House of Commons, introduced himself to him, and they became very intimate.   His lordship said to me one day afterwards, " I have never met with so thoroughly well-informed a gentleman as your friend Randolph, no matter what the subject—history, belles-lettres, biography; but, sir, the most astonishing part of all is, that he possesses a minute local knowledge of England and Ireland.   I thought that I knew them well, but I assure you I was obliged to yield the palm to him.   I have purposely tried to puzzle or confuse him, but all in vain.   His conversational powers are most dazzling, even in London, sir, where we pride ourselves on good talkers.   I never have been so much struck with any stranger; and although a high tory, I always forgot that *he* was a republican.   By the way, not a very *bigoted* one, sir.   I never heard him abuse the *aristocracy !*   I was so much pleased with him, on our first interview, I determined to pay him a mark of respect, which I was sure would gratify his Virginia pride.   I solicited permission from the Lord Chancellor, to introduce Mr. Randolph, as a distinguished American, into the House of Lords, by the *private* entrance, near the throne, instead of obliging him to force his way, with the crowd, at the common entrance.   Having obtained his lordship's consent, I then introduced Mr. Randolph to the door-keeper, and desired him to admit him whenever he presented himself, without requiring him to exhibit any special order.   His figure and whole appearance are so singular, I ran no risk in having any *counterfeit Randolphs,*— and I said so to the door-keeper, as some excuse for omitting our usual practice. When I told him of his privilege, I saw at once that I had won my way to his heart; and amply has he repaid me, sir, by the richness of his conversations whenever we have since met."

A few days after my arrival in London, continues Mr. Harvey, I had an opportunity of testing the value of this privilege of private entry. It will be recollected that George Canning, in the year 1822, just previous to his *intended* departure as governor-general of India (which never took place, owing to Lord Castlereagh's death), introduced, and carried through the House of Commons, the "Roman Catholic Peers' bill," as it was called, which he intended as a farewell legacy to his countrymen. It passed by a handsome majority, and was then sent to undergo the fiery ordeal of the House of Lords. The subject engrossed public attention, and there was great anxiety to attend the debate on the appointed night. The Marquis of L—— was kind enough to present me with an order to admit two persons—myself and friend—and I returned to our lodgings in great glee. There I found Randolph, told him of my good luck, and offered him the unoccupied half of my order.

"Pray, sir," said he " at which *door* do *you* intend to enter the House ?

"At the *lower* door, of course," replied I " where all strangers enter."

"Not *all* strangers if you please," said he, "for I shall enter at the *private* door, near the throne !" " Oh, my dear sir," replied I, " your privilege, I dare say, will answer on any common occasion; but to-night the members of the House of Commons will entirely fill the space around the throne, and *no* stranger, depend upon it, will be admitted there. So be wise, and don't refuse this chance, or you will regret it."

"What sir," retorted he, "do you suppose I would consent to struggle with and push through the crowd of persons who, for two long hours, must fight their way in at the *lower* door ? Oh no, sir! I shall do no such thing; and if I cannot enter as a gentleman commoner, I go not at all !"

After vainly endeavoring to induce him to change his mind, we separated; *he* for the aristocratic entrance, I for the common one. With great difficulty, and wondering how I had preserved my coat-tails whole, I finally squeezed myself into the House, half suffocated, and was fortunate enough (being then young and active) to secure a *stand* at the bar, from whence I could see my noble lord's face, and hear every word that was spoken. Casting a glance towards the throne soon after my entrance, to my no small surprise and *envy*, I beheld " Randolph of Roanoke " in all his glory, walking in most leisurely, and perfectly at home, along-side of Canning, Lord Castlereagh, Sir Robert Peel, and many other distinguished members of the House of Commons. Some of these gentlemen even selected for him a prominent position, where he could see and hear perfectly, and I observed many courtesies passing between them during the night. Very shortly after Mr. Randolph's arrival in London, a splendid ball was given, under the immediate patronage of George the Fourth and the principal nobility, for the benefit of the poor Irish peasantry of Munster and Connaught, who were suffering from the effects of famine, attended as usual by disease. It was a magnificent affair, Randolph attended, glad of an opportunity to give his mite, and to behold at the same time the congregated aristocracy of Great Britain. " It was cheap, sir, very cheap " said he to me, " actors and actresses innumerable, and all dressed out most gorgeously. There were jewels enough, sir, there, to make new crowns for all the monarchs of Europe! And I, too, *republican* though I am, must needs go in court-dress ! Well sir, don't imagine that I was so foolish as to *purchase* a new suit, at a cost of twenty-five or thirty guineas. Oh no! I have not studied London life for nothing. I have been told, sir, that many a noble lady would appear at the ball that night with jewels *hired* for the occasion ; and I took the hint, sir, and *hired* a full court-dress for five guineas. When I beheld myself in the glass, I laughed at the oddity of my appearance, and congratulated myself that I was three thousand miles from Charlotte Court-House. Had I played the harlequin *there*, sir, I think my next election would be doubtful. I stole into the room, with rather a nervous walk, and was about selecting a very quiet position in a corner, when your countryman, Lord Castlereagh, seeing my embarrassment, came forward, and with an air of the most finished politeness, insisted upon being my chaperon. For one hour he devoted himself to me, and pointed out all persons of notoriety in the crowd as they passed us in review. Such was the fascination of his manners, I forgot, for the moment, that I was speaking to the man who had sold his country's independence *and his own;* who had lent his aid to a licentious monarch to destroy his queen, who, if guilty, might point to her husband's conduct as the cause of her fall. But, sir, I was spellbound for that hour, for never did I meet a more accomplished gentleman; and yet he is a deceitful politician, whose *character* none can admire. An *Irish* tory, sir, I never could abide." Miss Edgeworth and Randolph met together for the first time at the breakfast-table of a very distinguished Irish member of Parliament (now a peer of the realm). The gentleman to whom I refer, told me that it was an intellectual feast, such as he had rarely enjoyed before. To use his own words:

"Spark produced spark, and for three hours they kept up the fire, until it ended in a perfect blaze of wit, humor, and repartee. It appeared to me that Mr. R. was more intimately acquainted with Miss Edgeworth's works than she was herself. He frequently quoted passages where her memory was at fault; and he brought forward every character of any note in all her productions: but what most astonished us was, his intimate knowledge of Ireland. Lady T—— and myself did nothing but listen; and I was really vexed when some public business called me away."

"Who do you think I met under the gallery of the House of Commons?" said Randolph to me one day. "You can't guess, and so I'll tell you. There was a spruce, dapper little gentleman sitting next to me, and he made some trifling remark, to which I replied. We then entered into conversation, and I found him a most fascinating witty fellow. He pointed out to me the distinguished members who were unknown to me, and frequently gave them a friendly shot. At parting, he handed me his card, and I read with some surprise, 'Mr. Thomas Moore.' Yes, sir, it *was* the 'Bard of Erin;' and upon this discovery I said to him, 'Well, Mr. Moore, I am delighted to meet you thus; and I tell you, sir, that I envy you more for being the author of the "Twopenny Post-bag" and "Tom Crib's Memorial to Congress," than for *all* your beautiful songs, which play the fool with young ladies' hearts.' He laughed heartily at what he called my 'singular taste,' and we parted the best friends imaginable."

Mr. Randolph was present at a large meeting of the African Institution at London. Mr. Wilberforce, after speaking with his usual ability and eloquence on the appropriate subjects of the occasion, concluded by pronouncing a warm panegyric upon the example set by the United States of America, in making the slave-trade piracy, and upon Mr. Randolph's great efforts in promoting that act.

Mr. Randolph then rose to return thanks for the mark of respect towards the United States of America. After a few appropriate remarks, he thanked the meeting for the grateful sense they had expressed towards America; and also assured them that all that was exalted in station, in talent, and in moral character among his countrymen, was (as was also to be found in England) firmly united for the suppression of this infamous traffic. It was delightful to him to know that Virginia, the land of his sires, the place of his nativity, had for half a century affixed a public brand and indelible stigma upon this traffic, and had put in the claim of the wretched objects of it to the common rights and attributes of humanity.

The plainness of Mr. Randolph's appearance, says a London paper, his republican simplicity of manners, and easy and unaffected address, attracted much attention, and he sat down amidst a burst of applause.

Mr. Randolph travelled extensively in England and Scotland, met a flattering and distinguished reception wherever he went, was pleased with every thing, and delighted every body with his cordial manner and fascinating conversation. He returned to the United States about the last of November, and was present during the last session of the seventeenth Congress, which, on the 3d of March, 1823, was closed; but he did not open his lips on any occasion whatever; indeed there was no discussion of any importance during the session. Immediately on the adjournment he hurried off to Virginia, and spent some days with his friend, William R. Johnson, in Chesterfield, who was then in high training for the great match race between the North and the South. The exercise and excitement of mind in anticipation of his favorite sport produced an evident change in Mr. Randolph's health; it was much improved; he slept better than he had for ten years.

"To that night," says he, "spent on a shuck matress in a little garret room at Chesterfield Court-house, Sunday, March the 9th, 1823, I look back with delight. It was a stormy night. The windows clattered, and William R. Johnson got up several times to try and put a stop to the noise, by thrusting a glove between the loose sashes. I heard the noise; I even heard him; but it did not disturb me. I enjoyed a sweet nap of eight hours, during which, he said, he never heard me breathe. N. B. I had fasted all day, and supped (which I have not done since) on a soft egg and a bit of biscuit. My feelings next day were as new and delightful as those of any bride the day after her nuptials, and the impression (on memory at least) as strong."

He was present (as most lovers of the turf were) at the celebrated race between Eclipse and Henry, on the Long Island Course, in the month of May. He stood in a very conspicuous place on the stand during the race, surrounded by gentlemen of the North and the South; and he evidently was very confident of the success of Henry. But after the result, to him so unexpected, and while the thousands of spectators were vociferously applauding the successful rider (Purdy), Mr. Randolph gave vent to his great disappointment by exclaiming to those around him in his most satirical tone:

"Well, gentlemen, it is a lucky thing for the country that the President of the United States is not elected by acclamation, else Mr. Purdy would be our next President, beyond a doubt."

He then left the ground, and spent the evening with Mr. Rufus King, at Jamaica. Next day he said to a friend, with a sigh:

"Ah, sir! only for that unfortunate vote on the Missouri question, *he* would be our man for the presidency. He is, sir, a genuine English gentleman of the old school; just the right man for these degenerate times. But, alas! it cannot be!"

Mr. Randolph, soon after this event, retired into his usual summer solitude, at Roanoke. Thence, on the 25th of July, he asks Dr. Brockenbrough, "You and Mr. Wickham are wise men, but a bystander, you know, sees the blots of better players than himself. Are you both resolved to die in harness? You may put the question to me, but I tell you NO. March 3, 1825, is the utmost limit of my servitude. But what's the use of talking?—' a man will do what he will do;' a saying, which, like some others, I once took to be rather silly, but which, I have since found out, contains much sense. * * *

"You wouldn't infer it from the tone of this epistle, but I too am sick—seriously sick, as well as home-sick, i. e. as Sir John Brute was wife-sick. My oaks send love and duty to you and the silent Madame, and hope you'll never be as tired of them as their master is. I would go among the *Selvidges*, beyond the 'mountings,' but I dare not encounter Pharaoh's plagues. I'd rather be swallowed up in the Red Sea at once.

"P. S. In sheer distress what to do with myself, I yesterday read Don Juan—the third, fourth and fifth cantos for the first time—fact, I assure you. It is diabolically good. The ablest, I am inclined to think, of all his performances. I now fully comprehend the cause of the odium plusquam theologicum of the lake school, toward this wayward genius. I am not sorry that I had not read the whole when I was in Southey's company. I could not have conversed so unreservedly as I did on the subject of Byron's writings."

In October, he says: "The life I lead here is enough to destroy the intellectual and moral faculty of any human being. It resembles, in many points, solitary confinement. It is the daily recurrence of the same dreary scene; and when evening sets in, so that I cannot read or ride, nothing can be imagined more forlorn. But I struggle through it, as the will of Providence.

"I've received from London some publications on the subject of slavery, that have awakened me more than ever to that momentous question. They are from Wilberforce, T. Clarkson, Adam Hodgson, and a larger pamphlet, entitled 'Negro Slavery as it exists in the U. S. and the West Indies, especially in Jamaica'—that being held up as the negro paradise, by the W. I. body in England."

CHAPTER XXII.

EIGHTEENTH CONGRESS—CONSOLIDATION IS THE ORDER OF THE DAY—"SPEAK A CHEERING WORD TO THE GREEKS."

IN 1822, a leading federalist, one who was conspicuous in the attempt to elect Burr over Jefferson, and was opposed to every measure of the Jefferson and of the Madison administrations, in 1822, made use of these words: "The federalists almost unanimously declared their approbation of the leading measures of the Government, and gave it their cordial support. The National Government, indeed, destroyed the federal party, in the only way it could be destroyed, *by adopting substantially its principles.*" This was true in that "era of good-feeling," when we were "all federalists and all republicans." The seeds of consolidation were sowed broad-cast. But at no period were more rapid strides made toward a prostration of all the barriers of the Constitution, than at the first session of the eighteenth Congress. A general distress pervaded all departments of business. The people were taught to look to Government for relief, and were ready to acquiesce in any measure that gave hopes of present alleviation, without regard to the consequences; and, besides this, there seemed to be a universal madness—a national and individual ambition that o'erleaped all bounds, and embraced the whole world in its aspiring grasp. The body politic seemed to be radically diseased. " You are right," said Randolph, to a friend who was deploring the state of things, " consolidation is the order of the day. The epidemic shows itself in a thousand Protean forms : so was despotism epidemic from the foundations of the world. In that state of the body politic the predisposition turns every pimple to cancer." With this belief, and in this spirit, he met and manfully, though often unsuccessfully, fought each Protean shape, as it successively arose to distil its leprous poison into the Constitution, or to develope the seeds of some gangrenous ulcer, deep festering in the body politic.

The first subject Mr. Randolph met and successfully opposed, was the measure proposed by Congress to be adopted on the Greek question. It will be recollected that the Spanish provinces, Mexico, Peru, New Granada, and others, had been struggling for a long time for their independence. They had been recognized by the United States as independent Republics, and ministers had been sent to reside near their respective governments. But Spain still persisted in her efforts to reconquer her revolted provinces; and it was rumored that aid would be granted her for this purpose, by the allied powers of Europe. In the mean time, the Greeks, also, had revolted from the odious yoke of Turkish despotism, and were fighting with a valor and a success worthy of the better days of Thermopylæ and of Marathon.

In this state of things, the President in his annual message to Congress expressed the opinion that there was reason to hope that the Greeks would be successful in the present struggle with their oppressors, and that the power that has so long crushed them had lost its dominion over them for ever. The same communication contained other matters of great importance, in relation to the rumored combination of foreign sovereigns to interfere in the affairs of South America. Under these circumstances, Mr. Webster thought it was proper and becoming that the communication of the President should receive some response from the House of Representatives. Accordingly, on Monday, December the 8th, 1823, he submitted for consideration a resolution: "That provision ought to be made, by law, for defraying the expense incident to the appointment of an agent, or commissioner, to Greece, whenever the President shall deem it expedient to make such appointment."

On the 19th of January the resolution was called up, and Mr. Webster delivered his sentiments on the subject embraced in it, in a speech of great power, eloquence, and feeling. When he sat down, Mr. Clay introduced a resolution: "That the people of these States would not see, without serious inquietude, any forcible interposition by the allied powers of Europe, in behalf of Spain, to reduce to their former subjection those parts of the continent of America which have proclaimed and established for themselves, respectively, independent governments, and which have been solemnly recognized by the United States." Thus the whole field of foreign politics was brought within the scope of the debate.

Next day Mr. Poinsett delivered his sentiments at length on the subject, and concluded by moving a modification of Mr. Webster's resolution, so as merely to express the sympathy of the nation for the suffering Greeks, and the interest felt by the Government in their welfare and success. Mr. Clay then followed and expressed himself with great force. It was, indeed, a glorious theme! wide as the sufferings of humanity; deep as the love of liberty in the breast of man. It was a subject that took hold on the hearts of the people; predisposed to sympathize with nations struggling against despotism every where, how could they resist the appeals of the glorious descendants of Leonidas, and of Epaminondas, and Philopœmen; aided, too, by the condensed logic of Webster, the varied learning of Poinsett, and the fervid eloquence of Henry Clay? A harvest of golden opinions was to be the destined reward of this day's exhibition. Webster was to be translated into Greek, to be read with rapture through the Peloponnesus, and to be pronounced side by side with Demosthenes from the heights of the Acropolis; while Clay was to receive the thanks and the gratitude of the South American Republics through the person of the great Liberator, the modern Washington.

Under such circumstances, it took a man of no ordinary strength of character to resist these seductive measures, and expose their true nature and tendency. John Randolph was the man for the times; he was then, as he had been for years past, " the solitary warder on the wall :" all others were asleep, or caught away by the enthusiasm; he saw the danger, and gave the alarm.

" This," said he, " is perhaps one of the finest and prettiest themes for declamation ever presented to a deliberative assembly. But it appears to me in a light very different from any that has as yet been thrown upon it.

" I look at the measure as one fraught with deep and deadly danger to the best interests and to the liberties of the American people; so satisfied, sir, am I of this, that I have been constrained by the conviction to overcome the almost insuperable repugnance I feel to throwing myself upon the notice of the House; but I feel it to be my duty to raise my voice against both these propositions.

My intention in rising at present, sir, is merely to move, that the committee rise, and that both of the resolutions may be printed. I wish to have some time to think of this business, to deliberate, before we take this leap in the dark into the Archipelago, or the Black Sea, or into the wide-mouthed La Plata. I know, sir, that the post of honor is on the other side of the House, the post of toil and of difficulty on this side, if, indeed, any body shall be with me on this side. It is a difficult and an invidious task to stem the torrent of public sentiment, when all the generous feelings of the human heart are appealed to. But I was delegated, sir, to this House, to guard the interests of the people of the United States, not to guard the rights of other people; and, if it was doubted, even in the case of England, a land fertile above all other lands (not excepting Greece herself) in great and glorious men—if it was doubted whether her interference in the politics of the continent, though separated from it only by a narrow strait, not so wide as the Chesapeake, as our Mediterranean Sea, had redounded either to her honor or advantage; if the effect of that interference has been a monumental debt that paralyzes the arm that might now strike for Greece, that certainly would have struck for Spain, can it be for us to seek, in the very bottom of the Mediterranean, for a quarrel with the Ottoman Porte? And this, while we have an ocean rolling between? While we are in that sea without a single port to refit a gun-boat; and while the powers of Barbary lie in succession in our path, shall we open this Pandora's box of political evils? Are we prepared for a war with these pirates? (not that we are not perfectly competent to such a war, but) does it suit our finances? Does it suit, sir, our magnificent projects of roads and canals? Does it suit the temper of our people? Does it promote their interests? will it add to their happiness? Sir, why did we remain supine while Piedmont and Naples were crushed by Austria? Why did we stand aloof, while the Spanish peninsula was again reduced under *legitimate* government? If we did not interfere then, why now?

"This Quixotism, in regard either to Greece or to South America, is not what the sober and reflecting minds of our people require at our hands. Sir, we are in debt as individuals, and we are in debt as a nation; and never, since the days of Saul and David, or Cæsar and Catiline, could a more unpropitious period have been found for such an undertaking. The state of society is too much disturbed. There is always, in a debtor, a tendency either to torpor or to desperation—neither condition is friendly to such deliberations. But I will suspend what I have further to say on this subject. For my part, I see as much danger, and more, in the resolution proposed by the gentleman from Kentucky, as in that of the gentleman from Massachusetts. The war that may follow on the one, is a distant war; it lies on the other side of the ocean. The war that may be induced by the other, is a war at hand; it is on the same continent. I am equally opposed to the amendment which has been since offered to the original resolutions. Let us look a little further at all of them. Let us sleep upon them before we pass resolutions, which, I will not say, are mere loops to hang speeches on, and thereby commit the nation to a war, the issues of which it is not given to human sagacity to divine."

The resolutions were postponed. When again taken up, Mr. Randolph spoke at large upon them. We must be content with a few paragraphs, only.

"It is with serious concern and alarm," said Mr. Randolph, "that I have heard doctrines broached in this debate, fraught with consequences more disastrous to the best interests of this people, than any that I ever heard advanced, during the five and twenty years since I have been honored with a seat on this floor. They imply, to my apprehension, a total and fundamental change of the policy pursued by this Government, *ab urbe condita*—from the foundation of the Republic, to the present day. Are we, sir, to go on a crusade, in another hemisphere, for the propagation of two objects as dear and delightful to *my* heart, as to that of any gentleman in this, or in any other assembly—Liberty and Religion—and, in the name of these holy words—by this powerful spell, is this nation to be conjured and beguiled out of the highway of heaven—out of its present compara-

tively happy state, into all the disastrous conflicts arising from the
policy of European powers, with all the consequences which flow from
them? Liberty and Religion, sir! Things that are yet dear, in spite
of all the mischief that has been perpetrated in their name. I believe that nothing similar to this proposition is to be found in modern
history, unless in the famous decree of the French National Assembly, which brought combined Europe against them, with its united
strength; and, after repeated struggles, finally effected the downfall
of the French power.

"I will respectfully ask the gentleman from Massachusetts,
whether, in his very able and masterly argument—and he has said
all that could be said on the subject, and much more than I supposed
could have been said by any man in favor of his resolution—whether
he, himself, has not furnished an answer to his speech. I had not
the happiness myself to hear his speech, but a friend has read it to
me—in one of the arguments in that speech, towards the conclusion,
I think, of his speech, the gentleman lays down from Puffendorff, in
reference to the honeyed words and pious professions of the Holy Alliance, that these are all surplusage, because nations are always supposed to be ready to do what justice and national law require. Well,
sir, if this be so, why may not the Greeks presume—why are they
not in this principle, bound to presume—that this Government is disposed to do all, in reference to them, that they ought to do, without
any formal resolutions to that effect? I ask the gentleman from Massachusetts, whether the doctrine of Puffendorff does not apply as
strongly to the resolution as to the declaration of the Allies—that is,
if the resolution of the gentleman be indeed that almost nothing he
would have us suppose, if there be not something *behind* this nothing,
which divides this House, (not *horizontally*, as the gentleman has
somewhat quaintly said—but *vertically*) into two unequal parties; one
the advocate of a splendid system of crusades, the other, the friends
of peace and harmony; the advocates of a *fireside policy*—for, as
long as all is right at the fireside, there cannot be much wrong elsewhere—whether, I repeat, does not the doctrine of Puffendorff apply
as well to the words of the resolution, as to the words of the Holy
Alliance?

"There was another remark that fell from the gentleman from
Massachusetts—of which I shall speak, as I shall always speak of
any thing from that gentleman, with all the personal respect that
may be consistent with the freedom of discussion. Among other
cases forcibly put by the gentleman, why he would embark in this
incipient crusade against Mussulmen, he stated this as one—that they
hold human beings as property. Aye, sir,—and what says the Constitution of the United States on this point?—unless, indeed, that
instrument is wholly to be excluded from consideration—unless it is

to be regarded as a mere useless parchment, worthy to be burnt, as was once actually proposed. Does not that Constitution give its sanction to the holding of human beings as property? Sir, I am not going to discuss the abstract question of liberty or slavery, or any other abstract question. I go for matters of fact. But I would ask gentlemen in this House, who have the misfortune to reside on the wrong side of a certain mysterious parallel of latitude, to take this question seriously into consideration—whether the Government of the United States is prepared to say, that the act of holding human beings as property, is sufficient to place the party so offending, under the ban of its high and mighty displeasure?

"Sir, I am afraid, that, along with some most excellent attributes and qualities—the love of liberty, jury trial, the writ of habeas corpus, and all the blessings of free government we have derived from our Anglo-Saxon ancestors, we have got not a little of their John Bull, or rather John Bull-dog spirit—their readiness to fight for any body, and on any occasion. Sir, England has been for centuries the game-cock of Europe. It is impossible to specify the wars in which she has been engaged for contrary purposes; and she will with great pleasure, see us take off her shoulders the labor of preserving the balance of power. We find her fighting, now for the Queen of Hungary—then for her inveterate foe, the King of Prussia—now at war for the restoration of the Bourbons—and now on the eve of war with them for the liberties of Spain.

"These lines on the subject, were never more applicable, than they have now become:

"'Now Europe's balanced—neither side prevails,
For nothing's left in either of the scales.'

"If we pursue the same policy, we must travel the same road, and endure the same burthens, under which England now groans. But, glorious as such a design might be, a President of the United States would, in my apprehension, occupy a prouder place in history, who, when he retires from office, can say to the people who elected him, I leave you without a debt, than if he had fought as many pitched battles as Cæsar, or achieved as many naval victories as Nelson. And what, sir, is debt? In an individual it is slavery. It is slavery of the worst sort, surpassing that of the West India Islands, for it enslaves the mind, as well as it enslaves the body; and the creature who can be abject enough to incur and to submit to it, receives, in that condition of his being, perhaps, an adequate punishment. Of course, I speak of debt, with the exception of unavoidable misfortune. I speak of debt caused by mismanagement, by unwarrantable generosity, by being generous before being just. I am aware that this sentiment was ridiculed by Sheridan, whose lamentable end was the best commentary upon its truth. No, sir; let us abandon these projects. Let us say to those seven millions of Greeks, 'We defended ourselves when we were but three millions, against a power, in comparison with which the Turk is but a lamb. Go and do thou likewise.' And so with the governments of South America. If, after having achieved their independence, they have not valor to maintain it, I would not commit the safety and independence of this country in such a cause. I will, in both these, pursue the same line of conduct which I have ever pursued, from the day I took a seat in this House, in 1799, from which, without boasting, I challenge any gentleman to fix upon me any colorable charge of departure.

"Let us adhere to the policy laid down by the second as well as the first founder of our republic—by him who was the Camillus, as well as Romulus, of the infant State—to the policy of peace, commerce, and honest friendship with all nations, entangling alliances with none; for to entangling alliances we must come, if you once embark in policy such as this. And, with all my British predilections, I suspect I shall, whenever that question shall present itself, resist as strongly an alliance with Great Britain, as with any other power. We are sent here to attend to the preservation of the peace of *this* country, and not to be ready, on all occasions, to go to war, whenever any thing like what, in common parlance, is termed a *turn up*, takes place in Europe.

"What, sir, is our condition? We are absolutely combatting shadows. The gentleman would have us to believe his resolution is all but nothing; yet, again, it is to prove omnipotent, and fill the whole globe with its influence. Either it is nothing, or it is something. If it be nothing, let it return to its original nothingness; let us lay it on the table, and have done with it at once; but, if it is that something, which it has been on the other hand represented to be, let us beware how we touch it. For my part, I would sooner put the shirt of Nessus on my back than sanction these doctrines—doctrines such as I never heard from my boyhood till now. They go the whole length. If they prevail, there are no longer any Pyrenees; every bulwark and barrier of the Constitution is broken down; it is become *tabula rasa*, a *carte blanche*, for every one to scribble on it what he pleases."

The resolutions were laid on the table, never afterwards to be called up.

CHAPTER XXIII.

INTERNAL IMPROVEMENTS.

IMMEDIATELY after the close of the foregoing debate, within a few days, there followed a discussion on an appropriation to defray the expenses of a survey of the country, with reference to an extended and connected scheme of roads and canals. But two years previous, May, 1822, Mr. Monroe had demonstrated, in the most elaborate manner, the unconstitutionality of any system of internal improvement by the Federal Government. Having duly considered the bill, entitled " An act for the preservation and repair of the Cumberland Road," he returned it to the House of Representatives, in which it originated, under the conviction that Congress did not possess the power, under the Constitution, to pass such a law.

A power to establish turnpikes, with gates and tolls, and to enforce the collection of the tolls by penalties, implies a power to adopt and execute a complete system of internal improvement. Mr. Monroe contended that Congress did not possess this power—that the States individually could not grant it. If the power exist, it must be either because it has been specifically granted to the United States, or that it is incidental to some power which has been specifically granted. It has never been contended that the power was specifically granted. It is claimed only as being incidental to some one or more of the powers that are specifically granted.

The following are the powers from which it is said to be derived : 1st. From the right to establish post-offices and post-roads. 2d. From the right to declare war. 3d. To regulate commerce. 4th. To pay the debts, and provide for the common defence and general welfare. 5th. From the power to make all laws necessary and proper for carrying into execution all the powers vested by the Constitution in the Government of the United States. 6th. From the power to dispose of, and make all needful rules and regulations respecting the territory and other property of the United States.

Mr. Monroe took up the power thus claimed, and by a most extended and elaborate review of the history and the principles of the Constitution, demonstrated that it could not be derived from either of those powers specified, nor from all of them united, and that in consequence it did not exist.

These views, so distinct and unequivocal, were set forth by Mr. Monroe on the 4th of May, 1822, in a special message, addressed to Congress. In December, 1823, a bill was introduced into the House of Representatives, by which the President of the United States was authorized to cause the necessary surveys, plans, and estimates to be made, of the routes of such roads and canals as he may deem of national importance, in a commercial or military point of view, or necessary for the transportation of the public mail. This bill, it was understood, contemplated a scheme of internal improvement on the most extended scale; as such, it was discussed and voted upon. The debate was long, and was ably conducted. Mr. Clay, as usual, was the great champion of this as of all the other brilliant schemes of the day. It was natural, therefore, that he and Randolph should come in collision on all occasions. The one was the bold leader of a new school of politicians, sprung up out of the ruins of the old Hamiltonian dynasty, who by interpolation or construction made the Constitution mean any thing and every thing their ardent minds chose to aspire to. The other was the clear-sighted, consistent, and upright statesman, that stood by the old landmarks of republicanism, as they were laid down by the fathers of the faith; and never could be induced to depart from them by the hope of reward or the fear of denunciation. They were the Lucifer and the Michael of contending hosts:

> " Now waved their fiery swords, and in the air
> Made horrid circles; two broad suns their shields
> Blaz'd opposite, while expectation stood
> In horror; from each hand with speed retir'd
> Where erst was thickest fight, the angelic throng,
> And left large field; unsafe within the wind
> Of such commotion."

Or Randolph, rather, was the faithful Abdiel—

> " Nor number, nor example with him wrought
> To swerve from truth, or change his constant mind,
> Though single. From amidst them forth he passed,
> And with retorted scorn his back he turned
> On those proud towers to swift destruction doomed."

Mr. Randolph, on the 31st of January, 1824, delivered his senti-ments at large on the bill.   The reader must here also be content with a few paragraphs:

"During no very short course of public life," said Mr. R., " I do not know that it has ever been my fortune to rise under as much em-barrassment, or to address the House with as much repugnance as I now feel.   That repugnance, in part, grows out of the necessity that exists for my taking some notice, in the course of my observations, of the argument, if argument it may be called, of an honorable mem-ber of this House, from Kentucky.   And, although I have not the honor to know, personally, or even by name, a large portion of the members of this House, it is not necessary for me to indicate the cause of that repugnance.   But this I may venture to promise the committee, that, in my notice of the argument of that member, I shall show, at least, as much deference to it, as *he* showed to the message of the President of the United States of America, on re-turning a bill of a nature analogous to that now before us—I say at least *as much;* I should regret if not *more.*   With the argument of the President, however, I have nothing to do.   I wash my hands of it, and will leave it to the triumph, the clemency, the mercy, of the honorable gentleman of Kentucky—if, indeed, to use his own lan-guage, amid the mass of words in which it is enveloped, he has been able to find it.   My purpose in regard to the argument of the gen-tleman from Kentucky is, to show that it lies in the compass of a nut-shell; that it turns on the meaning of one of the plainest words in the English language.   I am happy to be able to agree with that gentleman in at least one particular, to wit: in the estimate the gen-tleman has formed of his own powers as a grammarian, philologer, and critic; particularly as those powers have been displayed in the dissertation with which he has favored the committee on the inter-pretation of the word establish.

" 'Congress,' says the Constitution, 'shall have power to *establish* (ergo, says the gentleman, Congress shall have power to *construct*) post-roads.'

" One would suppose, that, if any thing could be considered as settled, by precedent in legislation, the meaning of the words of the Constitution must, before this time, have been settled, by the uniform sense in which that power has been exercised, from the commence-ment of the Government to the present time.   What is the fact? Your statute-book is loaded with acts for the 'establishment' of post-roads, and the post-master general is deluged with petitions for the 'establishment' of post-offices; and yet, we are now gravely debating on what the word 'establish' shall be held to mean !   A curious pre-dicament we are placed in: precisely the reverse of that of Molière's citizen turned gentleman, who discovered, to his great surprise, that he had been talking 'prose' all his life long without knowing it. A common case. It is just so with all prosers, and I hope I may not exemplify it in this instance. But, sir, we have been for five and thirty years establishing post-roads, under the delusion that we were exercising a power specially conferred upon us by the Constitution, while we were, according to the suggestion of the gentleman from Kentucky, actually committing *treason*, by refusing, for so long a time, to carry into effect that very article of the Constitution!

" To forbear the exercise of a power vested in us for the public good, not merely for our own aggrandizement, is, according to the argument of the gentleman from Kentucky, treachery to the Constitution! I, then, sir, must have commenced my public life in treason, and in treason am I doomed to end it. One of the first votes that I ever had the honor to give, in this House, was a vote against the *establishment*, if gentlemen please, of a uniform system of bankruptcy—a power as unquestionably given to Congress, by the Constitution, as the power to lay a direct tax. But, sir, my treason did not end there. About two years after the establishment of this uniform system of bankruptcy, I was *particeps criminis*, with almost the unanimous voice of this House, in committing another act of treachery in repealing it; and Mr. Jefferson, the President of the United States, in the commencement of his career, consummated the treason by putting his signature to the act of repeal.

" Miserable, indeed, would be the condition of every free people, if, in expounding the charter of their liberties, it were necessary to go back to the Anglo-Saxon, to Junius and Skinner, and other black-letter etymologists. Not, sir, that I am very skilful in language: although I have learned from a certain curate of Brentford, whose name will survive when the whole contemporaneous bench of Bishops shall be buried in oblivion, that *words*—the counters of wise men, the money of fools—that it is by the dexterous cutting and shuffling of this pack, that is derived one-half of the chicanery, and much more than one-half of the profits of the most lucrative profession in the world—and, sir, by this dexterous exchanging and substituting of words, we shall not be the first nation in the world which has been cajoled, if we are to be cajoled, out of our rights and liberties.

" In the course of the observations which the gentleman from Kentucky saw fit to submit to the committee, were some pathetic ejaculations on the subject of the sufferings of our brethren of the West. Sir, our brethren of the West have suffered, as our brethren throughout the United States, from the same cause, although with them the cause exists in an aggravated degree, from the acts of those to whom they have confided the power of legislation; by a departure— and we have all suffered from it—I hope no gentleman will under-

stand me, as wishing to make any invidious comparison between different quarters of our country, by a departure from the industry, the
simplicity, the economy, and the frugality of our ancestors. They
have suffered from a greediness of gain, that has grasped at the shadow while it has lost the substance—from habits of indolence, of profusion, of extravagance—from an aping of foreign manners and of
foreign fashions—from a miserable attempt at the shabby genteel,
which only serve to make our poverty more conspicuous. The way to
remedy this state of suffering, is, to return to those habits of labor
and industry, from which we have thus departed.

   "With these few remarks," continued Mr. R., "permit me now to
recall the attention of the committee to the original design of this
Government. It grew out of the necessity, indispensable and unavoidable, in the circumstances of this country, of some general
power, capable of regulating foreign commerce.   Sir, I am old
enough to remember the origin of this Government ; and, though I
was too young to participate in the transactions of the day, I have a
perfect recollection of what was public sentiment on the subject.
And I repeat, without fear of contradiction, that the proximate, as
well as the remote cause of the existence of the federal government,
was the regulation of foreign commerce.   Not to particularize all the
difficulties which grew out of the conflicting laws of the States, Mr.
R. referred to but one, arising from Virginia taxing an article
which Maryland then made duty-free; and to that very policy, may
be attributed, in a great degree, the rapid growth and prosperity of
the town of Baltimore. If the old Congress had possessed the power
of laying a duty of ten per cent. ad valorem on imports, this Constitution would never have been called into existence.

   " But we are told that, along with the regulation of foreign commerce, the States have yielded to the General Government, in as
broad terms, the regulation of domestic commerce—I mean the commerce among the several States—and that the same power is possessed
by Congress over the one as over the other.   It is rather unfortunate
for this argument, that, if it applies to the extent to which the power
to regulate foreign commerce has been carried by Congress, they
may prohibit altogether this domestic commerce, as they have here
tofore, under the other power, prohibited foreign commerce.

   "But why put extreme cases ?   This Government cannot go on
one day without a mutual understanding and deference between the
State and General Governments.   This Government is the breath of
the nostrils of the States.   Gentlemen may say what they please of
the preamble to the Constitution ; but this Constitution is not the
work of the amalgamated population of the then existing confede
racy, but the offspring of the States ; and however high we may
carry our heads and strut and fret our hour ' dressed in a little brief

authority,' it is in the power of the States to extinguish this Government at a blow. They have only to refuse to send members to the other branch of the legislature, or to appoint electors of President and Vice-President, and the thing is done. Gentlemen will not understand me as seeking for reflections of this kind; but, like Falstaff's rebellion—I mean Worcester's rebellion—they lay in my way and I found them."

" I remember to have heard it said elsewhere," said Mr. R., "that when gentlemen talk of precedent, they forget they were not in Westminster Hall. Whatever trespass I may be guilty of upon the attention of the Committee, one thing I will promise them, and will faithfully perform my promise. I will dole out to them no political metaphysics. Sir, I unlearned metaphysics almost as early as Fontenelle, and he tells us, I think, it was at nine years old. I shall say nothing about that word *municipal*. I am almost as sick of it as honest Falstaff was of 'security;' it has been like ratsbane in my mouth, ever since the late ruler in France took shelter under that word to pocket our money and incarcerate our persons, with the most profound respect for our *neutral* rights. I have done with the word *municipal* ever since that day. Let us come to the plain common sense construction of the Constitution. Sir, we live under a government of a peculiar structure, to which the doctrines of the European writers on civil polity do not apply; and when gentlemen get up and quote Vattel as applicable to the powers of the Constitution of the United States, I should as soon have expected them to quote Aristotle or the Koran. Our Government is not like the consolidated monarchies of the old world. It is a solar system; an *imperium in imperio ;* and when the question is about the one or the other, what belong to the *imperium* and what to the *imperio*, we gain nothing by referring to Vattel. He treats of an integral government—a compact structure, *totus teres atque rotundus.* But ours is a system composed of two distinct governments; the one general in its nature, the other internal. Now, sir, a government may be admirable for external, and yet execrable for internal purposes. And when the question of power in the government arises, this is the problem which every honest man has to work. The powers of government are divided in our system between the General and State Governments, except such powers which the people have very wisely retained to themselves. With these exceptions, all the power is divided between the two Governments. The given power will not lie unless, as in the case of direct taxes, the power is specifically given ; and even then the State ,has a concurrent power. The question for every honest man to ask himself is, to which of these two divisions of government does the power in contest belong ? This is the problem we have to settle: Does this power of internal improvement belong to the General or to the State

Governments, or is it a concurrent power? Gentlemen say we have, by the Constitution, power to establish post-roads; and, having established post-roads, we should be much obliged to you to allow us therefore the power to construct roads and canals into the bargain. If I had the physical strength, sir, I could easily demonstrate to the committee that, supposing the power to exist on our part, of all the powers that can be exercised by this House, there is no power that would be more susceptible of abuse than this very power. Figure to yourself a committee of this House determining on some road, and giving out the contracts to the members of both Houses of Congress, or to their friends, &c. Sir, if I had strength, I could show to this committee that the Asiatic plunder of Leadenhall street has not been more corrupting to the British Government than the exercise of such a power as this would prove to us.

"I said," continued Mr. R., "that this Government, if put to the test—a test it is by no means calculated to endure—as a government for the management of the internal concerns of this country, is one of the worst that can be conceived, which is determined by the fact that it is a government not having a common feeling and common interest with the governed. I know that we are told—and it is the first time the doctrine has been openly avowed—that upon the responsibility of this House to the people, by means of the elective franchise, depends all the security of the people of the United States against the abuse of the powers of this Government.

"But, sir, how shall a man from Mackinaw, or the Yellow Stone River, respond to the sentiments of the people who live in New Hampshire? It is as great a mockery—a greater mockery than it was to talk to these colonies about their virtual representation in the British Parliament. I have no hesitation in saying that the liberties of the colonies were safer in the custody of the British Parliament than they will be in any portion of this country, if all the powers of the States, as well as of the General Government, are devolved on this House; and in this opinion I am borne out, and more than borne out, by the authority of Patrick Henry himself.

"It is not a matter of conjecture merely, but of fact, of notoriety, that there does exist on this subject an honest difference of opinion among enlightened men; that not one or two, but many States in the Union see, with great concern and alarm, the encroachments of the General Government on their authority. They feel that they have given up the power of the sword and the purse, and enabled men, with the purse in one hand and the sword in the other, to rifle them of all they hold dear." . . . . . "We now begin to perceive what we have surrendered; that, having given up the power of the purse and the sword, every thing else is at the mercy and forbearance of the General Government. We did believe there were some parchment barriers—no! what is worth all the parchment barriers in the world—that there was, in the powers of the States, some counterpoise to the power of this body; but, if this bill passes, we can believe so no longer."

"There is one other power," said Mr. R., "which may be exercised, in case the power now contended for be conceded, to which I ask the attention of every gentleman who happens to stand in the same unfortunate predicament with myself—of every man who has the misfortune to be, and to have been born, a slaveholder. If Congress possess the power to do what is proposed by this bill, they may not only enact a sedition law—for there is precedent—but they may emancipate every slave in the United States, and with stronger color of reason than they can exercise the power now contended for. And where will they find the power? They may follow the example of the gentlemen who have preceded me, and hook the power upon the first loop they find in the Constitution. They might take the preamble, perhaps the war-making power, or they might take a greater sweep, and say, with some gentlemen, that it is not to be found in this or that of the granted powers, but results from all of them, which is not only a dangerous, but *the most* dangerous doctrine. Is it not demonstrable that slave labor is the dearest in the world, and that the existence of a large body of slaves is a source of danger? Suppose we are at war with a foreign power, and freedom should be offered them by Congress, as an inducement to them to take a part in it; or, suppose the country not at war, at every turn of this federal machine, at every successive census, that interest will find itself governed by another and increasing power, which is bound to it neither by any common tie of interest or feeling. And if ever the time shall arrive, as assuredly it has arrived elsewhere, and, in all probability, may arrive here, that a coalition of knavery and fanaticism shall, for any purpose, be got up on this floor, I ask gentlemen who stand in the same predicament as I do, to look well to what they are now doing, to the colossal power with which they are now arming this Government. The power to do what I allude to is, I aver, more honestly inferable from the war-making power than the power we are now about to exercise. Let them look forward to the time when such a question shall arise, and tremble with me at the thought that that question is to be decided by a majority of the votes of this House, of whom not one possesses the slightest tie of common interest or of common feeling with us."

The debate on this important question was kept up ten days longer. On the 10th of February, Mr. Randolph moved that the bill be indefinitely postponed. The motion was overruled, and the bill was passed by a majority of 115 to 86. So soon as the vote was announced, it was moved that the House go into committee of the whole on the state of the Union, with a view of taking up the bill for a revision of the tariff. Mr. Randolph exclaimed, "Sufficient for the day is the evil thereof," and hoped that the House would do no such thing; they, however, did go into committee, and made some progress in the bill.

The measure above adopted by the House, was sanctioned by the President, thus furnishing another instance of a most extraordinary and flagrant abandonment of first principles, on a vital point of the Constitution. Mr. Madison's arguments as to the unconstitutionality of the Bank, stand unanswered and unanswerable; yet, in 1816, Mr. Madison, under the pressure of circumstances, the plea of necessity, and the force of precedent, signed the Bank bill.

No man argued more clearly and conclusively than Mr. Monroe the unconstitutionality of a system of internal improvement; yet, under the influence of a yielding complacency, that was reluctant to oppose the encroaching spirit of the times, he sanctioned a measure that adopted the system in its broadest sense, and swept away every barrier of the Constitution.

CHAPTER XXIV.

SUPREME COURT—DULL DINNER—HUDDLESFORD'S OAK.

ABOUT the time the Roads and Canals bill was discussed in the House, a case was argued before the Supreme Court, involving the same principles. Aaron Ogden, under several acts of the Legislature of the State of New-York, claimed the exclusive navigation of all the waters within the jurisdiction of the State, with boats moved by fire or steam. Gibbons employed two steamboats in running between Elizabethtown, New Jersey, and New-York, in violation of the exclusive privilege. He was enjoined by the Chancellor of New-York, and in his answers stated, that the boats were *enrolled* and *licensed*, to be employed in carrying on the *coasting trade*, under the acts of Congress—and insisted on his right, in virtue of such licenses, to navigate the waters between Elizabethtown and the city of New-York, the acts of the legislature of the State of New-York to the contrary notwithstanding.

The question was, whether the laws of Congress, passed in virtue of the clause of the Constitution which confers on them the power to *regulate commerce* among the several States, shall con.ravene and supersede the laws of New-York, granting a monopoly to certain individuals to *navigate* steam vessels on the waters within the jurisdiction of that State.

The whole controversy turned on the interpretation of this clause of the Constitution—" Congress shall have power to regulate commerce with foreign nations, and among the several States, and with the Indian tribes."

The Chief Justice, to arrive at his conclusions, took the broadest latitude of construction. " It has been said, argues he, that these powers" (powers enumerated in the Constitution) " ought to be construed strictly. But why ought they to be so construed ? Is there one sentence in the Constitution which gives countenance to this rule ? In the last of the enumerated powers, that which grants expressly the means for carrying all others into execution, Congress is authorized ' to make all laws which shall be necessary and proper' for the purpose." With this broad principle as his rule of construction, he then goes on to argue that the power to regulate commerce with foreign nations, is full and absolute—and that it embraces the right to regulate *navigation*. The next step is to prove that the power to regulate commerce among the States is as broad and comprehensive as the power to regulate it with foreign nations. "; Commerce among the States," says he, " cannot stop at the external boundary line of each State, but may be introduced into the interior." . . . . . " The genius and character of the whole Government seem to be, that its action is to be applied to all the external concerns of the nation, and to those internal concerns which affect the States generally." . . . . " Commerce among the States must, of necessity, be commerce with the States. In the regulation of trade with the Indian tribes, the action of the law, especially when the Constitution was made, was chiefly within a State. The power of Congress, then, whatever it may be, must be exercised within the territorial jurisdiction of the several States." . . . . "This power, like all others vested in Congress, is complete in itself, may be exercised to its utmost extent, and acknowledges no limitations, other than are prescribed in the Constitution." . . . . . "The power of Congress, then, comprehends navigation within the limits of every State in the Union, so far as that navigation may be, in any manner, connected with 'commerce with foreign nations, or among the several States, or with the Indian tribes.'"

He goes on to apply these principles—self-evident *axioms* as he called them—to the case before the Court, and decided against the exclusive privilege of navigation granted by the laws and sustained by the Judiciary of New-York.

In conclusion, the Chief Justice says: "Powerful and ingenious minds, taking, as postulates, that the powers expressly granted to the government of the Union, are to be contracted by construction into the narrowest possible compass, and that the original powers of the States are retained, if any possible construction will retain them, may, by a course of well-digested, but refined and metaphysical reasoning, founded on these premises, explain away the Constitution of our country, and leave it, a magnificent structure indeed to look at, but totally unfit for use."

But the Chief Justice did not perceive, that, by pursuing the broad doctrines laid down by him, the several departments of government, especially the one over which he presided—the Judiciary, whose business it is to construe and interpret—might, step by step, absorb all the powers reserved to the States, and to the people, and make the government *a magnificent structure* indeed, not merely to look at, but one wielding all the concentrated powers of a consolidated empire. The true rule is to go neither to the one extreme nor to the other, but to give to each and to all that which rightfully belongs to them.

This opinion of the Chief Justice gave great umbrage to the States-rights men. They said he travelled out of the record, to make an elaborate argument in behalf of those principles which were then urged in Congress as a justification of a general system of internal improvement among the States.

Mr. Randolph says to Dr. Brockenbrough, the 3d of March:

"The Chief Justice yesterday delivered a most able opinion in the

great New-York steamboat case, fatal to the monopoly. It is said that
he decided in favor of the power of the General Government to make
internal improvements, but I don't believe it. He is too wise a
man to decide any point not before his court." No man admired
Marshall more than John Randolph; he held him up, as the reader
knows, as a model to the young—to the world; but he did not let
his partiality for the man blind his judgment as to the dangerous
doctrines of the Judge. When he had read "the opinion," he says:
"It is the fashion to praise the Chief Justice's opinion in the case of
Ogden against Gibbons. But you know I am not a fashionable man;
I think it is unworthy of him. Lord Liverpool has set him an example of caution in the last speech of the king: one that shames our
gasconading message. I said it was too long before I read it. It
contains a great deal that has no business there, or indeed any where.
Mr. Webster's phrase, 'unit,' which he adopts, is a conceit (concetto),
and a very poor one, borrowed from Dr. Rush, who with equal reason
pronounced disease to be a unit. Now, as this *theory* of the Doctor
had no effect whatever upon his *practice*, and that alone could affect his
patients, it was so far a harmless maggot of the brain. But when
that theory was imbibed at a single gulp by his young disciples,
who were sent out annually from Philadelphia, it became the means
of death not to units, or tens, or hundreds, but thousands, and tens
of thousands.

"A judicial opinion should decide nothing and embrace nothing
that is not before the court. If he had said that 'a vessel, having the
legal evidence that she has conformed to the regulations which Congress has seen fit to prescribe, has the right to go from a port of any
State to a port of any other with freight or in quest of it, with passengers or in quest of them, *non obstante* such a law as that of the State
of New-York under which the appellee claims,' I should have been
satisfied.

"However, since the case of Cohen *vs.* Virginia, I am done with
the Supreme Court. No one admires more than.I do the extraordinary powers of Marshall's mind: no one respects more his amiable
deportment in private life. He is the most unpretending and unas-
suming of men. His abilities and his virtues render him an ornament not only to Virginia, but to our nature I cannot, however,
help thinking, that he was too long at the bar before he ascended the
bench; and that, like our friend T——, he had injured, by the indiscriminate defence of right or wrong, the tone of his perception (if you
will allow so quaint a phrase) of truth or falsehood."

John Marshall was, "after the most straitest sect," a Federalist of the Hamilton school. The reader, doubtless, well remembers
his attempt to play at the game of Diplomacy with Talleyrand, and

the figure he cut in the X. Y. Z. business. Soon after his return to the United States he was elected a member of Congress, from the Richmond District, in the spring of 1799, after a most violent and bitter contest, beating John Clopton, the old republican representative. Mr. Adams, in 1800, removed Timothy Pickering from the head of his cabinet, and put General Marshall in his place; and in 1801, as one of the last acts of his administration, made him Chief Justice of the United States.

The man of great parts and of upright principles will perform justly and nobly the duties of whatever station he may be placed in. This maxim was well illustrated by Judge Marshall. As a partisan leader he was bold, fearless, uncompromising, and devoted to the principles of the cause he espoused. When elevated to the Bench he rose serenely above all party influences, and became the enlightened, wise, and upright Judge. But it is very clear, that wherever the powers of the Federal Government were concerned, he could not rise above those doctrines which had been so thoroughly inculcated on his mind. His federal principles, by long practice and thorough digestion, had so completely become a part of his mental system as to be a law of thought on all questions of constitutional interpretation. The tendency of the Supreme Court is now to the opposite extreme. The system of judicial reasoning, like all other moral systems built on the laws of the human mind, and not the principles of an exact science, revolves in a cycle; and in a series of years, will find itself occupying in regular succession the same positions which it had held at some former period. The mind progresses, but it is in a circle.

On the 20th of March, Mr. Randolph writes to his friend:

"Mr. King of N. Y., his colleague, Mr. Chief Justice, Tazewell and some three or four more dine with me to-morrow, so that I shall have good company, at least, if not a good dinner." Two days after, he says: "Mr. Chief Justice, Tazewell, Van Buren, Benton. Morgan, of N. Y., and George Calvert, dined with me yesterday (Mr. King was sick. of his late freak in the Senate, I shrewdly suspect); and your ' fat sall-ion party' was hardly more dull than we were. The Chief Justice has no longer the power ' d'être vif.' Tazewell took to prosing at the far end of the table to two or three, who formed a sort of separate coterie; V. B. was unwell, and out of spirits; and I was obliged to get nearly or quite drunk, to keep them from yawning outright."

Mr. Randolph was informed, about this time, that Miss Roane, the daughter of the late Judge Spencer Roane, was expected to visit Washington.

"If Miss Roane," says he, "should honor our metropolis with her presence, I shall make it a point to call upon her—if for no other cause, from the very high respect in which I held her father whilst living, and hold his memory, being dead. I consider him as a great loss to his country, not only in his judicial character, but as a statesman, who formed a rallying point for the friends of State-rights. Besides, he had the judgment to perceive, and the candor to acknowledge, the consistency of my public conduct with my avowed principles; and he had too much greatness of mind to lend himself to the long and bitter persecution with which I was assailed by two governments, by the press, by a triumphant party (many of whom were old sedition law federalists), until, Sertorius like, after having waged a long war upon my own resources, I was vanquished as much by treachery in my own camp, as by the courage or the conduct of the enemy My hopes (plans, I never had any) have been all blasted, and here I am, like Huddlesford's oak.

> " 'Thou, who unmoved hast heard the whirlwind chide
> Full many a winter, round thy craggy bed,
> And like an earth-born giant hast outspread
> Thy hundred arms, and Heaven's own bolts defied,
> Now liest along thy native mountain's side,
> Uptorn ! yet deem not that I come to shed
> The idle drops of pity o'er thy head,
> Or, basely, to insult thy blasted pride.
>
> " 'No, still 'tis thine, though fallen, imperial Oak,
> To teach this lesson to the wise and brave—
> That 'tis far better, overthrown and broke,
> In Freedom's cause to sink into the grave,
> Than in submission to a tyrant's yoke,
> Like the vile Reed, to bow and be a slave.'

CHAPTER XXV.

TARIFF—PROPHECY—LEWIS McLEAN.

THE Tariff question, during the spring of 1824, was thoroughly discussed, and for the first time distinctly recognized and placed on the footing of a protective policy. We pass over this subject, and

Mr. Randolph's great speech on its leading principles, for the present. Mr. Randolph, however, watched the bill in all its stages, and opposed many of its most objectionable parts in the incipient stage. Some of his best speeches are those short, comprehensive, and pithy discourses delivered on the spur of the occasion, on some isolated point under discussion. On the motion to reduce the duties on coarse woollens, Mr. Randolph said :—

"I am surprised that the votaries of humanity—persons who `an-not sleep, such is their distress of mind at the very existence of negro slavery—should persist in pressing a measure, the effect of which is to aggravate the misery of that unhappy condition, whether viewed in reference to the slave, or to his master, if he be a man possessing a spark of humanity ; for what can be more pitiable than the situation of a man who has every desire to clothe his negroes comfortably, but who is absolutely prohibited from so doing by legislative enactment ? I hope that none of those who wish to enhance to the poor slave (or what is the same thing—to his master) the price of his annual blanket, and of his sordid suit of coarse, but, to him, comfortable woollen cloth, will ever travel through the southern country to spy out the nakedness, if not of the land, of the cultivators of the soil. It is notorious that the profits of slave labor have been, for a long time, on the decrease ; and that, on a fair average, it scarcely reimburses the expense of the slave, including the helpless ones, whether from infancy or age. The words of Patrick Henry, in the Convention of Virginia, still ring in my ears : 'They may liberate every one of your slaves. The Congress possess the power, and will exercise it.' Now, sir, the first step towards this consummation, so devoutly wished by many, is to pass such laws as may yet still further diminish the pittance which their labor yields to their unfortunate masters, to produce such a state of things as will insure, in case the slave shall not elope from his master, that his master will run away from him. Sir, the blindness, as it appears to me—I hope gentlemen will pardon the expression— with which a certain quarter of this country—I allude particularly to the seaboard of South Carolina and Georgia—has lent its aid to increase the powers of the general government on points, to say the least, of doubtful construction, fills me with astonishment and dismay. And I look forward, almost without a ray of hope, to the time which the next census, or that which succeeds it, will assuredly bring forth, when this work of destruction and devastation is to commence in the abused name of humanity and religion, and when the imploring eyes of some will be, as now, turned towards another body, in the vain hope that it may arrest the evil, and stay the plague."

April 12, Mr. Randolph said : "If the House would lend me its attention five minutes, I think I can demonstrate that the argument of the gentleman from Delaware in favor of the increased duty on brown sugar, is one of the most suicidal arguments that ever reared its spectral front in a deliberative assembly.

" The gentleman objects to reducing the duty on sugar, because it will diminish the revenue, which he says we cannot dispense with, and yet he wishes to continue it as a bounty of $3 per 100 lbs. (not the long hundred of 112 lbs.), until the sugar planting and sugar manufacture should be extended, so as to supply the whole demand of our consumption. Then what becomes of the revenue from sugar, that we cannot dispense with? This is what I call a suicidal argument, it destroys itself.

Mr. McLean, at the commencement of his reply, appearing to be much irritated, Mr. Randolph rose and assured him that he intended not the slightest disrespect or offence—but Mr. McLean went on to say that the gentleman from Virginia had displayed a good head, but he would not accept that gentleman's head, to be obliged to have his heart along with it.

Mr. Randolph replied :

" It costs me nothing, sir, to say that I very much regret that the zeal which I have not only felt, but cherished, on the subject of laying taxes in a manner which, in my judgment, is inconsistent, not merely with the spirit, but the very letter of the Constitution, should have given to my remarks, on this subject, a pungency, which has rendered them disagreeable, and even offensive to the gentleman from Delaware. For that gentleman I have never expressed any other sentiment but respect—I have never uttered, or entertained, an unkind feeling towards that gentleman, either in this House or elsewhere, nor do I now feel any such sentiment towards him. I never pressed my regard upon him—I press it upon no man. He appears to have considered my remarks as having a personal application to himself. I certainly did not intend to give them that direction, and I think that my prompt disclaimer of any such intention ought to have disarmed his resentment, however justly it may have been excited. He has been pleased, sir, to say something, which, no doubt, he thinks very severe, about my head and my heart.

" How easy, sir, would it be for me to reverse the gentleman's proposition, and to retort upon him, that I would not, in return, take that gentleman's heart, however good it may be, if obliged, to take such a head into the bargain.

" But, sir, I do not think this—I never thought it—and, therefore, I cannot be so ungenerous as to say it: for, Mr. Speaker, who made me a searcher of hearts? of the heart of a fellow-man, a fellow-sinner? Sir, this is an awful subject! better suited to Friday or Sunday next (Good Friday and Easter Sunday), two of the most solemn days in the Christian calendar—when I hope we shall all consider it, and lay it to heart as we ought to do.

"But, sir, I must still maintain that the argument of the gentleman is suicidal—he has fairly worked the equation, and one-half of his argument is a complete and conclusive answer to the other. And, sir, if I should ever be so unfortunate as, through inadvertence, or the heat of debate, to fall into such an error, I should, so far from being offended, feel myself under obligation to any gentleman who would expose its fallacy, even by ridicule—as fair a weapon as any in the whole Parliamentary armory. I shall not go so far as to maintain, with my Lord Shaftesbury, that it is the unerring test of truth, whatever it may be of temper; but if it be proscribed as a weapon as unfair as it is confessedly powerful, what shall we say (I put it, sir, to you and to the House) to the poisoned arrow?—to the tomahawk and the scalping-knife? Would the most unsparing use of ridicule justify a resort to these weapons? Was this a reason that the gentleman sould sit in judgment on my heart?—yes, sir, *my* heart—which the gentleman (whatever he may say) in his heart believes to be a frank heart, as I trust it is a brave heart. Sir, I dismiss the gentleman to his self-complacency—let him go—yes, sir, let him go, and thank his God that he is not as *this* publican."

This is the finest retort of the kind to be found in the English language. Its admirable style and temper cannot be too strongly recommended to those who in the heat of debate may be tempted to say severe and irritating things. This is a model for them to follow: " A soft answer turneth away wrath." Mr. Randolph's conduct on this occasion was looked upon with admiration by all gentlemen.

" Mr. King, of New-York," says he to a friend, " came to me yesterday, and said that ' all the Georgetown mess were loud in their praises of my reception of McLean of Delaware's attack upon me on Monday (the day before yesterday), the 12th; that the Patroon (Van Rensselaer) was d·lighted,' &c., &c., &c. Tattnall of Georgia (a preux chevalier), told Mr. Macon that nothing could be more dignified or gentlemanly than my reply, and that it was just what it ought to have been. Many others tell me that this is the general sentiment."

Mr. Randolph frequently expressed to his friends his surprise at this attack upon him, and could not conceive the motive. He had a true regard for the gentleman from Delaware, though he might not have been aware of it; he pressed his regard upon no man. As far back as 1820, when Mr. McLean first took his seat in Congress, Mr.

Randolph, with characteristic accuracy and penetration, had described him to a friend, his origin and history, and that of his family, and concluded by saying, " He is the finest fellow I have seen here, by a double distance."

Mr. Randolph watched the tariff bill in all its stages, and resisted it so long as there was any hope. At length he wrote to a friend :

" I am satisfied (now) that nothing can avail to save us. Indeed I have long been of that opinion. ' The ship will neither wear nor stay, and she may go ashore, and be d—d,' as Jack says."

Friday, 25th April, he says:

" The tariff is finished, (in our House at least,) and so am I. I was sent for on Tuesday in all haste to vote upon it ; when I got there the previous question was taking, and the clerk reading the yeas and nays.

" At the end, Gilmore (a fine fellow, by the way, although a Georgian and a Crawford man) moved for a call of the House. When that was over, Wilde, from Georgia, moved to amend the title. I, as big a fool as he, got up to tell him what an ass he was. (By the way, for ' Smith's verses on the old continental money,' which the reporter put into my mouth—why or wherefore he only can tell—read what I actually did say : *Swift's verses on the motto upon Chief Justice Whitshed's coach.* So much for reporters. That over, Drayton, of S. C., who is the Purge of the House, got up to make another motion to amend. By this time the noisome atmosphere overcame me, and ι left the hall, Mr. D. on his legs ; but a copious effusion of blood from the lungs has been the consequence. It came on in about thirty minutes after I got home ; so that the debate on the amendment of the tariff bill has the honor of my coup de grace."

Mr. Randolph was appointed on the committee to investigate the charges of mismanagement brought by Ninian Edwards against the Secretary of the Treasury. In reference to this subject he writes to his constituents from on board the ship Nestor, at sea, May 17:

" Fellow-citizens, friends, and freeholders—A recurrence of the same painful disease that drove me from my post some two years ago again compels me to ask a furlough, for I cannot consent to consider myself in the light of a deserter. But no consideration whatever would have induced me to leave Washington, so long as a shadow of doubt hung over the transactions of the Treasury, which I was (among others) appointed to investigate. * * * * I confess that I was not without some misgivings that all was not right. Holding myself aloof from the intrigues and intriguers of Washington, I had remained a passive spectator of a scene such as I hope never again to witness. Not that I was without a slight, a very slight, preference in the choice of the evils submitted to us for our acceptance. I inclined towards Mr. Crawford, for some reasons which were private and personal, and with which it is unnecessary to trouble you; but, chiefly, because you preferred him to his competitors, and because, if elected, he would, in a manner, be compelled to throw himself into the hands of the least unsound of the political parties of the country; that he would, by the force of circumstances, be compelled to act with us (the people), whilst the rival candidates would, by the same force of circumstances, be obliged to act against us, and with the tribe of office hunters and bankrupts that seek to subsist upon our industry and means."

CHAPTER XXVI.

SECOND VOYAGE TO EUROPE.

MR. JACOB HARVEY, who died in 1848, was an Irishman by birth; he emigrated some thirty years ago from his native country, and made the city of New-York the place of his residence. He was a merchant by profession, and those who knew him in his business bear testimony to his extensive information, his skill and prudence, his integrity and liberality. He was a man of refined literary tastes, brilliant wit, genuine humor, and exquisite delicacy of feeling. These qualities rendered him, in the social relations of life, an instructive and fascinating companion. The acquaintance that commenced between him and Mr. Randolph, on his first voyage to Europe, grew into an unreserved intimacy that lasted to the day of his death. Speaking of him, in a letter to his niece from London, he says: "His name is Jacob Harvey, son of Joseph Massey H., a Limerick merchant, attached to the society of Friends—what is called a gay Quaker. His grandfather, Reuben H., was a merchant of Cork, and during the war of 1776 received a letter under General Washington's own hand, returning his thanks and those of Congress for his kindness to our countrymen in Ireland, prisoners and others. He was introduced to me by Mr. Colden, as we left the quay."

Having assisted Mr. Randolph, says Mr. Harvey, in making

his preparations for the voyage, I left him at Bunker's, and promised to call upon him next morning at half past nine o'clock, to accompany him to the steamboat, which was to convey him to the packet.

I charged him to have all his luggage ready, as the steamboat was to start precisely at ten o'clock, which he promised to do. Next morning, punctual to my appointment, I entered his sitting-room, expecting, of course, to find him. cap in hand, ready to walk to White-hall dock, the moment I appeared. Judge, then, of my utter astonishment to see him sitting at the table, in his dressing-gown, with a large Bible open before him, pen in hand, in the act of writing a letter; while 'John' was on his knees, most busily employed in emptying one trunk and filling another!

"In the name of heaven," said I, Mr. Randolph, what is the matter? Do you know that it will soon be ten o'clock, and the steamboat waits for nobody? You promised me last night to have every thing packed up and ready when I called, and here you are not even dressed yet!"

"I cannot help it, sir," replied he; "I am all confusion this morning; every thing goes wrong; even my memory has gone 'a good wool gathering.' I am just writing a farewell letter to my constituents, and, would you believe it, sir, I have forgotten the exact words of a quotation from the Bible, which I want to use, and, as I always quote correctly, I cannot close my letter until I find the passage; but strange to say, I forget both the chapter and verse. I never was at fault before, sir; what *shall* I do?"

"Do you remember any part of the quotation?" said I, " perhaps I can assist you with the rest, as time is precious."

"It begins," replied he, " ' How have I loved thee, oh Jacob;' but for the life of me, I cannot recollect the next words. Oh my head! my head! Here, do you take the Bible, and run your eye over *that* page, whilst I am writing the remainder of my address."

"My dear sir," said I, " you have not time to do this now, but let us take letter, Bible, and all on board the steamboat, where you will have ample time to find the passage you want, before we reach the packet."

After some hesitation and reluctance, he agreed to my proposition, and then, suddenly turning round, he said, in a sharp tone:

"Well, sir, I will not take John with me, and you will please get back his passage-money to-morrow. He must go home, sir."

"Not take John with you!" exclaimed I. "Are you mad? Do you forget how much you suffered last voyage for want of John or Juba, and how repeatedly you declared that you would never again cross the Atlantic without one of them? It is folly, and I cannot consent to it."

"I *have decided*, sir; the question is no longer open to discussion."

"At least," said I, "be so good as to give some reason for such a decision."

"Why, sir," replied he, "John has disobliged me. He has been spoiled by your *free blacks*, and forgets his duty; and I have no idea of having to take care of *him* all the way to Europe and back again!" Then, turning to poor John, who was completely crest-fallen, he went on: "Finish that trunk at once, and take it down to the steamboat, and on your return take your passage in the Philadelphia boat; and when you get to Philadelphia, call on Mr. ——, in Arch street, and tell him that I have sailed; then go on to Baltimore, and call on Mr. ——, in Monument Place, and say that I shall write to him from London; thence proceed to Washington; pack up my trunks, which you will find at my lodgings, and take them with you to Roanoke, and report yourself to my overseer." After a pause, he added, in a sarcastic tone, "Now, John, you have heard my commands; but you *need not obey them*, unless you choose to do so. If you prefer it, when you arrive in Philadelphia, call on the Manumission Society, *and they will make you free*, and I shall never look after you. Do you hear, sir?"

This unjust aspersion of John's love was too much for the faithful fellow; his chest swelled, his lips quivered, his eyes filled, as he replied, in much agitation:

"Master John, this is too hard. I don't deserve it. You know I love you better than every body else, and you know you will find me at Roanoke when you come back!"

I felt my blood rising, and said: "Well, Mr. Randolph, I could not have believed this had I not seen it. I thought you had more compassion for your slaves. You are positively unjust in this case, for surely, you have punished him severely enough by leaving him behind you, without hurting his feelings. You have made the poor fellow cry."

"What," said he quickly, "does he shed tears?" "He does," replied I, "and you may see them yourself." "Then," said he, "*he shall go with me!* John, take down your baggage, and let us forget what has passed. I was irritated, sir, and I thank you for the rebuke."

Thus ended this curious scene. John instantly brightened up, soon forgot his master's anger, and was on his way to the boat, in a few minutes, perfectly happy.

Just as the boat was casting off, Randolph called out to me—

"Good-by, my friend, and remember, I shall land at the Cove of Cork (the dangers of the sea always excepted), and go over to Limerick, and spend a day or two at your father's house."

I did not place much dependence upon this hasty promise, and was, therefore, agreeably surprised, a few weeks afterwards, by receiving a letter from home, informing me that "Randolph of Roanoke" had really paid my family a visit, of which they had not received the slightest intimation, until he entered the parlor and introduced himself. He made himself extremely agreeable, and they were very sorry to part with him the next day.

"Sir," said he, speaking of Ireland, "much as I was prepared to see misery in the South of Ireland, I was utterly shocked at the condition of the poor peasantry between Limerick and Dublin. Why, sir, John never felt so proud at being a *Virginia slave.* He looked with horror upon the mud hovels and miserable food of the *white slaves,* and I had no fear of *his* running away. The landlords, and the clergy of the established church, have a fearful account to give, some day or other, sir, of the five and ten talents intrusted to them. I could not keep silence, sir, but every where, in the stage-coaches and hotels, I expressed my opinions fearlessly. One morning, whilst breakfasting at Morrison's, in Dublin, I was drawn into an argument with half a dozen country gentlemen, all violent tories, who seemed to think that all the evils of Ireland arose from the disloyalty of the Catholics. I defended the latter, on the ground that they were denied their political rights; and I told them very plainly, in the language of Scripture, that until they 'unmuzzled the ox which treadeth out the corn,' they must expect insurrections and opposition to the government. I had no sooner uttered these words than they all endeavored to silence me by clamor, and one of them insinuated that I must be a 'foreign spy.' I stood up at once, sir, and after a pause, said, 'Can it be possible that I am in the metropolis of Ireland, the centre of hospitality, or do I dream? Is *this* the way Irish gentle men are wont to treat strangers, who happen to express sympathy for the wrongs of their countrymen? If, gentlemen, you cannot refute my arguments, at least do not drown my voice by noisy assertions, which you do not attempt to prove. If ever any of you should visit old Virginia, I shall promise you a fair hearing, at all events; and you may compare *our* system of slavery with yours—aye, and be the judges yourselves!' This pointed rebuke had the desired effect; the moment they discovered who I was they instantly apologized for their rudeness, insisted upon my dining with them; and never did I spend a more jovial day. The instant *politics* were laid aside, all was wit and repartee, and song. So ended my first and last debate with a party of *Irish tories.*"

Of England, he says, " there never was such a country on the face of the earth, as England; and it is utterly impossible that there ever can be any combination of circumstances hereafter, to make such another country as old England now is—God bless her! But in Ireland," he added, " the Government and the Church, *or the Lion and the Jackal,* have divided the spoils between them, leaving nothing for poor Pat, but the potatoes. The Marquis of Wellesley, sir, does his best to lessen the miseries of the peasantry, and yet he is abused by both factions—a pretty good proof that he acts impartially between them, sir."

From England, Mr. Randolph crossed over into France. From Paris, he addressed the following letter to his friend, Dr. Brockenbrough:

PARIS, July 24, 1824.

This date says every thing. I arrived here on Sunday afternoon, and am now writing from the Grand Hotel de Castile, rue Richelieu and Boulevard des Italiens—for, as the French say, it gives upon both, having an entrance from each.

I need not tell either of *you,* that it is in the very focus of gayety and fashion; and if the maitre d'hotel may be credited, it is always honored by the residence of " M. le Duc de Davuansaire," whenever his Grace pays a visit to his birthplace. The civilities which, through the good offices of my friend, Mr. Foster, were tendered to me two years ago, from 'Davuansaire House,' and 'Chisonig,' would render this circumstance a recommendation, if the neatness and comfort of my apartments did not supersede all necessity for any other recommendation.

Here, then, am I, where I ought to have been thirty years ago—and where I would have been, had I not been plundered and oppressed during my nonage, and left to enter upon life overwhelmed with a load of DEBT, which the profits of a nineteen years' minority ought to have more than paid; and ignorant as I was (and even yet am) of business, to grope my way, without a clue, through the labyrinth of my father's affairs, and brought up among Quakers, an ardent *ami des noirs*, to scuffle with negroes and overseers, for something like a pittance of rent and profit upon my land and stock.

" Under such circumstances, that I have not been utterly ruined, is due (under God) to the spirit I inherited from my parents, and to the admirable precepts, and yet more admirable example of my revered mother—honored and blessed be her memory.   Then I had to unravel the tangled skein of my poor brother's difficulties and debts.   His sudden and untimely death threw upon my care, helpless as I was, his family, whom I tenderly and passionately loved, and with whom I might be now living, at Bizarre, if the reunion of his widow with the ———— of her husband had not driven me to Roanoke; where, but for my brother's entreaty and forlorn and friendless condition, I should have remained; and where I should have obtained a release from my bondage more than twenty years ago.   Then I might have enjoyed my present opportunities; but time misspent and faculties misemployed, and senses jaded by labor, or impaired by excess, cannot be recalled any more than that freshness of the heart, before it has become aware of the deceits of others, and of its own.

" But how do you like Paris? for all this egotism you might have poured out from Washington."

Not in the least.   And I stay here only waiting for my letters, which are ———— to the return of this day's post from London.   To you I need not say one word of the Lions of Paris, but will, in a word, tell you, that crucifixes, and paintings of crucifixions, and prints of Charlotte Corday and Marie Antoinette, &c., are the fashion of the day.   That the present dynasty, infirmly seated in the saddle; and that by little and little every privilege, acquired not by the designs of its authors, but by the necessary consequences of such a revolution, will be taken from the people; nay, I am persuaded that the lands will be resumed, or (what is the same thing) an ample equivalent will be plundered from the public, to endow the losers with.   At the next session of the deputies, the measure of reimbursing the emigrants—a measure the very possibility of which was scouted, only three years ago. The Marquis de La Fayette had sailed for the United States about ten days before my arrival here. I am sorry he has taken the step. It will do no good to his reputation, which at his time of life he ought to nurse. I take it for granted, that Ned Livingston, or some other equally pure patriot, will propose *another* donation to him; the last, I think, was on the motion of Beau Dawson. I hope I may be there, to give it just such another reception as M. Figaro had at my hands. Although it is certainly a species of madness (and I hear that this malady is imputed to me) to be wearing out my strength and spirits, and defending the rights (whether of things or of persons) of a people who lend their countenance to them that countenance the general plunder of the public, in the expectation either that they may share in the spoil, or that their former peculations will not be examined into.

I consider the present King of France, and his family, to be as firmly seated on the throne of the Tuilleries, as ever Louis XIV. was at Versailles; all possibility of counter-revolution is a mere chimera of distempered imagination. It would be just as possible to restore the state of society and manners which existed in Virginia a half a century ago; I should as soon expect to see the Nelsons, and Pages, and Byrds, and Fairfaxes, living in their palaces, and driving their coaches and sixes; or the good old Virginia gentlemen on the assembly, drinking their twenty and forty bowls of rack punches, and madeira, and claret, in lieu of a knot of deputy sheriffs and hack attorneys, each with his cruet of whisky before him, and puddle of tobacco-spittle between his legs.

But to return to Paris. It is wonderfully improved since you saw it; nay, since the last restoration, but it is still the filthiest hole, not excepting the worst parts of the old town of Edinboro', that I ever saw *out of Ireland*. I have dined, for your sake, *chez Beauvilliers*, and had bad fare, bad wine, and even bad bread, a high charge and a surly *garçon*. Irving, whom you know by character (our ex-minister at Madrid), was with me. He says all the *Traiteurs* are bad, and the crack ones worst of all. I have also dined with Very, the first restaurateur of the Palais Royal, four times; on one of which occasions I had a good dinner and a *fair* glass of champagne—next door to Very, once, at the Café de Chartres—with Pravot—Pastel; all in the Palais Royal; all bad, dear, and not room enough, even at *Beauvilliers'* or Very's, to sit at ease. I can have a better dinner for half a guinea at the Traveller's, in a saloon fit for a prince, and where gentlemen alone can enter, and a pint of the most exquisite Madeira, than I can get here for fifteen francs. I have dined like a marketman for 5 fr. 10 sous; that is the cheapest. All the wine, except le vin ordinaire, is adulterated shockingly. The English, that made every thing dear, and spoiled the garçons and filles, whose greediness is only equalled by their impudence. Crucifixes, madonnas, and pictures and prints of that cast, with Charlotte Corday, &c., &c., are the order of the day. Paris swarms with old priests, who have been dug up since the restoration, and they manufacture young ones (Jesuits especially) by hundreds at a single operation.

Monsieur, whom you saw at Edinburgh, is remarkable, as I hear, for consuming a hat per day, when one is each morning put upon his toilet. Hats were not so plenty then.

I made a strange mistake in my order to Leigh. I intended to have given him control over all my funds, except the tobacco sold after that period, which I wished to reserve as a fund, on which to play here—I mean in Europe. Pray, let it be so, deducting my check for the passage money.

And now, my good friend, let me tell you that the state of my eyes, and of my health, and of my avocations too—for I have a great deal of writing to do—*may* cause this to be the last letter that you shall receive from me until my return, when we shall, I hope, chat about these and other matters once more.

In case you should not have gone to Kentucky, I expect a regular bulletin from you. There is one subject very near my heart that you must keep me informed about. I know that women (with great plasticity on other subjects) never will take advice upon that. I know that they rush into ruin with open eyes, and spend the rest of their lives in cursing, at least, the happier lot of their acquaintances, who have in the most important concern of life been governed by the dictates of common sense. The man is too old; he has not *nous* enough; he is helpless. If he had ten thousand a year, he would not be a match for her. I don't know who is worthy of her. But let him be of suitable age, with *mind* and *taste* congenial with her own, and of an *erect spirit* as well as carriage of body. They shall have my blessing.

Adieu,

J. R. OF R.

Except a few of the English, with which people Paris swarms, I have not seen, either in the streets or elsewhere, any thing that by possibility might be mistaken for a gentleman. The contrast in this respect with London is most striking; indeed I would as soon compare the Hottentots with the French as these last with the English. No Enquirer yet received, and I pine for news from home.

The latter part of the summer Mr. Randolph spent among the mountains of Switzerland. August the 25th he says: "I was at Lauterbrunnen gazing on the Stubbach, or seeing 'the soaring Jungfrau rear her never-trodden snow.'"

He arrived in New-York the 2d day of December, when the result of the Presidential election was still in doubt, and hastened on to Washington.

CHAPTER XXVII.

PRESIDENTIAL ELECTION.

THE Presidential election of 1824 was the legitimate result of the preceding " era of good feelings." In that contest there was not one political principle involved. In no State in the Union, Delaware alone excepted, did the people pretend to keep up their old party organization. The word federalist was not heard in political circles; it was a mark of rudeness to attach that epithet to any gentleman; the measures it represented had long since been exploded; the word itself, as calling up unpleasant reminiscences, had grown obsolete; and every body professed to belong to the great republican family. It was suspected there were many federalists in disguise, and that their profession of republicanism was merely a lip service; but no one could point them out, or identify them by their political acts. The party had been dissolved, the federalists themselves admitted; but they contended that it had only been dissolved by the republicans embracing their doctrines. And it is very true that all the leading measures of Congress were of a federal stamp, and that they were bottomed on principles of the most latitudinous kind; the very same that Hamilton used in defending his obnoxious schemes, that brought such discredit on the name of federalism. It was impossible to draw a line of distinction between men, or to set up any standard by which to judge their opinions. Old measures and the divisions they occasioned had passed away; new measures, under entirely new and variant circumstances, had been brought forward; but they involved the same principles of interpretation, and required the same line of argument in their defence, as the old ones: but men did not divide upon them as they had done heretofore. Those who professed to abhor the doctrines of Hamilton, when applied to the schemes of

his day, now embraced them as the only means of defending and sustaining their own measures. A change of circumstances was thought
to justify a change of political principle. In Hamilton's day, and
down to 1811, a national bank was unconstitutional; but now, in the
estimation of republicans, it had become "necessary and proper,"
and therefore constitutional. Those who came into power with Mr.
Jefferson, professing hostility to a national bank, and who refused in
1811 to re-charter the old one, established in 1816 a similar institu
tion. The latitudinous construction of the Constitution by the
Adams administration in 1798-99, and the odious measures based
thereon, such as the alien and sedition laws, constituted the principal
objection to that administration, and were the main cause of its overthrow; and the substitution of a party professing the contrary doctrines—a party that professed to interpret the Constitution literally,
and that would exercise no power that had not been specifically given
by some express grant in the Charter. This party pursued their
principles for some years, and furnished a model of a plain, just, and
economical government; but in 1816, while nominally in power, they
elected their President, and for eight years seemed to control the
measures of his administration; and yet those measures, as we have
abundantly seen, were founded on the same principles that had been
so loudly condemned and unequivocally repudiated under the Adams
dynasty: so easily are men deceived by names and appearances; so
hard is it to follow a rigid rule of abstinence, when appetite and
opportunity invite to indulgence.

A respectable minority, with John Randolph at the head, invariably opposed the consolidating measures of the times; demonstrated
their identity with the exploded doctrines of federalism, and warned
the people of the dangerous consequences; but it was a sort of Cassandra voice, that nobody heeded: it seemed impossible to restore the old
landmarks, and to convince the people that they had gone backwards,
and fallen into the old paths they had once abandoned. All were ex-
expecting some special advantage from the legislation of the day; the
hopes of profit had stifled the remonstrances of truth; and the popular
leaders were constantly dazzling the imaginations of the people with
some magnificent scheme, by which they hoped to gain renown for themselves, and to fasten to their fortunes by the ties of a common interest
some class or section of the community. The presidential candidates

were all committed, or in some way identified with those schemes. Mr. Adams, Mr. Calhoun, and Mr. Crawford, were members of the cabinet ; but they had not been slow in expressing themselves on all occasions, and had given unequivocal evidence of their devotion to those broad doctrines that swept away the barriers of the Constitution, and made it a convenient instrument to sanction whatever might be deemed for the time being to be necessary and proper.

Mr. Clay, as the leader in the House of Representatives, had been their most ardent, active, and eloquent champion. His position gave him the advantage of the initiative in all popular measures, and he never failed to identify himself with them by some bold and eloquent discourse. Not content with sweeping away the barriers within the narrow horizon of domestic politics, he embraced in the wide scope of his philanthropic regard all the oppressed and struggling nations of the earth; and, turning a deaf ear to the warning of the father of his country, he hastened to speak a word of encouragement, and to stretch out an arm of help without regard to the consequences to his own country. His ambition for public display, his thirst for present and personal applause, his frank and manly character, his sanguine temperament, and bold imagination, with a quick, comprehensive, yet undisciplined mind, made him just the character to be led off by any popular theme that might promise distinction and popularity—just the man to follow with undoubting faith the shining *ignis fatuus* of the hour, and to be dazzled by it and deceived.

General Jackson had not been in political life, and possessed great military renown ; this gave him an advantage over his competitors : but he was not known to differ materially from them in his politica opinions. There were no public acts to commit him ; but all his correspondence and conversations, so far as they were made known to the public, proved that at that time he had no clear conception of the principles that divided the old federal and republican parties, and that he was equally devoted to those new measures which had done so much to bring back in disguise the ascendency of federal doctrines.

In this state of things the partisans of each of the candidates for the presidency sought to impress on the public mind the idea that their friend was *par excellence* the true republican candidate. But it was impossible to persuade the people to this belief, when there was no political principle dividing them—no platform of doctrine on which they were called to stand, so as to be separated and distinguished from those around them.   The consequence was, the whole country was divided into sectional and personal factions.   The West and Southwest voted for a western and southwestern man; New-York and New England voted for a New England man; while the Southern and Middle States were divided between a northern, a southern, and a western man.   There was no principle to bring the discordant sections together, and to cause them to sacrifice their friend on the altar of the public good ; there was no such public good—nothing in the whole controversy that would justify any such immolation.   What advantage had Mr. Adams over Mr. Clay, or Mr. Crawford, or General Jackson ?   or what advantage had either of these over him, so as to induce the friends of one to surrender him that they might thereby secure the success of the other ?   It was not publicly pretended that one was sounder in his political opinions than the other ; and they all stood on their own personal merits as having done some service to the country and to the republican cause.   The friends of Mr. Crawford endeavored to gain an advantage for him by procuring a " regular nomination," according to the usages of the party.   It had been usual for a convention, or, as it was called, a caucus, of republican members at the proper time to assemble together, and to designate some suitable person for the presidency or whom the people might concentrate their votes, so as to prevent the triumph of those principles which they regarded as so obnoxious : so long as federalism continued in organized opposition, this concentration was the only means of securing the ascendency to the republican party.   But federalism had long ceased to exist as an opposing force. This party machinery, therefore, in the absence of those higher motives of combination, could only be made to subserve the purposes of faction, and to give an undue advantage where none was deserved.

The friends of Mr. Crawford, however, being mostly from Virginia and New-York, and considering themselves as the true standards of republican orthodoxy, persisted in their course, notwithstanding a formidable opposition, and called together their convention the 14th of February, 1824.   Out of two hundred and sixty-one members of Congress, only sixty-four attended the meeting in person, and two by proxy.   The two proxies and sixty-two members present voted for Mr. Crawford. Of the sixty-two votes, one-half were from New-York and Virginia. This convention did not exceed one-fourth of the members of Congress, and was composed entirely of the friends of one only of the candidates—there was no comparison of opinions— no sacrifices of personal preferences and mutual concessions for the good of a common cause. Under such circumstances, it is obvious that the meeting could make no pretensions to nationality, not even to a full and fair party organization. Yet it was proclaimed as "the regular nomination" according to the usages of the party, and the republicans called on to sustain it as such. In Virginia, the people gave it their support, because Mr. Crawford was their choice under all circumstances. But in New-York it met with a very different fate. Mr. Crawford was not a favorite with the people of New-York, though her delegation voted for him in the caucus of 1816 in oppo- sition to Mr. Monroe, and came near defeating by their skilful and secret management the only person seriously spoken of by the peo- ple. Finding that the "regular nomination," according to party usage, which carried such a potent spell with it heretofore, had lost its influence, and that if the people were left to themselves, Mr. Crawford was certain of defeat, his friends took refuge in the legis- lature, and determined to gain their point by keeping the election from the people. Up to this time the electors of President and Vice-President had been *nominated* by the legislature. The people now determined to take the election in their own hands. A bill to that effect passed the lower House with only four dissenting voices, such was the unanimity on the subject; but it was defeated in the Senate, where there were a majority of Mr. Crawford's friends. So great was the excitement in the State, that the Governor called an extra- session of the legislature to execute the will of the people. But the Senate again defeated the bill, and the Assembly adjourned without doing any thing. All this was done in the name of liberty. The majority of the Senate assumed to be the only true exponents of re- publicanism, and Mr. Crawford as its only true representative, and in order to carry their measures, committed great violence on their own principles. But even the legislature would not sustain this violent effort to force the State to cast her vote for one she did not prefer.

When the nominations were made, Mr. Crawford got only four out of the thirty-six electoral votes of New-York.

The events of this presidential campaign furnish an instructive page of history, which should be well considered by the people. It was just the combination of circumstances to tempt ambitious men to form coalitions for their own personal ends, and to make a regular bargain and sale of the rights of the people. In the absence of all political principle—in a mere contest between individuals for power—what was to prevent a union of the North and the South, or the East and the West, in a regular contract for a division of the spoils? There was no election by the people. Adams, Crawford, Clay and Jackson, were all voted for, but no one obtained a majority of the electoral colleges. The duty of making a choice between the three highest candidates now devolved on the House of Representatives. For a long time Mr. Clay was expected to be one of the three. The vote of Louisiana, which his friends expected, being given against him, caused Mr. Crawford to have a few more votes than he, and the contest was between Jackson, who had the highest number of votes in the electoral colleges, Adams, and Crawford. Mr. Clay, from his great influence, had entire control of the election. He decided in favor of Mr. Adams, and immediately accepted, at his hands, the office of Secretary of State. He was openly charged in the House of Representatives with bargain and corruption. He repelled the charge with becoming indignation. The reasons he gave for voting for Mr. Adams were just—situated as he was, he could not have voted otherwise—but the fact of his accepting office from the man he himself had elevated into the seat of power, condemned him. He should have given the vote, but declined the office. His own consciousness of innocence may have sustained him in the performance of the deed, but it could not screen him from the inferences that would be drawn from it by a censorious world. Men's motives are known only to themselves; language, says Talleyrand, was given to conceal them; and that which is avowed, is rarely the true cause of any action. Knowing these things, it is not surprising that a jealous and censorious world will at least *suspect* the motive, where the act and the circumstances might justify the imputation of a bad one.

During the time of the ballotting, an incident took place that was very characteristic of John Randolph; it showed his great accuracy in the statement of a fact, at the same time his jealous observance not only of the rights of the States, but even of the forms and expressions in which those rights might be involved. Mr. Webster was appointed by the tellers who sat at one table, and Mr. Randolph by those at the other, to announce the result of the ballotting. After the ballots were counted out, Mr. Webster rose, and said : Mr. Speaker, the tellers of the votes at this table have proceeded to count the ballots contained in the box set before them ; the result they find to be, that there are for John Quincy Adams, of Massachusetts, 13 votes; for Andrew Jackson, of Tennessee, 7 votes; for Wm. H. Crawford, of Georgia, 4 votes.

Mr. Randolph, from the other table, made a statement corresponding with that of Mr. Webster, in the facts, but varying in the phraseology, so as to say that Mr. Adams, Mr. Jackson, and Mr. Crawford, had received the votes of *so many States*, instead of *so many votes*.

CHAPTER XXVIII.

"SUCH CONSTITUENTS AS MAN NEVER HAD BEFORE, AND NEVER WILL HAVE AGAIN."

FROM Charlotte Court-house, Tuesday, April 5th, 1825, Mr. Randolph writes to Dr. Brockenbrough : "Much against my will—I do not deceive myself—I am involved in another election. Two more years, if I live as long, in that bear garden, the House of Representatives! You ask after my health, it is wretched in the extreme. Nothing but an earnest desire to avoid the imputation of giving myself airs, brought me here yesterday." He was at Prince Edward Court-house, also, on Monday, the 18th—the day of election in that county. It was the first time the writer of this memoir had the pleasure of seeing Mr. Randolph among his constituents, or hearing him on the hustings. He was then a lad at the neighboring college—Hampden Sydney. That day was given as a holiday to the students, and they all repaired at an early hour to the Court-house to see the wonderful man of whom they had heard so much. I saw Mr. Randolph when he arrived on the "court green;" he alighted from his sulky some distance from' the Court-house, and handed over the reins to Johnny, who was in an instant by his side. He was dressed in his old "uniform of blue and buff," with knee-buckles, and long fair-top boots. He seemed to limp slightly in his gait, which only added dignity and gravity to his carriage. The moment his arrival was known, the people came flocking from all directions towards him. The tavern-porches, the shops, and offices, were soon emptied, and every body went running towards the great object of attraction. His old acquaintances (and who were not old acquaintances there?) were eager to take him by the hand; they pressed forward without ceremony, and their greetings were most cordially reciprocated. To all the old men he had something to say, pointed and appropriate, that seemed to give them infinite satisfaction—a word of recognition, that meant more than it expressed, and went home to the heart. He marched slowly towards the Court-house, still greeting and talking with his friends, as they came up to take him by the hand. Many followed him, doubtless, from curiosity; but much the largest portion of the crowd that hovered around him, were men who had known him all their lives, and had seen him a hundred times before; yet they followed him with as much interest as the youngest school-boy there, and their eyes could not be sated by gazing upon him. Such is the magic influence of genius and of true greatness on the human mind. 'Tis said that Robert Burns could not arrive at an inn, at midnight, without its being known to all the inmates, who would come flocking, even in their night garments, to see, for the twentieth time, perhaps, the enchanting countenance of Scotland's noblest bard, who, like Randolph, from his earliest youth, had no other thought but to serve and adorn his native land.

> " E'n then a wish (I mind its power),
>   A wish, that to my latest hour
>   Shall strongly heave my breast—
>   That I, for poor auld Scotland's sake,
>   Some usefu' plan or book could make,
>   Or sing a sang at least."

Mr. Randolph was pressed to make a speech. He pleaded his wretched health, and begged to be excused. But no excuse would be taken; his old friends wanted to hear him; it was a long time since they had that pleasure; great changes had taken place in politics; they had heard much about them, but wanted to hear from his own lips how the matter stood. Finding that no apology would be taken, that such men as the Mortons, the Prices, the Watkins' and the Venables, were urging on him to say something to gratify the people, he at length consented; and retiring from the multitude, he sat down on an oaken bench in the corner of the Court-house yard, and rested his head on the end of his umbrella. No one approached or disturbed him. After sitting some ten or fifteen minutes, he arose, and asked the sheriff to make proclamation that he would address the people. There was no need of that; they were all there, pressing around, and waiting patiently his pleasure to speak to them. As he approached the stile, the crowd receded, and opened a way for him to pass. I followed in his wake, unconscious of what I was doing, and stood near his left side, where I could hear every word that was uttered, and see every motion of every muscle of the whole man. I was too young to remember what was said, at this distance of time. The newspapers said he "addressed his constituents in a *manner* and with *matter* which gave great and universal satisfaction. He descanted, with great eloquence and power, on the *alarming encroachments of the General Government upon the rights of the States.*" I have no doubt that was the theme of his discourse. But what I saw I shall never forget—the *manner* of the man. The tall, slender figure, swarthy complexion, animated countenance; the solemn glance, that passed leisurely over the audience, hushed into deep silence before him, and bending forward to catch every look, every motion and every word of the inspired orator; the clear, silver tones of his voice; the distinct utterance—full, round expression, and emphasis of his words; the graceful bend and easy motion of the person, as he turned from side to side; the rapid, lightning-like sweep of the hand when something powerful was uttered; the earnest, fixed gaze, that followed, as if searching into the hearts of his auditors, while his words were telling upon them; then, the ominous pause, and the twinkling of that long, slender forefinger, that accompanied the keen, cutting sarcasm of his words—all these I can never forget. My *beau ideal* of the orator was complete. What I had read of Demosthenes and Cicero, aided by the lights of Longinus and Quinctilian, was fulfilled in this man. I have heard him several times since from the same place. Those who have heard him elsewhere concur in the opinion, that before the people of Prince Edward he was peculiarly free and happy. These were the people that stood by him in the darkest hour of his fortunes; "when two administrations" and the whole political press made war upon him, they shielded him from the assaults of his enemies, and cheered him in the desolate and dangerous path he had to tread, by the light of their countenance and the voice of their approbation. It is not wonderful, then, that in the presence of such a people, the reminiscences of the olden time should· rekindle the slumbering fires of his heart, and inspire his thoughts with more than their wonted force and brilliancy.

From the stand, Mr. Randolph retired to the bench in the Court-house. The polls were opened, and the voting commenced. Each one, as he came up, pronounced with a clear and audible voice the name of John Randolph as the person voted for for Congress. There was not a dissenting voice. When any one of the old men gave his vote, Mr. Randolph partly rose from his seat, and in the most bland and affecting manner thanked him for his vote. He seemed to say, I am grateful, sir, and proud to have the approbation of a man of your independence, understanding, integrity, and weight of character. The old man returned the salutation with a look that said, I am proud, also, to have the privilege of voting for you, Mr. Randolph. There was no pretence, no affectation in all this; it was natural, spontaneous, and, to those who knew the history of the parties and their relations to each other, it was truly affecting. No one could look upon the scene without exclaiming, that with such constituents and such representatives, no danger or harm could befall the Republic. They were men, for the most part, owners of the soil, and living by its cultivation; men who, from their youth up, by the daily reading of the best conducted political journals, and their monthly conversations and discussions at the Court-house on political topics, had become familiar with the institutions of their country and the manner in which they had been conducted—who knew the characters of all public men that had risen above a neighborhood reputation, and could judge dispassionately and without enthusiasm of their objects and the tendency of their measures—they were models of republican simplicity, intelligence, and virtue. The same, for the most part.

may be said of all Mr. Randolph's district. He had represented them for five and twenty years; they all knew him—men, women, and children—and he knew them. These are the people of whom he spoke, when he said, on a memorable occasion in the House of Representatives:

"I will go back to the bosom of my constituents—to such constituents as man never had before, and never will have again—and I shall receive from them the only reward that I ever looked for, but the highest that man can receive—the universal expression of their approbation—of their thanks. I shall read it in their beaming faces; I shall feel it in their gratulating hands. The very children will climb around my knees, to welcome me. And shall I give up them, and this? And for what? For the heartless amusements and vapid pleasures and tarnished honors of this abode of splendid misery, of shabby splendor? for a clerkship in the war office, or a foreign mission, to dance attendance abroad, instead of at home—or even for a Department itself? Sir, thirty years make sad changes in man. When I first was honored with their confidence, I was a very young man, and my constituents stood almost in parental relation to me, and I received from them the indulgence of a beloved son. But the old patriarchs of that day have been gathered to their fathers—some adults remain, whom I look upon as my brethren: but the far greater part were children—little children—or have come into the world since my public life began. I know among them, grand-fathers, and men muster-free, who were boys at school when I first took my seat in Congress. Time, the mighty reformer and innovator, has silently and slowly, but surely changed the relation between us; and I now stand to them *in loco parentis*—in the place of a father—and receive from them a truly filial reverence and regard. Yes, sir, they are my children—who resent, with the quick love of children, all my wrongs, real or supposed. Shall I not invoke the blessings of our common Father upon them. Shall I deem any sacrifice too great for them? To them I shall return, if we are defeated, for all of consolation that awaits me on this side of the grave. I feel that I hang to existence but by a single hair—the sword of Damocles is suspended over me."

Mr. Randolph spent the summer in his usual solitude at Roanoke. In June, he says to Dr. Brockenbrough:

"You are very good in taking time to write to me, but I hope you will continue to do so, notwithstanding the drudgery of penmanship that you are subjected to—for your letters constitute the only link between me and the world, at present—a world where I have but a little while longer to stay. I feel those internal monitions (of which the patient alone is sensible) that convince me that I cannot hold out much longer, and although life has no one attraction left for me, I cannot but look towards its point of dissolution, with some mis-givings of mind. We shall probably never meet again on this side of the grave : beyond it, all is involved in obscurity. I have just as much expectation of living to the end of the century, as to the close of the year. There is nothing left now for regimen or medicine to act upon. I have never been in such a condition ; not even in 1817."

July 8th, he says :—" Your kind letter of the 3d has just arrived to throw a cheerful ray over my clouded mind. Although I stood in no need of any such assurance, yet the declaration it contained at the outset gave me most sensible gratification. I believe we have dealt as little in professions as any persons similarly circumstanced ever did ; and for a plain reason—neither of us distrusted the sincerity of his sentiments towards the other. My dear friend, my strength ebbs apace. My health (like the stocks) fluctuates, but gets worse. I have lost my grasp upon the world. If it be not mad—then I am. Its political, religious and commercial relationships are, in my view, irrational and contemptible ; but I still cherish a warm feeling of regard and of interest in the welfare of those who have manifested kindly dispositions towards me. Indeed, I wish well to all—I must except a few ' caitiffs'—and would do good to all, if it was in my power. Among those who have shown me favor, I set high value upon the attachment of Frank Gilmer ; and I too had a very strong desire for his sake, that he would take the professorship. I was concerned to learn by a late letter from Mr. Barksdale, that he looked very ill, and was more desponding than when B. saw him in March. When you write to him, name me among those who think often and always kind-ly of him.

" The rains have destroyed our crops of every description but In-dian corn, and that is much injured. If I live as long, which I do not at all look forward to, I shall assuredly take the voyage you mention. It is dreary enough to be in a land of strangers, a cipher and at sufferance ; but any thing is better than the horrors of this climate, and indeed our state of society and manners is so changed, that were I to remain here, it must be in a sort of dreamy existence, among my books and shades, ignorant of what might be passing in the world around me.

" Jarvis, I remember, some fourteen years ago, made me laugh very heartily at poor Nicholson's table in Baltimore ; but I might defy him now to raise even a smile, except of ' such a sort ' as Ju-lius Cæsar could not endure. You are right to be as convivial as you can ; *soberly*, as Lady Grace says. *Dulce est desipere.* I am persuaded that our self-righteous denouncers of our old-fashioned sports and pastimes have added nothing to the stock of our morali-ty ; our young men and boys have exchanged the five's-court, and other athletic exercises, for the tavern-bench, squirting tobacco-juice, and drinking whisky-grog. The girls, instead of balls and dress, &c., discourse of original sin—'fixed fate, free will, foreknowledge absolute.' But after all, we shall look in vain for the worth or manners of the last generation.

"I read little but Dr. Barrow, and not much of him. I have sometimes thought of attacking Atterbury and South; but after a short application, my eyes become dim and my head swims, and I have to take a turn or two about the room to recover myself. I would not trouble you with this long (for such it is) and stupid letter, but for the assurance that it is gratifying to you to hear from me in my present reduced condition. You may judge what it is, when I tell you that I have not seen my plantation since my return from Europe.

"Butler's Reminiscences I read two years ago, and was much disappointed in them. Do you note an article in the Edinburgh Review on the subject of the West Indies? It is written in a most ferocious spirit of philanthropy. My infirmity admonishes me to lay down my pen."

The monotony and tedium of his solitary life were greatly relieved by a visit from his friends, Dr. and Mrs. Brockenbrough, in the month of October. They spent a week with him. Most of his correspondence, before and after, was in reference to this visit. It was an important era in the chronicles of Roanoke. November 25th, he writes, "I am truly glad the agues fled before the thing with the hard name. Old Mrs. D. says of you, any body may see from his face that he is a mighty clever man. What say you to that, my dear madam? * * * * You know me well; 'distrust' is a sin that I cannot easily forgive. I can truly say that the pleasantest week by far that I have spent for years, was that that you and Mrs. B. spent here."

Mr. Randolph was detained at home on business till late in December. He did not arrive in Washington—"Babylon," as he called it—till Christmas. In the mean time, he had been elected to the Senate of the United States, to fill the vacancy occasioned by the resignation of Gov. James Barbour, who had been appointed, by Mr. Adams, Secretary of War.

The election took place the 17th of December. The candidates nominated were Judge Henry St. George Tucker, the half-brother of Mr. Randolph, William B. Giles, John Floyd, and John Randolph. On the first ballot, the vote stood: Tucker 65, Randolph

63, Giles 58, Floyd 40. According to the rule of the House, Mr Floyd was dropped, and the second ballot stood: Tucker 87, Randolph 79, Giles 60. Mr. Giles being likewise dropped under the rules, and the members having prepared and deposited their ballots in the boxes, Mr. Jackson on the part of the friends of Mr. Tucker, rose and stated to the House, that it was the desire of Mr. Tucker, in no event, to be placed in competition with Mr. Randolph. Considering that Mr. R. had no chance of being elected, they had on their own responsibility, put Mr. Tucker in nomination. But as the collision was now between these two gentlemen, they thought it due to Mr. Tucker's feelings and request to withdraw his name. Some conversation then ensued, in which it was suggested that the ballot-boxes ought to be emptied and the ballots again collected. Mr. Jackson declared he did not know the ballots had been put in the boxes, or he should have withdrawn Mr. Tucker sooner. One gentleman remarked that the person who had been last dropped, ought, under these circumstances, to be again before the House. But the chair decided, that as the ballots had been all deposited in the boxes, and there being no mistake or irregularity, they must be counted under the rule of the House. This was accordingly done, and the ballots stood, Randolph 104, Tucker 80. Mr. Randolph, having a majority, was declared duly elected.

On the reception of the news of this election, through a letter from Dr. Brockenbrough, Judge Tucker thus responds: "I have barely time before the closing of the mail to acknowledge the receipt of your friendly letter, and to express my hearty concurrence in the gratification you feel at the election of my brother. I could wish indeed that my name had been withheld, yet hope that its withdrawal even at the time it took place, was not too late to manifest my deference to him. God preserve him long as an honor to his station and the Old Dominion. I cannot but think that this occurrence will reanimate his spirit, and restore him to that activity in the public councils for which he was always remarkable, until he thought himself unkindly treated by his native State. He will now, I trust, see in himself her favorite son."

CHAPTER XXIX.

THE ADAMS ADMINISTRATION.

THE reader is already aware that Mr. Randolph took no interest in the late Presidential contest. There were circumstances that inclined him to favor the pretensions of Mr. Crawford; but it was a mere personal preference; and as there were no principles involved in the controversy, he left the country with rather a feeling of indifference as to the result of the election. But no sooner was the contest decided by the election of John Quincy Adams in the House of Representatives, than Mr. Randolph gave unequivocal evidences of hostility to the new administration. For this he has been blamed by many persons. It seemed like a pre-determination to condemn men when they as yet had perpetrated no act worthy of condemnation. But it must not be forgotten that we have a written Constitution, containing the fundamental law of all our political institutions. We have a Federal Government and State Governments, each with limited and specified powers, and acting as mutual checks and balances to each other. An over-action on the part of the one or the other would destroy the equilibrium, and endanger the existence of our complicated and nicely-adjusted system of Government. Hence the necessity of a scheme of doctrine, or rules of interpretation, by which the Constitution was to be construed, and the different departments guided in their administration of the Government. Our statesmen have something more to do than advise measures. They have to show that those measures are sanctioned by the Constitution, and that, in their final result, they will not disturb the harmony of the system.

In consequence of this necessity imposed on our public men, there had grown up at a very early period two distinct schools of politicians, differing widely in their doctrines and rules of interpretation. But, during the recent administration, as the reader is aware, these distinctions were effaced, and men seemed to stand on the same platform, professing a general, vague, undefined belief in the doctrines of republicanism. Mr. Adams, having acted a conspicuous part under Mr.

Monroe, had now to take an independent position, and to mark out a line of policy for himself. Rising from a subaltern station into the chief magistracy of the Republic, where he could not be restrained by the authority of superiors, one would naturally suppose that his mind would take the direction of its early thoughts and associations. Mr. Adams's early education unfitted him to associate with those statesmen who looked with jealousy on the Federal Government, who deprecated its over-action as dangerous to the Union, and who abstemiously exercised those powers that had been actually delegated to it. Being the son of the late President John Adams, he received his education mostly abroad, while his father, as Minister of the United States, attended the various courts of Europe. At a very early period, before he had performed any public service whatever, General Washington, doubtless, in compliment to his father, appointed him Minister Plenipotentiary to the Hague. During the eventful period of his father's administration, he continued abroad in daily connection with the habits, opinions, and associations of the royal courts to which he was successively transferred as Minister of the United States.

After the political revolution of 1800 had condemned the administration of John Adams, and driven him from the helm of affairs, one of his last acts was the recall of his son, to save him from the mortification of being dismissed by Mr. Jefferson.

Soon after his return, John Quincy Adams was elected to the Senate of the United States from Massachusetts. He was elected as a federalist by a federalist Legislature; and one of his first acts in the Senate was to oppose the purchase of Louisiana, then the favorite measure of the republican party. But he had not been in the Senate long before an eventful and radical change took place in his public conduct. The restrictive policy of Mr. Jefferson, as the reader is aware, was very much opposed in New England. It crippled their commerce, on which they were mainly dependent for support. The embargo, in 1808, capped the climax of restriction; and the opposition in New England, led on by the old federal leaders, knew no bounds in their denunciations of those measures, which they regarded as so destructive of their interests.

Mr. Adams conceived the idea, or was informed by what he deemed good authority, that his old friends and associates were about to commit an act of treason to the country; that so deep was their hostility to the measures of the Government, and so great their determination to get rid of the burthen, that they contemplated a separation from the Union. Through the interposition of a distinguished Senator, he called on the President, and communicated to him his apprehensions.

He spoke of the dissatisfaction of the eastern portion of our Confederacy with the restraints of the embargo. That there was nothing which might not be attempted to rid themselves of it. That he had information of the most unquestionable certainty, that certain citizens of the Eastern States (naming Massachusetts particularly) were in negotiation with agents of the British Government, the object of which was an agreement that the New England States should take no further part in the proceedings of the Federal Government; that, without formally declaring their separation from the union of the States, they should withdraw from all aid and obedience to them; that their navigation and commerce should be free from restraint or interruption by the British; that they should be considered and treated by them as neutrals, and as such might conduct themselves towards both parties. He assured Mr. Jefferson that there was imminent danger that a separation would take place; that the temptations were such as might debauch many from their fidelity to the Union. The course of Mr. Adams brought upon him the hostility of his own legislature: another person was elected to succeed him, and he was instructed, during the remnant of his term, to oppose the measures of the administration. He retired from a position he could no longer hold with honor. The purity of his motives was defended in the Senate by a member of the administration party against the denunciations of his late colleague, who manifested feelings of the deepest hostility towards him.

Soon after his retirement, Mr. Adams was tendered a mission to the court of St Petersburg, but the Senate did not think such a mission at that time was necessary, and did not confirm the appointment. He was renominated by Mr. Madison on his accession to the Presidency, and the appointment was confirmed by the Senate. Mr. Adams continued abroad in various diplomatic capacities till the summer of 1817, when he was recalled by Mr. Monroe, and placed at the head of his administration as Secretary of State.

During this "era of good feelings" nothing occurred to develope the opinions of Mr. Adams as to the true construction of the Constitution. He is known to have favored the magnificent schemes of that day, and is thought to have had much influence over the mind of Mr. Monroe in producing the great change of sentiment on the subject of internal improvement. Thus we perceive that the early education, and the diplomatic career of Mr. Adams in the midst of royal courts, and the strongly concentrated and despotic governments of an hereditary aristocracy, illy fitted him to appreciate the unpretending and abstemious doctrines of that republican school for which he abandoned his old friends, and, as they say, basely calumniated them. His change of position did not involve a change of politics. He merely exchanged a broken and divided party for one in the ascendant. There never was an occasion to test the sincerity of this change until he was elected President of the United States. In this exalted station, unrestrained by the routine of office, he was not long in manifesting the bold and ardent aspirations of his mind. Endowed with a poetic genius and an ardent imagination, possessing a quick, irascible, and obstinate temper, a man of the closet, wholly unused to the restraints and the caution of legislative experience, he mounted the chair of state with the boldness and the confidence of Phaeton into the chariot of the sun.

The great idea that filled the mind and kindled the imagination of Mr. Adams was a magnificent scheme of internal improvement, to be constructed by the General Government. In his inaugural address he recurs to the subject, as he says, *with peculiar satisfaction.* " It is that," he continues, "from which I am convinced that the unborn millions of our posterity who are in future ages to people this continent, will derive their most fervent gratitude to the founders of the Union; that on which the most beneficent action of its Government will be most deeply felt and acknowledged. The magnificence and splendor of their public works are among the imperishable glories of the ancient republics. The roads and aqueducts of Rome have been the admiration of all after ages; and have survived thousands of years after all her conquests have been swallowed up in despotism, or become the spoil of barbarians." Mr. Adams did not doubt the power of Congress to enter in this field of rivalry with the ancient republics; and to surpass even the Roman empire, with the spoils of a world in its treasury, in the magnificence and splendor of their roads and aqueducts. He impatiently rejects the contrary proposition as unworthy of consideration, and boldly and dogmatically announces "that the question of the power of Congress to authorize the making of internal improvements is, in other words, a question whether the people of this Union, in forming their common social compact as avowedly for the purpose of promoting the general welfare, have performed their work so *ineffably stupid* as to deny themselves the means of bettering their own condition. I have too much respect for the intellect of my country to believe it."

In his annual message, the President again dilates on this subject with his peculiar animation and earnestness : " The spirit of improvement is abroad upon the earth. It stimulates the heart, and sharpens the faculties, not of our fellow-citizens alone, but of the nations of Europe, and of their rulers. While dwelling with pleasing satisfaction upon the superior excellence of our political institutions, let us not be unmindful that liberty is power ; that the nation blessed with the largest portion of liberty, must, in proportion to its numbers, be the most powerful nation upon earth ; and that the tenure of power by man is, in the moral purposes of his Creator, upon condition that it shall be exercised to ends of benificence, to improve the condition of himself and his fellow-man. While foreign nations, less blessed with that freedom which is power, than ourselves, are advancing with gigantic strides in the career of public improvement, were we to slumber in indolence, or fold up our arms and proclaim to the world that we are palsied by the will of our constituents; would it not be to cast away the bounties of Providence, and doom ourselves to perpetual inferiority ?"

But the President was surpassed, if possible, in his ideas of a magnificent and all-powerful Government, by the Secretaries whom he had gathered around him, as constitutional advisers. The Secretary of State, while a popular orator on the floor of Congress, had never failed, when occasion offered, to describe in glowing terms, the benefits to be derived from a free and unrestrained exercise of all those powers that Congress, in its wisdom, might deem *necessary and proper* to promote the common good and general welfare. But the Secretary of the Treasury went beyond them both in defining the object and the duties of Government. In his annual report he says the duty of a provident Government is "to augment the number and variety of occupations for its inhabitants; to hold out to every degree of labor, and to every modification of skill, its appropriate object and inducement; to organize the whole labor of a country; to entice into the widest ranges its mechanical and intellectual capacities, instead of suffering them to slumber; to call forth, wherever hidden, latent ingenuity, giving to effort activity, and to emulation ardor; to create employment for the greatest amount of numbers, by adapting it to the diversified faculties, propensities, and situations of men, so that every particle of ability, every shade of genius, may come into requisition."

In the eye of these political economists, Government is every thing, the people nothing. In their estimation, Government is a unit, having absolute control over the property and the industry of the people; directing the resources of the one and the energies of the other, into this or that channel, as may seem best to its sovereign and omnipotent will.

Doctrines like these were not ventured even in the palmiest days of federalism. John Adams, the father, and Hamilton, the Secretary, could not hold a light to the son, and those luminaries around him, who drew their inspiration from some modern political philosophy, which taught that the prosperity of the people must be based upon, and measured by, the omnipotent and unlimited powers conferred on the Government. It is not surprising that the people awoke from their long dream of security, and that they were alarmed at the boldness and the confidence with which these extraordinary doctrines were announced by the highest authorities known to the Constitution. It is not surprising, that John Randolph, the champion of State-rights, should sound the tocsin to warn the people, and that in the midst of so much error of doctrine, and bold usurpation of authority, he should express doubts of a long continuance of our federative Government, as designed and constructed by our forefathers:

"We are now making an experiment," says he, "which has never yet succeeded in any region or quarter of the earth, at any time, from the deluge to this day. With regard to the antediluvian times, history is not very full; but there is no proof that it has ever succeeded, even before the flood. One thing, however, we do know, that it has never succeeded since the flood; and, as there is no proof of its hav ing succeeded before the flood, as *de non apparentibus et non existentibus eadem est ratio;* it is good logic to infer, that it has never succeeded, and never can succeed any where. In fact the *onus probandi* lies on them that take up the other side of the question ; for although *post hoc ergo propter hoc* be not good logic, yet, when we find the same consequences generally following the same events, it requires nothing short of the skepticism of Mr. Hume, to deny that there is no connection between the one and the other, whatever, metaphysically speaking, there may be of *necessary* connection between cause and effect.

" I say, then, that we are here making an experiment which has never succeeded in any time or country, and which—as God shall judge me at the great and final day—I do in my heart believe will here fail; because I see and feel that it is now failing. It is an infirmity of my nature ; it is constitutional ; it was born with me ; it has caused the misery (if you will) of my life ; it is an infirmity of my nature to have an obstinate constitutional preference of *the true* over the *agreeable ;* and I am satisfied, that if I had an only son, or, what is dearer, an only daughter—which God forbid !—I say, God forbid ! for she might bring her father's gray hairs with sorrow to the grave ; she might break my heart ; but, worse than that, what ! Can any thing be worse than that ? Yes, sir, I might break hers. I should be more sharp-sighted to her foibles than any one else. . . . . .

" I say, in my conscience and in my heart, I believe that this experiment will fail. If it should not fail, blessed be the Author of all Good for snatching this people as a brand from the burning, which has consumed as stubble all the nations—all the fruitfulness of the earth—which, before us, have been cut down, and cast into the fire. Why cumbereth it the ground ? Why cumbereth it ? Cut it down ! Cut it down !

" I believe that it will fail ; but, sir, if it does not fail, its success will be owing to the resistance of the usurpation of one man, by a power which was not unsuccessful in resisting another man, of the same name, and of the same race. And why is it that I think it will fail ? Sir, with Father Paul, I may wish it to be perpetual, *esto perpetua,* but I cannot believe that it will be so. I do not believe that a free republican government is compatible with the apery of European fashions and manners—is compatible with the apery of European luxury and habits ; but if it were, I do know that it is entirely incompatible with what I have in my hand—a base and baseless paper system of diplomacy, and a hardly better paper system of exchange.

" Now, sir, John Quincy Adams, coming into power under these inauspicious circumstances, and with these suspicious allies and connections, has determined to become the apostle of liberty, of un'versal liberty, as his father was, about the time of the formation of the Constitution, known to be the apostle of monarchy. It is no secret. I was in New-York when he first took his seat as Vice-President. I recollect—for I was a schoolboy at the time—attending the lobby of Congress, when I ought to have been at school. I remember the manner in which my brother was spurned by the coachman of the then Vice-President, for coming too near the arms emblazoned on the scutcheon of the vice-regal carriage. Perhaps I may have some of this old animosity rankling in my heart, and, coming from a race who are known never to forsake a friend or forgive a foe, I am taught to forgive my enemies; and I do, from the bottom of my heart, most sincerely, as I hope to be forgiven; but it is *my* enemies, not the enemies of my country, for, if they come here in the shape of the English, it is my duty to kill them; if they come here in a worse shape—wolves in sheeps' clothing, it is my duty and my business to tear the sheep-skins from their backs, and, as Windham said to Pitt, open the bosom, and expose beneath the ruffled shirt the filthy dowlas. This language was used in the House of Commons, where they talk and act like men; where they eat and drink like men; and do other things like men, not like Master Bettys. Adams determined to take warning by his father's errors; but in attempting the perpendicular, he bent as much the other way. Who would believe that Adams, the son of the sedition-law President, who held office under his father—who, up to December 6, 1807, was the undeviating, stanch adherent to the opposition to Jefferson's administration, then almost gone—who would believe he had selected for his pattern the celebrated Anacharsis Cloots, 'orator of the human race?' As Anacharsis was the orator of the human race, so Adams was determined to be the President of the human race, when I am not willing that he should be President of my name and race; but he is, and must be, till the third day of March, eighteen hundred and— I forget when. He has come out with a speech and a message, and with a doctrine that goes to take the whole human family under his special protection. Now, sir, who made him his brother's keeper? Who gave him, the President of the United States, the custody of the liberties, or the rights, or the interests of South America, or any other America, save, only, the United States of America, or any other country under the sun? He has put himself, we know, into the way, and I say, God send him a safe deliverance, and God send the country a safe deliverance from his policy—from his policy."

CHAPTER XXX.

THE PANAMA MISSION—BLIFIL AND BLACK GEORGE.

The American system of Mr. Clay was not confined to the mere domestic affairs of the United States, it contemplated a wider range,
and embraced within its scope an intimate political relationship with
all the republics and empires of North and South America. On
the floor of the House of Representatives, in 1820, he gave the first
outline of this American policy. " What would I give," says he,
" could we appreciate the advantages of pursuing the course I propose. It is in our power to create a *system* of which we shall be
the *centre,* and in which all South America will act with us. Imagine the vast power of the two continents, and the value of the intercourse between them, when we shall have a population of forty,
and they of seventy millions. In relation to South America, the
people of the United States will occupy the same position as the
people of New England do to the rest of the United States. We
shall be the *centre of a system,* which would constitute the *rallying
point* of human freedom against all the despotism of the old world.
Let us no longer watch the nod of any European politician. Let us
become real and true Americans, and place ourselves at the head of
the American system."

So soon as Mr. Clay took possession of the Department of State, he
had an ample field for the exercise of his passion for diplomacy. He
not only instilled his doctrines into the minds of our public functionaries abroad, but he immediately commenced a line of policy which
must soon consummate his cherished schemes, and place himself at
the head of an American Holy Alliance, to *defend human freedom
against the despotism of the old world.*

The Spanish American Republics, by various treaties among themselves, had determined to appoint delegates to meet in Congress at
Panama, for the purpose of devising means more effectually to prosecute the war with Spain, who had not yet acknowledged their independence ; to settle some principles of international law ; and to digest some plan of co-operation with the United States, to prevent the

interference of any other nation in the present war, on behalf of Spain, and to resist the further colonization of the American coast by the nations of Europe. There were many and serious difficulties in the way of any participation on the part of the United States in the deliberations and decisions of this Congress. Nor was their presence at first anticipated. But this Assembly furnished too favorable an opportunity for Mr. Clay to accomplish his schemes, to let it escape. He, as Secretary of State, intimated to the resident Ministers at Washington, in the name of the Government, that the United States, *if formally invited*, would, on their part, appoint a person to represent them. The invitation of course was extended; but before accepting it, the President thought that certain important preliminary questions should be settled. It appeared to him to be necessary, before the assembling of such a Congress, to settle between the different powers to be represented, several preliminary points; such as the subjects to which the attention of the Congress should be directed; the substance and the form of the powers to be given to the respective Representatives; and the mode of organizing the Congress. These subjects were discussed for many months in verbal conferences. They were not merely preliminary, but vital as to the propriety of accepting the invitation.

They were never settled. But the Secretary of State, and the President, whose imagination had now become inflamed with the same brilliant theme, were not to be diverted from their purpose by these grave difficulties. Two such ardent and obstinate tempers united on the same object, were not to be balked by ordinary obstacles.

But a few days before the meeting of Congress, the 30th of November, 1825, the Secretary wrote to the several Spanish American Ministers, residing at Washington. After expressing his regret that these subjects had not been arranged, he proceeds: "But as the want of the adjustment of these preliminaries, if it should occasion any inconvenience, could be only productive of some delay, the President has determined, at once, to manifest the sensibility of the United States to whatever concerns the prosperity of the American hemisphere, and to the friendly motives which have actuated your Governments in transmitting the invitation which you have communicated. He has, therefore, resolved, should the Senate of the United States, now expected to assemble in a few days, give their advice and consent, to send Commissioners to the Congress at Panama." Accordingly, in his annual message, the 6th of December, the President announces to Congress that "the invitation has been accepted, and ministers on the part of the United States will be commissioned to attend at those deliberations."

New offices were to be created, and the whole policy of the country, in despite of the warning of the father of his country, was to be changed, by mere Executive will, without the advice and consent of the Representatives of the States, or of the people.

This extraordinary measure was deemed by the President to be within the constitutional competency of the Executive; and, before ascertaining the opinion of the Legislature as to its expediency, by first obtaining a creation of the offices proposed to be filled, and then an appropriation for the salaries, he nominated Richard C. Anderson, of Kentucky, and John Sergeant, of Pennsylvania, to be Envoys Extraordinary and Ministers Plenipotentiary to the Assembly of American Nations, at Panama.

Mr. Randolph took his seat in the Senate a few days after the message containing these nominations was communicated to that body.

On the 4th of January, 1826, he writes to a friend, "We are here, as dull as the 'Asphaltic Pool.' Yet I think it possible (not to say probable) that we shall not continue so during the remainder of the session. . . . . If any check can be given to the Ex. Power, I have long believed that the Senate alone had the reins. The H. of R., from its character and composition, can never be formidable to a P. who has common sense." The "Asphaltic Pool" was soon driven and tossed by a mighty tempest.

After repeated calls on the President for fuller information, which he very mincingly dealt out to them, the Senate at length commenced in conclave to discuss the Panama question.

Mr. Van Buren, on the 15th of February, submitted a resolution, "That upon the question, whether the United States shall be represented in the Congress of Panama, the Senate ought to act with open doors; unless it shall appear that the publication of documents necessary to be referred to in debate will be prejudicial to existing negotiations."

He submitted a further resolution, "That the President be respectfully requested to inform the Senate whether such objection ex-

isted in the publication of the documents communicated by the Executive, or any portion of them ; and, if so, to specify the parts the
publication of which would, for that reason, be objectionable."

Mr. Randolph opposed these resolutions. He protested against
opening the doors, and contended that the President was a co-ordinate branch of the Government, and was entitled to all possible respect
from the Senate. "It is his duty," said he, "to lay before us information on which we must act; if he does not give us sufficient information, it is not our business to ask more." The resolutions, however, were
adopted ; and the next day, the President sent the following message
in reply : "In answer to the two resolutions of the Senate, of the 15th
instant, marked (Executive) and which I have received, I state respectfully, that all the communications from me to the Senate, relating to the Congress at Panama, have been made, like all other communications upon Executive business, in *confidence*, and most of them
in compliance with a resolution of the Senate, requiring them confidentially. Believing that the established usage of free confidential
communications between the Executive and the Senate ought, for the
public interest, to be preserved unimpaired, I deem it my indispensable duty to leave to the Senate, itself, the decision of a question involving a departure, hitherto, so far as I am informed, without example, from that usage, and upon the motives for which, not being informed of them, I do not feel myself competent to decide."

This message changed the tone of Mr. Randolph towards the
President. Some weeks afterwards, when addressing the Senate with
open doors, he alluded to this subject.

"I did maintain," said he, "the rights of the President ; but from
the moment he sent us this message, from that moment did my tone
and manner to him change ; from that moment was I an altered man,
and, I am afraid, not altered for the better.

"Sir, if he would leave to the Senate the decision of the question,
I would agree with him ; but the evil genius of the American house
of Stuart prevailed. He goes on to say that the question 'involves
a departure, hitherto, so far as I am informed, without example, from
that usage, and upon the *motives* for which, not being informed of
them, I do not feel myself competent to decide.' If this had been
prosecuted for a libel, what jury would have failed to have found a
verdict on such an inuendo ? That we were breaking up from our
own usages to gratify personal spleen ? I say nothing about our
movements, because he was not informed of them. The inuendo was,

that our motives were black and bad. That moment did I put, like Hannibal, my hand on the altar, and swear eternal enmity against him and his, politically. From that moment I would do any thing within the limits of the Constitution and the law; for, as Chatham said of Wilkes, ' I would not, in the person of the worst of men, violate those sanctions and privileges which are the safeguard of the rights and liberties of the best; but, within the limits of the Constitution and the law, if I don't carry on the war, whether in the Peninsula or any where else, it shall be for want of resources.' "

After further observations on the resolutions moved in conclave, Mr. Randolph repeated what he had then said in reference to the message of the President.

" Who made him a judge of our usages? Who constituted him? He has been a professor, I understand. I wish he had left off the pedagogue when he got into the Executive chair. Who made him the *censor morum* of this body? Will any one answer this question? Yes or no? Who? Name the person. Above all, who made him the searcher of hearts, and gave him the right, by an inuendo black as hell, to blacken our motives? Blacken our motives! I did not say that then. I was more under self-command; I did not use such strong language. I said, if he could borrow the eye of Omniscience himself, and look into every bosom here ; if he could look into that most awful, calamitous, and tremendous of all possible gulfs, the naked unveiled human heart, stripped of all its covering of self-love, exposed naked, as to the eye of God—I said if he could do that, he was not, as President of the United States, entitled to pass upon our motives, although he saw and knew them to be bad. I said, if he had converted us to the Catholic religion, and was our father confessor, and every man in this House at the footstool of the confessional had confessed a bad motive to him by the laws of his church, as by this Constitution, above the law and above the church, he, as President of the United States, could not pass on our motives, though we had told him with our own lips our motives, and confessed they were bad. I said this then, and I say it now. Here I plant my foot; here I fling defiance right into his teeth before the American people ; here I throw the gauntlet to him and the bravest of his compeers, to come forward and defend these miserable lines : ' Involving a departure, hitherto, so far as I am informed, without example, from that usage, and upon the motives for which, not being informed of them, I do not feel myself competent to decide.' Amiable modesty! I wonder we did not, all at once, fall in love with him, and agree *una voce* to publish our proceedings, except myself, for I quitted the Senate ten minutes before the vote was taken. I saw what was to follow; I knew the thing would not be done at all, or would be done unanimously. Therefore, in spite of the remonstrances of friends, I went away, not fearing that any one would doubt what my vote would have been, if I had staid. After twenty-six hours' exertion, it was time to give in. I was defeated, horse, foot, and dragoons—cut up, and clean broke down by the coalition of Blifil and Black George—by the combination, unheard of till then, of the puritan with the blackleg."

CHAPTER XXXI.

DUEL WITH HENRY CLAY.

THE remarks contained in the closing paragraph of the preceding chapter, were made in reference to the coalition between Mr. Clay and Mr. Adams. Mr. Randolph was fully persuaded that it was the result of corrupt motives; and being so persuaded, he did not hesitate to express himself in the strongest terms of denunciation. But, on the present occasion, he so far forgot himself as to indulge in language of the grossest personal insult. We do not believe that this was a premeditated and malicious assault on the private reputation of an absent rival. In the heat of debate, Randolph often used expressions that in cooler moments he regretted. Concentration of thought and intensity of expression were characteristic of his mind. Few men could say more pithy or pungent things. His sentences were aphorisms, without a superfluous ornament, and pregnant with meaning. On the present occasion, while the blood was up, and the mind glowing with intense action, we are persuaded that he looked only to the vividness of his illustrations and the aptness of his allusions. He felt only the strength of the orator giving intensity to his expressions; he perceived only the effect on his audience, and did not consider the wound he might inflict on the feelings of the subject of his allusions. If the thought flashed across his mind at the moment, it was too late; while "at the top of his bent," and in the eye of the Senate, he could not pause to weigh consequences. When, perhaps, in the next hour after taking his seat, he may have regretted that any offensive words had escaped his lips. So conscious was he

of his proneness to this license in the heat of debate, that he not unfrequently asked pardon of the House, or of the Senate, while a member of that body, for any unguarded and injurious expressions he
may have uttered. We can readily fancy that when his attention
was called to the subject by a friend, he would exclaim, " God forgive me! but it is too late now; it can't be helped." Having flung
down the gauntlet, and challenged the boldest champion of the administration to take it up, he was not the man to take back any insulting
expressions that might provoke an acceptance of his challenge. Having offered the insult, he calmly awaited the consequences, not doubt-
ing what those consequences would be. Mr. Clay was not a man of
such forbearance and Christian virtue as to permit a gross imputation on his motives to pass unnoticed. The circumstances by
which he was surrounded, and the quarter from which it came, forbade it on this occasion. He was compelled to act. He had reached
a crisis in his public career; a vast suspicion hung upon the integrity
of his late conduct; the public had fixed a jealous eye on his movements; had he then quailed, or even been silent, under the charge of
bankruptcy in morals, both public and private, his political fortunes
would have been ruined beyond the hope of redemption. Randolph,
too, was the man to confront. He had been the evil genius that from
the beginning stood in the way of his aspirations; not as the weird
sisters in the path of Macbeth, to cheer him on with prophecies of
future greatness, but as the angel with the flaming sword, that
checked the presumptuous Baalam as he went up to curse the children of God.

He strode from the vestibule to the speaker's chair, and from that
elevated position fixed his eye on a still more lofty seat. Randolph's
keen and practised perception saw the dangerous and the vaulting
ambition of the man, and from that moment marked him as an
object of especial notice. While the country yet paused, and her
fate still hung balanced between peace and war, Clay, with burning
zeal, urged on to strife, Randolph's voice was heard for peace. On
the political arena they met, and with ethereal weapons fought.
When the trophies of victory reared on the bloody field of combat
shall have mouldered into dust, the intellectual conflicts of these
great orators shall live in the memory of coming ages. Soon they
parted; one to the shades and the solitude of Roanoke, the other to the

achievement of still higher exploits in the cabinet of diplomacy
Again they met on the same arena. Peace had returned, and with
it a tide of prosperity that maddened the minds of the multitude,
and filled the imaginations of gravest statesmen with schemes of
magnificence and grandeur that brooked no constitutional restraint
in the way of their complete and immediate execution.   But the
towering genius of the young Apollo soared above them all, and
bore away the crown of victory, while the people stood charmed
with the melodious tones of his persuasive voice, and enchanted by
the magic spell he had thrown about their bewildered minds.   But
the eagle, towering in his pride, was doomed to fall.   The keen
archer sped an arrow, plumed with feathers fallen from his own wing,
that brought him wounded to the earth.   "From the time that I entered upon the subject of his conduct in relation to the Bank, in
1811 (renewal of the old charter) and in 1816 (the new Bank), and
on internal improvements, &c, (quoting his own words in his last
speech that ' this was a limited *cautiously restricted government,*) and
held up the ' compromise' in its true colors, he never once glanced
his eye upon me but to withdraw it, as if he had seen a basilisk."
But the glance of the basilisk, nor the archer's shaft, could quell his
aspiring mind.   Borne up on the popular breeze, he still mounted
aloft, and waved defiance to his enemies.   Scorning meaner things,
his wide vision stretched across the continent, and embraced far distant republics in the scope of his philanthropy.   A halo of glory
seemed to hover about his brow, and he rode like a sun, eclipsing the
beams of lesser luminaries.   But his hour had come ; the fatal blunder had been committed.   Proud and confident, he had never mis-
trusted his own infallibility.   The averted countenance of retiring
friends, the chilling breath of cold suspicion, taught him when too
late that he also was mortal.   In this hour of abandonment and
peril, his old enemy dealt him a deadly blow.   He had no right to
complain ; he could not exclaim *et tu, Brute!* for no friendship had
ever been professed : on the contrary, Randolph had ever deprecated
his ambition as dangerous, and felt justified in the use of any weapon
that might curb its career.   Embittered by the denunciations heaped
upon him on every hand, and chafed by the prospect of falling fortunes, Clay only saw in his ancient rival a cunning Mephistopheles,
heaping scornful words upon him, and smiling in triumph at his over-

throw. Stung to desperation, he sought revenge in the blood of his adversary. Pity he knew no other mode of vindicating an injured character than a resort to mortal combat. It is a reproach to civilization, if not to Christianity, that they have found no other means of wiping away the stains of dishonor than that which is exacted by the bloody code of a barbarous age.

These two remarkable men, so often meeting in the arena of debate, and now for the first time on the bloody field, were born within a day's ride of each other. One in the baronial halls of his ancestors, on the lofty banks of the Appomattox, the other in an humble dwelling amidst the slashes of Hanover. While the poor deputy clerk, in the intervals of toil, picked up his scanty crumbs of knowledge, the proud son of fortune enjoyed the richest repasts in the highest seminaries of learning. While the one yet a youth, was borne into the halls of Congress by the sweet voices of the people, the other was still fighting his uncouth way to fame and fortune among the hunters of Kentucky.

Born to command, each was reared in that school that best fitted him to perform the part Providence had assigned him. In daily contact with his fellows, the one became affable, courteous, winning in his ways, and powerful in his influence over the mind and the will of the admiring multitude; the other, in retirement and solitude, cherished those sterner virtues that made him the unbending advocate of truth, the unwavering defender of the Constitution, and the intrepid leader of those who rallied around the rights of the States as the only sure guarantee of the rights of the people.

The acknowledged champions of the two great political parties again reorganized, and with the hopes of the whole country resting upon them, these two men were about to meet for the purpose of extinguishing the lives of each other. Sad end to a bright career! But encompassed as they were by a false sense of honor, which they themselves had cherished, there was no other alternative but to fight. With a laudable desire to terminate the difference between the parties in a manner alike honorable to both, General Jesup and Colonel Tattnall mutually agreed to suspend the challenge and acceptance, in order that, if possible, satisfactory explanations might be entered into.

General Jesup, as the friend of Mr. Clay, stated that the injury of which that gentleman complained consisted in this: that Mr. Randolph had charged him with having forged or manufactured a paper connected with the Panama mission; also, that he had applied to him the epithet *black legs.* General Jesup considered it necessary that Mr. Randolph should declare that he had no intention of charging Mr. Clay, either in his public or private capacity, with forging or falsifying any paper, or misrepresenting any fact; and also, that the term *black legs,* if used, was not intended to apply to him.

Colonel Tattnall made the communication to Mr. Randolph. His reply cut off all hope of any satisfactory adjustment of the difficulty; "I have gone, says he, as far as I could in waiving my privilege to accept a peremptory challenge from a minister of the Executive Government, under any circumstances, and especially under such circumstances. The words used by me were, that I thought it would be in my power to show evidence, sufficiently presumptive, to satisfy a Charlotte jury, that this invitation was "manufactured" here—that Salagar's letter struck me as being a strong likeness in point of style, &c., to the other papers. I did not undertake to *prove* this, but expressed my suspicion that the fact was so. I applied to the administration the epithet, "puritanic, diplomatic, black-legged administration."

"I have no explanations to give—I will not give any—I am called to the field—I have agreed to go and am ready to go."

"The night before the duel," says General James Hamilton, of South Carolina, "Mr. Randolph sent for me. I found him calm, but in a singularly kind and confiding mood. He told me that he had something on his mind to tell me. He then remarked, 'Hamilton, I have determined to receive, without returning, Clay's fire; nothing shall induce me to harm a hair of his head; I will not make his wife a widow, or his children orphans. Their tears would be shed over his grave; but when the sod of Virginia rests on my bosom, there is not in this wide world one individual to pay this tribute upon mine.' His eyes filled, and resting his head upon his hand, we remained some moments silent. I replied, 'My dear friend (for ours was a sort of posthumous friendship, bequeathed by our mothers), I deeply regret that you have mentioned this subject to me; for you call upon me to go to the field and to see you shot down, or to assume the responsibility, in regard to your own life, in sustaining your determination to throw it away. But on this subject, a man's own conscience and his own bosom are his best monitors. I will not advise, but under the enormous and unprovoked personal insult you have offered Mr. Clay, I cannot dissuade. I feel bound, however, to communicate to Colonel Tattnall your decision.' He begged me not to do so, and said 'he was very much afraid that Tattnall would take the studs and refuse to go out with him.' I, however, sought Colonel Tattnall, and we repaired about midnight to Mr. Randolph's lodgings, whom we found reading Milton's great poem. For some moments he did not permit us to say one word in relation to the approaching duel; and he at once commenced one of those delightful criticisms on a passage of this poet, in which he was wont so enthusiastically to indulge. After a pause, Colonel Tattnall remarked, ' Mr. Randolph, I am told you have determined not to return Mr. Clay's fire; I must say to you, my dear sir, if I am only to go out to see you shot down, you must find some other friend.' Mr. Randolph remarked that it was his determination. After much conversation on the subject, I induced Colonel Tattnall to allow Mr. Randolph to take his own course, as his withdrawal, as one of his friends, might lead to very injurious misconstructions. At last, Mr. Randolph, smiling, said, ' Well, Tattnall, I promise you one thing, if I see the devil in Clay's eye, and that with malice prepense he means to take my life, I may change my mind.' A remark I knew he made merely to propitiate the anxieties of his friend.

" Mr. Clay and himself met at 4 o'clock the succeeding evening, on the banks of the Potomac. But he saw ' no devil in Clay's eye,' but a man fearless, and expressing the mingled sensibility and firmness which belonged to the occasion.

" I shall never forget this scene, as long as I live. It has been my misfortune to witness several duels, but I never saw one, at least in its sequel, so deeply affecting. The sun was just setting behind the blue hills of Randolph's own Virginia Here were two of the most extraordinary men our country in its prodigality had produced, about to meet in mortal combat. Whilst Tattnall was loading Randolph's pistols I approached my friend, I believed, for the last time ; I took his hand ; there was not in its touch the quivering of one pulsation. He turned to me and said, ' Clay is calm, but not vindictive—I hold my purpose, Hamilton, in any event; remember this.' On handing him his pistol, Colonel Tattnall sprung the hair-trigger. Mr. Randolph said, 'Tattnall, although I am one of the best shots in Virginia, with either a pistol or gun, yet I never fire with the hair-trigger; besides, I have a thick buckskin glove on, which will destroy the delicacy of my touch, and the trigger may fly before I know where I am.' But, from his great solicitude for his friend, Tattnall insisted upon hairing the trigger. On taking their position, the fact turned out as Mr. Randolph anticipated; his pistol went off before the word, with the muzzle down.

"The moment this event took place, General Jesup, Mr. Clay's friend, called out that he would instantly leave the ground with his friend, if that occurred again. Mr. Clay at once exclaimed, it was entirely an accident, and begged that the gentleman might be allowed to go on. On the word being given, Mr. Clay fired without effect, Mr. Randolph discharging his pistol in the air. The moment Mr. Clay saw that Mr. Randolph had thrown away his fire, with a gush of sensibility, he instantly approached Mr. Randolph, and said with an emotion I never can forget:—'I trust in God, my dear sir, you are untouched; after what has occurred, I would not have harmed you for a thousand worlds.'"

Thus ended this affair. None but the uncharitable will believe, after what passed on the field, that Randolph had any malicious motive in the words that fell from him on the floor of the Senate. Had a bloodthirsty spirit burned in his bosom, 'the best shot in Virginia' would not have permitted this opportunity to escape of levelling his weapon at the breast of an old rival, whose ponderous blows he had felt for fifteen years, and whose political opinions he considered so dangerous to the country. The true character of the man shone forth when he declared his intention not to injure a hair of Mr. Clay's head—and a gush of sensibility came over him at the thought of his forlorn condition. Mr. Clay had a wife and children to mourn his loss; but there was not one to shed a tear over his solitary grave. He knew the safety of his adversary—but with the immediate prospect of death before him, the sublime strains of the godlike Milton attuned his heart to softest influences; and the cords of affection so long silent and rusted by the chilling breath of a cold world, awakened by the soft echoes of long past memories, now vibrated a sweet, though mournful melody, that mingled its harmonious notes with the divine song of the poet:

"How mournfully sweet are the echoes that start
    When Memory plays an old tune on the heart."

John Randolph was not understood. Many who professed to
know him, and who considered themselves his friends, could not comprehend "the hair-trigger" sensibility of the man.

A few days after this affair, "Friday morning, April 14, 1826,"
he wrote thus to his friend, Dr. Brockenbrough:

"I cannot write—I tried yesterday to answer your letter, but I
could not do it. My pen *choked*. The *hysteria passio* of poor old
Lear, came over me. I left a letter for you in case of the worst. It
now lies on my mantel-piece. Perhaps you may, one time or other,
see it. I am a fatalist. I am all but friendless. Only one human
being ever knew me. *She* only knew me. Benton begins to understand and to love me. Nothing has stood in his way. No lions in
his path. Had I suffered it, he would have gone with me, as my
friend. In that case I should not have violated the laws of Virginia.
It was not my intention to do so. . . . . and . . . . were ardent,
honorable, devoted to my cause, but *obtuse*, wanted *tact*. I am a fatalist—on no one occasion of my life have I ever been in extremity, that
they, to whom my heart yearned and turned for aid, or at least for
comfort, have not appeared to hold aloof from me. I say *appeared*.
I am assured that it was appearance, only, in *both* instances, on the
part of the two persons in Virginia, who shared highest in my confidence and regard. But when a man comes home from the strife and
conflict of this wicked world, and its vile and sinful inhabitants, it is
then that a certain tone of voice—an averted look—or even the sweet
austere composure of our first mother, cuts him to the heart in the
reception of the wife of his bosom. The words are nothing—the
countenance and the tone of voice, the last especially, every thing.

"I again repeat, that I cannot write. But I shall be thankful for
your letters; as long as I could, I gave you what I had. I too am
bankrupt, and have as good a right to break as the rest. God bless
you both.'

CHAPTER XXXII.

NEGRO SLAVERY.

MR. RANDOLPH participated largely in the debates of the present session. The absence and illness of his colleague, Mr. Tazewell, imposed a double duty upon him. The extraordinary state of affairs

acting on a nervous sensibility, at all times acute--exasperated now by long protracted disease, made him more than commonly animated and eccentric in his manner and style of speaking. "The fever," says he, Feb. 27, 1826, "and the toast and water (I touch nothing else), keeps me more intoxicated (exhilarated, rather) than two bottles of champagne." Many thought him mad; but there was a method in his madness. All his speeches had a purpose bearing on the past history and the future destiny of the obnoxious incumbents in office. While many thought he was scattering sparks and even firebrands around him in wanton sport, he was forging weapons to be used in the coming contest with the men in power. Many of his speeches on these occasions were truly characteristic, some of them far-seeing and prophetic, especially the one delivered March 2, on "Negro Slavery in South America."

"I know there are gentlemen," said Mr. Randolph, "not only from the Northern, but from the Southern States, who think that this unhappy question—for such it is—of negro slavery, which the Constitution has vainly attempted to blink, by not using the term, should never be brought into public notice, more especially into that of Congress, and most especially here. Sir, with every due respect for the gentlemen who think so, I differ from them, *toto cœlo*. Sir, it is a thing which cannot be hid—it is not a dry-rot that you can cover with the carpet, until the house tumbles about your ears—you might as well try to hide a volcano in full operation—it cannot be hid; it is a cancer in your face, and must be treated *secundum artem;* it must not be tampered with by quacks, who never saw the disease or the patient—it must be, if you will, let alone; but on this very principle of letting it alone, I have brought in my resolution. I am willing to play what is called child's play—let me alone and I will let you alone; let my resolution alone, and I will say nothing in support of it; for there is a want of sense in saying any thing in support of a resolution that nobody opposes. Sir, will the Senate pardon my repeating the words of a great man, which cannot be too often repeated? 'A small danger, menacing an inestimable object, is of more importance, in the eyes of a wise man, than the greatest danger which can possibly threaten an object of minor consequence.' I do not put the question to you, sir. I know what your answer will be. I know what will be the answer of every husband, father, son, and brother, throughout the Southern States; I know that on this depends the honor of every matron and maiden—of every matron (wife or widow) between the Ohio and the Gulf of Mexico. I know that upon it depends the life's blood of the little ones which are lying in their cradles, in happy ignorance of what is passing around them; and not the white ones only, for shall not we too, kill—shall we not react the scenes which were acted in Guatamala, and elsewhere, except, I hope, with far different success; for if, with a superiority in point of numbers, as well as of intelligence and courage, we should suffer ourselves to be, as them, vanquished, we should deserve to have negroes for our task-masters, and for the husbands of our wives. This, then, is the inestimable object, which the gentleman from Carolina views in the same light that I do, and that you do too, sir, and to which every Southern bosom responds;—a chord which, when touched, even by the most delicate hand, vibrates to the heart of every man in our country. I wish I could maintain, with truth, that it came within the other predicament—that it was a small danger, but it is a great danger; it is a danger that has increased, is increasing, and *must* be diminished, or it must come to its regular catastrophe."

But it is not our purpose to make further allusion to Mr. Randolph's public acts during the present excited session. Let us turn to the inner man, and view him seated by his solitary fireside, communing with almost the only friend to whom he felt at liberty to unveil the secret workings of his heart. Friday, January 6, 1826, he writes to Dr. Brockenbrough:

Your letter, addressed to Petersburg, has just hove in sight; I should like "to have a word with *you* touching a certain subject." When I first heard of it I was thunderstruck. For that was the only person who had (repeatedly) urged this matter upon me, by the strongest expressions that our language affords. At first it revived very strongly the recollection of the "ratting" (as the English phrase it) among the "minority-men," some twelve or fourteen years ago; when this very person (and long before his seceding from us) wrote to me somewhat in this strain—"Let Monroe go over to the ministry, if he will—as for us," &c., &c. Well, what of all this; I have seen and conversed with the party, in the most familiar manner, without one bitter feeling. The event was too recent to be forgotten, but it did not tinge, in the slightest degree, the kindly intercourse between us. Am I to blame a man for being what nature and education made him? In this case, I am persuaded that all the blame lies at the door of the latter. What could be expected from such an example (to say nothing of the precepts) as this poor fellow had always before him. And again, is it not more than an even wager, that I have defects at least as great, although not of the same character? My horse Mark Anthony is fleeter than Janus, but Janus is the better horse. Why should I curse twenty poor devils that I could name, because they are mean? They can't help it. The leopard cannot change his spots.

Now, after all this philosophy, if it may be called such, do not suppose that I mean to compromise with fraud, and falsehood, and villany, in any shape. I only mean not to run a tilt against windmills or flocks of sheep. Yesterday I took a good long ride of eight or nine miles, and am now going to do likewise.   J. R. OF R.

To the same.

Saturday, January 14th, 1826.

Your letter of Thursday gives me very great relief: continue, I pray you, to write, if it be but a line. I noted Giles's " discovery;" but, this absurdity notwithstanding, it is a stinging piece. If he were not himself "particeps criminis," he would touch upon the libel against the whole West, in the case of John Smith, of Ohio ; and above all, the suspension of the habeas corpus.

On the whole, I am firmly persuaded that nothing but a paper, such as he would manage (and the vocation is as creditable as school-keeping), can arrest (if it can) the present current of affairs.

Your questions relating to the Senate I cannot (agreeably to our rule) answer. As to Mr. M——, I did not know, until I heard it from you, that he had been in the lachrymatory mood at all.

Poor Gilmer ! He is another of the countless victims of calomel. I had indulged a hope that he would at least live to finish his life of Fabricius. He told me some years ago, that if he survived me he meant to write a biography of me. But what he would have found to say that is not in the newspapers, I cannot conjecture.

You are right to like the Ch. J.'s Madeira, or any body's, if it be old and good. I ride every day from six to ten miles. A friend has just told me that M.'s pathos excited great laughter in the House.

    J. R. OF R.

To the same.

WASHINGTON, January 30th, 1826.

Your letter of the 28th—*Jam satis terris nivis.* It began to snow about an hour before day, and continues to fall fast and furious, reminding me of schoolboy and snow-bird days, " departed, never to return." I rode out yesterday some six or eight miles, and the day before as far (when I paid my devoirs to Madame la Presidente, I could do no less). I have even attended two days in the Senate, but if ever man was dying, I am. It does not take more than one hour for food, &c., to pass from my esophagus through the rectum, unchanged. This I have proved with various substances. The coffee passes off (not by the bladder) without a change of hue or smell. The least mental fatigue, above all, the jabber of Congress, prostrates me. My old friend, Mr. M——. comes " to keep me company," with the most amiable disposition in the world, and leaves me exhausted and worn down. If some one would sit by and say nothing, I could bear it; but conversation—no, no, no.

I have always believed that St. Thomas of Cantingbury's jewels were Bristol stones—in other words, that he was insolvent. What else could be expected from his gimcracks and crack-brained notions and "improvements?" Ah! that La Fayette business. Do you remember my Cassandra voice from Paris, about the time of his embarkation for the U. S.? I am more and more set against all new things. I only wanted to know who C. G. was, because in the Enquirer, of October the 25th last, F. Key published an answer to him; I have seen neither. I am against all Colonization, &c., societies—am for the good old plan of making the negroes *work*, and thereby enabling the master to feed and clothe them well, and take care of them in sickness and old age.

To the same.

Wednesday Morning, February st, 1826.

Yesterday we had a very interesting debate in the Senate, in which I took part. I verily believe it assisted the determination of my disease to the surface, for I was never more animated. A *superfical* speech, you will say. Be that as it may, it drew upon me a great many handsome and flattering compliments; and from one quarter, my friend Benton (for I was on his side), I believe sincere. We differed from the presiding officer upon what Mr. J. would call a "speck" in the political horizon; but it turned out to be of vital consequence as we probed it. It was laid over for mature consideration. After the debate, and while some Indian treaties were being read, Mr. C. sent for me, and said, that the question had assumed a new and important aspect—required solemn consideration and decision—my views were strong and important, &c., &c. He then sent for B. and told him much the same. He electioneers with great assiduity. Although it has no influence on the marked attention that I have received from *him*, yet the civilities of the palace have produced an evident effect on the manner of some others towards your humble servant. Indeed, since my call on Mrs. A (in return for her civility while I was confined), M., of Massachusetts, who is the ear-trumpet and mouthpiece of the palace in our House, has changed his demeanor from (not "sweet") "austere composure" to officious cordiality.

Your letter of Monday—my God! where will all this end? It will soon be disgraceful to be honest and pay one's debts. It is bitter cold, and I am suffering with it and erysipelas. Adieu!

To the same.

Monday Morning, February 6, 1826.

Your letters are my only comfort: that of the 4th was brought in just now on my breakfast tray. I can't help being sorry for that poor man to whom you were called the morning you wrote, although

he did, some twenty or thirty years ago (how time passes!) attempt
by a deep-laid scheme of   to beggar a family that I was much
attached to; one, too, with which he was nearly connected, and that
he kept upon the most friendly terms with—his debts have floored
him It is strange, passing strange—people will get in debt; and
instead of working and starving out, they go on giving dinners, keeping carriages, and covering aching bosoms with smiling faces, go
about greeting in the market-places, &c. I always think that I can
see the anguish under the grin and grimace, like old mother Cole's
dirty flannel peeping out beneath her Brussel's lace. This killed
poor H. H., and is killing like a slow poison all persons so circumstanced, who possess principle or pride. I never see one of these
martyrs to false pride writhing under their own reflections, that I am
not in some degree reconciled to the physical fire that I carry in my
bosom. The man whom H——'s fall will probably prostrate, would
himself have been no better off than his principal, but for
speculation and a lucky sale, just as the tide began to fall, a few
years ago.

I send you the "Citizen." The schoolmaster writes better than
his employer.   J. R. OF R.

To the same.

Monday, the 20th February, 1826.

For the first time during the last four or five days, I got a little
ride yesterday, sick as I was and am. I called on the Ch. J., and
told him what you said about L., and he joined me, in a hearty approbation of his refusal to become a candidate for the Assembly, or any
thing else, until he shall have secured "a competence, however moderate, without which no man can be independent, and hardly honest."
The words are Junius's to Woodfall, when he declined sharing any
part of the profits of his celebrated letters.

I told him, also, of my firm and positive refusal to present to the
Senate the petition of the Colonization Society, although earnestly
entreated to do so, by F. Key. That I thought the tendency of it
bad and mischievous; that a spirit of morbid sensibility, religious
fanaticism, vanity, and the love of display, were the chief moving
causes of that society.

That true humanity to the slave was to make him do a fair day's
work, and to treat him with all the kindness compatible with due
subordination. By that means, the master could afford to clothe and
feed him well, and take care of him in sickness and old age; while
the morbid sentimentalist could not do this. His slave was unpro-
vided with necessaries, unless pilfered from his master's neighbors;
because the owner could not furnish them out of the profits of the
negro's labor—there being none. And at the master's death, the
poor slaves were generally sold for debt (because the philanthropist

had to go to BANK, instead of drawing upon his crop), and were dispersed from Carolina to the Balize; so that in the end the superfine master turned out, like all other *ultras*, the worst that could be for the negroes.

This system of false indulgence, too, *educates* (I use the word in its strict and true meaning) all those pampered menials who, sooner or later, find their way to some Fulcher, the hand-cuffs, and the Alabama negro trader's slave-chain. How many such have I met within the different " coffles " (Mungo Park) of slaves that I had known living on the fat of the land, and drest as well as their masters and mistresses. I wished all the free negroes removed, with their own consent, out of the slave States especially ; but that, from the institution of the Passover to the latest experience of man, it would be found, that no two distinct people could occupy the same territory, under one government, but in the relation of master and vassal.

The Exodus of the Jews was effected by the visible and miraculous interposition of the hand of God ; and that without the same miraculous assistance, the Colonization Society would not remove the tithe of the increase of the free blacks, while their proceedings and talks disturbed the rest of the slaves. Enough ; enough. Rain—sleet—drizzle. J. R. OF R.

To the same.

Monday morning, February 27th, 1826.

Gaillard died yesterday, at 4 o'clock, P. M. Although, on this account, the Senate will transact no business to-day, yet, as I yesterday received from H. T. the sad news of his son's death, and have Tazewell to keep up with us, I can only acknowledge your letter of this morning (written on Saturday). Poor Gilmer ! he is only gone a little while before all that he loved or cared for. I am proud that I was one of the number.

As Dr. says, " I take" what you say about V. B.'s " address." I do assure you he has not warmed himself into my good graces by flattery, to which, like all men, I am accessible, and perhaps more so than men generally are, although I begin to think, that if they go on much longer as they do at present, I shall, like Louis Quatorze, not know when I am flattered. As to V. B. and myself, we have been a little cool; it was under that state of things that I mentioned him. He has done our cause disservice by delay, in the hope of getting first Gaillard, then Tazewell (while he was sick here), and since, while absent at Norfolk, and some other aid. I was for action, knowing that delay would only give time for the poison of patronage to do its office. His extreme delicacy upon all matters of money (upon which he never bestows a thought), having (as Junius says) secured a competency however moderate, his scorn of debt or obligation, won him first my good opinion. But if he has not, others have poured " the

leprous distilment into the porches of mine ears." The V. P. has
actually made love to me; and my old friend, Mr. Macon, reminds
me daily of *the old major*, who verily believed that I was a nonesuch
of living men.   In short, Friday's affair has been praised on all
hands, in a style that might have gorged the appetite of Cicero himself.   Mr. M. returned on Saturday from Lloyd's (he gave a party on
that day, and had invited Mr. M. three times before, who had excused himself), and asked me if my face did not burn.   I really did
not comprehend the question.   It was a saying, when I was a boy, that
when backbitten the ears burned.   He went on in a way that I shall
not repeat, as the sentiments of every man at table.

To the same.

March 4th, 1826; Washington, Saturday morn., four o'clock.
   I have been up an hour and a half, trying to kindle a fire, and have
at last succeeded.   I cannot sleep.   Death shakes his dart at me;
but I do not, cannot fear him.   He has already killed my friends—
Gilmer—Tazewell.   I fear that I shall never see the last again.   The
first is removed for ever.   This February and these ides of March
will live in future times, as the black year does yet in the North of
Europe—in Iceland particularly; *that* it depopulated of its enlightened, virtuous, and pious inhabitants; poor indeed, but pious and
good, and therefore happy; happy as mortality can be.   And what
is that?

   This cold black plague has destroyed the only two men that Virginia has bred since the Revolution, who had real claims to learning;
the rest are all shallow pretenders; *they* were scholars, and ripe and
good ones, and the soil was better than the culture.   Here the material surpassed the workmanship, tasteful and costly as it was.

   I had read " Burns and Byron" before I received the Compiler.
I am a passionate admirer of both.   I shall not pretend to decide
between them in point of genius.   They were the most extraordinary
men that England and Scotland have produced since the days of Milton and Napier of Merchiston, although there be no assignable relation between logarithms and poetry.   They are incommensurable.

   Write; but do not expect bulletins for some days.   I have no
phthisis, nor fear of it.   My cough is symptomatic, or sympathetic,
or some other " sym."

   McNaught is not the only suicide, even in Richmond.   Now,
when too late, I am a confirmed toast-and-water man.   My convivial-
ities for fifteen years (1807–1822) are now telling upon me.   If mankind had ever profited even by their own experience !   Now that poor
Frank is gone, and cannot execute his threat of writing my life, I
would turn autobiographer.   But he meant to dedicate to Tazewell !
That word, that name seems to petrify me.   If living, blind like

" Thamyris and blind Meonides," and like a greater than they—he who achieved " things unattempted yet in prose or rhyme."

I am really ill; the whole machine is rotten; the nails and screws that I drive will not take hold, but draw out with the decayed wood.   J. R. OF R.

CHAPTER XXXIII.

LETTERS FROM ABROAD.

EARLY in May, before the adjournment of Congress, Mr. Randolph sailed from the Delaware Bay on his third voyage to Europe. He arrived in Liverpool about the middle of June. " I have barely time to tell you," says he to a friend, " that I had a very disagreeable passage, finding B——n, the master of the Alexander, to be the most conceited and insufferable tyrant of the quarter-deck that I ever saw, and I have been to sea going on these three and forty years."

He remained in Liverpool for some time, enjoying the hospitalities of the place. " I am arrived in time for elections," says he. " You will see a lame report of an aquatic excursion, in which I bore a part, yesterday. Mr. Huskisson and Mr. John Bolton are just arrived to take me to the Mayor's to dinner." From Liverpool Mr. Randolph travelled extensively in England, Wales, and on the Continent. We are happy to have it in our power to allow him to speak of those travels in his own words.

To Dr. Brockenbrough.

HOLKHAM, Sunday, July 16th, 1826.

A month has now elapsed since I landed in England, during which time I have not received a line from any friend, except Benton, who wrote to me on the eve of his departure from Babylon the Great to Missouri. Missouri! and here am I writing in the parlor of the New Inn, at the gate of Mr. Coke's park, where art has mastered nature in one of her least amiable moods. To say the truth, he that would see this country to advantage must not end with the barren sands and flat infertile healths (strike out the *l*, I meant to write heaths) of the east country, but must reserve the Vale of Severn and Wales for a bonne bouche. Although I was told at Norwich that Mr. Coke was at home (and by a particular friend of his too), yet I find that he and Lady Anne are gone to the very extremity of this huge county to a wool fair, at Thetford, sixty-five miles off; and while my companion, Mr. Williams. of S. C. (son of David R. W.), is gone to the Hall, I am resolved to bestow, if not "all," a part at least of "my tediousness" upon you. Tediousness, indeed, for what have I to write about, unless to tell you that my health, so far from getting better, was hardly ever worse. Like the gallant General H., I am "pursued by a diarrhœa" that confines me to my quarters, and may deprive my native land of the "honor" of my sepulchre. The mischief is, that in this age of fools and motions in Congress, my ashes can have no security that some wiseacre may not get a vote (because no one will oppose him through mere *vis* inertia and ennui), that my "remains" too may be removed to their parent earth.

Mr. Williams has been very attentive and kind to me. I have been trying to persuade him to abandon me to the underwriters as a total loss, but he will not desert me; so that I meditate giving him' the slip for his own sake. We saw Dudley Inn and a bad race at Newmarket on our way to Norwich. There we embarked on the river Yare, and proceeded to Yarmouth by the steam packet. We returned to Norwich by land, and by different routes; he by the direct road, and I by *Beccles*, fifteen miles further; and yet I arrived first. Through Lord Suffield's politeness, who gave me a most hearty invitation to Gunton, I was enabled to see the Castle (now the county jail) to the best advantage. His lordship is a great prison discipline financier, and was very polite to me when I was in England four years ago. I met him by mere accident at the inn at Norwich, where the coach from Beccles stopped.

At this distance of time and place, our last winter's squabbles, over Panama itself, seem somewhat diminished in importance. For my part if I can get rid of that constitutional disease, which certain circumstances brought on last winter with symptoms of great aggravation, I shall care very little about the game, and nothing about them that play it.

With some of these circumstances, you are unacquainted—the chief one was the long absence of my coadjutor, which flung upon my shoulders a load that Atlas could not have upheld.

I see that Ritchie has come out against me. I looked for nothing better. But why talk of such things. M. H. knows more than he cares to tell. I was detained in town to attend the funeral of Mrs. Marx of Croydon. She was a charming woman, and her attention to poor Tudor, on his death bed, laid me under heavier obligations than this (equivocal) mark of respect to her memory can repay. God willing, I shall return to the United States with De Cost, who leaves Liverpool on the 24th of October, in the York. It is possible that I may be taken with a fit of longing to see Roanoke, (where I heartily wish that I now could be) that may accelerate my return. Meanwhile, you can have no conception of the pleasure that a long *gossiping* letter, from you, could give me. It would cheer my exile, which is no more voluntary than that of the Romans, who were forbidden the use of fire and water at Rome, and I was——but I can't write now, for my heart is heavy to sadness. It well may be so, for it has not been kindly treated. God bless you both—I hope that the experience of last year has not been thrown away upon you. Here the climate has been almost as bad as ours is in a favorable summer. The drought has been unparalleled and the distress impending over the land, tremendous. A failure of the potato crop, in Ireland, threatens to thicken the horrors of the picture. The ministers are not upon a " bed of roses." Musquitoes abound here. I have just killed a " gallinipper." Adieu!   J. R. OF R.

To the same.

THE HAGUE, Tuesday, August 8, 1826.
" The Portfolio reached me in safety." So much had I written of a letter to you in London, but I was obliged to drop my pen in G. Marx's compting-house, and here I am, and at your service at the Hague. My dear friend, I wish you could see,—and why can't you ? for I wear a window in my breast—what is passing in my bosom. You could find there, thoughts black as hell sometimes, but nothing of the sort towards any one of the few—the very few—who, like you, have clung to me, through good and evil reports. What an ill starred wretch have I been through life—a not uneventful life—and yet, how truly blest have I been in my friends ; not one, no, not one has ever betrayed me, whom I have admitted into my sanctum sanctorum. * Bryan, Benton, Rutledge—let me not forget him, whom I knew before either of the others, although for the last thirty years we have met but once. . The last letter that I received on my departure from Washington, was from him. In the late election, he was the warm supporter of General J., whom he personally knew and esteems ; and I confess that the testimony of one whom I have known intimately for more than six and thirty years, to be *sans peur et sans reproche*, and who is an observer and an excellent judge of mankind, weighs as it ought to weigh with me, in favor of the veteran. I know him (Genl. J.) to be a man of strong and vigorous mind, of dignified deportment, and is, I believe, *omni fœnore solatus*. I think this is no small matter. In the olden time, when credit existed, because there was real capital, a man in debt—I mean a landed man in debt—might be trusted. But not so now, for reasons that are curious and amusing ; which (were I to state them) would cause this letter to run into an essay on the progress of society, that would require quires instead of pages.

In my passage from London I met with a serious accident, that might have been fatal. We broke our engine, and when the pilot boarded us, I was desirous to get on board of his boat; to do this, I had to cross the quarter-deck. The sky-light of the ladies' cabin was open, but (*pour bienséance*) the "orifice" was covered with our colors, and the grating being removed only about 18 inches, a complete pit-fall or trap was made, into which I fell, and my right side, immediately below the insertion of the false ribs into the spine, was "brought up by the combings of the sky-light." I lay for some minutes nearly senseless, and it was more than an hour before I could be moved from the deck. My whole side, kidney and liver, are very much affected. It has obliged me to suspend n.y course of Swain's Panacea, upon which I entered a few days before I left London.

I have not seen Mr. Gallatin. Mr. John A. King, our *chargé d'affaires*, was very polite to me. We met on neutral ground, at the Traveller's Club-House, in Pall Mall, No. 49.

I am pleased with Holland. Cleanliness here becomes a virtue. My companion's, Mr. Wm's passport wanting some formularies, and our *chargé* (Mr. C. Hughes! oh for some of Giles' notes of admiration!!!!) not being present, Sir Charles Bagot has been good enough to do the needful. I waited upon him in Mr. Wm's behalf and was received by him with the greatest warmth, asked to dine *en famille*, (as I leave the Hague to-morrow for Leyden), and told that any letters brought to dinner would be forwarded by his courier to London. To him, therefore, I am obliged for a conveyance for this.

Apropos to Giles. I think I know him to the bottom, if he has any bottom. I know also the advantages that will be taken of me, the formidable array of enemies that I have to encounter. I might have neutralized some of them; but as Bonaparte said on another occasion. "it is not in my character" Whatever may be the decision of the Virginia Assembly on my case, I shall always say that a capricious change of her public agents has never been the vice of the Government or the people of Virginia, and that whenever a man is dismissed from the service of either, it is strong presumptive evidence (*prima facie*) of his unfitness for the place.

I hope, however, that no report of my speeches will be taken as evidence of what I have uttered, for I have never seen any thing further from a just representation than the report of one that G. and S. say I in part revised, and so I did, and if they had printed it by their own proof-sheet now in London, I should have been better satisfied with that part; the first, that I did not revise, is mangled and hardly intelligible even to me. The warning, which they make me give to my friend from Missouri, is to poor little Miles of Mass., and the whole affair is as much bedevilled as if they had at random picked out every other word. So much for that.—Neither Gales (whom I solicited) nor Seaton took down my speeches.

Your intelligence about the election, about W. S. A., and W. R. J., and W. B. G., was highly gratifying.   I hope that my *initials* are intelligible to you, for your Miss S., upon whom you say Mr. M. D. was attending, is *une inconnue à moi.*   I did not know that you had any Richmond Belles, of whom the Beaux could say, " I love my love with an S., because," &c., &c.

Poor Stephenson, I think, has no daughter, or child, even.   Remember me kindly to him and the Lord Chief, and do not forget my *best* love and duty to madame.   Tell her, and mark it yourself, that you at home may and can write long gossiping letters, but a man at the end of a journey, harassed by a *valet de place*, and *commissionaire pour le passeporte,* has no stomach but for his coffee at 1 bed.   Such is my case (this day excepted, and even to-day I am a good deal wearied by a jaunt to Scheveling, and Mr. Wm's business), and such has it been since I set my foot on the quay at Liverpool.

And so old Mr. Adams is dead ; on the 4th of July, too, just half a century after our Declaration of Independence ; and leaving his son on the throne.   This is Euthenasia, indeed.   They have killed Mr. Jefferson, too, on the same day, but I don't believe it.

Great news from Turkey.   That country is either to be renovated as a great European power, or it is to be blotted from the list of nations, at least on this side the Hellespont.   It is a horse medicine now in operation.   It will kill or cure.

I am sensible that this letter is not worth sending across the Atlantic.   But what am I to do ; you expect me to write.

Pray, has the *Enquirer* come out against me.   I see something that looks like it in the matter of Mr. D., of M——s.   *Le vrai n'est pas toujours le vraisemblable.*   There is a *dessous de cartes* there, that is not understood.   But who does really understand any thing ?   The English know us only through the medium of New-York and Yankee newspapers, and which is worse, through the Yankees themselves.   The only Virginia papers that I saw at the North and South American Coffee House, were the *Norfolk Beacon,* ditto *Herald,* and *Richmond Whig.* They don't take the *Enquirer.*   What a pretty notion they must have of us in Virginia.   Adieu for the present.

To the same.

PALL MALL, Sept. 22, 1826. Friday.
I write because you request me to do so ; but really, my dear friend, I have nothing to tell you, that you may not find in the newspapers ; and they are as dull and as empty as the town.   They who can take pleasure in the records of crime, may indeed find amusement in Bow Street and other criminal reports   It is now agreed on all hands, that misery, crime and profligacy are in a state of rapid and alarming increase.   The Pitt and paper system (for although he

did not begin it, yet he brought it to its last stage of im perfection), is now developing features that "fright the isle from its propriety."

Your letter reached me in Paris, where I was in a measure compelled to go, in consequence of my having incautiously set my foot in that huge man-trap, France. I had there neither time nor opportunity to answer it, and now I have not power to do it. The dinner to M. does, I confess, not a little surprise me. I know not what to think of these times, and of the state of things in our country. The vulgarity and calumny of the press I could put up with, if I could see any tokens of that manly straight-forward spirit and manner that once distinguished Virginia. Sincerity and truth are so far out of fashion that nobody now-a-days seems to expect them in the intercourse of life. But I am becoming censorious—and how can I help it, in this canting and speaking age, where the very children are made to cry or laugh as a well-drilled recruit shoulders or grounds his firelock.

I dined yesterday with Mr. Marx. It was a private party—and took additional cold. This morning my expectoration is quite bloody, but I do not apprehend that it comes from the lungs. It is disagreeable, however, not only in itself, but because I have promised my Lord Chief Justice Best to visit him at his seat in Kent, and another gentleman, also, in the same county; "*invicta*," "unconquered Kent."

Mr. Marx has shipped my winter clothing to his brother. By this time you will be thinking of a return to Richmond; and before this reaches you, I hope that you and madame will be restored to the comforts of your own fireside, where I mean to come and tell you of my travels. God bless you both.   J. R. OF R.

To the same.

PALL MALL, October 13, 1826.

Another packet has arrived, and no letter for me. The last that I received from you was (in Paris) dated July. How is this, my good friend? you, who know how I yearn for intelligence from the other side of the Atlantic, and that I have no one to give it to me but yourself.

Mr. W. J. Barksdale writes his father, that a *run* will be made at me by G——s, this winter. On this subject, I can only repeat what I have said before—that when the Commonwealth of Virginia dismisses a servant, it is strong presumptive evidence of his unfitness for the station. If it shall apply to my own case, I cannot help it. But I should have nothing to wish on this subject, if the Assembly could be put in possession of a tolerably faithful account of what I have said and done. I have been systematically and industriously misrepresented. I had determined to devote this last summer to a revision of my speeches, but my life would have paid the forfeit, had I persisted in that determination. Many of the misreprescntations proceed from the "ineffable stupidity" of the reporters, but some must, I think, be intentional. Be that as it may, the mangled limbs of Medëa's children, were as much like the living creations as the *disjecta membra* of my speeches resemble what I really did say. In most instances my meaning has been mistaken. In some it has been reversed. If I live, I will set this matter right. So much for *Ego.*

I see that Peyton R. advertises his land on —— River. This was the last of my name and race left whom I would go and see. The ruin is no doubt complete. Dr. Archer has "resumed the practice of the bar;" and poor Mrs. Tabb, by the death of Mrs. Coupland, is saddled with two more helpless grand-children. She is the best and noblest creature living; and I pray God that I may live once more to see her—a true specimen of the old Virginia matron.

On the 24th, God willing, I depart with DeCost, in the York. My health is by no means so good as it has been since my arrival on this side the Atlantic; but I have made up my mind to endure life to the last.

My best regards to Mr. and Mrs. Rootes. I exerted myself to see her protegés, Jane and Marianna Bell, but they were at Ramsgate, out of my reach. Mr. Barksdale talks of returning to Virginia next autumn. I fear that he will put it off till it is too late.

Town is empty, and I live a complete hermit, in London. If you see the English newspapers, you will see what a horrible state of society exists in this strange country, where one class is dying of hunger and another with surfeit. The amount of crime is fearful; and cases of extreme atrocity are not wanting. The ministry will not find themselves upon a bed of roses when Parliament meets.

———•••———

CHAPTER XXXIV.

HIS DEFEAT FOR THE SENATE.

AT the opening of Congress, in December, 1826, Mr. Randolph took up his winter quarters at his old lodgings, Dowson's, No. 2, on Capitol Hill. His health was extremely bad during the winter. Almost his only companion, was his old and tried friend, Mr. Macon, of North Carolina—a man whose matured wisdom, simplicity of manners, and integrity of character, distinguished him as the admired relict of a purer age, and the venerable patriarch of a new genera tion. How pleasant it is to look into the quiet parlor of those two remarkable men! While the busy and anxious politicians were holding their secret conclaves, and plotting the means of self-advancement, they sat, whole hours together, in the long winter nights, keeping each other company. In silence they sat and mused, as the fire burned. Each had his own private sorrows and domestic cares to brood over; both felt the weight of years pressing upon them, and still more, the wasting hand of disease. They had long since learned to look upon the honors of the world as empty shadows, and to value the good opinion of the wise and good more than the applause of a multitude. Nothing but the purest patriotism, an ardent devotion to their country and her noble institutions, could hold them to the discharge of their unpleasant duties, while every admonition of nature warned them to lay aside the harness of battle, and be at rest.

What eventful scenes had they passed through! Side by side they stood and beheld the young eagle plume himself for flight, and mount into the sky, with liberty and universal emancipation inscribed on his star-spangled banner. With anxious eye they saw him plunge into the dark clouds, and battle with the storms, and hailed him with delight as he emerged from the perils that encompassed his path, and glanced his outspread wing in the sunbeams of returning day, and wafted himself higher and still higher in his ethereal flight.

But now, behold! in mid-career a mortal foe encounters him in fiercest battle—"An eagle and a serpent wreathed in fight!"—and like the maiden on the sea-shore did they watch, with suppressed heart, "the event of that portentous fight."

> "Around, around, in ceaseless circles wheeling,
>   With clang of wings and screams, the Eagle sailed
> Incessantly—sometimes on high, concealing
>   Its lessening orbs—sometimes, as if it failed,
>   Dropp'd through the air; and still it shrieked and wailed,
> And casting back its eager head, with beak
>   And talon unremittingly assailed
> The wreathed Serpent, who did ever seek
> Upon his enemy's heart a mortal wound to wreak.

> "What life, what power, was kindled and arose
>   Within the sphere of that appalling fray!
> *	*	*	*	*	*	*	*	*

Swift changes in that combat—many a check,
And many a change, a dark and wild turmoil;
Sometimes the Snake around his enemy's neck
Lock'd in stiff rings his adamantine coil,
Until the Eagle, faint with pain and toil,
Remitted his strong flight, and near the sea
Languidly flutter'd, hopeless so to foil
His adversary, who then rear'd on high
His red and burning crest, radiant with victory.

"Then on the white edge of the bursting surge,
Where they had sunk together, would the Snake
Relax his suffocating grasp, and scourge
The wind with his wild writhings; for to break
That chain of torment, the vast bird would shake
The strength of his unconquerable wings,
As in despair, and with his sinewy neck,
Dissolve in sudden shock those linked rings,
Then soar, as swift as smoke from a volcano springs."

So may our country, like her noble symbol, triumph over every enemy! So may she shake the strength of her unconquerable wings, and dissolve, in sudden shock, the adamantine coil of that wreathed serpent that now seeks upon her heart a mortal wound to wreak!

After this manner, we may suppose that those venerable sages, seated by their solitary fireside, looked back on the rapid career of their country—its dangers and triumphs of past years, in which they had participated—and meditated with awe and trembling on the many difficulties that now beset her path. What a treasure of wisdom, could those meditations have been embodied in words, and handed down for our instruction! But a faint glimmering of what passed in the mind of one of those men, may be found in the letters at the close of this chapter.

Mr. Randolph continued faithful in the discharge of his duties in the Senate. He rarely opened his mouth during the session, but made it a point never to miss a vote. He suffered martyrdom during many a tedious and protracted debate; but, however painful, he never abandoned his post when action was required.

But his enemies would not allow the old Commonwealth of Virginia long to be honored by the services, and adorned by the illustrious character, of her most devoted and faithful son. Too faithful in his devotion, she again was made to deal out to him his accustomed reward—" a step-son's portion."

Mr. Randolph's doctrine was too stern, abstemious, and unpalatable to the lovers and the parasites of power. His restrictive system had grown obsolete. Lulled in the lap of prosperity, the people had ceased to listen to his warning voice. Too often had he repeated to unwilling ears, "that the inevitable tendency of this system, by even a fair exercise of the powers of the Federal Government, has a centripetal force—the centrifugal force not being sufficient to overcome it; and at every periodic revolution, we are drawing nearer and nearer to the final extinguishment that awaits us." They ceased to listen to him, or returned such answer as was given to the prophets of old: Are not things now as they were before, and have always been? then hush your babblings, and disturb not the people with your idle prophecies.

Even in his native State, that had been the standard-bearer of the doctrine of State-rights, he now found, to his mortification, a woful degeneracy. In the days of Hamilton and the elder Adams, when the centripetal force of the Federal Government, by an intense over-action, was rapidly hurrying the system to its final catastrophe, the counterpoise of Virginia, almost alone, restored the rightful balance, and gave it once more an onward and harmonious movement. But now, in these latter days, when the legitimate successors of old federalism, under a new name, were in the ascendent, the position of Virginia in regard to them was not merely doubtful, but she was about to throw her whole weight on the side of centralism, by rejecting from her councils the only man that could arrest the rapid tendencies of the Government in that direction. From 1800 to the present time, there had been scarcely a show of opposition in Virginia to the conservative States-rights doctrine of George Mason and Thomas Jefferson. But during the "era of good feelings," and the undisturbed repose of Mr. Monroe's administration, the pernicious doctrines of a contrary school had been widely disseminated. And now that the elements of party strife were again set in motion, mainly through the exertions of Mr. Randolph himself; now that the great fountains of the political deep were broken up, and men were struggling to re-form themselves around some fixed principles, according to their natural affinities, without regard to former associations, which had long since been obliterated, it was discovered that the old federalism of John Adams, newly baptized, had numerous and powerful friends in a land where it could never have flourished under its original name. Many who were the followers of Mr. Jefferson, and still professed his doctrine when applied to the alien and sedition law, adopted the American system in all its parts. Bank, protective tariff, internal improvement by the Federal Government, and political alliances with foreign republics—which system could only be supported by the same doctrine that justified those obnoxious laws.

Mr. Randolph did not spare those men. Neither age nor station could escape his burning indignation. He knew them all—their history, both public and private—his denunciations were often bitter, personal, and sometimes insulting.

This drew upon him not only a political, but a rancorous and unrelenting personal opposition. Old reminiscences were revived, and many sought to wreak their vengeance upon him for wounds inflicted in days long gone by; instead of yielding their private feelings to the public good, they preferred the unholy incense of personal revenge to the rich oblation of a self-sacrifice on the altar of their country.

But Mr. Randolph, after all, could not be defeated without taking some man from his own ranks, who could carry off some personal friends to his support. Mr. Floyd, Mr. Giles, and others of the Republican party, were spoken of as his competitors. During all this excited canvass, in which so much personal and bitter feeling was permitted to enter, Mr. Randolph remained calm and unmoved. New Year's day he writes to his friend, Dr. Brockenbrough:

"I am greatly obliged to Mr. May and my other friends and supporters; but no occasion has yet presented itself, on which I could, with propriety, have said any thing; and to be making one, would, I think, be unworthy of my character and station. The fabrications of my enemies, I cannot help. I can only say that there exists not the slightest foundation for them. I feel, perhaps, too keenly for the state of the country. I have (as who has not?) my own private sorrows; and I have participated in the deep affliction of my poor brother. If it be any crime to be *grave*, I plead guilty to the charge, but, at the same time, thank heaven! I feel myself to be calm, composed and self-possessed. To pretend indifference to the approaching election, would be the height of affectation and falsehood—but, go how it may, I trust that I shall bear myself under success or defeat, in a manner that my friends will not disapprove. I have ever looked up to Virginia, as to a mother. whose rebukes I was bound to receive with filial submission; and no instance of her displeasure, however severe, shall ever cause me to lose sight of my duty to her."

At length an available candidate was found in the person of Mr. Tyler, then Governor of the State.

When the friends of Mr. Randolph learned that he was to be opposed by that gentleman, they addressed him a note, the 18th January, 1827, in which they say—"We understand that the friends of the Administration and others will support you for the Senate in opposition to Mr. Randolph. We desire to understand destinctly, whether they have your consent or not."

Mr. Tyler replied—"My political opinions on the fundamental principles of the Government, are the same as those espoused by Mr. Randolph, and I admire him most highly, for his undeviating attachment to the Constitution, manifested at all times, and through all the events of a long political life; and if any man votes for me under a different persuasion, he most grievously deceives himself. You ask me whether I have yielded my consent to oppose him. On the contrary, I have constantly opposed myself to all solicitations." Mr. Tyler, however, was run against Mr. Randolph, and was successful in defeating him. With what magnanimity Mr. Randolph bore this defeat, and how cheerfully he submitted to the rebuke, coming from his native State—venerated and beloved, with all her unkindness, may be seen from the following letters, addressed to Dr. Brockenbrough, that range from the first of January, to the close of Congress.

Wednesday, Jan. 3, 1827.

Yesterday I had the gratification of seeing my old friend Mr. Macon elected to the Presidency of the Senate. He had not a single vote to spare. I apprehend that he owed his election chiefly to the absence of Chambers of Maryland, who had gone to the eastern shore, and who arrived from Baltimore not ten minutes after Mr. M. had taken the chair. Mr. Silsbee of Massachusetts voted for him. So did Mr. Noble of Indiana, and H. of Ohio. The other vote, I conjecture, was given by Mr. Mills, for one of our side (King) was also absent, although it was not generally known. This is the greatest and almost the only gratification that I have received here. It was altogether unexpected.

Friday, Jan. 5, 1827.

I write, although I have nothing in the world to say. Yesterday letters were received stating that P. P. B. would receive the vote of the administration men, notwithstanding his refusal to be nominated by them. I wish with all my heart the thing was decided one way or other; although I am sensible that the precipitation of one of my friends on a former occasion did mischief. I have neither the right nor the will to dictate, but to you (who are not a member) I can say that my present situation is far from being agreeable. General Smythe has not at all disappointed me—he has acted magnanimously and like a patriot. I looked for such a course from him—I never had a feeling of enmity against him—nothing ever passed between us, beyond a single spar.

Sunday morning, Jan. 7, 1827.

Mr. Macon is highly gratified at your mention of him. I could not resist the inclination to show him that part of your letter. He is to me, at this time, a treasure above all price; but that consideration apart, he richly deserves every sentiment of respect and veneration that can be felt for his character.

The news *here* is that the administration folks are chuckling at the prospect of my discomfiture. They are, or affect to be, in high spirits upon that subject. It must be confessed that my situation is awkward enough.

Monday morning, Jan. 8, 1827.

Your letters and Mr. Macon's society are my greatest resources against the miserable life we lead here. Tazewell tells me that he is well convinced that the article in question was written here. Mr. Macon, who reads the paper to his daughter, flung it into the fire with great indignation. I cannot understand Mr. R.'s reasons, and therefore they cannot be satisfactory to me, although no doubt they are perfectly so to himself.

Poor old S. will, I think, be re-elected. His masters have shaken the whip over him to secure his future unconditional obedience.

This morning was ushered in by a salute of cannon. A great dinner is to be eaten in honor of the day. Mr. M. and I foreswore public dinners ever since one that we gave Monroe in 1803, on his departure for France. Consequently, neither of us go. The day is wet and dirty, if there be such a word, and we shall lose nothing by staying at home.

I should like very well to see the antique you mention. It ought to be preserved with care. How little, in fact, do we know of our early history. Perhaps there was nothing to tell; but all the plantations seem to have been considered as a *terra incognita* by the mother country. I am sorry for what you mention respecting Mr. M., of F'k. But it can't be helped.

Friday morning, Jan. 12, 1827.

Another mail, and no letter from you. I can't help feeling anxious and uneasy.

My old friend is a good deal better; but I, after many days of premonition, from pains in the right side, &c., have had a very smart attack. My constitution is so worn out that it can resist nothing, and cannot recover itself as it once could. It seems to be the prevailing opinion here that the friends of the powers that be are somewhat despondent. Pennsylvania they say has given the most decisive indications of her adherence to Jackson. The dinner, although the military men slunk away from it, was attended by a formidable array of adversaries.

The weather is excessively gloomy, and sheds its malign influence upon my spirits. I can't read, and my old friend's cough is excited by talking; so we sit, and look at the fire together, and once in half an hour some remark is made by one or the other.

Saturday, Jan. 13, 1827.

Your letter of Thursday gives me much relief, although it contains intelligence of a very unpleasant nature. I allude to the publication you mention. I know that such things—to one especially not at all inured to them—are most unpleasant; but I trust that the impudent excuse of the printer will not be entirely thrown away, for it is as true as it is shameless. My good friend, I have long been of the opinion, that we are fast sinking into a state of society the most loathsome that can be presented to the imagination of an honorable man. Things, bad as they are, have not yet reached the lowest deep. If I had health and strength, I think that I would employ a portion of them in an inquiry into the causes that propel us to this wretched state. Why is it that our system has a uniform tendency to bring forward low and little men, to the exclusion of the more worthy? I have seen the operation of this machine from the beginning. The character of every branch of the Government has degenerated. In point of education and manners, as well as integrity, there has been a frightful deterioration every where. In this opinion I am supported by the experience of one of the most sagacious and observing men, himself contemporary with the present system from the commencement. My dear friend, I cannot express to you the thousandth part of the disgust and chagrin that devour me. When I landed at New-York the complexion of the public journals made me blush for the country. There was a respectable foreigner, my fellow-passenger, and I thought I could see the dismay which he attempted to conceal, at certain matters that passed, as things of course, in one of the first boarding-houses in that city. To me, the prospect is as cheerless and desolate as Greenland. Yourself, and one or two others, separated by vast distances and execrable roads, form here and there, as it were, an oäsis in the Sahara. My soul is "out of taste," as people say of their mouths after a fever. I dream of the snow-capped Alps, and azure lakes and waterfalls, and villages, and spires of

Switzerland, and I awake to a scene of desolation such as one might look to find in Barbary or upper Asia. But the *morale*, as the French would say, is worse than the *physique* and the *materiel.* I remember well when a member of Congress was respected by others and by himself. But I cannot pursue this theme.

The Government is as you describe it to be. They have nearly monopolized the press; and if the opposition prints lend themselves to their views the cause is hopeless. However, such is the growing conviction of their depravity, that I believe the people will throw them off at the next election. I shall expect your letters, of course, with eagerness.   Yours truly,   J. R. of R.

Sunday morning, January 14, 1827.
Your letter of Friday is just received. The artifices resorted to are worthy of the tools of such an administration as ours. By this time to-morrow I shall know the result. Be it what it may, it will exercise a very decisive influence over what may remain of my life to come. Success I *know* cannot elate me, and I hope that defeat will not depress me: but I have taken a new view of life, of public life especially; and if I am not a wiser and a better man for my last year's experience, you may pronounce me an incorrigible, irreclaimable fool.

Yesterday Mr. Chief Justice paid me a very friendly visit. His manner said more than his words. I am not vain but proud of the distinguished marks of regard which I have received on many occasions from this truly good and great man. Our conversation was interrupted by the unexpected and undesired visit of another person.
Yours truly,   J. R. of R.

Friday, January 19, 1827.
Your most welcome letter of Wednesday is just now received. Every syllable in the way of anecdote is gratifying in a high degree.

My first impression was to resign. There were, notwithstanding, obvious and strong objections to this course; my duty to my friends, the giving of a handle to the charges of my enemies that I was the slave of spleen and passion, and many more that I need not specify. There was but one other course left, and that I have taken, not without the decided approbation of my colleague, and many other friends here. I find, too, that it was heartily desired by my enemies that I should throw up my seat. They even propagated a report on Monday, that I had done so in a rage, and left the city. Numerous concurring opinions of men of sense and judgment, who have had no opportunity of consulting together, have reached me, that fortify me in the line of conduct that I have taken. Nothing, then, remains but a calm and dignified submission to the disgrace that has been put upon me [his ejection from the Senate]. It is the best evidence that I can give my friends of the sense which I feel, and will for ever cherish, of their kind and generous support.   J. R. of R.

Saturday, January 20, 1827.

" Bore me ?" Your letter has become more necessary to me than my breakfast; and it is almost as indispensable for me to say a few words to you upon paper, as soon as I have finished it. It consists of a cup of tea and a cracker, without butter, which I never touch. My constitution is shaken; nerves gone, and digestive powers almost extinct. I look forward to hopeless misery. As to a " firm and dignified" discharge of my duty, I hope that I shall be equal to it, so far as attendance and voting goes. I can't go farther, because I am unable. What I shall do with myself I am at a loss to conjecture. I have already found the solitude of Roanoke insupportable. With worse health, and no better spirits, how can I endure it? But too much of this egotism.

I would give not a little to know the reply of Mrs. B. to the member in question. The tear shed by her eyes for my defeat is more precious in my own than the pearl of Cleopatra. I beseech you not to omit writing whenever you can. I require all the time that you can bestow upon me. Except Mr. M., I am desolate.

Sunday morning, February 11, 1827.

I have not written as usual, because I almost made it a matter of conscience to oppress you with my gloom. I have never been more entirely overwhelmed with bad health and spirits. I look forward without hope, and almost without a wish, to recover. What can be more cheerless and desolate than the latter days that are left to me? I am, however, relieved from one apprehension—the fear of surviving all who may care for me. I feel that this can hardly be, for without some almost miraculous change in a worn-out constitution, I shall hardly get through the year. The thoughts of returning here torment and harass me by day and by night. Little do you even know of the character and composition of the House. If I were even able to exert myself, I should never obtain the floor. The speech which I made on the tariff was owing to a waiving of the right of another to speak. I feel that my public life ought to terminate with this session of Congress. These thoughts are for you, and you alone. I have risen from a sleepless bed to give utterance to them.

I saw the V. P. yesterday. He is in good spirits; he is sustained by a powerful passion. For my part, I am far from thinking a seat in the S. very desirable, although, certainly, to be preferred to any other position in this Government. If I could have done it with propriety, I should not have hesitated to retire voluntarily from mine.

Wednesday, Feb. 14, 1827.

Yesterday the Senate gave no equivocal evidence on behalf of the woollen bill from the other House. My colleague is, I think, more disgusted and wounded than I am. We are bound hand and foot, and the knife is at our throat. There is no help but from the

people through the State Legislatures.   We are sold before our faces
in open market.

Thursday, Feb. 15, 1827.

The V. P. has pressed me very warmly to take a seat in his carriage, which will travel the direct road by Carter's Ferry. This temptation is a very strong one in my present feeble condition. A pleasant companion, easy stages, and exemption from all the cares of a
journey that will bring me to my own door. But then I shall not
see you. This consideration would determine me to forego his invitation if I could see you and one or two others without bustle in a
quiet way. But I take it that the close of a session of Assembly is
(like one in Congress) as the last days of a long voyage.

Among my afflictions and privations, I cannot read. I have absolutely lost all taste for reading of every sort, except the letters of my
friends. Books, once a necessary of life, have no longer a single
charm for me. How this has happened I know not; but it is so. I
should not talk so eternally of myself if I felt at liberty to speak of
other people : I do not mean in the way of censure, but in any way.
I think I see a great deal more than meets the usual eye; but then
I may be mistaken. Of one thing I am certain, that nothing can
surpass the disgust of my colleague. His countenance speaks volumes.
Indeed I cannot blame him. I know that there is nothing in this
thing that, from its length, seems a letter; but I can't help it. Adieu
to you both.

Saturday, February 17, 1827.

Your last was dated this day week. Yesterday we had no mail
in consequence of the storm of Thursday. That storm nearly demo-
lished me. I took a violent cold at the door of the Senate waiting
until two hackney coaches could disengage themselves from a *jam*.
I have since been much worse. I hope to get a line from you to-day.

I mentioned to you the V. P.'s invitation to accompany him. You
will think me a strange, inconsistent creature, when I tell you that I
am at a loss what to do. Home I must go; and yet for me home has no
charms. I think of its solitude, which I can no longer relieve by
field-sports, or books, and my heart dies within me. Stretched on a
sick-bed, alone, desolate, cheerless. I must devise some other plan,
and I want to see you and consult you about it. You see what little
mercy my querulous selfishness has upon you.

The prospect here is far from brightening. I know others, and
abler men than myself, who think differently; but they take counsel
of their hopes and wishes. I, who have neither to bias me, can see
more plainly, with weaker vision. Not that I am at all indifferent
(far from it) to the question of change of the bad and corrupt men at
the head of our affairs. I allude to wishes of a different sort.

What you say about the spirit of the times and the state of society, has "often and over", occurred to me. I want to be at rest; with Gray's prophetess, I cry out "leave me, leave me to repose!" I am almost as well convinced that I shall not live twelve months, as twelve times twelve, and I wish to die in peace. My best love to Mrs. B. God bless you both, my dear friends.

Wednesday, Feb. 21, 1827.

I have omitted for some days to bore you with my querulous notes, because I knew that you had better use for your time than to read them. And now, that I have taken up my pen, what shall I say? Still harp upon the old string? My good friend, you will, I am sure, bear with my foolishness. I am incapable of business. I have not been so sensible of the failure of my bodily powers since 1817, when you saw me at Mr. Cunningham's; and in my dreary and desolate condition I naturally turn to you.

My view of things in Richmond coincided with your own, before I knew what your impressions were. I think that I shall make my escape, with the V. P., via Cartersville. It is the very road that I travelled here, and is the obvious way back again.

I shall have again to attend a six hours' sitting to-day. It absolutely murders me. The H. of R. sat late last night. Mr. Rives gained great, and I believe deserved praise. Mr. Archer passed a severe rebuke upon one of his colleagues from beyond the Blue Ridge, who spoke very irreverently, 'tis said, of his native State.

I fear that when we do meet, I shall teaze you to death with my egotism. A man with a tooth-ache thinks only of his fang. I am become the most inert and indolent of creatures. I want to get into port. Nothing would suit me so well as an annuity, and nothing to do. You see how selfish I am. But all my selfishness vanishes when I think of you. God bless you both. Adieu.

Thursday, Feb. 22, 1827.

General S. Smith, of Maryland, made a very strong speech yesterday on the colonial trade bill and the report accompanying it. He exposed, without reserve, the ignorance and incapacity of our cabinet, and particularly of the Secretary of State; and pointed out many manifest errors in the bill and report, between which he showed more than one instance of discrepancy. His speech was so much approved that a subscription for its publication was immediately set on foot and filled. I think it will have great effect on the public opinion. I listened to it with great attention, and after he had concluded, the old gentleman came and thanked me for it. He said that my occasional nods of assent to what he said was a great support to him, and enabled him to get through with what he had to say with more animation and effect than he had anticipated. The applause bestowed upon him by very many members of the Senate, seemed to warm the old man's heart.

Friday, Feb. 23, 1827.

Yesterday we adjourned much earlier than usual, on the motion of Mr. Johnson, of Louisiana, who means to inflict upon us a speech of unconscionable length, if I am to judge from the apparatus of notes and books which he has collected. It will, no doubt, receive contribution from the S. of S. It is strange that the administration should be reduced to rely upon so feeble and confused an understanding as that of J., whom no one can listen to, and who is unanswerable because he is unintelligible. His friend and patron passes my window every morning, arm in arm with M. C.'s, whom he appears to be vainly engaged in drilling. My good friend, politics remind me of Goldsmith's character of a schoolmaster—any other employment seems "genteel" in comparison to it.

Saturday, Feb. 24, 1827.

Your letter of Thursday and the Enquirer of the same date are just now brought in. I am truly sensible of the kind partiality of my friends, but I feel that my career is drawing to a close. My system is undermined and gone, and a few months must, I should think (and almost hope) put an end to my sufferings. God only knows what they have been. I think it probable that I shall take the steamboat to Richmond; in which case I shall have the pleasure to see you once more. I don't like to hear of your being "unwell," and hope that the approaching adjournment of the Assembly will relieve you from your harassing employment at the Bank.

I have lain all night listening to the rain. I have not passed one quite so bad this winter. I shall, nevertheless, go to the Senate, for I have made it a point not to miss a vote. I tasked myself beyond my strength in retaining my seat. and am by no means quite satisfied that I took the right course in that matter. It is not now, however, to be remedied.

Many thanks for your news of my niece. God bless her! I wrote to her the day before yesterday.

We had yesterday a confused jumble of two and a half hours from J., of L. But I have no doubt that the best face that the administration can put on the matter will appear in *print*. The chairman of foreign relations has been weighed and found wanting. The man has not a shadow of pretension to ability or information. Adieu.

Sunday, Feb. 25, 1827.

My lamentations must, I am sure, weary you, and not a little. Like Dogberry, I bestow all my tediousness upon you. I have had another bad night. Not so bad however as the preceding one. But I am in a state of utter atony. I think that you medical men have such a term. I have lost all relish for every thing, and would willingly purchase exemption from all exertion of body and mind at almost any price. My old friend, Mr. M., remarks my faint and languid aspect, but even he little knows of what is passing within. If change of scene brings no relief, and I have little hope that it will, I cannot long hold out under it; and why do I reiterate this to you? Because I have no one else to tell it to, and out of the fulness of the heart the mouth speaketh. I can no longer imagine any state of things under which I should not be wretched. I mean a possible state. I am unable to enter into the conceptions and views of those around me. They talk to me of grave matters, and I see children blowing bubbles.

Monday morning, Feb. 26, 1827.

Your letter of Friday, which ought to have arrived yesterday morning, came in with the northern mail. No two instruments of music ever accorded more exactly than our opinions do, concerning public men and measures. I am heartily sick of both, and only wish to find some resting-place, where I may die in peace. I saw a letter from Crawford to Mr. M., a day or two ago, that affected me most deeply. Nothing can be more simple and touching than the manner in which he speaks of himself and his affairs. What a fate his has been!

I agree with you, about the great man of Richmond. His antagonist I know well. He is a frog at the utmost degree of distention. How I shall get home I can't yet tell. My helplessness is inconceivable. I want a dry nurse—somebody to pick me up and take me away. I have passed another horrid night. Garnett writes me that he obtained relief from Dr. Watson, during his late visit to Richmond. There is some talk of a fight in the other House, but I conjecture that it will end in smoke. I listen, but say nothing.

Your letter of Saturday, and the Enquirer of Wednesday, are just now put into my hands. "Old Prince Edward has come out manfully" indeed; and if any thing could exhilarate me, it would be such a manifestation of the confidence of those who know me best; but to the dead fibre all applications are vain.

SENATE, Thursday, March 1, 1827.

I can only thank you for your letter of Tuesday. We meet at ten; and yesterday we adjourned at the same hour. It almost killed me, and has worsted my old friend, Mr. M., a good deal. In common with all the honest and sagacious men here, he partakes of the general disgust; and I think it not at all unlikely that he will throw up his commission before the next winter. S. of S. C., one of the most sterling characters, and of untiring zeal and labor hitherto, begins also to despond, seeing, as he does, that the administration is more effectually served by its professed opponents than by its friends. They are utterly insufficient. This is for you only.

This is probably the last note that you will receive from me until we meet. You must be prepared for a great change in me—greater in temper, &c., than in health. You *both*, I know, will put up with my tediousness. I feel that I am becoming a burthen to others, as well as to myself, and the thought depresses me not a little. "Time and the hour run through the longest day." What a fate ours would have been if we had been condemned to immortality here.

Saturday, March 3, 1827.

We sat until after two this morning. The House of Representatives, by a very thin vote, adhered to their amendment to the Colonial Bill. Had it been put off until to-day, it would not have been done. We shall, I take it for granted, also adhere, and so the bill will be lost. I have made my arrangements to go in the Potomac to-morrow, at 9 o'clock. When I consider, that at this session the Bankrupt Bill, the Woollen Bill, the Naval School, and two Dry Docks, and the Colonial Bill, have all failed, I am of opinion that (as we say in Virginia) we have made a "great break." In fact, the administration have succeeded in no one measure.

CHAPTER XXXV.

ELECTION TO THE HOUSE OF REPRESENTATIVES.

So soon as it was known in Washington that Mr. Randolph had been defeated for the Senate, Dr. George W. Crump, who represented his district, published a letter to his constituents, declining a re-election, and united with Mr. Randolph's other friends, in announcing him as a candidate for Congress.

The legislature was still in session, as he passed through Richmond. His friends in that body invited him, as a token of their respect, to partake of a public dinner. He said, in reply:—" The feebleness of my health admonishes me of the imprudence I commit in accepting your very kind and flattering invitation, but I am unable to practise the self-denial which prudence would impose. I have only to offer my profound acknowledgment, for an honor to which I am sensible of no claim on my part, except the singleness of purpose with which I have endeavored to uphold our common principles, never more insidiously and vigorously assailed than now, and never more resolutely defended and asserted." To a complimentary toast, call-ing him " the constant defender of the principles of the Constitution, the fearless opponent of a mischievous administration," he made a very brief but appropriate answer—"He knew that of late years it had become a practice, that the person thus selected as the object of distinction and hospitality, should make his acknowledgments in a set speech; but as a plain and old-fashioned Virginian, it was, he must be permitted to say, a custom more honored in the breach than the observance. He felt assured that no declaration of his principles was called for on the occasion. It would, indeed, be too severe a tax upon the courtesy of that intelligent auditory, for him to attempt to gloss over what he had done or omitted to do. He did not expect them to judge of those principles from any declarations that he might see fit to make, instead of inferring them from the acts of his public life, which had commenced in the last century, and had terminated but a few days ago." Mr. Randolph received several similar invitations from his old constituents, but he was constrained to decline them all. He expressed his regret at being unable to partake of the hospitality and festivity of his friends, "to whom," says he, "I am bound by every tie that can unite me to the kindest and most indulgent con-stituents that ever man had."

It is almost needless to say, that at the April elections he was returned to Congress by his old constituents, without opposition. The summer was spent in his accustomed solitude at Roanoke; and as to the thoughts and feelings that occupied and harassed him during that monotonous period, we leave him to speak for himself, in the fol-lowing letters to his friend, Dr. Brockenbrough:

ROANOKE, March 30, 1827; Friday.

MY DEAR FRIEND—My worst anticipations have been realized. I got home on the 22d (Thursday), and since then I have scarcely been off my bed except when I was in it. My cough has increased very much, and my fever never intermits; with this, pain in the breast and all the attendant ills. Meanwhile I am, with the exception of my servants, as if on a desert island. I feel that my doom is sealed, as it regards this life at least. I do not want to distress you, or to make you gloomy; but you had a right to know the truth, and I have told it to you.

My best regards to Mrs. B. Write to me when you have nothing better to do. I shall be detained here all the summer, if I last as long. Like other spendthrifts, I have squandered my resources, and am pennyless.

ROANOKE, May 15th, 1827; Tuesday.

Your letter gives me much concern. These sudden and repeated attacks alarm me. Pray do not fail to write and let me know how you are. I would readily embrace Mrs. B.'s kind invitation (God bless her for it); but, my good friend, I am unfit for society. My health is better—more so in appearance than in reality; but my spirits are (if any thing) worse. In other words, a total change has been effected in my views and feelings, and nothing can ever restore the slightest relish for the world and its affairs. If property in this country gave its possessor the command of money, I would go abroad immediately. But I feel that I am fixed here for life. I am sensibly touched by the kind interest expressed for my welfare by the Wickhams (and others). Make my best acknowledgments to them. Yesterday I received a present of fish from a man whom I haraly know, who sent it eight miles. On Saturday, for the first time, I made an essay towards riding, and got as far as Mrs. Daniel's, who, I heard, was very unwell. I repeated the experiment on Sunday; but yesterday was cold and cloudy, and the rain, I am persuaded, saved us last night from another frost.

By this time, I conjecture that my niece is in Richmond. Give her my best love, and Mrs. B. and Mary also. Remember me most kindly to Leigh, Stevenson, and all who ask after me.

Reading over what I have written, I find that I have expressed myself unhappily, not to say ungraciously, on the subject of Mrs. B.'s invitation. What I meant was, that I could not be in Richmond without being thrown into society. It is inexpressibly fatiguing and irksome to me to keep up those forms of intercourse which usage has rendered indispensable. He who violates them deserves to be kicked out of company. This is one among many reasons why I like to go abroad. You may ask

patria qui exsul
Sequoque fugit?

but I have no such vain expectation.

Five, P. M.—Since writing the above I have felt so peculiarly desolate and forlorn, that I would be glad to transport myself any where from this place. For some days this feeling has been gaining the mastery over me. What wouldn't I give to be with you at this moment, or to see you drive up to my door! The pain in my right side and shoulder has increased, and that, no doubt, occasions, in part at least, my wretched sensations. To-morrow will bring but the same joyless repetition of the same dull scene.

ROANOKE, May 22, 1827; Tuesday.

Your last (14th) gives me considerable relief on the subject of your health. Now that you have hit upon the remedy, I hope to hear no more of your spasmodic paroxysms. I have followed your advice with sensible benefit; but nothing seems to relieve the anxiety, distress, and languor to which I am by turns subjected, or the pains, rheumatic or gouty, that are continually flying about me.

I have passed a wretched week since my last. Why my letters are so long getting to hand, I cannot tell—perhaps it would be well for you if they should miscarry altogether, for they are little else besides lamentations. I cannot express to you the horror I feel at the idea of a winter in Washington. I have used a very improper word, for it is a feeling of loathing, of unutterable disgust. I am (of course) obliged to "every body" for their inquiries and "apparent concern" respecting my health; but there are some individuals towards whom I entertain a warmer feeling, and I beg you to express it for me to Leigh, the Wickhams, and others whom I need not name, although I will name Mr. and Mrs. T. Taylor.

Whichever way I look around me, I see no cheering object in view. All is dark, and comfortless, and hopeless : for I cannot disguise from myself, that the state of society and manners is daily and not slowly changing for the worse. After making every allowance for the gloom of age and disease, there are indications not to be mistaken of general deterioration. If I survive this winter I must try and hit upon some plan of relief, for I would not spend another year 1827 for any imaginable earthly consideration. This is not a bull, although it may look like one.

I have some conveniences here (not to say comforts) that I cannot always meet with from home; and this consideration, and the *vis inertiæ* which grows daily stronger, have detained me here, where I vegetate like the trees around me. Give my best love to Mrs. B., and Mary. I most heartily wish that I could see you all.

ROANOKE, Tuesday, June 12, 1827.

Your letter of the 5th was received last night. When I wrote that to which you refer, I had not received Mr. Chiles's and Mr. Allen's, with your P. S. They came about a week afterwards. I wrote you a few hardly legible lines on Friday evening. The next morning I got into my chair and drove to W. Leigh's, whence I returned yesterday. I would have stayed longer, but there were young people in the house, and I felt as if I was a damper upon their cheerfulness. Luckily I had a cool morning for my return home.

I have had a visit from a *Stouldburg*—old Mr. Archibald B. It almost made me resolve never to leave my own plantation again. I hardly think that I shall go to the Springs. I have a decided aversion to mixing with mankind, especially where I am known. I have been obliged to give up riding on horseback altogether. It crucified me, and I did not get over a ride of two miles in the course of the whole day. I will stay at home, and take your prescription. I wish I could see your Dr. Johnston's book. There are other reasons why I should stay at home: I have no clothes, and no money. In fact, I never was in so abject a state of misery and poverty since I was born. They who complain are never pitied. But I have so true a judgment of the value of this world and its contents, that I would not give the strength and health of one of my negro men for the wisdom of Solomon, and the wealth of Crœsus, and the power of Cæsar.

> "Though Solomon, with a thousand wives,
> To get a wise successor strives,
> But one, and he a fool, survives."

So much for the pleasure of offspring.

My best love to Mrs. B. and Mary, and to my niece, who is with you, I hope. Tell her that I got her two last letters a great while after they were written; and that I should have written in return, but that I was never in a frame of mind for it. My life is spent in pain and sorrow. "We passed in maddening pain life's feverish dream," was said of poor Collins. It is almost true of me. I have a thousand things to attend to, many duties to perform, and all are neglected. I know and feel that I am incurring an awful responsibility, but that only serves to add to the miseries of the day and night.

ROANOKE, September 4, 1827.

I certainly took it for granted that you were at the Springs, or I should have written, although I have been particularly unwell of late, and have had a great deal of company, most of which I could have gladly dispensed with. Indeed, I have more than once regretted that *not at home* was inadmissible in the country. At this time I am laboring under a sharp attack of bile, and am hardly able to direct my pen. All those symptoms of anxiety, distress, &c., I need not recapitulate to you. I had anticipated your caution respecting wine, but am not the less thankful for it. Kidder R. was here, and had no one to join him in a glass of claret, so that, as Burns says, I helped him to a slice of my constitution, although my potation was very moderate. If people would not harass me with their unmeaning visits I should do much better.

ROANOKE, Nov. 6, 1827; Tuesday.

I write because you request it. I got home on Friday evening (the 2d), and Sam and the wagons arrived here next night. This morning I received your letter of the 1st, Thursday. In answer to your inquiry, I am worse, decidedly worse than when I wrote from Amelia. I wrote you a long letter from thence, which I afterwards threw into the fire—and like it, I am withering, consuming away. I will try and see you if I can, on my way to W. Nothing but the circumstance attending my election, prevents an immediate resignation of my seat. My good friend, I can't convey to you—language can't express—the thousandth part of the misery I feel.

I found a long letter from you, at Charl. C. H. You say that "without something of the sort (cotton spinning), Richmond is done over." My dear friend, she is "done over," and past recovery. She wears the *facies Hippocratica.* That is not the worst—the country is also ruined—past redemption, body and soul—soil and mind.

My friend, Mr. Barksdale, has resolved to sell out and leave Amelia. He is right, and would be so, were he to give his establishment there away. If I live through the coming year, I too, will break my fetters. He was almost my only resource. They have dried up, one by one, and I am left in the desert alone.

Mrs. B. "wants to see me"—God bless her. When I come, you must hide me. I can write no more, even of this nonsense. Farewell.

WASHINGTON, Dec. 15, 1827; Saturday.

I confess that I have been disappointed, nay almost hurt, at not hearing from you. My good friend, I am sore and crippled, mind and body—and I might add estate. These, according to the Liturgy, embrace all the concerns of man, but there is another branch in which I am utterly bankrupt.

You say that you have nothing to communicate, and yet Stevenson tells me that *the* election made a great sensation with you.

Quant à moi. I am dying as decently as I can. For three days past, I have rode out, and people who would not care one groat, if I died to-night—are glad that I am so much better, &c., &c., with all that wretched grimace that grown-up makers of faces call, and believe to be, politeness, good-breeding, &c. I had rather see the children or monkeys mow and chatter.

My diet is strict. Flesh once a day (mutton, boiled or roasted), a cracker and cup of coffee, morning and night, no drink but toast water. But it will not do. For the first time in my life, I now begin to drink in the night, and copiously. I would give fifty pounds if no one would ask me again, "how I do?"

Mr. Macon, who was strictly neutral last year, is now decided for Jackson. Perhaps this may give some relief to our friend, Christopher Quandary. From some Fanquier and other symptoms, I fear that the Chief J. is quandaryish too.

Tazewell talks of going home, and has asked me to go with him. If I could bear the beastly abominations of a steamboat, I would do it, for here I cannot stay. Mr. M. recruited very much after his arrival, but within a few days he has been complaining, and in very bad spirits. The fact is, that his grand-children torture my old friend almost to death. I bless God that I have none. Of all the follies that man is prone to, that of thinking that he can regulate the conduct of others, is the most inveterate and preposterous. Mr. Macon has no such weakness; but the aberrations of his descendants crucify him. What has become of all the countless generations that have preceded us? Just what will become of us, and of our successors. Each will follow the devices and desires of its own heart, and very reasonably expect that its descendants will not, but will do, like good boys and girls, as they are bid. And so the papas and mammas, and grand-papas and grand-mammas flatter themselves—utterly regardless of their own contumacy. If ever I undertake to educate, or regulate any thing, it shall be a thing that cannot talk. I have been a Quixotte in this matter, and well have I been rewarded—as well as the woful Knight in the Galley slaves in the Brown mountain.

WASHINGTON, Friday, Dec. 21, 1827.

At last I have a letter from you. Your epistles are like angels' visits, "short and far between." I have one too from the Chief Justice, whom Mrs. B. will smile to hear me describe as one of the best-bred men alive. I sent him the King's speech and documents, and here in return is a letter that I would not exchange for a Diploma from any one of our Universities.

Nothing was further from my intention than to touch any nerve in Watkins, &c., when I mentioned his having written a book. At that time, I thought C. Q. was ascribed to Garnett. I referred to his publications some years ago against Jackson. Do you remember that Dr. Johnson, who hardly rose to the dignity and polish of a bear, told Boswell that he thought himself a very well-bred man? Now, I thought that I rallied our friend that night, with playful good humor, incapable of wounding even as sensitive a person as he on that occasion seemed to be.

Although I rode out on Wednesday, I am no better. Yesterday the atmosphere was loaded with *rheum*, and to-day it is hardly better. The first good spell of weather that seems settled, I shall leave this place, *pour jamais*. I have yet some confidence left in mankind, and much in my constituents. Now, let me beg you not to mention this to any one. I have heard of my conversation with W. L. at your house with alterations, I can't say with emendations. How every idle word I utter flies abroad upon the wings of the wind, I know not. I could not help smiling at the version given of my retort, that " J. could not write because he had never been taught, and Adams because he was not teachable "—the two last words were changed into " a man of abilities." This is like the National Intelligencer's reports of me.

I am sensible that these effusions of querulous egotism can have no value in your eyes. I will therefore try something else.

Mr. Barbour's motion is, to say the least of it, ill-timed. I believe that he consulted no one about it. Our play is to win the game; to keep every thing quiet; to give no handle for alarm, real or pretended; to finish the indispensable public business, and to go home.

As you make no mention of Mrs. B. or of Mary, I conclude that they are both well. My love to them both. I have been not a little amused with hearing a gentleman describe the artful and assiduous, and invidious court paid to a certain lady, the year before last, at the Springs, by a certain great, very great man. I now understand why she introduced the subject of General Jackson to *me* of all the people in the world, when I last saw her—the only instance of want of good taste that I ever remarked in that lady. *Quant à moi*, I was (as became me) mute as a fish.

I agree that it is a *serious* objection to any man that he has such a hanger-on as C. B. But when I am determined upon turning off a very bad overseer, I shall not be deterred, because I can't get exactly him whom I would prefer. This squeamishness does for girls, but with men, you must act as a man upon what is, and not upon what ought to be. I have seen no man but Genl. W., and there were strong objections to him, that I think fit for the office.

WASHINGTON, Saturday, Dec. 22, 1827.

My cough and pain in the breast are both much worse, owing to my being a few minutes in the House yesterday, from which I was speedily driven by the atmosphere. I cannot believe it possible that the Ch. J. can vote for the present incumbent. To say nothing of his denunciation of all the most respectable federalists; the implacable hatred and persecution of this man and his father of the memory of Alexander Hamilton (the best and ablest man of his party, who basely abandoned him for old Adams' loaves and fishes), would, I suppose, be an insuperable obstacle to the C. J.'s support of the younger A. When I say the best and ablest of his party, I must except the Ch. J. himself, who surpassed H. in moral worth, and although not his equal as a statesman, in point of capacity, is second to none. Hamilton has stood very high in my estimation ever since the contest between Burr and Jefferson; and I do not envy a certain Ex.-P. or your predecessor, the glory of watching his stolen visits to a courtezan, and disturbing the peace of his family by their informations. I have a fellow-feeling with H. He was the victim of rancorous enemies, who always prevail over lukewarm friends. He died because he preferred death to the slightest shade of imputation or disgrace. He was not suited to the country, or the times; and if he lived now, might be admired by a few, but would be thrust aside to make room for any fat-headed demagogue, or dextrous intriguer. His conduct, too, on the acquisition of Louisiana, proved how superior he was to the Otises and Quincys, and the whole run of Yankee federalists.

Yours are the only letters that I receive from Richmond—the one mentioned yesterday, from the Ch. J., excepted. Indeed I have had but three others; one from Mr. Leigh, and two from Barksdale. It is now snowing fast, and I fear that I shall be detained here much longer than I could wish. I left the House yesterday, after an hour's stay in it, and, as I finished my ride, I saw the flag waving over the Hall of the Representatives. I thought what fools men were, to be there listening to jackanapes, and what fools we, the people, were, to submit to their rule. I must get away, or die outright.

WASHINGTON, Wednesday, Dec. 26, 1827.

MY DEAR FRIEND,—Your letter, too, looks a little more like "past times" than those which I have received from you of late. I wonder that you should be at a loss for something to write about, for Mr. Speaker, whom I saw some days ago, for a single minute, related to me that you had given a splendid party; for so I interpreted the word fandango, used by him.

But for a visit last evening from Frank Key, who came and sat about three hours with me, yesterday would have been the dullest Christmas day that I can recollect. We want a synonym for the French *triste*. I was invited to dine, *en famille*, with Mr. Hamilton, of South Carolina, but the day was so particularly detestable, that I could not stir abroad. The Pennsylvania Avenue is a long lake of mud. I go nowhere, and see nobody but Mr. Macon. He is so deaf that he picks up none of the floating small trash in the Senate, and I am hard put to it to make him hear my hoarse whispers.

I understood the whole matter of Mr. H., of Kentucky, and the "very great man," and I readily comprehended the lady's scruples; one, especially, that was to be looked for in a female of delicacy and right feeling; for I have felt, and I do feel the same, myself. But there is no alternative.

You say that "all the world are amazed *how the devil I know every thing before any body else.*" I got that piece of information from Lynchburg, a long while ago, through my silent, discreet friend, W. L., who, I verily believe, never mentioned it to any body else, but, as the Waverly man says, "kept a calm sough." I have paid more money of my own for intelligence than, I believe, any other public man living; but this came *gratis*. Apropos to the Waverly man. His last work (Canongate) is beneath contempt. The mask is off, and he stands confessed a threadbare jester, repeating his worn-out stories. I wish that some one would take pen in hand, and abolish him quite. It might be easily done.

I pray you write to me as often and as fully as you can. I have no other epistolary aliment, except from Harry Tucker. God bless you *both*.

My most respectful and friendly regards to Mr. Wickham, whenever you see him. He has won upon my esteem. I made the very same remark upon the Ch. J——'s dignified and simple manners, that evening, that Mrs. B. did. Pray tell him that I hope soon to see him here.

CHAPTER XXXVI.

LEADER OF THE OPPOSITION—A WISE AND MASTERLY INACTIVITY.

MR. RANDOLPH's opposition commenced with the administration. His objection was not confined to the measures, but extended to the men—the principles they avowed—and the manner in which they came into power. In his judgment they were condemned in the beginning, and it was folly to wait to strike the first blow until they could safely intrench themselves behind the walls of patronage, and the well furnished batteries of a pensioned press. Like a skilful leader, he dashed at once on the foe, and gave him a stunning and fatal blow, ere he was aware of the near approach of an enemy. Two years ago, in the Senate, we observed his bold and vigorous onset; and now, in another field, his charges on the intrenchments of the enemy are still more fearless and effective. "I shall carry the war into Africa," said he, " *Delenda est Carthago!* I shall not be content with merely parrying. No, Sir, if I can—so help me God!—I will thrust also ; because my right arm is nerved by the cause of the people and of my country."

It was conceded, on all hands, that he was the leader of the opposition in Congress.

A member from Ohio, in responding to a rhetorical inquiry propounded by himself—"Who is it that manifested this feeling of proscription towards us and our posterity ?" answered, ' Sir, it is the man who is now at the head of the opposition to this administration; it is the man who was placed by you, Sir, at the head of the principal committee of this House. Yes, Sir, he was placed there by aid of the vote of the very people that he has derided and abused; and if ill health had not prevented, would have been in that exalted station. It is the man that is entitled to more credit—if it is right that this administration should go down—for his efficiency in effecting that object, than any three men in this nation. This is not a hasty opinion of mine; it is one long held, and often expressed. I have been an attentive observer of his course ever since the first organization of the party to which he belongs. From the moment he took his seat in the other branch of the legislature, he became the great rallying officer of the South. Our southern brethren were made to believe that we, of the North, were political fiends, ready to oppress them with heavy and onerous duties, and even willing to destroy that property they held most sacred. Sir, these are not exaggerated statements relative to the course of this distinguished individual. He is certainly the ablest political recruiting sergeant that has been in this or any other country."

Another member " considered him the commanding general of the opposition force, and occupying the position of a commander, in the rear of his troops, controlling their movements; issuing his orders ; directing one subaltern where and how to move his forces; admonishing another to due and proper caution, and to follow his leader; nodding approbation to a third, and prompting him to extraordinary exertion; examples of which he has given us in this debate."

Mr. Randolph was eminently fitted to be the leader of the republican party, at this time. The time-serving policy, and the " centripetal " tendency of the last twelve or fifteen years, had utterly obliterated all traces of its former existence. The old principles that constituted it, were effaced from the memory. He was the " Old Mortality," whose sharp chisel could retrace the lines on the whited sepulchres, and bring them out in bold relief, in all their original strength and freshness. His was the prophet's voice, to stir the dry bones in the valley.

In the first place, he was purely disinterested. He filled the station assigned him by his beloved constituents ; his ambition extended not beyond. His age, his wretched health, and " church-yard cough," admonished him that he might not live to witness the triumph of his cause. None but the most uncharitable could suspect his motives, or doubt that his right arm was nerved by the cause of the people and of his country. The history of all nations, and of their governments, was well known to him ; the causes of their rise, progress, and decline, were thoroughly studied and digested. He knew the Constitution of his own country—its strength, its weakness, and the dangers that beset it. Possessing a thorough acquaintance with human character, and a keen insight into the motives of individuals, he was familiar with the history, both public and private, of every prominent man connected with the Government. Nothing escaped his observation. No "Senior Falconi" could work the wires in his presence, without being detected and exposed. He possessed a fearless spirit, that dared to look at the naked truth—to confront it boldly, and to speak to it.

He called things by their right names; he called a spade a spade, offend whom it might. His mind was untrammelled by professional habits: nor was it fettered to the narrow round of an inferior trade. His comprehensive genius, with a free and fearless spirit, travelled over every field of knowledge, and appropriated to itself the richest fruits of ancient and modern lore. While others were poring over their books, or plodding through a labored and methodical speech, striving by a slow inductive process to arrive at their conclusion, he, with a comprehensive glance surveyed the whole field, and by an intuitive perception leapt to the conclusion without an apparent effort. No man more completely fulfilled his own beautiful fable of the caterpillar and the huntsman. "A caterpillar comes to a fence; he crawls to the bottom of the ditch, and over the fence; some one of his hundred feet always in contact with the object upon which he moves : a gallant horseman, at a flying leap, clears both ditch and fence. 'Stop !' says the caterpillar, 'you are too flighty, you want connection and continuity; it took me an hour to get over; you can't be as sure as I am, who have never quitted the subject, that you have overcome the difficulty, and are fairly over the fence.' 'Thou miserable reptile,' replies our huntsman, 'if, like you, I crawled over the earth slowly and painfully, should I ever catch a fox, or be any thing more than a wretched caterpillar?' " With these qualities of head and of heart—a profound statesman, a ready debater, a resolute will, *possessing the spirit of command*—he was eminently fitted to be the leader of a great party. While others were bewildered, or timidly waited the coming of events, he was quick to perceive and prompt to act.

His policy during the present session was a *wise and masterly inactivity*. The administration was in a minority, and with a "sardonic sneer" had told the leaders of the opposition that they had become "responsible for the measures of the Government." But Mr. Randolph urged his friends to do nothing—stand still and observe a wise and masterly inactivity. He often used that expression: "We ought," said he, " to observe that practice which is the hardest of all, especially for young physicians—we ought to throw in no medicine at all—to abstain—to observe a wise and masterly inactivity." That was not only his policy then, but at all times. We are indebted to him for a political maxim that embraces the whole duty of an American statesman. Let the Government abstain as much as possible from legislation; interfere not at all with individual interests; leave all they can to the States, and to the boundless energies of a free and enlightened people. In a word, the true constitutional spirit of the Federal Government would prompt it at all times (there are exceptions of course to all rules) to observe a wise and masterly inactivity; it would fulfil its whole duty in that. Whither would the contrary doctrine of the men then in power—that *Government must do every thing*— have carried us? to what a condition has it brought the nations of Europe? Let their enormous standing armies, bankrupt treasuries, irredeemable national debts, wretched and impoverished people, *answer the question!*

All of Mr. Randolph's speeches during the present session were interesting and instructive. Some of them are tolerably fair specimens of his style of thought and composition; especially the one in answer to Mr. Everett, of Massachusetts, on the first of February, which was revised by himself and dedicated to his constituents : " To my constituents, whose confidence and love have impelled and sustained me under the effort of making it, I dedicate this speech."

It is a great mistake to suppose that he had no method in his discourse. His was not a succession of loose thoughts and observations strung together by the commonplace rules of association, but the profound method of a mind of genius, that looked into the very heart of a subject, and drew forth the *law* of association by which its *ideas* are bound together in an adamantine chain of cause and effect. Like the musician who draws from a simple ballad an infinite variety of harmonies, in all of which may be traced the elements of the original song—so, Randolph, in his speeches, expanded the original thought into a rich and copious variety; but every illustration was suggested by the subject; each episode tended to accomplish the purpose he had in view. Let the following extract from the speech now under consideration, suffice as a specimen of his large acquaintance with history; profound knowledge of human character; his copiousness of illustration, and the rapidity, beauty, strength, and purity of his style. After reviewing the observations of other speakers that had gone before him, suggested by a former speech of his, he comes directly to the subject in hand—the unfitness of the present rulers: we wanted statesmen who could wisely direct the helm of State, and not orators to make speeches, or logicians to write books:

Sir, said he, I deny that there is any instance on record, in history, of a man not having military capacity, being at the head of any Government with advantage to that Government, and with credit to himself. There is a great mistake on this subject. It is not those talents which enable a man to write books and make speeches, that qualify him to preside over a Government. The wittiest of poets has told us that

> "All a rhetorician's rules
> Teach only how to name his tools."

We have seen professors of rhetoric, who could no doubt descant fluently upon the use of these said tools, yet sharpen them to so wiry an edge as to cut their own fingers with these implements of their trade. Thomas à Becket was as brave a man as Henry the Second, and, indeed, a braver man—less infirm of purpose. And who were the Hildebrands, and the rest of the papal freebooters, who achieved victory after victory over the proudest monarchs and States of Christendom? These men were brought up in a cloister, perhaps, but they were endowed with that highest of all gifts of Heaven, the capacity to lead men, whether in the Senate or in the field. Sir, it is one and the same faculty, and its successful display has always received, and always will receive, the highest honors that man can bestow: and this will be the case, do what you will, cant what you may about military chieftains and military domination. So long as man is man, the victorious defender of his country will, and ought to receive, that country's suffrage for all that the forms of her government allow her to give.

A friend said to me not long since: "Why, General Jackson can't write." "Admitted." (Pray, Sir, can you tell me of any one that can write? for, I protest, I know nobody that can.) Then, turning to my friend, I said: "It is most true that General Jackson cannot write," (not that he can't write his name or a letter, &c.,) "because he has never been taught; but his competitor cannot write, because he was not teachable;" for he has had every advantage of education and study. Sir, the Duke of Marlborough, the greatest captain and negotiator of his age, which was the age of Louis the Fourteenth, and who may rank with the greatest men of any age, whose irresistible manners and address triumphed over every obsta-

cle in council, as his military prowess and conduct did in the field—
this great man could not spell, and was notoriously ignorant of all
that an undergraduate must know, but which it is not necessary for
a man at the head of affairs to know at all.   Would you have superseded him by some Scotch schoolmaster ?   Gentlemen forget that it
is an able helmsman we want for the ship of state, and not a professor of navigation or astronomy.

Sir, among the vulgar errors that ought to go into Sir Thomas
Brown's book, this ought not to be omitted: that learning and wisdom are not synonymous, or at all equivalent. Knowledge and wisdom, as one of our most delightful poets sings—

> " Knowledge and wisdom, far from being one,
> Have ofttimes no connection : Knowledge dwells
> In hearts replete with thoughts of other men;
> Wisdom in minds attentive to their own.
> Knowledge is proud that he has learned so much ;
> Wisdom is humble that he knows no more.
> Books are not seldom talismans and spells,
> By which the magic art of shrewder wits
> Holds the unthinking multitude enchained."

And not books only, Sir.   Speeches are not less deceptive.   I not
only consider the want of what is called learning, not to be a disquali-
fication for the commander-in-chief in civil or military life ; but I do
consider the possession of too much learning to be of most mischievous consequence to such a character, who is to draw from the cabinet
of his own sagacious mind, and to make the learning of others, or
whatever other qualities they may possess, subservient to his more
enlarged and vigorous views.   Such a man was Cromwell ; such a
man was Washington : not learned, but wise.   Their understandings
were not clouded or cramped, but had fair play.   Their errors were
the errors of men, not of schoolboys and pedants.   So far from the
want of what is called education being a very strong objection to a
man at the head of affairs, over-education constitutes a still stronger
objection.   (In the case of a lady it is fatal.   Heaven defend me from
an over-educated accomplished lady !   Yes, accomplished indeed ; for
she is *finished* for all the duties of a wife, or mother, or mistress of a
family.)   We hear much of military usurpation, of military despotism, of the sword of a conqueror, of Cæsar, and Cromwell, and Bonaparte.   What little I know of Roman history has been gathered
chiefly from the surviving letters of the great men of that day, and
of Cicero especially; and I freely confess that if I had then lived,
and had been compelled to take sides, I must, though very reluctantly, have sided with Cæsar, rather than have taken Pompey for
my master.   It was the interest of the House of Stuart—and
they were long enough in power to do it—to blacken the character
of Cromwell, that great, and, I must add, bad man.   But, Sir, the

devil himself is not so black as he is sometimes painted. And who would not rather have obeyed Cromwell than that self-styled Parliament, which obtained a title too indecent for me to name, but by which it is familiarly known and mentioned in all the historians from that day to this. Cromwell fell under a temptation, perhaps too strong for the nature of man to resist; but he was an angel of light to either of the Stuarts, the one whom he brought to the block, or his son, a yet worse man, the blackest and foulest of miscreants that ever polluted a throne. It has been the policy of the House of Stuart and their successors—it is the policy of kings—to villify and blacken the memory and character of Cromwell. But the cloud is rolling away. We no longer consider Hume as deserving of the slightest credit. Cromwell "was guiltless of his country's blood;" his was a bloodless usurpation. To doubt his sincerity at the outset from his subsequent fall would be madness. Religious fervor was the prevailing temper and fashion of the times. Cromwell was no more of a fanatic than Charles the First, and not so much of a hypocrite. It was not in his nature to have signed the attainder of such a friend as Lord Strafford, whom Charles meanly, and selfishly, and basely, and cruelly, and cowardly repaid for his loyalty to him by an ignominious death—a death deserved indeed by Strafford for his treason to his country, but not at the hands of his faithless, perfidious master. Cromwell was an usurper—'tis granted; but he had scarcely any choice left him. His sway was every way preferable to that miserable corpse of a Parliament that he turned out, as a gentleman would turn off a drunken butler and his fellows; or the pensioned tyrant that succeeded him a dissolute, depraved bigot and hypocrite, who was outwardly a Protestant and at heart a Papist. He lived and died one, while pretending to be a son of the Church of England— aye, and sworn to it—and died a perjured man. If I must have a master, give me one whom I can respect, rather than a knot of knavish attorneys. Bonaparte was a bad man; but I would rather have had Bonaparte than such a set of corrupt, intriguing, public plunderers as he turned adrift. The Senate of Rome, the Parliament of England, " the Council of Elders and Youngsters," the Legislature of France—all made themselves first odious and then contemptible; and then comes an usurper and this is the natural end of a corrupt civil government.

There is a class of men who possess great learning, combined with inveterate professional habits, and who, *ipso facto*, or perhaps I should rather say *ipsis factis*, for I must speak accurately, as I speak before a professor, are disqualified for any but secondary parts any where, even in the cabinet. Cardinal Richelieu was, what? A priest. Yes, but what a priest! Oxenstiern was a chancellor. He it was who sent his son abroad to see *quam parva sapientia regitur mundus*—with how little wisdom this world is governed. This administration seemed to have thought that even less than that little would do for us. The gentleman called it a strong, an able cabinet—second to none but Washington's first cabinet. I could hardly look at him for blushing. What, Sir! is Gallatin at the head of the Treasury—Madison in the department of State? The mind of an accomplished and acute dia-lectician, of an able lawyer, or, if you please, of a great physician, may, by the long continuance of one pursuit—of one train of ideas—have its habits inveterately fixed, as effectually to disqualify the pos-sessor for the command of the councils of a country. He may, never-theless, make an admirable chief of a bureau—an excellent man of details, which the chief ought never to be. A man may be capable of making an able and ingenious argument on any subject within the sphere of his knowledge; but every now and then the master sophist will start, as I have seen him start, at the monstrous conclusions to which his own artificial reasoning had brought himself. But this was a man of more than ordinary natural candor and fairness of mind. Sir, by words and figures you may prove just what you please; but it often and most generally is the fact, that, in propor-tion as a proposition is logically or mathematically true, so it is poli-tically and commonsensically (or rather nonsensically) false. The talent which enables a man to write a book, or make a speech, has no more relation to the leading of an army or a senate, than it has to the dressing of a dinner. The talent which fits a man for either office is the talent for the management of men: a mere dialectician never had, and never will have it; each requires the same degree of courage, though of different kinds. The very highest degree of moral courage is required for the duties of government. I have been amused when I have seen some dialecticians, after assorting their words —" the counters of wise men, the money of fools"—after they had laid down their premises, and drawn, step by step, their deductions, sit down completely satisfied, as if the conclusions to which they had brought themselves were really the truth—as if it were irrefragably true. But wait until another cause is called, or till another court sits—till the bystanders and jury have had time to forget both argu-ment and conclusion, and they will make you just as good an argu-ment on the other side, and arrive with the same complacency at a directly opposite conclusion, and triumphantly demand your assent to this new truth. Sir, it is their business—I do not blame them. I only say that such a habit of mind unfits men for action and for decision. They want a client to decide for them which side to take; and the really great man performs that office. This habit unfits them for government in the first degree. The talent for government lies in these two things—sagacity to perceive, and decision to act. Genuine statesmen were never made such by mere training; *nas cuntur non fiunt:* education will form good business men. The maxim, *nascitur non fit,* is as true of statesmen as it is of poets. Let a house be on fire, you will soon see in that confusion who has the talent to command. Let a ship be in danger at sea, and ordinary subordination destroyed, and you will immediately make the same discovery. The ascendency of mind and of character rises and rises as naturally and as inevitably where there is fair play for it, as material bodies find their level by gravitation. Thus, a great logician, like a certain animal, oscillating between the hay on different sides of him, wants some power from without, before he can decide from which bundle to make trial. Who believes that Washington could write a good book or report as Jefferson, or make an able speech as Hamilton? Who is there that believes that Cromwell would have made as good a judge as Lord Hale? No, Sir; these learned and accomplished men find their proper place under those who are fitted to command, and to command them among the rest. Such a man as Washington will say to Jefferson, do you become my Secretary of State; to Hamilton, do you take charge of my purse, or that of the nation, which is the same thing; and to Knox, do you be my master of horse. All history shows this; but great logicians and great scholars are, for that very reason, unfit to be rulers. Would Hannibal have crossed the Alps, when there were no roads—with elephants—in the face of the warlike and hardy mountaineers, and have carried terror to the very gates of Rome, if his youth had been spent in poring over books? Would he have been able to maintain himself on the resources of his own genius for sixteen years in Italy, in spite of faction and treachery in the Senate of Carthage, if he had been deep in conic sections and fluxions, and the differential calculus, to say nothing of botany and mineralogy, and chemistry? "Are you not ashamed," said a philosopher to one who was born to rule; "are you not ashamed to play so well upon the flute?" Sir, it was well put. There is much which becomes a secondary man to know—much that it is necessary for him to know, that a first-rate man ought to be ashamed to know. No head was ever clear and sound that was stuffed with book learning. You might as well attempt to fatten and strengthen a man by stuffing him with every variety and the greatest quantity of food. After all, the chief must draw upon his subalterns, for much that he does not know and cannot perform himself. My friend, Wm. R. Johnson, has many a groom that can clean and dress a race-horse, and ride him too, better than he can. But what of that? Sir, we are, in the European sense of the term, not a military people. We have no business for an army; it hangs as a dead weight upon the nation, officers and all. All that we hear of it is through pamphlets—indicating a spirit that, if I was at the head of affairs, I should very speedily put down. A state of things that never could have grown up under a man of decision of character at the head of the State, or the Department—a man possessing *the spirit of command ;* that truest of all tests of a chief, whether military or civil. Who rescued Braddock when he was fighting, *secundem artem,* and his men were dropping around him on every side? It was a Virginia militia major. He asserted in that crisis, the place which properly belonged to him, and which he afterwards filled in a manner we all know.

CHAPTER XXXVII.

LETTERS FROM ROANOKE.

WE again leave the reader to follow Mr. Randolph into his accustomed summer quarters, there to commune with him alone, and to commiserate his unhappy lot. With a heart most exquisitely attuned, as the reader has learned to know, to love and friendship, he had no wife nor children to share his home and fortune, and to fill that aching void, that none but domestic affection can fill. Wholly dependent on outward friendship, he found the world all too busy for that, and was desolate. The reader will not be at a loss to perceive that the following letters were addressed to Dr. Brockenbrough.

ROANOKE, Tuesday evening. May 27. 1828.

My dear friend, I hope to hear from you by Sam on Saturday night, and to receive Lord Byron in a coffin, where I shall very soon be. I daily grow worse ; if that can be called "growth" which is diminution and not increase. My food passes from me unchanged. Liver, lungs, stomach (which I take to be the original seat of disease), bowels, and the whole carnal man are diseased to the last extent. Diarrhœa incessant—nerves broken—cramps—spasms—vertigo. Shall I go on ?—no, I will not.

I have horses that I cannot ride—wine that I cannot drink—and friends too much occupied with their own affairs to throw away a day (not to say a week) upon me. Of these, except Mr. Macon. yourself and Barksdale, who has entangled himself with Mrs. Tabb's estates, are all that I care to see *here.* Meanwhile, my dear friend, I am not without my comforts, such as they be. I have a new passion arising within me, which occupies me incessantly—the improvement of my estate. But for three men :—A. B. V. (your old master), Creed Taylor, and Patrick Henry, I should have commenced thirty years ago, what now I can hardly begin—finish, never. Don't you smile at my array of names ? *" Le vrai n'est pas toujours le vraisem-*

blable." Perhaps I might say, without hazarding more than public speakers (of whom I have been one) often do, *"jamais"* for *"toujours"*

My cough is tremendous. The expectoration from mucus has become purulent. My dear friend, you and I know that the cough and diarrhœa, and pain in the side and shoulder, are the last stage of my disorder, whether of lungs in the first instance, or of liver.

I send you the measure of my thigh at the thickest part. Calves I have none, except those that suck their dams; but then I have ankles that will out-measure yours or any other man's as far as you beat me in *thighs*.

I am super-saturated with politics; care nothing about convention or no convention, or any thing but the P. election, and no great deal about that. The country is ruined, thanks to Mr. Jefferson and Mr. Ritchie, who, I suppose, is ashamed of sending me the Enquirer, for I never get it. It is a temporizing, time-serving print, which I heartily despise, and should not care to have it, except that it is the Moniteur of the poor old, ruined and degraded Dominion. Nevertheless, ask *somebody* (for Ritchie is too much of a Godwinian to attend to facts) to send it to me.

ROANOKE, Friday, May 30, 1828.

Although I wrote to you so short a time ago by Sam, as well as by the post, yet as my frank has not expired (at one time indeed I expected not to live out my 60 days' leave), I write again to tell you that extremity of suffering has driven me to the use of what I have had a horror of all my life—I mean opium; and I have derived more relief from it than I could have anticipated. I took it to mitigate severe pain, and to check the diarrhœa. It has done both; but to my surprise it has had an equally good effect upon my cough, which now does not disturb me in the night, and the diarrhœa seldom, until towards daybreak, and then not over two or three times before breakfast, instead of two or three and thirty times. Yet I can't ride—but I hobble with a stick, and scold and threaten my lazy negroes who are building a house between my well and kitchen, and two (a stable boy and under gardener) mending the road against you come—or Barksdale. I want to see nobody else, that will come, except Leigh and Mr. Wickham, and they won't. Yes, let me except W. M. Watkins, who has been twice to see me; once spent the day from early breakfast, until after dinner—and seemed to feel a degree of interest in my life, that I thought no one took, except my "woman kind," and my friend Wm. Leigh.

Disgusted to loathing with politics, I have acquired a sudden taste for improving my estate, and my overseers are already aghast at my inspection of their doings. My servants here had been corrupted, by dealing with a very bad woman, that keeps an ordinary near me.

Twenty odd years ago, I saw her, then about 16, come into Charlotte court to choose a very handsome young fellow of two and twenty, for her guardian, whom she married that night. She was then as beautiful a creature as ever I saw (some remains yet survive). They reminded me of Annette and Lubin, but alas! Lubin became a whisky sot, and Annette a *double you.* Her daughters are following the same vocation, and her house is a public nuisance. I have been obliged to go there and lecture her—at first she was fierce, but I reminded her of the time when she chose her guardian, extolled her beauty—told her that I could not make war upon a woman—and that with a widow—that if she wanted any thing, she might command much more from me as a gentleman, by a request, than she could make by trafficking with my slaves. She burst into tears, promised to do so no more, and that I might, in case of a repetition of her offence, " *do with her as I pleased.*" Her tears disarmed me, and I withdrew my threat of depriving her of her license, &c., &c.: *Voila un roman.*

ROANOKE, Aug. 10, 1828.

Your brother Tom, who dined here and lay here last Tuesday tells me that you say " you believe that I have forgot you." I told the colonel to reply in jockey phrase, that " the boot was on the other leg." Until I saw him, I took it for granted that you had gone on from Charlottesville to the Springs, and I should as soon think of addressing a letter to Tombuctoo, as to our watering places. Moreover, he tells me that " he does not think that you will go at all." Now all the circumstances of the case taken together, I think I have some right to complain ; but as that is a right which I had much rather waive than exercise, I shall content myself with laughing at you most heartily, for the part you had in the accouchment of Carter's mountain, which, after violent throes, has not produced even a mouse. My good friend, you and your compeers, Ex-P—s, Ch. J—s, and learned counsellors (to say nothing of the little tumbler), remind me of my childhood, when we used to play at " ladies and gentlemen," and make visits from the different corners of the room, and cut our bread or cake into dishes of beef, mutton, &c. What is all this for ?—a menace ? Then it must be treated with contempt ; a persuasive, or argument ? then *I* should treat it *likewise.* Against all self-created associations, taking upon themselves the functions of government, I set my face ; and I should disregard the propositions of the convention, however reasonable or just, because of the manner in which they had been got up. Richardson and Gaines and Joe Wyatt are my political attorneys ; in fact, and by them only, I mean to be bound—one set is enough, and I am vain enough to believe that my opinion and wishes are entitled to as much respect from the assembly (*ceteris paribus*) as that of any member of the Charlottesville convention. In truth we are a fussical and fudgical people.' We do stand in need of "In-ternal Improvement"—beginning in our own bosoms, extending to our families and plantations, or whatever our occupation may be; and the man that stays at home and minds his business, is the one that is doing all that can be done (rebus existentibus) to mitigate the evils of the times.

"Well, after all this expectoration, how is your cough?" Steadily getting worse; *d'allieurs*, I am better—I mean as to the alimentary canal. Why can't you and madam come and see me? We are burnt to a cinder; although I had beautiful verdure this summer, until late in July. But if you could but see my colt Topaz, out of Ebony; my filly Sylph, out of Witch; or my puppy Ebony, you would admit that the wonders of the world were ten, and these three of them. Adieu!

J. R. OF R.

P. S. My frank being out, I subject you to double postage, to tell you that I clearly see in the C. C. a sort of tariffical log rolling between Ja. R. and the "mounting men," to tax the rest of the State and spend the money among themselves. I expect to live to see the upper end of Charlotte combine to oppress and plunder the lower end; or vice versa. The *cui bono* Mr. Mercer can tell, so can such contractors as his friend J. G. G. &c.

Did you read Mr. J.'s letter? I could not get through with it. Who does these things? It is exhumation.

ROANOKE, Tuesday, September 30, 1828.

MY DEAR FRIEND—Your letter, which I received last night, was a complete surprise upon me. I had begun to think that I was never to hear from you again. I have been here five cheerless months. Two letters from you, and one from Barksdale, written early in May! Did you get one from me in reply to your penul-timate, addressed to Philadelphia? Since my return home from W. I have not once slept out of my own bed; neither have I eaten from any other man's board, except when carried to Char-lotte C. H. by business. With the exception of a few visitors, I have been solitary, or worse—being occasionally *bored* with company that I would have been glad to dispense with. There is a disease prevailing on Dan river, which they call the cold plague. It is very fatal and speedy; the patient dying on the second or third day. In Virginia we have a moral cold plague, that has extinguished every social and kindly feeling. I do not believe that there ever existed a state of society—no, not even in Paris—so selfish and heartless as ours; and then the pecuniary distress that stares you in the face, whichsoever way you turn! The like has never been seen and felt in this country before. If I had the means of insuring a mutton cutlet and a bottle of wine in a foreign land, I would take shipping in the next packet.

My good friend, my health is very bad. My disease is eating me away, and for the last month I have been sensible of a dejection of mind that I can't shake off. Perhaps some interchange of the courtesies and civilities of life might alleviate it; but these are unknown in this region.

ROANOKE, Tuesday, October 28, 1828.

You are very good, but I cannot accept your kind invitation. I have lived here six solitary months in sickness and sorrow, until I find myself unfit for general converse with mankind. Mr. Barksdale presses me to go to How Branch, but I cannot. Sometimes, in a fit of sullen indignation, I almost resolve to abjure all intercourse with mankind; but the yearnings of my heart after those whom I have loved, but who, in the eagerness of their own pursuits, seem to have cast me aside, tell me better.

My good friend, I am sick, body and mind. I am without a single resource, except the workings of my own fancy. Fine as the weather is and has been all this month, I have not drawn a trigger. I often think of the visit you and madame made me three years ago just at this time. Although I never get a word from her, give her my best love. God bless you, may you never feel as I do. J. R. OF R.

CHARLOTTE C. H., November 4, 1828.

I got here to-day with some difficulty, and attempted to return home, but have been compelled to put back into port. Yesterday I was unable to attend. Indeed I have been much worse for the last five or six days.

Vote of the county at 4 P. M., Tuesday—Jackson 270; Adams 57.

The sun is more than an hour high, but I am obliged to go to bed. No letters from you for a long time. J. R. OF R.

CHAPTER XXXVIII.

PRESIDENTIAL ELECTION—RETIREMENT FROM CONGRESS.

GENERAL JACKSON was elected, by a large majority, President of the United States. No man contributed more than Mr. Randolph to this result—none expected to profit less from the triumph of his cause. His sole object was to turn out men from office who had climbed up the wrong way, and whose principles were ruinous to the Constitution, and to the Union as a union of co-equal and independent States. Having accomplished this end, he had nothing more to desire. Whether the new men in office would fulfil his expectations remained to be seen. One thing was certain, if they did not, they would find no support, from him. The spoils of office had no charm to lull him into forgetfulness of his duty—the sop of Cerberus could not close his watchful eye, nor silence his warning voice. *Principles, not men,* were not empty sounds on his lips, but a rule of action from which he never deviated; friend or foe alike shared his indignation whenever they betrayed a perverseness in their opinions, or a selfishness in their motives. His course was understood from the beginning. "The gentleman from Massachusetts warns us," says he, "that if the individual we now seek to elevate shall succeed, he will in his turn, become the object of public pursuit; and that the same pack will be unkennelled at his heels, that have run his rival down. It may be so. I have no hesitation to say, that if his conduct shall deserve it, and I live, I shall be one of that *pack;* because I maintain the interests of stockholders against presidents, directors, and cashiers."

After the election Mr. Randolph, as he had always done, kept aloof from political intrigues; took no *personal* interest in the formation of the new cabinet; nor did he open his mouth during the session of Congress that closed the day General Jackson was inaugurated President of the United States.

He had nothing more to do; his work was finished. He announced his intention not to be a candidate for re-election, and to bid adieu for ever to public life. It was certainly the last time he ever appeared on the floor of Congress. The question has often been asked, where are the monuments of his usefulness? what important measure did he ever advocate? The answer to this inquiry can only be found in contrasting the results of his labor with those of his great rival. Mr. Clay exerted all his great faculties and commanding influence to build up his American system. Randolph labored with equal assiduity to prevent its being built up; and after it was established, was unremitting in his exertions to tear it down. It has been torn down; and none did more than he in the work of demolition. One prop after another was taken from beneath this magnificent structure, and it now lies a heap of ruins. The American system is a mouldering ruin—the very memory of it has grown obsolete; but the American people were never more prosperous, and the American Constitution was never more ardently cherished by their grateful hearts. The American system, whatever might have been the design of the great projector, worked only for the benefit of the presidents, directors, and cashiers; the destruction of it has resulted to the infinite advantage of the stockholders. But this is a service the people do not appreciate—a negative virtue, in their estimation, for which there is no reward. He is more valued who invites them to a feast, than he who holds them from the poisoned chalice. We have labored, throughout the Life of Mr. Randolph, to show that there are principles of the Constitution behind all measures and all administrations, of infinitely more importance than the temporary advantage that might be obtained by an infringement of them. These principles he studied with unremitting assiduity, and drew from them the golden rule that a statesman must abstain from much legislation, and leave every thing to the unrestrained energies of the people. He taught, as the soundest maxim of philosophy, not only in the practice of the medical art, but of political science, *a wise and masterly inactivity.*

But these lessons of wisdom have fallen like seed by the wayside, and many are tempted to ask, Where are the fruits of the long life and labors of this man? If the doctrine of State-rights, engrafted on the Constitution by George Mason, and expounded by Jefferson and by Madison, be an essential element in our federative system, then what a debt of gratitude do we owe to John Randolph, who ever defended those principles through evil as well as through good report; never swerved from their practice; and finally, when the centripetal tendencies of the present administration were rapidly hastening their destruction, rescued them from ruin, and gave the federative system a new impulse, which we trust will restore it to its original balance, and a just and harmonious action.

The people are beginning to awake from their delusions. When they shall fully perceive and understand the fact that all those brilliant schemes that so much dazzled their fancy and made such potent appeals to their interests, were not only calculated to corrupt, oppress, and bankrupt the community, but to sweep away all the landmarks and barriers that stood in the way of lawless power, then will the name of John Randolph, whose prophetic voice had warned them of these consequences, be fondly cherished by them, and handed down from generation to generation as one of the greatest benefactors a kind Providence had vouchsafed to their country.

The following letters were written by Mr. Randolph to his friend, Dr. Brockenbrough, during the session of Congress:

WASHINGTON, Nov. 29, 1828.

MY GOOD FRIEND—Your kind letter reached me yesterday, but too late to thank you for it by return mail. At Fredericksburg I received such representations of the Dumfries road, as to induce me to take the steamboat. As there was only one other passenger, the cabin was quite comfortable. The boat is a new one, and a very fine one, and always gets up to the wharf. Her deck is roofed. We got here at two o'clock, but I lay until eight. Found Dr. Hall (N. C.) here (at Dawson's), and this morning Colonel Benton and Mr. Gilmer have arrived.

My cough is very much worse, and the pain in my breast and side increased a good deal. God bless you both. Pray write as often as you conveniently can. Yours, ever.   J. R. OF R.

Dr. BROCKENBROUGH.

WASHINGTON, Dec. 7, 1828.

You have no doubt heard that Mr. A. does not return to Quincy. *On dit*, that a very ungracious reception awaits him in Boston. A great deal has been said of the " philosophy" with which he bears his defeat, but a friend of mine, who saw him yesterday, tells me that he is emaciated to a great degree, and looks ten years older than he did last winter; that his features are sunken, and his coat, although buttoned, hanging about him like a man's coat upon a boy. In short, said my informant, your epithets "lank and lean," applied to the administration, were forcibly recalled to my mind by the personal appearance of the P. Clay, too, he added, endeavors to put a good face on the matter; but after working himself up into one of these humors, the collapse is dreadful. Such are the rewards of ambition.

> "Ambition thus shall tempt to rise,
> Then whirl the wretch on high,
> To bitter scorn a sacrifice,
> And grinning infamy."

You see I have nothing to write, when I send you stale poetry. My duty and love to Madame, and kind and respectful remembrance to Mr. Wickham. Yours, ever.   J. R. OF R.

WASHINGTON, Dec. 11, 1828; Wednesday.

Your letter shows on the face of it how much you are straitened for time. I wish I could spare you some of mine, that hangs heavy on my hands. In addition to my other annoyances, I am laboring under a severe influenza, and might sit for the picture of a weeping philosopher, although I have as few claims to philosophy as Mr. J. Q. A. himself. He rides or walks around the square in front of the Capitol, every day. I have not seen him, but Hall tells me that he does very often, and that the sight makes him feel very queerly. " *He* looks," says Hall, " as if he did not know me, and I look as if I did not know him." His appearance is wretched. An acquaintance of mine called on him a few days ago ; he was much dejected, until some one made an allusion to Giles, when, in great wrath, he pronounced G.'s statements respecting him to be utterly false ; said G.'s memory was inventive, &c. ; and, on the whole, conducted himself very undignifiedly.

WASHINGTON, Dec. 17, 1828.

Your letter, although dated four days ago, did not come to hand until this morning. It needed no excuse, for I am, now-a-day, glad to get a letter from you on any terms.

Yesterday I dined with our old acquaintance, Dennis A. Smith, at Gadsby's. He spoke with great interest and regard of you. He introduced me to a Dr. McAulay, who has married a lady of fortune, in Baltimore. He was formerly of Virginia, and I conjecture, a son of McAulay, of York. I am glad that you are pleased with your adopted daughter. I pray that she may realize your fondest expectations. I have long since done with forming any. If my " body" and " estate" would permit, my " mind" is bent on spending the rest of my life in travelling—not in search of happiness ; that, I know, is not to be found—but of variety, which may be found ; and in which I consider the chief pleasure of life to consist. Habit, I know, can reconcile the gin-horse to his lot ; but I never could have made a gin-horse.

This place is exceedingly dull. As no purpose can now be answered, by giving entertainments, none are made. I am nearly as much alone as I was at Roanoke ; and, with the exception of the daily mails, I am full as much at a loss for resources to break the monotony of the day ; each day being, with the exception of the weather, exactly alike. If there be any news, I am in the dark. I only hear that some ladies of the heads of departments have, for the first time during the present reign, condescended to visit ladies of M C., who have passed several winters here, unnoticed by those grand dignitaries. This was told me by my friend Benton, who sometimes knocks at my door, and sits a few minutes with me—but for whom, I should be utterly ignorant of what's going on.

As to G.'s " religion," I shall be sorry to pass upon it or him. My quondam neighbor, Peter J., has, I am certain, mistaken his wants, whatever may be the lady's case. My niece is now in Richmond, attending the wedding of some female friend. *She* is an admirable creature, susceptible of high and generous sentiments; but

I have a most pitiful opinion of the friendship of girls generally; marriage is a touch-stone that few of them can bear. Indeed, it is too much the case with our sex, also. By this time you must be tired of my prosing. Let me hear from you, when you can find leisure to write.   Yours truly,   J. R. OF R.

WASHINGTON, Dec. 22, 1828.

After a dreadful night, I am greeted by your letter of Saturday. I am truly concerned to hear of Mrs. B.'s afflicting indisposition. In this climate, as we advance in life, that disorder becomes more common and more formidable. Make my best respects to her.

My good friend, few persons of my age, have thought more on the subject of government, and my situation for the last forty years has been highly favorable for watching the operations of our own. The conclusions that I have come to, do not very widely differ from your own; they are any thing but cheering. What you say upon the authority of Mr. Short, of the condition of "a solitary itinerant," I know by some thousands of miles' experience, to be true; but bad as it is, it is better, far better, than the life I lead here or at home.

Mr. J. is again in the newspapers. I think this course very ill-advised; but perhaps I am wrong, and do not take into consideration the very low state into which our society has fallen.

The influenza has left my eyes weak and inflamed; but if there was any thing worth communicating, I would tax them to give it to you. I hear nothing and see nobody. I cannot work myself up to take any interest in what is going on, or said to be going on.

There is not, at this time, on the face of the earth, one spot where a man of sense, attached to the principles of free government, would wish to live. Governments have poisoned every thing.

Farewell! I can truly repeat after you, "Whether at home or abroad," God bless you.   J. R. OF R.

January 6, 1829.

Mr. Bell, of the House of Representatives, from Tennessee, has received a letter from Nashville, informing him that Mrs. Jackson died on the 23d December; the day for the dinner and ball to Gen. J. While awaiting his arrival at the festival, a messenger brought the news of Mrs. Jackson's death.

I shall probably not be in the Convention. I am sick of public affairs and public men, and have no opinions of constitutions ready made or made to order.

If it would do any good, I would wish most heartily that your connection with the B. of V. was dissolved. You have been a slave to that company; and after wearing yourself down, and devoting to it time and abilities and acquirements more than enough to amass an independent fortune (otherwise applied). where is your reward? I tell you plainly and fairly that, in public opinion, a banking-house is a house of ill fame, and that all connection with it is discreditable. This, whether just or not, is the general sentiment of the country.

My sufferings, for the last three days especially, have been such that if it were lawful I would pray for death.

You are sadly misinformed as to the "heroism of our men in office here." Their affectation, like all other affectation, defeats its object. Mrs. A., who has been fuming and fretting all the year past, and who went to bed sick upon the catastrophe being announced, now " is glad that she is no longer the keeper of a great national hotel." Mr. A. is quite rejoiced, and Mr. Clay delighted at the result. A keen and close observer tells me that C. is, on the contrary, down, down, down; that he cannot support himself; that he sinks under the effort to bear up against his defeat.

WASHINGTON, . anuary 12, 1829; Monday.

MY DEAR DOCTOR—It won't do for a man, who wishes to indulge in dreams of human dignity and worth, to pass thirty years in public life. Although I do believe that we are the meanest people in the world, I speak of this "court" and its retainers and followers. I am super-saturated with the world, as it calls itself, and have now but one object, which I shall keep steadily in view, and perhaps some turn of the dice may enable me to obtain it: it is, to convert my property into money, which will enable me to live, or rather to die, where I please; or rather where it may please God.

As to State politics I do not wish to speak about them. The country is ruined past redemption: it is ruined in the spirit and character of the people. The standard of merit and morals has been lowered far below "*proof.*" There is an abjectness of spirit that appals and disgusts me. Where now could we find leaders of a revolution? The whole South will precipitate itself upon Louisiana and the adjoining deserts. Hares will hirdle in the Capitol. "Sauve qui peut" is my maxim. Congress will liberate our slaves in less than twenty years. Adieu.

Friday, February 6, 1829.

"This," you will say, "is nothing to you." You know better; it is a great deal to me, and I sit up in bed to tell you that when you wrote that you did know better. My dear friend, I can hardly write or breathe. I was attacked last Monday about noon. I am now better; that is, not in extremity. My best love and duty to madame. The itch to know and attach one's self to the great is an inherent vice of our nature. Have you seen Lockhart's Life of Burns? Adieu for the present.

WASHINGTON, February 9, 1829; Monday.

MY GOOD FRIEND—I scratched a few lines to you on Thursday (I think) or Friday, while lying in my bed. I am now out of it, and

somewhat better; but I still feel the barb rankling in my side. Whether, or not, it be owing to the debility brought on by disease, I can't
contemplate the present and future condition of my country without
dismay and utter hopelessness.   I trust that I am not one of those
who (as was said of a certain great man) are always of the opinion of
the book last read.   But I met with a passage in a Review (Edinburgh) of the works and life of Machiavelli that strikes me with great
force as applicable to the whole country south of Potapsco : " It is
difficult to conceive any situation more painful than that of a great
man condemned to watch the lingering agony of an exhausted country, to tend it during the alternate fits of stupefaction and raving which
precede its dissolution, to see the symptoms of its vitality disappear
one by one, till nothing is left but coldness, darkness, and corruption."

You see that whatever temporary amendment there may be in
my health, there is none in my spirits.   On the contrary, they were
never worse.   It is not, I assure you, for the want of such feeble effort as I can make against the foul fiend.

The operation of this present Government, like a debt at usurious interest, must destroy the whole South.   It eats like a canker
into our very core.   South Carolina must become bankrupt and depopulated.   She is now shut out of the English market for her rice,
with all the premium of dearth in Europe.   I am too old to move,
or the end of this year should not find me a resident of Virginia,
against whose misgovernment I have full as great cause of complaint as
against that of the U. S.   It has been one mass of *job* and abuse—
schools, literary funds, internal improvements, Charlottesville conventions, and their spawn.   I have as great horror of borrowing as
you have ; but a friend having made the offer of some money, on
good security, I think I shall take up some on mortgage, and make
one more trial for life.   If you lived in the country, I would come
and stay with you ; but when I go to see you, you make dinners, and
put yourself out of the way, and to unnecessary expenses, which I
don't like to be the occasion of.

The snow is all gone, and the sun is seen once more.   God bless
you *both*.

Thursday, February 12, 1829.

MY GOOD FRIEND—Your letter of Monday came to hand yesterday, after I had written, and too late to thank you for it.   Tom Mil-
ler writes this morning that the convention bill has passed, and that
my friends expect me to be a candidate for a seat in that body.   If
any one can and will devise a plan by which abler and better men
shall be necessarily brought into our councils, I will hail him as my
Magnus Apollo!   But as I have no faith in any such scheme, and a
thorough detestation and contempt for political metaphysics, and for

an arithmetical and geometrical constitution, I shall wash my hands of all such business. The rest of my life, if not passed in peace, shall not be spent in legislative wrangling. I am determined, absolutely, not to expose myself to collision where victory could confer no honor. No, my dear friend, let political and religious fanatics rave about their dogmas, while the country is going to ruin under the one, and the others are daily becoming worse members of society. " I'll none of it." " By their fruits shall ye know them."

P. S. By the time you receive this, you will have seen the Boston correspondence of Mr. Adams. The reply is, I'm told, by Mr. Jackson. Meanness is the key-word that deciphers every thing in Mr. Adams' character.

Saturday, February 14, 1829.

MY DEAR FRIEND—Your opinions concerning the operation of this incubus, miscalled Government, I confess surprise me. I have made every allowance for the dearness of slave labor, and the monstrous absurdities of our own State legislation. But I cannot shut my eyes to the fact, that a community that is forbidden to buy, cannot sell. " The whole southern country will buy less, and make their own clothing, without making smaller crops." *Cui bono* this last operation, except to wear out their lands and slaves gratuitously ? It is this very " buying less," that lies at the root of our mischief. If we bought more, we would sell more in proportion, and become rich by the transaction. To pursue a Chinese policy, which we did not want, this Government, by cutting us off from our best customer, England, inflicts a dead loss of $15,000,000 this very year on one southern State alone (South Carolina) ; as returns cannot be made in her commodities, England, in time of dearth, refuses to receive her rice. Formerly she would not eat India rice. In like manner, she will soon become independent of us for her supply of cotton. She is also planting tobacco ; so that the conflagration of the factories, at which I heartily rejoice, will take from us the mite received for their consumption. Again, all the expenditure of this machine of ours is made (Norfolk and Point Comfort excepted) north of the Chesapeake. All of the dividends of the debt of the bank are received there. No country can withstand such oppression and such a drain.

As to W. H., I should not pay the slightest regard to any thing that he can say. I am well acquainted with the West Indies, and I have been told by some of the principal proprietors, that with all their heavy charges for provisions, lumber, mules, &c., from which Louisiana is exempt, the sugar crop is clear of all expenses ; these being defrayed by the molasses and rum. Moreover, you are to consider that the West Indies suffer under grievous commercial restrictions, and that Wilberforce and Co. have very much impaired the value of their slaves. (The same thing is at work here.) Nevertheless,

I was assured, by the most intelligent and opulent of the " West India Body," that the mortgages and embarrassments of Jamaica, &c., grew chiefly out of the proprietors residing in England, and trusting to agents; sometimes to colonial ostentation and extravagance; but that there was scarcely an instance of a judicious and active planter personally superintending his affairs, who did not amass a fortune in a very few years.

England was our best customer, because we were her best custo ers. This is the law of trade, and the basis of wealth; instead of which, we have the exploded " mercantile system," as it was ridiculously called, revived and fastened, like the Old Man of the Sea, around our necks.

Monday, February 16, 1829.

I abstained saying any thing about the convention, seeing no cause to change my first impression on that subject. I once told you that every man was of some importance to himself. I found out this too late—after I had poured myself out like water for others. From my earliest childhood, I have been toiling and wearing my heart out for other people, who took all I could do and suffer for them as no more than their just dues. My dear friend, I am super-saturated with disgust. My bodily infirmities do not contribute to relieve the feeling; and if I mix in affairs, I must be content to be set aside, with contemptuous pity, for a testy, obstinate old fool. To this I do not mean to subject myself. " Let the dead bury their dead." I shall not dig or throw one shovel full of earth. Adieu !

Thursday, February 19, 1829.

Your letter of Tuesday (17) is just received. I did not " mistake you very much," for I did not attribute to you opinions favorable to the tariff. The causes of disparity between the East and South, are to be found, among other things, in the former charging and being paid for every militia man in the field during the Revolutionary war, and for every bundle of hay and peck of oats furnished for public service; in the buying up the certificates of debt for a song, and funding them in the banks; in the bounty upon their navigation, and the monopoly of trade which the European wars gave them. If the militia services, losses, and supplies of the Carolinas had been brought into account, all New England would not have sold for as much as would have paid them. In regard to the West Indies, the great law of culture prevails—that the worst soils hardly reproduce the expense of cultivation. If even in Georgia, where the cane does not yield one-half the *strength* of syrup, sugar can be made to profit, what must be the yield of the rich. fresh lands of Jamaica, St. Kitts, or Juvinau? The syrup of New Orleans is, by the proof, 8—of the West Indies, 16.

I have not seen the picture. No steamboat can, I am persuaded, approach within fifty miles of this place.

From what I hear, public expectation will be much disappointed in regard to the composition and character of the new cabinet. This is for you alone. "As you have done with political economies," so am I with politics, and politicians too. I went yesterday to vote, ineffectually, against "the Gate Bill." I shall be agreeably disappointed if it does not pass the Senate.

Monday morning, February 23, 1829.

My Good Friend—I don't know why I write to you, unless it be to assuage or divert the chagrin by which I am devoured. I have never witnessed so complete a discomfiture as is expressed in the faces of such of my friends as I see, and they tell me that there is not one exception among the eminent men who lately acted together. The countenances of the adverse party beam with triumph, as might be expected.

I am making my arrangements to get away, and yet, I am better off here than I shall probably ever be again. I have a comfortable apartment and receive the most kind attentions from all the gentlemen under this roof, particularly Major Hamilton, Col. Benton and D. Hall. I shall never again know the comforts of society. The Ch. Justice was good enough to sit an hour with me yesterday ; and I had afterwards a visit from Mr. Quincy, my old fellow-laborer. He said that if Gen. J. had called to his councils *high* men, the East would be satisfied. He then asked who the present men were ? adding, "They say that this is C——'s arrangement." It continues to be intensely cold. Have I lost ground in Madame's good graces ? I shall be sorely mortified if it be so.

Thursday morning. Feb. 26, 1829.

My dear friend, I've been thinking of you all night, awake or asleep, and to-morrow, I hope to hear from you. You will see a most extraordinary announcement in this day's Telegraph. I am credibly informed by my friend H., that the V. P. is as much astounded by these results as any body, and is as indignant. This is most private and particular. Every body shocked, except Clay and Co. Strangers partake of these feelings.—My highest regards to Madame.

CHAPTER XXXIX.

ELECTED TO THE CONVENTION.

On his retirement from Congress, Mr. Randolph hoped to disconnect himself from public affairs, and to spend the remainder of his days in travelling abroad. But his old constituents were not so willing to give up his services. They had lost him for ever on the floor of Congress, but they now wished him to represent them on another theatre. The people of Virginia had determined on a convention to amend the Constitution of the State. Mr. Randolph was called to serve them in that body.

The reader will perceive, from the following letters, addressed to Dr. Brockenbrough, that he was nominated as a candidate without his knowledge, and greatly against his wishes. He was much embarrassed by this procedure, but at length consented to the sacrifice, that he might save the feelings of one friend and aid in the election of another who was a candidate also for the convention.

The letters were written before the election. He was returned of course as a member of the convention, and took his seat in that body when it assembled, on the first Monday of October, in the Hall of Representatives, in the capitol at Richmond.

ROANOKE, Tuesday, April 21, 1829.

To my friend Wm. Leigh, who called at the P. O. yesterday after the stage had left it, I am indebted for your kind letter of the 15th. He was riding post haste from P. Edward election to Halifax Superior Court, for which place he set out this morning by day-light. Such is the life of those who are at the head of the liberal professions in this country.

Whilst I was expressing to him my surprise at that passage of your letter which referred to my having consented to serve in the convention, if elected; he told me, to my utter astonishment, that a proclamation to that effect had been made at the last Charlotte Court, and by a staunch friend of mine too, and a man of honor and truth. Now, I have held but one language on this subject from first to last, and you know what that is. To you, to B., W., L., and others, in writing and orally, I have explicitly avowed my determination to have nothing to do with this matter. The more I have reflected on my retirement from public life, the better satisfied I am of the propriety and wisdom of the step. Before I take any in reference to this last matter, I shall see the gentleman who made the declaration in my behalf. He will be here about the last of this week.

My dear friend, we shall not "meet in October." I am anchored for life. My disease every day assumes a more aggravated character. I have been obliged to renounce wine altogether. Coffee is my only cheerer. A high fever every night, which goes off about day break with a colliquative sweat; violent pain in the side and breast; incessant cough,—with all my tenacity of life this can't hold long. I have rode once or twice a mile or two, but it exhausts me.   The last three days have been warm, but last night we had a storm, and it was cold again.   Luckily I have no appetite, for I have hardly any thing to eat except asparagus, which is very fine and nice.   I tried spinach *à la Française*, but it disagrees with me.   You see that, like Dogberry, " I bestow all my tediousness upon you."   You know my maxim, " that every man is of great consequence to himself."   The trees are budding and the forest begins to look gay, but when I cast my eyes upon the blossoms, the sad lines of poor Michael Bruce recur to my memory :—

> " Now Spring returns, but not to me returns
> The vernal joy my better years have known ;
> Dim in my breast, life's dying taper burns,
> And all the joys of life with health are flown."

Remove Mr. Manvy !   You amaze me.   What, the friend and school-fellow and class-mate of Jefferson, the first appointment to that consulate by Washington !   Pray, what is the matter ?   And who is to be the successor ?

ROANOKE, Tuesday, April 28, 1829.

MY DEAR FRIEND—You and I, if I mistake not, have long ago agreed that there is no such thing as free agency.   I am at this moment a striking example of the fact.   In short, to save the feelings of a man of as much truth and honor as breathes, who believed himself to be doing right, and to avoid injuring certain friends and interests, which the withdrawal of my name would, it seems, occasion, I am fain even to let it stand, at the risk of incurring the imputation of fickleness (for the world will never know the true version), and at what I shrink from with unutterable disgust, the prospect of again becoming a member of a deliberative, i. e. spouting assembly.

ROANOKE, Friday, May 22, 1829.

MY DEAR FRIEND—It is a long while since I heard from you, and I am in a condition that requires all the aid my friends can give.   If I could have been permitted to remain in the privacy I thought I had found, my life might have been prolonged some months—possibly years : but the kindness of my friends has destroyed me.   I have been in a manner, forced upon exertions to which my strength was utterly unequal, and at an expense of suffering, both body and mind, of which none but the unhappy victim can have a conception.   I have not been so ill since this month last year.

As I have not the least prospect of attending Halifax election, I count upon being left out, a result which I by no means deprecate ; having already attained the only two objects that I had at heart, and which prevented my withdrawing my name in the out set—the saving the feelings of one friend, who had " declared me," and promoting the election of another (W. L.). I am an entire stranger in Halifax, and personal courtship is as necessary to success in Politics as in Love. They have four candidates of their own.

To be killed by kindness is, to be sure, better than to be murdered, and it is some consolation to know that you have done service to one friend, and gratified many: but I have been most keenly sensible of the cruelty of which I could not complain.

My kindest regards to Mrs. B. and to Mr. Wickham when you see him. Your much afflicted but sincere friend.

CHAPTER XL.

THE VIRGINIA CONVENTION—EVERY CHANGE IS NOT REFORM.

No body of men that ever assembled in Virginia, created more interest than this convention. The State had been agitated for many years, on the subject of constitutional reform. Most of the slave property, and other wealth, were in the eastern section, extending from the Allegany to the sea shore, while a large free population were scattered over the western section, among the mountains. These people were almost unanimous in favor of an amendment of the Constitution, fixing the basis of representation on free white population. The result of such a measure, would be to change the balance of power, by giving the right of taxation to one portion, while the property to be taxed, for the most part, belonged to another portion of the Commonwealth; thus divorcing taxation and representation, which, according to American doctrine, should be inseparable. The eastern counties, who were to be the sufferers, strenuously opposed so radical a change in the fundamental law. It was not a mere question of reform, that might affect all parts alike, but it was one of power between two sections of the State, essentially different in feelings, habits, and interests; it was a question, too, that deeply involved that most difficult and delicate of all subjects, the right of slave representation. For these reasons, a deep and absorbing interest was felt in the deliberations of the convention now assembled in the capitol, at Richmond. Each section put forth its strength. The ablest men were selected without regard to locality. Gentlemen living in the lower part of the State, were elected by districts beyond the mountains, because of their coincidence of opinion with their distant constituents.

Perhaps no assembly of men ever convened in Virginia, displaying a larger amount of genius and talent—certainly none that contained a greater number of individuals whose reputation had extended beyond the borders of the State, and reached the farthest limits of the Union. There were many of less renown, who, in after years, acquired equal eminence in their professional and political career. Indeed, of the one hundred men that composed that Convention, much the larger portion were above the ordinary standard of talents, experience, and weight of character. The Editor of the " Proceedings and Debates" of the Convention, says, " that an assembly of men was drawn together, which has scarcely ever been surpassed in the United States."

What strange groups, and awkward meetings, took place on that occasion! Madison and Marshall side by side, in the same deliberative body! Giles and Monroe! Randolph, Tazewell, Garnett, Leigh, Johnson, Taylor, Mercer! Old Federalists, old Democrats, *Tertium Quids*, and modern National Republicans! What a crowd of recollections must have pressed on the mind of John Randolph, as he cast an eye around that assembly. For thirty years he had been on the political stage; for full one-third of that time, the whole of the political press, and two administrations—State and Federal, made war upon him! He was like an Ishmaelite; his hand against every man, and every man's hand against him. Then a friend was a friend indeed! and an enemy was one to be remembered! Now, behold around him so many that were friends, so many that were enemies, and so many who, pretending to be friends, in his hour of need betrayed him!

Randolph's manner and bearing, on this extraordinary occasion, was in some respects peculiar, even for him; but before the Convention adjourned, his bland and conciliatory course exalted him in the estimation of the country, and gratified his devoted friends, even beyond their most sanguine expectations.

The first thing done in the Convention, was to divide out to committees different parts of the Constitution, for revision. The most important was the Legislative Committee, to whom was assigned the duty of revising the " Right of Suffrage," the basis of representation.

Randolph was a member of this committee. Mr. Madison was chair man. In the committee room (Senate chamber) he took his seat at the head of a long table, and the members arranged themselves promiscuously along down the sides. Mr. Randolph, on the contrary, took his seat at some distance, in a corner, where he could observe every thing and every body that was passing. Erect in his seat, and his arms folded across his breast, he sat almost motionless, while his keen eye might be observed watching like a cat. Now and then his shrill voice, as if coming from some unseen being, would startle those in the room, and the crowd around would press forward to see from what quarter so startling a sound had emanated.

Of all the men assembled there on that great occasion, he was certainly the observed of all observers. The multitude were soon satisfied with seeing Madison, Marshall, Monroe, and other distinguished men, but no gratification could abate their desire to watch every movement, and to catch every word that fell from the lips of John Randolph. They crowded around him whenever he emerged from the capitol; through the throng of eager admirers he passed, hat in hand, with an ease, and grace, and dignity of manner, that struck every beholder with admiration.

Few men escaped with the reputation they brought into that assembly. They found that professional attainments, however extensive, or political studies confined to the measures or the politics of the day, did not qualify them to discuss those great principles which lie at the foundation of all government. Quite other habits of thought than the professional, and a far different training were necessary for the discussion of those questions that involved all the interests of man, past, present, and to come. That, however, was the field for John Randolph to display, in a pre-eminent degree, his commanding genius. His profound knowledge of men, of history, of government; the causes of the growth and decay of nations; his patient attention and wonderful faculty of winnowing the chaff, and collecting together the substantial grains of a protracted debate; his concentrated, pointed, and forcible expressions, making bare in a few words the whole of a complicated subject; and his vast experience in parliamentary proceedings, gave him an unexpected and controlling influence over the proceedings of the Convention.

He watched those proceedings with unremitted attention, partook largely in the debates, and before the close of the Convention, was the acknowledged leader of a powerful party, embracing the most distinguished men, who opposed all changes in the old Constitution, and actually prevented many that were contemplated by the reformers, and who, when they first assembled, supposed themselves in a decided majority. Mr. Randolph's speeches, with one exception (and that did not exceed two hours), were generally short, but to the purpose. They were well reported by Mr. Stansberry, the best stenographer of his time, and some of them are very fair specimens of his peculiar style.

The cardinal rule that governed his whole political life may be found in the following short speech:

"Mr. Randolph said, he should vote against the amendment, and that on a principle which he had learned before he came into public life; and by which he had been governed during the whole course of that life—that it was always unwise, yes, highly unwise, to disturb a thing that was at rest. This was a great cardinal principle, that should govern all statesmen—never, without the strongest necessity, to disturb that which was at rest. He should vote against the amendment on another, and an inferior consideration. Whatever opinion might have been expressed as to a multitude of counsellors, there was but one among considerate men as to a multiplicity of laws. The objection urged by the gentleman from Richmond, over the way (Mr. Nicholas), to the existing clause, was precisely one of the strongest motives with him for preferring the amendment. I am much opposed, said Mr. R., except in a great emergency—and then the legislative machine is always sure to work with sufficient rapidity—the steam is then up—I am much opposed to this 'dispatch of business.' The principles of free government in this country (and if they fail, if they should be cast away, here, they are lost for ever, I fear, to the world), have more to fear from over legislation than from any other cause. Yes, sir, they have more to fear from armies of legislators, and armies of judges, than from any other, or from all other causes. Besides the great manufactory at Washington, we have twenty-four laboratories more at work, all making laws. In Virginia, we have now two in operation—one engaged in ordinary legislation, and another *hammering* at the fundamental law. Among all these lawyers, judges, and legislators; there is a great oppression on the people, who are neither lawyers, judges, nor legislators, nor ever expect to be; an oppression barely more tolerable than any which is felt under the European governments. Sir, I never can forget, that in the great and good Book to which I look for all truth and all wisdom, the Book of Kings succeeds the Book of Judges."

On a proposition being made to ingraft in the new Constitution a mode in which future amendments shall be made therein, Mr. Randolph addressed the Convention:

"Mr. President, I shall vote against this resolution : and I will state as succinctly as I can, my reasons for doing so. I believe that they will, in substance, be found in a very old book, and conveyed in these words : 'Sufficient unto the day is the evil thereof.' Sir, I have remarked since the commencement of our deliberations, and with no small surprise, a very great anxiety to provide for *futurity*. Gentlemen, for example, are not content with any present discussion of the Constitution, unless we will consent to prescribe for all time hereafter. I had always thought him the most skilful physician, who, when called to a patient, relieved him of the existing malady, without undertaking to prescribe for such as he might by possibility endure thereafter.

Sir, what is the amount of this provision? It is either mischievous, or it is nugatory. I do not know a greater calamity that can happen to any nation than having the foundations of its government unsettled.

Doctor Franklin, who, in shrewdness, especially in all that related to domestic life, was never excelled, used to say that two movings were equal to one fire. And gentlemen, as if they were afraid that this besetting sin of republican governments, this *rerum novarum lubido* (to us a very homely phrase, but one that comes pat to the purpose), this *maggot* of innovation, would cease to bite, are here gravely making provision that this Constitution, which we should consider as a remedy for all the ills of the body politic, may itself be amended or modified at any future time. Sir, I am against any such provision. I should as soon think of introducing into a marriage contract a provision for divorce, and thus poisoning the greatest blessing of mankind at its very source—at its fountain head. He has seen little, and has reflected less, who does not know that "necessity" is the great, powerful, governing principle of affairs here. Sir, I am not going into that question, which puzzled Pandemonium—the question of liberty and necessity :

"Free will, fixed fate, foreknowledge absolute;"

but I do contend that necessity is one principal instrument of all the good that man enjoys. The happiness of the connubial union itself depends greatly on necessity; and when you touch this, you touch the arch, the key-stone of the arch, on which the happiness and well-being of society is founded. Look at the relation of master and slave (that opprobrium, in the opinion of some gentlemen, to all civilized society and all free government). Sir, there are few situations in life where friendships so strong and so lasting are formed, as in that very relation. The slave knows that he is bound indissolubly to his master, and must, from necessity, remain always under his control. The master knows that he is bound to maintain and provide for his slave so long as he retains him in his possession. And each party accommodates himself to his situation. I have seen the dissolution of many friendships—such, at least, as were so called; but I have seen that of master and slave endure so long as there remained a drop of the blood of the master to which the slave could cleave. Where is the necessity of this provision in the Constitution? Where is the use of it? Sir, what are we about? Have we not been undoing what the wiser heads—I must be permitted to say so—yes, sir, what the wiser heads of our ancestors did more than half a century ago? Can any one believe that we, by any amendments of ours, by any of our scribbling on that parchment, by any amulet, any legerdemain—charm—Abrecadabra—of ours can prevent our sons from doing the same thing—that is, from doing as they please, just as we are doing as we please? It is impossible. Who can bind posterity? When I hear of gentlemen talk of making a Constitution for "all time," and introducing provisions into it for "all time," and yet see men here that are older than the Constitution we are about to destroy— (I am older myself than the present Constitution—it was established when I was boy)—it reminds me of the truces and the peaces of Europe. They always begin : " In the name of the most holy and undivided Trinity," and go on to declare, " there shall be perfect and perpetual peace and unity between the subjects of such and such potentates for all time to come;" and in less than seven years they are at war again.

Sir, I am not a prophet nor a seer ; but I will venture to predict that your new Constitution, if it shall be adopted, does not last twenty years. And so confident am I in this opinion, that if it were a proper subject for betting, and I was a sporting character, I believe I would *take ten* against it. It would seem as if we were endeavoring (God forbid that I should insinuate that such was the intention of any here)—as if we were endeavoring to corrupt the people at the fountain head. Sir, the great opprobrium of popular government is its *instability*. It was this which made the people of our Anglo-Saxon stock cling with such pertinacity to an independent judiciary, as the only means they could find to resist this vice of popular governments. By such a provision as this, we are now inviting, and in a manner prompting, the people to be dissatisfied with their government. Sir, there is no need of this. Dissatisfaction will come soon enough. I foretell now, and with a confidence surpassed by none I ever felt on any occasion, that those who have been the most anxious to destroy the Constitution of Virginia, and to substitute in its place this *thing*, will not be more dissatisfied now with the result of our labors, than this new Constitution will very shortly be opposed by all the people of the State. I speak not at random. I have high authority for what I say now in my eye. Though it was said that the people called for a new state of things, yet the gentleman from Brooke himself (Mr. Doddridge), who came into the Legislative Committee armed with an axe to lay at the root of the tree, told the Convention that he would sooner go home and live under the old Constitution than adopt some of the provisions which have received the sanction of this body. But I am wandering from the point.

Sir, I see no wisdom in making this provision for future changes. You must give governments time to operate on tne people, and give the people time to become gradually assimilated to their institutions. Almost any thing is better than this state of perpetual uncertainty. A people may have the best form of government that the wit of man ever devised ; and yet, from its uncertainty alone, may, in effect, live under the worst government in the world. Sir, how often must I repeat, that *change* is not *reform*. I am willing that this new Constitution shall stand as long as it is possible for it to stand, and that, believe me, is a very short time. Sir, it is vain to deny it. They may say what they please about the old Constitution. The defect is not there. It is not in the form of the old edifice, neither in the design nor the elevation—it is in the *material*—it is in the people of Virginia. To my knowledge that people are changed from what they have been. The four hundred men who went out to David, were *in debt*. The partisans of Cæsar were *in debt*. The fellow-laborers of Cataline were *in debt*. And I defy you to show me a desperately indebted people any where, who can bear a regular sober government. I throw the challenge to all who hear me. I say that the character of the good old Virginia planter—the man who owned from five to twenty slaves, or less, who lived by hard work, and who paid his debts, is passed away. A new order of things is come. The period has arrived of living by one's wits—of living by contracting debts that one cannot pay—and above all, of living by office-hunting. Sir, what do we see ? Bankrupts—branded bankrupts, giving great dinners—sending their children to the most expensive schools—giving grand parties—and just as well received as any body in society. I say, that in such a state of things, the old Constitution was too good for them; they could not bear it. No, sir, they could not bear a freehold suffrage and a property representation. I have always endeavored to do the people justice, but I will not flatter them ; I will not pander to their appetite for change. I will do nothing to provide for change, I will not agree to any rule of future apportionment, or to any provision for future changes, called amendments of the Constitution. They who love change—who delight in public confusion—who wish to feed the caldron and make it bubble, may vote, if they please, for future changes. But by what spell—by what formula are you going to bind the people to all future time? *Quis custodiet custodes?* The days of Lycurgus are gone by, when we could swear the people not to alter the Constitution until he should return—*animo non revertendi.* You may make what entries on parchment you please. Give me a Constitution that will last for half a century—that is all I wish for. No Constitution that you can make will last the one-half of half a century. Sir, I will stake any thing short of my salvation, that those who are malcontent now, will be more malcontent three years hence, than they are at this day. I have no favor for this Constitution. I shall vote against its adoption, and I shall advise all the people of my district, to set their faces—aye, and their shoulders against it. But if we are to have it, let us not have it with its death warrant in its very face: with the *facies hypocratica*—the sardonic grin of death upon its countenance."

The resolution was rejected by a large majority, and the Convention determined that the new Constitution should contain in itself no provision for future amendments.

As the most distinguished member on the floor, Mr. Randolph was assigned the duty of closing the business of the Convention.

" Mr. Chairman," said he, " for the last time, I throw myself upon the indulgence and courtesy of this body. I have a proposition to submit, which, I flatter myself—which I trust—I believe, will be received with greater unanimity than any other which has been offered in the course of our past discussions, with perfect unanimity. You will perceive, sir, that I allude to your eminent colleague, who has presided over our deliberations. When I shall have heard him pronounce from that chair, the words—' This Convention stands adjourned *sine die,*' I shall be ready to sing my political *nunc dimittis,* for, it will have put a period to three months, the most anxious and painful of a political life, neither short nor uneventful. Having said thus much, I hope I may be permitted to add, that, notwithstanding any heat excited by the collision of debate, I part from every member here, with the most hearty good-will to all. But I cannot consent that we shall separate, without offering the tribute of my approbation, and inviting the House to add theirs—infinitely more valuable—to the conduct of the presiding officer of this Assembly. If it were a suitable occasion, I might embrace within the scope of my motion, and of my remarks, his public conduct and character elsewhere, with which I have been long and intimately acquainted; but this, as it would be misplaced, so would it be fulsome. I shall, therefore, restrict myself to the following motion:

"' *Resolved,* That the impartiality and dignity with which Philip P. Barbour, Esq, hath presided over the deliberations of this House, and the distinguished ability whereby he hath facilitated the dispatch of business, receive the best thanks of this Convention.' "

At the time of this adjournment, no man stood higher than John Randolph in the estimation of the members or of the people. He had won greatly on their affections. A more familiar contact, and closer observation of the man, had served to remove many prejudices. They began to comprehend and appreciate one who had been so long the victim of wilful misrepresentation, and of calumny. Notwithstanding the boldness with which he spoke unpleasant truths in the Convention, his manner, on the whole, was so mild and conciliatory, his wisdom and his genius so conspicuous, that they won for him the esteem and the veneration of every body. His friends, delighted with this state of things, wrote to him from all quarters, congratulating him on this agreeable termination of his labors in the Convention. Here is one of his letters in answer to a friend who had written him on this subject:

" How I have succeeded in gaining upon the good opinion of the public—as you and others of my friends tell me I have done—I cannot tell. I made no effort for it, nor did it enter into my imagination to court any man, or party, in or out of the Convention. It is most gratifying, nevertheless, to be told by yourself and others, in whose sincerity and truth I place the most unbounded reliance, that I have, by the part I took in the Convention, advanced myself in the estimation of my country. With politics I am now done; and it is well to be able to *quit winner.*"

CHAPTER XLI.

MISSION TO RUSSIA.

BEFORE Mr. Randolph took his seat in the Convention he had been offered the mission to the Court of St. Petersburgh. The President's letter, making the offer, was highly flattering to him. It was in the following words:

WASHINGTON, Sept. 16, 1829.

DEAR SIR: The office of Envoy Extraordinary and Minister Plenipotentiary to Russia will soon become vacant, and I am anxious that the place should be filled by one of the most capable and distinguished of our fellow-citizens.

The great and rapidly increasing influence of Russia in the affairs of the world, renders it very important that our representative at that Court should be of the highest respectability; and the expediency of such a course at the present moment is greatly increased by circumstances of a special character. Among the number of our statesmen from whom the selection might with propriety be made, I do not know one better fitted for the station, on the score of talents and experience in public affairs, or possessing stronger claims upon the favorable consideration of his country, than yourself. Thus impressed, and entertaining a deep and grateful sense of your long and unceasing devotion to sound principles, and the interest of the people, I feel it a duty to offer the appointment to you.

In discharging this office I have the double satisfaction of seeking to promote the public interest, whilst performing an act most gratifying to myself, on account of the personal respect and esteem which I have always felt and cherished towards you.

It is not foreseen that any indulgence as to the period of your departure, which will be required by a due regard to your private affairs, will conflict with the interests of the mission: and I sincerely hope that no adverse circumstances may exist, sufficient to deprive the country of your services.

I have the honor to be, with great respect,

Your most ob't serv't,

ANDREW JACKSON.

The Hon. JOHN RANDOLPH OF ROANOKE.

This letter, as it must necessarily have been, was general, and diplomatic in its terms; but it was sufficiently explicit to show that Mr. Randolph was needed for a special service; that his great talents and experience rendered him, in the judgment of the President, peculiarly fitted for the service, and that no delay which might be required for his private affairs, would affect the interests of the mission.

The Secretary of State, Mr. Van Buren, who inclosed the above communication, stated in his letter that "the vacancy spoken of by the President will be effected by a recall which he feels it to be his duty to make, and the notice of which will be sent the moment your answer is received."

To the President's invitation Mr. Randolph replied:

ROANOKE, Sept. 24, 1829.

SIR: By the last mail I received, under Mr. Van Buren's cover, your letter, submitting to my acceptance the mission to Russia.

This honor, as unexpected as it was unsought for, is very much enhanced in my estimation, by the very kind and flattering terms in which you have been pleased to couch the offer of the appointment. May I be pardoned for saying, that the manner in which it has been conveyed could alone have overcome the reluctance that I feel at the thoughts of leaving private life, and again embarking on the stormy sea of federal politics. This I hope I may do without any impeachment of my patriotism, since it shall in no wise diminish my exertions to serve our country in the station to which I have been called by her chief magistrate, and under those " circumstances of a special character" indicated by your letter. The personal good opinion and regard, which you kindly express towards me, merit and receive my warmest acknowledgments.

I have the honor to be, with the highest respect, sir, your most obedient and faithful servant,

JOHN RANDOLPH OF ROANOKE.

To ANDREW JACKSON, Esq., President of the U. S.

Mr. Randolph was not called upon to assume the duties of his mission till the month of May, 1830, when the appointment was first made known to the public. This was not occasioned by any expressed wish on his part for a delay. It was caused by circumstances over which the President himself had no control; and which were to him the source of much vexation.

Every thing was done by the President and Mr. Van Buren to render the appointment agreeable. General Hamilton, and others, had solicited the post of Secretary of Legation for Mr. Cruger, of South Carolina. The reply was that the President had decided to leave that matter altogether to Mr. Randolph. In a letter to him, February 25, 1830, Mr. Van Buren says: "If he (Cruger) will accept, and you approve, no objections will be made from any quarter."

About a month afterwards he was informed that the friends of Mr. Cruger had declined for him, he not being yet returned from Europe; and was requested to look about him to suit himself.

What followed is thus explained by him in a letter to Dr. Brockenbrough, dated Friday, June 4, 1830:

"Thanks for your caution; but I was forearmed. This matter was left entirely to me. I had a full account of the late incumbent long ago. I waited as long as was practicable for Mr. Cruger, and this day sevennight I sent off Clay, who received the appointment the morning of his arrival. He says: 'He (the P.) told me he wished you to sail by the 15th of June, as the vessel would be ready at Norfolk by that time. As I could not get an audience before eleven o'clock, I have no time to add more. The P. will write to

you to-day.' (I shall not receive this until Monday.) 'The commission for me will be made out to-morrow or next day, and your instructions as soon as possible. He told me, that although he would
have liked very much to have shaken you by the hand, yet he would
not put you to the inconvenience of coming to this place.'

"This is vigorous proceeding. Last Friday I broached the subject of my appointment to this youth. After talking of my disappointment in regard to Mr. Cruger, I most unexpectedly offered it
to him. It was an electric shock. That evening (in two hours after
the mail arrived) he left me; and about the same time at the termination of the week I have his letter, which must have been mailed at
twelve on the noon of his arrival in Washington."

About the latter part of the month of June Mr. Randolph sailed
from Hampton Roads. His acceptance of this mission has been
much condemned : many of his best friends disapproved of it ; they
thought it was inconsistent with his former professions. They seemed
to wish that it might be always said of him—he never accepted office—
lived and died in the service of the people,—the great commoner.
But this was taking a limited view of the subject. It must be remembered that Mr. Randolph had retired from public life ; the session that closed the 4th of March, 1829, put an end to his legislative
career; his health was feeble; and his only hope of a prolonged
existence was in travelling and sojourning in a better climate than
that of his native land. All his plans had a reference to that object;
he looked for nothing, expected nothing, from the Government. In
this state of things a distinguished and important appointment was
offered him.

On whom could the President have more appropriately bestowed
the most signal evidence of his approbation and confidence? He was
by far the most illustrious man in the ranks of the administration,
and had done more than any other individual to pull down the former, and to build up the present dynasty. As the President most
happily expressed himself, he was moved to make the appointment
from "a deep and grateful sense of Mr. Randolph's long and unceasing devotion to sound principles and the interest of the people." To
have neglected bestowing some mark of distinguished honor on such
a man, would have betrayed such a spirit of injustice and ingratitude
as to arouse the indignation of the country.

What more appropriate office could have been assigned him?
The departments at Washington, the missions to London and to

Paris, were too confining, laborious, and vexatious in their details for his feeble health. At the distant court of St. Petersburgh he could not be much perplexed with business ; while, at the same time, to give dignity and importance to his mission, he had assigned him a special duty, the results of which might greatly redound to the good of the country, while it required only occasional attention, and could not suffer by delay.

In accepting this appointment, he only carried out his original design of going abroad in search of health ; while, at the same time, he served his country in a station she had pressed upon him as an evidence to foreigners of her distinguished regard. But he had said, office had no charms for him ; in his condition, a cup of cold water would be more acceptable. All this was true. Had he sought a change of administration for the sake of office—had he retired from the service of the people " to drudge in the laboratories of the departments, or to be at the tail of the corps diplomatique in Europe," he might have been charged with inconsistency. But no one could justly accuse him of seeking to overthrow the administration of Mr. Adams from personal considerations. " Sir," said he, " my ' churchyard cough' gives me the solemn warning, that, whatever part I shall take in the chase, I may fail of being in at the death. I should think myself the basest and the meanest of men—I care not what the opinion of the world might be—I should know myself to be a scoundrel, and should not care who else knew it, if I could permit any motive connected with division of the spoil, to mingle in this matter with my poor, but best exertions for the welfare of my country."

None but the most uncharitable, could doubt the truth and the sincerity of this declaration. But it so happened that Mr. Randolph did survive, and that the new administration called on him to leave his retirement, and to perform an important service for the country, in the diplomatic department. What answer could he give ? I have no desire for office ; its drudgery would be intolerable to me, in my feeble health. I am aware of that, says the President, but there is a special object to be accomplished at one of the most important courts in Europe. I can think of no one more able than yourself, or that will bring more weight of character into the service. I beg of you, for the sake of the country, to accept the office. What answer could he give, to this appeal to his patriotism ? Sir, I am the champion of the people, and will only serve them. I will not accept your bribe, to close my eyes and silence my tongue. Such an answer would have been worthy of Diogenes (whose part he was expected to play on this occasion), but not of a patriot and a statesman, who is willing to serve his country in any capacity; and who knows that a faithful discharge of his duties, in whatever station, is a good service performed for the benefit of the people. Mr. Randolph gave the only answer that was becoming in him to give—"May I be pardoned for saying that the manner in which it has been couched (the appointment) could alone have overcome the reluctance that I feel at the thoughts of leaving private life, and again embarking on the stormy sea of federal politics. This I hope I may do, without any impeachment of my patriotism, since it shall in no wise diminish my exertions to serve our country in the station to which I have been called by her Chief Magistrate." Had Mr. Randolph declined the office so warmly pressed upon him, it would have been a condemnation of the administration in the beginning. It would have been a declaration to the world that he had no faith, no confidence in the man he had been so instrumental in elevating to the presidency. As he did not thus feel, it would have been unpatriotic and unwise, to take a course that would manifest such distrust. Indeed, Mr. Randolph had no other alternative, without doing great violence to his true sentiments, but to accept the appointment, at whatever cost to his private interests; and it was a great sacrifice; "it has been my ruin," says he, "body and estate, this Baltic business."

Mr Randolph arrived in St. Petersburgh about the last of August. He writes to Dr. Brockenbrough, 4th September:

"My reception has been all that the most fastidious could wish. You know I always dreaded the *summer* climate, when my friends were killing me with the climate of Russia before my time. Nothing can be more detestable. It is a comet; and when I arrived it was in perihelion. I shall not stay out the aphelion. Heat, dust impalpable, pervading every part and pore, and actually sealing these last up, annoying the eyes especially, which are farther distressed by the glare of the white houses. Insects of all nauseous descriptions, bugs, fleas, mosquitos, flies innumerable, gigantic as the empire they inhabit; who will take no denial. Under cover of the spectacles, they do not suffer you to write two words, without a conflict with them. This is the land of Pharaoh and his plagues—Egypt, and its ophthalmia and vermin, without its fertility—Holland, without its wealth, improvements, or cleanliness. Nevertheless, it is beyond all comparison, the most magnificent city I ever beheld. But you must not reckon upon being laid in earth; there is, properly speaking, no such thing here. It is rotten rubbish on a swamp; and at two feet you come to water. This last is detestable. The very ground has a bad odor, and the air is not vital. Two days before my presentation to the Emperor and Empress, I was taken with an ague. But my poor Juba lay at the point of death. His was a clear case of black vomit; and I feel assured that in the month of August, Havana or New Orleans would be as safe for a stranger as St. Petersburgh. It is a Dutch town, with fresh-water-river canals, &c. To drink the water is to insure a dysentery of the worst type.

"In consequence of Juba's situation, I walked down one morning to the English boarding-house, where Clay had lodged, kept by a Mrs. Wilson, of whom I had heard a very high character as a nurse, and especially of servants. I prevailed upon her to take charge of the poor boy, which she readily agreed to do. I put Juba, on whom I had practised with more than Russian energy, into my carriage, got into it, brought him into the bedroom taken for myself, had a blazing fire kindled, so as to keep the thermometer at 65° morning, 70° afternoon; ventilated well the apartment; poured in the quinine, opium, and port wine; snake-root tea for drink, with a heavy hand (he had been previously purged with mercurials), and to that energy, under God, I owe the life of my dear faithful Juba."

Mr. Randolph very soon learnt, on his arrival, that the special object of his mission could not at that time be accomplished. "There has been," says he, "a game playing between my predecessor and a certain great man, in which M. has fairly beaten him, at his own weapons; most disgracefully 'tis true for M., but not less so for the other party. This is the secret of that delay so vexatious to General Jackson, so injurious to me, and so destructive to the success of my mission. The day before I left Hampton Roads, Count Nesselrode's star sunk temperately to the West, and Prince Lieven became the Lord of the ascendent. The waters of Carlsbad are only like young unmarried ladies' dropsical affections, for which they are sent down to their friends in the country, a decent cover for what all consider a virtual superseding of the minister."

Add to this change in the Ministry, the revolution in France, and in Belgium, the rebellion in Poland, and the cholera then raging through Europe, and it may readily be imagined that Russia was not in a condition to deliberate on such matters, as might without prejudice be postponed.

The Emperor had as much as he could do to attend to affairs at home. The *special subject* of Mr. Randolph's mission was delayed, and as he had no particular object connected with his public duties to detain him, he sought refuge in a more genial climate.

He writes from London, Wednesday, Sept. 29, 1830: " I write merely to tell you that after having been lifted on board the coach and steamboat at St. Petersburgh on the 7th—19th instant, I landed this morning at 8 on the Custom-House Wharf, able to walk a few steps."

October 28, he writes : " I have letters from St. Petersburgh, one a ' note' from Count Nesselrode, as late as the 6th of this month, and I am daily in expectation of others from the same quarter. On Sunday, if I have strength, we go to New Market, to attend the 3rd October or Houghton meeting. This will be a fine theme for the coalition presses. No matter. Let the curs bark since they cannot bite. I have been so often left for dead and rose again, that they may despair of victory over my feline political lives."

Many ridiculous stories were told in the United States about Mr. Randolph's conduct and reception in Russia. In allusion to this subject, he writes to his friend :

" The yearnings of my heart after home, have been stifled by the monstrous and malignant calumnies which have been heaped upon my unoffending head. To them I have but to oppose the honor of a gentleman, upon which I declare them to be utterly false and groundless.

" My official correspondence will flatly contradict the most mischievous of them, as regards the public interest.

" Nothing could be more cordial than my reception in Russia. It was but yesterday (Dec. 19, 1830) that I had my first interview with Prince Lieven since his return to this court, and my reception was like that of a brother.

" On my arrival at St. Petersburgh I took up my abode at the principal Hotel, Demouth's. where I staid one week.

" Furnishing myself with a handsome equipage and four or five horses, I called promptly on every diplomatic character, whether Ambassador, Envoy, or Chargé, or even Secretary of Legation, from the highest to the lowest. Not content with sending round my carriage and servants, I called in person and left my cards.

" Count Athalin, the new representative of France. promptly called on me (being a later comer), and the next day, being ill a-bed, I sent my coach and Secretary of Legation to return his visit. I had previously called on the Chargé d'Affaires of France under Charles X.

"I had not, during my sojourn in St. Petersburgh, the slightest difference with any one, except a British subject, and that was on the construction of a contract. This man (my landlord) and his niece were my fellow-passengers from Cronstadt, and we parted on the most civil and friendly terms.

"He is not the author of these slanders.

"Before I thought of cancelling the bargain with Smith, I had applied to Mrs. Wilson to receive and nurse my poor Juba. I removed to her house myself, not as a boarder, but a lodger, and took a room on the *ground floor*. Except Clay and Capt. Turner, of the ship Fama of Boston, to whom I intrusted my faithful Juba, I did not set eyes upon one of the inmates of the house. Capt. T. at my request was often in my apartment, and to him I fearlessly appeal for the falsehood of these calumnies, so far as I came under his observation. They are utterly false.

"'The Court Tailor.' A day or two after I got to Demouth's Hotel, a person very unceremoniously opened my parlor door and advanced to my bed-room, where I was lying on a sofa. He was the *American Consul's Tailor*, and said, 'he had been sent for,' but seemed abashed at finding the Consul with me. I, seeing through the trick (it is universally practised there), told him he had been misinformed, and the man apologized and withdrew. He was sent for about ten days afterwards, and made some clothes for Mr. Clay.

"I did not refuse to land at Cronstadt. The authorities came on board to visit me, and when they returned, I entered the steamboat and proceeded up to St. Petersburgh.

"My dress, on presentation to their Imperial Majesties, was a full suit of the finest black cloth that London could afford; and, with the exception of a steel-cap sword, was the dress of Mr. Madison during the late Convention. (I had indeed no diamond buckles.) In the same dress, never worn except upon those two occasions (with the exception of gold shoe and knee buckles, adopted out of pity to Mr. McLane, and laying aside, at his instance, the sword), I was presented at court here On neither occasion did I think of my costume after I had put it on; nor did it attract observation; and I am well satisfied that the love of display on the part of some of our own foreign agents, and the pruriency of female frontlets for coronets and tiaras, have been at the bottom of our *court-dress abroad*. It is not expected or desired, that a foreign minister shall have exacted from him what is the duty of a subject. I saw Prince Talleyrand at the King's levee as plainly dressed as I was. But what satisfies me on the subject is, that Prince Lieven, on whose goodness I threw myself for instruction at St. Petersburgh, and who saw me in the dress (chosen by Polonius's advice), never hinted any thing on the subject; but truly said that 'his Majesty the Emperor would receive me as one gentleman receives another;' and such was the fact."

Mr. Randolph afterwards described this interview to some of his friends. He said he went to the Palace, passed through a number of guards and officers splendidly dressed, and was introduced to the Emperor alone. He was a handsome young man, dressed in uniform. But a difficulty arose from Mr. Randolph's speaking French imperfectly, and the Emperor not speaking English. The Emperor sent for some one that could interpret for them; but after a little time they managed to understand each other—Mr. Randolph speaking French very slowly, and the Emperor answering in the same manner. At length, the Emperor asked him if he wished to see the Empress? Mr. R. replied that he did. The Emperor then bowed, and Mr. Randolph bowed himself out of the presence backwards, according to the etiquette of the court. He was then conducted to another part of the Palace, and introduced, among a large assemblage of ladies, where he was presented to the Empress, she being in advance of the rest. He described her as being very handsome. She questioned him whether he had ever been at court before. He said he had not; that it was the first time he had ever been in the presence of royalty. She asked him if he knew Mr. Monroe, who had been aide-de-camp to Prince Constantine, and afterwards to the Emperor? He said he did not. She said he was a very fine young man, and a great favorite with the Emperor ; and asked if he was not the son of the Postmaster-General? He replied that he was not; but was the son of the postmaster at Washington. She asked him if he was not a relation of ·President Monroe? He told her he was not. After some further conversation, Mr. Randolph said something which made the Empress laugh " most vociferously." The audience soon ended, and Mr. Randolph had again to bow himself out backwards ; " and it was lucky," said he, " that I happened to be near the door."

On the 22d of January, 1831, Mr. Randolph wrote to his friend, Mark Alexander, Esq., a late colleague from the Mecklenburgh District, then in Washington :

" I am daily and hourly in the hope of hearing from Russia. My absence from that country has not been of the slightest detriment to our affairs in that quarter. Before my departure, I had put the imperial ministry in full possession of our propositions and views, and have since been awaiting their answer, which the revolutions in France and Belgium and the insurrection of Poland (to say nothing of the cholera morbus) have retarded. The Russian government have been

too much engrossed by these events, and by the feverish state of
Europe, to attend to subjects which may as well be settled next year
as now, not being of pressing necessity, and Russia having but a
secondary interest in them. If my health shall permit, and there
be the most remote prospect of success in the objects we have in
view (or any of them), I shall return as soon as the Baltic is open."

On the 19th of February he writes to Dr. Brockenbrough:

" Count Nesselrode, who says that ' Mr. Randolph has justly anticipated the cause of delay on the part of the Imperial Ministry,'
promises me as speedy an answer as the present disturbed state of
Europe will permit them to give. It commenced in July last, and
the political atmosphere seems to thicken. I shall probably return
to Russia in April or May, and I fear that I shall have to pass another winter in Europe—south of the Alps, of course. The barking
of the curs against me in Congress I utterly despise. I think I can
see how some of them, if I were present, would tuck their tails between their hind legs, and slink—aye, and stink too. Perhaps the time
may come when I may see some of them, not face to face, for their
eyes could not meet mine, I know by experience.

" I could give you a great deal of speculation upon the present
state of Europe ; for when I please, I can be as dull as another ; but
perhaps the next advices might overthrow all my conjectural estimates, and leave me, like other builders of theories, a laughing-stock,
until some new folly took off attention from my case. It remains to
be seen whether Philip Louis, who is no Philip Augustus, can arrest
the march of the revolution of July, and chain France to the car of
the Holy Alliance. Here I am in the focus of European intrigue,
and watching like a cat. I think, however, it requires not the eyes
of a lynx, or any other of the feline tribe, to see that this present
' government,' as 'tis the fashion to call it, have no stomach to reform
or to *iberalism*, or to any thing but the emoluments and patronage
of office. There are illustrious exceptions—Lord Althorp and Sir
James Graham, for example—but my Lord Grey & Co. are of a very
different temper."

May 2d, he writes: " The heroic resistance of the Poles has
found ample occupation for the councils as well as the arms of Russia ; but I fear that the contest cannot be prolonged beyond the
present season. It makes one's heart sick to think of the catastrophe. My thoughts are shared between the Poles and my friends
at home ; a sinking of the heart comes over me when I think of
either ; a sensation inexplicable, but most painful."

June 4th, he speaks of the late political changes at home : " Yesterday, with your letter, I received the intelligence of the resignation
of our cabinet. The course of events during the past year is enough
to perplex and puzzle abler judgments than mine. I have read the

letters of V B. and the P. more than once, and with intense interest. At this distance, and with my imperfect knowledge of the state of affairs, it may be presumptuous in me to give an opinion; but by such lights as I have, the step taken by V. B. seems manly and judicious—worthy of his character, and of his attachment to Gen'l Jackson, whose reply is worthy of all praise. I cannot help feeling the deepest concern for the old hero, thus, as it were, left to struggle alone against his foes; and I sincerely and devoutly pray, that he may form an administration that will contribute to his repose and glory, as well as the welfare of his country. . . . .

"Lord Palmerston entertained the corps diplomatique, in honor of the king's birth-day, and did me the honor to include me in his invitation. I went, because I did not feel at liberty to decline. It was, as you may suppose, very grand, but very dull. I was flattered by his lordship's polite attentions, and gratified by the cordial reception of P. Lieven, with whom I had a good deal of conversation."

"If I abstain," says he, June 16, "from saying any thing on politics, it is not because I feel indifferent to the state of public opinion at home. Far from it; and I hope, when you get to New-York, that your promised letter will enlighten me on that head. The events which have taken place during my absence, seem to have unhinged and unsettled every thing. It is a matter of self-gratulation to all who are unconnected with them."

In the autumn, Mr. Randolph returned to the United States, much reduced in health. When he landed in New-York, his old friend, Mr. Harvey, hastened to see him, and was greatly shocked at his emaciated appearance. "His eagle-eye," says he, "detected, by my countenance, what was passing in my mind, and he said, in a mournful tone of voice : 'Ah, Sir, I am going at last ; the machine is worn out; nature is exhausted, and I have tried in vain to restore her.' 'Why,' replied I, forcing a smile, 'you told me the same thing some years ago, and yet here you are still.' 'True,' rejoined he, 'but I am seven years *nearer the grave.*'"

CHAPTER XLII.

OPIUM EATER.

On his way home, October, 1831, Mr. Randolph spent a few days in Richmond. He was entirely prostrate—never left his bed-room—

rarely his bed; but his friends visited him frequently, and they speak in raptures of his brilliant and instructive conversation. None of them detected in his discourse any thing more than an occasional "flightiness," produced by fever—aggravated, perhaps, by the use of opium, to whose soothing qualities he had been compelled to resort, to quiet the pangs of that inexorable disease, which, like the vulture in the heart of Prometheus, had plunged its talons in his vitals, and consumed them with remorseless fangs, from the cradle to the grave.

Mr. Randolph made no secret of his use of opium at this time. "I live by, if not upon opium," said he to a friend. He had been driven to it as an alleviation of a pain to which few mortals were doomed. He could not now dispense with its use. "I am fast sinking," said he, "into an opium-eating sot, but, please God! I will shake off the incubus yet before I die; for whatever difference of opinion may exist on the subject of suicide, there can be none as to '*rushing into the presence of our Creator*' in a state of drunkenness, whether produced by opium or brandy." To the deleterious influence of that poisonous drug, may be traced many of the aberrations of mind and of conduct, so much regretted by his friends, during the ensuing winter and spring. But he was, by no means, under its constant influence. During this period, h. wrote almost daily to his friend, Dr. Brockenbrough. Those letters furnish incontestable evidence that, when they were written at least, his feelings were calm, and his judgment as unclouded as it ever had been.

He hastened up from Richmond to Charlotte Court-house, to address the people on court day, the first Monday in November. The subject of his speech, among other things, was his conduct while minister to the Court of St. Petersburgh. His anxiety to explain this matter, so unusual with him, and his coldness of manner towards his friends, caused many of them to suspect that he was not altogether himself at that time. The next Monday, he addressed the people of Buckingham. On his return next day, Nov. 15, he wrote from Charlotte Court-house to Dr. Brockenbrough:

"On my road to Buckingham, I passed a night in Farmville, in an apartment which in England they would not have thought fit for my servant; nor on the continent did he ever occupy so mean a one. Wherever I stop, it is the same—walls black and filthy—bed

and furniture sordid—furniture scanty and mean, generally broken—
no mirror—no fire-irons—in short, dirt and discomfort, universally
prevail, and in most private houses the matter is not mended.   The
cows milked half a mile off—or not got up, and no milk to be had at
any distance—no jordan—in fact, the old gentry are gone and the
nouveaux riches, where they have the inclination, do not know how to
live.   *Biscuit* not half *cuit*, every thing animal and vegetable, smear-
ed with melted butter or lard.   Poverty stalking through the land,
while we are engaged in political metaphysics, and, amidst our filth
and vermin, like the Spaniard and Portuguese, look down with contempt on other nations, England and France especially.   We hug
our lousy cloaks around us, take another *chaw* of *tvbbacker*, float the
room with nastiness, or ruin the grate and fire-irons, where they
happen not to be rusty, and try conclusions upon constitutional
points."

The great degeneracy of the times, was the constant theme of his
discourse.   He could not shake the sad reflection from his mind.
When he thought of what Virginia had been and what she was, he
was stung to the quick.   His late experience of the high cultivation,
the comforts, and the refinements of English society, brought the
contrast of·the past and the present more vividly to his recollection.
Many thought him mad on this subject.   But little could they comprehend the depth of his feelings, or the anguish of his soul, when
he so often exclaimed, "Poor old Virginia! poor old Virginia!" What
they conceived to be the ebullitions of a diseased fancy, were the lamentations of a statesman and patriot over the ruins of his country,
which his prophetic eye had long foreseen, and his warning voice had
in vain foretold!   *The old gentry are gone*; none knew better than
he, the force of this truth.   He saw what others could not see; he
saw, from the sea-board to the mountains, nothing but desolation and
poverty, where the fires of a noble and generous hospitality had burned on a thousand hearths.   He remembered sires and grandsires,
whose degenerate sons, like the Roman youth, pointed to the statues
and the monuments of their noble ancestors, instead of achieving a
monument for themselves by their own great deeds.

This was the theme of Mr. Randolph's discourse at Prince Ed
wards Court-house, where, on the third Monday in November, he
addressed the people.   He passed in review all the old families of Virginia, alluded to the fathers and grandfathers of many then standing
around him; spoke of their energy, sagacity, and efficient usefulness

of character.   Then, addressing himself to one individual in particular, as was his custom, he said : You, sir, "will be the first to admit
the higher claims of your father on the country, for general utility
and energy of character.   I am too old (he sportively added) to know
much of his sons personally, but I will venture to affirm, that placed
in your father's shoes, and *having to keep off the calf whilst the wife
milked the cow*, you never would have achieved what he has done in
point of character and fortune.   The young people, now-a-days,
have too much done for them, for them to exert themselves as their
fathers and grandfathers have done."   He then spoke of many illustrious men, whose names adorn many pages of our earliest and brightest history.   Henry, Mason, and others; not one has left a son equal
to their father.   "In short," said he, "look at the Lees, Washingtons,
Randolphs—what woful degeneracy !"

What had all this to do with the politics of the day ? on which
he was expected to talk to the people.   Was there ever such a scat-
ter-brain speech ?   Some turned away, shook their heads, and said,
"the man is mad;" others maliciously misrepresented what he said,
and went about telling people that he had slandered his old friends
and neighbors.   He struck at the root of the disease, however—probed
the wound to its core; the *men of seventy-six* were gone; their sons,
if not degenerate, were not equal to their fathers !

It cannot be denied, that Mr. Randolph attributed this great
change in the condition of Virginia, mainly to the policy of Mr. Jefferson.   The destruction of the law of inheritance, followed by the
embargo and the non-intercourse system, he conceived, gave the finishing stroke to her prosperity.   "The embargo," he said, "was the
Iliad of all our woes."   The blind fidelity with which the people of
Virginia followed Mr. Jefferson in all his schemes, is thus humorously described: "I cannot live (says ʌe, March, 1832,) in this miserable, undone country, where, as the Turks follow their sacred
standard, which is a pair of Mahomet's green breeches, we are governed by the old red breeches of that prince of projectors, St. Thomas, of Can*ting*bury; and surely, Becket himself never had more pil-
grims at his shrine, than the saint of Monticello."

Another source of great annoyance and excitement to Mr. Randolph, was the conduct of his negroes and overseers during his absence.   He suspected that they had taken up a notion he would never

be able to return home again, and that they might do as they pleased, without the fear of his displeasure. His sudden appearance among them took them by surprise, and they were not prepared to give an account of their stewardship. Whether he had just cause of complaint, is not for us to determine. One thing is certain, he had to spend near two thousand dollars to buy provisions for their support. One would suppose that three hundred negroes, on the best lands in Virginia, might support themselves.

"I have been in a perpetual broil (says he, November 15th, 1831,) with overseers and *niggers*. My head man I detected stealing the wool that was to have clad his own and the other children; the receiver the very rascal (one of Mr. Mercer's 'housekeepers,') who flogged poor Juba, who had no wool except upon his head. I have punished the scoundrel exemplarily, and shall send him to Georgia or Louisiana, at Christmas. He has a wife and three fine children. Here is a description of his establishment: a log house of the finest class, with two good rooms below, and lofts above; a barrel half-full of meal (but two days to a fresh supply); steel shovel and tongs, better than I have seen in any other house, my own excepted; a good bed, filled with hay; another, not so good, for his children; eight blankets; a large iron pot, and Dutch-oven; frying-pan; a large fat hog, finer than any in my pen; a stock of large pumpkins, cabbages, &c., secured for the winter. His house had a porch, or shed, to it, like my own."

Mr. Randolph had an old servant by the name of Essex, the father of John. "He was the most genteel servant I ever saw," says Mr. Marshall. Mr. Randolph called him familiarly, "Daddy Essex. Although the relation of master and servant was kept up between them, it was done with more cordiality and kindness in the manner of each, than had ever been witnessed between master and slave. It was the custom of Essex, when leaving his master's service at night, to give him the usual salutations, and this civility was returned by Mr. Randolph. But on the present occasion, whenever Essex came into his presence, he immediately flew into a passion, accused him of keeping a tavern in his absence, entertaining a pedler, and once or twice, even went so far as to strike him with a stick. Every body knows the inestimable value he set on John and Juba, but they now shared his wrath. "When I arrived in New-York," said he, "I would not have taken for John or Juba, or the smallest child either of them had, two thousand guineas; but now, I would as soon sell them to a negro-trader as not." They were actually driven out of the house, into the corn-field, and other awkward fellows taken into their places. " Moses goes rooting about the house like a hog." Mr. Randolph's friends witnessed, during the winter, many ludicrous scenes between him and his servants. But his fits of excitement did not last long. His extreme irritability, occasioned by disease, and the stimulants he was compelled to use to alleviate pain, may have caused him to magnify the offences of his slaves. But he was prompt in making reparation. His favorite body-servants were soon restored to their proper station. About the first of February, he called on the overseer, and asked him to ride out with him; said he was going to make friends with his head man, Billy, whom he had put to work in the ditch. They rode to the ditch, and Mr. Randolph said, " Your servant, Billy." " Your servant, master," replied Billy. ' Well, Billy," said he, " I have come to make friends with you." " Thank you, master," said Billy. " Billy," said Mr. Randolph, " you stole my wool, and sold it for fifty cents." " Yes, master." " But I think I am in debt to you, Billy, for I took your pumpkins and your house, and hog, turned you out of a comfortable house, and gave you three damned whippings. And now, I think I owe you something, and I have come up to settle with you." As the result of the settlement Billy was restored to his place and to his property.

Mr. Randolph's mind continued to be disordered, and his health to grow more and more feeble, till the month of April, when many of his friends expected he would die. About the twenty-fifth of that month, he was moved to the house of his friend, Mr. John Marshall, at Charlotte Court-house. He frequently sent for Mr. Marshall into his room ; when that gentleman entered, he would say, " You are too late—it is all over." Sometimes he had a small bell in his hand, which he would ring slowly, saying, " It is all over." Sometimes he would make John ring the bell. He would sometimes ask Mr. Marshall, " Will you stand by me ?" as if he was apprehensive of some personal conflict. He continued much in this condition till the middle of May, with this difference, that his memory gave way almost entirely, and he had sunk into a kind of stupor.

About the middle of May, after being reduced almost to a skeleton, his mind began to clear away, his memory returned, and his feelings were calm and kind towards every person of whom he spoke. In a very short time he seemed to be perfectly himself. The first time Mr. Marshall saw him, when a change in his mind was distinctly marked, they were in the room alone. Mr. Randolph burst into tears, and said, " Bear with me, my friend; this is unmanly, but I am hard pressed." He seemed to be in great pain, and said, " It is impossible—I speak it reverently—that the Almighty himself, consistent with his holy counsel, can withhold this bitter cup. It is neces sary to afflict me thus, to subdue my stubborn will." He then prayed a few words audibly, shut his eyes, and seemed to be praying in a low whisper. From this time his spirits were good; he uni· formly appeared cheerful and in good temper, conversed handsomely, and spoke of men, whether his political enemies or others, in good humor; his appetite seemed to have improved, and he gradually gained flesh. From this time forth, with rare exceptions, his mind continued unclouded to the day of his death. But it is astonishing how one in his condition, could prolong for a twelve-month, an existence so attenuated, so feeble.

In August he writes—" My lungs made a noble resistance, but, like the Poles, they were over-powered. The disease is now phthisis, and the tubercles are softening for breaking out into open ulcers; liver, spleen, heart (I hope the pericardium), but above all, the *stomach.* diseased, and this last, I fear, incurable. My diet is water-grûel, for breakfast; tomatoes and crackers for dinner, and no supper. Yet, these taken in the very smallest quantities that can sustain life, throw me into all the horrors of an indigestion; so that I put off eating as long as possible, and thereby make a dinner of my breakfast, and a sort of supper at five or six o'clock, of my dinner. Sleep I am nearly a stranger to. Many nights I pass bolt upright in my easy chair; for when propped up by pillows in bed, so as to be nearly erect from the hips upwards, I cough incessantly and am racked to death."

Some weeks after this, he says to Dr. Brockenbrough—" After I wrote to you on Sunday night, the next day I had a most violent fit of hysteria. I was so moved by the ingratitude of my servants, and my destitute and forlorn condition, that I ' lifted up my voice and wept;' wept most bitterly. Yet I am now inclined to think that I did the poor creatures some injustice, by ascribing to ingratitude, what was the insensibility of their condition in life. But every body, you only excepted, abandons me in my misery."

CHAPTER XLIII.

THE CONSUMMATION.

ANDREW JACKSON was elected by State-rights men. There were many others united under his banner, who agreed only in their sentiments of opposition to the ruling powers; but the political principles that transformed and harmonized the discordant elements into a consistent whole, were the doctrines of the old Republican party. The centripetal tendency of the administration of Adams and Clay, had awakened and alarmed the country. Mr. Clay, with a boldness and an energy peculiar to himself, had pressed forward his American sytem to its final and full consummation. The Bank was omnipotent; the principle of Protection for protection's sake, was distinctly recognized, and nothing remained to complete and to fasten the system on the country, but to carry out those magnificent plans of Improvement which had been projected.

Randolph, Van Buren, Tazewell, and other distinguished leaders of the old Republican party, sounded the alarm, and raised the standard of opposition. Andrew Jackson was the man selected as their leader. Whether he fully concurred with them in principles and in purposes, could not be known—his past life had not been in the line of politics—he was pledged to no system—the great object was to defeat the present dynasty, and to take the chances of directing his course by wise counsel, hereafter. Their object is explained by the familiar and homely illustration used by Mr. Randolph, to satisfy his own constituents. "When you have a faithless, worthless overseer," said he, "in whom you could place no confidence, and have resolved to dismiss him, did you ever change your mind, because, for no matter what reason, you could not get the man that you preferred, to every other? or have you been satisfied to turn him off, and employ the best man that you could get?"

Jackson well fulfilled the expectations of those who elevated him to the Presidency. The first great measure of his administration, was to put an end to a system of Internal Improvement, which had been commenced by the Federal Government, and was rapidly growing up into a magnificent scheme of fraud, speculation and expenditure, far surpassing the South Sea or Mississippi scheme, that ingulfed all Europe in bankruptcy and ruin. The veto to the Maysville Road bill, arrested this great evil, and did much to bring back the people to a just and sound interpretation of the Constitution.

All reflecting men, who have any regard to the words and the spirit of a written, limited, and well-defined grant of power to a Federative Union of States, are now satisfied that the construction of roads and canals, and other means of intercommunication, properly belongs to the States. To take it from them and to exercise jurisdiction within their borders, in the construction of highways, was so gross a violation of the Constitution, and so bold an assumption of the reserved rights of the States, as to render all other usurpations of minor consideration. Like Aaron's rod, it swallowed up every thing else. Besides, the States are better acquainted with their own resources, and can conduct the means of their development more economically, more judiciously, and more extensively. If they, in the prosecution of their plans, have involved themselves in so large a debt, suffered so much from fraudulent legislation, as to be driven, some to the necessity of repudiation, others to the verge of bankruptcy, what would have been the condition of the whole Union, had they contin-ued those plans so zealously commenced, and entered on the prosecution of those magnificent surveys which their engineers had reported as practicable, necessary and proper? The States ceasing to be sovereign and independent—ceasing to act as a counterweight to the centralizing influence of the Federal Government, would have been clamorous suppliants for its bounty; fraudulent combinations would have carried every thing in the national legislature—some of the States would have had large improvements conducted through their borders, while others would have none; and all would have been loaded with a debt, only surpassed by the crushing burthen of England. Resorting to that tribunal power, intrusted to the Executive, not only for the preservation of its own independence and dignity but for the protection of the rights reserved to the States and the people, Andrew Jackson, by the simple exercise of its authority, arrested the centralizing tendency of the Republic, restored the States to their proper equilibrium, rebuked the spirit of Federal usurpation, and saved his country from ruin.

When Jackson took in his hand the helm of State, the Bank of the United States was in the plenitude of its power ; its numerous branches, in close affiliation and absolute dependence on a central power, occupied the most important and commanding positions. Its influence over the currency and the commercial operations of the country, was unbounded. It could make or unmake, build up or destroy, at pleasure. Its directory, seated in their marble palace at Philadelphia, like the gods on Olympus, could make rain or sunshine, as it pleased their sovereign will. Even the Representatives of the people, sent to examine into the abominations and sorceries of this red harlot, were dazzled with her brightness. They bowed obsequiously before her golden altars, and returned rejoicing, and told the people that she was not only pure, but worthy of all trust and confidence. No greater combination of power ever existed under any government. The East India Company, that held an Empire under its sway, and burthened the seas with its treasures, could not boast of greater authority. To possess the money influence in a commercial country, is to control its movements, not only in the affairs of government, but in the remotest ramifications of society. It is holding Leviathan with a hook. This power, all pervading and absolute, was unquestionably held by the Bank of the United States. The time had come, not to supplicate, but to demand a renewal of her charter, and a continuation of her enormous power for another generation. Shall the demand be granted? was the question now submitted to the Representatives of the people, and to the President.

January 10th, 1832, Randolph says, "I *know* Jackson to be firm on the Bank of the United States; and I believe the tariff too. In United States Bank stock there will be a fall, for every thing is settled by the London prices; and *there* will be a panic. But the Bank will bribe through I detest it, and shall do all I can to defeat it, even by coming into Congress next election *si le Roy* (Peuple) *le veut*. When the Union shall crumble to pieces, the Bank will stand. The *courts* and its *debtors* will sustain it, in each grain of our rope of sand." In one particular, this prediction has happily not been verified. The Bank is an " obsolete idea," while the Union still survives, we trust, to live for ever. But the other part of the prophecy was literally fulfilled ; the Bank did create a panic, and did bribe through. While the bill was under discussion, Mr. Randolph wrote to his friends, urging them to resistance. Some of them from the South were offended with Jackson, and he was afraid they would suffei their feelings to influence them on this occasion. To Mark Alexander, Esq., his old colleague, he says, " I have just received (June 26, 1832) your blank envelope, covering the *Telegraph* of the 21st. I write to entreat you to tell Warren R. Davis and his colleagues (alas ! for poor Johnston), that if, by their votes, the United States Bank bill shall pass the House of Representatives, they will receive the curses, loud and deep, of every old school Republican of the South. To embarrass Jackson is a small game, compared with saddling the country with that worst and most flagrant of the usurpations of the Federal Government, and the most dangerous engine against the rights, and very existence of the States. I am warm and abrupt, but I am dying, and have not time to be more courtly and circumlocutory. The Tariff, the Internal Improvement jobs, and the Supreme Court, combined, are not to be put into the scale against this accursed thing. The man who supports the Bank and denounces the Tariff as unconstitutional, may take his choice between knave or fool, unless he admits that he is both.

" In one case, the power to lay duties, excises, &c., is granted ; in the other, no such power is given. The true key is, that the *abuse, under pretence of exercise of any power* (midnight judiciary, &c.) is unconstitutional. This unlocks every difficulty. Killing a man may be justifiable homicide, chance-medley, manslaughter or murder, according to the motives and circumstances of the case. An unwise, but honest, exercise of a power, may be blamed, but it is not unconstitutional. But every usurped power (as the Bank) is so."

The Bank bill, however, passed both Houses of Congress, and was submitted to the President, for his approval. Randolph was not mistaken in his man. " I *know* Jackson to be firm on the Bank of the United States." Against that formidable institution, he stood up and battled alone. In his reading of the Constitution, there was no authority for it ; to his observation and experience, the existence of such a power was dangerous to a free republic. Satisfied in his mind that the Bank of the United States was both unconstitutional and inexpedient, it was vain to remonstrate. It was idle to tell him that Washington had sanctioned it ; he had as clear a judgment, as pure a patriotism, as Washington. It was useless to tell him, that good and wise men, yielding to the cry of distress, had, for the second time, established a Bank ; and that Madison, surrendering his own judgment to precedence and authority, had approved it. No such distress existed now; no such plea of necessity could be urged. Now was the time, in profound peace, to apply the knife and the cautery, to cut out and destroy the cancer that was threatening to consume the Constitution of the country. Deserted by all his friends, as he had been on many trying occasions before, while a military chieftain, he was left alone to rely on his own clear judgment and unshaken fortitude. When he vetoed the Bank bill, and caused the public money to be removed from the custody of that institution, his friends earnestly entreated him not to do it. But there was one that stood by him—a kindred spirit, that would perish with him in the ruins rather than have yielded.

Had Randolph been on the floor of Congress, the Bank bill would never have passed. He would have scourged the money-changers from the temple. But the veto saved the Republic, and he was rejoiced at it. "Tell Leigh (says he, August 2,) that the veto message, and some other things, have made a Jackson man of me, and that I shall be delivered of my vote without *forceps*, or the Cæsarean operation."

But another deed, still greater, if possible, had yet to be performed, before the Government could be rescued from its centripetal tendency, and those features of a federative republic that, in the vicissitudes of forty years, had well nigh been effaced, could be restored to their original distinctness and beauty. A tariff of duties, onerous to the agricultural interests, and laid solely for the protection of other interests, and as a bounty, had been imposed. The protective policy was distinctly recognized as a principle 'of legislation ; its friends regarded it as firmly established, and proclaimed it to be as *fixed as fate*. But this principle of protection, according *to States-right doctrine,* which was the basis and the essential element of the old Republican party, could only be looked upon as a violent interpolation. The most eminent statesmen of the strict-construction school denounced it as an unwarrantable abuse of power, if indeed it was not a plain infraction of the letter of the Constitution, which gave power to lay and collect duties, imports, and taxes, merely for the purposes of revenue. But one of the States of the Confederacy, believing that the right to impose a tax on one class of industry, as a bounty to another, had not been granted, and hearing a stern majority assert the doctrine, and pronounce it as *fixed as fate*, proclaimed that the only safety of the Republic lay in State interposition.

Our fathers did not complain of the burthen of their taxes, but contended against the right of taxation without representation. But South Carolina contended that her grievances were even greater than those of our ancestors; she protested against the tariff system, as founded in usurpation and injustice, and at the same time complained of the onerous nature of the taxes imposed She was heavily taxed for the benefit of others, and yet had no voice in the imposition. Feeling herself aggrieved, and having appealed, as she thought, in vain for redress, she took the remedy of her wrongs in her own hands. The only conservative power of this Confederative Republic is in the States. What matters it how nicely adjusted may be the balance of power between the executive, legislative, and judicial departments at Washington, when they have swallowed up all the powers that were reserved to the States and to the people. Take away the rights that belong to Virginia and the other States as *bodies politic*, and those that belong to their people, as citizens of each State respectively (strictly speaking, there is no such thing as an American citizen); take away these domestic guards, destroy these home securities that we hold in our own hands, and where is the guaranty for our liberties? We should no longer be a federative republic of equal and sovereign States, but the miserable, degraded provinces of a consolidated empire, where a sectional and selfish majority will rule the nation with a rod of iron. The States would be recreant to their trust, and unworthy the veneration of their sons, did they not stand by those rights so essential to their own existence, and so invaluable as the means of protecting and preserving the liberties of their people. This is what Massachusetts did in the days of the embargo; it is what South Carolina did on the present occasion. She asserted (and surely she was the best judge) that the tariff which had been forced upon her, was not only ruinous, but as unjust and as unwarrantable as the right claimed by the British parliament to tax the Colonies without their consent. She protested that the tax was forced upon her by those who had no common interest, and declared her resolution to refuse obedience to the law. Whether she acted wisely—whether she threw herself upon those constitutional rights reserved to her as a State—or whether she resorted to the ultimate right of the oppressed under every form of government, is for the general historian and the political philosopher to determine. The biographer of John Randolph has only to say that he sympathized with the State, and went with her, heart and soul, in the fearful struggle that ensued. He had battled with this tariff system from the beginning, and foresaw the dangerous consequences to which it would lead. When the subject was under discussion in 1824, he said, on the floor of the House of Representatives:

"And what, sir, are we now about to do? For what was the Constitution formed? To drive the people of any part of this Union from the plough to the distaff? Sir, the Constitution of the United States never would have been formed, and if formed, would have been scouted *una voce* by the people, if viewed as a means of effecting purposes like this. The Constitution was formed for external purposes, to raise armies and navies, and to lay uniform duties on imports, to raise a revenue to defray the expenditure of such objects. What are you going to do now? To turn the Constitution wrong-side out; to abandon foreign commerce and exterior relations—I am sorry to use this Frenchified word—the foreign affairs which it was established to regulate, and convert it into a municipal agent; to carry a system of espionage and excise into every log-house in the United States. * * * * But no *force*—no, sir, no force short of Russian despotism—shall induce me to purchase, or, knowing it, to use any article from the region of country which attempts to cram this bill down our throats. On this we of the South are as resolved, as were our fathers about the tea, which they refused to drink; for this is the same old question of the stamp act in a new shape, viz. : whether they who have no common feeling with us shall impose on us not merely a burdensome but a ruinous tax, and that by way of experiment and sport. And, I say again, if we are to submit to such usurpations, give me George Grenville, give me Lord North, for a master. It is in this point of view that I most deprecate the bill. If from the language I have used, and gentlemen shall believe I am not as much attached to this Union as any one on this floor, he will labor under a great mistake. But there is no magic in this word *Union;* I value it as the means of preserving the liberty and happiness of the people. Marriage itself is a good thing; but the marriages of Mezentius were not so esteemed. The marriage of Sinbad, the Sailor, with the corse of his deceased wife, was an union; and just such an union will this be, if, by a bare majority in both Houses, this bill shall become a law. And I ask, sir, whether it will redound to the honor of this

House, if this bill should pass, that the people should owe their escape to the act of any others, rather than to us? How will it answer for the people to have to look up for their escape from oppression, not to their immediate representatives, but to the representatives of the States, or, possibly, to the Executive? * * * * In case this bill should be, unhappily, presented to him (the President) for his signature, I hope, sir, he will scout it as contrary to the genius of our government, to the whole spirit and letter of our Confederation. I say of our Confederation. Blessed be God, it is a Confederation, and that it contains within itself the redeeming power, which has more than once been exercised, and that it contains within itself the seeds of preservation, if not of this Union, at least of the individual commonwealths of which it is composed."

In another part of the same speech (1824), Mr. Randolph declared:

" This is not the last tariff measure; for, in less than five years, I would, if I were a betting man, wager any odds that we have another tariff proposition, worse by far than that, amendments to which gentlemen had strangled yesterday by the bowstring of the previous question. * * * * * When I recollect that the tariff of 1816 was followed by that of 1819–20, and that by this measure of 1823–4, I cannot believe that we are at any time hereafter long to be exempt from the demands of those sturdy beggars, who will take no denial. Every concession does but render every fresh demand and new concession more easy. It is like those dastard nations who vainly think to buy peace."

They did follow in rapid succession; the tariff of 1828 and of 1832, each based on the principle of protection, each more burthensome than those that had gone before, and proclaimed *as fixed as fate*. Mr. Randolph watched the crisis brought on by this unwise and oppressive legislation with intensest interest. South Carolina had taken her position, and he knew well she would maintain it. Though in retirement, he was in daily correspondence with the chief actors on the scene; he knew they were in earnest, that they had counted the costs, and would not lightly hazard the dangers of a rupture and a civil war. In March, 1832, before any decisive steps had been taken, he spoke freely to his friends on the subject of South Carolina nullification. He said that dreadful times were coming, the United States Bank would be broken, and troops would be marching through the country; he said that South Carolina would not yield—that she would fight; that General Jackson would be glad to get Hamilton, Calhoun, McDuffie, and Hayne into his power; that he had no doubt if a war came, as come he feared it must, General Jackson would hang those gentlemen, if he could get hold of them; but that the whole South would unite, for it was their interest to do so, and there would be a bloody war of it. He read letters from gentlemen in South Carolina, and became highly excited on the subject. He said that if the war took place, he would have himself buckled on his horse, Radical, and would fight for the South to the last breath. These expressions, the reader is aware, were used by Mr. Randolph under peculiar circumstances, when he was not altogether himself. In his cooler moments no man looked more calmly or more judiciously on this momentous subject. On the 6th of December, before he knew of the ordinances of South Carolina, or the proclamation of the President, he writes:

" A letter from my friend Hamilton indicates the most morbid state of excitement in South Carolina. The truth is, I have no doubt, that imprudent and rash declarations have been made on both sides, and have been carried from one to the other by the earwigs that, more or less, infest all political parties. This has put the leaders of the two hostile divisions into the worst state of mind imaginable for cordial and dignified reconciliation. But I have great faith in Jackson's magnanimity, and I trust that, as soon as he finds himself in a situation to recede without dishonor, he will make the preliminary advances with graceful cordiality."

Had Randolph himself been on the floor of Congress, events might have been different. No man had more the confidence of both parties than he had; but unfortunately there was no one of sufficient weight and influence, to give affairs this pacific direction, and they were consequently hurried on to their catastrophe.

South Carolina, by her ordinance, proclaimed that she would not obey a law of the United States. It was the duty of the President to see that the laws were faithfully executed. General Jackson, by his proclamation, pronounced his determination to see that the Tariff law was properly enforced in South Carolina. The Proclamation contains an elaborate argument in justification of his conduct. It cannot be denied that his duty required him to take some such course, but he sustained and justified it, by a resort to the exploded doctrines and reasonings of the old federal school; if his arguments were true, then the principles of the Republican party, on which he had hitherto acted, were false.

It may have been a right action, but a wrong reason. All power ema‧ nates from the people, they are sovereign; but the general undefined mass of individuals, told by the head within the borders of the United States, are not the people known to our Institutions: the citizens of each State acting through the *body politic*, or a convention, or in their primary assemblies, are the people. Whatever they shall do in their sovereign capacity, as the people of a State, may be a revolution, but it can never be a rebellion; a sovereign cannot rebel against himself, nor against his coequal sovereigns; he may violate a compact with them, or they may commit a breach of faith towards him, so as to justify resistance and even war, a revolution if you please of all the relations existing between them, but no act of omission or aggression between coequal and independent parties can be construed into a rebellion.

Here was Jackson's great mistake; he did not have a clear perception of a federative union between coequal and independent States; he regarded the ordinance of the people of South Carolina, issuing from the highest authority known to a State—their sovereign will expressed in Convention—as an act of rebellion, and the men and officers appointed to execute their will as rebels that ought to be hung whenever taken.

So soon as Randolph heard of this fatal proclamation, so pregnant with pestilent heresies, his indignation knew no bounds. The Editor of the Richmond Enquirer endeavored to discriminate between the act itself and the reasoning in defence of it; but Randolph involved both perpetrator and defender in one common denunciation. The 16th of December he says:

"Your letter of the 12th was received late last night whilst I was under the influence of morphine and blue-pill, but such was the interest I took in it, and in the jesuitical comments of Mr. Enquirer Ritchie on the ferocious and blood-thirsty proclamation of our Djezzar Pacha, that I did not close an eye until daybreak. I am now just out of bed (1 o'clock, P. M.), and not more than half alive, indeed not so much.

"The apathy of our people is most alarming. If they do not rouse themselves to a sense of our condition and put down this wretch ed old man, the country is irretrievably ruined. The mercenary troops who have embarked for Charleston, have not disappointed me they are working in their vocation, poor devils! I trust that no quar‧ ter will be given to them.

"Pray tell William Leigh to write to me forthwith, and to give me his full, unreserved opinion upon the state of affairs. I sometimes distrust my own judgment in my present diseased condition.

"I am heartily glad that my brother refuses to go to the Senate of the U. S. I should not be sorry to see him in our Legislature, where, as 1798–9, the resistance must be made." January 4, 1833, he writes to Mr. Harvey: "My life is ebbing fast. What will the New-York Evening Post say to Ritchie's apology for the Proclamation, in his 'Enquirer' of the first instant? Never was there so impudent a thing. It seems, then, that the President did not know, good, easy man, what *his* Proclamation contained. Verily, I believe it. He is now all for law and the civil power, and shudders at blood. 'Save me from my friends' is a good old Spanish proverb. But his *soi-disant* friends are his bitterest enemies, and use him as a tool for their own unhallowed purposes of guilty ambition. They have first brought him into odium, and then sunk him into contempt. Alas! alas!" January 31st he says: "I am now much worse than when I wrote you last, and see no probability of my ever recovering sufficiently to leave this place. The springs of life are worn out. Indeed, in the abject state of the public mind, there is nothing worth living for. It is a merciful dispensation of Providence, that death can release the captive from the clutches of the tyrant. I was not born to endure a master. I could not brook military despotism in Europe, but *at home* it is not to be endured. I could not have believed that the people would so soon have shown themselves unfit for free government. I leave to General Jackson, and the Hartford men, and the ultra-federalists and tories, and the office-holders and office-seekers, *their triumph over the liberties of the country. They will stand damned to everlasting fame.*"

But the dying statesman resolved to make another effort to rouse the people, and to pluck the fallen liberties of the country from the grasp of military despotism. The veteran of a hundred fields harnessed himself for his last battle. The same cause that nerved his youthful arm, now shook the palsy from his aged limbs, and kindled in his bosom once more its slumbering fires. The sight of mercenary troops levied to uphold the usurpations of Government first called forth that bold and manly eloquence, that revealed to the people the future champion of their cause, and made John Thompson exclaim—*he will become an object of admiration and terror to the enemies of liberty.* True to the destiny thus foretold, for more than thirty years he had successfully contended against the minions of power. But now, behold the same appalling scenes re-enacted before him—the hirelings of Government marching through the land to trample down the rights of the States and of the people—the same doctrines avowed—the same excuses offered for the interposition of military authority—while the people, sunk into a deep lethargy like that of sleep, are unconscious of the "leprous distilment" that has poisoned the fountains of truth, and are forgetful of the threatening dangers that surround them. "The apathy of our people is alarming!"

But there was no apathy in him: he saw, he felt, he acted. Lifted into his carriage like an infant, he went from county to county, and spoke with a power that effectually aroused the slumbering multitudes. Too weak to stand, he addressed them from his seat: but like Jupiter seated on Olympus, he shot forth his thunderbolts on every hand, blasting and withering whatever stood in the way. The sublime energies of a patriot soul were his; they could not be repressed, and all the faculties of a dying frame were summoned to this last effort. It was like a voice coming from beyond the tomb: there was the skeleton of a man before them, but the people saw the fires of an immortal spirit beaming forth from its blazing sockets; they heard the trembling accents of an expiring tongue, but felt the living words of an inspired prophet fall upon their tingling ears. Their fathers had heard that clear ringing voice in the days of his youth echo sweet music through their hearts, and had clasped him to their bosoms as their most cherished son: *they* now listened to his solemn tones, like the knell of a death-bell, with silence and awe; and re ceived his warning admonitions with the duty and reverence of affec tionate children.

He did not speak in vain. Throughout his old district, with scarcely a dissenting voice, they adopted his resolutions condemning the tone, the temper, and the doctrines of the Proclamation. In the course of his speech at Buckingham, Mr. Randolph is reported, on what seems to be good authority, to have said: "Gentlemen, I am filled with the most gloomy apprehensions for the fate of the Union. I cannot express to you how deeply I am penetrated with a sense of the danger which at this moment threatens its existence. If Madison filled the Executive chair, he might be bullied into some compromise. If Monroe was in power, he might be coaxed into some adjustment of this difficulty. But Jackson is obstinate, headstrong, and fond of fight. I fear matters must come to an open rupture. If so,

this Union is gone !" Then pausing for near a minute, raising his fin
ger in that emphatic manner so peculiar to his action as a speaker,
and seeming, as it were, to breathe more freely, he continued—" There
is one man, and one man only, who can save this Union—that man
is HENRY CLAY. I know he has the power, I believe he will be
found to have the patriotism and firmness equal to the occasion."

Mr. Clay did not disappoint his expectations. Whatever may be
said of him as a statesman, none can deny that he is a true-hearted
patriot. With parental fondness he cherished his American system
—with unyielding pertinacity contended for it to the last extremity—
but when it became a question between that and the integrity of the
Union, he did not hesitate; like Abraham, he was ready to sacrifice
his own offspring on the altar of his country, and to see the fond idols
he had cherished perish one by one before his lingering eyes. Mainly
through his efforts the Compromise bill of 1833 was passed, the
principle of protection abandoned, the duties reduced, South Carolina
satisfied, her honor preserved, and the Union saved. But let not
Jackson be too lightly condemned. He had a difficult task to perform; aside from the heresies of his Proclamation we have not condemned him. There were the laws on the statute book; he had
labored to get them modified: but however much he might disapprove of their character, or sympathize with those on whose shoulders
they fell as a grievous burthen, so long as they were laws, he was
bound to see them enforced. He was not the man to shrink from
his duty, and promptly declared that they should be enforced. This
was an awful moment for the Republic.

The most important experiment in the history of government had
to be tried. The trial had to be made, whether State sovereignty
was of any avail, or the Federal Government absolute and omnipotent.
Had Carolina failed, we should have gone down like the Roman Republic, into a consolidated empire, with all power concentrated in the
capitol, and governed by venality and corruption. Had Jackson failed in his duty, and suffered the laws to be put at defiance with impunity, the fraternal bonds of this Union would have been dissolved,
and we should have existed for a time as petty States, in perpetual
warfare, until some master should arise to govern them, or they should
fall, as exhausted provinces, into the hands of European power. In
this awful moment, when disrupture and civil war seemed inevitable,

that magnanimous spirit of compromise, in which the Constitution was framed, again rescued it from destruction. And so will it ever be while the States have independence and courage to assert their rights, and patriot souls shall guide the helm of affairs.

This was the auspicious moment for John Randolph to depart. He died in the midst of the battle, but the victory had been won. The doctrine of State rights, ingrafted on the Constitution by George Mason, developed by Jefferson, expounded by Madison, and practised by himself, had once more triumphed—a strict construction of the Constitution, a total abstinence from the exercise of all powers not specifically granted, an abandonment to the States of the right to control all things affecting their internal and domestic affairs, was once again to become the rule of action to the Federal Government, and to be the means of developing a prosperity in the several States, unparalleled in the annals of history, and of exciting among them a generous spirit of emulation, causing each to strive with all the means of this inventive age, to excel the other in the various walks of industry, in the arts of peace, in the deeds of arms, and in noble acts of chivalry, that will cast a lustre over this great Republic, uneclipsed by the most brilliant achievements of ancient or modern times.

For this glorious consummation, we are indebted to John Randolph, more than to any other man. His bold and masterly efforts arrested that centripetal tendency which was rapidly destroying the counterbalance of the States, and making them, instead of what they are, proud independent sovereignties, jealous of their peculiar rights, and prompt to defend them, mere abject provinces, bowing patiently to encroachment so long as largesses were bestowed by the bountiful hand of an all-powerful and concentrated empire.

Let not the absurd notion then be repeated, that he was powerful to pull down, but feeble to build up. There it was, already built up, that beautiful system, unknown to the world before, *an imperium in imperio ;* he had nothing to add to the design of those who projected it—leave it to its own beautiful and simple operations, and like the solar system, we should scarcely know of its existence save by the genial influence shed on the various planets that composed it; he taught *a wise and masterly inactivity*—add nothing to clog its motion—nothing to hurry it to rack and ruin, like an unbalanced horologue, and the States and the Union in perpetual harmony, will move,

> " Like a star that maketh not haste,
> That taketh not rest;
> —— each one fulfilling
> His God-given hest."

CHAPTER XLIV.

"I HAVE BEEN SICK ALL MY LIFE."—DEATH.

MR. RANDOLPH attempted to go to the different counties of his old district, in the month of April, and to address the people on the days of election, but he did not succeed. On the 14th of April, he writes to Dr. Brockenbrough. "Your letter of the 4th was received here (Charlotte Court-house) last night, on my return from Buckingham. I made an effort to attend that election, but was obliged to return *re infecta*, and reached this place so done up by fatigue, that I have not been able to get on to Roanoke. Exercise by *gestation* is indispensable to my existence; from *ten* to *twenty* miles are requisite to enable me to support life. I am now scuffling to get to England in the May packet. Whether I shall succeed or not, I propose being in Richmond immediately after the Cumberland election, if not sooner." He was at Cumberland on the day of election, and started that evening for Richmond; but was compelled to turn in at Clay Hill, the residence of his friend Barksdale in Amelia. On the 23d, he says: "Although more than half dead when taken out of my carriage, and enduring excessive pain, I passed a better night than I have had for two months, and was in every respect far better this morning, than I had been within that period; and I feel satisfied that exercise by gestation, if I take enough of it, will greatly remit my exhausted system. However, while I was chuckling over my success, I suffered a fatal relapse, and the day has been spent in stupor and pain, which did not allow me to dispense with Johnny's presence and services. *Deo volente*, he will set out to-morrow by day with this letter." From George W. Johnson's, near Moody's, Chesterfield, Thursday, May 2d, he writes: "I am here very ill. I have little expectation of ever leaving this apartment, except on men's shoulders; an act of imprudence on the night of my arrival has nearly sealed my doom. Yet with my characteristic reaction, I may go to Petersburg to-morrow, and on Monday, to Richmond. Pray, secure me, if practicable, a parlor and bedroom adjoining, on a lower floor, and speak to Ball to reserve stalls for five horses and three servants.

"If my dear brother Harry be not gone, entreat him to come to me on the receipt of this. If I can, I will take the packet from the Delaware for London, avoiding the Irish Channel, which is the worst as the English S. Coast is the best of climates."

He did go on to Petersburg, attended the races, made a speech, passed through Richmond, and from the Merry Oaks, Friday, May 17, he writes:

"Arrived here last night, through torrents of rain that deluged the roads, and made them run like rivers, John and Juba, as wet as drowned rats, but it was an admirable *sedative* (you are an ' Embro' man, and possibly a disciple of Cullen) for John's over stimulant. *Quant à moi*, I came every foot of the way in torture, having been so lumbered by John, that I might as well have been in the pillory, and each jolt over stone, stump, or pole, or old fence rails left in the road, when the new one was made, or the old one ' upset' for the benefit of travelling carriages, those of gentlemen in *especial*, as the Waverly man has it.

"At Botts's gate, Half Sink, I was fain to call and ask the price of his land, and sponge upon him for the night, for I was in agony, but he was gone to the Baltimore races. So, after making some better arrangements, and watering the tits which were half choked with thirst, I proceeded on over the slashes and ' *cross* ways' with *peine forte et dure*, to the old oaks, ignorant until then that the stage road had been changed, or I would have taken the other, except on account of the house. If Botts's land lay in any other county, except Henrico, and especially if it were on the south side, I would buy it and take my chance for selling Spring Hill, which except in point of soil, has every advantage over Half Sink."

This was the last letter ever written by Mr. Randolph, to his most cherished and confidential friend. He had, in his last journey, passed rapidly by most of the scenes rendered dear to him by the recollections of youth, and by the fond associations of love and friendship; and it so happened that he saw most of the few friends that were left him this side of the grave. What recollections were called up, as he passed for the last time through Amelia—love! love! blighted love! deeply buried in his heart's inmost core! as he passed through Chesterfield, and looked for the last time on the tombs of his beloved father and mother, at old Matoax, where he had so long wished to lie down and be at rest—Petersburgh—Richmond—there were a few left that still cared for him, that loved him, and warmly pressed his fevered hand as he passed rapidly by, on his last journey. They were now all behind him, and he might exclaim, as he did on a former occasion, when he heard of the death of one endeared by early, though mournful recollections:

> "Days of my cherished youth,
> When all unfelt Time's footsteps fell,
> And all unheeded flew,
> Dreams of the morn of life, farewell! a long, a last farewell!"

Mr. Randolph reached the landing at Potomac creek, before the arrival of the steamboat, and considerably in advance of the Fredericksburg stage-coaches, which could not keep pace with his fleet horses.

When the approach of the boat was announced, he was brought out of the room by his servants, on a chair, and seated in the porch, where most of the stage passengers were assembled. His presence seemed to produce considerable restraint on the company; and though he appeared to solicit it, none were willing to enter into conversation; one gentleman only, who was a former acquaintance, passed a few words with him; and so soon as the boat reached the landing, all hurried off, and left him nearly alone, with his awkward servants as his only attendants. An Irish porter, who seemed to be very careless and awkward in his movements, slung a trunk round and struck Mr. Randolph with considerable force against the knee. He uttered an exclamation of great suffering. The poor Irishman was much terrified, and made the most humble apology, but Mr. Randolph stormed at him—would listen to no excuse, and drove him from his presence. This incident increased the speed of the by-standers, and in a few minutes not one was left to assist the dying man.

Dr. Dunbar, an eminent physician, of Baltimore, witnessing what happened, and feeling his sympathies awakened towards a man so feeble, and apparently so near his end, walked up to the chair, as the servants were about to remove their master, and said, "Mr. Randolph, I have not the pleasure of your acquaintance, but I have known your brother from my childhood; and as I see you have no one with you but your servants—you appear to require a friend, I will be happy to render you any assistance in my power, while we are together on the boat." He looked up, and fixed such a searching gaze on the doctor as he never encountered before. But having no other motive but kindness for a suffering fellow man, he returned the scrutinizing look with steadiness. As Mr. Randolph read the countenance of the stranger, who had thus unexpectedly proffered his friendship, his face suddenly cleared up; and with a most winning smile, and real politeness, and with a touching tone of voice, grasping the Doctor's hand, he said. "I am most thankful to you, sir, for your kindness, for I do, indeed, want a friend."

He was now, with the Doctor's assistance, carefully carried on board, and set down in the most eligible part of the cabin. He seemed to be gasping for breath, as he sat up in the chair; having recovered a little, he turned to the Doctor, and said, "Be so good, sir, if you please, as to give me your name." The Doctor gave him his name, his profession, and place of residence.

"Ah! Doctor," said he, "I am passed surgery—passed surgery!" "I hope not, sir," the Doctor replied. With a deeper and more pathetic tone, he repeated, "*I am passed surgery.*"

He was removed to a side berth, and laid in a position where he could get air; the Doctor also commenced fanning him. His face was wrinkled, and of a parched yellow, like a female of advanced age. He seemed to repose for a moment, but presently he roused up, throwing round an intense and searching gaze. The Doctor was reading a newspaper.

"What paper is that, Doctor?"

"The —— *Gazette*, sir."

"A very scurrilous paper, sir—a very scurrilous paper."

After a short pause, he continued, "Be so good, sir, as to read the foreign news for me—the debates in Parliament, if you please."

"As the names of the speakers were mentioned, he commented on each; "Yes," said he, "I knew him when I was in England;" then went on to make characteristic remarks on each person.

In reading, the Doctor fell upon the word budget; he pronounced the letter *u* short, as in *bud*—búdget. Mr. Randolph said quickly, but with great mildness and courtesy, "Permit me to interrupt you for a moment, Doctor; I would pronounce that word bûdget; like *oo* in book." "Very well, sir," said the Doctor, pleasantly, and continued the reading, to which Mr. Randolph listened with great attention. Mr. Randolph now commenced a conversation about his horses, which he seemed to enjoy very much; Gracchus particularly, he spoke of with evident delight. As he lay in his berth, he showed his extremities to the Doctor, which were much emaciated. He looked at them mournfully, and expressed his opinion of the hopelessness of his condition. The Doctor endeavored to cheer him with more hopeful views. He listened politely, but evidently derived no consolation from the remarks. Supper was now announced; the captain and the steward were very attentive, in carrying such dishes to Mr. Randolph as they thought would be pleasing to him. He was plentifully supplied with fried clams, which he ate with a good deal of relish. The steward asked him if he would have some more clams. "I do not know," he replied; "Doctor, do you think I could take some more clams?" "No, Mr. Randolph; had you asked me earlier, I would have advised you against taking any, for they are very injurious; but I did not conceive it my right to advise you." "Yes you had, Doctor; and I would have been much obliged to you for doing so. Steward, I can't take any more; the Doctor thinks they are not good for me."

After the table was cleared off, one of the gentlemen—the one referred to as a former acquaintance of Mr. Randolph's, observed that he should like to get some information about the boats north of Baltimore. "I can get it for you, sir," replied Mr. Randolph. "Doctor, do me the favor to hand me a little wicker-basket, among my things in the berth below." The basket was handed to him; it was full of clippings from newspapers. He could not find the advertisement he sought for. The gentleman, with great politeness, said, "Don't trouble yourself, Mr. Randolph." Several times he repeated, "Don't trouble yourself, sir." At length Randolph became impatient, and looking up at him with an angry expression of countenance, said, "I do hate to be interrupted!" The gentleman, thus rebuked, immediately left him.

Mr. Randolph then showed another basket of the same kind, filled with similar scraps from newspapers, and observed that he was always in the habit, when any thing struck him in his reading, as likely to be useful for future reference, to cut it out and preserve it in books, which he had for that purpose; and that he had at home several vol umes of that kind.

He showed his arrangements for travelling in Europe; and after a while, seeing the Doctor writing, he said, "Doctor, I see you are writing; will you do me the favor to write a letter for me, to a friend in Richmond?" "Certainly, sir." "The gentleman," he continued, stands A. No. 1, among men—Dr. Brockenbrough, of Richmond." The letter gave directions about business matters, principally, but it contained some characteristic remarks about his horses. He exulted in their having beaten the stage; and concluded, "So much for blood. Now," said he, "sign it, Doctor."

"How shall I sign it, Mr. Randolph? sign it John Randolph of Roanoke?"

"No, sir, sign it Randolph of Roanoke."

It was done accordingly. "Now, Doctor," said he, ' do me the favor to add a postscript." The postscript was added, "I have been so fortunate as to meet with Dr. ———, of ——, on board this boat, and to form his acquaintance, and I can never be sufficiently grateful for his kind attentions to me."

So soon as the letter was concluded, Mr. Randolph drew together the curtains of his berth; the Doctor frequently heard him groaning heavily, and breathing so laboriously, that several times he approached the side of the berth to listen if it were not the beginning of the death-struggle. He often heard him, also, exclaiming, in agonized tones, "Oh God! Oh Christ!" while he was engaged in ejaculatory prayer.

He now became very restless, was impatient and irascible with his servants, but continued to manifest the utmost kindness and courtesy towards Dr. Dunbar.

When the boat reached the wharf at Alexandria, where the Doctor was to leave, he approached the side of the berth, and said, "Mr. Randolph, I must now take leave of you." He begged the Doctor to come and see him, at Gadsby's, then, grasping his hand, he said, "God bless you, Doctor; I never can forget your kind attentions to me."

Next day he went into the Senate chamber, and took his seat in rear of Mr. Clay. That gentleman happened at the time to be on his feet, addressing the Senate. "Raise me up," said Randolph, "I want to hear that voice again." When Mr. Clay had concluded his remarks, which were very few, he turned round to see from what quarter that singular voice proceeded. Seeing Mr. Randolph, and that he was in a dying condition, he left his place and went to speak to him; as he approached, Mr. Randolph said to the gentleman with him, " Raise me up." As Mr. Clay offered his hand, he said, " Mr. Randolph, I hope you are better, sir." " No, sir," replied Randolph, " I am a dying man, and I came here expressly to have this interview with you."

They grasped hands and parted, never to meet more.

Having accomplished the only thing that weighed on his mind, having satisfied Mr. Clay, and the world, that, notwithstanding a long life of political hostility, no personal animosity rankled in his heart, he was now ready to continue on his journey, or to meet, with a lighter conscience, any fate that might befall him.

He hurried on to Philadelphia, to be in time for the packet, that was about to sail from the Delaware. But he was too late; he was destined to take passage in a different boat, and to a land far different from that of his beloved England. It was Monday night when he reached the city, and the storm was very high. His friends found him on the deck of the steamboat, while Johnny was out hunting for a carriage. He was put into a wretched hack, the glasses all broken, and was driven from hotel to hotel in search of lodgings, and exposed all the time to the peltings of the storm. He at length drove to the City Hotel, kept by Mr. Edmund Badger. When Mr. Badger came out to meet him, he asked if he could have accommodations. Mr. Badger replied that he was crowded, but would do the best he could for him. On hearing this, he lifted up his hands, and exclaimed, " Great God! I thank thee; I shall be among friends, and be taken care of !"

Mr. Randolph was very ill. Dr. Joseph Parish, a Quaker physician, was sent for. As he entered the room, the patient said, " I am acquainted with you, sir, by character. I know you through Giles." He then told the Doctor that he had attended several courses of lectures on anatomy, and described his symptoms with medical accuracy, declaring he must die if he could not discharge the puriform matter.

" How long have you been sick, Mr. Randolph?"

" Don't ask me that question; I have been sick all my life. I have been affected with my present disease, however, for three years. It was greatly aggravated by my voyage to Russia. That killed me, sir. This Russian expedition has been a Pultowa, a Beresina to me."

The Doctor now felt his pulse. "You can form no judgment by my pulse; it is so peculiar."

"You have been so long an invalid, Mr. Randolph, you must have acquired an accurate knowledge of the general course of practice adapted to your case."

"Certainly, sir; at forty, a fool or a physician, you know."

"There are idiosyncracies," said the Doctor, "in many constitutions. I wish to ascertain what is peculiar about you."

"I have been an idiosyncracy all my life. All the preparations of camphor invariably injure me. As to ether, it will blow me up. Not so with opium; I can take opium like a Turk, and have been in the habitual use of it, in one shape or another, for some time."

Before the Doctor retired, Mr. Randolph's conversation became curiously diversified. He introduced the subject of the Quakers; complimented them in his peculiar manner for neatness, economy, order, comfort—in every thing. "Right," said he, "in every thing except politics—there always twistical." He then repeated a portion of the Litany of the Episcopal church, with apparent fervor. The following morning the Doctor was sent for very early. He was called from bed. Mr. Randolph apologized very handsomely for disturbing him. Something was proposed for his relief. He petulantly and positively refused compliance. The Doctor paused and addressed a few words to him. He apologized, and was as submissive as an infant. One evening a medical consultation was proposed; he promptly objected. "In a multitude of counsel," said he, "there is confusion; it leads to weakness and indecision; the patient may die while the doctors are staring at each other." Whenever Dr. Parish parted from him, especially at night, he would receive the kindest acknowledgments, in the most affectionate tones: "God bless you; he does bless you, and he will bless you."

The night preceding his death, the Doctor passed about two hours in his chamber. In a plaintive tone he said, "My poor John, sir, is worn down with fatigue, and has been compelled to go to bed. A most attentive substitute supplies his place, but neither he nor you, sir, are like John; he knows where to place his hand on any thing, in a large quantity of baggage prepared for a European voyage."

The patient was greatly distressed in breathing, in consequence of difficult expectoration. He requested the Doctor, at his next visit, to bring instruments for performing the operation of bronchotomy, for he could not live unless relieved. He then directed a certain newspaper to be brought to him. He put on his spectacles, as he sat propped up in bed, turned over the paper several times, and examined it carefully, then placing his finger on a part he had selected, handed it to the Doctor, with a request that he would read it. It was headed " Cherokee." In the course of reading, the Doctor came to the word " omnipotence," and pronounced it with a full sound on the penultimate—omni*po*tence. Mr. Randolph checked him, and pronounced the word according to Walker. The Doctor attempted to give a reason for his pronunciation. " Pass on," was the quick reply. The word impetus was then pronounced with the *e* long, ' im-*petus.*" He was instantly corrected. The Doctor hesitated on the criticism. " There can be no doubt of it, sir." An immediate acknowledgment of the reader that he stood corrected, appeared to satisfy the critic, and the piece was concluded. The Doctor observed that there was a great deal of sublimity in the composition. He directly referred to the Mosaic account of creation, and repeated " ' Let there be light, and there was light.' There is sublimity."

Next morning (the day on which he died), Dr. Parish received an early and an urgent message to visit him. Several persons were in the room, but soon left it, except his servant, John, who was much affected at the sight of his dying master. The Doctor remarked to him, " I have seen your master very low before, and he revived ; and perhaps he will again." " John knows better than that, sir." He then looked at the Doctor with great intensity, and said in an earnest and distinct manner, " I confirm every disposition in my will, especially that respecting my slaves, whom I have manumitted, and for whom I have made provision."

" I am rejoiced to hear such a declaration from you, sir," replied the Doctor, and soon after, proposed to leave him for a short time, to attend to another patient. " You must not go " was the reply; " you cannot, you shall not leave me. *John !* take care that the Doctor does not leave the room." John soon locked the door, and reported, " Master, I have locked the door, and got the key in my pocket : the Doctor can't go now."

He seemed excited, and said " If you do go you need not return."
The Doctor appealed to him as to the propriety of such an order, inasmuch as he was only desirous of discharging his duty to another
patient. His manner instantly changed, and he said, " I retract
that expression." Some time afterwards, turning an expressive look,
he said again, " I retract that expression."

The Doctor now said that he understood the subject of his communication, and presumed the Will would explain itself fully. He
replied in his peculiar way—" No, you don't understand it ; I know
you don't. Our laws are extremely particular on the subject of
slaves—a Will may manumit them, but provision for their subsequent
support, requires that a declaration be made in the presence of a
white witness ; and it is requisite that the witness, after hearing the
declaration, should continue with the party, and never lose sight of
him, until he is gone or dead. You are a good witness for John.
You see the propriety and importance of your remaining with me ;
your patients must make allowance for your situation. John told me
this morning—' master, you are dying.' "

The Doctor spoke with entire candor and replied, that it was rather a matter of surprise that he had lasted so long. He now made
his preparations to die. He directed John to bring him his father's
breast button ; he then directed him to place it in the bosom of his
shirt. It was an old fashioned, large-sized gold stud. John placed
it in the button hole of the shirt bosom—but to fix it completely, required a hole on the opposite side. " Get a knife, said he, and cut
one." A napkin was called for, and placed by John, over his breast.
For a short time he lay perfectly quiet, with his eyes closed. He
suddenly roused up and exclaimed—" Remorse ! remorse !" It was
thrice repeated—the last time, at the top of his voice, with great agitation. He cried out—" let me see the word. Get a Dictionary, let
me see the word." " There is none in the room, sir." Write it down
then—let me see the word." The Doctor picked up one of his cards,
" Randolph of Roanoke"—" shall I write it on this card ?" " Yes,
nothing more proper." The word *remorse*, was then written in pencil. He took the card in a hurried manner, and fastened his eyes on
it with great intensity. " Write it on the back," he exclaimed—it
was so done and handed him again. He was extremely agitated—" Remorse ! you have no idea what it is ; you can form no idea

of it, whatever; it has contributed to bring me to my present situation—but I have looked to the Lord Jesus Christ, and hope I have obtained pardon. Now let John take your pencil and draw a line under the word," which was accordingly done. " What am I to do with the card?" inquired the Doctor. " Put it in your pocket—take care of it—when I am dead, look at it."

The doctor now introduced the subject of calling in some additional witnesses to his declarations, and suggested sending down stairs for Edmund Badger. He replied—" I have already communicated that to him." The doctor then said—" With your concurrence, sir, I will send for two young physicians, who shall remain and never lose sight of you until you are dead; to whom you can make your declarations—my son, Dr. Isaac Parish, and my young friend and late pupil, Dr. Francis West, a brother of Capt. West."

He quickly asked—" Capt. West of the Packet?" " Yes, sir, the same." " Send for him—he is the man—I'll have him."

Before the door was unlocked, he pointed towards a bureau, and requested the Doctor to take from it a remuneration for his services. To this the Doctor promptly replied, that he would feel as though he were acting indelicately, to comply. He then waived the subject, by saying—" in England, it is always customary."

The witnesses were now sent for, and soon arrived. The dying man was propped up in the bed, with pillows, nearly erect. Being extremely sensitive to cold, he had a blanket over his head and shoulders; and he directed John to place his hat on, over the blanket, which aided in keeping it close to his head. With a countenance full of sorrow, John stood close by the side of his dying master. The four witnesses—Edmund Badger, Francis West, Isaac Parish, and Joseph Parish, were placed in a semi-circle, in full view. He rallied all the expiring energies of mind and body, to this last effort. " His whole soul," says Dr. Parish, " seemed concentrated in the act. His eyes flashed feeling and intelligence. Pointing towards us, with his long index finger, he addressed us."

" I confirm all the directions in my Will, respecting my slaves, and direct them to be enforced, particularly in regard to a provision for their support." And then raising his arm as high as he could, he brought it down with his open hand, on the shoulder of his favorite John, and added these words—" especially for this man." He then asked each of the witnesses whether they understood him. Dr. Joseph Parish explained to them, what Mr. Randolph had said in regard to the laws of Virginia, on the subject of manumission—and then appealed to the dying man to know whether he had stated it correctly. "Yes," said he, and gracefully waving his hand as a token of dismission, he added—" the young gentlemen will remain with me."

The scene was now soon changed. Having disposed of that subject most deeply impressed on his heart, his keen penetrating eye lost its expression, his powerful mind gave way, and his fading imagination began to wander amid scenes and with friends that he had left behind. In two hours the spirit took its flight, and all that was mortal of John Randolph of Roanoke was hushed in death. At a quarter before twelve o'clock, on the 24th day of June, 1833, aged sixty years, he breathed his last, in a chamber of the City Hotel, No. 41 North Third Street, Philadelphia.

His remains were taken to Virginia, and buried at Roanoke, not far from the mansion in which he lived, and in the midst of that " boundless contiguity of shade," where he spent so many hours of anguish and of solitude. He sleeps quietly now; the squirrel may gambol in the boughs above, the partridge may whistle in the long grass that waves over that solitary grave, and none shall disturb or make them afraid.

That innumerable funeral bells were not tolled, and eulogies pronounced, and a monument was not erected to his memory in the capitol of his native State, is because Virginia has not yet learned to " understand" and to appreciate her wisest statesman, truest patriot, and most devoted son.

THE END.